itv SPORT *The Complete Encyclopedia of*

FORMULA ONE

12TH EDITION

First published in 2004

This revised and updated edition published in 2010

10 9 8 7 6 5 4 3 2 1

A CIP catalogue record for this book is available from the British Library

ISBN: 978-1-84732-304-0

Editor: Nigel Matheson
Project Art Direction: Jim Lockwood
Design: Vicki Smith
Picture Research: Stephen O'Kelly
Production: Lisa French and Kate Pimm

Printed in Dubai

The publishers would like to thank the following sources for their kind permission to reproduce the images in this book:

Action Images: /Michael Hewett/Sporting Pictures: 36, 39, 44, 45, 53, 132 bottom, 143 bottom, 157 top, 171; /Carlos Matos: 81; /Sporting Pictures: 79, 83; /Crispin Thurston: 56, 58, 67, 71, 80, 88, 95, 128, 176, 182 bottom

Colorsport: 156 bottom, 177, 184, 189; /Stuart MacFarlane: 155 bottom

Corbis: /Bettmann: 124 left

Fotosports International: /Roger Parker: 179 bottom

Getty Images: 161 top, 164 top, 257; /Pierre Andrieu/AFP: 217; /Paolo Cocco/AFP: 185 top, 268; /Michael Cooper: 93, 248; /Mike Hewett: 167; /Stan Honda/AFP: 195 bottom; /Hulton Archive: 124 right, 125, 132 top, 136 top; /John Krutop: 75; /Bryn Lennon: 253; /J.P. Moczulski/AFP: 258; /Mike Powell: 65; /Pascal Rondeau: 76-77, 82, 185 bottom, 187 top; /Clive Rose: 127, 137, 198, 249; /STR/AFP: 259; /Ronald Startup: 206; /Mark Thompson: 170, 197, 250, 264

LAT Photographic: 3, 6-7, 12, 13 bottom, 14, 16, 17, 18-19, 20, 21, 22, 23, 24, 25, 26, 27, 28, 29, 30-31, 32, 33, 34, 35, 38, 40, 41 42-43, 46, 47, 48, 49, 51, 52, 54-55, 57, 59, 60, 61, 62, 63, 64, 66, 68, 69, 70, 72, 73, 74, 78, 84, 85, 86, 87, 89, 90, 91, 92, 94, 96, 97, 98-99, 100, 101, 102, 103, 104, 105, 106, 107, 108, 109, 110, 111, 112, 113, 114, 115, 116, 118, 119, 122, 123, 126, 130, 131, 133, 134, 135, 136 bottom, 138, 139, 140, 141, 142, 143 top, 144, 145, 146, 148, 149, 150, 152, 153, 154, 156 top, 157 bottom, 158 top, 159, 160, 162, 163, 164 bottom, 166, 168, 169, 172, 173 174, 175 top, 178, 179 top, 180 , 181, 182 top, 183, 188, 190, 192, 194, 196, 199, 200, 201, 202, 203, 207, 208, 209, 210, 211, 212, 213, 214, 215, 216, 218, 219, 220, 221, 222, 223, 224, 225, 226, 227, 228, 229, 230, 231, 232, 233, 234, 235, 236, 237, 238, 239, 240, 241, 243, 251, 252, 254, 255, 256, 260, 262, 263, 265, 266, 267, 269, 270, 271, 272, 273, 274, 275, 276, 277, 278, 279, 280, 281, 282, 283

Mary Evans Picture Library: 11 top right, 11 bottom

National Motor Museum Beaulieu: 13 top

Press Association Images: /Barratts/ALPHA: 165, 191; /James Bearne: 186, 193; /Empics Sport: 37, 50; /Steve Etherington: 129, 187 bottom; /John Marsh: 147, 151 top, 155 top, 195 top; /Steve Mitchell: 151 bottom; /S&G/ALPHA: 158 bottom, 161 bottom

Topfoto.co.uk: 10, 11 top left; /National Motor Museum/HIP: 15, 175 bottom

Every effort has been made to acknowledge correctly and contact the source and/or copyright holder of each picture and Carlton Books Limited apologises for any unintentional errors or omissions, which will be, corrected in future editions of this book.

itv SPORT | *The Complete Encyclopedia of*
FORMULA ONE

12TH EDITION

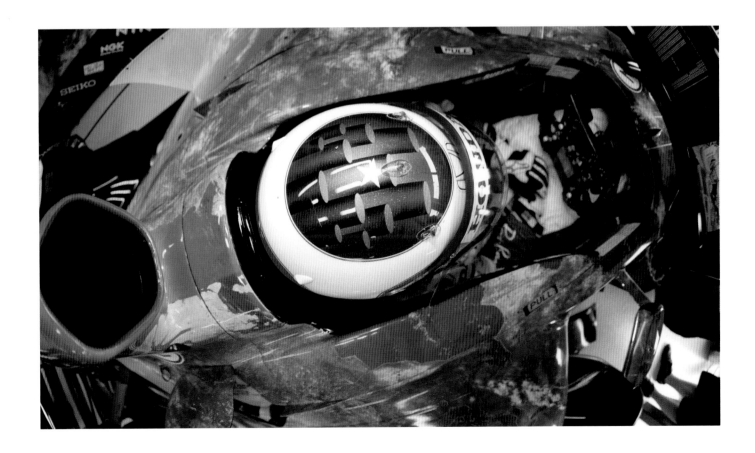

CARLTON
BOOKS

CONTENTS

FOREWORD
NIGEL MANSELL

Formula One has evolved since Nigel Mansell won his title in 1992, but it still takes the same magic to be a world champion.

I've found it fascinating to delve into *The ITV Sport Complete Encyclopedia of Formula One*. The pictures really take you back and some great moments came flooding back to me, especially from the early eighties and even before that. The great thing is that, in many of the photographs, you can see the cars actually moving and sliding, and power-sliding and twitching. That's what it was really like.

With this book, the teams, cars, drivers and especially the atmosphere all come back to you: you can almost smell the high-octane fuel and sense the expectation coming off the crowd. I'm also a little sad at the thought of the number of people who are no longer with us.

Grand prix racing is the absolute pinnacle of motor sport and there's no feeling like being behind the wheel of a competitive car, in with a real chance of winning a World Championship race. And being in the hunt against five to seven fellow world champions, with a full grid of 26 cars, that's very special. Few things are more exhilarating.

I love Formula One, and still follow it closely but I can't help noticing how much it has changed. In my day, the depth of competition was immense. Circuits were really ballsy and you could run flat-out over large sections of the track; you didn't have run-offs or sandtraps. It really was dicing with death. We used to go round corners at 180 or 200mph – you had to be extremely stupid as well as brave to take part because if something went wrong you knew you were going to be in very serious trouble.

I believe safety is paramount, although I think it may have gone too far now and some of the circuits have become a little tame.

Seeing how far F1 has evolved, all ex-grand prix drivers must look at the current age with a tinge of regret. Most of the current lot take home an immense wage packet without having to win a race. And you don't even have to change gear: everything is done by computers in the garage. In days gone by, the drivers had tremendous input into how to set up the car. Maybe we are about to go

back to the future with a new set of rules that will bring sheer driving skills to the fore again.

In the meantime, the sport remains massively popular all over the world and the crowd's expectations remain unabated. The cars continue to develop technically, as do the rules that govern them. But the desire to be the best driver in the world, in the best car, that will never change. It's that special combination of cutting-edge technology and the fundamental human desire to win that makes Formula One the most desirable sport on the planet.

Nigel Mansell in action during the 1992 South African GP, on his way to the first of his nine victories in his championship-winning season

PART 1:

THE STORY OF FORMULA ONE

Little can the original brave _pilotes_ have known as they took part in the first-ever car race in 1894 that they were the forerunners to a sport that would become global currency; a sport that would be watched the world over, its stars household names and rich beyond their wildest dreams.

That first race between Paris and Rouen set the ball rolling and motor racing now has so much momentum behind it at the start of the 21st century that it rivals football as the world's most popular sport; its 16 or so grands prix watched by television audiences outstripped only by the Olympic Games. It's safe to say that everything has changed from that

first race in 1894: the circuits, the drivers, the cars and most certainly the speed at which they travel. The involvement of the manufacturers has ebbed and flowed, but all have benefitted from the technological gains unearthed by the engineers' quest to make their cars go faster. However, one thing has remained unchanged: the fame of the drivers,

with the greats of every decade worthy of respect, from Tazio Nuvolari to Juan Manuel Fangio to Jackie Stewart to Alain Prost to Ayrton Senna and to the most successful driver of all, Michael Schumacher, as well as recent champions Lewis Hamilton and Jenson Button.
All statistics are correct to the end of the 2009 World Championship.

1894
» First-ever car race held in France on public roads between Paris and Rouen, with a stop for lunch; 21 drivers, each with a mechanic, set out from Paris aiming to win the 5,000 Franc prize
» Count de Dion was first to Rouen, but he had not carried a mechanic, so the prize went to Peugeot driver Georges Lemaitre instead

1895
» There-and-back races become popular with Panhards and Peugeots fighting for honours in a successful Paris-Bordeaux-Paris race
» Emile Levassor was first to the finish, but his Panhard was ineligible as it was a two-seater, with only four-seaters allowed

1896
» The Automobile Club de France organizes a race from Paris to Marseilles and back, a distance of over 1,000 miles

1898
» First racing fatalities suffered in Paris-Nice race when the Marquis de Montaignac is killed, along with the Marquis de Montariol's riding mechanic
» A Paris-Amsterdam-Paris race takes motor racing outside France for the first time, with a record-winning average of 26.88mph, emphasizing the rapid rate of progress in the machinery as extraneous weight is shed

1899
» *New York Herald* European editor Gordon Bennett announces a special race, later to be known as the Gordon Bennett Trophy, with national teams of up to three drivers piloting cars built in their country

1900

» First Gordon Bennett Trophy, held between Paris and Lyon, is won by the French team with Fernand Charron first home in a Panhard at an average speed of 38.617mph

1901

» First spectator fatality endured as a boy steps out to watch a car in the Paris-Berlin road race, only to be hit by the next one along the road

» The French government bans all racing, but later relents

1903

» Paris-Madrid race is stopped when it reaches Bordeaux due to numerous accidents involving both drivers and spectators

1904

» A record six national teams contest the Gordon Bennet Trpohy, with victory going to Frenchman Leo Thery at Homburg in Germany in front of the Kaiser

1906

» The French refuse to organize the Gordon Bennett Trophy race, instead holding the first French Grand Prix with a race at Le Mans on public roads, with each lap 65 miles in length. This is the start of grand prix racing

» Hungarian driver Ferenc Szisz wins in a Renault. This is the first race on a closed circuit and his winning average speed is 62.887mph in a race that takes 12 hours 14 minutes and 7 seconds

THE EARLY YEARS

The first ever motor race, in France in 1894, bemused onlookers, but road racing was soon all the rage, until ever-increasing speeds confined racing to specially built circuits. And the cars just went faster and faster...

The Pioneering Racers

Motor racing has changed a great deal since the first competition took place in 1894, but its essential nature has not: brave and talented men (and occasionally women) do battle in the fastest and most sophisticated machinery of the day. Motor racing has always been dangerous and, although the attitude to safety has become less cavalier (especially in the last few years) and the likelihood of injury has become increasingly less common, danger still exists – and that is part of the sport's undying attraction for its ever-growing legion of fans.

1894 Paris to Rouen: 21 drivers, each with a mechanic aboard, raced on public roads for a 5,000 Franc purse, with a stopover for lunch

Grand prix racing has been many things to many people over the years, but to those who take part in it and are involved in it, whether as drivers, team managers, owners or mechanics, it remains one of the last great challenges left on this earth.

Almost as soon as the car was invented, enthusiasts began to create competitions for it. It was less than ten years from the appearance of the first car to the organization of the first race, an exceedingly gentlemanly affair, far removed from the intense competition of the grands prix of today. It was arranged by Pierre Gifard of the newspaper *Le Petit Journal*, and the winner of the trip from Paris to Rouen – with a stop for lunch! – was to be the vehicle which covered the

80 miles "without danger, was easy to handle and cheap to run".

Although the internal-combustion engine had been invented in Germany and Britain had led the Industrial Revolution, both countries were initially hostile to the car. But the French immediately took to it and soon established the largest industry in the world, at a time when racing on public roads was banned in the other two leading European nations. This enthusiasm and technical prowess, combined with rivalry between manufacturers and the existence of many straight roads, produced the first age of motor racing. With cars like Peugeot and the Panhard, the French dominated racing until the end of the nineteenth century and, despite the gentle ethos behind the first race, it didn't take long for racing to distil

to today's "fastest wins" philosophy.

While the idea behind racing may have been essentially similar to today, the cars were not. Early Panhards were steered by a lever, not unlike the tiller on a boat, and Peugeots had a handlebar. The steering wheel soon replaced them, although it took rather longer for pneumatic tyres to supersede the solid ones.

In the early years racing took the form of town-to-town events, organized in the same way as rallies are today – cars started individually, and the winner was decided on aggregate time. In 1896 the Automobile Club de France (ACF) organized a race from Paris to Marseilles and back, and by 1897 there was the first sign that racing cars were becoming different to road cars: the professionals stripped off non-essentials like mudguards and

"Accident Terrible": the first racing fatality as Marquis de Montaignac dies in the 1898 Paris to Nice

Out in Front: Ferenc Szisz hurls his Renault round this uphill left en route to his first grand prix win

GREAT RACE

French Grand Prix 1906

The modern Formula One fan would not have recognized the first grand prix ever held. First of all, the circuit was all of 65 miles long, running around a triangular course of closed-off public roads to the east of Le Mans. Secondly, there was no qualifying competition, just the race itself. Or, more to the point, the races, as there was one on the Saturday and another on the Sunday, each lasting six laps. Thirdly, the cars were started at 90-second intervals. Fourthly, there was a massive disparity between the appearance and the performance of the cars, with the largest powered by 18-litre engines. And, finally, each car carried two people: a driver and a riding mechanic. The bulk of the field was made up of three-car teams from Mercedes, Fiat and Itala, with Mercedes' Camille Jenatzy expected to set the pace. The French were quietly confident, though, with a clutch of teams entered by Panhard, de Dietrich, Hotchkiss, Darracq and Renault. And they were proved right to be so as Hungarian Ferenc Szisz - former riding mechanic to the late Louis Renault - drove one of their Renaults to first place at the end of the first day and outright victory on the second, helped on both days by using detachable rims that sped up tyre changing.

seat cushions, and manufacturers developed more powerful engines.

During these first forays into racing power outputs grew enormously, and there was growing unease about cars hurtling along public roads lined with crowds, most of whom had not the faintest idea of what a car was capable of. This unease was heightened by racing's first fatality.

Shortly after the start of the 1898 Paris-Nice race, Benz driver M de Montariol waved through his friend, the Marquis de Montaignac, who took his hands off the tiller to wave back. The car swerved, and took de Montariol's machine off the road. It shot up a bank and overturned. De Montariol was thrown clear, but his mechanic suffered fatal head injuries. De Montaignac turned to watch the accident, and overturned his own car. He survived long enough to accept the blame.

While the deaths could be put down to incompetence, that did little to mollify the Paris police chief who tried to stop the running of the Paris-Amsterdam race later that year. He failed, outfoxed by the competitors who decided to take their cars on a train to a starting point outside his jurisdiction, and again at the end when he realized it was ill-advised to interfere with a huge crowd celebrating the triumph of the winner, Fernand Charron.

By the turn of the century, a British newspaper magnate, John Gordon Bennett, had decided that it was time the motor industry in Britain was

given a kick-start, and he conceived the idea of organizing a race between teams representing countries rather than manufacturers.

The French were hostile, because entries were limited per country but, after a few years of being run alongside the great town-to-town races, in 1904 the Gordon Bennett race received a considerable boost when it was hosted by Germany for the first time. The event enjoyed a couple of years of glory before it was killed off by the French in 1906, when they refused to organize it alongside their new Grand Prix de l'ACF.

Meanwhile, the infant motor racing had ridden out a crisis - twice. In the 1901 Paris-Berlin event a boy had been killed as he stepped into the road to watch a passing car and was hit by the next one. The French government banned racing, but it eventually bowed to pressure from the influential motor industry and allowed it to start again.

A worse tragedy was to follow. In 1903 the ACF organized the Paris-Bordeaux-Madrid event, three million people lined the route. But cars crashed into trees, their drivers' views obscured by dust. Spectators, having difficulty in allowing for the speed of the cars (Louis Renault averaged 65mph on the first leg), were hit, and the event was cancelled when it reached Bordeaux after the Spanish and the French governments stepped in to ban it.

Again, though, the French government gave way to pressure and allowed racing, provided the roads

1921

» French Grand Prix at Le Mans - this time on a 10.7-mile circuit - sets the ball rolling again, with American Jimmy Murphy winning in a Duesenberg, showing how the European manufacturers had lost ground during the First World War
» First Italian Grand Prix at Brescia, this the first non-French grand prix on European soil, with Jules Goux winning around the 10.75-mile circuit in a Ballot

1922

» Introduction of 2-litre engine capacity limit is the first international regulation
» Italian Grand Prix moves to Monza, where it has been hosted almost continuously ever since. Pietro Bordino wins in a Fiat, with the 6.2-mile circuit following the current route, but also including a banked loop that can still be seen today

1923

» First win for a British driver - Henry Segrave - in a British car, a Sunbeam (right), at the French Grand Prix at Tours
» Fiat 805 is first grand prix car to be developed in a wind tunnel then promptly driven on the road from Turin across the Alps to take part in the French Grand Prix
» First Spanish Grand Prix, at Sitges, brings the number of grands prix up to three along with the French and Italian races. Divo triumphs in a Sunbeam

1924

» Alfa Romeo launches P2 racer, a car modelled largely on the Fiat
» Alfa Romeos carry the four-leafed clover borne by Richard-Barsiers before the First World War
» Giuseppe Campari wins the French Grand Prix at Lyon and Antonio Ascari the Italian Grand Prix at Monza for the Italian team
» Alfa Romeo stays away from San Sebastien Grand Prix at Lasarte in northern Spain and Segrave wins for Sunbeam

were sealed by barriers and races were held in sparsely populated areas. This was the start of racing on closed roads, a form that was to develop into circuit racing as we know it.

The First Golden Age

Ironically, the first grand prix, organized by the Automobile Club de France, was to mark the end of the era of French domination of racing. The sport became more professional and, together with cars from Germany, Italy, Britain and America, came a new generation of professional drivers - men like Felice Nazzaro, Georges Boillot and Jules Goux.

Germany, Italy and Britain wanted races on their own soil but, when the first purpose-built track was opened at Brooklands in Surrey in 1907, racing was already heading towards a crisis. There was an economic recession, and conflicting interests over the regulations and the sites of races led to the French pulling out in 1909.

In America, however, racing was beginning to boom. During the first decade of the twentieth century the Americans were consistently humiliated by the successes of imported European cars, and often of European drivers, but the opening of the Indianapolis Motor Speedway in 1909 gave a glimpse of the future. Racing spread westwards, and more and more speedways - or tracks - were constructed. Most popular were the one- or two-mile ovals built quickly and relatively cheaply out of wood. The promoters loved them because it meant that the spectators were all in one place and could be charged admission, while the spectators also approved: they could see the entire track and, better still, the racing was close, fast and dangerous. By 1917 the American Automobile Association's

Happy Days: Christian Lautenschlager and riding mechanic kick up the dust in the 1914 French GP

RULES OF THE GAME
American Grand Prize

The French had their grand prix so, within two years, the Americans had launched their Grand Prize. This annual race was a road race held at an assortment of tracks around the country, starting at Savannah around a 25-mile circuit in 1908 when, following a leisurely ten days of practice, Louis Wagner won for Fiat ahead of the Benzes. Two years later, Benz took the glory, with American hero David Bruce-Brown at the wheel, with the same driver winning for Fiat in 1911. The race ran through until 1916, being held at Santa Monica twice as well as at Milwaukee and San Francisco, but then racing on purpose-built ovals took over and these great road races were confined to the history books as American motor racing fans demonstrated their preference for circuits on which drivers turned only to the left.

GREAT RACE
1911 Indy 500

With their national pride battered by being beaten in road races, even on their own soil, the Americans responded by launching the famous 500-mile race on the banked oval at the Indianapolis Motor Speedway. The first of these came in 1911, starting a sequence that runs unbroken (save for 1942-45 during the Second World War) through to today. Victory in that first race went to Ray Harroun in a Marmon Wasp, winning by 1 minute and 43 seconds from Ralph Mulford's Lozier at an average speed of 74.6mph (the current record is 185.9mph). Fully 46 cars turned out, 40 passed the 75mph qualifying requirement and 80,000 spectators turned out to watch them. David Bruce-Brown led until mid-distance when Harroun - the only driver without a riding mechanic - took over, gaining advantage from the fact that his car was both narrower and lighter than those of his rivals. He rested for 100 miles, being relieved by Cyril Patshcke, then resumed to win, with, impressively, 11 other cars ending the race on the winning lap.

1925
>> Riding mechanics are banned
>> First Belgian Grand Prix, at Spa-Francorchamps, won by Alfa Romeo's Ascari. The 8.7-mile lap through the Ardennes forests remained little changed until 1978
>> Alfa Romeo team-mate Campari is only other finisher, 22 minutes adrift
>> Ascari crashes to his death when leading the French Grand Prix at Montlhery

1926
>> Engine capacity is reduced to 1.5 litres with Delage introducing a car - the 15S8 - that keeps on improving until it wins the first British Grand Prix at Brooklands in the hands of Robert Senechal and Louis Wagner
>> Season starts with just three cars turning up for French Grand Prix at the Miramas autodrome in the south of France. Jules Goux is the only finisher in his Bugatti and thus wins the race...

1927
>> Cars are no longer required to carry two seats, and an immediate narrowing and streamlining of their design ensues
>> Robert Benoist's winning speed in Italian GP at Monza is the first above 100mph
>> Benoist is also winner of three of the other four grands prix: France, Spain, Brooklands
>> German Grand Prix is held to sports car regulations and Otto Merz wins in a Mercedes. This is the first time that the Nurburgring hosts a grand prix

1928
>> Free engine capacity rule is introduced to attract more manufacturers to go racing, something that is important as the economy slides towards depression
>> Bugatti driver Louis Chiron (right) wins the San Sebastien, Spanish and Italian Grands Prix with Bugatti and Mercedes sharing the honours in the other two grands prix, both of which are run to sports car regulations

Push Start: Ascari's Alfa P2 fails to get going after a pitstop when leading the 1924 French GP

LANDMARK CAR

Alfa Romeo P2

Designer: **Vittorio Jano**   Years raced: **1924-29**
Grand prix wins: **5**   Pole positions: **1**   Fastest laps: **2**
Engine type: **Alfa Romeo supercharged straight 8**
Engine size/power: **1987cc/155bhp, later 175bhp**

The Italians really got into their stride in racing circles in the 1920s, when, in 1924, Alfa Romeo responded to Fiat's dominance of the previous two years by introducing the P2. Although a car exclusively for the works Alfa Romeo, this was fielded by none other than Enzo Ferrari's Scuderia Ferrari right the way through to the end of the 1930s. Giuseppe Campari gave the P2 a winning debut in the French Grand Prix and then, in its second year, 1925, the Vittorio Jano-designed car walked away with the newly organized World Championship for Manufacturers - with Antonio Ascari the man to beat until he was killed at Montlhery in the second ever race in which drivers no longer had to be accompanied by riding mechanics. The P2s were rendered outmoded in the late 1920s by cars from Bugatti, Delage and Mercedes, but bounced back in 1929 with Achille Varzi at the wheel.

national championship was made up entirely of oval races, many on these wooden "roaring boards".

Popular they may have been, but these ovals were lethal. Yet the drama and danger merely added to the interest of watching heroes like Ralph de Palma and Dario Resta battle it out. Back in Europe, the recession lifted again in 1911 and, in the couple of years before the First World War, racing enjoyed a brief flowering, and car design underwent a revolution.

Circuits were becoming more winding and twisting, whereas before most had been little more than triangles, and so emphasis switched from brute power to manoeuvrability, much better brakes and more flexible engines. By 1914 the racing car had arrived at a basic form it would keep more or less unchanged for the next 40 years.

The war, however, left racing in Europe in a parlous state, and it took some time to re-establish itself. The effects of the war can be judged by the 1921 ACF Grand Prix at Le Mans, in which the American visitors wiped the floor with the Europeans. Engineers, though, had learnt a great deal during the war and their knowledge was about to open the way to a period of technical advancement. This was to have two results: the domination of European racing by Italy and a technological divorce between the Americans and Europeans.

In America, cars like the slim-line Miller 122 were being developed exclusively for use on speedways, while in Europe, Fiat worked on the high-revving overhead camshaft engine and mated it to the lightweight 805 chassis. The cars bettered 105mph, and Felice Nazzaro, driving one, dominated the 1922 French Grand Prix at Strasbourg, the scene of racing's first mass start.

The 1923 Fiat 805.405, the first grand prix car to have a supercharger, was developed in a wind-tunnel.

It handed a first victory to a British car in the French Grand Prix, though, after its supercharger ingested dust. Henry Segrave won in a Sunbeam, which, ironically, had been copied off the previous year's Fiat. But after that the Fiats were in a class of their own, driven by Pietro Bordino and Nazzaro.

Alfa Romeo, keen not to lose out to its rivals, designed for 1923 the P1, which was superseded in 1924 by the P2, a seminal grand prix car. It easily won the newly organized World Championship for Manufacturers in 1925, and was unbeaten until Antonio Ascari's all-out style caused him to clip the fencing at the French Grand Prix at Montlhery. The car rolled and Ascari was killed.

The Golden Age ended as abruptly as it had begun. Alfa pulled out, declaring that racing was too expensive, and in 1926 the world was heading towards one of its biggest economic slumps.

The Great Depression was to have a devastating effect on many aspects of European political, economic and social life, not least on motor racing.

1929

>> First Monaco Grand Prix is won by British driver "Williams" in a Bugatti

>> Like Monza, Monaco's current circuit layout is scarcely different from the original 1.9-mile circuit

>> "Williams" wins the French GP at Le Mans

>> Chiron wins Spanish GP and also German (sports car) GP, also for Bugatti

>> Achille Varzi gives Alfa Romeo its first win since 1925 when he triumphs at the Italian Grand Prix

1930

>> Czechoslovakia is the latest country to host a grand prix, doing so at Brno, a tricky 18-mile-long track

1931

>> Three grands prix are run for ten-hour durations with two drivers sharing each car. The rules are soon changed to make races shorter again

1933

>> Italy's most popular driver, Giuseppe Campari, is killed in the Monza Grand Prix on what was billed as his final race before retiring to be an opera singer. He crashed on a patch of oil on the banked South Curve, with Baconin Borzacchini also killed in the same accident

1934

>> Cars are limited to a maximum weight of 750kg and so starts an era that runs through to 1951, aka "the early moderns"

>> Auto Union runs its cars with their engines mounted behind the driver

>> First Swiss Grand Prix, at 4.5-mile Bremgarten, is won by Hans Stuck for Auto Union

>> Algerian driver Guy Moll scores a shock win at Monaco, driving for Alfa Romeo

Depression and Fascism, War and Peace

As the Great Depression took effect, the sport's governing body tried to impose a formula for 1.5-litre cars. Following the death of Ascari and those American heroes Resta, Jimmy Murphy and Joe Boyer, safety concerns assumed paramount importance. In the United States the American Automobile Club introduced a stock car formula for Indianapolis (dubbed the "Junk Formula" by purists) in an attempt to attract manufacturers back. By 1930, with the Depression lifting, it was beginning to work.

In Europe there was a similar situation, with most promoters accepting come-as-you-are entries in an attempt to fill grids. Far from causing a period of stagnation in racing, the years of the Depression were a breeding ground for some of the greatest drivers ever, as well as for one of the most fabulous cars. The Formula Libre races provided the ideal training opportunities for professional, independent drivers racing quasi-works cars.

This was the era of Achille Varzi, Louis Chiron, Rudolf Caracciola and, the greatest of the time, Tazio Nuvolari. These drivers plied their trade on classics like the daunting Targa Florio road race in Sicily and the Mille Miglia (literally "1,000 miles") which was an epic journey on public roads through the mountains from Brescia to Rome and back.

The 1930 Mille Miglia saw Nuvolari and Varzi pitched against each other in the same Alfa-Romeo team. At dawn on the second day Varzi, three minutes ahead of Nuvolari on the road, but behind on aggregate time, saw the pattern of Nuvolari's headlights on the road behind him. The race, he thought, was lost. But then the lights disappeared, and Varzi allowed himself to dream that Nuvolari had dropped out. He was startled, less than 30 miles from the finish, by a flash of lights and the blast of a horn. Nuvolari had been behind him, lights off, as they plunged through the mountain passes...

Nuvolari enjoyed heroic status in Italy. His driving was all flair and verve, which reflected his personality. Varzi, by contrast, was ice-cool of nerve, and smooth and clinical in the car. Enzo Ferrari said of the early 1930s: "The outstanding man was Nuvolari, but he found a worthy adversary in Varzi, who surpassed him in his cool, perfect style." These greats raced for manufacturers from their native countries. Nuvolari for Alfa,

Journey to the Pole: Fagioli's Alfa P3B is pushed to the starting grid for the 1933 Italian GP, a race it would go on to win from Tazio Nuvolari's Maserati

1935

>> Auto Union enters the transfer market and signs Italian ace Achille Varzi, but he fails to win as Rudolf Caracciola dominates for Mercedes

>> Top teams start using a locking differential to harness increasing power of their engines

>> Grand prix racing returns to Britain for first time since 1927, this time to Donington Park, with Richard Shuttleworth winning in an Alfa Romeo ahead of Earl Howe's Bugatti

1936

>> Bernd Rosemeyer is the star of the season as he wins the German, Swiss and Italian Grands Prix for Auto Union

>> Mercedes, Alfa Romeo and Bugatti are also victorious, with Bugatti's win coming in the French Grand Prix that is run to sports car regulations, as it will be the following year

1937

>> German teams attend Donington Grand Prix for the first time and massive crowds turn out to watch Rosemeyer win for Auto Union, averaging more than 13mph faster than the winning speed in 1936

>> This is one of Auto Union's two wins all year as Mercedes dominate with four wins for Caracciola and one for Manfred von Brauchitsch

1938

>> Cars with 3.0-litre supercharged or 4.5-litre normally aspirated engines are allowed, with minimum weight varying between 400 and 850kg according to engine capacity

>> Dick Seaman (right) wins German GP for Mercedes, becoming the first British driver to win a grand prix

>> Auto Union's Nuvolari is the only driver to win more than once - at Monza and Donington Park

1939

>> Mercedes makes it three European championship titles in succession

>> Racing is interrupted by the outbreak of the Second World War

>> The Yugoslavian Grand Prix at Kalemagdan Park in Belgrade the last to be held before hostilities commence

Put Out More Flags: Brooklands hosted the first British GP, with chicanes breaking the flow

Brooklands

Built as the first permanent circuit in Europe back in 1907, at a time when road racing was all the rage, it made its debut a year after the first grand prix. This was a circuit with a difference, though, as the banked venue was not a closed-off section of roads but a purpose-built facility with banked turns cut into the Surrey hillsides, enabling cars to corner at far greater speeds. The circuit, on the outskirts of Weybridge, proved an instant hit, with a combination of layouts that included different routes around the flat infield offering great flexibility so that the circuit could be tailor-made for each type of category. Brooklands hosted the first British Grand Prix, in 1926, with Robert Senechal and Louis Wagner sharing the winning Delage. Their winning average speed was 71.661mph, but Robert Benoist pushed that out to 85.586mph in his similar car the following year. Brooklands then entered its most famous period in the 1930s when cars with massive engines were raced all the way around the outer banking, with John Cobb setting a record lap speed of 143mph in his Napier Railton in 1935. Donington Park then assumed the upper hand as far as grand prix racing was concerned and Brooklands was never to rise again after being closed for the Second World War, with only a museum and some of the banking still remaining today.

Caracciola for Mercedes and Chiron for Bugatti. Only Varzi would change from car to car, searching for the best drive, although Caracciola drove Alfas when Mercedes pulled out in 1932.

For five years, from the late 1920s to the early 1930s, these drivers dominated racing. And, in 1932, Nuvolari and Caracciola battled it out in one of the greatest racing cars ever, the Alfa-Romeo P3. It handled like a dream, and in the hands of Nuvolari, Caracciola and Baconin Borzacchini it won nearly every race it contested. But, almost as soon as it had begun, the era of P3 domination was over. The Alfa board pulled out, and left its team, Scuderia Ferrari, to carry on with older Monza cars.

Technological Revolution

In January 1933 Adolf Hitler and the Nazi party were elected to power. The new German chancellor was a fast-car enthusiast, and wanted to use racing as a platform for Nazi propaganda. A new formula was announced, with a minimum weight of 750kg, and the German government's subsidy was split between Mercedes and Auto Union. The German public relations drive was to lead to a rapid evolution in the technology, power, speed and spectacle of racing.

It also led to a time of complete domination by the German teams, whose first cars, the Mercedes W25 and Auto Union Type A, were in a class of their own when they appeared at Avus in Berlin in mid-1934. Mechanical teething troubles caused them some problems, although Hans Stuck won

at the Nurburgring for Auto Union, and Manfred von Brauchitsch at the Eifelrennen for Mercedes.

No one recognized the challenge more than Nuvolari who, since Mercedes had a full team (Caracciola, Luigi Fagioli and von Brauchitsch), asked Auto Union for a drive. Astonishingly, it turned him down. It had signed up Varzi who, despite his great respect for his rival - probably because of it - had always said that he would never drive in the same team as Nuvolari. Since Stuck, too, was not very keen to have the greatest driver of the era signed up, Nuvolari had to return to Ferrari and Alfa. But he was to exact revenge at the race which mattered most to the Germans.

The Italian Job in Germany

The year was a Mercedes benefit, with Auto Union picking up some of the pieces along the way, and Caracciola won all the important races to take the first European Drivers' Championship. All except one, that is - at the classic and daunting Nurburgring in Germany, when 300,000 spectators witnessed a German victory. At the end of the first lap, though, Nuvolari's P3 was behind the leader Caracciola. By lap nine he had fallen behind new Auto Union recruit Bernd Rosemeyer, Fagioli and Chiron's Alfa as well, and had to stop for tyres.

There now began one of the greatest drives ever seen. From a seemingly impossible position, the little Italian clawed his way to second place, battling for four hours on the tortuous mountain circuit, with only his natural

The Man Who Knew No Fear: Bernd Rosemeyer takes the chequered flag, having won the Donington Grand Prix in his rear-engined Auto Union in 1937

ability, aided by a fine drizzle, keeping him in touch. Nuvolari made up 45 seconds on the final lap, before a tyre blew on leader von Brauchitsch's Mercedes, handing Nuvolari a victory for genius over technology in front of a silent German crowd.

The following year it was Auto Union's turn to dominate, with the European Championship surrendering to Rosemeyer, a former motorcycle ace, in a revised, better-handling car, the Type B. Rosemeyer was the personification of Hitler's Aryan dream – blond, good-looking and heroic. "Bernd literally did not know fear," said Caracciola, "and sometimes that's not good. We actually feared for him in every race. Somehow I never thought a long life was on the cards for him."

Sadly, Caracciola was right. Rosemeyer was killed in a speed record attempt in 1938 and was replaced by Nuvolari. Caracciola won his third European title in four years.

Although Rosemeyer was a dream for Hitler, he also was a reminder that, while the drivers of these teams were picked for propaganda purposes, they did not always fulfil them as readily as might have been hoped. In the 1937 German Grand Prix Rosemeyer had again been the star, finishing third, less than a minute behind winner Caracciola, despite losing more than three minutes in the pits over repairs and then a further minute in another off-road incident. On the rostrum, Caracciola was presented with an effigy of the goddess of speed by Adolf Huhnlein, a Brown Shirt appointed as Hitler's man in the field. When Huhnlein momentarily had his back turned, Rosemeyer stuck his cigarette between its lips and, as the crowd laughed, Huhnlein spun around again, only to see Rosemeyer with his cigarette back in his mouth and the picture of innocence.

The Aftermath of War

The era of German domination ended with the Second World War and, although motor racing started again soon after the bomb had been dropped on Hiroshima, it took some time to re-establish itself, since there was a shortage of oil.

By 1947 racing was again under a formula and by 1948 it was back on its feet. The year was a turning point. It was to see Nuvolari's last great drive (in the Mille Miglia) when, at 56, he showed that all his skill remained – leading, and carrying on despite spitting blood from his lungs, destroyed from years of breathing noxious car fumes, until his Alfa's brakes failed at Parma.

Later in the year Varzi was killed in a wet practice session at the Swiss Grand Prix at Berne. And 1948 was also the year in which a little-known driver from Argentina, Juan Manuel Fangio, scored his first win in Europe, in the Pau Grand Prix.

A World Drivers' Championship was just around the corner, and the world of motor racing had a new sense of purpose.

1950s

1950 British Grand Prix
MARQUE OF RESPECT

Under the gaze of the royal family, the first-ever World Championship kicked off at Silverstone. Alfa Romeo dominated, with its cars filling the first four places on the grid. Giuseppe Farina won from Luigi Fagioli and Reg Parnell, with only Juan Manuel Fangio's retirement in the fourth Alfa spoiling the Italians' day.

1951 British Grand Prix
ENTER THE PRANCING HORSE

Alfa Romeo's run came to an end after nine races, with Jose Froilan Gonzalez giving Ferrari its first win. This came thanks to the chunky Argentinian taking over from Alfa's first-lap leader Felice Bonetto. Fangio also had a couple of spells in the lead, but an extra fuel stop left him second.

1954 French Grand Prix
BUILT FOR VICTORY

Alfa Romeo had dominated and then Ferrari, but both were put into the shade by the arrival of Mercedes midway through 1954, with Fangio giving the silver cars victory on their debut at Reims. Their streamlined, wheel-encasing body shapes gave them an aerodynamic advantage on the long straights.

1955 British Grand Prix
CATCHING YOUR SHADOW

Fangio seemed to be all but unbeatable, with understudy Stirling Moss faithfully finishing in his wheeltracks at Spa-Francorchamps and Zandvoort before coming to Aintree. He chased Fangio in the early laps, then took over the lead and remained in front to the finish, with Fangio acting as his shadow. Was it a gift? No one knows.

1957 German Grand Prix (left)
FOLLOW THAT CAR

If you like a chase, then this was the race for you, as Mike Hawthorn and Peter Collins seemed to have it under control for Ferrari after Fangio had made a lengthy fuel stop. But the Argentinian treated every lap like a qualifying lap, hauling both of the Ferrari drivers in and passing them with just over a lap to go, making up 45 seconds.

1958 Argentinian Grand Prix
PACKING IT ALL IN THE BACK

British designers threatened to transform Formula One in the late 1950s when they pitted their rear-engined cars against the established front-engined cars. And the little cars struck gold in Buenos Aires, with Stirling Moss piloting Rob Walker's privately entered Cooper to victory ahead of Luigi Musso's Ferrari.

1950

The World Championship was held for the first time in 1950, linking the established grands prix of just six countries. Alfa Romeo and its drivers Farina, Fangio and Fagioli dominated, but Ferrari was waiting to pounce.

Leader of the Pack: Giuseppe Farina (second from left) at the start of the British GP, Silverstone, 1950

In the years after the end of the Second World War it did not take long for motor racing to re-establish itself, and by 1950 the governing body had decided the time was right to launch a World Championship. There was plenty of pre-war equipment available and also no shortage of drivers who had raced in the 1930s. True, they had lost some of the best years of their careers but, despite the enforced break, were at the top of their game.

Alfa Romeo's superb squad comprised the legendary "three Fs": Dr Giuseppe "Nino" Farina, Juan Manuel Fangio and Luigi Fagioli. Equipped with an update of the pre-war Tipo 158, they steamrollered the opposition, led by Ferrari.

Ferrari had been disappointing in 1949 and the team was absent from the very first race of the new series, held at a bleak Silverstone on 13 May in the presence of the royal family. There were 21 cars in the field for this first race, and Farina had the honour of taking the first pole position. Old stager Fagioli led initially, but dropped to third behind Farina and Fangio. When the latter's engine failed, Fagioli took second, ahead of local star Reg Parnell.

A week later at Monaco Farina's luck changed when he triggered a nine-car pile-up, which also took out Fagioli. Fangio was ahead of the carnage, and somehow survived when he came across it on the next lap. He went on to score a memorable win. Ferrari entered the championship for the first time, and 31-year-old Alberto Ascari was rewarded with second place, one lap down. Farina and Fagioli scored a one-two in the Swiss Grand Prix at the tricky Bremgarten road circuit, and once again Fangio suffered an engine failure – as did all three works Ferraris. At Spa, Fangio fought back with his second win of the year, ahead of Fagioli. Variety was provided by Raymond Sommer, who led in his Talbot before blowing up.

The first championship, like so many to follow, came to a head in the final round at Monza. Fangio had 26 points to the 24 of the consistent Fagioli, and the 22 of Farina. Fangio and Farina had the new and more powerful 159 model, but the title was settled when Fangio retired with a seized gearbox. Farina won the race, and with it the championship. Ferrari had been working hard on a new unsupercharged engine during the season, showing well in non-championship races, and Ascari was on the pace with the latest model. When his car retired, he took over the machine of team-mate Dorino Serafini and finished second, ahead of Fagioli. The most talked-about car never appeared at a grand prix race. The much-vaunted BRM V16 made an ignominious debut in the International Trophy at Silverstone in August, retiring on the line with driveshaft failure.

LANDMARK CAR
Alfa Romeo 158

Designer: **Gioacchino Colombo**   Years raced: **1950**
Grand prix wins: **6**   Pole positions: **6**   Fastest laps: **6**
Engine type: **Alfa Romeo supercharged straight 8**
Engine size/power: **1479cc/350bhp at 9,000rpm**
Such was the ability of this Gioacchino Colombo-penned car that it filled all four places on the front row of the grid for the opening round of the first World Championship at Silverstone in 1950, before going on to claim all three positions on the podium. On top of that, the 158 was designed before the Second World War, won the first grand prix after the war, at Bremgarten in 1947, and was still the cream of the crop three years later. Changes for its successor, the 159, were few and far between, and this car was also an immediate winner in Juan Manuel Fangio's hands in 1951, with the power from its supercharged engine being boosted to 425bhp. Both the 158 and 159 were known as "Alfettas".

DRIVERS' WORLD CHAMPIONSHIP 1950

	Driver (NATIONALITY)	Make	Pts
1	**Giuseppe Farina** (ITA)	Alfa Romeo	30
2	**Juan Manuel Fangio** (ARG)	Alfa Romeo	27
3	**Luigi Fagioli** (ITA)	Alfa Romeo	24
4	**Louis Rosier** (FRA)	Talbot	13
5	**Alberto Ascari** (ITA)	Ferrari	11
6	**Johnnie Parsons*** (USA)	Kurtis-Offenhauser	8
7	**Bill Holland*** (USA)	Deidt-Offenhauser	6
8	**Prince Bira** (THAI)	Maserati	5
9	**Reg Parnell** (GB)	Alfa Romeo	4
	Louis Chiron (MON)	Maserati	4
	Peter Whitehead (GB)	Ferrari	4
	Mauri Rose* (USA)	Deidt-Offenhauser	4

Best four scores from seven races to count   *denotes points scored in Indy 500

1951

Alfa Romeo continued to set the pace, but Ferrari came close to toppling the champions. Mechanical problems had robbed him the previous year, but now Juan Manuel Fangio was dominant and claimed his first title.

For 1951 Alfa Romeo broke up the "three Fs" team, replacing Fagioli with 48-year-old Felice Bonetto. Froilan Gonzalez, who had previously driven a Maserati, joined Ascari and Luigi Villoresi at Ferrari. The stocky young Argentinian, known as the "Pampas Bull", was to become a major force during the season.

The championship was expanded to seven races, with Monaco missing and events in Germany and Spain added. This time the series began in Switzerland, and in soaking conditions Fangio scored a fine win.

Meanwhile, a promising young Englishman made his debut in a British HWM, qualifying 14th and finishing eighth. His name was Stirling Moss.

Farina and Fangio dominated the Belgian Grand Prix at Spa, but when Fangio pitted, a rear wheel stuck on and his race was ruined. Farina won from the Ferraris of Ascari and Villoresi, while a fired-up Fangio set the fastest lap – but finished ninth.

Fagioli was back in an Alfa at Reims, and went on to score his first victory – but only after Fangio took over his car when his own mount had retired in a race of high attrition. Another shared car, the Ferrari of Gonzalez and Ascari, took second, ahead of Villoresi. After tyre troubles, Farina was a distant fifth.

A Ferrari win seemed on the cards, and the first finally came at Silverstone where Gonzalez put in a fine performance to take the lead from countryman Fangio when the Alfa driver pitted and stalled when he tried to rejoin. The BRM made its first championship appearance, with Reg Parnell taking a promising fifth and Peter Walker seventh.

Ferrari proved the dominant force at the Nurburgring, the first champ-ionship race held on the long, tortuous circuit. Ascari notched up his first win, despite a late stop for rear tyres. Fangio, who required an extra scheduled fuel stop, took second for Alfa. Third to sixth places were filled with Ferraris, while Farina retired with gearbox trouble.

Monza was the penultimate round, and Ascari and Gonzalez celebrated a fine one-two for Ferrari. Alfa had a much-modified car, the 159M, and Fangio was battling for the lead until a tyre failed. His storming recovery drive ended with engine failure. Farina retired early, but took over Bonetto's car and eventually earned third place.

The final race at Pedrables in Spain proved to be Alfa's swansong. Despite his Monza retirement, Fangio led Ascari by 28 points to 25 going into the race, and a dominant win secured Juan Manuel's first crown. The Ferraris suffered tyre troubles, with Gonzalez and pole man Ascari taking second and fourth, split by Farina's Alfa. At the end of the year Alfa withdrew from grand prix racing, unable to finance a new car to challenge Ferrari in 1952. Partly in response to Alfa's Romeo's departure, the Fédération Internationale de l'Automobile announced that, for 1952, the World Championship would run to less powerful Formula Two rules. It was hoped this would encourage a wider variety of cars and avoid a Ferrari walkover.

The Champ: Fangio acknowledges the applause as he wins the Spanish GP to clinch his first world title

GREAT RACE
Indianapolis 500

Between 1950 and 1960, the Indianapolis 500 was a round of the Formula One World Championship. This seemed to make sense as it was America's biggest race, attended by 400,000 spectators. In actual fact it made no sense whatsoever, as it was not a race attended by the Formula One teams, merely one contested by the American oval racers in their vastly different cars. Some grand prix drivers including, notably, Andre Boillot and Louis Chiron, had had a crack in the 1920s, but the only cross-pollination in this period came in 1952 when Alberto Ascari qualified his Ferrari mid-grid, and then at the first United States Grand Prix, in 1959, when that year's Indy 500 winner Rodger Ward entered a short oval racer at Sebring and was roundly beaten.

DRIVERS' WORLD CHAMPIONSHIP 1951

	Driver (NATIONALITY)	Make	Pts
1	**Juan Manuel Fangio** (ARG)	Alfa Romeo	31
2	**Alberto Ascari** (ITA)	Ferrari	25
3	**Froilan Gonzalez** (ARG)	Ferrari	24
4	**Giuseppe Farina** (ITA)	Alfa Romeo	19
5	**Luigi Villoresi** (ITA)	Ferrari	15
6	**Piero Taruffi** (ITA)	Ferrari	10
7	**Lee Wallard*** (USA)	Kurtis-Offenhauser	8
8	**Felice Bonetto** (ITA)	Alfa Romeo	7
9	**Mike Nazaruk*** (USA)	Kurtis-Offenhauser	6
10	**Reg Parnell** (GB)	Ferrari/BRM	5

Best four scores from eight races to count   *denotes points scored in Indy 500

1952

Ferrari responded to the Formula Two rule changes by dominating the season. Alberto Ascari won every race he entered and became world champion. An injured Fangio could only watch these events from the sidelines.

Double Delight for Ferrari: Alberto Ascari (centre) and Piero Taruffi celebrate at Silverstone

Despite the change of regulations, Ferrari entered 1952 as the major force. The marque had already been highly successful in Formula Two, and had a first-class driver squad. Ascari, Villoresi and Piero Taruffi were joined by Farina – on the market after Alfa's withdrawal. The main opposition should have come from reigning champion Fangio, who had switched from Alfa Romeo to Maserati to drive the new A6GCM. However, he was forced to miss the entire season after breaking his neck in a crash during a non-championship race at Monza.

The rule change achieved its aim of attracting a variety of cars to take on the red machines. From France came the Gordinis of Jean Behra and Robert Manzon, while in Britain there was a host of projects under way, including the Cooper-Bristol, Connaught, Alta, Frazer Nash and ERA. The most successful of these would prove to be the Cooper-Bristol, an underpowered but superb-handling machine. Its brilliant young driver was the flamboyant Englishman, Mike Hawthorn, who was the find of the year.

The championship began with the Swiss Grand Prix, notable for the absence of Ascari, who was busy with Ferrari commitments at Indianapolis. Taruffi scored an easy win, well ahead of local Ferrari privateer Rudi Fischer. The Gordini showed promise, with Behra taking third. That place was held by Moss in the HWM, but his car was withdrawn after two of its sister entries suffered hub failures.

Ascari returned at Spa, and scored his first win of the new Formula Two era in soaking conditions, ahead of team-mate Farina. Manzon gave Gordini another third, but all eyes were on Hawthorn, making his championship debut. He ran third and, after a fuel leak delayed him, finished a fine fourth. It was the highest place to date for a British car, and the first sign of great things to come from John Cooper's small company.

Behra's Gordini beat the Ferraris at Reims but, sadly in this particular year, it was a non-championship race.

The French Grand Prix moved to Rouen a week later, and Ascari, Farina and Taruffi finished one-two-three, with Manzon fourth. At Silverstone Ascari and Taruffi were one-two, but Hawthorn was the darling of the crowd, finishing third. Dennis Poore also impressed with his Connaught, leading Hawthorn until a long fuel stop, before coming fourth.

The German Grand Prix at the Nurburgring was a complete Ferrari whitewash, with Ascari heading Farina, Fischer and Taruffi. Ascari had to work hard for his win: a late pit stop for oil dropped him to second and forced him to catch and repass Farina. The new Dutch event at Zandvoort saw Ascari heading home Farina and Villoresi, with Hawthorn again leading the challenge in a gallant fourth with his Cooper-Bristol.

Ascari had clinched the title before the finale at Monza, where he scored his sixth win from six starts.

LANDMARK CAR
Ferrari 500

Designer: Aurelio Lampredi   Years raced: **1952-53**
Grand prix wins: **14**   Pole positions: **13**   Fastest laps: **13**
Engine type: **Ferrari 4 cylinder**
Engine size/power: **1985cc/180bhp at 7,800rpm**
With the rules changing dramatically for 1952, Ferrari wanted a car to run a 2-litre engine rather than the V12s that went before it, so this was it, with constant development boosting its initial power output of 165bhp to 180bhp in 1953. The 500 was one of the most successful Formula One cars ever as it won every World Championship race - bar one - in which it appeared over two seasons, with Piero Taruffi setting the ball rolling in Switzerland in 1952. But then Alberto Ascari took over to claim both drivers' titles. Mike Hawthorn and Giuseppe Farina also won one apiece in 500s. The 500 was later reworked as the 625.

DRIVERS' WORLD CHAMPIONSHIP 1952

	Driver (NATIONALITY)	Make	Pts
1	**Alberto Ascari** (ITA)	Ferrari	**36**
2	**Giuseppe Farina** (ITA)	Ferrari	**24**
3	**Piero Taruffi** (ITA)	Ferrari	**22**
4	**Rudi Fischer** (SWI)	Ferrari	**10**
	Mike Hawthorn (GB)	Cooper-Bristol	**10**
6	**Robert Manzon** (FRA)	Gordini	**9**
7	**Troy Ruttman*** (USA)	Kuzma-Offenhauser	**8**
	Luigi Villoresi (ITA)	Ferrari	**8**
9	**Froilan Gonzalez** (ARG)	Maserati	**6.5**
10	**Jim Rathmann*** (USA)	Kurtis-Offenhauser	**6**
	Jean Behra (FRA)	Gordini	**6**

Best four scores from eight races to count   *denotes points scored in Indy 500

1953

Alberto Ascari claimed his second crown as Ferrari were again supreme in the second and final year of the Formula Two category. However, Fangio raced strongly for Maserati, signalling the start of four years of domination by the maestro.

Fangio was fit and back at the start of 1953, and heading a Maserati outfit which looked as if it might upset the Ferrari bandwagon.

Joining him in a strong Argentinian line-up were Gonzalez and Onofre Marimon. Meanwhile, Hawthorn's performances with the Cooper had not gone unnoticed, and he had earned a seat with Ferrari, alongside Ascari, Farina and Villoresi.

With Hawthorn gone Cooper lacked a driver of substance, and Gordini provided the only real opposition to the Italian cars.

For the first time the World Championship tag was justified by a race outside Europe, with the series kicking off at Buenos Aires. Unfortunately the race was marred by undisciplined spectators, and Farina was involved in a tragic incident when he hit a boy who crossed the track. Nine people were killed in the mayhem that followed. They were the first fatalities in a championship race.

Meanwhile, Ascari and Villoresi scored a Ferrari one-two, ahead of debutant Marimon. Hawthorn had a steady race to fourth, while local hero Fangio ran second, before retiring. Maserati's new car arrived for Zandvoort.

It showed promise, but Ascari and Farina took the usual Ferrari one-two, with the best Maserati – which was shared by Bonetto and Gonzalez –

in third. Fangio broke a rear axle. At Spa the Maseratis were the cars to beat. Gonzalez and Fangio led the field until retiring. Inevitably Ascari was there to pick up the pieces, scoring his ninth consecutive win.

The French race was back at Reims, and proved to be a classic encounter which saw Hawthorn come of age. After taking two fourths and a sixth in the opening races, he emerged as a front-runner, getting the better of a sensational duel with Fangio to score his first win – and the first for any British driver.

Strangely, Hawthorn could not repeat his French form at Silverstone, where Ascari was utterly dominant. Fangio chased very hard, and finished ahead of Farina, Gonzalez and Hawthorn.

At the Nurburgring, Ascari was again the man to beat, but he lost a front wheel early on. He made it back to the pits, and later took over Villoresi's fourth-placed car.

Farina maintained Ferrari's record, winning ahead of Fangio and Hawthorn. In his new car Ascari was closing in on the British driver when the engine blew.

Ascari clinched his second title at the penultimate race in Switzerland, yet it was anything but easy. Fangio led Ascari initially until gearbox and engine troubles intervened, and then Ascari lost the lead with a plug

change. He dropped to fourth, but worked his way back to the lead, heading home Farina and Hawthorn.

Maserati had threatened to win all year, and it eventually happened in the finale at Monza – in bizarre circumstances. After a great slipstreaming battle Ascari looked all set to triumph, but on the last lap he spun and forced Farina wide. Somehow the lapped Marimon also got involved, and through the dust cloud emerged Fangio, to score his first win since 1951.

Hot Pursuit: Fangio gives chase but Ascari (10) led all the way to win the first Argentinian GP for Ferrari

DRIVERS' WORLD CHAMPIONSHIP 1953

	Driver (NATIONALITY)	Make	Pts
1	**Alberto Ascari** (ITA)	Ferrari	**34.5**
2	**Juan Manuel Fangio** (ARG)	Maserati	**27.5**
3	**Giuseppe Farina** (ITA)	Ferrari	**26**
4	**Mike Hawthorn** (GB)	Ferrari	**19**
5	**Luigi Villoresi** (ITA)	Ferrari	**17**
6	**Froilan Gonzalez** (ARG)	Maserati	**13.5**
7	**Bill Vukovich*** (USA)	Kurtis-Offenhauser	**8**
8	**Emmanuel de Graffenried** (SWI)	Maserati	**7**
9	**Felice Bonetto** (ITA)	Maserati	**6.5**
10	**Art Cross*** (USA)	Kurtis-Offenhauser	**6**

Best four scores from nine races to count   *denotes points scored in Indy 500

1954

Mercedes finally returned to racing and the "blank cheque" operation set new standards. Juan Manuel Fangio and his wonderful W196 Silver Arrow were unstoppable. However, Britain found a new star in Stirling Moss.

Winning Start: Mercedes began brilliantly at the French GP when Fangio and Kling were first and second

After two years of Formula Two it was all change for 1954, with the introduction of new 2.5-litre regulations. The big story was the decision by Mercedes-Benz to return to grand prix racing for the first time since the Second World War. The legendary Alfred Neubauer was still at the helm, and he snapped up Fangio to join Hans Herrmann and Karl Kling. The new W196 was a technical marvel, but was not ready until the third race of the year.

Also on the way was Lancia's new D50. The marque hired Ascari and Villoresi to drive it, but it was ready even later than the Mercedes. After two consecutive titles, Ascari effectively wasted the season. Fangio was luckier, for he was allowed to start the year in the new Maserati, the 250F. An attractive and effective car, it would be one of the mainstays of grand prix racing for the next few seasons. Ferrari had lost Ascari and Villoresi, but Hawthorn, Farina, Gonzalez and Frenchman Maurice Trintignant were on hand to drive the latest model.

Fangio's decision to start the year in a Maserati was a wise one, for he duly won the opening events in Argentina and Belgium. The first race was a chaotic, rain-hit affair with the track changing several times. Quick in the wet, Fangio won through ahead of the Ferraris of Farina, Gonzalez and Trintignant. Farina led the early laps in Belgium, but when he hit trouble Fangio went by, and headed home Trintignant. Moss showed he would be a force to be reckoned with by taking third.

Mercedes finally appeared at Reims with three of the magnificent W196s in streamlined, full-bodied form. The cars were perfectly suited to the fast track, and Fangio and Kling finished one-two, with Herrmann setting the fastest lap. However, Mercedes came down to earth with a bang at Silverstone, for the streamlined bodies did not like the airfield circuit. Fangio finished fourth in his battered car, while Gonzalez scored his second British Grand Prix win.

Tragedy struck at the Nurburgring when Marimon was killed in practice; he was the first driver to die at a World Championship event. Countrymen Fangio and Gonzalez were distraught but, to his credit, Fangio got on with the job and won the race, his Mercedes now using the new open-wheel body.

In Switzerland Fangio led from start to finish. Moss pursued him until retiring, and then Gonzalez took up the challenge. Monza established Moss as a star of the future. His performances had earned him a works Maserati seat, and he led until nine laps from the end when the oil tank split. He would eventually push the car over the line in 11th. Meanwhile, Fangio swept by to win in the streamlined Mercedes from Hawthorn. The Lancia team was finally ready for the last race in Spain. The car showed promise, for Ascari led for ten laps before retiring, and set the fastest lap. Hawthorn went on to score his second win, ahead of Maserati's young find, Luigi Musso. Mercedes had a bad day, and Fangio finished only third. But his second title was in the bag.

DRIVERS' WORLD CHAMPIONSHIP 1954

	Driver (NATIONALITY)	Make	Pts
1	**Juan Manuel Fangio** (ARG)	Maserati/Mercedes	42
2	**Froilan Gonzalez** (ARG)	Ferrari	25.14
3	**Mike Hawthorn** (GB)	Ferrari	24.64
4	**Maurice Trintignant** (FRA)	Ferrari	17
5	**Karl Kling** (GER)	Mercedes	12
6	**Bill Vukovich*** (USA)	Kurtis-Offenhauser	8
	Hans Herrmann (GER)	Mercedes	8
8	**Jimmy Bryan*** (USA)	Kuzma-Offenhauser	6
	Giuseppe Farina (ITA)	Ferrari	6
	Luigi Musso (ITA)	Maserati	6
	Robert Mieres (ARG)	Maserati	6

Best five scores from nine races to count   *denotes points scored in Indy 500

1955

Mercedes, Fangio and Moss dominated the season, but the appalling tragedy at Le Mans, which cost over 80 lives, overshadowed absolutely everything. Mercedes later announced that it was withdrawing from grand prix racing.

Perhaps the blackest day in motor racing history is 11 June 1955. More than 80 people were killed when Pierre Levegh's Mercedes crashed into the crowd during the early laps at Le Mans. Grand prix stars Fangio and Hawthorn were both peripherally involved in the incident, which had major repercussions for the sport. The grands prix in France, Germany, Switzerland and Spain were all cancelled. In fact, motor racing would never return to Switzerland.

The German team went into the season with morale high. Neubauer had signed up Moss to partner Fangio, and now had two top-level drivers in his Silver Arrows. Maserati signed up Jean Behra to replace Moss, while Mike Hawthorn left Ferrari to drive the patriotic Vanwall. The season opener

in Argentina was run in sweltering conditions which saw Fangio score a comfortable victory. He was one of only two drivers able to go the full distance solo, as each of the three pursuing cars were shared by three drivers apiece as the energy-sapping heat took its toll.

At Monaco Ascari was in the headlines, after flipping his car into the harbour. He escaped with minor injuries. At the time he was leading, for Fangio and Moss had both retired their Mercedes. Trintignant proved a popular and surprise winner, ahead of the Lancia of Eugenio Castellotti.

Four days later Ascari was killed in a bizarre accident at Monza, while testing a Ferrari sports car. Lancia announced its withdrawal from the sport, regrettably before the D50 had been able to fulfil its initial promise.

Mercedes bounced back at Spa, where Fangio and Moss ran one-two with ease. Castellotti was allowed a final fling in a Lancia – as a privateer – and ran third before retiring from racing.

The following weekend came the Le Mans tragedy and, despite the outcry, the grand prix circus reconvened at Zandvoort just a week later. Fangio and Moss scored another Mercedes one-two, chased by Musso's Maserati. By now Hawthorn had given up on the Vanwall project, and his return to Ferrari was rewarded with seventh place.

The British Grand Prix moved to Aintree for the first time, and Mercedes scored a crushing one-two-three-four. This time Moss headed home Fangio, with Kling and Taruffi following on. It was Stirling's first win, but for years

people wondered if Fangio had allowed him to take the glory at home. At the back of the grid in a little Cooper was a rookie called Jack Brabham...

With all the cancellations, only the Monza race remained to be run, this time on the banked circuit. After Moss retired, Fangio headed Taruffi in another Mercedes one-two finish, with Castellotti third in a Ferrari. Fangio's third title was already secure, with Moss a distant second. But both men would be hit hard when Mercedes announced its withdrawal.

A hugely significant result came in a non-championship race held at the end of the season, when Tony Brooks took his Connaught to victory at Syracuse on Sicily. This famous victory was the first major British win of the World Championship era.

Off to a Flyer: Fangio leads away in the British GP at Aintree, with eventual winner Moss on his shoulder

DRIVERS' WORLD CHAMPIONSHIP 1955

	Driver (NATIONALITY)	Make	Pts
1	**Juan Manuel Fangio** (ARG)	Mercedes	40
2	**Stirling Moss** (GB)	Mercedes	23
3	**Eugenio Castellotti** (ITA)	Lancia	12
4	**Maurice Trintignant** (FRA)	Ferrari	11.33
5	**Giuseppe Farina** (ITA)	Ferrari	10.33
6	**Piero Taruffi** (ITA)	Mercedes	9
7	**Bob Sweikert*** (USA)	Kurtis-Offenhauser	8
8	**Robert Mieres** (ARG)	Maserati	7
9	**Jean Behra** (FRA)	Maserati	6
	Luigi Musso (ITA)	Maserati	6

Best five scores from seven races to count   *denotes points scored in Indy 500

1956

Following the withdrawal of Mercedes, Fangio switched to Ferrari and won his fourth World Championship. But the Argentinian needed some luck – and the incredible generosity of his sensational new team-mate, Peter Collins.

Driving Force: Fangio leads from Moss and Collins, whom he overtook to secure a vital second place

The two Mercedes stars did not spend much time contemplating unemployment. Fangio joined Ferrari, where another fresh face was talented British youngster Collins, along with Musso and Castellotti. The promising Lancias had also found a new home at Ferrari. They had, in fact, been entered by the Scuderia at Monza the previous year, but had non-started owing to tyre troubles. Modified over the winter, they became Lancia-Ferraris.

Meanwhile, Moss returned to Maserati to race the still competitive 250F alongside Behra. Prospects looked good for the British teams. Hawthorn and Tony Brooks joined BRM, while Vanwall had modified cars for Trintignant and Harry Schell. Connaught hoped to build on the Syracuse success.

Fangio won the opener in Argentina, but he had to take over Musso's car after his own retired. The Maseratis struggled, although Behra took second place. Maserati hit back at Monaco, where Moss scored a fine second grand prix victory. A seemingly very off-form Fangio damaged his own car and this time took over the sister machine of Collins, which he maintained in second place.

At Spa Fangio and Moss both hit trouble, and Collins scored a famous victory in his Lancia-Ferrari. He became the third British race winner in as many seasons. Local star Paul Frère earned a fine second place, while Moss took over another car and recovered third. Collins scored his second win at Reims a month later, heading home Castellotti, Behra and

Fangio, the champion, delayed by a pit stop. Surprise of the race was Harry Schell, who flew in the Vanwall after an early delay.

Collins went into the British Grand Prix leading the championship from the consistent Behra and Fangio. His thunder was stolen by Hawthorn and Brooks, who led the field on the return of BRM. Both hit trouble early on, however. Moss and Roy Salvadori each led until retiring, which allowed Fangio to take the honours. Collins took over the car of Alfonso de Portago and was runner-up, ahead of Behra. Fangio was an easy winner at the Nurburgring.

For the first time in several seasons the title fight went down to the wire at Monza. Fangio was well placed on 30 points, but Collins and Behra were eight behind – and could take the title by

winning the race and setting the fastest lap. Schell again surprised everyone by running at the front in the Vanwall and, when he retired, Moss, Fangio and Collins were left to fight it out.

Fangio's hopes faded with steering trouble, but he was saved when Collins – who could still have won the title – stopped and handed his car over. It was a remarkable gesture, which Fangio would never forget.

Despite a scare when he ran out of fuel, Moss just held on from Collins/Fangio in an exciting finish. With BRM and Vanwall having already shown well during the year, it was Connaught's turn to earn some success as Ron Flockhart took advantage of a high attrition rate to come in third. Further British success seemed just around the corner.

LANDMARK CAR
Vanwall

Designer: **Frank Costin**   Years raced: **1956-58**
Grand prix wins: **9**   Pole positions: **7**   Fastest laps: **6**
Engine type: **Vanwall 4 cylinder**
Engine size/power: **2,490cc/285bhp at 7,600rpm**

Vanwall remains one of the worst constructors when it comes to numbering its cars. So, even though its VW range ran from 1954 to 1960, this landmark car was used by this most British of teams between 1956 and 1958, with Stirling Moss and Tony Brooks both winning races. With bodywork by Frank Costin and suspension by Colin Chapman, the Vanwalls were the slipperiest cars in the field and thus the fastest in a straight line. They won the inaugural Constructors' championship in 1958 and might have won the drivers' title with better engines.

DRIVERS' WORLD CHAMPIONSHIP 1956

	Driver (NATIONALITY)	Make	Pts
1	**Juan Manuel Fangio** (ARG)	Ferrari	30
2	**Stirling Moss** (GB)	Maserati	27
3	**Peter Collins** (GB)	Ferrari	25
4	**Jean Behra** (FRA)	Maserati	22
5	**Pat Flaherty*** (USA)	Watson-Offenhauser	8
6	**Eugenio Castellotti** (ITA)	Ferrari	7.5
7	**Sam Hanks*** (USA)	Kurtis-Offenhauser	6
	Paul Frère (BEL)	Ferrari	6
	Francesco Godia (SPA)	Maserati	6
	Jack Fairman (GB)	Connaught	6

Best five scores from eight races to count   *denotes points scored in Indy 500

1957

Fangio acquired his fifth and last title for Maserati, but Stirling Moss and Vanwall were the true stars of a year in which the all-British team took a remarkable three wins. Ferrari was struggling desperately to keep up.

There was plenty of activity during the winter, the most notable being Fangio's switch from Ferrari to Maserati. It was a coup for Maserati to entice the reigning champion back to drive its latest 250F, and it proved to be a wise choice for Juan Manuel.

Meanwhile, Moss, always keen to drive British cars wherever possible, headed to Vanwall. He had already won the previous year's International Trophy for Tony Vandervell's promising concern. Hawthorn continued to hop back and forth across the English Channel, rejoining Ferrari for a third spell after a bad time with BRM. He teamed up with his great buddy Collins, plus Musso and Castellotti.

Once again Fangio won his home race in Argentina, heading home a Maserati one-two-three-four as the Ferrari challenge fell apart. Vanwall did not enter the race, and Moss had trouble at the start in his borrowed Maserati. He set the fastest lap as he recovered to seventh. After the Argentine race the talented Castellotti lost his life in a testing crash at Modena, and he was replaced by Trintignant. Then the enigmatic Alfonso de Portago was killed in the Mille Miglia. It was a bleak period indeed for Enzo Ferrari.

Monaco saw a spectacular pile-up at the start which eliminated Moss, Collins and Hawthorn. Fangio scored an easy win, while Brooks took his Vanwall to second after extricating it from the mess. Star of the race was Jack Brabham, who got his underpowered Cooper up to third before the fuel pump failed. The plucky Australian pushed it home sixth.

The French Grand Prix returned to Rouen and Fangio stormed to victory. The next race was at Aintree and it proved to be a memorable day for Britain. After Moss retired his leading Vanwall, he took over the sixth-placed car of team-mate Brooks. The opposition wilted, and when Behra blew his engine – and Hawthorn punctured on the debris – Moss swept home to a wonderful victory.

The Nurburgring race is remembered as one of the all-time classics, as Fangio came storming back to win after a fuel stop, leaving Collins and Hawthorn in his wake. Fangio would always regard the race in Germany as his greatest ever.

Because Spa and Zandvoort had been cancelled, an extra Italian race, the tortuous Pescara Grand Prix, was added. Enzo Ferrari did not enter Hawthorn and Collins, but loaned a "private" car to Musso. He was in front at first before Moss took the lead and scored his second win of the year. Fangio finished second, and sealed his fifth and final title. The Monza finale saw a spectacular fight between Vanwall and Maserati. Moss headed Fangio home, with the promising German, Wolfgang von Trips, upholding Ferrari honour in third. It was a lame year for the Prancing Horse. Ferrari had not won a race all year, and clearly needed to resolve that situation in 1958. The job was made easier when Maserati withdrew its works team at the end of the season, owing to lack of funds.

Partners in Crime: a thirsty Stirling Moss shared victory in the British GP with team-mate Brooks

---

LANDMARK CAR
Coventry Climax
Designers: **Walter Hassan and Harry Mundy**
Years raced: **1957-61**
Grand prix wins: **18**
Pole positions: **15**
Fastest laps: **16**
Engine type: **Straight 4**
Engine size/power: **1,500-2,500cc/141-240bhp**
Look at the gilded successes of the Coventry Climax engine and few would guess that it started life as a lightweight fire pump. Such was the ingenuity in British engineering in the mid-1950s, however, that it was identified as a compact engine just right for the compact British cars that were taking the battle to the continental racers of the time. Jack Brabham drove his to the 1959 and 1960 world titles.

DRIVERS' WORLD CHAMPIONSHIP 1957

	Driver (NATIONALITY)	Make	Pts
1	**Juan Manuel Fangio** (ARG)	Maserati	**40**
2	**Stirling Moss** (GB)	Vanwall	**25**
3	**Luigi Musso** (ITA)	Ferrari	**16**
4	**Mike Hawthorn** (GB)	Ferrari	**13**
5	**Tony Brooks** (GB)	Vanwall	**11**
6	**Harry Schell** (USA)	Maserati	**10**
	Masten Gregory (USA)	Maserati	**10**
8	**Peter Collins** (GB)	Ferrari	**8**
	Sam Hanks* (USA)	Epperly-Offenhauser	**8**
10	**Jean Behra** (FRA)	Maserati	**6**
	Jim Rathmann* (USA)	Epperly-Offenhauser	**6**

Best five scores from eight races to count   *denotes points scored in Indy 500

1958

Mike Hawthorn pipped Stirling Moss to the title, but his title success was over-shadowed by the death of his team-mate and friend, Peter Collins. Mike retired from racing at season's end, only to lose his life in a road accident soon afterwards.

Just the One: Hawthorn won only once, so results like second in the British GP made him champion

The departure of Maserati was a major blow to the sport, although the cars survived in the hands of privateers. The marque's withdrawal coincided with that of Fangio. He would run just two races in 1958, before calling it a day.

Ferrari abandoned the old Lancia-based cars, and had a new model, the 246 Dino, with Hawthorn, Collins and Musso the star drivers. Moss, Brooks and Stuart Lewis-Evans stayed with Vanwall, while John Cooper mounted a serious effort with Brabham and Roy Salvadori. Rob Walker entered a private Cooper-Climax for Trintignant, and Behra and Schell headed a revived BRM effort. The season started off with a surprise in Argentina. Most of the British teams were absent, including Vanwall, so Moss was free to replace Trintignant in Walker's Cooper. He duly won the race in a canny display, although his tyres were worn out by the end.

At Monaco Trintignant was in Walker's car and, amazingly, he scored his second success in the street race. The British success continued at Zandvoort, where Vanwall swept the front row. Moss won, while the BRMs of Schell and Behra finished second and third. Ferrari had been without a win since 1956, but the waiting ended at Reims where Hawthorn scored what would be his only victory of the season. However, there was no celebrating. Team-mate Musso, who had qualified second, was killed in the race. Fangio finished fourth in his last race. At Silverstone it was the turn of Collins to win for Ferrari, with Hawthorn second. A fortnight later tragedy struck again when Collins died in the German Grand Prix. Brooks went on to score a hollow victory.

Moss had retired while leading in Germany, and he gained some revenge at the new event in Portugal, winning from pole position with Hawthorn second. In one of the closest points battles ever, Moss led all the way and set the fastest lap in the final race in Casablanca. But, with Brooks blowing up, Hawthorn eased into second, which was all he required to take the crown. It was a terrible day for both Vanwall and Stirling, made worse when Lewis-Evans crashed and later succumbed to his injuries. The only consolation for Vanwall was the inaugural constructors' title. Then, after quitting the sport, Hawthorn was killed in a road accident in January 1959. He was just 29 years old.

CONSTRUCTORS' CUP 1958

	Make	Pts
1	Vanwall	48
2	Ferrari	40
3	Cooper	31
4	BRM	18
5	Maserati	6
6	Lotus	3

GREAT RACE

Moroccan Grand Prix 1958

This was the championship decider in a season dominated by British drivers – only the Monaco GP went to a non-British driver – with Ferrari's Mike Hawthorn taking on Vanwall's Stirling Moss and Tony Brooks, who only had an outside chance as they arrived at the circuit outside Casablanca. Hawthorn started on pole, but was immediately jumped by Moss who raced clear to win. Phil Hill gave chase for Ferrari, with Brooks making up the places to be third by mid-distance, a result that would have made Moss champion. But, just after mid-distance, Brooks' engine failed allowing Hawthorn to advance. Knowing he only needed second place, even if Moss won, he was let past by team-mate Phil Hill and so became Britain's first World Champion, by a single point from Moss. Sadly, Vanwall's Stuart Lewis-Evans crashed late in the race and, although flown to England for treatment at the famous East Grinstead burns unit, he was to die of his injuries six days later.

DRIVERS' WORLD CHAMPIONSHIP 1958

	Driver (NATIONALITY)	Make	Pts
1	Mike Hawthorn (GB)	Ferrari	42
2	Stirling Moss (GB)	Cooper/Vanwall	41
3	Tony Brooks (GB)	Vanwall	24
4	Roy Salvadori (GB)	Cooper-Climax	15
5	Harry Schell (USA)	BRM	14
	Peter Collins (GB)	Ferrari	14
7	Luigi Musso (ITA)	Ferrari	12
	Maurice Trintignant (FRA)	Cooper-Climax	12
9	Stuart Lewis-Evans (GB)	Vanwall	11
10	Phil Hill (USA)	Ferrari	9
	Wolfgang von Trips (GER)	Ferrari	9
	Jean Behra (FRA)	BRM	9

Best six scores from 11 races to count

1959

The old order changed for ever when Jack Brabham took his Cooper-Climax to the 1959 championship. It was the first title for a rear-engined car, marking a triumph of handling over power. The revolution started here.

The big news of the winter was the surprise withdrawal of the Vanwall team, just as it had reached full competitiveness. But Cooper, BRM and Lotus upheld British honour. After the previous year's tragedies there were big changes at Ferrari. Brooks joined from Vanwall and Behra from BRM, while Phil Hill – an occasional Ferrari driver in 1958 – went full time. Moss kept his options open, and would appear in both Walker's Cooper-Climax, and a BRM in the colours of the British Racing Partnership.

With Argentina cancelled, the series opened at Monaco. Behra's Ferrari led until retiring, and then Moss's nimble Cooper expired, leaving Brabham to score his first win in the works Cooper. Zandvoort saw a major surprise, as Jo Bonnier notched up BRM's first victory, nine years after the marque made its first, stumbling steps. Ferrari fought back with a fine win for Brooks at Reims, team-mate Hill following him home. Moss was in the BRP BRM on this occasion, and was battling for second when he went off the road. Three marques had won the first three races, but Cooper was back in the frame at Aintree as Brabham scored his second win, ahead of Moss's BRM. Stirling just held off young Kiwi Bruce McLaren – the second works Cooper driver was starting to make a name for himself. Ferrari did not turn up, blaming Italian industrial action.

For the first and only time the German Grand Prix was held on the daunting, banked Avus circuit in Berlin and, uniquely, the result was an aggregate of two 30-lap heats. Missing Aintree had obviously done Ferrari some good, for Brooks dominated the event. But, as at Reims the year before, Ferrari's celebration was muted by tragedy. Veteran Behra, who had been a mainstay of the championship since its inception, died after a crash in the sports car support race.

Moss had to wait until the Portuguese race to pick up his first win of the year in Walker's Cooper. Brabham crashed out, but still led the championship as the circus moved to the penultimate race at Monza. Moss won again, ahead of Hill, while third place for Brabham kept his title challenge alive. It was a full three months before the final race, the first ever US Grand Prix, and the only one to be held on the Sebring airfield track in Florida, home of the famous 12 hours sports car race. Moss could still lift the crown and, after taking pole, he was leading comfortably when his gearbox failed.

Brabham ran out of fuel and had to push his car home in fourth place, but the title was his. A surprise win went to his team-mate McLaren, who at 22 became the youngest grand prix winner – a record which still stands. Trintignant was second in another Cooper, ahead of Brooks.

CONSTRUCTORS' CUP 1959

	Make	Pts
1	Cooper	40
2	Ferrari	32
3	BRM	18
4	Lotus	5

Tough Luck: Brabham was heading for victory in the final round at Sebring, but ran out of fuel

DRIVERS' WORLD CHAMPIONSHIP 1959

	Driver (NATIONALITY)	Make	Pts
1	**Jack Brabham** (AUS)	Cooper-Climax	31
2	**Tony Brooks** (GB)	Ferrari	27
3	**Stirling Moss** (GB)	BRM/Cooper-Climax	25.5
4	**Phil Hill** (USA)	Ferrari	20
5	**Maurice Trintignant** (FRA)	Cooper-Climax	19
6	**Bruce McLaren** (NZ)	Cooper-Climax	16.5
7	**Dan Gurney** (USA)	Ferrari	13
8	**Jo Bonnier** (SWE)	BRM	10
	Masten Gregory (USA)	Cooper-Climax	10
10	**Rodger Ward*** (USA)	Watson-Offenhauser	8

Best five scores from nine races to count   *denotes points scored in Indy 500

1960s

1961 Italian Grand Prix
TRAGEDY AT MONZA

This was the race where the German aristocrat, Wolfgang von Trips, hoped to wrap up the World Championship, but it all went wrong on the opening lap when he clashed with Jim Clark's Lotus and his Ferrari speared off into the crowd, killing both him and 12 spectators. Team-mate Phil Hill duly won both the race and the title.

1963 Italian Grand Prix
THE DETERMINED SCOT

Jim Clark was already the brightest star in Formula One's firmament when he arrived at Monza, but a victory here would make him champion with three grands prix still to run. In a slipstreaming special, the lead changed hands 21 times, with Clark pushing his Lotus in front six times before he finally made it stick.

1966 French Grand Prix
MASTER OF DIY

Winning a grand prix is a feat in anyone's books, but doing it in a car designed and built by your company and bearing your name is something else. To date, only Jack Brabham and Bruce McLaren have achieved this. Jack did so first, at Reims in 1966, after Lorenzo Bandini's Ferrari failed; what's more, Brabham went on to win the title, too.

1967 Dutch Grand Prix (left)
BRITISH GRUNT

This was the moment that made Formula One what it is today. The success, on its debut, of the Ford Cosworth DFV engine at Zandvoort (thanks to Jim Clark and Lotus) paved the way for the development of an engine that would enable the British specialist teams that rival Ferrari today to come into existence.

1968 British Grand Prix
SHAPING UP

One minute Formula One cars looked like cigar tubes, the next they appeared entirely different. This is what happened in the summer of 1968. The first aerodynamic fins had appeared a month before. However, these nose tabs and low rear wings were replaced by aerofoils mounted high on supports over the rear suspension.

1969 Spanish Grand Prix
WINNING COMBINATION

The alliance of Jackie Stewart, a Ford DFV and the Ken Tyrrell-run Matra team was always going to be hard to beat and so it proved as they swept to the 1969 title. This, his second win of the year, wasn't his finest, as perennial bad luck denied Chris Amon the glory at Montjuich Park, but it put him clear of the rest of the pack.

1960

Jack Brabham scored his second consecutive title win for Cooper, with Lotus emerging as a major force. But for a mid-season accident putting him out for several races, Stirling Moss might have won that elusive title.

By 1960 the rear-engined machines were completely dominant. For the time being Ferrari stuck with its old car and won at Monza – but only because the British teams boycotted the event.

Colin Chapman's Lotus team had been in grand prix racing for two years with very little success, but all that was to change with the new 18, the first rear-engined model.

BRM also had a new rear-engined car, which had debuted at Monza the previous year. Bonnier stayed on, joined by Graham Hill from Lotus and American Dan Gurney from Ferrari. Phil Hill and von Trips stayed with the Italian team, while Brabham and McLaren maintained their successful partnership at Cooper.

McLaren won the opening race in Argentina and Cliff Allison did well to get his Ferrari home second. Bonnier and Moss (still in Walker's old Cooper) had both led before retiring. Allison was seriously injured in practice at Monaco.

Meanwhile, Moss got his hands on the new Lotus, and won in fine style in the rain, ahead of McLaren and Phil Hill. Once again, Bonnier's BRM led before retiring, while a notable newcomer was motorbike star John Surtees in a works Lotus.

Brabham had failed to score in either race, but bounced back by winning at Zandvoort. Innes Ireland took his Lotus to second, ahead of Graham Hill. For the second consecutive race Chapman gave a first chance to a future world champion.

At Monaco it was Surtees and in Holland it was a young Scot called Jim Clark. He was battling for fourth when the gearbox broke, ruling him out of the race.

Spa was one of the blackest weekends ever in grand prix history. During practice Moss crashed heavily, breaking his legs. Then two young Britons, Chris Bristow and Alan Stacey, were killed in separate accidents. Brabham and McLaren went on to score a Cooper one-two, but only after Graham Hill's BRM blew up while running second.

At Reims Brabham took a third consecutive win, and on this fast track the front-engined Ferraris of Phil Hill and von Trips gave him a hard time until they broke.

Graham Hill was the star at Silverstone. He stalled on the line, and drove superbly through to the lead before spinning off. Brabham came through to score his fourth straight win, followed by the very impressive Surtees and Ireland.

Brabham scored a fifth win in Portugal and with it clinched the title with two races still to run in the championship. After missing two races Moss was back, and ran second before he had problems.

Monza was a disappointment. The race was on the banked track once again, and the British teams boycotted it on safety grounds. Ferrari turned up in force, and Phil Hill scored a hollow victory. The US Grand Prix moved from Sebring to Riverside, and Moss won. The race marked the demise of the 2.5-litre formula which had seen the transfer of power from Mercedes to the British rear-engined machines.

CONSTRUCTORS' CUP 1960

	Make	Pts
1	**Cooper-Climax**	48
2	**Lotus**	34
3	**Ferrari**	26
4	**BRM**	8
5	**Cooper-Castellotti**	3
	Cooper-Maserati	3

The Riviera Touch: Jo Bonnier keeps his BRM ahead of Jack Brabham and Stirling Moss at Monaco

DRIVERS' WORLD CHAMPIONSHIP 1960

	Driver (NATIONALITY)	Make	Pts
1	**Jack Brabham** (AUS)	Cooper-Climax	43
2	**Bruce McLaren** (NZ)	Cooper-Climax	34
3	**Stirling Moss** (GB)	Cooper/Lotus-Climax	19
4	**Innes Ireland** (GB)	Lotus-Climax	18
5	**Phil Hill** (USA)	Ferrari	16
6	**Wolfgang von Trips** (GER)	Ferrari	10
	Olivier Gendebien (BEL)	Cooper-Climax	10
8	**Richie Ginther** (USA)	Ferrari	8
	Jim Clark (GB)	Lotus-Climax	8
	Jim Rathmann* (USA)	Watson-Offenhauser	8

Best six scores from ten races to count   *denotes points scored in Indy 500

1961

Ferrari was better prepared than anybody else for the new formula, and dominated the season. Phil Hill took the title, but in the most tragic circumstances after his team-mate, Wolfgang von Trips, lost his life at Monza.

Horse Power: Ferraris to the fore once more as Phil Hill, von Trips and Ginther power clear at Reims

It was all change for 1961 with the introduction of a 1.5-litre formula. The British manufacturers had been slow to respond, but not so Ferrari. Effectively sacrificing the previous season, the Italian team developed a rear-engined car, dubbed the "sharknose" – and a new V6 engine. Climax and BRM lagged behind; the only engine available for the British teams was the four-year-old 1475cc Climax F2.

Von Trips, Phil Hill and American Richie Ginther were lucky to have works Ferrari seats. Welcome variety was provided by Porsche. Already successful in Formula Two, the German marque signed Gurney and Bonnier from BRM. Lotus had an excellent new chassis, the 21, and the promising Jim Clark and Ireland to drive it. Graham Hill and Brooks led the BRM

attack, while once again Brabham and McLaren teamed up at Cooper.

More than ever before, Moss had underdog status. Walker was not allowed to buy a new Lotus 21, and had to make do with the old 18 model. And yet in Monaco Moss turned in one of the drives of his career, to brilliantly beat the Ferraris of Ginther and Phil Hill.

Ferrari took its revenge when von Trips scored his first win at Zandvoort, with Phil Hill in second. The result was reversed at Spa, where Ferrari finished one-two-three-four and Phil Hill took his first win against a representative field, following that boycotted Monza race the previous year. Reims was a sensational race. Phil Hill, Ginther and von Trips retired, and Giancarlo Baghetti – making his first start in a private Ferrari – just

pipped Gurney's Porsche to the line. Baghetti remains the only driver to have won on his grand prix debut.

It was back to normal at Aintree as von Trips, Phil Hill and Ginther finished one-two-three in the rain. Moss had tried to mix it with the Italian cars before his brakes failed, but then struck back at the Nurburgring.

Nobody objected to the banks at Monza this time. Ironically the race, which should have seen the title fight between von Trips and Phil Hill reach a crucial stage, turned to tragedy. Clark and von Trips tangled early on, and the German star was killed, along with 12 spectators. Phil Hill won the race, and with it the title.

The US Grand Prix moved to a third new venue in as many years in the form of Watkins Glen. With Ferrari not

entering, Moss and Brabham battled for the lead. When they both retired, Ireland came through to score his first (and only) win, and the first for the works Lotus team. Gurney was again second, ahead of the BRM of Brooks. At the end of the year Brooks announced his retirement, after a distinguished career which was often overshadowed by the exploits of Moss and Hawthorn.

CONSTRUCTORS' CUP 1961

	Make	Pts
1	**Ferrari**	40
2	**Lotus**	32
3	**Porsche**	22
4	**Cooper**	14
5	**BRM**	7

LANDMARK CAR
Ferrari Dino 156

Designer: **Mauro Forghieri**   Years raced: **1961-64**
Grand prix wins: **7**   Pole positions: **7**   Fastest laps: **8**
Engine type: **Ferrari V6**
Engine size/power: **1480cc/190bhp at 9,500rpm**
One of the most evocative racing Ferraris of all time, the 156 was a classic case of a team being prepared for a change in the rules and hitting the ground running. The change was to engine size, again, with the adoption of a 1.5-litre formula and Ferrari had finally followed the British lead by fitting its engine in the tail. Better known as the "Sharknose", the 156 was beaten in its first race, but then Wolfgang von Trips and Phil Hill started to win at will. Although von Trips was killed at Monza – with Hill taking the title – the 156 raced on, but never won a race again.

DRIVERS' WORLD CHAMPIONSHIP 1961

	Driver (NATIONALITY)	Make	Pts
1	**Phil Hill** (USA)	Ferrari	34
2	**Wolfgang von Trips** (GER)	Ferrari	33
3	**Stirling Moss** (GB)	Lotus-Climax	21
	Dan Gurney (USA)	Porsche	21
5	**Richie Ginther** (USA)	Ferrari	16
6	**Innes Ireland** (GB)	Lotus-Climax	12
7	**Jim Clark** (GB)	Lotus-Climax	11
	Bruce McLaren (NZ)	Cooper-Climax	11
9	**Giancarlo Baghetti** (ITA)	Ferrari	9
10	**Tony Brooks** (GB)	BRM-Climax	6

Best five scores from eight races to count

1962

Ferrari's star faded in the most dramatic fashion, as BRM and Lotus battled it out for the championship. Graham Hill beat Jim Clark to score his first title win at the beginning of another golden era for the British teams.

The biggest story of the 1962 season occurred in a non-championship race at Goodwood on Easter Monday. Stirling Moss suffered multiple injuries when he crashed his Lotus, and he was never to race at the top level again. Ferrari self-destructed over the winter, as some of the top staff walked out. The team carried on with virtually unchanged cars and drivers Phil Hill and Baghetti.

BRM had a new V8 engine, and Graham Hill was joined by Ginther from Ferrari. Meanwhile, the Climax V8 was the choice of many top teams. Brabham quit Cooper to design his own car, so McLaren became team leader.

Lotus had another new car, the 25, which featured a revolutionary monocoque chassis. Clark and Trevor Taylor were the works drivers. An interesting newcomer was the Lola, entered by the Bowmaker team for John Surtees and Roy Salvadori, while Porsche had a new flat-eight engine for Gurney and Bonnier.

The season opened at Zandvoort in May. Graham Hill scored his first win, and the first for BRM since Bonnier's victory at the same track three years earlier. Taylor finished second in only his second grand prix. McLaren won at Monaco, chased home by Phil Hill in the Ferrari driver's best race of the year.

Spa was a historic occasion, as it marked the first win for Jim Clark. Three marques had won the first three races, and it became four when Gurney gave Porsche its maiden victory at Rouen – but only after three leaders, Clark, Surtees and Graham Hill, had all retired.

Clark became the first repeat winner, dominating the British Grand Prix at Aintree ahead of Surtees and McLaren. Surtees continued his good form at the Nurburgring, finishing second behind Graham Hill's BRM, and just ahead of Gurney's Porsche.

Monza was the turning point in the title battle, for Graham Hill and Ginther gave BRM a one-two after a thrilling race, and Clark failed to finish. Clark fought back at Watkins Glen, heading Graham Hill home. For the first time the finale was held at East London in South Africa in December. Clark took pole position, and was leading the race until his engine failed.

Graham Hill took the win and the championship crown. It was to be BRM's only success. McLaren finished second, and took third in the points after a consistent season as Cooper's top man. It had been a poor year for Ferrari, and the team did not even enter the two final races. Even worse, up-and-coming star driver Rodriguez, who finished fourth at Spa, was killed in practice for the non-championship Mexican Grand Prix. He was just 20.

Breaking New Ground: South Africa joined the World Championship and Graham Hill took his first title

TECHNICAL INNOVATION
Race Suits and Helmets

Looking at the clothing of modern-day Formula One drivers, it is hard to imagine that the grand prix gladiators of the 1950s still went out in cork helmets and short-sleeved shirts. Racesuits were only just coming onto the scene, with single-layer cotton or silk overalls carrying minimal advertising. Today's four-layer racesuits are covered with sponsors' names, each helping to pay that driver's retainer. Helmets have also been transformed, from an open-faced, glue-soaked canvas dome lined with cork and offset by a pair of goggles to a full-face helmet made from Kevlar and carbonfibre padded with polystyrene lining, tailor-made to fit the driver's head. Not only fitted with a near bullet-proof visor (with rip-off strips to improve vision if oily) and a tube to a drinks bottle, each one must now have an emergency oxygen supply.

DRIVERS' WORLD CHAMPIONSHIP 1962

	Driver (NATIONALITY)	Make	Pts
1	**Graham Hill** (GB)	BRM	42
2	**Jim Clark** (GB)	Lotus-Climax	30
3	**Bruce McLaren** (NZ)	Cooper-Climax	27
4	**John Surtees** (GB)	Lola-Climax	19
5	**Dan Gurney** (USA)	Porsche	15
6	**Phil Hill** (USA)	Ferrari	14
7	**Tony Maggs** (RSA)	Cooper-Climax	13
8	**Richie Ginther** (USA)	BRM	10
9	**Jack Brabham** (AUS)	Lotus/Brabham-Climax	9
10	**Trevor Taylor** (GB)	Lotus-Climax	6

Best five scores from nine races to count

1963

The year proved to be a memorable one for Jim Clark and Lotus. Clark won seven races in all. It was the most devastating display of craftmanship by a single driver since the great triumph of Alberto Ascari 11 years previously.

Team Talk: Jim Clark confers with Lotus team-mate Peter Arundell before the French Grand Prix

Absent from the tracks in 1963 was the Porsche team, which had withdrawn to concentrate on sports car racing. The German marque would be back as an engine-supplier more than 20 years later. The Lotus, BRM and Cooper line-ups were unchanged but, as usual, the off-season had been busy. Having lost his Porsche ride, Gurney teamed up with Jack Brabham to drive the double champion's own cars. The promising Bowmaker/Lola team withdrew, and the cars were bought by Reg Parnell for young Kiwi, Chris Amon.

With Bowmaker out, Surtees moved to Ferrari. He joined Belgian Willy Mairesse, who had shown some promise in the past. The Ferrari breakaway had spawned a new team, ATS, and a pair of works Ferrari drivers, Phil Hill and Baghetti, both jumped ship. They would come to regret their decision.

Clark led the opener at Monaco, but retired when the gearbox broke. It was to be his only retirement in an exceptionally reliable year for Lotus. With Clark out, Graham Hill and Ginther scored a one-two. Clark's luck changed at Spa, and he took a memorable win in the rain, ahead of McLaren and Gurney (scoring the Brabham team's first top-three finish).

It was the same story at Zandvoort, where Clark led all the way to win from Gurney and Surtees, and at Reims, where even a misfire could not stop him. Clark scored his fourth win in a row at Silverstone, while Surtees took second after Graham Hill ran out of fuel on the last lap. Surtees had threatened to win for a couple of years, and he finally came good at the Nurburgring, scoring Ferrari's first success since Monza in 1961. Clark took second, ahead of BRM's Ginther.

At Monza Ferrari had a new chassis, which was designed to accept the forthcoming 1964 spec V8 engine. Clark headed home Ginther and McLaren, and clinched the championship – even though there were still three races to run. Graham Hill headed Ginther and Clark home at Watkins Glen. Clark was stymied by a flat battery, and had to start from the back.

The Mexican Grand Prix was in the championship for the first time, and Clark scored his sixth win of the year. He added a record seventh in South Africa in December to cap an amazing season. Before dropped scores were taken into account, he had amassed 73 points.

Brabham finished second in Mexico and then team-mate Gurney repeated the feat in South Africa, showing that "Black Jack" had got his sums right, and would be a force to reckon with.

CONSTRUCTORS' CUP 1963

	Make	Pts
1	Lotus	54
2	BRM	36
3	Brabham	28
4	Ferrari	26
5	Cooper	25
6	BRP-BRM	64

LANDMARK CAR
Lotus 25

Designer: **Colin Chapman**   Years raced: **1962-64**
Grand prix wins: **13**   Pole positions: **17**   Fastest laps: **13**
Engine type: **Coventry Climax V8**
Engine size/power: **1,496cc/1,95bhp at 9,800rpm**
Many people of a certain age still consider the Lotus 25 to be the most beautiful Formula One car of all time. Indeed, its shape is incredibly pure, though, the lines crafted by Colin Chapman were all the mightier as they scored win after win in the hands of the incomparable Jim Clark en route to the 1963 world title. It was groundbreaking, too, as the 25 was the first Formula One car to use a monocoque. It was a basic one, being little more than a metal bathtub flanked by pontoons containing the fuel tanks, but it was the first car to break away from making its chassis out of a framework of tubes clad in body panels.

DRIVERS' WORLD CHAMPIONSHIP 1963

	Driver (NATIONALITY)	Make	Pts
1	**Jim Clark** (GB)	Lotus-Climax	54
2	**Graham Hill** (GB)	BRM	29
	Richie Ginther (USA)	BRM	29
4	**John Surtees** (GB)	Ferrari	22
5	**Dan Gurney** (USA)	Brabham-Climax	19
6	**Bruce McLaren** (NZ)	Cooper-Climax	17
7	**Jack Brabham** (AUS)	Brabham-Climax	14
8	**Tony Maggs** (RSA)	Cooper-Climax	9
9	**Innes Ireland** (GB)	BRP-BRM	6
	Lorenzo Bandini (ITA)	Ferrari	6
	Jo Bonnier (SWE)	Cooper-Climax	6

Best six scores from ten races to count

1964

John Surtees made racing history when he became the first man to win a World Championship on both two wheels and four. In a truly thrilling finale in Mexico City, Surtees, in his Ferrari, just outscored Graham Hill and Jim Clark.

Four-Wheel Drive: John Surtees had to make do with third at Brands Hatch but still became champion

Ferrari hopes looked up for 1964 as the new V8 engine was mated to the chassis which had shown promise at Monza the previous year. Surtees stayed on to lead the team alongside Lorenzo Bandini. Lotus produced an updated car for Clark, the 33. Peter Arundell was the team's new number two. Hill and Ginther stayed at BRM, and had a revised car, while Cooper tried to keep up with the new monocoque technology, updating a Formula Three chassis by welding on panels.

Clark started on a high by leading at Monaco, but he had to pit when his rear roll-bar broke. Hill and Ginther scored another one-two for BRM and a late engine failure for Clark handed third place to team-mate Arundell. Clark made amends with a demonstration run to victory at Zandvoort, while

Surtees gave notice of Ferrari's intentions with second place, ahead of the newcomer Arundell.

The Brabham team did not fare well in the early races, but at Spa Gurney led comfortably. In a farcical turn of events, Hill took the lead and suffered fuel pump failure; then McLaren ran out of gas. This allowed a surprised Clark – who had made an early stop – to take victory. At least McLaren was able to coast home in second.

Gurney made amends at Rouen, by scoring a fine first win for the Brabham team. Graham Hill pipped Brabham for third, while again Clark led the early stages, before his engine failed.

For the first time the British Grand Prix moved to Brands Hatch, and Clark kept up his tradition of winning at home. Hill was second and Surtees

was happy to get third after two consecutive retirements. Surtees then began his surge towards the title by winning at the Nurburgring. The first Austrian Grand Prix was held at Zeltweg, and took a high toll on machinery. Hill, Surtees, Clark, McLaren and Gurney were among the retirements, leaving Bandini to score his first grand prix win.

Ferrari's run of success continued at Monza, where Surtees scored his second win of the year. McLaren and Bandini completed the top three. Hill broke his clutch on the line in Italy, but kept his title challenge afloat by winning at Watkins Glen after Clark suffered engine problems. Surtees was second, ahead of an impressive Jo Siffert.

Three drivers went to the finale in

Mexico City with a crack at the title. Hill led on 39 points, Surtees had 34 and outsider Clark 30. Hill was soon out of contention for points, and Clark looked set for the title. But with just two laps to go, he struck engine trouble. Surtees had worked his way up, and was waved into second behind Gurney by team-mate Bandini – it was enough to take the title from Hill.

CONSTRUCTORS' CUP 1964

	Make	Pts
1	Ferrari	45
2	BRM	42
3	Lotus	37
4	Brabham	30
5	Cooper	16

GREAT RACE

Mexican Grand Prix 1964

Just like the 1958 finale, this race in Mexico City was a three-way British title shoot-out. This time it was between Graham Hill, John Surtees and Jim Clark, with the Scot nine points down on leader Hill. Clark gave it his best shot by qualifying his Lotus on pole and then blasted off into the lead. No one was able to live with him that day. Hill was hampered when Surtees' Ferrari team-mate Lorenzo Bandini pitched him into a spin and a pitstop took him out of contention. This left Surtees in fourth place and he could only hope something went wrong for Clark. Which it did, when his engine seized with just over a lap to go. Dan Gurney swept by to win in his Brabham, with Clark parking up and Bandini waving team-mate Surtees through to second place to get the extra points he needed to take the title by a point from Hill.

DRIVERS' WORLD CHAMPIONSHIP 1964

	Driver (NATIONALITY)	Make	Pts
1	**John Surtees** (GB)	Ferrari	40
2	**Graham Hill** (GB)	BRM	39
3	**Jim Clark** (GB)	Lotus-Climax	32
4	**Lorenzo Bandini** (ITA)	Ferrari	23
	Richie Ginther (USA)	BRM	23
6	**Dan Gurney** (USA)	Brabham-Climax	19
7	**Bruce McLaren** (NZ)	Cooper-Climax	13
8	**Jack Brabham** (AUS)	Brabham-Climax	11
	Peter Arundell (GB)	Lotus-Climax	11
10	**Jo Siffert** (SWI)	Brabham-BRM	7

Best six scores from ten races to count

1965

After retirements had robbed him during 1964, Jim Clark bounced back to win the 1965 title – and the Indy 500 – for Lotus. Once again a change of engine regulations at the end of the year signalled the passing of an era.

The British teams struck back against Ferrari in 1965, with Lotus and Brabham using a new 32-valve version of the Climax V8. Clark was joined by another new team-mate in the form of Mike Spence, who had driven at Monza for the team the previous year. Brabham and Gurney were joined by a newcomer from New Zealand called Denny Hulme, while Rob Walker entered Brabhams for Bonnier and Siffert.

Ferrari continued with Surtees and Bandini, and there was new competition, too, from Honda, who launched a full effort with Ginther and the little-known Ronnie Bucknum. Ginther's departure from BRM left a seat open alongside Graham Hill, and it was very ably filled by a promising young Scot who had never driven in a grand prix; his name was Jackie Stewart. Talented Austrian Jochen Rindt joined McLaren at Cooper.

South Africa became the first race of the season rather than last, and Clark, still using the older Climax engine, scored a runaway win. Surtees continued his championship form with second, ahead of Hill. Debutant Stewart finished sixth.

Lotus was missing from the second race at Monaco. The team was competing instead at Indianapolis, where Clark notched up a historic first win for a rear-engined car. In his absence Hill scored a wonderful victory in the street classic, recovering from an early incident to pass Surtees and Bandini. Clark came back with a win at Spa in the wet, ahead of Stewart and McLaren, while Ginther picked up a point in the improving Honda. Clark and Stewart then repeated their double act in the French Grand Prix, held this year on the mountainous Clermont-Ferrand track.

Clark won the British Grand Prix at Silverstone for the fourth consecutive time. Clark continued his winning ways at Zandvoort, and for the third time countryman Stewart followed him home. The big surprise was the performance of Ginther, who led for two laps in the Honda. At the Nurburgring Clark scored his sixth win of the year and his first on the daunting German track. With only six scores counting, he had reached maximum points, and the championship was his.

He was in the lead pack at Monza and, after he retired with fuel pump trouble, Stewart scored a marvellous maiden win, fractionally ahead of Hill and Gurney. However, with the title sewn up, Clark's luck seemed to have deserted him. At Watkins Glen he retired with engine problems, and Hill scored BRM's third win of the year.

The season had a twist in the tail. In Mexico City Ginther gave Honda (and tyre maker Goodyear) a first win, leading from start to finish. It was the Californian's only win. The race also marked the end of the 1.5-litre formula after four seasons.

CONSTRUCTORS' CUP 1965

	Make	Pts
1	Lotus	54
2	BRM	45
3	Brabham	27
4	Ferrari	26
5	Cooper	14
6	Honda	11

Top Scot: Jim Clark on his way to victory in the British GP at Silverstone in his works Lotus Climax

THE GREAT CIRCUITS

Monaco Yachts

When people think of Formula One, most think of its glamorous image, and nowhere conjures up this image better than Monaco. Stand on the quayside and look out at the opulence of the yachts all around and it is hard to imagine this is the same sport that also plies its trade at windswept circuits all over northern Europe. The principality of Monaco on the French Riviera tends to be sun-drenched when the grand prix comes to town – as it has since 1929 – and to some, is just a background for all the posing. The flashy yachts that usually berth in the harbour are sent away for the week and replaced by even larger ones that host party after party, which stop only so the guests can trawl the boutiques and go to the casino. Oh, and watch the race...

DRIVERS' WORLD CHAMPIONSHIP 1965

	Driver (NATIONALITY)	Make	Pts
1	Jim Clark (GB)	Lotus-Climax	54
2	Graham Hill (GB)	BRM	40
3	Jackie Stewart (GB)	BRM	33
4	Dan Gurney (USA)	Brabham-Climax	25
5	John Surtees (GB)	Ferrari	17
6	Lorenzo Bandini (ITA)	Ferrari	13
7	Richie Ginther (USA)	Honda	11
8	Bruce McLaren (NZ)	Cooper-Climax	10
	Mike Spence (GB)	Lotus-Climax	10
10	Jack Brabham (AUS)	Brabham-Climax	9

Best six scores from ten races to count

1966

It was all change in 1966 as the 3-litre formula was introduced and there was a race to get new engines ready in time. Jack Brabham was better prepared than most and earned a deserved third championship title in his own car.

Teams and engine builders were busy through the winter as they prepared for the new formula. There was no pukka new engine from Climax, so existing customers had to find their own solutions.

The man who did the best job was Jack Brabham. He announced he was using a new V8 from the Australian Repco company. The engine was not the most powerful, but it was reliable, light and compact, and mated well with an updated version of Brabham's existing chassis. Jack had not won a race himself since 1960, and the package was to give his career a new lease of life. With Dan Gurney moving on, Denny Hulme became his number two. Cooper had a more exotic solution, mating a Maserati V12 to a new chassis. Richie Ginther and Jochen Rindt were the works drivers, and Rob Walker bought one for Siffert.

Ex-Cooper driver Bruce McLaren followed Brabham's example and set up his own team. Another driver to copy the Brabham example was Gurney, whose All-American Racers concern built the neat Eagle.

It was no surprise to see Ferrari follow the V12 route, and the Scuderia produced a promising new car for John Surtees. Lorenzo Bandini stayed on as his team-mate. Both BRM and Lotus had to use uprated 2-litre versions of their V8 and Climax engines. BRM had an unusual H16 under development, but it did not race until late in the year. That said, it started very well at Monaco where less powerful cars proved a match for the new machinery. Clark took pole but had an unlucky race, while Stewart won for BRM. Spa turned to chaos when eight cars retired on the wet first lap, among them Stewart, who had the worst crash of his Formula One career. Surtees won after overcoming a challenge from Rindt's Cooper-Maserati. A few weeks later John fell out with the Italian team and left to join Cooper.

The new Brabham-Repco came good at Reims, Jack winning after Bandini had retired. Brabham won again at Brands Hatch, with team-mate Hulme second. Jack picked up a third win at Zandvoort.

Brabham's winning streak continued at the Nurburgring, where he held off the Coopers of Surtees and Rindt. His luck ran out at Monza, where he retired. Ferrari newcomer Ludovico Scarfiotti won.

Despite retiring in Italy, Brabham had clinched his third title. He was on pole at Watkins Glen, but retired. Clark won. Cooper-Maseratis finished second, third and fourth, and their form continued in the finale in Mexico, won by Surtees.

CONSTRUCTORS' CUP 1966

	Make	Pts
1	**Brabham**	42
2	**Ferrari**	31
3	**Cooper**	30
4	**BRM**	22
5	**Lotus-BRM**	13
6	**Lotus-Climax**	8
7	**Eagle-Climax**	4
8	**Honda**	3
	McLaren	3

His Cup Floweth Over: Jack Brabham celebrates at Reims after victory in a car bearing his name

---

LANDMARK CAR

Brabham BT19

Designer: **Ron Tauranac**   Years raced: **1966-67**
Grand prix wins: **4**   Pole positions: **3**   Fastest laps: **1**
Engine type: **Repco V8**
Engine size/power: **2994cc/315bhp at 7,250rpm**

It is said that a change in regulations leads to a changing of the guard. This was certainly true in 1966 when the 1.5-litre engine regulations gave way to those for engines twice that size. Jack Brabham had planned for the BT19 chassis to take a flat-16 Coventry Climax, but the rule changes meant he sourced the Repco V8 and had it bored out from 2.5-litres to 3.0. Jack powered to the title and became the first driver to win a grand prix in a car bearing his own name. The BT20 that followed helped the team to a drivers' title courtesy of Denny Hulme.

DRIVERS' WORLD CHAMPIONSHIP 1966

	Driver (NATIONALITY)	Make	Pts
1	**Jack Brabham** (AUS)	Brabham-Repco	42
2	**John Surtees** (GB)	Ferrari/Cooper-Maserati	28
3	**Jochen Rindt** (AUT)	Cooper-Maserati	22
4	**Denny Hulme** (NZ)	Brabham-Repco	18
5	**Graham Hill** (GB)	BRM	17
6	**Jim Clark** (GB)	Lotus-Climax/BRM	16
7	**Jackie Stewart** (GB)	BRM	14
8	**Lorenzo Bandini** (ITA)	Ferrari	12
	Mike Parkes (GB)	Ferrari	12
10	**Ludovico Scarfiotti** (ITA)	Ferrari	9

Best five scores from nine races to count

1967

Brabham and Repco scored a second win through the efforts of Denny Hulme, but the story of the year was the arrival of the new Cosworth DFV engine. Packaged with the Lotus 49, it marked the beginning of an era.

Kiwi in Flight: Denny Hulme set his successful campaign rolling with this victory at the Monaco GP

Lotus had struggled through 1966, but in March that year Colin Chapman had persuaded Ford to invest in a new engine, to be built by Cosworth. The British firm embarked on an all-new V8 design for 1967, which would initially be for the exclusive use of Lotus. Chapman drew a simple but effective car, the 49, to exploit it. He further strengthened his package by bringing Graham Hill back to join Clark.

That elevated Stewart to team-leader status at BRM, where he was joined by Spence. Chris Amon joined Bandini at Ferrari. Ex-Ferrari star Surtees was signed to lead Honda's effort, while Pedro Rodriguez joined Rindt at Cooper.

The season opened at the new Kyalami track in South Africa, and the race nearly saw a sensational win for privateer John Love in an old Cooper-Climax. A late stop for fuel dropped him to second, behind the Cooper-Maserati of Rodriguez.

Grand prix racing had been through a safe – or lucky – couple of seasons, but Ferrari ace Lorenzo Bandini was to lose his life at Monaco. He was leading when he crashed, and the car caught fire. Hulme won for Brabham, ahead of Hill and Amon.

Zandvoort saw the long-awaited debut of the Ford Cosworth and the Lotus 49. Clark took the win after poleman Hill's engine failed. At Spa Hill retired; then leader Clark had to pit for a plug change. Gurney took the often unreliable Eagle-Weslake to a memorable first (and only) win.

For one time only the French Grand Prix was staged at the Bugatti circuit at Le Mans. Brabham and Hulme finished one-two, ahead of Stewart. Lotus fortunes looked up at Silverstone, where Clark won the British Grand Prix for the fifth time in six years. Kiwis Hulme and Amon finished second and third. Lotus gremlins struck again at the Nurburgring, where Clark and Hill were both sidelined by suspension failures. Hulme and Brabham scored a one-two.

For the first time the circus moved to the scenic Mosport track in Canada. Ignition problems put Clark out and – surprise surprise – Brabham and Hulme were there to take another one-two, with Hill a distant fourth. Clark was the hero at Monza, coming back from early problems to lead until he ran out of fuel. In a typically exciting finish, Surtees pipped Brabham to give Honda its first win of the 3-litre age. Luck swung to Lotus once again in Watkins Glen, where Clark and Hill managed a one-two. Hulme had been a steady performer all year, and he just pipped his boss to the title in Mexico. Clark won from Brabham, but third was enough to keep Denny ahead.

CONSTRUCTORS' CUP 1967

	Make	Pts
1	Brabham	63
2	Lotus	44
3	Cooper	28
4	Ferrari	20
	Honda	20
6	BRM	17
7	Eagle	13

LANDMARK CAR
Ford Cosworth DFV

Designer: **Keith Duckworth**   Years raced: **1967-85**
Grand prix wins: **155**   Pole positions: **131**   Fastest laps: **138**
Engine type: **V8**
Engine size/power: **2,993cc/408-530bhp**
No engine has ever done so much to change Formula One. Without it, Formula One could have crumpled in the early 1970s. What it offered was not only an engine that could fight with the best, but one that could be bought off the shelf for around £5,000. McLaren and Williams wouldn't be here today if it hadn't been for the Double Four Valve. Ford paid engine specialists Cosworth £100,000 to badge the engine, and it was the most successful commercial deal ever as it won on its debut in 1967, then won title after title and went on right through until mid-1985.

DRIVERS' WORLD CHAMPIONSHIP 1967

	Driver (NATIONALITY)	Make	Pts
1	**Denny Hulme** (NZ)	Brabham-Repco	51
2	**Jack Brabham** (AUS)	Brabham-Repco	46
3	**Jim Clark** (GB)	Lotus-BRM/Climax/Ford	41
4	**John Surtees** (GB)	Honda	20
	Chris Amon (NZ)	Ferrari	20
6	**Pedro Rodriguez** (MEX)	Cooper-Maserati	15
	Graham Hill (GB)	Lotus-BRM/Ford	15
8	**Dan Gurney** (USA)	Eagle-Weslake	13
9	**Jackie Stewart** (GB)	BRM	10
10	**Mike Spence** (GB)	BRM	9

Best nine scores from 11 races to count

1968

Sponsorship and wings arrived on the Formula One scene, but the new developments were overshadowed by the death of Jim Clark in a Formula Two race. In the sad aftermath, Graham Hill bravely won his second title for the grieving Lotus team.

Left in the Dark: Graham Hill drives on in the murk as Jackie Stewart blasts to victory in Germany

Several things happened in 1968 which were to have long-term effects on Formula One, but nothing shook the racing world quite as much as Jim Clark's death in a Formula Two race at Hockenheim. The season was perhaps most notable for the introduction of overt commercial sponsorship. The previously green and yellow Lotuses were now red, white and gold, thanks to backing from Gold Leaf cigarettes.

Early in the year Lotus, Brabham and Ferrari began to experiment with downforce-enhancing wings, which soon became standard equipment.

Other big news was the arrival of Ken Tyrrell to run Matra-Fords. He scooped up Stewart as his driver, and the partnership would blossom for the next six seasons. Meanwhile Matra's own team, with Henri Pescarolo and Jean-Pierre Beltoise, became a serious force. Talented Belgian youngster Jacky Ickx joined Amon at Ferrari, while Hulme moved to join Bruce McLaren.

Clark and Hill continued to lead the Lotus challenge, with Siffert in a private Rob Walker car. A sign of what might have been came at Kyalami, when Clark dominated the race, ahead of team-mate Hill. By the next race, at the new Jarama track in Spain, Clark was gone. Jackie Oliver replaced him, and Hill revived Lotus morale with his first win with the 49. Graham then scored another victory at Monaco.

At Spa McLaren gave his marque its first victory after Stewart ran out of fuel. It was also the first win for a DFV in something other than a Lotus 49. The next was not long in coming, for Stewart gave Tyrrell's Matra-Ford its first win at Zandvoort. At Rouen, young Ickx gave Ferrari its only win of the year in pouring rain. Surtees was second for Honda, but veteran team-mate Jo Schlesser was killed.

At Brands Hatch the popular Siffert gave Walker his first win in seven years with the private 49, heading home the Ferraris of Amon and Ickx after early leaders Hill and Oliver retired.

The Nurburgring saw one of the greatest drives of all time, Stewart winning with a virtuoso performance in atrocious conditions. Hulme showed that his 1967 crown was deserved by winning the next two events at Monza and the Mont Tremblant circuit in Canada. At Watkins Glen newcomer Mario Andretti earned a sensational pole for Lotus, but Stewart took his third win of the year. In the Mexico City finale Graham Hill scored his third win of the year. If the losses of Clark and Schlesser were not enough, BRM's Mike Spence was killed during practice at Indianapolis, and former Italian Grand Prix winner Ludovico Scarfiotti died in a hillclimb.

CONSTRUCTORS' CUP 1968

	Make	Pts
1	**Lotus**	62
2	**McLaren**	49
3	**Matra**	45
4	**Ferrari**	32
5	**BRM**	28
6	**Cooper**	14
	Honda	14
8	**Brabham**	10

TECHNOLOGICAL INNOVATION

Aerofoils

Aerofoils burst onto the grand prix scene in the late 1960s and offered the cars massive improvement in handling and road-holding. These wings sprouted on the cars' cigar-shaped bodies and provided the downforce needed for better traction. The wings started as small tabs either side of the nose, but Lotus boss Colin Chapman mounted wings on pillars onto the suspension, front and rear, producing downforce equivalent to the weight of two adult males. However, these high-mounted aerofoils were banned after breakages and resultant accidents in the 1969 Spanish GP, with aerofoils henceforth having to be lower and sturdier. Designers now had to get the most out of less wing both front and rear, with aerodynamic pioneer Lotus utilizing the wedge-shape of the monocoque of its 72 chassis to add further downforce.

DRIVERS' WORLD CHAMPIONSHIP 1968

	Driver (NATIONALITY)	Make	Pts
1	**Graham Hill** (GB)	Lotus-Ford	48
2	**Jackie Stewart** (GB)	Matra-Ford	36
3	**Denny Hulme** (NZ)	McLaren-Ford	33
4	**Jacky Ickx** (BEL)	Ferrari	27
5	**Bruce McLaren** (NZ)	McLaren-Ford	22
6	**Pedro Rodriguez** (MEX)	BRM	18
7	**Jo Siffert** (SWI)	Lotus-Ford	12
	John Surtees (GB)	Honda	12
9	**Jean-Pierre Beltoise** (FRA)	Matra	11
10	**Chris Amon** (NZ)	Ferrari	10

All scores counted

1969

Jackie Stewart marched forward to take the title with Ken Tyrrell's Matra-Ford, since there was virtually no one else who could offer a consistent challenge. It looked certain that now Stewart would be the man to beat.

Jackie Stewart had come close to the title the previous year, and in 1969 everything went his way. With Matra withdrawing its own team, all efforts were concentrated on Tyrrell's outfit. Stewart and team-mate Johnny Servoz-Gavin were joined by Jean-Pierre Beltoise. Rindt took up a golden opportunity and joined Hill at Lotus, while Ickx left Ferrari to replace him at Brabham. Jack had finally given up on Repco and joined the DFV bandwagon. Surtees was available because Honda had withdrawn at the end of 1968. The DFV supremacy had taken its toll. Also gone from the scene were Eagle-Weslake and Cooper-Maserati.

The big development of the year was four-wheel drive. Matra, McLaren and Lotus all tried it, but it was a white elephant and none of the cars really worked. Stewart started the season in fine form, dominating the opening race at Kyalami. Andretti, who would have occasional drives in a third Lotus, gave him a hard time early on. Stewart won again at the Montjuich Park circuit near Barcelona. First Hill and then Rindt had huge crashes after their wings failed.

Rindt would have to miss Monaco, where the FIA announced an immediate ban on the high-mounted aerofoils which had proliferated. They soon crept back in, but in a new and less outrageous form, attached to the bodywork. Stewart and Amon both led but retired, allowing Hill to score a historic fifth win. Piers Courage finished second in a Brabham entered by Frank Williams – the first significant result for the British team owner.

The race at Spa was cancelled, and Rindt was fit enough to return at Zandvoort. He took pole and led until retiring, so Stewart scored another win. Jackie's fourth victory came at Clermont-Ferrand in France, where team-mate Beltoise did a good job to finish second.

Stewart won once more at Silverstone, where he battled hard with Rindt until the Austrian had to pit with a loose wing. Ickx had a good run to second with the Brabham, and two weeks later he went one better at the Nurburgring, where he gave the team its first win since 1967.

The Scot clinched the title with a sixth win in an epic, slipstreaming battle at Monza, where he headed home Rindt, Beltoise and McLaren. But, after such a run of success, Stewart failed to win any of the last three races.

Ickx triumphed in Canada, Rindt scored his first success at Watkins Glen and Hulme provided more variety with a win for McLaren in Mexico. Missing from the Mexican race was Graham Hill, who had broken his legs in a massive accident at Watkins Glen. He was fit for the following season, but would never again win a grand prix.

Reign in Spain: Jackie Stewart made it two wins in a row when he raced to victory in the Spanish GP

GREAT RACE
Monaco Grand Prix 1969

Graham Hill was known as "Mr Monaco" and he seemed incapable of being beaten here. This was his fifth win, a record at the time, on one of the real tests for drivers. The race was notable for the FIA banning the high-mounted wings that had proliferated that season and which had led to Jochen Rindt being hospitalized at the previous race, at Barcelona's Montjuich Park. As in so many races that year, Jackie Stewart was dominant and led from the start, but a failed transmission shaft took him out. By then, Hill, who had already overtaken Jean-Pierre Beltoise, was up to second place as Amon had also pulled off, with differential failure. And so Graham raced on to the easiest of his five wins on this narrow and tricky street circuit, with the post-race partying going on long into the night.

DRIVERS' WORLD CHAMPIONSHIP 1969

	Driver (NATIONALITY)	Make	Pts
1	Jackie Stewart (GB)	Matra-Ford	63
2	Jacky Ickx (BEL)	Brabham-Ford	37
3	Bruce McLaren (NZ)	McLaren-Ford	26
4	Jochen Rindt (AUT)	Lotus-Ford	22
5	Jean-Pierre Beltoise (FRA)	Matra-Ford	21
6	Denny Hulme (NZ)	McLaren-Ford	20
7	Graham Hill (GB)	Lotus-Ford	19
8	Piers Courage (GB)	Brabham-Ford	16
9	Jo Siffert (SWI)	Lotus-Ford	15
10	Jack Brabham (AUS)	Brabham-Ford	14

All scores counted

DEFINING MOMENTS
1970s

1970 Dutch GP
THE DEATH OF COURAGE
One of Formula One's most dashing drivers perished at Zandvoort when Piers Courage crashed his Frank Williams-run de Tomaso on lap 23 when he was seventh. The car rolled over after hitting one of the banks surrounding the track and burst into flames. No one was able to get close enough to save him.

1973 British GP
ENFANT TERRIBLE
If people accuse you of being a little wild, the last thing you want to do is what Jody Scheckter did at Silverstone in his fourth race. He qualified his McLaren in sixth, but lost control at the end of the opening lap and triggered a multi-car accident that stopped the race, leaving ten cars *hors de combat* and Andrea de Adamich with two broken legs.

1974 Spanish GP (left)
RED WITH EMBARRASSMENT
It seems hard to imagine Ferrari ever being down, but they were in the early 1970s. Then Niki Lauda arrived from BRM and had the guile and application to make it competitive, with the first of his wins coming at Jarama as he and team-mate Clay Regazzoni found themselves on the right tyres on a drying track.

1976 German GP
LAUDA ESCAPES DEATH
You can still drive the old Nurburgring in your road car today, revelling in its bucking and twisting 14-mile lap. However, by 1976, Ferrari's Niki Lauda was leading a campaign to have it dropped as it was too dangerous for Formula One. The race went ahead, though, and he nearly lost his life in a fiery accident.

1977 British GP
GETTING TURBOCHARGED
People always stand and watch when new technology arrives in Formula One, waiting to see whether it's good or not. Turbocharging was no different when Renault launched it midway through 1977. Jean-Pierre Jabouille qualified just 21st and retired, but it set rival teams' engineers thinking and, soon, everyone had them.

1978 Swedish GP
GLUED TO THE ROAD
The Brabham BT46B caused a stink on its debut at Anderstorp, for rival teams said that its system of sealing off the area under the engine and gearbox and sucking the air within out with a large fan was illegal. The ease with which Lauda won, after harrying Mario Andretti, made him weep at its subsequent banning.

1970

Jochen Rindt was leading the World Championship for Lotus when he lost his life at Monza, but the popular Austrian became the sport's first posthumous champion. In a dark year, Bruce McLaren and Piers Courage were also killed.

Taking the Applause: Rindt couldn't believe his luck at winning the Monaco GP after Brabham crashed

The big story of the winter was the arrival of March Engineering. Seemingly out of nowhere, the British company appeared at the first race with no fewer than five DFV-powered cars. The works March team had strong drivers in Amon and Siffert. Ferrari looked well placed with the all-new 312B, and Ickx returned to drive it. BRM attracted backing from Yardley, and produced the much-improved P153.

Brabham had not won since the 1967 Canadian Grand Prix, but he started the year with a fine win in South Africa with his new BT33.

At Jarama Stewart gave March a win in the marque's second-ever race. He was hounded by the rejuvenated Brabham, until Jack's engine broke. Brabham was to the fore at Monaco, holding off Rindt in a fine battle for the lead. But the Aussie slid off at the last corner, allowing Rindt to win. Tragedy struck before the next race in Belgium when Bruce McLaren was killed while testing a CanAm car at Goodwood. He had been a mainstay of Formula One since 1959.

BRM had not won since Monaco in 1966, but at Spa Rodriguez gave the team a sensational victory after holding off Amon's March. Zandvoort saw the delayed appearance of Chapman's slick new Lotus 72, and it scored a debut win in the hands of Rindt. Alas, Piers Courage perished when the De Tomaso crashed and caught fire. Another new face was dashing young Frenchman François Cevert, who joined Tyrrell when Servoz-Gavin abruptly retired. Rindt and the 72 won at Clermont-Ferrand,

and then again at Brands Hatch after Brabham ran out of fuel, while leading rookie Brazilian Emerson Fittipaldi drove a works Lotus 49C to eighth.

Ickx was having a bad season, with just four points on the board. He fought back with second in the German Grand Prix, held at Hockenheim, while Rindt took his fifth win. In Austria Ickx gave Ferrari a much-needed victory, heading home new team-mate Clay Regazzoni.

Tragedy struck again in practice at Monza when Rindt crashed fatally after a mechanical failure; he was just 28 years old. The race went ahead without Lotus, and Regazzoni scored a fine win in only his fifth start. Ickx led Regazzoni in a Ferrari one-two in Canada, finished fourth in Watkins Glen and then won in Mexico. It was not enough, but even he really did

not want to win by default. Canada saw the first appearance of another new marque. Ken Tyrrell had built his own car to replace the March. It showed promise in Stewart's hands, but would have to wait until 1971 for its first success.

CONSTRUCTORS' CUP 1970

	Make	Pts
1	Lotus	59
2	Ferrari	52
3	March	48
4	Brabham	35
	McLaren	35
6	BRM	23
	Matra	23
8	Surtees	3

LANDMARK CAR
Lotus 72

Designer: **Maurice Philippe**   Years raced: **1970-75**
Grand prix wins: **20**   Pole positions: **18**   Fastest laps: **9**
Engine type: **Ford DFV V8**   Engine size/power: **2,993cc/415bhp at 10,000rpm improving to 470bhp at 11,000rpm**
This wedge-shaped wonder is yet another epochal design from Lotus and one of the longest-lasting, serving through six seasons and winning grands prix from 1970 to 1974. Chief among its radical design features was having its radiators mounted mid-ships. As a result, the nose could be low line, with an obvious aerodynamic advantage. Although launched in Gold Leaf colours, and soon a winner in Jochen Rindt's hands, the 72 will always be remembered in the black and gold of John Player Special, with Emerson Fittipaldi's first world title in 1972.

DRIVERS' WORLD CHAMPIONSHIP 1970

	Driver (NATIONALITY)	Make	Pts
1	**Jochen Rindt** (AUT)	Lotus-Ford	45
2	**Jacky Ickx** (BEL)	Ferrari	40
3	**Clay Regazzoni** (SWI)	Ferrari	33
4	**Denny Hulme** (NZ)	McLaren-Ford	27
5	**Jack Brabham** (AUS)	Brabham-Ford	25
	Jackie Stewart (GB)	March/Tyrrell-Ford	25
7	**Chris Amon** (NZ)	March-Ford	23
	Pedro Rodriguez (MEX)	BRM	23
9	**Jean-Pierre Beltoise** (FRA)	Matra	16
10	**Emerson Fittipaldi** (BRA)	Lotus-Ford	12

All scores counted

1971

Jackie Stewart earned his second title with a dominant performance for Tyrrell. But once again, the year was tinged with sadness as racing recorded the deaths of two of the fastest and most popular stars on the circuit.

Jack Brabham was missing from the grids, having retired at the end of the previous year after 126 starts and three championships. He settled into life as a team owner, and Graham Hill signed up to drive.

The works March team had endured a poor first season, and the star drivers left. Siffert joined Porsche sports car colleague Rodriguez at BRM, while Amon went to the promising Matra-Simca outfit. The third STP March driver, Mario Andretti, joined Ickx and Regazzoni to become Ferrari's third driver. Early in the year the Italian team lost Ignazio Giunti in a terrible sports car crash in Argentina.

To lead its challenge March signed up Ronnie Peterson, who had done a solid job in a private car the year before. The Swede soon emerged as a leading contender, although he would never actually win a race.

Ferrari drew first blood in South Africa when Andretti scored his maiden triumph, although Hulme had looked set to win for McLaren. Stewart finished second and followed it up with wins in Barcelona and Monte Carlo. Peterson scored a fine second in the latter event.

Stewart struggled at a wet Zandvoort, finishing a disappointing 11th while Ickx won for Ferrari. The French Grand Prix moved to the modern Paul Ricard facility, where Stewart and Cevert scored a fine one-two. Not long afterward BRM star Rodriguez, who had finished second in Holland, was killed in a minor sports car race at the Norisring.

Stewart won again at Silverstone, followed home by Peterson and then, at the Nurburgring, he and Cevert picked up their second one-two; it was a repeat of the Scot's 1969 form. BRM bounced back in fine style with a sensational win for Siffert in Austria and an even more spectacular one for Peter Gethin at Monza.

In Austria few noticed the low-key debut of Niki Lauda in a rented March, while at Monza Amon looked set to finally score his first win in the Matra-Simca – until he accidentally ripped off his visor in the closing laps. He finished sixth.

Stewart's engine had broken in Italy, but he bounced back with a win in Canada, Peterson again coming second.

In the finale at Watkins Glen it was the turn of Cevert to score his maiden win, after Stewart slipped back to fifth with tyre troubles.

The title had long since been in Stewart pocket, although Peterson was the big find of the year, finishing second in the championship thanks to his consistent results. Cevert, another brilliant youngster, took third.

Lotus had a disappointing year, the marque failing to win a race for the first time since 1960. A lot of effort was wasted with an Indy-derived gas turbine car, which never lived up to expectations.

In October tragedy struck again: Siffert was killed when his BRM crashed and caught fire in a non-championship race at Brands Hatch. It was a sad end to the season.

Sui Generis: Jackie Stewart was in a class of his own as he won for Tyrrell at Silverstone

CONSTRUCTORS' CUP 1971

	Make	Pts
1	Tyrrell	73
2	BRM	36
3	March	33
4	Ferrari	33
5	Lotus	21
6	McLaren	10
7	Matra	9
8	Surtees	8

DRIVERS' WORLD CHAMPIONSHIP 1971

	Driver (NATIONALITY)	Make	Pts
1	Jackie Stewart (GB)	Tyrrell-Ford	62
2	Ronnie Peterson (SWE)	March-Ford	33
3	François Cevert (FRA)	Tyrrell-Ford	26
4	Jacky Ickx (BEL)	Ferrari	19
	Jo Siffert (SWI)	BRM	19
6	Emerson Fittipaldi (BRA)	Lotus-Ford	16
7	Clay Regazzoni (SWI)	Ferrari	13
8	Mario Andretti (USA)	Ferrari	12
9	Chris Amon (NZ)	Matra-Simca	9
	Peter Gethin (GB)	BRM	9
	Denny Hulme (NZ)	BRM	9
	Pedro Rodriguez (MEX)	BRM	9
	Reine Wisell (SWE)	Lotus-Ford	9

All scores counted

1972

Lotus returned once again to the top of the podium. Its rising star, Emerson Fittipaldi, who had shown much promise the previous year, became the youngest world champion. There was no-one else able to offer a season-long challenge.

The Man in Black and Gold: victory in the Austrian GP set Emerson Fittipaldi fair for his first world title

Lotus went into 1972 armed with an updated version of the appropriately named 72 chassis, plus a dramatic new colour scheme. Gold Leaf had been replaced by the black and gold hues of John Player Special. Other sponsors had been in the news as well. Yardley left BRM to join a revitalized McLaren effort, in which Hulme was partnered by Peter Revson, returning some eight years after a shaky debut in the mid-1960s.

Meanwhile BRM found major backing from Marlboro and, in what proved to be an over-ambitious plan, ran up to five cars per race. Brabham was acquired by Bernie Ecclestone. Hill was joined by Argentina's Carlos Reutemann, the first talent to emerge from that country since the 1950s.

Newcomer Reutemann stunned the field when he took pole for his debut at Buenos Aires, but it was back to normal when he had to pit for tyres and Stewart won from Hulme. The Kiwi went one better in South Africa, giving McLaren its first win since the 1969 Mexican Grand Prix.

Fittipaldi dominated the Spanish Grand Prix for JPS. Monaco brought a total surprise when, in wet conditions, Beltoise drove a fine race for BRM. It was to be the marque's last-ever win.

Fittipaldi won at the new and boring Nivelles track in Belgium, and Stewart triumphed at Clermont-Ferrand after Amon again lost a race in the late stages – this time with a puncture. Ickx's Ferrari led the British Grand Prix until the Belgian was stricken with an oil leak, allowing Fittipaldi to win. Ickx fought back with victory at the Nurburgring, ahead of team-mate Regazzoni. Fittipaldi won the next race in Austria and then triumphed again at Monza to clinch the title.

Stewart had not had much luck, but a new car, introduced in Austria, improved his form. He finished the season with wins at Mosport and Watkins Glen, heading home Revson in the first race and Cevert in the latter. It was enough for Jackie to make a late run to second place in the championship, ahead of Hulme. The previous year's runner-up, Peterson, had a poor season. March's new car failed and a slightly more successful replacement was hastily built. However, Peterson had impressed the right people: for 1973 he earned himself a Lotus ride, alongside champion Fittipaldi. But there was sad news for Ronnie's country as well. In June veteran Jo Bonnier was killed when his Lola crashed at Le Mans. He raced from 1957 to 1971, but never matched the form which had given him BRM's first win in 1959.

CONSTRUCTORS' CUP 1972

	Make	Pts
1	Lotus	61
2	Tyrrell	51
3	McLaren	47
4	Ferrari	33
5	Surtees	18
6	March	15
7	BRM	14
8	Matra	12
9	Brabham	7

LANDMARK CAR
Tyrrell 005/006

Designer: **Derek Gardner**   Years raced: **1972-74**
Grand prix wins: **7**   Pole positions: **4**   Fastest laps: **4**
Engine type: **Ford DFV V8**
Engine size/power: **2,993cc/450bhp at 10,800rpm**
Confusingly, Tyrrell's 005 and 006 were effectively the same chassis. Smaller in almost every dimension from the 002/004 range they superseded, 005/006 gained small sidepods to house oil radiators either side of the cockpit, with fluted ends to the wide nose wing that housed the water radiators. By 1973, when 006 was in its pomp as Jackie Stewart raced to his third drivers' title, the car's appearance had been altered by the sprouting of an ever taller airbox behind the driver's head. These chassis continued to be used by the team into 1974.

DRIVERS' WORLD CHAMPIONSHIP 1972

	Driver (NATIONALITY)	Make	Pts
1	**Emerson Fittipaldi** (BRA)	Lotus-Ford	61
2	**Jackie Stewart** (GB)	Tyrrell-Ford	45
3	**Denny Hulme** (NZ)	McLaren-Ford	39
4	**Jacky Ickx** (BEL)	Ferrari	27
5	**Pete Revson** (USA)	McLaren-Ford	23
6	**François Cevert** (FRA)	Tyrrell-Ford	15
	Clay Regazzoni (SWI)	Ferrari	15
8	**Mike Hailwood** (GB)	Surtees-Ford	13
9	**Chris Amon** (NZ)	Matra	12
	Ronnie Peterson (SWE)	March-Ford	12

All scores counted

1973

Jackie Stewart acquired his third title after a hard battle with Lotus and decided to quit while he was at the top. Once again the season was blighted, with the deaths of François Cevert and newcomer Roger Williamson.

Colin Chapman's fortunes certainly looked good. Fittipaldi and Peterson represented a Lotus team of two top drivers, but some people remembered the previous time the team tried that with Rindt and Hill in 1969 – and Stewart won the championship.

Stewart and Cevert had developed into a fine partnership, and Hulme and Revson looked good at McLaren.

Ickx was joined at Ferrari by little Arturo Merzario, who had run a few races in 1972, while Regazzoni left to join Marlboro BRM.

An intriguing new marque was the American-financed Shadow. The sinister black cars were handled by Jackie Oliver and George Follmer, an American veteran with no Formula One experience. Graham Hill quit Brabham to set up his own team.

Fittipaldi had a dream start to his title defence, winning in both Argentina and his native Brazil. The first was by no means easy, since Regazzoni and Cevert both led before having problems.

In South Africa McLaren introduced the sleek and very modern-looking M23, which would ultimately have a lifetime of six seasons. Hulme put it on pole, but fell to fifth as Stewart scored a fine win after a heavy practice crash. Mike Hailwood became a hero in the race as he rescued Regazzoni from his burning car.

Fittipaldi scored a third win in Spain, and then Stewart added a second in Belgium, where the track broke up and many cars skated off. Jackie won again in Monaco to make it three each for the main contenders. The race saw the debut of Briton James Hunt, in a March run by aristocrat Lord Hesketh.

For the first time Sweden hosted a race at the Anderstorp circuit and, although local hero Peterson was on pole, Hulme gave the M23 its maiden victory. Ronnie got his revenge in France, finally scoring his first win after suffering appalling luck in the early races. It did not help him much at Silverstone, where the race was stopped after a multi-car pile-up was triggered by Jody Scheckter. Revson won the restarted race after Stewart spun out.

Tragedy returned to Zandvoort, when Roger Williamson – in only his second race – was killed in a fiery crash. Stewart and Cevert scored a one-two, a feat they repeated in Germany. In Austria, Peterson waved Fittipaldi through, but won anyway when Emerson retired. At Monza Peterson and Fittipaldi finished one-two, but the title went to Stewart. After an early stop he charged through the field to an amazing fourth place.

Revson won the chaotic, rain-hit Canadian race, which saw the first use of a pace car in Formula One. The circus moved to Watkins Glen where Stewart planned to have his 100th and last grand prix. But Cevert was killed in practice, and Tyrrell withdrew.

It was a bitter end to a fantastic farewell season for Stewart. In the race Peterson picked up a fourth win, but he was pushed hard by the fast-improving Hunt.

CONSTRUCTORS' CUP 1973

	Make	Pts
1	**Lotus**	92
2	**Tyrrell**	82
3	**McLaren**	58
4	**Brabham**	22
5	**March**	14
6	**BRM**	12
	Ferrari	12
8	**Shadow**	9
9	**Surtees**	7
10	**Iso Williams**	2

Winning Smile: Jackie Stewart looks delighted, having put the title in the bag by winning in Gemany

DRIVERS' WORLD CHAMPIONSHIP 1973

	Driver (NATIONALITY)	Make	Pts
1	**Jackie Stewart** (GB)	Tyrrell-Ford	71
2	**Emerson Fittipaldi** (BRA)	Lotus-Ford	55
3	**Ronnie Peterson** (SWE)	Lotus-Ford	52
4	**François Cevert** (FRA)	Tyrrell-Ford	47
5	**Pete Revson** (USA)	McLaren-Ford	38
6	**Denny Hulme** (NZ)	McLaren-Ford	26
7	**Carlos Reutemann** (ARG)	Brabham-Ford	16
8	**James Hunt** (GB)	March-Ford	14
9	**Jacky Ickx** (BEL)	Ferrari	12
10	**Jean-Pierre Beltoise** (FRA)	BRM	9

All scores counted

1974

This was one of the closest championships for years, in which Fittipaldi and Regazzoni battled for top position. In a dramatic finale Fittipaldi claimed his second title – a first for McLaren. At the year's end Denny Hulme retired.

Homegrown Hero: Fittipaldi moved from Lotus to McLaren and won on his second outing in Brazil

The winter of 1973-74 was one of the busiest in memory. The big news was that Fittipaldi quit Lotus to join McLaren, along with substantial new backing from Texaco and Marlboro. Hulme stayed on as his team-mate, while a third car – in Yardley colours – was entered for Hailwood.

Ickx left Ferrari to join Peterson at Lotus, while Tyrrell found himself needing two new drivers. He hired Scheckter from McLaren and French newcomer Patrick Depailler. Revson also left McLaren, joining French youngster Jean-Pierre Jarier at Shadow. Hill's team swapped from Shadow to Lola chassis, while Hesketh built its own car for Hunt. BRM had new French sponsors, and Beltoise led a squad of three French drivers.

Amon's career took another dive as he tried to run his own team.

Regazzoni rejoined Ferrari after a year at BRM, and brought with him Lauda. From the start the revised Ferrari line-up was competitive. Hulme won the first race in Argentina, but Regazzoni qualified on the front row and Lauda took second in the race.

In Brazil Peterson and Fittipaldi duelled for the lead until the Swede punctured, leaving Emerson to score McLaren's second. At last, Reutemann came good by winning in Kyalami – Brabham's first success for exactly four years. Sadly, in pre-race testing Revson was killed when he crashed the Shadow.

At Jarama Ferrari's promise produced results when Lauda won.

Fittipaldi scored a second win in Nivelles, and then Peterson triumphed at Monaco. Two weeks later Tyrrell new boys Scheckter and Depailler scored a brilliant one-two in Sweden.

Lauda and Regazzoni scored a Ferrari one-two in the French Grand Prix, and then Scheckter took his second at Brands Hatch. At the Nurburgring Lauda threw it away on the first lap, leaving Regazzoni to save face for Ferrari. Reutemann won in Austria, and then Peterson was on top at Monza when the Ferraris failed.

Fittipaldi made his claim in the penultimate race at Mosport, winning ahead of Regazzoni. Incredibly, they went into the final race on equal points. In the end a fourth place was enough for Emmo, with neither of his rivals scoring. McLaren also beat Ferrari to the constructors' title. But the race was marred by the death of rookie Helmuth Koinigg.

CONSTRUCTORS' CUP 1974

	Make	Pts
1	**McLaren**	73
2	**Ferrari**	65
3	**Tyrrell**	52
4	**Lotus**	42
5	**Brabham**	35
6	**Hesketh**	15
7	**BRM**	10
8	**Shadow**	7
9	**March**	6
10	**Iso Williams**	4

McLaren M23

Designer: **Gordon Coppuck**   Years raced: **1973-78**
Grand prix wins: **16**   Pole positions: **14**   Fastest laps: **10**
Engine type: **Ford DFV V8**
Engine size/power: **2,993cc/475bhp at 10,750rpm**
This is the chassis that took over from the Lotus 72 as the pick of the pack in the early 1970s and went on to help two drivers, Emerson Fittipaldi and James Hunt, to win two titles, in 1974 and 1976 respectively. Amazingly, this was Gordon Coppuck's first full Formula One design. Just as the Lotus 72 evolved from the rounded 49, so the M23 followed the curvaceous M19, with its wedge nose and broad sidepods. The M23 started with its airbox high above the driver's head, but this was chopped down early in 1976 when such airboxes were outlawed, leaving an inverted L-shaped vent either side of his helmet.

DRIVERS' WORLD CHAMPIONSHIP 1974

	Driver (NATIONALITY)	Make	Pts
1	**Emerson Fittipaldi** (BRA)	McLaren-Ford	55
2	**Clay Regazzoni** (SWI)	Ferrari	52
3	**Jody Scheckter** (RSA)	Tyrrell-Ford	45
4	**Niki Lauda** (AUT)	Ferrari	38
5	**Ronnie Peterson** (SWE)	Lotus-Ford	35
6	**Carlos Reutemann** (ARG)	Brabham-Ford	32
7	**Denny Hulme** (NZ)	McLaren-Ford	20
8	**James Hunt** (GB)	Hesketh-Ford	15
9	**Patrick Depailler** (FRA)	Tyrrell-Ford	14
10	**Mike Hailwood** (GB)	McLaren-Ford	12
	Jacky Ickx (BEL)	Lotus-Ford	12

All scores counted

1975

Niki Lauda dominated the season in brilliant style. Amazing to record, it was Ferrari's first championship since Surtees had triumphed 11 years earlier. Graham Hill's death in a plane crash brought a tragic end to the year.

The winter season saw few changes among the front-runners. Graham Hill planned a switch from Lola to his own Hill team. Following the first two races, he announced his retirement after an incredible 176 starts.

Fittipaldi won in Argentina for McLaren, ahead of Hunt's Hesketh after the Englishman lost the lead with a mistake. In Brazil, Pace scored a popular first win in his home country, ahead of local hero Fittipaldi. Pace and Reutemann shared the front row in South Africa, but Scheckter scored a home win for Tyrrell.

At the Spanish race the Ferraris were the pacesetters, with Lauda and Regazzoni on the front row. But the event was beset by a dispute over safety standards at the Montjuich Park track. Eventually a boycott was avoided, but the race turned to chaos. Half the field crashed, including the Ferraris. Rolf Stommelen led in the Hill, but crashed when the rear wing broke, killing several onlookers. The race was stopped early with Mass leading.

In a soaking wet race at Monaco Lauda and the 312T came good, winning from Fittipaldi. Lauda followed that with wins at Zolder and Anderstorp. Zandvoort brought a popular first win for Hunt and the Hesketh team. James had developed into a top-rank driver, and in Holland beat Lauda in a dramatic wet/dry fight. The result was reversed when Lauda won at sunny Paul Ricard.

The rain returned at Silverstone – for another dramatic weekend which saw 15 cars crash. Pryce stunned everyone with pole and he, Pace, Regazzoni, Jarier and Hunt all took turns in the lead. When the crashes finally forced a red flag, Fittipaldi was ahead. Surprisingly, it was to prove his last ever Formula One victory.

In Germany, Reutemann survived as most of the front-runners had punctures, and then in Austria rain and confusion struck once more. The popular Brambilla was ahead when the race was curtailed to give the works March team its first win – and the first for any March since 1970. Tragically, however, American driver Mark Donohue crashed in the warm-up and subsequently succumbed to head injuries.

Lauda had been quietly racking up the points, and clinched his first title with a third at Monza, as team-mate Regazzoni won. Just Watkins Glen remained, and Lauda added yet another win.

November brought a tragedy which shocked the racing world. On the way back from a test session at Paul Ricard, Graham Hill crashed his light plane. The double world champion and several of his team were killed.

French Polish: victory at Paul Ricard put Niki Lauda on the road to the title in his Ferrari 312T

GREAT RACE

Dutch Grand Prix 1975

This was a race in which David put one over on Goliath. David was played by James Hunt, racing for aristocratic British privateers Hesketh, and Goliath by soon-to-be world champion Niki Lauda for Ferrari. Lauda qualified on pole and led the way on a wet track. Hunt was lying in fourth. However, the track soon started to dry and Hunt was the first to pit for slick tyres. Hunt emerged in the lead, revelling in a car that had been set up for dry conditions. After overtaking Jarier with 30 laps to go, Lauda locked on to the Hesketh. Hunt's advantage was whittled away and, with 20 laps to run, Lauda was a second behind. Hunt's white Hesketh then came under huge pressure, but the Englishman held his ground all the way to the chequered flag to trigger riotous partying from Lord Hesketh and his entourage.

DRIVERS' WORLD CHAMPIONSHIP 1975

	Driver (NATIONALITY)	Make	Pts
1	Niki Lauda (AUT)	Ferrari	64.5
2	Emerson Fittipaldi (BRA)	McLaren-Ford	45
3	Carlos Reutemann (ARG)	Brabham-Ford	37
4	James Hunt (GB)	Hesketh-Ford	33
5	Clay Regazzoni (SWI)	Ferrari	25
6	Carlos Pace (BRA)	Brabham-Ford	24
7	Jochen Mass (GER)	McLaren-Ford	20
	Jody Scheckter (RSA)	Tyrrell-Ford	20
9	Patrick Depailler (FRA)	Tyrrell-Ford	12
10	Tom Pryce (GB)	Shadow-Ford	8

All scores counted

1976

This season will go down as one of the most dramatic in the history of Formula One. Niki Lauda survived a terrible accident in Germany and was quickly back in harness, but James Hunt beat him to the title in the Japanese finale.

As in 1974, Emerson Fittipaldi was at the centre of the news. After two years he decided to quit McLaren and join his brother's team, Copersucar. McLaren was left stranded without a number one driver, but the timing was perfect. Lord Hesketh had decided to pull the plug on his very competitive team, and Hunt was unemployed. It did not take long for him to find his way to McLaren.

Brabham secured Alfa engines, while Tyrrell stunned everyone by announcing a six-wheeled car, the P34. At Lotus, Chapman designed a new car, the 77. Ickx left for Wolf-Williams, and Peterson was joined at the first race by Andretti, a Lotus driver back in 1968-69. Neither was certain to stay, and matters were not helped when they collided in the first race in Brazil.

Lauda started, as he had finished the previous season, with a win.

Hunt was on pole in Kyalami, but again Lauda won. An exciting addition to the calendar was a street race at Long Beach, dubbed the US Grand Prix West. Regazzoni led the whole way.

The European season began at Jarama. All the cars were different since new rules banned tall air boxes, and the race saw the debut of the six-wheeler. Hunt beat Lauda, but was disqualified when the car was found to be fractionally too wide. Lauda won in Belgium and Monaco, and at neither race did Hunt score. Sweden saw a fabulous one-two for the six-wheelers, Scheckter heading home Depailler. Hunt's luck turned at Paul Ricard, when the Ferraris broke and he won easily. The same week he was

reinstated as Spanish winner, but at Brands Hatch fortune did not favour him. Lauda and Regazzoni collided at the first corner, and the race was stopped. Hunt won the restart in style, but was disqualified because he had not been running at the time of the red flag. It gave Lauda another win.

In Germany disaster struck when Lauda crashed heavily and was badly burned. Hunt won the race, but the world waited for news on Lauda. Somehow he pulled through and began a remarkable recovery. Unbelievably, Lauda was back in Monza, where Peterson won for March and Niki finished fourth. Hunt scored nothing, but struck back with wins at Mosport and Watkins Glen. That put him to within three points of Lauda as the circus moved to Fuji for the

first Japanese Grand Prix. The weather was atrocious, and Lauda immediately pulled out. In a thrilling chase, Hunt came storming back from a tyre stop to take the third place he required.

Victory Roll: James Hunt celebrates winning the British GP but it wasn't a result that would stand

LANDMARK CAR

Tyrrell P34

Designer: **Derek Gardner**   Years raced: **1976-77**
Grand prix wins: **1**   Pole positions: **1**   Fastest laps: **3**
Engine type: **Ford DFV V8**
Engine size/power: **2,993cc/470bhp at 10,800rpm**
Six-wheelers could have been the way to go, but although a winner, Tyrrell's P34 never quite caused designers of rival teams to follow suit. The P34 had a pair of small front wheels fitted one behind the other supported by regular-sized wheels at the rear. The idea was that the car's reduced frontal area would lead to less drag and create better airflow to the rear wing. The extra rubber would also improve road-holding and braking. It was good enough for Jody Scheckter to win the Swedish GP in its first year, but even Ronnie Peterson could not win with one in 1977.

DRIVERS' WORLD CHAMPIONSHIP 1976

	Driver (NATIONALITY)	Make	Pts
1	**James Hunt** (GB)	McLaren-Ford	69
2	**Niki Lauda** (AUT)	Ferrari	68
3	**Jody Scheckter** (RSA)	Tyrrell-Ford	49
4	**Patrick Depailler** (FRA)	Tyrrell-Ford	39
5	**Clay Regazzoni** (SWI)	Ferrari	31
6	**Mario Andretti** (USA)	Parnelli/Lotus-Ford	22
7	**Jacques Laffite** (FRA)	Ligier-Matra	20
	John Watson (GB)	Penske-Ford	20
9	**Jochen Mass** (GER)	McLaren-Ford	19
10	**Gunnar Nilsson** (SWE)	Lotus-Ford	11

All scores counted

1977

Niki Lauda was most certainly not the fastest driver, but he was consistent and the Ferrari proved to be extremely reliable. He succeeded in beating off strong challenges from Andretti, Hunt and Scheckter to win his second title.

After three seasons Scheckter quit Tyrrell to join an intriguing new team, Walter Wolf Racing. Hunt and Mass stayed at McLaren to drive the new M26, the replacement for the ageing M23 and, even before the end of 1976, Reutemann left Brabham to join Ferrari. Peterson replaced Scheckter at Tyrrell, and Watson left the now defunct Penske team to replace Reutemann at Brabham.

Chapman had pulled another surprise, providing Andretti and his new team-mate, Gunnar Nilsson, with the stunning 78, the first "ground-effects" car. It had prominent side pods with sliding skirts which produced masses of downforce. The latest Brabham-Alfa was quick, Watson leading the opening race in Argentina until it broke. Team-mate Carlos Pace and Hunt also led, but victory went to Scheckter and the new Wolf. Ferrari was also competitive. Reutemann won in Brazil, and then at Kyalami Lauda scored his first success since his accident. The race was marred by the death of Tom Pryce, the Welshman hitting a marshal who ran across the track. Before the next race Pace lost his life in a plane crash.

Scheckter led most of the way at Long Beach but, when he punctured, Andretti went ahead to give the Lotus 78 its first win. He quickly added a second in Spain.

Scheckter took his second of the season in Monaco, which marked the 100th win for the Cosworth DFV. In Belgium there was a typically confusing wet race and it resulted in a fine win for Nilsson in the second Lotus. Hunt had had no luck in his title defence, but at Silverstone he beat Watson in a splendid duel. The race saw the debut of Jean-Pierre Jabouille's Renault and its V6 turbocharged engine.

Lauda scored Goodyear's 100th win in Hockenheim, and once again Austria produced an unusual result, Alan Jones giving Shadow its first win in another damp encounter.

The summer witnessed a spate of Cosworth engine failures. Andretti had four in a row, and Hunt and Scheckter also suffered. Meanwhile, Lauda quietly racked up the points, scoring another win in Holland. Andretti's car held together long enough for him to win in Monza. At a wet Watkins Glen Hunt won after Stuck crashed, but Lauda's fourth place clinched the title. With that, he upped and left Ferrari.

There were still two races left. Scheckter won in Canada, after Mass tipped team-mate Hunt off. James ended on a high note with a win in Japan, where this time the sun shone. But the race was marred by the deaths of two spectators after Ferrari new boy Gilles Villeneuve tangled with Peterson and the car flipped over the barrier.

Fittipaldi had another bad season with his own car, although he occasionally broke into the top six, while Peterson and Depailler struggled all year with the latest six-wheeler. At the end of the year Tyrrell ditched the concept. In contrast, fellow veteran Regazzoni did great things with the little Ensign team, picking up a few points.

CONSTRUCTORS' CUP 1977

	Make	Pts
1	Ferrari	95
2	Lotus	62
3	McLaren	60
4	Wolf	55
5	Brabham	27
	Tyrrell	27
7	Shadow	23
8	Ligier	18
9	Fittipaldi	11
10	Ensign	10

DRIVERS' WORLD CHAMPIONSHIP 1977

	Driver (NATIONALITY)	Make	Pts
1	**Niki Lauda** (AUT)	Ferrari	72
2	**Jody Scheckter** (RSA)	Wolf-Ford	55
3	**Mario Andretti** (USA)	Lotus-Ford	47
4	**Carlos Reutemann** (ARG)	Ferrari	42
5	**James Hunt** (GB)	McLaren-Ford	40
6	**Jochen Mass** (GER)	McLaren-Ford	25
7	**Alan Jones** (AUS)	Shadow-Ford	22
8	**Patrick Depailler** (FRA)	Tyrrell-Ford	20
	Gunnar Nilsson (SWE)	Lotus-Ford	20
10	**Jacques Laffite** (FRA)	Ligier-Matra	18

All scores counted

Up for It: James Hunt and Niki Lauda fight for supremacy on the run to the first corner at Kyalami

1978

Mario Andretti won the title after a brilliant run with Chapman's wonderful Lotus 79. But it was a year of mixed feelings for Mario, as team-mate Ronnie Peterson died from injuries received in a first-lap accident at Monza.

Quick off the Mark: Lotus aces Andretti and Peterson show the pack a clean pair of heels at Zandvoort

Nobody seemed to cotton on to the secrets of the Lotus 78, and rival teams were in for a shock when Colin Chapman introduced the beautiful 79. He had a new second driver, too, with Peterson back at Lotus, eager to restore his name. Meanwhile, Nilsson left to join Arrows, but he never got to drive as cancer set in, leaving the team to sign up Riccardo Patrese. Another former Shadow driver, Alan Jones, also linked up with what was effectively a new team: Williams.

Newcomer Didier Pironi joined Depailler in the four-wheel Tyrrell 008, while Patrick Tambay replaced Mass at McLaren. Villeneuve landed a full-time seat at Ferrari, alongside Reutemann. The new 312T3 was a superb machine, and the team changed to Michelin.

Starting the season with the old 78, Andretti won in Argentina. In Brazil Reutemann won for Ferrari, and Fittipaldi finally came good with second in the "family car". Kyalami was a classic. The race culminated in a fabulous duel between Peterson and Depailler, Ronnie just winning. Villeneuve starred at Long Beach, leading until he hit back marker Regazzoni and allowed Reutemann to score. Monaco saw Depailler finally earn his first win. In Belgium Mario debuted the 79, disappeared into the distance, with Peterson taking second in the 78. They scored another one-two in Jarama.

By now the others were reacting. Scheckter had a proper ground-effect Wolf, and Brabham responded with the amazing "fan car". Lauda dominated in its only race at Anderstorp before it was abruptly banned. Andretti and Peterson scored a one-two in France. At Brands Hatch they both retired, and Reutemann passed Lauda to win.

Rain struck in Austria, and Peterson drove brilliantly to win the red-flagged race. At Monza, only Peterson could now beat Mario to the title, but he was happy to obey orders. He had to take the start in the old 78, and got in a massive pile-up. The race was restarted and Andretti won from Villeneuve, but both were penalized for jumped starts. Lauda took the honours. Peterson died the following morning and the racing world was stunned.

Jean-Pierre Jarier replaced him, and was the star of the last two races, although he retired in both events. Reutemann held off Jones in Watkins Glen, while Villeneuve won on a new track in Montreal. There was more sadness when Nilsson succumbed to cancer 12 days after the Canadian race. He was just 29 years old.

CONSTRUCTORS' CUP 1978

	Make	Pts
1	**Lotus**	86
2	**Ferrari**	58
3	**Brabham**	53
4	**Tyrrell**	38
5	**Wolf**	24
6	**Ligier**	19
7	**Fittipaldi**	17
8	**McLaren**	15
9	**Arrows**	11
	Williams	11

LANDMARK CAR
Lotus 79

Designer: **Martin Ogilvie**   Years raced: **1978-79**
Grand prix wins: **6**   Pole positions: **10**   Fastest laps: **5**
Engine type: **Ford DFV V8**
Engine size/power: **2,993cc/4,85bhp at 10,800rpm**
Its forerunner, the Lotus 78, introduced ground effects to Formula One but it was the more rounded and cohesive 79 that perfected them. In short, harnessing ground effects helped channel and contain airflow under the car under lengthy sidepods with undersides shaped like inverted wings to create an area of negative pressure that effectively sucked the car down to the track. As with the 78, this air flowing under the car was stopped from escaping to the sides by small skirts made of brushes. Mario Andretti, in particular, made the car sing.

DRIVERS' WORLD CHAMPIONSHIP 1978

	Driver (NATIONALITY)	Make	Pts
1	**Mario Andretti** (USA)	Lotus-Ford	64
2	**Ronnie Peterson** (SWE)	Lotus-Ford	51
3	**Carlos Reutemann** (ARG)	Ferrari	48
4	**Niki Lauda** (AUT)	Brabham-Alfa Romeo	44
5	**Patrick Depailler** (FRA)	Tyrrell-Ford	34
6	**John Watson** (GB)	Brabham-Alfa Romeo	25
7	**Jody Scheckter** (RSA)	Wolf-Ford	24
8	**Jacques Laffite** (FRA)	Ligier-Matra	19
9	**Emerson Fittipaldi** (BRA)	Fittipaldi-Ford	17
	Gilles Villeneuve (CAN)	Ferrari	17

All scores counted

1979

Ground-effect cars took over the Formula One scene, although some worked better than others. In a very competitive season the reliability of the Ferraris gave them top place and helped Jody Scheckter to scoop the title.

Things looked good at Lotus as Ferrari ace Reutemann joined Andretti, Martini replaced JPS as title sponsor and Chapman still had the inside line on new technology. Or did he? The wingless Lotus 80 was supposed to be a leap forward, but it did not work.

Williams was also spot on with its new car, the FW07. It was not ready at the start of the season, so Jones and new team-mate Regazzoni started out in the old machine. Ferrari was also late with the 312T4. Scheckter quit Wolf to join Villeneuve. After 18 months in the background, Renault expanded to a second entry for René Arnoux and built the effective RS10.

Ligier started the season with a bang, and Laffite won the races in Argentina and Brazil. The new Ferrari arrived at Kyalami, and Villeneuve and Scheckter finished one-two. Significantly, Jabouille's Renault took its first pole. Villeneuve and Scheckter repeated the result at Long Beach. Ligier bounced back in Spain, sweeping the front row; Depailler led throughout. Lotus had a rare good day, Reutemann and Andretti taking second and third. Zolder saw the debut of the Williams FW07. Jones led easily until retiring, leaving victory to Scheckter. Jody won again in Monaco, chased home by Regazzoni's FW07. After retiring in this race, Hunt decided he had had enough and hung up his helmet. Wolf signed fiery Finn Keke Rosberg to replace him.

In France, Renault's Jabouille gave the team its first win. And, in a thrilling finale, Villeneuve just edged Arnoux out of second. Then luck went the way of Williams. Regazzoni gave the team a fabulous first win at Silverstone, which was followed by successes for Jones at Hockenheim, the Osterreichring and Zandvoort.

Scheckter kept collecting points, and by winning at Monza he had amassed enough to claim the title with two races to go. By Montreal, Brabham had abandoned the awful BT48 and replaced it with the neat DFV-powered BT49. It did not interest Lauda, who announced he was quitting.

The race saw a fine battle between Jones and Villeneuve, which went the way of the Williams driver. The pair fought again at a wet Watkins Glen, but Jones lost a wheel after a pit stop, and the gutsy little Canadian won with another display of Ferrari reliability.

Triple Treat: Scheckter's victory at Monaco was one of his three wins as he became champion

CONSTRUCTORS' CUP 1979

	Make	Pts
1	Ferrari	113
2	Williams	75
3	Ligier	61
4	Lotus	39
5	Tyrrell	28
6	Renault	26
7	McLaren	15
8	Brabham	7
9	Arrows	5
10	Shadow	3

TECHNICAL INNOVATION

Turbocharging

Turbo badges were all the rage in the 1980s, with almost all performance cars, save for those with massive engines, using turbochargers to produce extra horsepower. The concept was all about utilizing the engine's exhaust gases and re-routing them through a compressor to push the petrol/air mix through at a greater rate. Although this was a technique first tried at the start of the 20th century, it wasn't until 1977 that it made it into Formula One, with Renault in the vanguard of a technique that was to take engine outputs to record horsepower figures of 1300bhp. Renault's early steps were tentative, with Jean-Pierre Jabouille seldom reaching the end of the race, but it was soon clear that this was the way to go. Jabouille finally scored that first turbo win in 1979, with Nelson Piquet becoming the first turbo-powered World Champion in 1983. Turbo engines raced on until 1988, after which only normally aspirated engines were permitted.

DRIVERS' WORLD CHAMPIONSHIP 1979

	Driver (NATIONALITY)	Make	Pts
1	Jody Scheckter (RSA)	Ferrari	51
2	Gilles Villeneuve (CAN)	Ferrari	47
3	Alan Jones (AUS)	Williams-Ford	40
4	Jacques Laffite (FRA)	Ligier-Ford	36
5	Clay Regazzoni (SWI)	Williams-Ford	29
6	Carlos Reutemann (ARG)	Lotus-Ford	20
	Patrick Depailler (FRA)	Ligier-Ford	20
8	René Arnoux (FRA)	Renault	17
9	John Watson (GB)	McLaren-Ford	15
10	Mario Andretti (USA)	Lotus-Ford	14
	Jean-Pierre Jarier (FRA)	Tyrrell-Ford	14
	Didier Pironi (FRA)	Tyrrell-Ford	14

Best eight scores from 15 races to count

DEFINING MOMENTS
1980s

1980 Spanish Grand Prix
DIFFERENCE OF OPINION

Politics make the world go around, but this wasn't the case at Jarama when the FISA-supporting teams Ferrari, Renault and Alfa Romeo withdrew after the race promoter sided with the FOCA teams over a long-running argument. The race went ahead, but it wasn't to count for the championship. More squabbles would follow.

1982 San Marino Grand Prix (left)
LEADING MAN

The next race at which the FISA v FOCA battle led to teams withdrawing was at Imola, but it will always be remembered for the bad blood that came out of Didier Pironi apparently going back on a pre-race agreement with Ferrari team-mate Gilles Villeneuve that whoever was leading at the start of the final lap would win.

1984 Monaco Grand Prix
TOTAL WASH-OUT

If wet weather sorts the men from the boys, Clerk-of-the-Course Jacky Ickx saved McLaren's Alain Prost from the boys when he stopped the race early because of heavy rain. This deprived the fast-closing Ayrton Senna of a shot at victory in his Toleman, with Tyrrell's Stefan Bellof catching both at an even greater rate.

1986 Australian Grand Prix
SO NEAR AND YET SO FAR

A second can make a massive difference as Nigel Mansell discovered in Adelaide when running third and set to land the world title. Then he had a blow-out at 180mph and did well to guide his snaking car down an escape road. With Alain Prost going on to win, the sidelined Brit would have to wait another six years to become champion.

1987 British Grand Prix
BEST OF ENEMIES

A few drivers like each other, most tolerate each other, but some, like Nigel Mansell and Nelson Piquet, hate each other. This is why the Williams duo's battle was so fierce at Silverstone, with Mansell making up 28 seconds after an unplanned pitstop and all but touching a swerving Piquet as he blasted past with less than three laps to go.

1988 Portuguese Grand Prix
GOING FOR GOLD

As with Mansell and Piquet, driving for the same team as your chief rival isn't easy, and so McLaren's Alain Prost and Ayrton Senna came close to blows at Estoril when going for gold as the season wound down. Senna led at the end of the first lap but, as Prost tried to pass him, Senna all but squeezed him into the pitwall.

1980

Alan Jones triumphed in the 1980 World Championship despite a strong challenge from Nelson Piquet. However, for the first time in its history, Formula One politics began to attract almost as much attention as the sport itself.

Williams FW07

Designer: **Patrick Head** Years raced: **1979-82**
Grand prix wins: **15** Pole positions: **8** Fastest laps: **16**
Engine type: **Ford DFV V8**
Engine size/power: **2,993cc/475bhp at 10,800rpm**

This was the car that took Williams into the big time. It was the team's first ground-effect car and came on stream part way into the 1979 season, once the races reached Europe. Clay Regazzoni gave the car its breakthrough win, on its fifth outing, at the British GP. Then Alan Jones won four of the next five races, outpacing the previously dominant Ferraris and the Lotus 79 that had introduced ground-effect, thanks to superior chassis rigidity. The FW07 was remodelled into the FW07B in 1980, helping Jones to five wins and the world title, and later became the FW07C in 1981, when under-car skirts had been banned.

Just as Colin Chapman failed to follow up his 1978 success, so Enzo Ferrari's team lost its way in 1980. The new 312T5 was not a very efficient ground-effect car.

Indeed, reigning champion Jody Scheckter failed to win a race or even reach the podium, with one fifth place his solitary score all year. Team-mate Gilles Villeneuve fared little better and they could only look on in admiration

as Alan Jones and Williams continued the form that made them the dominant force in the second half of the 1979 season.

While Ferrari was heading down the charts, Brabham was getting its act together thanks to dropping Alfa Romeo engines and joining most of the other teams in using Ford Cosworth DFV power. With Niki Lauda having retired, it was very much a team built

around Nelson Piquet, supported in little more than sharing a garage by Ricardo Zunino then Hector Rebaque. Another change among the top teams was that former Ligier driver Patrick Depailler had recovered from the injuries he sustained in a hang-glider accident and stepped from the physio's bench to Alfa Romeo, to be replaced by Didier Pironi who moved across from Tyrrell.

The number of teams was starting to decline after the boom days of the late 1970s, with the Merzario, Rebaque and Kauhsen teams not returning for any further action, but with Osella stepping up from Formula Two.

The Wolf and Fittipaldi teams merged but retained their respective drivers. Rosberg and Emerson started the season in the rebadged 1979 Wolfs, while a new F8 came on stream later.

Queue Jumper: Australia's Alan Jones leads the way for Williams at the start of the Dutch Grand Prix, Zandvoort, chased by René Arnoux and Jacques Laffite

Alfa Romeo now returned with two Marlboro-backed machines for Bruno Giacomelli and Depailler.

Jones began the season much as he finished 1979. Indeed, with the season kicking off in January, it was only 14 weeks after the last race of 1979, giving little time for things to change. He dominated in Argentina, despite spinning twice on a crumbling track. Piquet scored his best result to date with second, while Rosberg gave some hint of his potential with third for the Fittipaldi team. René Arnoux won for Renault in Brazil, then repeated the feat in South Africa ahead of the Ligiers of Laffite and Pironi at a meeting that interrupted Marc Surer's season as he broke his ankles in practice, with Jan Lammers filling in until his return.

Long Beach saw the end of Clay Regazzoni's career. He crashed his Ensign at the end of Shoreline Drive and was paralysed. Meanwhile, Piquet took pole and scored his first win, ahead of Patrese and Fittipaldi. Most of the big names retired, including Depailler, who held a fine second with the new Alfa. The Williams FW07B

Tight Corner: even the champions get it wrong as Jones shows by crashing out of the Dutch GP

made its bow at Zolder and, although it was quick, Jones and Reutemann were led home by Pironi, another first-time winner. Pironi was on form again at Monaco but, after he hit the barrier, the steady Reutemann took victory.

At Jarama politics and racing collided head on, as FOCA was in dispute with FISA. A confusing weekend ended with a "Formula DFV" race going ahead without Ferrari, Alfa and Renault. It was not to count for World Championship points. Jones won there and won again at

Paul Ricard and Brands Hatch. The Renaults were quick but fragile in Germany and, when leader Jones had a puncture, Laffite took the victory. Sadly, in pre-race testing Depailler crashed fatally in the Alfa.

France took another win in Austria, Jabouille scoring his second success as he held off the determined Jones. Lotus test driver Nigel Mansell was finally given his chance in a third car, only to have to start the race in a fuel-soaked race suit. In Holland, Jones threw it away by damaging a skirt on a kerb. Piquet, who was developing into a deadly rival, took the win, ahead of Arnoux.

The Italian Grand Prix moved to Imola for the first time, and Piquet

scored another win from a brake-troubled Jones.

The situation was tense going to Montreal, and it blew up when Piquet and Jones tangled on the first lap and caused a huge pile-up.

For the restart, Piquet had to ride in the spare, and his qualifying engine duly failed. Pironi led all the way, but was penalized for a jumped start. Jones sat in second and took maximum points, and the title.

Two big names drove their final races at the Glen. Having failed to qualify the dreadful Ferrari in Canada, Scheckter finished 11th and last. Meanwhile, Fittipaldi broke his suspension on lap 15, ending another trying season with his own team.

THE POLITICS OF FORMULA ONE

FISA v FOCA Wars

The early 1980s witnessed a power struggle between the Federation Internationale du Sport Automobiles (sporting arm of the FIA) and the Formula One Constructors' Association. Manufacturer-entered teams Alfa Romeo, Ferrari and Renault sided with FISA and the British "garagistes" took FOCA's side. FOCA had grown strong through the 1970s with Brabham supremo Bernie Ecclestone at its helm. Indeed, race organizers gave him the prize fund to distribute. This led to the FISA-supporting teams withdrawing from the 1980 Spanish GP when the organizer backed the FOCA teams in an argument. The race went ahead with 22 cars and was subsequently declared null and void. Round two was at Kyalami in 1981 when the FOCA teams raced with the skirts that FISA had banned. Again the race was to count for nothing. After a flare-up in Brazil in 1982, the final skirmish was at Imola, with the FOCA teams refusing to turn out in response to two of them being excluded from first and second in Brazil for running underweight. In their quest to match the turbo cars, the FOCA teams dumped their coolant soon after the start, then had it topped up again before the cars were scrutinized. Their no-show left just 14 cars, but the race was allowed to count towards the World Championship. Matters were never this bad again.

1981

Nelson Piquet successfully turned the tables on Alan Jones in 1981, winning his first World Championship title and the first for Brabham since Bernie Ecclestone took control. Unfortunately, off-track disputes dominated the headlines.

McLaren MP4

Designer: **John Barnard**   Years raced: **1981-83**
Grand prix wins: **6**   Pole positions: **0**   Fastest laps: **5**
Engine type: **Ford DFV V8 and later TAG Porsche turbo V6**
Engine size/power: **2,993cc/480bhp at 11,000rpm and later 1,499cc/700bhp at 11,500rpm**
No more than once a decade is an epochal car created, and the MP4 is one of the most groundbreaking. The brainchild of John Barnard, this was not only the first car with a carbonfibre monocoque, but also the one that put McLaren back on the rails following the Ron Dennis takeover. Harnessing this material from the aerospace industry was inspired, as it offered strength and rigidity and yet was lighter than traditional materials. A race winner for John Watson in 1981 and 1982, it was re-adapted for Niki Lauda in 1983, when a TAG Turbo was fitted.

After the disaster of 1980, Ferrari switched to a new V6 turbo engine, the Italian team becoming the first to follow Renault's pioneering route, with Didier Pironi joining from Ligier to replace the retired Jody Scheckter.

The other big news of the winter was the takeover of McLaren by Ron Dennis, with John Barnard immediately setting to work on a revolutionary carbon fibre chassis and Alain Prost leaving to replace Jean-Pierre Jabouille at Renault, with his seat alongside John Watson being filled by Andrea de Cesaris, who had made his Formula One debut with Alfa Romeo at the end of 1980. Alfa Romeo had a more than capable replacement in the form of 1978 champion Mario Andretti who would partner Bruno Giacomelli. The other main changes on the driving front were at Tyrrell, with Michele Alboreto and Eddie Cheever taking over from Derek Daly and Jean-Pierre Jarier, with Marc Surer now Ensign's team leader.

The Shadow team was no longer part of the show, having folded early in 1980. But numbers were up as March returned for the first time since 1977, Theodore joined in using largely ex-Shadow stock and Toleman stepped up from Formula Two, keeping drivers Brian Henton and Derek Warwick who had dominated the 1980 season.

The championship began at Long Beach and with sliding skirts officially banned. Patrese took a surprise pole with the Arrows, but victory went to champion Jones, ahead of Reutemann and Piquet.

The Ferraris were quick, but fragile. Amazingly, Patrick Tambay brought his unfancied Theodore home sixth. Lotus had its nose out of joint as its twin-chassis 88 was turned away after first practice as it was considered outside the spirit of the rules.

In Brazil the new rules turned to farce. Brabham had perfected a hydro-pneumatic suspension system – the car was legal in the pits, but on the track it sat down and the skirts touched the ground. Piquet took pole, started the wet race on slicks and blew it. Reutemann controversially

Hitting the Jackpot: Brabham driver Nelson Piquet sprays champagne as he celebrates winning the Drivers' World Championship title finale at Las Vegas

led Jones home, because he was supposed to let Jones past. In Argentina Piquet made no mistake, winning easily, while unrated team-mate Hector Rebaque ran second until his car broke.

The European season started at Imola with the newly invented San Marino Grand Prix – an excuse to have two races in Italy. Villeneuve and Pironi both led the wet race early on, but Piquet came through to win from Patrese and Reutemann.

At Zolder, a mechanic from the small Osella team died after being struck by a car in practice, and an Arrows mechanic suffered broken legs when hit attending Patrese's stalled car on the grid – just as the race started. Pironi led until his brakes went, Jones crashed out after earlier knocking Piquet off and the win went to Reutemann.

Wings of Victory: a win in the German GP came Nelson Piquet's way when his rivals hit trouble

TECHNICAL INNOVATION

Twin Chassis (Lotus 88)

Lotus founder Colin Chapman possessed the most fertile imagination in Formula One. He might not have been the greatest designer, but he was the one with the guts to chase any new notion that might provide his team with an advantage. With Lotus's introduction of ground-effects still fresh in everyone's minds, Chapman tried to take matters further in 1981 with the Lotus 88 chassis – or, more accurately, two chassis, as this was the car's revolutionary concept. The idea was that one chassis – comprising the bodywork, front and rear wings and sidepods – would be attached by coil springs to the other (via the wheel uprights), and be forced down at speed to offer greater downforce without the suspension itself having to be as stiff as it was on "regular" cars, leaving the sprung chassis free. The car caused a stir on its unveiling at Long Beach and was banned after practice for stepping outside the spirit of the rules banning cars from running with their bodywork within 6cm of the track surface. Chapman tried to get around the unrest by defining the chassis as "sprung structures". The organizers of the British GP accepted this, but the sport's governing body decided that this was one interpretation of the rules too far, and prevented it from making its debut at Silverstone or ever racing thereafter. Chapman was furious and, indeed, failed ever to be as ingenious again.

Mansell was in great form at Monaco, qualifying third behind Piquet and Villeneuve. Nelson led, but Jones put him under pressure and the Brazilian crashed out.

Jones suffered a fuel pick-up problem and Villeneuve sped by to score a superb win in the unwieldy Ferrari. Amazingly, he repeated that success at Jarama. After Jones fell off, Gilles led a train comprising Laffite, Watson, Reutemann and de Angelis, none of whom could pass his unwieldy car on this narrow and twisty track as it had the grunt to drop them down the main straight.

The French Grand Prix at Dijon-Prenois was another odd race. Rain split the event into two parts, and Prost scored his first win in the Renault. Watson and Piquet completed the top three.

Wattie's big day came at Silverstone. Prost and Arnoux took turns in the lead, but when they failed John was in the right place. It was his first win since Austria in 1976.

Villeneuve, Prost and Arnoux all took turns in the lead in Germany. Jones and Reutemann both had engine problems of varying degrees. Piquet took a canny win, with Prost second. Austria brought a popular win for Laffite.

At Zandvoort Prost and Jones fought hard in the early stages, until Jones's tyres went off. Prost pulled away to win from Piquet, with Jones third. Reutemann tangled with Laffite, so Piquet took the title lead. Prost led all the way at Monza, winning from Jones and Reutemann. Piquet looked set for third until his engine went on the last lap.

The Canadian Grand Prix was an exciting, wet event. Jones spun off while leading, Prost took over, then Laffite got to the front and held on to win. So they headed for the finale with Reutemann on 49 points, Piquet on 48, and Laffite on 43.

The race was held in a car park in Las Vegas. Reutemann took pole, but in the race he faded away. Jones won the race with Piquet fifth and Laffite sixth – which gave Piquet the title by a point. After surprising everyone at the previous race, Jones stood by his word and quit Formula One, for the time being...

1982

The 1982 season proved to be one of the most turbulent - and tragic - in the long history of Formula One. Keke Rosberg became the first man since 1964 to secure the championship with just a single victory to his name.

GREAT RACE

Monaco Grand Prix 1982

This was the race no one appeared to want to win. The ever-changing order at the front in the closing laps nearly pitched commentator Murray Walker into meltdown. The early laps were largely irrelevant, save for Bruno Giacomelli retiring his Alfa, and René Arnoux spinning out of the lead. Arnoux's Renault team-mate, Alain Prost, was in complete control with ten laps to go as light drizzle fell. Then, entering the 74th lap out of 76, Prost crashed at the chicane and everything went wild. Patrese was heading for his first win, but he spun and stalled at the Loews hairpin. Then Didier Pironi was in front with a lap and a half to go, but his electrics failed. Andrea de Cesaris was leading, but his car ran out of fuel. Derek Daly could have profited, but his gearbox seized, and so it was that Patrese, who had had his car pushed out of a dangerous position by marshals, took the chequered flag. It was his lucky day...

Lauda was back after two years setting up his charter airline, joining John Watson at McLaren. Williams replaced Jones with Keke Rosberg, and Brabham looked better than for a long time, with Riccardo Patrese as Piquet's team-mate. The other changes in the cockpit included Andrea de Cesaris moving across from McLaren after a destructive season to join Alfa Romeo, Eddie Cheever moving from Tyrrell to Ligier and Marc Surer hooking up with Arrows.

Piquet crashed in the opening race at Kyalami, and the Renaults dominated until Prost had a puncture. But he charged back from eighth to win from Reutemann and Arnoux. Piquet was first across the line in Brazil, too, but he and Rosberg were disqualified after protests lodged by Ferrari and Renault for their cars being under the minimum weight at the end of the race. This was due to a loophole allowing the teams to top up the water tank for brake cooling after the race. In effect, this tank was for nothing of the sort, with the water simply being dumped at the start. Victory was thus handed to Renault's Alain Prost.

Lauda won at Long Beach from Rosberg. The retrospective disqualifications of first and second in Brazil, had led FOCA teams to boycott San Marino, and it was a half-hearted

Finnish End of the Wedge: Keke Rosberg won but once for Williams, in the Swiss Grand Prix at Dijon-Prenois, but he was to end the year as Formula One champion

event with just 14 cars entering. Tyrrell, bound by Italian sponsors, broke ranks to join the manufacturer outfits. Pironi and Villeneuve dominated and traded places in what many thought was a show for the fans. Pironi passed the Canadian on the last lap to take the victory, and so a deadly feud began.

The feud rumbled on to Zolder where, in final qualifying, desperate to outgun Pironi, tragedy struck. Villeneuve hit the back of Jochen Mass's March and was launched into a frightening roll. The most entertaining driver of the era was killed. The race went ahead without Ferrari, and Watson won after passing Rosberg with two laps to go as brake and tyre troubles afflicted the Finn's Williams.

Monaco was dramatic. Arnoux led until spinning, Prost took over until crashing heavily with three laps to go; Patrese then led, but spun, and Pironi and de Cesaris went by. With one lap to go, Pironi stopped with electrical problems, de Cesaris ran out of fuel and Williams replacement Derek Daly retired after clouting the barrier. Patrese recovered to win.

Destructive Feud: Didier Pironi and Gilles Villeneuve during their fateful battle at Imola

Detroit was next – this street circuit in the home of the American automotive industry being visited for the first time – and Watson drove a storming race to victory from 17th on the grid, his hard Michelin tyres helping him to pass 12 cars.

In Montreal, now named the Circuit Gilles Villeneuve, Pironi stalled from pole and was hit by Osella driver Riccardo Paletti, who was killed. Piquet won the race, Patrese came in second. At Zandvoort, Ferrari finally had some good news, Pironi winning

in fine style as new second driver Patrick Tambay settled in well.

Brands Hatch saw Lauda win but the star of the race was Warwick, who got the tank-like Toleman up to second before retiring. The race was notable for Brabham waiting in the pitlane with pressurized fuel tanks and tyre ovens for a pit stop at mid-distance, the first of the modern age. Trouble was, neither Patrese nor de Cesaris made it that far...

Arnoux headed home Prost in a Renault one-two in the French Grand Prix with Pironi finishing third to head to Hockenheim leading by nine points. But in wet practice Pironi struck the back of Prost's Renault and was launched into a career-ending accident that broke his legs. In the race Tambay scored his first win in the second Ferrari, ahead of Arnoux and Rosberg.

The Austrian Grand Prix was one of the best of the year, with Lotus driver Elio de Angelis holding off a lunge from Rosberg's Williams in one of the closest finishes ever to win by 0.05 seconds.

In the Swiss Grand Prix, held at Dijon-Prenois in France, the Renaults led, but Rosberg came through to win from Prost. After Arnoux won at Monza, from Tambay, Watson then had to win the final race, at Las Vegas, to deprive Rosberg of the title. Arnoux and Prost both led, but a shock victory went to Tyrrell's Alboreto. Watson was second, but it was not enough and fifth-placed Rosberg took the honours. Amazingly, 11 drivers won races in 1982, making it a season like none before or since. So competitive was it up front that Rosberg became champion despite winning only once, backing this up with three second places.

CONSTRUCTORS' CUP 1982

	Make	Pts
1	Ferrari	74
2	McLaren	69
3	Renault	62
4	Williams	58
5	Lotus	30
6	Tyrrell	25
7	Brabham-BMW	22
8	Ligier	20
9	Brabham-Ford	19
10	Alfa Romeo	7

TECHNICAL INNOVATION

Refuelling

For the first three decades of Formula One, the pits were visited only to replace a punctured tyre or have a mechanical malady fixed. But this all changed in 1982, when the Brabham team introduced pitstops for refuelling. This came about as the team's lusty BMW engines were particularly thirsty and couldn't go the distance on one tank of fuel. So, Gordon Murray decided that a stop would be needed and that the tyres might as well be changed while the car was stationary, meaning that softer tyre compounds could be used in either half of the race, with an obvious performance advantage. By the turn of the 21st century, pitstops could make or break a race. As a result, it is crucial that everyone knows what they are doing. The pit crew is split so that there is a member on the front jack and another on the rear. A third person holds up a "lollipop" to give the driver stop-and-go instructions. A fourth wipes the driver's visor. Three people attend each of the four wheels, with one on the air-hammer, one removing the wheel and the third applying the new one. The refuelling crew comprises one holding the nozzle, another supporting the hose, a third standing ready with a fire extinguisher and a fourth holding the "dead man's handle" on the fuel pump.

DRIVERS' WORLD CHAMPIONSHIP 1982

	Driver (NATIONALITY)	Make	Pts
1	Keke Rosberg (FIN)	Williams-Ford	44
2	Didier Pironi (FRA)	Ferrari	39
	John Watson (GB)	McLaren-Ford	39
4	Alain Prost (FRA)	Renault	34
5	Niki Lauda (AUT)	McLaren-Ford	30
6	René Arnoux (FRA)	Renault	28
7	Michele Alboreto (ITA)	Tyrrell-Ford	25
	Patrick Tambay (FRA)	Ferrari	25
9	Elio de Angelis (ITA)	Lotus-Ford	23
10	Riccardo Patrese (ITA)	Brabham-Ford	21

All scores counted

1983

Nelson Piquet notched up his second world title as Alain Prost and Renault threw away their chances during what was a safe season, without strikes or technical squabbles. The action on the track was all that mattered.

Brabham BT52

Designer: **Gordon Murray**   Years raced: **1983**
Grand prix wins: **4**   Pole positions: **5**   Fastest laps: **1**
Engine type: **BMW 4 cylinder turbo**
Engine size/power: **1499cc/640bhp at 11000rpm**

This was one of the more unusual-looking chassis of its era in that its weight was concentrated largely to the rear. This was emphasized by its short, triangular-fronted sidepods that started only behind the driver's shoulders, that is to say directly in front of the engine. Gordon Murray clearly knew what he was doing, as this not only won grands prix for Nelson Piquet and Riccardo Patrese, but helped the Brazilian to his second title in two years. Although the BMW engine is listed as pushing out 640bhp, this figure was thought to be around 750bhp when in qualifying trim, with the turbo boost turned right up.

New flat-bottom regulations that banned ground-effect underwing sections under the sidepods cut downforce, while turbos became essential. As did a pit crew that knew how to refuel in a hurry, as Brabham's introduction of this tactic meant cars could start a race with half a tank of fuel, with its obvious advantages of speed and tyre wear.

Williams, for whom champion Keke Rosberg was joined by Jacques Laffite, wasn't ready and would have to spend another year with Ford Cosworth DFV power until its Honda-powered car was ready. The Japanese manufacturer was back after a 15-year break, making a low-key start with the small Spirit team, which had employed Stefan Johansson as its driver, giving him another chance after his aborted start with Shadow in 1980. McLaren, too, had to be patient. It had arranged for sponsor TAG to pay for Porsche's V6 and, until that was ready, Lauda and Watson were stuck with the DFV.

Colin Chapman had scored a coup by securing Renault engines for Lotus. Although he died suddenly, Lotus carried on: de Angelis had the new car for race two, while Mansell used DFV power until mid-season.

Of those with turbo experience, Brabham's Piquet and Patrese had stuck with BMW engines, while Arnoux left Renault to join Tambay at Ferrari, being replaced by Eddie Cheever who had moved on from Ligier, with the French team having to make do with ageing Jean-Pierre Jarier and Raul Boesel who joined from March. Toleman had a much-improved car for Warwick and Giacomelli. The other leading teams were stuck with DFV power, these including Ligier, Arrows and Tyrrell.

Theodore and Ensign combined, with the Theodore name remaining, while Fittipaldi failed to last into 1983.

Piquet won in impressive style in Rio, but Rosberg drew all the attention. He led, had a fire at his pit stop, recovered to second and was then excluded for a push start. Lauda and Laffite thus took the other podium places.

Long Beach was a rare opportunity for the DFV cars to shine. Watson and Lauda qualified 22nd and 23rd, but they got the race set-up right and came charging through to finish one-two, with Arnoux third. Unusually, the European season kicked off at Paul Ricard and Renault continued its habit of winning at home, with Prost coming first.

Tambay scored an emotional win for Ferrari at Imola, well aware that a year earlier his friend Villeneuve had been robbed by Pironi. Monaco was another chance for the DFVs to shine. Rosberg qualified sixth behind the turbos, but it rained and he chose to start on slicks. He was in the lead by lap two

Run Off the Road: there was trouble at the front at Zandvoort, with Alain Prost taking out Piquet

The Italian Job: Nelson Piquet put himself in the driving seat by winning at Monza ahead of Ferrari's René Arnoux and Renault's Eddie Cheever

CONSTRUCTORS' CUP 1983

	Make	Pts
1	Ferrari	89
2	Renault	79
3	Brabham	72
4	Williams	36
5	McLaren	34
6	Alfa Romeo	18
7	Lotus	12
	Tyrrell	12
9	Toleman	10
10	Arrows	4

and pulled away as the others pitted.

After a 13-year break, the Belgian Grand Prix returned to Spa-Francorchamps. It was rebuilt and much shorter than the original, but it was instantly regarded as the best on the calendar. De Cesaris took the lead, but retired with engine problems.

Prost took over and held on to the flag.

Detroit gave the DFV runners another chance and Alboreto scored his second win for Tyrrell, taking the lead when Piquet had to pit with a puncture. This was the 155th victory for the Ford Cosworth DFV, and no one could guess that it would also be the last. In Canada Arnoux dominated for Ferrari, ahead of Cheever and Tambay.

Prost scored a brilliant win at Silverstone. The Ferraris led, but Prost pushed them as they used up their tyres. Piquet came through to take second, with Tambay third.

Arnoux scored another win at Hockenheim, although he defied team orders at the start when he was supposed to let Tambay stay ahead. Tambay retired, while Piquet lost out with a major fire and de Cesaris took a lucky second. Prost had to work hard to win in Austria, passing Arnoux with six laps to go. Piquet kept his title hopes alive with third, and Prost's lead was now 14 points. He got it wrong in Holland, sliding into Piquet, putting them both out. Arnoux drove a good race to win from tenth.

Monza brought the worst possible result for Prost: retirement, while Piquet won and Arnoux was second. Britain hosted the Grand Prix of Europe, at Brands Hatch. Piquet won again, but Prost kept his hopes alive with second.

Just South Africa remained, and Piquet was quick in the first half, while Arnoux stopped early and Prost became stuck in a battle for third. But his turbo was failing and he retired. Piquet dropped to third, as Patrese won from de Cesaris, but ensured that he scored the vital points needed for the title.

TECHNICAL INNOVATION

Flat-Bottom Chassis

Lotus upset the apple cart when it introduced ground-effect to Formula One in the late 1970s, helping the cars to corner as if on rails and raising their lap speeds at a remarkable rate. Considering this to be dangerous, saying that the cars had "outgrown" the tracks, the sport's governing body thought that something had to be done to limit speeds. Their answer was to insist that the cars ran with flat bottoms. This meant that no car was allowed to have the aerodynamic skirts and sculpting on their undersides that helped to form the vortex shape that was key to ground-effect working.

The implementation of this – from the rear of the front wheels and the front of the rear ones for the start of 1983 – caused a quarrel between FOCA (supporting the British teams that pioneered and mastered ground-effect) and the FISA (supporting teams such as Ferrari and Renault who enjoyed more powerful turbocharged engines but who had failed to produce a chassis good enough to harness them effectively). It was a time of much political fighting, but flat bottoms have been a feature of Formula One ever since, albeit with the designers finding other ways to make the airflow under the car work for them once more.

DRIVERS' WORLD CHAMPIONSHIP 1983

	Driver (NATIONALITY)	Make	Pts
1	Nelson Piquet (BRA)	Brabham-BMW	59
2	Alain Prost (FRA)	Renault	57
3	René Arnoux (FRA)	Ferrari	49
4	Patrick Tambay (FRA)	Ferrari	40
5	Keke Rosberg (FIN)	Williams-Ford	27
6	Eddie Cheever (USA)	Renault	22
	John Watson (GB)	McLaren-Ford	22
8	Andrea de Cesaris (ITA)	Alfa Romeo	15
9	Riccardo Patrese (ITA)	Brabham-BMW	13
10	Niki Lauda (AUT)	McLaren-Ford	12

All scores counted

1984

Niki Lauda once again took advantage of the opportunity to display his judgement and guile when he beat his faster and younger team-mate, Alain Prost, to take the title. This was to be the first of many great years for McLaren.

McLaren MP4/2

Designer: **John Barnard**   Years raced: **1984-86**
Grand prix wins: **23**   Pole positions: **7**   Fastest laps: **16**
Engine type: **TAG Porsche V6 turbo**
Engine size/power: **1,496cc/750bhp and later 850bhp at 12,000rpm**
The MP4 was revolutionary, but it struggled to win more than a few grands prix. It was only when the MP4/2 was introduced in the second year, in which flat bottom rules were mandatory, that McLaren began to dominate. With ample power from its TAG Turbo, the MP4/2 raced for three years, evolving into the MP4/2C and winning 23 races for Niki Lauda and Alain Prost, with Lauda winning the 1984 title and Prost the next two. Outwardly little different from the MP4 Barnard said the reason it was so good was that it was developed with its turbo in situ rather than on the dyno as with other teams.

Alain Prost stunned the Formula One world when he upped and joined McLaren, after falling out with Renault's management. With the TAG/Porsche engine up to speed, McLaren looked to be the best bet.

There was a clean sweep at Renault, with Tambay and Warwick joining as Cheever found a new home at Alfa, where he was joined by Patrese.

Ligier had sourced Renault and attracted de Cesaris from Alfa. He joined French newcomer François Hesnault. Arrows had a BMW deal, and two good drivers in Boutsen and Surer, although they would start the year with DFVs. Tyrrell produced a nimble car and was blessed with two great rookies, Stefan Bellof and Martin Brundle. Gone fom the frame for 1984 was Theodore, with owner Teddy Yip opting instead to run a car in the Indy Car championship.

One ruling was to give the teams a headache. This was the reduction of the fuel allowed for a car in a race, from 250 litres to 220, with refuelling pit stops banned. Teams took to cooling their fuel pre-race so that it reduced in volume and thus more could be squeezed into the tank.

New Ferrari signing Michele Alboreto led in Brazil, but spun out, letting Lauda and Warwick take turns in front, but the English driver's

A Chequered Career: Niki Lauda was in a class of his own in winning the second race of the campaign, the South African Grand Prix at Kyalami

Top of the World: Marlene Lauda hugs Niki after his title-winning second place at Estoril

suspension broke, Prost came through to win, while Rosberg showed the Honda's potential with second.

McLaren was dominant in South Africa. Piquet led until encountering turbo problems, and Lauda sailed to an easy win. Prost had to start in the spare, and stormed through from the back to take second. Toleman's Ayrton Senna scored his first point.

The European season kicked off in Belgium and a return to the unloved Zolder. Alboreto led all the way from pole for his first win in a Ferrari. Warwick was second for Renault.

McLaren was on form at Imola, as Prost led all the way, despite a spin. Lauda retired with engine failure and Piquet held second until a turbo failed, so Arnoux inherited the place. Renault desperately wanted to win in France, and Tambay led most of the race, but had brake and clutch problems, letting Lauda by to win.

Monaco was wet, and Renault's Tambay and Warwick crashed at the first corner, while poleman Prost led Mansell. Mansell took the lead and pulled away, only to crash. Prost regained the lead and was still in front

when the race was red-flagged, and half points were awarded.

At Montreal Piquet was back on form. The Brabham had a new oil cooler in the front, intended to help with weight distribution, but the side effect was that Piquet burned his feet while leading from start to finish!

Detroit started with a shunt between Piquet, Prost and Mansell, for which Nigel got the blame. All three were back for the restart, and Piquet led all the way. Star of the race was Brundle, who climbed to second.

Next was Dallas for yet another race on a temporary track. It was ragingly hot, the track broke up, many crashed and the circus never went back. Rosberg was the hero, winning in style. Mansell led, but his gearbox broke and he collapsed while pushing the car to the line. Sanity returned when the circus returned to Europe for Brands Hatch, although the race was stopped after Jonathan Palmer crashed his RAM. Prost led until his gearbox failed, leaving Lauda to win from Warwick and the improving Senna.

De Angelis and Piquet retired while leading at Hockenheim, leaving Prost to win from Lauda. In Austria Prost spun off when second, and a gearbox-troubled Lauda won from Piquet and Alboreto. Piquet led early on in Holland, until he suffered an oil leak, so Prost and Lauda completed another demo run. By now the

McLaren stars had a lock on the title: Lauda 54, Prost 52.5. Prost's engine blew in Monza, and once Piquet did his usual trick of retiring while leading, Lauda cantered to victory ahead of Alboreto. By now Tyrrell had been banned for irregularities found in Detroit, losing their points. Many saw sinister undertones in the way the sole "atmo" runner was thrown out.

For the first time Formula One went to the new Nurburgring for the European Grand Prix. Prost led all the way, while Alboreto and Piquet – both out of fuel – were second and third. Lauda finished fourth after a spin, making it Lauda 66, Prost 62.5.

The finale was at Estoril, and Prost won, while Lauda did all he needed to do and came second to secure the title by the closest-ever margin.

CONSTRUCTORS' CUP 1984

	Make	Pts
1	**McLaren**	143.5
2	**Ferrari**	57.5
3	**Lotus**	47
4	**Brabham**	38
5	**Renault**	34
6	**Williams**	25.5
7	**Toleman**	16
8	**Alfa-Romeo**	11
9	**Arrows**	6
10	**Ligier**	3

TECHNICAL INNOVATION

Engine Management

As engines became increasingly complicated, the engineers decided in the 1980s as turbocharged engines pushed horsepower figures through the roof that the best way to make them perform to their full potential was to use a system of engine management. This would control and optimize the rate of ignition and injection to ensure optimum power. Using its road car-building knowledge, Porsche was the first company to introduce engine management to Formula One, when Bosch was brought in to help make the most of McLaren's TAG turbo engines. Harnessing computerized electronics in place of their transistorized forerunners, these systems used a microprocessor in their Electronic Control Units to adjust fuel injection into each cylinder according to speed rather than to load. These "brains" could be programmed to an "engine map" so that they would initiate the optimum ignition and injection settings across a range of speeds, something that was as important for fuel economy as much as for outright performance following the introduction of fuel capacity limitations in 1984, and then more stringently in 1985. Accurate engine management also prevented some of the spectacular blow-ups of the early turbo years whenever the boost was wound up for a flying lap.

DRIVERS' WORLD CHAMPIONSHIP 1984

	Driver (NATIONALITY)	Make	Pts
1	**Niki Lauda** (AUT)	McLaren-Porsche	72
2	**Alain Prost** (FRA)	McLaren-Porsche	71.5
3	**Elio de Angelis** (ITA)	Lotus-Renault	34
4	**Michele Alboreto** (ITA)	Ferrari	30.5
5	**Nelson Piquet** (BRA)	Brabham-BMW	29
6	**René Arnoux** (FRA)	Ferrari	27
7	**Derek Warwick** (GB)	Renault	23
8	**Keke Rosberg** (FIN)	Williams-Honda	20.5
9	**Nigel Mansell** (GB)	Lotus-Renault	13
	Ayrton Senna (BRA)	Toleman-Hart	13

All scores counted

1985

Alain Prost finally made it to the top in 1985. After being squeezed out in the previous two years, the Frenchman secured his first title at the end of a highly competitive year in the McLaren-TAG. Nothing could stop him now.

Two future World Champions made big career moves for 1985. Nigel Mansell left Lotus to join Williams. While Ayrton Senna quit Toleman for Lotus. Jacques Laffite returned to Ligier from Williams, while Arrows signed Gerhard Berger, who had shone for ATS, and Teo Fabi led a reorganized Toleman from Monaco on. Tyrrell finally joined the turbo club, landing Renault engines for Brundle and Bellof, albeit starting the year with trusty Ford Cosworths. New teams Minardi, Haas Lola and Zakspeed joined the show.

Michele Alboreto began in fine form, taking pole for Ferrari in Rio de Janeiro. Keke Rosberg was alongside, and both led, but victory went to Prost, while Alboreto took second, ahead of Elio de Angelis's Lotus.

René Arnoux finished fourth in the second Ferrari, but fell out with Enzo and refused to turn out for a test session and was replaced by Stefan Johansson.

There had been flashes of brilliance in 1984 with Toleman, so no one was too surprised when Senna put his Renault-powered Lotus on pole in Portugal. The race was soaking wet, but the weather only emphasized his skills as others aquaplaned off the track as he stormed to his first win. Alboreto was a distant second, finishing more than a minute behind.

Senna was again on pole at Imola, and led for 56 laps, then ran out of fuel. Johansson took over, but he too ran dry.

So Prost was first home, only to be disqualified for being underweight. Thus victory went to de Angelis with the rest a lap behind...

In Monaco, Senna made it three straight poles, and he and Alboreto took turns in the lead, but Prost came through for his second win of the year. Alboreto kept up his scoring rate with second.

Fun in the Sun: Alain Prost was a clear champion and this victory at Monaco was the second of five wins for McLaren which eventually took him to the title

Lotus swept the front row in Canada, this time with de Angelis ahead of Senna. Elio led for 15 laps before Alboreto took over and won, while Johansson made it a Ferrari one-two. Senna was back on pole in Detroit, but he was one of many to crash, along with Mansell and Prost. Rosberg took the lead early on to give Williams its first win of the year.

Rosberg took pole at Paul Ricard, but it was Brabham's day as Piquet won and gave Pirelli its first success since 1957! Rosberg took second, ahead of Prost.

Silverstone saw the most impressive qualifying lap of the year as Rosberg stormed to pole at over 160mph. Yet Senna led for 58 laps until he ran out of fuel. Prost took over and won by a lap from Alboreto, while Rosberg dropped out of third with exhaust problems.

The all-new Nurburgring played host to the German Grand Prix for the first time, and Toleman's Teo Fabi took a surprise pole.

Ferrari men Alboreto and Johansson tangled at the first corner, but Alboreto fought back to win after Rosberg and Senna had spells in front. Prost continued to pile up points with second place.

The Austrian Grand Prix had to

One-two: Alain Prost and Michele Alboreto (left) celebrate finishing first and second at Silverstone

be restarted after a first-lap crash. Lauda led for the first time this year but retired and Prost went on to win. Senna and Alboreto were next up.

The race was notable as it was the first one with an all-turbo field, Tyrrell finally ceasing to use its Ford Cosworths and running both of its cars with Renault turbos hereafter after several races of experimentation.

Zandvoort hosted a grand prix for

the final time, and Piquet took pole, but Rosberg led early on.

Prost took over when Rosberg retired yet again, but it was Lauda who came through the field to notch up his first win of the year – and what turned out to be the last victory of his career.

Monza was a familiar story, with Senna on pole and Rosberg leading early on. But Prost won from Piquet and Senna. Prost was on pole at Spa-Francorchamps, but Senna won from Mansell.

As in 1983, Brands Hatch hosted the European Grand Prix, and Mansell came good in front of his home crowd, scoring his first win ahead of Senna and Rosberg.

Meanwhile, fourth place clinched the title for a cautious Prost. Mansell was on top form now, and at Kyalami he took pole and led Rosberg home, with Prost third.

The season ended with a new race on the streets of Adelaide. Senna took pole, but Prost won, while Ligier ended the season on a high note, with Laffite and Streiff taking second and third. Lauda led a couple of laps, but crashed.

Although Formula One had enjoyed a relatively safe season, two talented drivers lost their lives in sports cars: Manfred Winkelhock, of ATS, died at Mosport Park, while Tyrrell's Bellof was killed at Spa-Francorchamps.

CONSTRUCTORS' CUP 1985

	Make	Pts
1	McLaren	90
2	Ferrari	82
3	Lotus	71
	Williams	71
5	Brabham	26
6	Ligier	23
7	Renault	16
8	Arrows	14
9	Tyrrell	7

LANDMARK CAR
TAG Turbo
Designer: **Hans Mezger**   Years raced: **1983-87**
Grand prix wins: **25**   Pole positions: **7**   Fastest laps: **18**
Engine type/size/power: **V6/1,499cc/600bhp**
This was the engine that took McLaren into the turbo world, superseding its Ford DFVs towards the end of 1983. At the behest of John Barnard, McLaren eschewed fitting established turbo engines from BMW or Renault and looked to Porsche, a company with huge turbo experience in its road cars and racers. McLaren's sponsor, the TAG group, financed the project. One of the key design features on which Barnard insisted was a narrow shape with the plumbing kept high to aid a clean flow of air underneath to offer maximum ground-effect potential. This caused Hans Mezger a nightmare, but he got there in the end, only for ground-effect to be banned for 1984... However, it was to help the team to three titles, although it was outpaced in 1986 by both the Honda and Renault units.

DRIVERS' WORLD CHAMPIONSHIP 1985

	Driver (NATIONALITY)	Make	Pts
1	**Alain Prost** (FRA)	McLaren-Porsche	73
2	**Michele Alboreto** (ITA)	Ferrari	53
3	**Keke Rosberg** (FIN)	Williams-Honda	40
4	**Ayrton Senna** (BRA)	Lotus-Renault	38
5	**Elio de Angelis** (ITA)	Lotus-Renault	33
6	**Nigel Mansell** (GB)	Williams-Honda	31
7	**Stefan Johansson** (SWE)	Ferrari	26
8	**Nelson Piquet** (BRA)	Brabham-BMW	21
9	**Jacques Laffite** (FRA)	Ligier-Renault	16
10	**Niki Lauda** (AUT)	McLaren-Porsche	14

Best 11 scores from 16 races to count

1986

This saw one of the most dramatic conclusions of recent years. Mansell and Piquet had fought hard all year, but in the final race Mansell blew a tyre, Piquet made a precautionary stop, and a dis-believing Prost sped through to the title.

LANDMARK CAR

Brabham BT55

Designer: **Gordon Murray**   Years raced: **1986**
Grand prix wins: **0**   Pole positions: **0**   Fastest laps: **0**
Engine type: **BMW 4 cylinder turbo**
Engine size/power: **1499cc/900bhp at 11,200rpm**

Known as a "low-line" chassis, the BT55 could easily have been known as "low-lying", as that's exactly what drivers Elio de Angelis, Riccardo Patrese and Derek Warwick had to do in the cockpit. Sadly, many of the advantages of its small frontal area that ought to have helped the airflow were negated by faults which included the turbocharged BMW engine not working at its best when canted over to fit into the low engine bay. While looking odd worked well for the title-winning BT52, it did nothing for the BT55, with a pair of sixth places its best results. The idea was never pursued with later chassis, from any of the manufacturers...

Having lost Niki Lauda to retirement, McLaren replaced him with another champion: Keke Rosberg. The Finn was also replaced by a champion with Nelson Piquet moving across from Brabham. Lotus wanted to hire Derek Warwick, but Ayrton Senna didn't want a top name alongside him, so they chose Johnny Dumfries.

With Renault having pulled out, Warwick headed for Brabham where he was joined by Elio de Angelis.

Over the winter the Toleman team turned into Benetton - named after the Italian knitwear company that had been backing the Alfa Romeo team until it folded at the end of 1985 - and the talented Gerhard Berger joined Teo Fabi with BMW engines, perhaps the most powerful in the field. RAM and Spirit also failed to make it through the close season, but numbers were boosted by the arrival of the one-car entry from the French AGS team, with Ivan Capelli having the "honour" of driving the Motori Moderni-engined device.

Fuel consumption was again an issue, as the fuel allowed per car per race was reduced from 220 litres to 195. In qualifying at least, though, drivers didn't have to think of consumption and would wind their turbo boost up five bar for a flying lap.

Piquet got off to the best possible start, winning his home grand prix

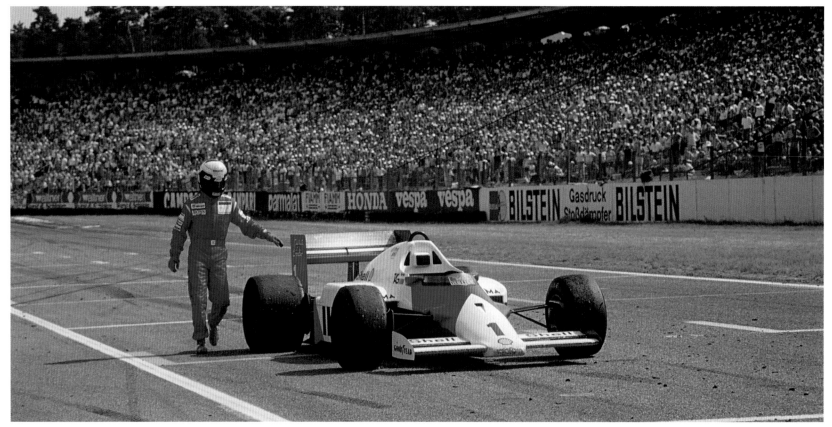

Early Exit: Alain Prost suffers an embarrassing end to the German Grand Prix at Hockenheim, with his car dry of fuel and falling from third place to sixth

The Three Amigos: Piquet, Prost and Mansell before the Adelaide shoot-out that Prost won

at Rio de Janeiro. Senna took pole, and he and Prost led before Piquet took over.

After a five-year break, Spain had a grand prix again, on the twisty Jerez track in the country's far south. And it produced a thrilling race, with Senna holding off Mansell by 0.014 seconds.

Senna was on pole at Imola, but a jammed wheel bearing forced him out, while Rosberg fell from second to fifth, his tank dry of fuel. Piquet and Rosberg led, but the reliable Prost was there to win from Piquet.

Prost broke Senna's string of poles at Monaco, and led Rosberg home. Senna led briefly, but fell to third.

The meeting was a landmark for Ford as it returned for the first time since the demise of the Cosworth DFV, introducing its first turbo in the rear of the Haas Lolas of Alan Jones and Patrick Tambay.

Tragedy struck when de Angelis was killed in testing at Paul Ricard, the Italian driver being asphyxiated when his car inverted after rear wing failure.

Piquet took pole at Spa, but Mansell came through to win from Senna and Johansson.

In a black weekend in June, former Osella driver Jo Gartner was killed at Le Mans, while Arrows star Marc Surer was injured in a rally, with Christian

Danner upgrading from Osella to replace him.

Brabham was back up to strength in Canada, Warwick returning from the Jaguar sports car team. Mansell took pole and won from Prost.

Senna won from pole in Detroit, but both Ligiers took a turn in the lead, with Laffite finishing second.

Mansell won at Paul Ricard, ahead of Prost, Piquet and Rosberg. And nobody was going to stop him at home, although Piquet pipped him for pole at Brands Hatch.

Nigel had a drive shaft break, but his day was saved by a red flag as Johansson and Laffite collided and Laffite hit a barrier, breaking both his legs and ending his career. Mansell went and won the restart after a tussle with Piquet.

The German Grand Prix returned to Hockenheim. On this power track it was a surprise to see Rosberg and Prost on the front row, but Keke led before Piquet took over and won to keep his title challenge alive.

The twisty and slow Hungaroring circuit made its debut, as Formula One made its first visit to the Eastern bloc and Piquet outran Senna to win in front of 200,000 spectators.

BMW power ruled in Austria as Fabi and Berger grabbed the front row for Benetton. Berger led until his turbo blew, and in a race of high attrition it was inevitably Prost who kept it flowing to win from Alboreto.

Fabi took pole at Monza with what was quite possibly the most powerful car ever seen in Formula One. He shared the front row with Prost, but Piquet led Mansell to a Williams one-two.

Senna was on pole in Portugal, but Mansell led all the way to win from Prost and Piquet.

The campaign's third new track was in fact an old one – but the circus had not visited Mexico City since 1970. Benetton finally came good and Berger scored his first win.

In a dramatic finale in Adelaide, with both Williams drivers and Prost up for the title, Mansell was perfectly placed to take the title when a rear tyre blew.

Williams made Piquet pit for a precautionary change, and he fell to second behind Prost. Victory gave the Frenchman his second title.

CONSTRUCTORS' CUP 1986		
	Make	Pts
1	Williams	141
2	McLaren	96
3	Lotus	58
4	Ferrari	37
5	Ligier	29
6	Benetton	19
7	Tyrrell	11
8	Haas Lola	6
9	Brabham	2

GREAT RACE

Australian Grand Prix 1986

The image of Nigel Mansell's Williams snaking out of control with a strip of rubber flailing off its left rear wheel will long remain with British fans who were up early to turn on the television and watch him become Britain's first World Champion since James Hunt in 1976. Mansell had arrived at Adelaide with a six-point advantage over Prost, with Piquet a further point behind. Although starting from pole, Mansell drove a cautious first lap, falling to fourth as Piquet led from Ayrton Senna's Lotus and Keke Rosberg's McLaren, with Prost lying in fifth. Anxious to end his career on a high, Rosberg was soon in front, with Prost reaching second by lap 23 after Piquet spun. The McLarens were looking good, but Prost could do nothing about Mansell. Then Prost clipped a slower car and picked up a puncture, rejoining in fourth. All changed on lap 63, though, as Rosberg thought he had heard his engine fail. It was, in fact, a delaminated tyre hitting the bodywork. This threw up a dilemma: whether the Williams would go the distance on their similar rubber. A lap later, they had their answer, as Mansell had his 180mph blow-out. Piquet was called in for new tyres and Prost won both the race and the title.

DRIVERS' WORLD CHAMPIONSHIP 1986			
	Driver (NATIONALITY)	Make	Pts
1	Alain Prost (FRA)	McLaren-Porsche	72
2	Nigel Mansell (GB)	Williams-Honda	70
3	Nelson Piquet (BRA)	Williams-Honda	69
4	Ayrton Senna (BRA)	Lotus-Renault	55
5	Stefan Johansson (SWE)	Ferrari	23
6	Keke Rosberg (FIN)	McLaren-Porsche	22
7	Gerhard Berger (AUT)	Benetton-BMW	17
8	Michele Alboreto (ITA)	Ferrari	14
	René Arnoux (FRA)	Ligier-Renault	14
	Jacques Laffite (FRA)	Ligier-Renault	14

Best 11 scores from 16 races to count

1987

Team-mates Nelson Piquet and Nigel Mansell fought for the title, and the Englishman was a strong contender until an accident sidelined him in Japan. Piquet accepted the laurels for the third time, even before the race started.

LANDMARK CAR
Williams FW11B
Designer: **Patrick Head**   Years raced: **1987**
Grand prix wins: **9**   Pole positions: **12**   Fastest laps: **7**
Engine type: **Honda turbo V6**
Engine size/power: **1,500cc/850bhp at 10,000rpm**
If the Williams FW11 was a great car which helped the team bounce back from Frank Williams' paralysing accident, its drivers Nigel Mansell and Nelson Piquet were still pipped at the post in 1986. However, the car that followed, the FW11B, was a development of this. While it offered improved cooling and a more powerful, fuel-efficient V6 turbo from Honda, the key to its leap forward was its active suspension, which helped the drivers to nine wins, with Piquet taking the title. The active suspension kept the car level whatever it hit, and helped when cornering. Lotus had been the first team to use it, but Williams was ahead of most.

With the FIA considering turbos now too powerful and engine development too expensive, it made something of a U-turn and a new formula was announced: from 1989, Formula One would return to atmospheric (normally aspirated) engines, this time of 3.5-litre capacity. There would be two interim years, however, and to encourage teams to change the Jim Clark Cup was introduced for drivers of "atmo" cars.

In response, Cosworth produced the "atmo" DFZ which was used by Tyrrell, March, AGS and Larrousse. For those sticking with turbo engines, boost would be restricted to four bar and minimum weight would be 540kg, with 500kg allowed for "atmo" cars. With Pirelli having quit in 1986, Goodyear had a tyre monopoly and elected not to produce a qualifying tyre, in order to keep costs in check.

On the engine front, Renault had withdrawn and Lotus had attracted Honda, with Satoru Nakajima as part of the package. Ford moved to Benetton, with Thierry Boutsen joining Teo Fabi as Gerhard Berger had moved to Ferrari to partner Michele Alboreto after Stefan Johansson had joined Alain Prost at McLaren. Williams continued with Mansell and Piquet.

Elsewhere, Eddie Cheever and Derek Warwick lined up for Arrows, Andrea de Cesaris stepped up from Minardi to Brabham, Jonathan Palmer

Good Day's Work: victory in the Italian Grand Prix set Nelson Piquet fair for his third Formula One world title, this his first for Williams

joined Tyrrell from Zakspeed, leaving Martin Brundle to head the other way. March returned with a single Leyton House-liveried car for Ivan Capelli.

Mansell and Piquet shared the front row in Rio de Janeiro and, although Piquet led early on, Prost won with Piquet second and Johansson third. In Imola luck went against Piquet when he crashed and was unable to start. Mansell powered past poleman Senna to win.

Mansell and Piquet shared the front row at Spa-Francorchamps. The race was stopped after Tyrrell's Streiff and Palmer crashed. So did Mansell and Senna later on, leading to a confrontation. Prost won after Piquet retired, with Johansson second and de Cesaris a surprise third for Brabham, albeit running out of fuel before the finish and only staying ahead of Cheever's fourth-placed Arrows as it was a lap behind.

Mansell led at Monaco until his turbo broke, leaving Senna to score the first of his many wins there. Piquet was second ahead of Alboreto – who'd survived a clatter with the barriers after colliding with Christian Danner's Zakspeed in qualifying – and Berger. Danner was disqualified from the meeting for not showing sufficient

In Agony: Nigel Mansell shows how much pain he is suffering after crashing at Suzuka, Japan

care after exiting the pits. In Detroit, Mansell led from pole, but Senna took over as he was hit by cramp and won from Piquet and Prost.

Mansell won the French Grand Prix at Paul Ricard. Then, after a late tyre stop at Silverstone, Mansell beat Piquet in an inspired charge that culminated in him taking the lead with just over two laps to go with a bold dive into Stowe. Senna and Nakajima followed the Williams pair home, albeit a lap in arrears, for a Honda top-four.

Mansell's engine failed in Germany and Piquet won while Johansson came second with a flat tyre as just seven cars finished. Then Mansell took pole in Hungary but failed to finish when he lost a wheel nut, and Piquet won from Senna and Prost. Senna dropped a bombshell on Lotus that weekend, announcing that his dissatisfaction with the 99T was making him quit the team at the end of the year.

The Austrian Grand Prix was stopped twice by crashes on the pit straight before Mansell won easily from Piquet. Johansson hit a deer in qualifying. Had he done so head-on, he would undoubtedly have met the same fate as the deer.

Piquet pipped Mansell to pole at Monza, and then won with Mansell third, the pair split by Senna. Berger led most of the way in Portugal but Prost won with Piquet third, while Mansell retired.

Mansell won at Jerez ahead of Prost, Johansson and Piquet. Then he won in Mexico, in a race interrupted by an accident from which Warwick emerged unscathed. Piquet was second.

For the first time since 1977 Japan had a grand prix, this time at Suzuka. Mansell crashed in practice and hurt his back. Piquet celebrated, for Mansell was out for the weekend, and was to miss the final race too, making Piquet champion. Ironically, Piquet didn't score in either. Instead, Berger won both. Senna and Johansson followed him home in Japan, then Berger led all the way in Australia from Senna. However, the Lotus was disqualified for having illegal brakes, and it cost Senna second place overall.

Palmer won the Jim Clark Cup, while Tyrrell won the constructors' version. Not that many people noticed, with Palmer 11th overall.

TECHNICAL INNOVATION

Active Suspension

To be strictly accurate, what is about to be described here is reactive suspension, but active suspension is how it was referred to in Formula One circles. Whatever the name, it was introduced by Lotus in 1987 and was a computer-operated system that controlled the movement of a car's suspension through the use of sensors at each corner of the car that reacted to any bump or dip in the track and adjusted the suspension so that the car remained stable on the track. In effect, it was a self-damping, self-levelling system that helped the car maintain a level attitude at all times, and which also provided an obvious benefit in cornering. It also prevented the driver from receiving a tiring buffeting. Lotus led the way, using the suspension expertise that it had developed through its construction of high-performance road cars, with Williams et al following as soon as they were able. There had been previous attempts to make such a system work, with BRM having a go in the 1950s then Ligier and Renault in the early 1980s, but this was the first time that it did work.

1988

Alain Prost scored more points than McLaren team-mate Ayrton Senna, but the Brazilian claimed the drivers' title because he could count his best 11 results from the 16 rounds and, moreover, had eight wins to Prost's seven.

Honda V6 turbo

Designer: **Ichida**   Years raced: **1985-88**
Grand prix wins: **15**   Pole positions: **15**   Fastest laps: **10**
Engine type/size/power: **V6/1,496cc/810-1,077bhp**

Honda had a history in Formula One in the 1960s. However, its greatest success came when it returned as an engine supplier. Kicking off with Williams in the final race of 1983, the turbo engine was notable for its power delivery across a wide rev band, and it was a winner in 1984 before really finding its feet in 1986, with Ayrton Senna adding more wins when Lotus also ran the engine in 1987. Extra power was found as its injection system was improved, with turbo boost turned up in qualifying to hit 1077bhp in 1985, thanks in part to its unusually large piston area. McLaren poached the Japanese manufacturer for 1988 and Senna and Alain Prost won 15 of the 16 races between them.

This was the final year for cars with turbocharged engines and turbo fuel allowance was slashed to just 150 litres per race with a maximum of 2.5 bar boost. McLaren was the only team to bother building a new chassis for this final turbo year and this, as well as lusty Honda power, meant that it ruled the roost.

There was a good deal of change among the top teams, with Senna quitting Lotus for McLaren and his compatriot Nelson Piquet filling the seat that he'd vacated after leaving Lotus for Williams, something that wasn't seen as a good move as Williams no longer had Honda engines but Judd units instead, as did Ligier and March. It was McLaren and Lotus that were to enjoy Honda power. Stefan Johansson left McLaren for Ligier, with Piercarlo Ghinzani making way by heading to Zakspeed to fill the seat left open by Martin Brundle standing down to chase success in sports cars with Jaguar. Alessandro Nannini was rewarded for strong form with Minardi by a drive at Benetton.

Brabham dropped to the sidelines, but the British team was replaced by three new teams: Dallara, Eurobrun and Rial. March, meanwhile, doubled its presence, adding Mauricio Gugelmin to its driving strength alongside Ivan Capelli.

Making a flying start for McLaren, Senna qualified on pole from

So Far So Good: Ayrton Senna's McLaren leads the way down to Mirabeau on the opening lap at Monaco, but he was to make a minor error...

Mansell's Williams in Brazil, with Prost third, but had to start from the pits. Prost passed Mansell. So did Ferrari's Berger. And no one headed Prost again. Senna reached second, but was disqualified for using the spare car when the race had been delayed rather than restarted after his car had become jammed in first gear on the grid. Thus Berger came second and Nelson Piquet third for Lotus.

Senna led all the way at Imola, helped by Prost being slow off the line and being forced to be his shadow. Senna was almost a minute up on Prost with 12 laps to go at Monaco, when he grazed the barriers. It was several hours before he re-emerged from his apartment, by which time Prost had won from Berger and Alboreto.

Prost beat Senna in Mexico with only Berger on the same lap. In Canada it was another McLaren one-two, although this time Senna won from Prost. Senna and Prost finished in the same order in Detroit, while Mansell retired for the sixth race in a row. In France, anxious that Senna was eroding his lead, Prost won with Senna a distant second, suffering from gearbox problems.

So difficult were the wet conditions at Silverstone that few will recall that Senna passed the Ferraris to win. What people will recall is that Prost pulled off, saying the conditions were too dangerous. Mansell was second and Nannini third.

Senna won in Germany with Prost second. Then Senna led in Hungary, but hit traffic on the straight. Prost dived inside him, but Senna let him slide by and regained the lead. Senna won again in Belgium, where he overcame a poor start to move into the points lead. Prost was second with Benetton's Boutsen and Nannini third and fourth.

Berger broke McLaren's run. And to make matters better, it was a Ferrari one-two, with Alboreto half a second behind. Better still, the race was in Italy... But what of McLaren? Prost retired when second with engine failure, while Senna was leading on the penultimate lap, but struggling with fuel consumption.

Then he found Williams replacement driver Schlesser at the chicane. They touched, sending Senna into retirement and the crowd wild. Eddie Cheever and Derek Warwick were third and fourth for Arrows.

McLaren won in Portugal, Prost taking the spoils. The race had to be restarted and Senna led the first lap then swerved at Prost when he pulled alongside as they passed the pits. Prost kept his foot in and took the lead. Senna fell back with handling problems and Ivan Capelli became Prost's challenger. Driving his March like never before, the Italian was the star of the race, but settled for second.

Prost won again in Spain with Senna struggling home fourth, troubled by a computer that gave confusing readings about his fuel consumption. Mansell was a distant second with Nannini third.

Senna stalled in Japan and was in 14th going into the first corner. Prost found himself in the lead, but he had to contend with Capelli, who led briefly before his electrics failed. Senna then caught and passed Prost for his eighth win to claim the title. Prost was second, with Boutsen third yet again. Prost won the last race of the turbo era in Australia from Senna and Piquet.

Red is the Colour: Prost stands atop the Paul Ricard podium, flanked by Senna and Alboreto

CONSTRUCTORS' CUP 1988

	Make	Pts
1	McLaren	199
2	Ferrari	65
3	Benetton	39
4	Arrows	23
	Lotus	23
6	March	22
7	Williams	20
8	Tyrrell	5
9	Rial	3
10	Minardi	1

DRIVERS' WORLD CHAMPIONSHIP 1988

	Driver (NATIONALITY)	Make	Pts
1	Ayrton Senna (BRA)	McLaren-Honda	90
2	Alain Prost (FRA)	McLaren-Honda	87
3	Gerhard Berger (AUT)	Ferrari	41
4	Thierry Boutsen (BEL)	Benetton-Ford	27
5	Michele Alboreto (ITA)	Ferrari	24
6	Nelson Piquet (BRA)	Lotus-Honda	22
7	Ivan Capelli (ITA)	March-Judd	17
	Derek Warwick (GB)	Arrows-Megatron	17
9	Nigel Mansell (GB)	Williams-Judd	12
	Alessandro Nannini (ITA)	Benetton-Ford	12

Best 11 scores from 16 races to count

1989

The McLaren steamroller rolled on inexorably. This time it was the turn of Alain Prost to take the world title, and join the serried ranks of three-time winners. The trouble was that he was no longer on speaking terms with Senna...

Japanese Grand Prix 1989

Alain Prost arrived in Japan with the title all but in the bag, but his McLaren team-mate, Ayrton Senna, had other plans. With a 16-point advantage, Prost did not need a win to claim his third world title. To keep his hopes alive, however, Senna did. The Frenchman still gave it his all in qualifying to lap faster than qualifying king Senna. In the race, no one could touch them as they sped into the distance. On lap 47 out of 53, Senna made a dive up the inside into the chicane. Prost chose not to make any room for him and they collided. Prost was out, while Senna had to be pushed clear and pit for a new nose to maintain any chance of winning the race. However, he was then disqualified for having received outside assistance and Benetton's Alessandro Nannini was handed the victory. Prost remained champion for five days until an appeal took the matter to court, albeit for the judgement to be found in his favour.

The battle between Prost and Senna raged on, with the rest of the field reduced to a supporting role. Nigel Mansell had quit Williams for Ferrari to drive alongside Berger, while Williams had got rid of its Judd engines and signed with Renault. Ferrari had another trump up its sleeve as it introduced semi-automatic gearboxes, allowing it to do away with a gear lever and letting its drivers keep both hands on the steering wheel at all times, flicking paddles on its flanks to change up and down the gearbox.

Thierry Boutsen arrived at Williams, his place at Benetton being filled by Formula 3000 hotshot Johnny Herbert. Also on the move was Michele Alboreto, stepping down from Ferrari to join his former team, Tyrrell.

The late 1980s continued to be good for new teams, with Brabham returning after a year away, this time with Swiss financier Joachim Luhti at the helm and Martin Brundle and Stefano Modena on the driving force, and Onyx stepping up to join them with Stefan Johansson trying his luck with yet another team.

Senna claimed pole from Patrese in Brazil, but he went off at the first corner and Patrese took an early lead, although Mansell was able to control the race as Prost hit trouble. Prost kept going to finish second, with Mauricio Gugelmin hard on his heels and Herbert right with the pair of them in one of the most impressive Formula One debuts of all time. It was even more so when Johnny's foot and ankle injuries suffered in 1988 were taken into consideration.

Senna led at Imola, but the race was stopped when Gerhard Berger crashed at Tamburello, the Austrian suffering second-degree burns to his hands and a broken rib in an accident that demonstrated the progress teams had made in strengthening their cars' cockpits. Prost got away better at the restart but Senna overturned a pre-race deal and snatched the lead. Senna and Prost started from the front row in Monaco and Senna led all the way to win easily from Prost, while Brundle was denied third by electrical failure that let Brabham team-mate Modena through.

Senna dominated in Mexico, while Prost chose the wrong tyres and fell to fifth. Mansell ran second, but his gearbox

Best of Enemies: Alain Prost leads team-mate Senna and Ferrari's Berger at the start of the Japanese Grand Prix, but trouble was to follow...

Rain Dance: Alain Prost and Ayrton Senna lead away through the spray in Adelaide

TECHNICAL INNOVATION
Semi-Automatic Gearboxes

Performance in a sports car always suggests a manual gearbox, so it is something of a surprise that Formula One cars do not contain a gear lever. Indeed, since 1989, their gearboxes have been semi-automatic. Racing with an automatic gearbox would have been unthinkable to Juan Manuel Fangio or Jim Clark, as changing gears effectively was part of their armoury of skills. Niki Lauda says that removing the function of changing gear renders today's cars so simple to drive that anyone of average ability could drive them semi-competitively. Alain Prost also says he wishes for a move back to manuals, as they help overtaking since all drivers miss several gear changes per race. They made their debut in 1989, when Ferrari introduced the semi-automatic gearbox, an electro-hydraulic system activated by the driver flicking paddles mounted on the steering wheel, with one for changing up and the other for down, with an electronic impulse being sent to a control box and on to a hydraulically operated gearbox. This instantly removed the need for a driver's right hand to move to a gear lever, with obvious safety gains. There was also no longer any need for a clutch, leaving the driver just two pedals. Furthermore, drivers would no longer miss gears and gear changes were far faster than when done manually, taking 20-40 milliseconds. This speed of operation enabled teams to fit a greater number of gear ratios, with most teams running seven-speed gearboxes by 2000.

failed and this promoted Patrese and Tyrrell's Alboreto to complete the rostrum. Prost won on the streets of Phoenix as Senna's electrics failed, leaving Prost free to beat Patrese.

McLaren domination was broken in Canada when Boutsen scored his first win after the McLarens retired. Patrese made it a Williams one-two. Herbert failed to qualify and was dropped by Benetton, to be replaced by Emanuele Pirro. There was drama in France as Mauricio Gugelmin got it very wrong at the start and his Leyton House March took off over the pack, forcing the race to be stopped. Then, on the restart, Senna's transmission failed and this left Prost clear to lead all the way. Mansell was second despite starting from the pits after his car was damaged at the first start.

Senna failed to score at the British Grand Prix, spinning out of the lead to let Prost win again. Mansell delighted the crowd with second, despite delays with a puncture. Senna struck back in Germany, recovering from a slower pitstop to retake the lead when Prost's gearbox started balking. Mansell was third.

Mansell was in fighting form when he tigered from 12th to win in Hungary, while Senna came second with Boutsen third. It was wet at Spa-Francorchamps, and Senna led all the way. The sun was out at Monza – well, for Prost at least, as he won from Berger and Boutsen.

In Portugal, Berger won from Prost and Johansson. Mansell missed his pit, reversed and was black flagged. This he ignored and then spun out with Senna, later being given a one-race ban, so he took no part in Spain. This left Senna to win with Berger second and Prost third. Prost and Senna clashed in Japan and settled the title race in Prost's favour. Senna dived up the inside into the chicane, but Prost refused to cede and they spun. Prost retired on the spot, but Senna was push-started before pitting for a new nose and still was first to the finish. But he was disqualified for receiving external assistance, giving Nannini his first win. Boutsen won again in Adelaide from Alessandro Nannini after Senna had stormed clear but ploughed into Brundle's spray-hidden Brabham.

CONSTRUCTORS' CUP 1989

	Make	Pts
1	McLaren	141
2	Williams	77
3	Ferrari	59
4	Benetton	39
5	Tyrrell	16
6	Lotus	15
7	Arrows	13
8	Brabham	8
	Dallara	8
10	Minardi	6
	Onyx	6

DRIVERS' WORLD CHAMPIONSHIP 1989

	Driver (NATIONALITY)	Make	Pts
1	**Alain Prost** (FRA)	McLaren-Honda	76
2	**Ayrton Senna** (BRA)	McLaren-Honda	60
3	**Riccardo Patrese** (ITA)	Williams-Renault	40
4	**Nigel Mansell** (GB)	Ferrari	38
5	**Thierry Boutsen** (BEL)	Williams-Renault	37
6	**Alessandro Nannini** (ITA)	Benetton-Ford	32
7	**Gerhard Berger** (AUT)	Ferrari	21
8	**Nelson Piquet** (BRA)	Lotus-Jaudd	12
9	**Jean Alesi** (FRA)	Tyrrell-Ford	8
10	**Derek Warwick** (GB)	Arrows-Ford	7

Best 11 scores from 16 races to count

DEFINING MOMENTS
1990s

1990 Japanese Grand Prix
RED RAG TO A BULL

With no drivers able to match their craft, Alain Prost and Ayrton Senna were at each other's throats at Suzuka in 1990, just as they had been at the same venue the previous year. This time Prost was driving for Ferrari, so perhaps that was red rag to a bull as Senna simply drove him off the track at the first corner.

1991 Belgian Grand Prix
INAUSPICIOUS START

It's strange that Michael Schumacher got his Formula One break only because Jordan driver Bertrand Gachot was jailed for assaulting a taxi driver. However, he shocked everyone by qualifying seventh at Spa-Francorchamps. Trouble was, his debut was short – his clutch burned out as he waited for the start.

1993 European Grand Prix
FOUR IN ONE

Pure artistry is how most would describe Senna's opening lap at Donington Park in 1993. He fluffed his start, falling to fifth but then, on a wet track, the McLaren ace did what few have ever done and picked off the four drivers ahead of him in four passing manoeuvres before the lap was complete.

1994 San Marino Grand Prix
RACE OF DISASTER

This was a grand prix at which everything that could go wrong did. Rubens Barrichello was fortunate to survive a huge crash on the Friday. Roland Ratzenberger was killed in qualifying on the Saturday. Then Ayrton Senna (right, before the race) was killed after his steering column sheared off and a spectator was also hit by flying debris.

1996 Japanese Grand Prix
FAMILY BUSINESS

There have been many racing sons of racing fathers, but Damon Hill was the first to follow his father in becoming World Champion, doing so at Suzuka in 1997 when he emulated the feat of his deceased father Graham who had been World Champion in 1962 and 1968.

1999 Malaysian Grand Prix
RE-ORIENTATION

Formula One was very Euro-centric at the end of the 20th century, and so it was with great excitement that Malaysia became one of the countries privileged to host a grand prix. Its first event was at Sepang in 1999, with Michael Schumacher keeping Mika Hakkinen back in third to help team-mate Eddie Irvine score a valuable win.

1990

It was Ayrton Senna versus Alain Prost for the third season in a row. As in 1988, the Brazilian took the spoils, with no-one else in sight. But at one time it looked as though he wasn't going to be allowed to start the World Championship at all.

The trouble between Senna and the authorities stemmed from his clash with Prost in Japan in 1989, and the fact that he then accused FISA president Jean-Marie Balestre of manipulating the title and was subsequently refused entry for 1990. It was only with the first race in sight that Senna was readmitted.

With no love lost between Prost and Senna after their collision at Suzuka at the end of 1989, perhaps it was a good thing that they were no longer in the same team, with the Frenchman having left McLaren to join Ferrari to partner Nigel Mansell, with Gerhard Berger going in the opposite direction.

Williams kept Thierry Boutsen and Riccardo Patrese on its books, while Benetton welcomed Nelson Piquet from Lotus, with Satoru Nakajima also leaving to race for Tyrrell, joining Jean Alesi who'd been impressing the team since he finished fourth on his debut half way through 1989. In their place,

Lotus signed Derek Warwick and rookie Martin Donnelly who'd made a one-off appearance for Arrows in the 1989 French Grand Prix.

Michele Alboreto had also left Tyrrell and he moved to Arrows, while Ligier replaced Rene Arnoux and Olivier Grouillard with Philippe Alliot and Nicola Larini, with Grouillard downgrading to Osella. Rial and Zakspeed had quit, with only the Life team coming in, albeit to make almost no impression as neither Gary Brabham nor Bruno Giacomelli could qualify their car. This Italian team failed to see out the season.

Trick fuels were all the rage, with the top teams and the fuel suppliers introducing "aromatics" as they played around with fuel chemistry in their quest for extra horsepower. For most teams, though, what they really needed was the Honda engine enjoyed by McLaren or that in the Ferraris.

It came as no surprise that Senna starred at the opening race around the streets of Phoenix. However, he was pushed hard by Alesi, who put his Tyrrell into the lead on the opening lap and stayed there until the halfway point. Senna tracked him down, took the lead, was re-passed, but then pulled clear. Boutsen was third in his Williams, while Prost climbed to fourth then retired.

Senna was set for victory in Brazil when contact with Nakajima forced

Victory Bonus: Ayrton Senna stopped a three-race winning streak for Ferrari's Prost by winning the German Grand Prix at Hockenheim for McLaren

CONSTRUCTORS' CUP 1990

	Make	Pts
1	**McLaren**	121
2	**Ferrari**	110
3	**Benetton**	71
4	**Williams**	57
5	**Tyrrell**	16
6	**Lola**	11
7	**Leyton House**	7
8	**Lotus**	3
9	**Arrows**	2
	Brabham	2

Fighting Tooth and Nail: Alain Prost and Ayrton Senna were at it again at Suzuka in the Japanese Grand Prix, this time at the first corner

him to pit for a new nose, confining him to third behind Prost and Berger.

Patrese ended a seven-year drought to win at Imola. Senna led from pole but a stone jammed in his brakes and he spun off, while Prost came fourth behind Berger and Benetton's Nannini. Then Senna dominated at Monaco, chased by Alesi's nimble Tyrrell.

Berger jumped the start in Canada and was penalized a minute. With time to make up, Senna waved Berger by. Yet, although he finished 45 seconds clear, he was classified only fourth, as Senna won.

Prost qualified 13th in Mexico, but he drove a patient race to win on a track that ate tyres. Senna led for 60 laps, but had a puncture, with Mansell completing a Ferrari one-two. Prost won at Paul Ricard after Capelli had led for Leyton House, a team that had never scored a point, taking the lead with three laps to go.

Mansell announced at Silverstone that he would retire at the end of the year, while Prost won after Mansell had retired with gearbox problems and Boutsen took second with Senna coming back from a spin for third.

Hockenheim was next, and it was Senna's turn to win after struggling to re-pass Nannini who ran non-stop to the Brazilian's one planned stop. Senna was pipped by Boutsen in Hungary, having taken off Nannini shortly before the flag.

The Brazilian then won as he pleased in Belgium, with only Prost keeping him company.

Warwick's Lotus was destroyed at Monza. Amazingly, he ran back to the pits and took the spare car for the restart, which Senna won from Prost. Senna then beat Prost in Belgium.

Mansell left his mark in Portugal by chopping Prost at the start, causing him to lift off and fall to fifth. This left Mansell to motor to victory, from Senna and Prost, with the French ace winning at Jerez, gaining valuable points as Senna retired.

The meeting was marred by Donnelly suffering really dreadful injuries when he crashed in practice, being thrown headlong from his obliterated Lotus.

Senna and Prost clashed again at Suzuka, this time on the first lap. Both were out on the spot, giving Senna the title. Then the quarrels began.

Almost obscured by this drama, Piquet led home a Benetton one-two ahead of Roberto Moreno who had replaced Nannini who had severed one of his hands in a helicopter accident.

Piquet won in Australia. Mansell and Prost were second and third, Senna having crashed from the lead.

GREAT RACE
Japanese Grand Prix 1990

The bitterness that had arisen between Alain Prost and Ayrton Senna following their clash in the 1989 title showdown was still evident when the circus returned to Suzuka in 1990. This time Prost was racing for Ferrari, adding a further element to their already explosive relationship. Reversing their positions from the previous year, Senna was ahead on points, nine up with two races to go. He duly qualified on pole, and action was guaranteed as Prost placed his Ferrari next to him at the front of the grid. With the stewards standing firm against Senna's pre-qualifying request to move pole position from the dirty pit wall side of the track, Prost knew that his best chance to pass the Brazilian would be off the grid. And so it proved, as he moved ahead on the run to the first corner. He turned in from the outside line, but Senna kept coming and speared the Frenchman off the circuit. It was a year before he owned up to doing this intentionally. Nigel Mansell took control for Ferrari, but driveshaft failure left Nelson Piquet to win, ahead of childhood friend Roberto Moreno who had stepped in to replace Alessandro Nannini who had suffered terrible injuries in a helicopter accident.

DRIVERS' WORLD CHAMPIONSHIP 1990

	Driver (NATIONALITY)	Make	Pts
1	**Ayrton Senna** (BRA)	McLaren-Honda	78
2	**Alain Prost** (FRA)	Ferrari	71
3	**Nelson Piquet** (BRA)	Benetton-Ford	43
4	**Gerhard Berger** (AUT)	McLaren-Honda	43
5	**Nigel Mansell** (GB)	Ferrari	37
6	**Thierry Boutsen** (BEL)	Williams-Renault	34
7	**Riccardo Patrese** (ITA)	Williams-Renault	23
8	**Alessandro Nannini** (ITA)	Benetton-Ford	21
9	**Jean Alesi** (FRA)	Tyrrell-Ford	13
10	**Ivan Capelli** (ITA)	Leyton House-Judd	6
	Roberto Moreno (BRA)	Benetton-Ford	6
	Aguri Suzuki (JAP)	Lola-Lamborghini	6

Best 11 scores from 16 races to count

1991

Ayrton Senna and McLaren made it two World Championship titles in succession, while Nigel Mansell elected not to quit Formula One but to race for Williams, who were in strong form. He would challenge Senna, but would fall short.

McLaren kept its driver line-up of Ayrton Senna and Gerhard Berger, but there was a different engine behind their shoulders. It was still a Honda, but now a V12 in place of the V10.

Mansell's move from Ferrari to Williams opened the door for Jean Alesi to join Ferrari, leaving his seat at Tyrrell to Stefano Modena. His ride at Brabham and that of team-mate David Brabham, went to Mark Blundell and Martin Brundle.

Unhappy with uncompetitive machinery, Derek Warwick had stepped down from Formula One to race sports cars, with Formula Three hotshot Mika Hakkinen joining Johnny Herbert who'd stood in for Martin Donnelly for the final two races of 1990. With Ligier having failed to score a point, it also elected for a clean-out, with Thierry Boutsen and Formula 3000 champion Erik Comas replacing Philippe Alliot and Nicola Larini and Lamborghini engines taking over from Cosworths.

At the back of the grid, Eurobrun opted out of Formula One, Osella was taken over and re-emerged as Fondmetal while Modena Lambo made its entrance.

A cut above these Italian teams was a third newcomer: Jordan. Entered by Formula 3000 team owner Eddie Jordan, it showed its hand at the first race when Bertrand Gachot qualified mid-grid. With all of these new teams plus Coloni and Dallara having to pre-qualify for the right to enter qualifying proper, team-mate Andrea de Cesaris failed to make the grid but, before the year was out, would run second at Spa-Francorchamps.

Senna left his opposition standing by winning the first four races. The first, the US Grand Prix at Phoenix, was won by 16 seconds from Alain Prost's Ferrari and Nelson Piquet's Benetton. It was closer in Brazil, as

Gracious Loser: Nigel Mansell congratulates Ayrton Senna after the Brazilian slowed to finish second at Suzuka, a result that was sufficient to make him champion

Senna pipped the Williams of a fast-closing Riccardo Patrese with his own team-mate Gerhard Berger close behind. However, only one thing mattered to Senna: he'd won his home race at his eighth attempt.

The San Marino Grand Prix was easier, with only Berger finishing on the same lap. Patrese became the first driver to lead Senna, but his Williams suffered engine problems. Mansell went off on the first lap after colliding with Brundle. The cruellest luck of all struck Eric van de Poele when his Lambo's fuel pump failed with two laps to go when he was running fifth. Amazingly, this was the only race for which he qualified.

Next up was Senna's stamping ground: Monaco. He duly won. The closest anyone got to him was Modena. But his Tyrrell's engine blew, taking out Patrese who went off on its oil slick.

Mansell had the Canadian Grand Prix in his pocket, but his engine died when he waved to the crowds on the final lap, letting Piquet by for victory.

Pit Problem: Nigel Mansell's season took a dive when one of his wheels escaped at Estoril

Patrese hit the top in Mexico after a late-race challenge from Mansell. Senna followed them home, then attacked Honda for not having an engine able to match the Renaults.

Mansell took his first win of the year when Magny-Cours held the French Grand Prix for the first time, having swapped the lead with Prost. Senna resisted a challenge from Alesi for third. Mansell repeated his success at Silverstone. Senna should have been second, but he ran out of fuel on the last lap, letting Berger and Prost past. Mansell made it three in a row at Hockenheim. Amazingly, Senna ran out of fuel on the last lap again, this time losing fourth place.

Senna won in Hungary. With the power circuits to come, it was to be his last likely victory until a return to the twistier tracks. Spa-Francorchamps favours those with power, so it was a surprise to see Senna win. He had been outpaced by Mansell and Alesi, but both retired.

De Cesaris was set for second, but his engine failed. His team-mate was debutant Michael Schumacher, who outqualified him, but was out on lap one. By the next race he was driving for Benetton in place of Roberto Moreno. Senna led for many laps at Monza, but was eating his tyres so

fell to second place behind Mansell. Schumacher scored his first points, coming fifth.

Patrese won in Portugal, but this was handed to him when Mansell lost a wheel leaving the pits. The wheel was reapplied, but in an illegal place, so Mansell was kicked out. Senna grabbed second. Mansell won at Barcelona from Prost and Patrese with Senna fifth. It was Berger's turn to win in Japan, albeit only after Senna slowed to let him pass. By then, the title was already his, having seen Mansell crash out of the race.

The season closed in Adelaide where Senna dominated in torrential conditions in a race that was halted after 14 laps. The race took place without Prost who'd been fired by Ferrari. He was leaving the team anyway, tired of the politics.

CONSTRUCTORS' CUP 1991

	Make	Pts
1	McLaren	139
2	Williams	125
3	Ferrari	55.5
4	Benetton	38.5
5	Jordan	13
6	Tyrrell	12
7	Minardi	6
8	Dallara	5
9	Brabham	3
	Lotus	3

DRIVERS' WORLD CHAMPIONSHIP 1991

	Driver (NATIONALITY)	Make	Pts
1	Ayrton Senna (BRA)	McLaren-Honda	96
2	Nigel Mansell (GB)	Williams-Renault	72
3	Riccardo Patrese (ITA)	Williams-Renault	53
4	Gerhard Berger (AUT)	McLaren-Honda	43
5	Alain Prost (FRA)	Ferrari	34
6	Nelson Piquet (BRA)	Benetton-Ford	26.5
7	Jean Alesi (FRA)	Ferrari	21
8	Stefano Modena (ITA)	Tyrrell-Honda	10
9	Andrea de Cesaris (ITA)	Jordan-Ford	9
10	Roberto Moreno (BRA)	Benetton-Ford	8

All scores counted

1992

This was the year when Nigel Mansell finally showed the racing world he could be a World Champion, and not just a melodramatic bit-player. Seldom has any driver dominated the Formula One championship to such an extent as he did.

Williams FW14B

Designers: **Patrick Head and Adrian Newey**   Years raced: **1992**
Grand prix wins: **10**   Pole positions: **15**   Fastest laps: **11**
Engine type: **Renault V10**
Engine size/power: **3,493cc/760bhp at 14,400rpm**
Anyone who witnessed the manner in which Nigel Mansell steamrollered the opposition in 1992 will appreciate that the FW14B was something special. Fitted with a semi-automatic gearbox and packed with gadgets, some would say it was the ultimate Formula One car. Mod-cons included active suspension and traction control, making the drivers' job of putting down the class-leading power of their Renault V10 engines all the easier. These driver aids were later outlawed, thus the "ultimate" tag. This was the second chassis designed by both Head and Newey and it was so good that it scorched to ten victories.

It was the sixth race before Nigel Mansell was beaten and his tally stood at eight wins after the first ten. He wrapped up the title at the next race, with five still to run.

By year's end, he had almost double the score of the second-placed driver, Williams team-mate Riccardo Patrese. Nigel's driving was from the top drawer, but he was given a huge help by Williams with its fabulous chassis and world-beating Renault engine.

There was an unusual degree of continuity among the top teams, with Williams, McLaren and Lotus keeping their driver line-ups from 1991. Struggling Ligier did too. But the most talked-about change was Alain Prost being replaced at Ferrari by Ivan Capelli, that rare thing, an Italian driver racing for this most Italian of teams.

With Brabham having achieved precious little in 1991, Martin Brundle was keen to move on and did so by joining Benetton to race alongside Michael Schumacher, a driver already seen as a future champion.

Mark Blundell was not so lucky and found himself without a drive as the Brabham team continued to slide, offering Eric van de Poele and Formula One newcomer Damon Hill little chance. Having ranked a hugely commendable fifth overall in its maiden season, Jordan was back

for more, but this time with new drivers in Mauricio Gugelmin and Stefano Modena at the wheel, both of whom would curse the team's decision to affiliate itself with a motor manufacturer: Yamaha. They would spend the season wishing they still had Cosworth power.

Tyrrell was another team that swapped everything, with Andrea de Cesaris and Olivier Grouillard assuming the driving duties and Ilmor

Will o' the Wisp: Nigel Mansell was all but untouchable for Williams in 1992. Here he opens out a massive lead on the opening lap at Silverstone in the British Grand Prix

engines taking over from Honda. Likewise, Minardi changed Ferrari power for Lamborghini and inserted Formula 3000 champion Christian Fittipaldi and Gianni Morbidelli.

March was called March again after its spell of being Leyton House, and it too was a case of all-change, with Capelli and Gugelmin being replaced by Karl Wendlinger and actor's son Paul Belmondo.

The merry-go-round at the tail of the field continued, with AGS, Coloni and Lambo not reappearing, and the Andrea Moda taking up the challenge, half-heartedly.

The season started in South Africa and Mansell enjoyed his reacquaintance with Kyalami, for he won by 24s from Patrese. Mexico was next, and it was the same story, with Mansell heading a Williams one-two.

Schumacher made his first podium visit, finishing third for Benetton. At Interlagos, Williams were first and second again, Mansell winning by 30s.

With Mansell dominant in Spain, the major surprise was that it was Schumacher not Patrese who came second after Patrese spun. Mansell took his fifth win at Imola, with Patrese

First of Many: Schumacher enjoys his first podium celebration with Patrese and Mansell in Mexico

second again. Senna fought to third, but his input had been so great that it was 20 minutes before he was able to climb from his McLaren.

Mansell's run came to an end at Monaco, losing to Senna. But only just, with Mansell only 0.2s away after a struggle to re-pass Senna after he'd pitted to replace a puncture.

Senna had led past half-distance in Montreal, but his electrics failed, by which time Mansell had spun and Berger came through to win. The French Grand Prix should have been Patrese's, but the race was halted by

rain and he lost out on the restart as team orders forced him to wave Mansell past. Patrese wasn't happy.

There was only going to be one winner at Silverstone: Mansell. Pole, fastest lap and victory by 40s was proof of that.

Patrese was second, with Brundle taking third when Senna pulled off. Mansell won again at Hockenheim, this time ahead of Senna, with Schumacher third.

Mansell hoped to wrap up the title with a win at the Hungaroring, but had to play second fiddle to Senna. However, that was enough for him to claim the coveted crown.

Schumacher scored his first win, at Spa-Francorchamps. Despite light rain, everyone started on slicks.

But the rain grew worse and only Senna stuck with slicks. If the rain

had stopped, it would have been a masterstroke, but it didn't and Senna would finish fifth. Schumacher judged conditions best to win from Mansell and Patrese.

Mansell ceded the lead at Monza so that Patrese could win, but both hit gearbox problems, with Patrese limping home fifth as Senna came through to win.

Mansell was back to winning form at Estoril, but he was nearly caught out by wreckage from Patrese's car after the Italian had flipped after clipping Berger.

Mansell waved Patrese into the lead at Suzuka, but his engine blew. The season came to an end in Adelaide, with Berger grabbing his second win ahead of Schumacher in a race that lost Mansell and Senna in a shunt when contesting the lead.

CONSTRUCTORS' CUP 1992

	Make	Pts
1	**Williams**	164
2	**McLaren**	99
3	**Benetton**	91
4	**Ferrari**	21
5	**Lotus**	13
6	**Tyrrell**	8
7	**Footwork**	6
	Ligier	6
9	**March**	3
10	**Dallara**	2

TECHNICAL INNOVATION

Wind Tunnels

With aerodynamics being the key to success in Formula One, the wind tunnel is one of the most valuable assets for any team in the 21st century. Indeed, for all the computer modelling that can be undertaken, including Computational Fluid Dynamics, the wind tunnel is still where the donkey work is done in shaping the car to reap its potential, with many teams operating their wind tunnels 24 hours per day, seven days per week throughout the winter. A wind tunnel is used to assess how a car reacts to aerodynamic forces at different speeds, with air being pumped through this tightly controlled environment (a giant cylinder in shape) by aluminium blades in a 4m high fan. Each model, whether full size or scale, has a load cell attached to it that measures drag, downforce, side force, roll, pitch (rotation of the car about its lateral axis) and yaw (side movement of a car under acceleration, braking or cornering). As yet, no wind tunnel can provide cornering or braking forces to make the test fully comprehensive. However, it's said that a ten per cent improvement in the relationship between drag and downforce will lead to a one second lap time improvement which, in Formula One terms, is huge.

DRIVERS' WORLD CHAMPIONSHIP 1992

	Driver (NATIONALITY)	Make	Pts
1	**Nigel Mansell** (GB)	Williams-Renault	108
2	**Riccardo Patrese** (ITA)	Williams-Honda	56
3	**Michael Schumacher** (GER)	Benetton-Ford	53
4	**Ayrton Senna** (BRA)	McLaren-Honda	50
5	**Gerhard Berger** (AUT)	McLaren-Honda	49
6	**Martin Brundle** (GB)	Benetton-Ford	38
7	**Jean Alesi** (FRA)	Ferrari	18
8	**Mika Hakkinen** (FIN)	Lotus-Ford	11
9	**Andrea de Cesaris** (ITA)	Tyrrell-Ilmor	8
10	**Michael Alboreto** (ITA)	Footwork-Honda	6

All scores counted

1993

Domination by one driver was the name of the game. And yet again the driver was in a Williams, but this time it was Alain Prost, who had been helped by a year away from the cockpit to regain his composure and passion for racing.

European Grand Prix 1993

This race was a "I was there when..." moment, for no one who saw Ayrton Senna's mesmerizing opening lap at Donington Park will ever forget it. The weather may have been cold and the track wet, but what happened in the first 90 seconds was electric. Starting fourth behind Alain Prost and Damon Hill, as well as Michael Schumacher, Senna fluffed his getaway and slipped behind to fifth by the first corner, Redgate. Then his charge began, with Schumacher picked off by the exit of Redgate. Karl Wendlinger's Sauber was next, at the daunting Craner Curves. Hill was demoted before McLeans and then Prost at the Melbourne Hairpin. Senna then made a mockery of his rivals as he sprinted away in difficult conditions, lapping all but Hill on this day of days. Jordan's Rubens Barrichello shone by running second in only his third grand prix before retiring with mechanical problems, but the day belonged only to Senna.

It was known in 1992 that Frank Williams was anxious to have Prost or Ayrton Senna in place of Mansell, triggering his departure to Indycars. Williams duly began 1993 with Prost and Damon Hill upgraded from the test team. McLaren signed Indycar racer Michael Andretti to replace Gerhard Berger who'd left for Ferrari, the Italian team anxious to find a driver who'd do better than Ivan Capelli had in 1992. Capelli found a ride with Jordan, but he was soon replaced by Thierry Boutsen who also wasn't to keep the drive for long, with Marco Apicella, Emanuele Naspetti and Eddie Irvine all having a go in the second Jordan. Rookie Rubens Barrichello was the team's star.

Having lost his ride with Williams, Riccardo Patrese had joined Benetton alongside Michael Schumacher, with Martin Brundle moving to Ligier, where he was partnered again by Mark Blundell. Tyrrell had a Japanese feel with Yamaha engines and Ukyo Katayama in its second car.

One driver who nearly didn't join in was Senna, as he'd been anxious at Honda engines giving way for Ford power and finally agreed to start the season on a race-by-race basis. This left Mika Hakkinen on the sidelines as he'd reckoned on Senna quitting and joined from Lotus. He'd spend the year on the sidelines until Andretti quit.

Brilliant Effort: Alain Prost was in a class of his own for Williams, as demonstrated by this photo of him waltzing to victory in the British Grand Prix at Silverstone, his 50th win in Formula One

Brabham, Fondmetal and March all failed to return, while the Dallara team run by BMS Scuderia Italia was back, but now known as Lola BMS Scuderia Italia in deference to the fact that its chassis were now built by Lola not Dallara. They weren't a success, with even Michele Alboreto struggling to qualify them. Far more successful was a new team from Switzerland: Sauber. Having run sports cars successfully, latterly for Mercedes, Peter Sauber's team arrived with Ilmor engines and a strong driver line-up of JJ Lehto and Karl Wendlinger.

Senna made the early running for McLaren at Kyalami, but Prost hit the front and beat Senna by 20s, with Ligier's Blundell a surprise third.

Prost was leading in Brazil when rain started and he hit a car that had spun. This put Hill in front, but he became Senna's prey and lost out to finish second. Rain hit the European Grand Prix at Donington Park, but Senna starred as he forced his way from fourth into the lead by the end of a stunning first lap and roared away as his rivals tiptoed in his wake. The other star was Barrichello who was heading for third place when his engine failed.

Hill led the early laps at Imola but spun off, leaving Prost to triumph.

Blowing Everyone Away: Ayrton Senna put on the most stunning drive of the year at Donington Park

CONSTRUCTORS' CUP 1993

	Make	Pts
1	**Williams**	168
2	**McLaren**	84
3	**Benetton**	72
4	**Ferrari**	28
5	**Ligier**	23
6	**Lotus**	12
	Sauber	12
8	**Minardi**	7
9	**Footwork**	4
10	**Jordan**	3
	Larrousse	3

Hill led from the start at Barcelona, dropped behind Prost but reapplied the pressure and was looking good until his engine blew, leaving Prost to win from Senna and Schumacher. Andretti finally finished a race for McLaren, doing so in fifth. Prost led at Monaco, but was given a stop-and-go and magnified this by stalling. This put Schumacher in front, but his hydraulics failed, and so Senna took over for his sixth win in the principality. Hill came second, with Alesi third for Ferrari.

The Canadian Grand Prix marked the start of a four-race streak for Prost. Considering the superiority of Williams, it was surprising that it took until round eight before they scored a one-two. Fittingly, it was on Renault's home patch in France. Hill led from pole, but was delayed in the pits and was demoted by Prost. Hill led at Silverstone until two-thirds distance when his engine blew, letting Prost motor on to his 50th win. Schumacher and Patrese finished second and third.

Hill was set for victory in Germany until a tyre blew two laps from home. Prost – 10s behind after a stop-and-go – flew past as Hill tried to struggle back to the pits, with Schumacher and Blundell second and third. Hill finally won at the Hungaroring, leading throughout after Prost was forced to start from the rear of the grid after

stalling on the parade lap. Senna shadowed Hill, but retired.

Schumacher and Prost trailed Hill at Spa-Francorchamps, while Alesi and Andretti were second and third behind Hill at Monza. Prost should have won to clinch his fourth world title, but his engine blew five laps from home.

Schumacher won at Estoril, but he really had to work for it, as Prost was on his tail. Second was enough for Prost to claim the title and he duly announced his retirement

Senna won in Japan, but then punched debutant Irvine who he felt had blocked him en route to sixth. Prost and Hakkinen – in at McLaren in place of Andretti – ran second and third all race. The season ended in Adelaide, with a win for Senna. Prost was second and Hill third.

DRIVERS' WORLD CHAMPIONSHIP 1993

	Driver (NATIONALITY)	Make	Pts
1	**Alain Prost** (FRA)	Williams-Renault	99
2	**Ayrton Senna** (BRA)	McLaren-Ford	73
3	**Damon Hill** (GB)	Williams-Renault	69
4	**Michael Schumacher** (GER)	Benetton-Ford	52
5	**Riccardo Patrese** (ITA)	Benetton-Ford	20
6	**Jean Alesi** (FRA)	Ferrari	16
7	**Martin Brundle** (GB)	Ligier-Renault	13
8	**Gerhard Berger** (AUT)	Ferrari	12
9	**Johnny Herbert** (GB)	Lotus-Ford	11
10	**Mark Blundell** (GB)	Ligier-Renault	10

All scores counted

1994

It was a very bad year, a championship horribly marred by Senna's death and further spoiled by controversy. The title race went down to the wire in Adelaide and then Michael Schumacher clinched the crown – in questionable fashion.

San Marino Grand Prix 1994

Formula One was rocked at Imola: two drivers were killed, two more escaped frightening accidents, a wheel flew into the grandstands and another struck mechanics in the pitlane. It was the meeting from hell. To start things off, Rubens Barrichello was hospitalized on the Friday. Then novice Roland Ratzenberger suffered a fatal injury when he crashed his Simtek in qualifying. Then Benetton's JJ Lehto, nursing a broken neck, stalled on the grid and was struck by Pedro Lamy's Lotus. Wreckage flew into the grandstand opposite, injuring eight spectators. The safety car was deployed and Ayrton Senna held station ahead of Michael Schumacher. When the cars were released three laps later, Senna got the jump on Schumacher. Tragically, as they entered the left-hand Tamburello kink on the next lap, Senna's Williams twitched on a bump and then speared straight into the retaining wall.

For the second year running, Williams started the year without its World Champion, with Alain Prost having been replaced by Ayrton Senna, a driver who Frank Williams had been trying to get to sign for his team for a decade. His ride at McLaren was taken by Martin Brundle, but he and Mika Hakkinen weren't to enjoy a strong year as the team's Peugeot engines were poor. With Riccardo Patrese having retired after 17 seasons, there was a vacancy at Benetton and this was filled by JJ Lehto, with his seat at Sauber going to Heinz-Harald Frentzen who came as part of the deal with Mercedes engines.

Ferrari retained Jean Alesi and Gerhard Berger. Here the main change was that team boss Jean Todt – who had arrived midway through 1993 – was transforming the way that this team ran in an attempt to stop it squandering its budget and become truly competitive again.

Despite enjoying a decent 1993 campaign, Ligier changed both drivers again, with Eric Bernard and Formula 3000 champion Olivier Panis replacing Mark Blundell and Brundle, with Blundell moving on to Tyrrell.

After his strong showings at the end of 1993, Eddie Irvine stayed with Jordan as team-mate to Rubens Barrichello. As finding a budget was proving a perennial problem, Minardi and the Lola BMS Scuderia Italia combined forces, with Pierluigi Martini coming from the former and Michele Alboreto from the latter.

Again, there were new teams, this time with Pacific stepping up after great success in the junior formulae, with Bertrand Gachot and Paul Belmondo as its drivers. Another British team, Simtek, joined them, but this was one created from scratch, with David Brabham and Roland Ratzenberger.

Senna seemed sure to win the title now that he'd joined Williams, but this isn't how it worked out. Indeed, by the time of his death, the Brazilian had scored no points from the first two races, while Schumacher had two wins to his credit for Benetton.

With driver aids such as traction control banned and refuelling now a prerequisite, Senna led in Brazil, but Benetton were kings of the pit stop and had Schumacher back out in the lead. Senna spun into retirement in his efforts to keep up, letting team-mate Damon Hill finish second in a race that lost Bernard, Brundle, Irvine and Jos Verstappen in a spectacular shunt for which Irvine was blamed.

The new TI Circuit in Japan was next, but Senna was tipped into the gravel at the first corner by former team-mate Mika Hakkinen. This left Schumacher clear to win from Berger and an ecstatic Barrichello.

Perfect Start: Michael Schumacher's victory at Monaco for Benetton was his fourth from the first four races and it put him on course for the title

Dicing with Death: Michael Schumacher and Ayrton Senna were the main men at the start of the year, but Senna was to die at Imola

Then came Imola. Ratzenberger hit a wall at 190mph in qualifying and died. Then Senna crashed out of the lead at the Tamburello kink, suffering fatal injuries, leaving Schumacher to score a cheerless win.

At Monaco, Schumacher made it four from four, with Martin Brundle 37s behind and Berger third. Sauber's Karl Wendlinger had crashed in qualifying and was in a coma for three weeks before making a full recovery. At Barcelona, Schumacher became stuck in fifth gear. Hill went by, but the German hung on to finish second, with Blundell third for Tyrrell.

Schumacher then beat Hill by 40s in Montreal, where Senna's replacement David Coulthard scored his first points, even leading early on. Renault paid for Nigel Mansell to make a one-off return for Williams at Magny-Cours. Despite qualifying on the front row with Hill, Schumacher blasted past both at the start to win.

Schumacher broke grid order at Silverstone, passing poleman Hill on the parade lap. He was shown the black flag, but ignored it, earning a two-race suspension.

Eventually, he came in for his stop-and-go penalty, so Hill won. His suspension was deferred, but victory at Hockenheim went to Berger, breaking a 58-race drought for Ferrari. The race is recalled more for a pit fire that engulfed Verstappen's Benetton.

Schumacher and Verstappen sandwiched Hill in first and third in Hungary. Then Schumacher won from Hill and Hakkinen in Belgium, but he'd ground away too much of his "plank" (a strip on the underside of the car), and was disqualified.

Schumacher missed Monza and Estoril, with Hill winning both.

Then Schumacher beat Hill at Jerez when the Williams wouldn't take on its fuel. Schumacher led at Suzuka, but the wet race turned when he chose to pit twice, Hill just once. It was a vital win, as Schumacher's points lead was cut to one.

Just before mid-distance in the Adelaide shoot-out, Schumacher grazed a wall. Hill dived for a gap and the German, knowing that his car was damaged, drove into him. This made Schumacher champion, as Hill's car was also too damaged to go on, leaving Mansell to win from Berger.

TECHNICAL INNOVATION
Driver Safety

Until the 1980s, drivers knew that they could be killed if they crashed. Now, they seem to survive literally any impact. To understand why drivers can afford to race closer to the edge, you only need to compare their cockpits with those of the 1950s. First you would notice that the drivers in the 1950s sat "on" the car rather than "in" it. The steering wheel was huge and wooden – whereas contemporary ones are tiny – and the drivers were held in by six-point harnesses. In the 1950s, few cars were fitted with rollhoops, as drivers preferred to be thrown clear. Today's monocoques must absorb a lateral impact of 30kN. They are also fitted with an impact-absorbing section, the "survival cell", to withstand a rear impact. Higher cockpit sides protect the driver's head and neck. These were first seen in 1994, following Karl Wendlinger's crash at the Monaco chicane that left him in a coma. These would deform if the driver's head hit it. In 1996, teams were told to include a 75mm deformable section around the driver's head, reducing the maximum g-force figure from 192g – at which point the driver's head would weigh more than a ton – to 75. All cars are now fitted with fire extinguishers that discharge into the cockpit and onto the engine. There are also kill switches – to cut ignition and fuel pumps – on the dashboard and on the rollhoop.

<table>
<thead>
<tr><th colspan="4">DRIVERS' WORLD CHAMPIONSHIP 1994</th></tr>
<tr><th></th><th>Driver (NATIONALITY)</th><th>Make</th><th>Pts</th></tr>
</thead>
<tbody>
<tr><td>1</td><td>Michael Schumacher (GER)</td><td>Benetton-Ford</td><td>92</td></tr>
<tr><td>2</td><td>Damon Hill (GB)</td><td>Williams-Renault</td><td>91</td></tr>
<tr><td>3</td><td>Gerhard Berger (AUT)</td><td>Ferrari</td><td>41</td></tr>
<tr><td>4</td><td>Mika Hakkinen (FIN)</td><td>McLaren-Peugeot</td><td>26</td></tr>
<tr><td>5</td><td>Jean Alesi (FRA)</td><td>Ferrari</td><td>24</td></tr>
<tr><td>6</td><td>Rubens Barrichello (BRA)</td><td>Jordan-Hart</td><td>19</td></tr>
<tr><td>7</td><td>Martin Brundle (GB)</td><td>McLaren-Peugeot</td><td>16</td></tr>
<tr><td>8</td><td>David Coulthard (GB)</td><td>Williams-Renault</td><td>14</td></tr>
<tr><td>9</td><td>Nigel Mansell (GB)</td><td>Williams-Renault</td><td>13</td></tr>
<tr><td>10</td><td>Jos Verstappen (NDL)</td><td>Benetton-Ford</td><td>10</td></tr>
</tbody>
</table>

All scores counted

1995

Williams versus Benetton. Damon Hill against Michael Schumacher. The top qualifier vying with the world's best racer. There was action aplenty, but it was all over with a race to spare as the German claimed his second straight world title.

Michael Schumacher was never expected to win the 1994 world title. But then Ayrton Senna died and he sneaked it from Damon Hill. For 1995, though, it looked as though it would be the Englishman who had the last laugh. Staying on at Williams, he had the best chassis and the top engine: Renault's V10.

Schumacher would also be armed with a Renault. Equal on horsepower after fighting with a deficit in 1994, the German's Benetton looked a brute on the handling front. Indeed, Schumacher's team-mate Johnny Herbert would attest to the car's twitchiness. And, like many Benetton number twos before him, he couldn't tame it. On pole in the Brazilian opener, Hill was leading from Schumacher when his suspension collapsed, allowing the German to win from Hill's team-mate David Coulthard. But then the first pair were ejected for using fuel that was deemed illegal. They were later reinstated.

Argentina was next, hosting a grand prix for the first time in 14 years and Hill dominated from Jean Alesi's Ferrari and an off-form Schumacher. Alesi was fortunate, indeed, as he'd lost control at the start and brought out the red flags by triggering a pile-up. Luckily for Alesi, it was his turn to have the spare Ferrari, so it was set-up for him and not for team-mate Gerhard Berger's lankier frame.

The next race in Europe was a poignant return to Imola just a year after the meeting claimed the lives of Ayrton Senna and Roland Ratzenberger. This time, all went well, and Hill won from the Ferraris, Alesi beating Berger.

It all came right for Benetton in Spain, with Schumacher heading Herbert home. Indeed, Schumacher started on pole and led every lap. Hill should have been second, but his hydraulics failed on the last lap, dropping him to fourth. A similar failure eliminated Coulthard from third.

Monaco used to be Senna's property. Nowadays, one looks to Schumacher for victory around the streets. But this was challenged when Hill took pole convincingly. In the race, though, Benetton's one-stop tactics helped Schumacher beat the twice-stopping Hill by 35 seconds.

In Canada, Schumacher again opted for one stop, but he ducked in for an unscheduled one because of gearchange problems and Alesi nipped through for his first grand prix win after 91 attempts to trigger a wave of pitlane emotion, especially for his former manager Eddie Jordan whose cars came home second and third, Rubens Barrichello ahead of Eddie Irvine.

Schumacher beat Hill to win in France, taking control with his pitstop strategy rather than with a piece of

Pacific Heights: Michael Schumacher celebrates after taking his Benetton to victory in the first-ever Pacific Grand Prix at the TI Circuit

overtaking on the track. Hill was caught in backmarkers when Schumacher first pitted and then couldn't call into his own pits as his team-mate was already there. Coulthard just resisted Martin Brundle's Ligier for third.

Historians will recall 1995 as the year in which Hill and Schumacher collided a lot. The first of the famous clashes came at Silverstone as Hill fought to pass Schumacher for the lead after his second pitstop. The move came at Priory and was hugely optimistic and took both out. Coulthard thus looked set for his first win, but was called in for a 10-second penalty for speeding in the pitlane and Herbert came through to win from Alesi.

Germany follows Britain on the calendar and thus Hill was greeted angrily by the hordes who packed Hockenheim. Starting from pole, he opened a cracking lead on the first lap and promptly lost control and crashed starting the second lap. Schumacher took over and was able to win as he pleased from Coulthard to open up a 21-point lead.

Hill made amends in Hungary with the perfect performance: pole, fastest lap and victory, backed up by Coulthard in second and Schumacher in retirement after a late-race fuel pump failure when second.

Coulthard dominated in Belgium, but his gearbox failed and through came Hill and Schumacher (up from 16th on the grid...) for a fierce battle.

Fast Finish: in Canada, Schumacher had problems and Jean Alesi nipped in for his first GP win

There was slight contact as the German (on slicks) did his utmost to block Hill (on new wets), both to stay in the lead and to negate the new tyres' advantage. And it worked, although Schumacher was given a one-race ban suspended for four races.

In Italy, Coulthard again made the early running before retiring, and Schumacher and Hill collided again. This time the fault was Hill's as he clouted the rear of the Benetton as they passed a tail-ender while chasing Berger. But he too was to retire. Alesi took over, yet there was to be no home win for Ferrari, as he too parked up. Through it all came Herbert to win from Mika Hakkinen's McLaren and Heinz-Harald Frentzen's Sauber.

Coulthard finally got his reward in Portugal, with Schumacher demoting Hill to third in the dying laps. Ukyo

Katayama caused the race to be restarted when he barrel-rolled his Tyrrell at the start.

The Grand Prix of Europe, at the Nurburgring, was a belter. Run in damp conditions, Alesi amazed everyone by not only starting on slicks but by working his way through into the lead. Some tough racing ensued with Hill clipping his car and then Hill and Schumacher touching. Hill crashed out and this left Schumacher to chase and catch Alesi with three laps to run. His victory all but wrapped up the title.

Not one but two Japanese races followed, with the Pacific Grand Prix at the TI Circuit first. This was won by Schumacher for his second world title in a row. Coulthard led the first 50 laps, but Schumacher's three-stop strategy to the Scotsman's two was the key. That and his amazing speed.

Hill was a distant third. Schumacher rubbed it in at Suzuka, taking his ninth win of the year, enough to give Benetton its first constructors' crown. Hill and Coulthard both spun off, and this helped Hakkinen (back after a race away to have an appendectomy) to second ahead of Herbert.

And so to Adelaide for the final time. Coulthard wanted to end his last race for Williams with victory, but he left them aghast when he pitted (in the lead) and crashed into the pitlane entrance. Hill then won as he pleased, while Schumacher was chopped by Alesi and retired as a result. Frentzen moved into second and retired. Then Herbert did likewise. In fact, almost all of the frontrunners dropped out, and Hill won by two laps from Olivier Panis's Ligier and Gianni Morbidelli's Arrows.

GREAT RACE

Canadian Grand Prix 1995

It's always pleasing when a driver wins for the first time, but when that driver is doing so at his 91st attempt, then the emotion is all the more heartfelt. The driver in question was Jean Alesi. He was in his fifth year with Ferrari and still winless, so he travelled to Montreal more in hope than expectation. Fifth place on the grid did not augur well, but he was soon up to third after passing team-mate Gerhard Berger and benefiting after David Coulthard had spun off. He passed Damon Hill's Williams by quarter distance, but Michael Schumacher's pole-starting Benetton was well clear. With ten laps to go, however, Schumacher trickled into the pits with his car stuck in third. And so Alesi was bound for glory, crying into his visor at the realization that he would finally achieve his ambition.

DRIVERS' WORLD CHAMPIONSHIP 1995

	Driver (NATIONALITY)	Make	Pts
1	**Michael Schumacher** (GER)	Benetton-Renault	102
2	**Damon Hill** (GB)	Williams-Renault	69
3	**David Coulthard** (GB)	Williams-Renault	49
4	**Johnny Herbert** (GB)	Benetton-Renault	45
5	**Jean Alesi** (FRA)	Ferrari	42
6	**Gerhard Berger** (AUT)	Ferrari	31
7	**Mika Hakkinen** (FIN)	McLaren-Mercedes	17
8	**Olivier Panis** (FRA)	Ligier-Mugen Honda	16
9	**Heinz-Harald Frentzen** (GER)	Sauber-Ford	15
10	**Mark Blundell** (GB)	McLaren-Mercedes	13

All scores counted

1996

It was a case of mission accomplished for Damon Hill. For, in 1996, he landed the World Championship that Michael Schumacher had kept out of his grasp in the previous two seasons. He had made the might of Williams pay.

LANDMARK CAR
Williams FW18
Designers: **Patrick Head and Adrian Newey**   Years raced: **1996**
Grand prix wins: **12**   Pole positions: **12**   Fastest laps: **11**
Engine type: **Renault V10**
Engine size/power: **3,000cc/750bhp at 14,500rpm**
Damon Hill has a soft spot for the FW18, the car with which he secured his world title in 1996. Like the FW14B, this was the work of Head and Newey, with the latter responsible for its aerodynamics, the former for the engineering. It was a combination other teams could only aspire to. High-nosed, like its predecessor the FW17B, there were two main factors that helped the FW18 win all but four of the season's 16 races in the hands of Hill and Jacques Villeneuve: its balance (found after two years of struggle to find a balance without active suspension) and the class-leading delivery of horsepower from its Renault V10 engine.

The Fat Lady Sings: Damon Hill is delighted as this victory for Williams at Magny-Cours puts his championship challenge back on track

The 1996 season was the one in which Damon Hill was going to put the record straight. With 1994 and 1995 World Champion Michael Schumacher moving to Ferrari, the idea was that there would be no one who could stop the Englishman from emulating his late father, Graham Hill by becoming World Champion.

Four wins from the first five races gave the lie to this as the Williams team flexed its muscles. But then the fates struck and deprived Hill of a clear victory at the Monaco Grand Prix, a race he had desperately wanted to win since he arrived in Formula One. On that strange day, just three cars finished, with Olivier Panis a surprise winner for Ligier. Then retirement in the Spanish Grand Prix also meant no points for Hill, and a full-house for Schumacher who put on a masterful display in the wet.

It should be pointed out, though, that from the very first race in Australia Hill found there was a threat from within, new Williams team-mate and IndyCar Champion Jacques Villeneuve having made the most of a comprehensive winter of testing to get to grips with Formula One. The little Canadian even had the temerity to show Hill the way in Melbourne until an oil leak forced him to slow and cede his maiden victory. Villeneuve had to wait only until the fourth race,

the Grand Prix of Europe at the Nurburgring, to hit the big time, winning a great chase to the line ahead of Schumacher.

Victories in Canada and France put Hill back on track. But there was no such luck on home ground at Silverstone where he fell off and Villeneuve won. Hill's world appeared to cave in at the next race, in Hockenheim, when a story broke that he was to lose his ride at Williams to Heinz-Harald Frentzen, sending the newspaper hacks into a frenzy. He was able to leave Germany wearing a smile, though, as he picked up a fortunate win when Benetton's Gerhard Berger had his Renault engine blow up with three laps to go, giving Hill a 21 point lead over Villeneuve who was third that day.

This was soon whittled down, however, as Villeneuve won in Hungary by a short head from Hill, then reduced Hill's advantage to 13 at the Belgian Grand Prix as he was placed second behind Schumacher with Hill only fifth after a serious mix-up over when to come in for tyres. A few days later, Frank Williams announced that Frentzen would be replacing Hill. Even if Hill landed the world title, he would be looking elsewhere for his employment for 1997. And all the top drives were now filled.

When Hill crashed out of the lead in Italy, matters looked serious. But

Villeneuve also failed to score, so Hill was in a position to wrap it all up in Portugal, and he led, bar pitstops, until lap 48 of the 70-lap race distance. But then Villeneuve motored past him after a fabulous drive that saw him pass Schumacher around the outside of the fearsome last corner, and this took the title race down to the wire at the final round in Japan, albeit with Hill needing just one point to clinch the coveted prize.

Hill and British racing fans will all remember the outcome of that one as Damon stamped his authority on proceedings at Suzuka and led all the way to sign out in style with a win. However, he had already become the first ever second-generation World Champion as Villeneuve had lost a wheel and crashed out 15 laps from the finish. For Hill, this was a life's goal reached at last. For Villeneuve, it was just the beginning.

Villeneuve was a revelation to many in 1996, his four wins not only impressing those who watched them, but also raising the stock of IndyCar drivers which had taken a battering when Michael Andretti drove for McLaren in 1993 and was not a factor. Villeneuve's racer's instinct is not displayed in the flamboyant style of his late father Gilles, but is effective all the same, and his ability to attack in traffic is not far short of Schumacher's. Many saw 1996 as his dress rehearsal and the feeling

The Rivals: Damon Hill has every reason to smile as he tells Schumacher that he is now champion

was no-one would prevent him from landing the big one in 1997.

Beyond this golden duo, Schumacher stood supreme whenever he could coerce his wayward Ferrari to behave. And, mid-season, this was not often at all, with both he and team-mate Eddie Irvine failing to go very far in the consecutive Canadian, French and British Grands Prix. He won, though, in Spain, Belgium and Italy, with his drive in torrential rain in the first of these the most impressive of the season, but his home win at Monza being the one closest to the heart of the *tifosi*. Trouble was, having started the season with a low-nose format and then changed mid-season to a high-nose format, the team was always playing catch-up. And, if there was development work to be done, Schumacher did it. Frustrated by a

lack of track time, Irvine's third place in the opening round was his best finish. Berger and Jean Alesi deserved to win races for Benetton, but were ever deprived. Berger revealed that he had been suffering from a virus early in the year, and his improved form from the summer on proved his return to health. Alesi was almost always on the pace, but remained prone to mad moves that would send boss Flavio Briatore into a rage, such as when he crashed on the opening lap of the Japanese Grand Prix to help Ferrari steal second place in the Constructors' Cup from Benetton.

Mercedes had high hopes of finding grand prix glory for the first time since 1955 with McLaren, but while Mika Hakkinen and David Coulthard gave their all and made progress, they were still not quite there yet. Jordan moved up a position on its 1995 ranking

to be fifth overall, swapping places with Ligier, and rewarded its drivers Rubens Barrichello and Martin Brundle by firing them. So you could see where Eddie Jordan put the blame for the team continuing winless.

Ligier, on the other hand, did win. But, the freak win at Monaco aside, Panis scored just twice more, and Pedro Diniz got just two sixth places. Frentzen remained Sauber's blue-eyed boy, but Johnny Herbert pushed him hard in the second half of the year, albeit only for the minor places.

Tyrrell, Footwork and Minardi continued to field two cars apiece and pray for the odd point. But their seasons were more about survival than success. Survive they did, which is more than the Italian Forti team which was pitched into oblivion by a financial crisis mid-season, leaving Formula One with just 20 cars.

CONSTRUCTORS' CUP 1996

	Make	Pts
1	**Williams**	175
2	**Ferrari**	70
3	**Benetton**	68
4	**McLaren**	49
5	**Jordan**	22
6	**Ligier**	15
7	**Sauber**	11
8	**Tyrrell**	5
9	**Footwork**	1

DRIVERS' WORLD CHAMPIONSHIP 1996

	Driver (NATIONALITY)	Make	Pts
1	**Damon Hill** (GB)	Williams-Renault	97
2	**Jacques Villeneuve** (CAN)	Williams-Renault	78
3	**Michael Schumacher** (GER)	Ferrari	59
4	**Jean Alesi** (FRA)	Benetton-Renault	47
5	**Mika Hakkinen** (FIN)	McLaren-Mercedes	31
6	**Gerhard Berger** (AUT)	Benetton-Renault	21
7	**David Coulthard** (GB)	McLaren-Mercedes	18
8	**Rubens Barrichello** (BRA)	Jordan-Peugeot	14
9	**Olivier Panis** (FRA)	Ligier-Mugen	13
10	**Eddie Irvine** (GB)	Ferrari	11

All scores counted

1997

Champion in 1994 and 1995, Schumacher came close to a third title in 1997, but he failed to land the one Ferrari craved by clashing with Jacques Villeneuve at the final round, leaving the Canadian to win for Williams.

European Grand Prix 1997

It is sad to say so, but many races that stand out do so because of a collision between the leading protagonists. The stage was set with Ferrari's Michael Schumacher leading by a point from Williams' Jacques Villeneuve. Freakishly, both were given the same time in qualifying, down to 0.001s. As he had set his time first, Villeneuve claimed pole, but he slipped to third at the start. After the first round of pit stops, he was second behind Schumacher. Sauber stand-in Norberto Fontana blocked Villeneuve and cost him two seconds, but Villeneuve closed in again. On lap 47, he made a dive at the Dry Sack hairpin. It worked, but Schumacher looked across and simply swerved into him. Taking both out would have made him champion, but Villeneuve survived and continued in the lead, right until the final lap when he let the McLaren drivers through, safe in the knowledge that he was champion.

Ferrari spent the bulk of the 1990s chasing the World Championship, frequently being coy pre-season about its chances of achieving its holy grail. Few believed the team when they said their plan was to win races then go for the crown the following year. Surely, insiders said, if you couldn't win with Michael Schumacher aboard, then you were never going to win. So 1997 was definitely a year in which they were going for gold.

But, between Schumacher and the crown lay Williams with its Renault engines and Jacques Villeneuve, joined by Heinz-Harald Frentzen.

So, it was a mighty shock at the opening race in Melbourne when David Coulthard took McLaren back to the winner's circle for the first time since Ayrton Senna won at Adelaide at the end of 1993. However, the speed Villeneuve had shown when he qualified on pole by over a second

from Frentzen with Schumacher a further third of a second back was a pointer. Shame then that he was tipped off by Schumacher's team-mate Eddie Irvine at the first corner, as was Sauber's Johnny Herbert. Frentzen was catching Coulthard in the closing laps but a brake disc exploded. And so Schumacher salvaged second ahead of Hakkinen despite having to make an extra stop as his car hadn't taken on enough fuel.

Villeneuve won the next two races in Brazil and Argentina, the first ahead of Gerhard Berger's Benetton and Olivier Panis's Prost. His win in Buenos Aires was hard-fought as he battled both with an upset stomach and with a fired-up Irvine. With Frentzen not having scored, the pressure was on his shoulders when they visited Imola. And he came good to win ahead of the Ferraris. Villeneuve led early on but lost out at the first stops and lost third when his gearbox failed.

Monaco was next and on past form this ought to mean victory for Michael Schumacher. And so it was to prove as he got the jump on polesitter Frentzen and led all the way in the wet. The Williams drivers made the wrong tyre choice and Rubens Barrichello claimed an emotional second place for the new Stewart team.

Tyres were again crucial in Spain. But not because it rained, rather because the Catalunya track ate them. And here Villeneuve showed his guile while Frentzen struggled, winning ahead of Panis and Benetton's Jean Alesi.

The Canadian Grand Prix will be recalled for two events: firstly Panis breaking his legs in a high-speed collision with the barriers, and secondly for Coulthard dominating until his engine fluffed at a pit stop when leading on the very same lap, handing the race to Michael Schumacher and leaving the Scot seventh.

The Moment of Truth: Jacques Villeneuve dives his Williams up the inside at Jerez and Michael Schumacher starts to turn into him at the European GP

Schumacher won again at Magny-Cours. There were just over six laps to go at Silverstone and Hakkinen was heading for his first win, but his engine failed and so Villeneuve collected a lucky 10 points.

Berger returned at Hockenheim. And what a return! He not only claimed pole, but also set fastest lap and led almost every lap to win... His chief challenger was Fisichella, who led after Berger pitted, but retired when a puncture damaged a radiator.

The Hungarian Grand Prix very nearly produced the oddest result of the year, if not of all-time, as Damon Hill not only qualified the previously unimpressive Arrows third, but he passed Michael Schumacher for the lead and then led until halfway around the final lap when Villeneuve swept past his ailing Arrows to win. His gearbox barely working, Hill limped home a still astonishing second, with Herbert third.

Spa-Francorchamps, like Monaco, is a drivers' track. And thus Michael Schumacher was tipped to win. And he didn't disappoint, winning by almost half a minute in the wet after overcoming early leader Villeneuve and Alesi once the safety car peeled off after controlling the field for the first four laps. Having also fitted intermediates, Fisichella was second ahead of Frentzen, while Villeneuve was frustrated by having pitted too early for his tyre change.

Calm before the Storm: Villeneuve and Schumacher contemplate the battle that lies ahead

The Italian Grand Prix was won in the pits, as Coulthard used his only stop to find a way past long-time leader Alesi, with Frentzen falling from second to third in the scramble.

Jarno Trulli started the season with one and a half year's Formula Three experience to his name since starring in karting. After starting the season with Minardi, he stepped up to Prost when Panis was injured.

All useful experience people thought, but he rocked the boat when he led the first 37 laps of the Austrian Grand Prix before being passed by eventual winner Villeneuve, with his engine blowing 13 laps from the flag. The Stewarts also showed well, but Coulthard and Frentzen completed the podium.

The sight of the Jordans clashing at the first corner of the Luxembourg Grand Prix at the Nurburgring was shocking, but when Ralf Schumacher cannoned into his brother and took him out of the race the championship battle was truly opened up. But the McLaren's were dominant on the home ground of engine supplier Mercedes until first Coulthard blew up when second and then Hakkinen was again denied while leading. And so Villeneuve won from Alesi and Frentzen to open a nine-point lead over Schumacher.

Ferrari had to fight back at the penultimate race, and Schumacher and Irvine duly qualified second and third behind Villeneuve at Suzuka. But Villeneuve (along with several others) was punished for not slowing past yellow flags. With a suspended ban hanging over him, he was able to start the race only under appeal.

Irvine soon demoted him and then Schumacher hit the front to win from Frentzen and Irvine, with Villeneuve fifth. Williams then decided to drop its appeal and start the final race a point behind Schumacher.

And it was at Jerez that Schumacher famously pulled across on Villeneuve, with the collision leaving him both in the gravel trap and in disgrace, while Villeneuve was able to bring his lightly damaged car home, ceding the lead only on the final lap when he let Hakkinen and Coulthard through, as third place gave him the points needed for the title. And thus the Finn finally scored a long overdue first win. The FIA didn't bow to pressure to ban Schumacher from the first two races of 1998, instead removing him from second place in the 1997 rankings.

RULES OF THE GAME

Crash Testing

Crash testing has become more and more stringent. There are two types of crash testing: impact and static-load testing. The first is when the car is accelerated into a wall on a sled on a sloping track. Static-load testing is when the car is stationary and weights are swung into it. For frontal impact testing, the amount of deformation can be examined by markings every 50mm along the nose, with the impact filmed at 3,000 frames per second. Further assessment comes from a pair of accelerometers which measure deceleration. In lateral impact tests, the car is hit at 12m/s by a 25kg cone. To check the strength of the sidepods, a 500mm x 500mm square of aluminium honeycomb is clamped to a metal frame before the cone is dropped. In all testing, the car's safety cell must remain intact, with safety harness and fire extinguisher mounting points staying firm.

1998

The Formula One World Championship has always been about a clash of individuals, and 1998 will go down as one of the epic encounters as it was Mika Hakkinen versus Michael Schumacher and McLaren versus Ferrari. And no quarter was given.

To have a season-long battle for World Championship honours, one usually needs to have the likely protagonists squaring up to each other all year in evenly matched cars. However, it didn't look as though there was a ghost of a chance of this happening in 1998 between Hakkinen and Schumacher after the opening race in Melbourne when the McLarens creamed the opposition, lapping the entire field. McLaren had responded best to the incoming regulations that insisted on narrower chassis and the use of grooved tyres.

Yet, on that day back in March an important thing happened: Hakkinen thought he'd been called into the pits after mishearing a radio message and made a stop that cost him the lead. However, Coulthard kept to a pre-race agreement that whichever of them led into the first corner on the first lap would win the race and so let Hakkinen past for victory. The difference between first and second was four points, and these would become truly crucial for the Finn. At the time, however, it looked as though they would only be useful in his fight against Coulthard.

The Brazilian Grand Prix came and went with Hakkinen followed home by Coulthard. Yet Schumacher made progress by not only finishing the race, but finishing it in third place.

But still it was hard for the German to harbour any title aspirations.

After You, Mika: the moment that caused a storm in Melbourne when Coulthard (right) let Hakkinen through for victory in the season opener

Yet the arrival of a wider Goodyear front tyre, in conjunction with the first of a raft of aerodynamic changes from Ferrari, achieved the seemingly impossible in the Argentinian Grand Prix. Schumacher won after muscling Coulthard out of the lead. Hakkinen could only trail home second with Eddie Irvine making it a doubly good day for Ferrari by finishing third while Coulthard endured a further accident, with 1997 champion Jacques Villeneuve's Williams, before finishing sixth.

This appeared to have been something of a false dawn, however, when McLaren dominated at Imola. Certainly, Hakkinen dropped out, but Coulthard won, albeit cruising to the finish ahead of Schumacher.

Lest Ferrari were thinking that Hakkinen's retirement at Imola showed a chink in McLaren's armour, Hakkinen and Coulthard dominated the Spanish Grand Prix. Then Hakkinen won at Monaco after Coulthard's engine blew when right with him. Schumacher, though, had a disastrous time, losing laps in the pit for repairs after clashing with Alexander Wurz. Still, he came off better than the young Austrian whose Benetton later collapsed in the tunnel and he was fortunate to escape the ensuing ride along the barriers. At least Benetton had a smile at the end of the day, though, as Giancarlo Fisichella survived a spin to bring their other car home in second place.

However, when the circus headed for Canada, McLaren had looked set for another maximum haul of points, but then Hakkinen found himself without a drive at the second start, after Wurz had triggered a restart after a further aerobatic moment. Then Coulthard dropped out of the lead when his car also failed, leaving the way open for Schumacher to win, despite taking in a stop/go penalty for forcing Heinz-Harald Frentzen's Williams off the track.

When Schumacher and Irvine got ahead of the McLarens at the second start of the French Grand Prix they bottled them up there and finished first and second.

Amazingly, Schumacher made it a hat-trick in the British Grand Prix after Hakkinen lost a 40 second lead when the safety car was deployed as the track was so wet that cars were aquaplaning. Hakkinen then spun and Schumacher took the lead. But he was called in for a stop/go penalty and this ought to have handed the win back to Hakkinen, although he somehow got around this by taking this penalty in the pits after passing the chequered flag. Amazingly, he was allowed to keep his win because of a procedural cock-up.

McLaren bounced back with Hakkinen and Coulthard finishing first and second in both Austria and Germany. They should have repeated this in Hungary, too, but Ferrari

Shake On It: Hakkinen is congratulated by Schumacher on winning the World Championship in Japan

CONSTRUCTORS' CUP 1998

	Make	Pts
1	**McLaren-Mercedes**	156
2	**Ferrari**	133
3	**Williams-Mecachrome**	38
4	**Jordan-Mugen Honda**	34
5	**Benetton-Mecachrome**	33
6	**Sauber-Petronas**	10
7	**Arrows**	6
8	**Stewart-Ford**	5
9	**Prost-Peugeot**	1

tactician Ross Brawn put Schumacher on a three-stop strategy that worked a treat for a famous win.

Schumacher should have won at Spa-Francorchamps as well, but he slammed into the back of a delayed Coulthard and ripped off a wheel, throwing away a 30-second lead over Damon Hill's Jordan which went on to the team's first win ahead of team-mate Ralf Schumacher and Jean Alesi's Sauber. He was gifted a win on home ground at Monza, though, when Coulthard dropped out of the lead and Hakkinen fell to fourth with brake problems. Amazingly, this brought him level on points with Hakkinen and although he led at the Nurburgring, Hakkinen came from behind to win and thus head for the last round four points ahead with momentum behind him.

Yes, those four gifted points from Australia had come home to roost. And this put the pressure on Schumacher, knowing that he had to win to be champion. And, even if he did, Hakkinen was going to have to finish third or lower. So he was relying heavily on team-mate Eddie Irvine. Then Schumacher stalled at the start and was forced to start the race from the back of the grid. The battle was over and Hakkinen raced off to his eighth win and the World Championship that had looked his right from his early days in racing.

And what of the rest? Well, 1998 marked a three-way shoot-out for third in the Constructors' Cup between Williams, Benetton and Jordan. Villeneuve and Frentzen struggled all year, finishing no higher than third, while Fisichella scored Benetton's best results with a pair of second place finishes.

But it was relative newcomers Jordan who hit the jackpot, with their day of days coming when they scored their famous one-two in the crash-torn Belgian Grand Prix. This, combined with a run of strong results, propelled the team that failed to score until the second half of the season past Benetton into fourth place overall.

Sauber had a lacklustre time in 1998 despite the arrival of Alesi, who got the better of Johnny Herbert. Arrows normally saw drivers Mika Salo and Pedro Diniz pulling off in a cloud of smoke, although they both finished in the points at Monaco. Stewart dropped Jan Magnussen to introduce Jos Verstappen alongside Rubens Barrichello with little effect. Minardi soldiered on to no real glory. While Tyrrell showed flashes of speed through mercurial Japanese driver Toranosuke Takagi, but had a dismal end to its 30-year career. From now on it will be effectively a completely new team: British American Racing.

TECHNICAL INNOVATION
Grooved Tyres

After 27 years of Formula One cars racing on treadless ("slick") tyres, grooved tyres were introduced in 1998 to slow cars through corners and to make drivers brake earlier as they had less grip, thus increasing the possibility of overtaking. Grooved tyres were expected to add four to five seconds to a lap time. However, cars lapped just 2s slower at the start of the year and almost as fast within a year. As for boosting overtaking, drivers felt this had not worked as the grooved tyres made the cars more twitchy, forcing them to take fewer risks. If rain falls, teams have to decide if it's worth adding an extra stop to swap grooved rubber for intermediates or wets. Unless the track is soaked, wets will overheat as their tread generates more heat than is good for the tyres.

DRIVERS' WORLD CHAMPIONSHIP 1998

	Driver (NATIONALITY)	Make	Pts
1	**Mika Hakkinen** (FIN)	McLaren-Mercedes	100
2	**Michael Schumacher** (GER)	Ferrari	86
3	**David Coulthard** (GB)	McLaren-Mercedes	56
4	**Eddie Irvine** (GB)	Ferrari	47
5	**Jacques Villeneuve** (CAN)	Williams-Mecachrome	21
6	**Damon Hill** (GB)	Jordan-Mugen Honda	20
7	**Heinz-Harald Frentzen** (GER)	Williams-Mecachrome	17
8	**Alexander Wurz** (AUT)	Benetton-Mecachrome	17
9	**Giancarlo Fisichella** (ITA)	Benetton-Mecachrome	16
10	**Ralf Schumacher** (GER)	Jordan-Mugen Honda	14

1999

This was 1998 all over again: Mika Hakkinen versus Michael Schumacher. But then the German broke a leg and Hakkinen faced a new challenge from Eddie Irvine, one that raged all the way to the final round in Japan.

Little had changed for 1999, as McLaren and Ferrari had retained their driver line-ups and design teams. All cars had to race on tyres with an extra groove in them, but this failed to shuffle the order, with Jordan, Williams and Benetton still fighting to be best of the rest, and Arrows and Minardi fighting not to be last. The major novelty was the arrival of a new team: BAR. Jacques Villeneuve had moved from Williams to join his friend Craig Pollock, with Ricardo Zonta in the number two seat.

McLaren filled the front row at Melbourne, with Hakkinen 1.3s clear of Schumacher's best. Fortunately for Ferrari and the others, the new McLaren was fragile and both retired. Schumacher wasn't to benefit, as he'd failed to get away on the parade lap before the second start – the first having been aborted after both Stewarts caught fire – and had to start from the rear. And so team-mate Eddie Irvine came away with his first win, followed home by Jordan newboy Heinz-Harald Frentzen and the driver with whom he'd changed places, Ralf Schumacher, now of Williams.

Hakkinen overcame a gearbox problem to overhaul Schumacher for victory at Interlagos. Rubens Barrichello led in front of his home-town fans when Hakkinen slowed without gears. He was on a two-stop strategy, the others planning to stop just once, but it showed how the Stewart team was making progress. However, his engine failed, leaving Frentzen to finish on the podium for the second straight race.

It was an all-McLaren front row at Imola, but the Ferraris were right with them. This pressure paid in the race, when Hakkinen pressed too hard in his attempts to build up a lead, running over the kerbs out of the Traguardo chicane and clouting the wall. The crowd became even more excited when Schumacher outran David Coulthard to win. Ferrari's improving form was emphasized with a first and second at Monaco.

Lest Ferrari think they had taken the upper hand, McLaren meted out its traditional one-two in Spain, but with Schumacher just 11s down on Hakkinen in third after he'd been delayed by a fast-starting Villeneuve until his first pitstop. Still, though, BAR sought its first point.

If Hakkinen had slipped at Imola, then Schumacher did likewise at Montreal, sticking his Ferrari into the wall when leading. Hakkinen took maximum points, while Coulthard came away with nothing after tangling with Irvine when fighting for third.

The best race of the year came at Magny-Cours, with five drivers leading the race as rain affected play. At the end, it was Frentzen in front thanks to a clever refuelling tactic when the

Cat and Mouse: Eddie Irvine leads Hakkinen in the early laps of the first ever Malaysian Grand Prix

team put in sufficient fuel to see him through to the end. Hakkinen, who was ahead in the closing stages, had to pit for a second time with seven laps remaining. He thus fell to second, ahead of Barrichello who'd started on pole after a quick lap before the skies opened in qualifying and led for half of the race. With Schumacher only fifth behind his brother, Hakkinen was now eight points to the good.

The title battle was to change at Silverstone as Schumacher crashed on the first lap and broke his right leg. Hakkinen was unable to benefit as a wheel fell off his car and Coulthard came through to win from Irvine. However, Coulthard tipped Hakkinen into a spin on the first lap at the A1-Ring. Although Hakkinen fought back from last to third, he had every reason to be unhappy.

To make matters worse, Coulthard had been outpaced by Irvine who was now just two points down on Hakkinen. This became even more of a nightmare for Hakkinen at Hockenheim when he lost the lead when there was a problem with his refuelling rig. On rejoining in fourth, his fightback came to an end when he had a blow-out and crashed coming into the stadium. Again Irvine won, this time courtesy of Schumacher's stand-in Mika Salo letting him through.

McLaren stopped the red tide in Hungary with a Hakkinen–Coulthard one-two. Still two points behind Irvine

Aftermath of Battle: Eddie Irvine congratulates Mika Hakkinen on his second world title

going to Spa, Hakkinen didn't enjoy the Ulsterman's advantage of having number one treatment, as McLaren boss Ron Dennis refused to ask Coulthard to be subservient. And this showed when the pair touched at the first corner. Coulthard emerged ahead and stayed ahead, with Frentzen keeping Irvine back in fourth.

The pressure was on at Monza and again Hakkinen cracked when leading, spinning out. Fortunately for him, Irvine was able only to finish sixth and thus they were level on points with three rounds to go. For the record, Frentzen drove a great race to win at Monza with Ralf Schumacher second ahead of Salo to give Williams its best result since 1997. Even Ralf's team-mate Alessandro Zanardi ran third before his wretched comeback season after winning two IndyCar crowns was

hit by a detached undertray and he slipped back to seventh.

Rain shuffled the order at the European GP at the Nurburgring. Frentzen had been set for victory, but his electrics failed. This left Coulthard in front, but he spun off, as did Fisichella. So Ralf Schumacher led, but a puncture cost him time and Johnny Herbert profited, thanks to staying on dry tyres in the changing conditions. With Barrichello finishing third behind Jarno Trulli's Prost, team boss Jackie Stewart had every reason to be delighted.

His team had proved itself to be a winning outfit before being handed over to new owners Jaguar. Hakkinen finished fifth, with Irvine missing out with a run to seventh not helped when his pitcrew lost a tyre at a pitstop. Minardi's Marc Gene split the

two on a day that saw team-mate Luca Badoer lose fourth place when his gearbox failed.

There had been talk of Schumacher being ready to return at the Belgian GP, but he didn't fancy assisting Irvine to become the first Ferrari driver since 1979 to be World Champion. So he delayed his comeback until F1's first visit to Malaysia. And there he dutifully held back Hakkinen so that Irvine could win the first race at Sepang.

Arriving at Suzuka with a four-point deficit, Hakkinen knew that the best way of claiming his second title on the trot was to win. And this he did, leading all the way from Schumacher, with Irvine a distant third. Even if Irvine had been let through to second and ended the year equal on points, Hakkinen would have taken the title by having five wins to Irvine's four.

RULES OF THE GAME

Start Procedure

The waving of the national flag used to signal the start of a grand prix in the 1950s, but this has long since been consigned to history. In the 21st century, the procedure runs as follows: the pitlane opens 30 minutes before start time and cars are free to drive the lap around to the grid. At three minutes to the start time, everyone except race officials and team personnel must leave the grid. At one minute, all engines must be started and all personnel must leave the grid. At the top of the hour, the five lights on the starting gantry turn green and cars must leave for their formation lap. When the cars have returned to the grid and are lined up to the satisfaction of the starter, the start sequence begins with each of five pairs of red lights illuminating at one second intervals before they are all flicked out and the race is under way.

DRIVERS' WORLD CHAMPIONSHIP 1999

	Driver (NATIONALITY)	Make	Pts
1	**Mika Hakkinen** (FIN)	McLaren-Mercedes	76
2	**Eddie Irvine** (GB)	Ferrari	74
3	**Heinz-Harald Frentzen** (GER)	Jordan-Mugen Honda	54
4	**David Coulthard** (GB)	McLaren-Mercedes	48
5	**Michael Schumacher** (GER)	Ferrari	44
6	**Ralf Schumacher** (GER)	Williams-Supertec	35
7	**Rubens Barrichello** (BRA)	Stewart-Ford	21
8	**Johnny Herbert** (GB)	Stewart-Ford	15
9	**Giancarlo Fisichella** (ITA)	Benetton-Playlife	13
10	**Mika Salo** (FIN)	BAR-Supertec & Ferrari	10

All scores counted

DEFINING MOMENTS
2000s

2000 Japanese GP
FORZA FERRARI
The wait was over for Ferrari, as the eighth of Michael Schumacher's nine wins, at Suzuka, was enough to parry McLaren driver Mika Hakkinen's outside title shot and land the team its first title since 1983 and its first drivers' title since Jody Scheckter came top in 1979. The celebrations went on long into the night both in Japan and at home in Maranello.

2002 Austrian GP
RED CARS, RED FACES
Michael Schumacher had almost total control over the early races, winning four of the first five. Then came the A1-Ring where his Ferrari team-mate Rubens Barrichello led all the way from pole, only to be asked by team chief Jean Todt to pull over and let Schumacher through. He did, on the run to the chequered flag, and an uproar ensued.

2005 United States GP
FORMULA ONE'S SHAMEFUL DAY
A second crash into the wall at Turn 13 in two years by Ralf Schumacher triggered concern for all of the teams using Michelin tyres. Not convinced that their tyres would survive the g-loadings of this banked bend, the seven teams on these tyres withdrew before the race, leaving just six Bridgestone-shod cars to perform in front of a livid crowd.

2006 Spanish GP
FOR THE FANS
Winning grands prix is great, but what really excites a driver is winning in front of their home fans and Fernando Alonso did this at the fifth time of asking at the Circuit de Catalunya. His arrival as World Champion added tens of thousands to the crowd, but it was his run from pole position to victory in his Renault that sent them home happy.

2008 Brazilian GP
TO THE BITTER END
Lewis Hamilton had lost the title in the last race of his rookie season at Interlagos and he returned with another title to win. Just as he was set to lose out again, he came across Timo Glock's Toyota struggling for grip and flashed by into the final corner to deny Ferrari's race-winner Felipe Massa.

2009 Australian GP
RISING FROM THE ASHES
Honda Racing was shut down at the end of 2008, but technical director Ross Brawn revived it as Brawn GP and Jenson Button and Rubens Barrichello celebrate saving their careers by starting their season with a one-two finish at Melbourne's Albert Park circuit. Their rivals could only gawp and start designing their own double diffusers in a bid to keep up.

2000

So, Ferrari can rest at last, its countless millions have yielded the drivers' title for the first time since 1979 when Jody Scheckter won. And who more fitting to bring them the glory they have sought so passionately than Michael Schumacher?

Pedal to the Metal: Michael Schumacher powers his Ferrari around the outside of David Coulthard's Mclaren on the famous Indianapolis banking

Schumacher was brought in to Ferrari in 1996 on the sport's largest retainer with one aim: to give the team its 10th drivers' title. However, it was no easy matter. Apart from Barrichello swapping rides with Eddie Irvine, with the Ulsterman leaving Ferrari for the Stewart team that was rebadged as Jaguar, the top two teams had remarkable stability in personnel. Williams had signed 20-year-old

Jenson Button straight from Formula Three and changed its Supertec engines for ones from the returning BMW. Another team that had ditched Supertec engines was BAR, back for a second year with Honda engines. Arrows took up one of the Supertec deals and brought in Jos Verstappen. Jordan signed Jarno Trulli from Prost to replace Damon Hill, with Prost signing Jean Alesi and Nick Heidfeld to replace Trulli and Olivier Panis.

As for the previous two years, the battle for honours was between Ferrari and McLaren, and honours looked set for McLaren when the season kicked off at Melbourne, with Hakkinen and Coulthard on the front row. But both McLarens broke and Schumacher led Barrichello home for a Ferrari one-two. Notably, third place went to Ralf Schumacher, the BMW in his Williams stronger than people had been led to believe. Perhaps the

largest cheer was from the BAR pit, as they put their point-free debut season behind them with Jacques Villeneuve fourth and Ricardo Zonta sixth.

Ferrari's dream start continued when Hakkinen retired from the lead at Interlagos, with Coulthard disqualified from second, handing the place to Benetton's Giancarlo Fisichella ahead of Jordan's Heinz-Harald Frentzen and Trulli, with Button scoring in only his second race. Better still, Schumacher then beat the McLarens fair and square at Imola. So, three races in, and Schumacher had 30 points to Hakkinen's six and Ferrari 39 to McLaren's 10.

Hakkinen had three poles from three before he arrived for the British Grand Prix at a waterlogged Silverstone, but his chance of keeping a 100 per cent record was scuppered when Barrichello mastered drying conditions best to pip Frentzen to pole. Barrichello led to mid-distance, but Coulthard was right on his tail and took over with a great move around the outside at Stowe. The Brazilian then retired with hydraulic failure and Coulthard went on to beat Hakkinen and Schumacher.

Reigning champion Hakkinen wouldn't have reckoned on waiting until the fifth round for his first win, but he got his show on the road with victory in Spain. Coulthard was fortunate to be there, having survived a plane crash that killed his pilot and co-pilot, and showed great bravery in racing with cracked ribs. After the second round of pitstops, Hakkinen took the lead, facilitated by a slow stop for Schumacher. Coulthard then moved into second as Schumacher slowed with a puncture.

The pendulum swung Ferrari's way at the Nurburgring when conditions were perfect for Schumacher to show his wet-weather skills. Hakkinen had rocketed from third on the grid to lead into the first corner. However, five laps in, rain started to fall, and Schumacher took over, staying ahead for his fourth win ahead of the McLaren duo.

Schumacher looked set to make it five wins at Monaco but a leaking exhaust made his suspension collapse. Coulthard was left clear to win.

Schumacher's escape from pole in Canada was boosted when Coulthard was called in for a stop-go penalty as his car had been worked on past the 15 second board on the grid. Rain hit mid-race and Schumacher was told to slow because of a possible brake problem. Barrichello closed in, but team orders dictated that he finished behind his team leader.

Coulthard gained his revenge at Magny-Cours when he outraced Schumacher for the honours, with Hakkinen claiming second when Schumacher's engine failed. Hakkinen bounced back at the A1-Ring by leading from start to finish ahead of Coulthard.

The Warm Glow of Victory: Schumacher shows his delight at becoming Ferrari's first champion since 1979

Schumacher had further first lap disappointment at Hockenheim, this time swerving to the outside after failing to pass Coulthard, only to put himself into the path of Fisichella. Then, with rain setting in, but only at the stadium end of the track, Barrichello elected to stay out and won as Hakkinen pitted for wets. Hakkinen assumed control at the Hungaroring, by making a blinding getaway to lead from start to finish, while Coulthard harried Schumacher to the line.

The greatest overtaking move of 2000 was performed at Spa-Francorchamps when Hakkinen slipstreamed Schumacher up to Les Combes, then squeezed through a tiny gap inside Zonta as Schumacher went outside the Brazilian. It was inch-perfect and his reward was victory.

The Italian Grand Prix was marred by the death of a marshal following a huge accident into the second chicane on the opening lap, leaving Schumacher to win from Hakkinen, with Ralf Schumacher claiming his second consecutive third.

Formula One and the United States were reacquainted after a nine-year break when the circus moved to the Indianapolis Motor Speedway. Schumacher won easily after the chasing Hakkinen's engine failed.

Arriving at Suzuka with an eight-point disadvantage, Hakkinen got the jump at the start, but slick tactics, traffic and a brief shower as Hakkinen emerged from his second stop put Schumacher in front where he stayed to the finish. Schumacher then made it four wins in succession when he pipped Coulthard to the line at Sepang.

Michael had moved ahead in the pitstop sequence, when leader Coulthard was forced to pit early after running wide and debris caused his engine to overheat. Hakkinen, on the other hand, moved before the start and his stop-go dropped him to 18th before he advanced to fourth behind Barrichello.

So, Ferrari lifted the Constructors' Cup and Williams proved best of the rest. Jordan fell from third to sixth behind Benetton and BAR who finished equal on points, with Arrows not quite receiving the reward that its marked improvement deserved. Jaguar scored just four points compared to the 36 they scored as Stewart in 1999, but Prost and Minardi failed even to score a point, with the French team looking in particular disarray.

CONSTRUCTORS' CUP 2000

	Make	Pts
1	Ferrari	170
2	McLaren-Mercedes	152
3	Williams-BMW	36
4	Benetton-Playlife	20
5	BAR-Honda	20
6	Jordan-Mugen Honda	17
7	Arrows-Supertec	7
8	Sauber-Petronas	6
9	Jaguar	4
10	Minardi-Fondmetal	0
	Prost-Peugeot	0

GREAT RACE

United States Grand Prix 2000

According to the records, races at Indianapolis had counted towards the championship from 1950 to 1960, but this was just a case of including the Indy 500 rather than a proper US GP. Michael Schumacher mastered the part oval-part infield circuit to claim pole, but was headed into the first corner by David Coulthard. Even with Mika Hakkinen on his tail, Schumacher was able to take the lead after six laps, rubbing wheels as he did so. Coulthard dropped back as he was penalized for jumping the start and so it was up to Hakkinen to challenge. This he did, chipping away at an 11-second deficit until his engine blew. And so Schumacher won as he pleased from team-mate Rubens Barrichello and so in the process set himself up to go on to the final round and become Ferrari's first World Champion since Jody Scheckter in 1979.

DRIVERS' WORLD CHAMPIONSHIP 2000

	Driver (NATIONALITY)	Make	Pts
1	Michael Schumacher (GER)	Ferrari	108
2	Mika Hakkinen (FIN)	McLaren-Mercedes	89
3	David Coulthard (GB)	McLaren-Mercedes	73
4	Rubens Barrichello (BRA)	Ferrari	62
5	Ralf Schumacher (GER)	Williams-BMW	24
6	Giancarlo Fisichella (ITA)	Benetton-Playlife	18
7	Jacques Villeneuve (CAN)	BAR-Honda	17
8	Jenson Button (GB)	Williams-BMW	12
9	Heinz-Harald Frentzen (GER)	Jordan-Mugen Honda	11
10	Jarno Trulli (ITA)	Jordan-Mugen Honda	6

All scores counted

2001

If anyone thought that they could prevent Michael Schumacher from winning two titles in a row, they were fooling themselves. Indeed, the German trounced all-comers, leaving McLaren's David Coulthard as best of the rest.

Michael Schumacher started the year as reigning World Champion. And, unusually for Ferrari, but depressingly for the opposition, the team in red hit the ground running, with Michael winning the opening race in Australia. He followed this up with victory in Malaysia, but this owed a lot to fortune as rain fell just after he'd slipped off the track and out of the lead, with the fitting of intermediate tyres when all others fitted wets proving inspired.

However hard the opposition tried, with both McLaren and Williams getting in on the act, Ferrari remained the team in control and the remainder of Michael's year was one of domination as he won fully seven more times, wrapping up his fourth title as early as the Hungarian GP, with four races still to run.

David Coulthard was consistent in the first two races, then inspired in victory in Brazil, but McLaren's failure to develop its launch control sufficiently left him stranded at the start at Barcelona. David then produced his lap of the year to qualify on pole at Monaco, only to have his launch control fail again, meaning he'd have to start from the back of the grid on this track on which overtaking is so difficult. As at Barcelona, he was restricted to a fifth-place finish, with Michael taking a maximum score both times to stretch his points advantage. Despite winning the French

GP, David then spent the rest of the year very much in Michael's wake.

Coulthard's team-mate Mika Hakkinen was seemingly uninspired and not firing on all cylinders. Much of this was down to mechanical failure, and this never hit him harder than at the Spanish GP where he was half a lap away from a dominant win when his car broke, allowing Michael Schumacher through to victory. However, Mika was reinvigorated by winning at Silverstone,

then one race after announcing his intention to take a sabbatical, he won again at Indianapolis. Despite Mika's protestations at the final round at Suzuka that he'd be taking just one year out to recharge his batteries, many felt that the curtains had just been drawn on the great Finn's illustrious career.

Rubens Barrichello came out of Michael's shadow more in the second Ferrari. But he was put back in his place when told to cease his pursuit of Coulthard for the lead in the closing laps of the Austrian GP to let Michael through. This Rubens did, grudgingly, coming out of the final corner. Only when Michael had wrapped up the title did the team start to help his challenge to beat Coulthard and Ralf Schumacher to be the season's runner-up. His form picked up noticeably, although strong runs at Monza and Indianapolis didn't produce the points the Brazilian's input deserved, as Coulthard collected sufficient points to end the year as runner-up.

Running on Michelins was always going to be a gamble for the Williams team, as the French tyre manufacturer

was making its return to the grand prix scene against the vastly more experienced Bridgestone. However, with ever more powerful engines from BMW, Williams was confident. Off the pace whenever the conditions were cold and wet, they struggled at Imola, until it warmed up and Ralf Schumacher romped clear of the McLarens for his first win. This was repeated at Montreal, and a further win was added at Hockenheim.

However, by this stage in the season, new team-mate Juan Pablo Montoya had stopped making mistakes. The Colombian had showed his speed as early as the third race, muscling his way past Michael Schumacher in Brazil, later being deprived of victory at Hockenheim by a delayed pit stop that led to a blown engine. However, the former Champ Car star's day of days came at Indianapolis when he scored what will surely be the first of many wins.

Fourth overall in the Constructors' Cup was Sauber, the little-fancied team surprising everyone by being consistent point-scorers. Equipped

A Quiet Drive along the Coast: Schumacher raced to his fifth Monaco win. Here he's shown steering his Ferrari through the Nouvelle Chicane

A Vintage Year: Schumacher takes the title for Ferrari and equals Alain Prost's 51 career wins

2002. Heinz-Harald Frentzen also left the team, but before the year was out, being dropped to make way for Jean Alesi.

Renault tried to be different in 2001, returning to Formula One with a radical, wide-angle engine in the back of the Benettons of Fisichella and Jenson Button. They were off the pace and their running was restricted, leaving them perilously close to the rear of the grid in the first half of the season. However, Renault upped the power and promise was revealed in the German GP when both scored points. Two races later, in Belgium, Fisichella ran second for much of the race before being demoted to an eventual third by Coulthard. This left everyone sure that when the team was rebranded as Renault for 2002, it would be running much closer to the pace of Formula One's big three: Ferrari, McLaren and Williams. BAR, like Jordan, lacked the ultimate grunt from their Honda engines, but their main worry was the chassis, leaving Jacques Villeneuve and Olivier Panis to scrap for points, although the Canadian twice lucked into a podium position.

Jaguar was another team that failed to shine, with team boss Bobby Rahal being shown the door to make way for Niki Lauda taking sole charge. Eddie Irvine claimed a surprise third at Monaco, but neither he nor Pedro de la Rosa had much else to smile about.

Arrows lacked power and budget,

but Jos Verstappen often showed well in the early stages of races, although this pace was artificial as he would start the race on a two-stop strategy and thus be running with a light fuel load while others planned to stop just the once.

While the arrival of Australian airline magnate Paul Stoddart brought the finance to save tailenders Minardi, Alain Prost's team spent the season heading for meltdown. Financial top-ups kept it going and the battle for survival continued into the close-season, but the French team folded in the New Year, with various rescue bids doomed for hard-to-understand reasons, meaning that Alesi's hard-won points were to count for nothing. At least the numbers on the grid wouldn't drop in 2002 as their place was being taken by a new team: Toyota.

CONSTRUCTORS' CUP 2001

	Make	Pts
1	Ferrari	179
2	McLaren-Mercedes	102
3	Williams-BMW	80
4	Sauber-Petronas	21
5	Jordan-Honda	19
6	BAR-Honda	17
7	Benetton-Renault	10
8	Jaguar-Cosworth	9
9	Prost-Ferrari	4
10	Arrows-AMT	1

with the previous year's Ferrari engines – badged as Petronas engines – they had power aplenty. But the fact that designer Sergio Rinland quit before the opening race didn't augur well for this team that traditionally loses ground through the year through lack of development. However, the chassis was a good one and not only did Nick Heidfeld finally have a car in which to shine, but his rookie team-mate Kimi Raikkonen did too. The Finn arrived with just 23 car races to his name, having bypassed not only Formula 3000 but Formula Three as well. FIA president Max Mosley wasn't happy about this,

putting the Finn under observation, but this proved unneccessary when he scored a point on his debut and continued to impress. In fact, so much so that Hakkinen urged McLaren's Ron Dennis to take on his compatriot during his year off in 2002.

Considering that Jordan had hoped to finish at least fourth overall, 2001 was a disappointment. Indeed, they ended up fifth only after Jarno Trulli's disqualification from fourth in the US GP was overturned on a technicality. It was the least that the luckless Italian deserved before effecting a straight swap with Giancarlo Fisichella for

DRIVERS' WORLD CHAMPIONSHIP 2001

	Driver (NATIONALITY)	Make	Pts
1	Michael Schumacher (GER)	Ferrari	123
2	David Coulthard (GB)	McLaren-Mercedes	65
3	Rubens Barrichello (BRA)	Ferrari	56
4	Ralf Schumacher (GER)	Williams-BMW	49
5	Mika Hakkinen (FIN)	McLaren-Mercedes	37
6	Juan Pablo Montoya (COL)	Williams-BMW	31
7	Nick Heidfeld (GER)	Sauber-Petronas	12
	Jarno Trulli (ITA)	Jordan-Honda	12
	Jacques Villeneuve (CAN)	BAR-Honda	12
10	Kimi Raikkonen (FIN)	Sauber-Petronas	9

All scores counted

2002

Not since Jim Clark swept all before him in 1963 has the World Championship been so dominated by one driver. Michael Schumacher and his Ferrari controlled proceedings so much that the drivers' title was wrapped up by mid-season.

Ferrari F2002

Designer: **Rory Byrne** Years raced: **2002-03**
Grand prix wins: **15** Pole positions: **11** Fastest laps: **15**
Engine type: **Ferrari V10**
Engine size/power: **2997cc/865bhp at 18,200rpm**
This Rory Byrne-designed beauty won 11 of the 15 grands prix that it entered in 2002 and was still good enough to win one of the four grands prix in which it was entered in the following season. The F2002 was again from the pen (computer stylus) of Rory Byrne, with the biggest difference from the F2001 being in the sloping shape of the tail of its sidepods, these punctuated by tall, periscope exhausts. Under the skin, the main change was the introduction of traction control and launch control. Finally, the car was able to receive engine management adjustments from the pits while circulating...

Jawohl: Michael Schumacher is greeted by his mechanics as he crosses the finish line in Germany

The problem with total excellence in any sport is that it usually belittles the stature of what has been achieved. This was the case in 2002 as, instead of applauding Michael's string of victories, they were adjudged dull. Indeed, such was his superiority that the driver's title was already his as early as the French Grand Prix in July – with six of the 17 grands prix still to run. This wasn't a year in which the promoters could look forward to the massive television ratings that a last-round shoot-out attracts. That the German had also been champion in 2000 and 2001 added to the sense of predictability and viewing figures dropped away. As a result, the fact that he had equalled 1950s' star Juan Manuel Fangio's tally of five world titles went largely ignored.

The only real change among the top squads going into 2002 was that Mika Hakkinen was now on the sidelines, happy to be at home by a lake in Finland, with fellow Finn Kimi Raikkonen taking his seat at McLaren. It wasn't until mid-season, though, that Mika announced that rather than simply taking a sabbatical, he had retired from Formula One.

Among the teams hoping to escape from the midfield was Renault, now having metamorphosed from Benetton, with Jenson Button being partnered by Jarno Trulli who had joined from Jordan in a straight swap with Giancarlo Fisichella. Although the Prost team had failed to last the winter, the numbers on the grid were kept up by Toyota and its brand new and very well-funded team.

Ferrari had ended 2001 in control, and Michael Schumacher set the ball rolling in Australia after an extremely dramatic start that saw brother Ralf's Williams fly over the back of Barrichello's pole-sitting Ferrari - the ensuing melee took out six other drivers. Juan Pablo Montoya finished second for Williams. The story of the race, though, was centred on Mark Webber as the Formula One debutant raced home fifth in the little-fancied Minardi.

Ralf made amends in the second round in Malaysia and his victory gave Williams every reason to smile as, with Montoya second, it was their first one-two since 1996. Montoya and Michael Schumacher had clashed at the first corner, with both dropping down the order as a result. Michael had to come in for a new nose and finished third.

Having delayed the introduction of its 2002 chassis until the Brazilian Grand Prix, Ferrari then shocked its rivals by shifting up a gear. Revelling in the balance of the F2002, Michael produced a run of four wins in four grands prix, demoralizing his rivals at Interlagos, Imola, Barcelona and at the A1-Ring. It was at the last of these, though, that Ferrari's top brass ought to have ended up with faces as red as their cars; for this is where they ordered Barrichello – who had been fastest all weekend – to give up what would only have been his second-ever win in Formula One to let Michael through to win. As a result, the FIA reconsidered the role of team orders and how their manipulation could cast the sport in a bad light. As it was, the "win" gave Michael a lead of 27 points over Montoya, 54 to 27.

Looking back at those four races, Montoya would have had every reason to regret running too close to Michael in Brazil. A fifth-place finish behind Ralf, McLaren's David Coulthard and Button's Renault was largely the result of him losing his nose on the opening lap. Ralf put up a brave charge at Imola, but fell to third behind Barrichello as Montoya finished a lacklustre fourth. The Colombian gave it his best shot in Spain finishing second, albeit 35 seconds behind Michael. He was third in Austria, a race remembered for a dreadful shunt in which Nick Heidfeld's Sauber T-boned Takuma Sato's Jordan without serious injury to the Japanese driver.

Having been outgunned early on,

After You: controversy reared its head when Barrichello let team-mate Schumacher through in Austria

McLaren came up trumps at Monaco, with Coulthard getting the jump on poleman Montoya and then leading every lap, with Michael rising to second after Montoya's engine failed. Michael resumed his winning ways in Montreal, chased by Coulthard, with Barrichello third as engine failures left the Williams drivers on the sidelines.

A good start for Barrichello at the Nurburgring and a spin for Michael ensured that the Brazilian triumphed. When Michael won the next race at Silverstone, however, he headed to the French GP with a chance of becoming

champion. And that is precisely what happened, as he profited from a slip by Raikkonen that let him into the lead with five laps to go, leaving him with an unassailable tally of 96 points, with Montoya fully 62 points behind.

Michael then took to the re-shaped Hockenheim, scoring his first win at the German circuit since 1995. It may have been payback for Austria, but Michael played second fiddle to Barrichello at the Hungaroring, thus easing his team-mate into second place overall as Montoya failed to score.

Perhaps the most notable event in Hungary, however, was the non-appearance of Arrows, after severe financial difficulties meant that the team was never to appear again on the Formula One circuit.

The wins kept coming for Ferrari, as Michael dominated at Spa-Francorchamps. There were two Ferrari drivers on the podium at Monza, too, this time with Barrichello first and Michael second. Eddie Irvine was up there with them in third.

The penultimate race at Indianapolis was another Ferrari one-two, but Michael made a mistake in trying to stage a dead-heat, with Barrichello nosing ahead for victory. Coulthard ran strongly to finish third ahead of Montoya.

Michael then completed his season by winning at Suzuka – his 11th win from 17 starts – in a race in which homeboy Sato scored his first points of the year, finishing in fifth place for Jordan.

CONSTRUCTORS' CUP 2002

	Make	Pts
1	**Ferrari**	221
2	**Williams-BMW**	92
3	**McLaren-Mercedes**	65
4	**Renault**	23
5	**Sauber-Petronas**	11
6	**Jordan-Honda**	9
7	**Jaguar**	8
8	**BAR-Honda**	7
9	**Arrows-Cosworth**	2
	Minardi-Asiatech	2
	Toyota	2

RULES OF THE GAME

Team Orders

Ferrari found itself in hot water at the 2002 Austrian Grand Prix when it ordered Rubens Barrichello to slow on the run to the finish and let Michael Schumacher through to win. It was unfair on Rubens, but Ferrari said that it was merely doing its job in ensuring that its lead driver gathered the most points available. Team orders were up for discussion, but they were nothing new. Drivers in the 1950s often shared cars, with a team's lead driver taking over that of a team-mate when their own broke so that they could carry on scoring towards hoped-for championship glory. With cars breaking down frequently, it was seen as the norm. However, when Schumacher was handed that win in Austria, it was not the norm and many said that they would have accepted it had it been in the final round, with the title hanging on the outcome, but this was before the halfway point in the season, with Schumacher enjoying a tally double that of his closest rival. It made Formula One look very silly. McLaren and Williams take an opposite approach to Ferrari, favouring neither of its drivers, indeed expecting them to race each other until one no longer has a mathematical chance of the title.

DRIVERS' WORLD CHAMPIONSHIP 2002

	Driver (NATIONALITY)	Make	Pts
1	**Michael Schumacher** (GER)	Ferrari	144
2	**Rubens Barrichello** (BRA)	Ferrari	77
3	**Juan Pablo Montoya** (COL)	Williams-BMW	50
4	**Ralf Schumacher** (GER)	Williams-BMW	42
5	**David Coulthard** (GB)	McLaren-Mercedes	41
6	**Kimi Raikkonen** (FIN)	McLaren-Mercedes	24
7	**Jenson Button** (GB)	Renault	14
8	**Jarno Trulli** (ITA)	Renault	9
9	**Eddie Irvine** (GB)	Jaguar	8
10	**Giancarlo Fisichella** (ITA)	Jordan-Honda	7
	Nick Heidfeld (GER)	Sauber-Petronas	7

All scores counted

2003

Michael Schumacher was crowned World Champion for the fourth year in succession, but this was no cakewalk. It was the most competitive season for years as Williams, McLaren and even Renault took the fight to Ferrari.

British Grand Prix 2003

The big excitement happened on the opening lap when Fernando Alonso tried to pass Michael Schumacher at 190mph into Stowe, only to be squeezed onto the grass. Coulthard, both Toyota drivers and Ralph Firman pitted, but were soon laughing as the safety car came out as a lunatic had run onto the Hangar Straight. The teams instantly brought forward their first planned stops, with the second driver in each team having to wait, meaning that Michael Schumacher and Juan Pablo Montoya fell to 14th and 12th. Thus Toyota's Cristiano da Matta led a grand prix for the first time in his career. Then Raikkonen took the lead at mid-distance, but Barrichello slashed the Finn's lead and then passed him with a move that started at Stowe and lasted until the exit of Bridge. Montoya then reeled in Barrichello, but the Brazilian had matters under control.

Ready for the Off: Michael Schumacher strapped into the cockpit of his Ferrari F2003 GA in preparation for the French Grand Prix at Magny-Cours

in Malaysia and Brazil. The race at Sepang went to team-mate Kimi Raikkonen, his first grand prix victory, while the one at Interlagos was a masterful performance by the Scot in changing conditions that was brought to a premature end when Mark Webber crashed his Jaguar just after Coulthard had made his final pit stop and was left fourth by the premature end. It was declared that Raikkonen had made it two wins in a row, but the countback ruling proved that Jordan's Giancarlo Fisichella had finally scored a grand prix win. He was given the trophy at the following race.

Ferrari's rivals awaited the arrival of the F2003-GA at the Spanish Grand Prix with trepidation and Michael duly won first time out, albeit only after a mighty battle with Alonso's Renault; the appearance of the local hero brought in an extra 20,000 fans to the race. Another win followed for Michael in Austria, this time without the interference of team orders, but then it was Juan Pablo Montoya's turn for glory, as the Colombian gave the Williams team its first win of the year, and started a run of results for both himself and his team-mate Ralf Schumacher.

Michael interrupted their fun by winning in Canada, a race in which Ralf was slated for not going for the kill, but following his brother meekly to the finish, even though Michael's Ferrari

Two things stand out when you consider the 2003 World Championship. The first is that the top teams were all tremendously competitive and that Michael Schumacher only claimed the title in the closing laps of the final round. The second is that a new generation of drivers finally took the battle to Schumacher, with both Kimi Raikkonen and Fernando Alonso throwing down the gauntlet. The latter became the youngest driver ever to

win a grand prix when he triumphed in Hungary at the age of 22 years and 26 days, beating Bruce McLaren's record that had stood since 1959.

The biggest change of all, though, was to qualifying. This was now a one-at-a-time affair, with each driver going out in an order determined by their speed in a session on Friday, for three laps each – an out lap, a flying lap and an in lap. One slip and their flying lap would be ruined, as David

Coulthard, in particular, would find out time and again. In a further attempt to spice up the championship, points were awarded for the first time to the first eight drivers home rather than just to the first six, with a 10-8-6-5-4-3-2-1 scoring system.

The opening grand prix was a shambles, and David Coulthard was fortunate to come away as victor. However, his fortune deserted him when he lost deserved wins both was struggling with fading brakes. Montoya and Alonso were right with them at the end, the quartet covered by a margin of just 4.48 seconds.

Anxious to make amends, Ralf struck back by winning at the Nurburgring and then at Magny-Cours. At the first of these, Raikkonen had blown up when streaking clear of the chasing pack and Michael spun when Montoya passed him around the outside at the Dunlop hairpin, falling to fifth. The second of these, at Magny-Cours, was Ralf from start to finish, and he led every lap ahead of his team-mate. Williams was in complete control.

The British Grand Prix – a race under threat on the Formula One calendar – confounded its critics by hosting the best race of the year. Barrichello came away as winner following a race that had seen the order of the cars scrambled when the safety car came out while a track invader was escorted off the racing line and then witnessed the Brazilian chase and pass Raikkonen in a move that lasted for four corners... Montoya also passed the Finn to finish second. The Colombian then went one better and dominated the German GP, a race that was spoiled when Ralf, Barrichello and Raikkonen clashed at the first corner. After Michael suffered

Home and Hosed: Rubens Barrichello produced one of the drives of the year at Silverstone

a late-race puncture, Coulthard claimed second, over a minute down on Montoya and Renault's Jarno Trulli came in third to secure his first podium visit.

Renault was finally rewarded for its improving form when Alonso won in Hungary, a race that saw Ralph Firman fortunate to survive a huge crash when his Jordan's rear wing snapped and Rubens Barrichello walk away from his Ferrari unscathed after his rear suspension failed during the race. Michael finished a lapped eighth after his engine stalled during a pit stop, and the World Champion's points lead was down to just one over Montoya and two over Raikkonen.

All through the summer, McLaren talked of finally unveiling its 2003

chassis, the MP4-18, but it was eventually shelved altogether and Raikkonen and Coulthard struggled at Monza, where only Montoya could challenge Michael and Barrichello held off Raikkonen. This set the stage for Indianapolis where the three-way title fight lost Montoya when he was given a drive-through penalty for a clash with Barrichello. A damp track favoured the Michelin-shod runners, but as soon as the rain intensified Michael was in a class of his own and won ahead of his only remaining title rival Raikkonen.

And so to Suzuka, where Michael only had to finish eighth to claim his record-setting sixth title. Raikkonen had to win, but Barrichello stepped up a gear and won to help Michael to the title, which was indeed fortunate as Michael drove a wretched race from 14th on the grid to eighth, including a clash with Takuma Sato – standing

in at BAR after Jacques Villeneuve had elected not to race, having been dropped for 2004 – and being hit up the rear by his own brother at the chicane. Raikkonen's second-place finish was his seventh in 16 starts and he later let people know that the McLaren MP4-17D simply hadn't been good enough to win. Coulthard completed the podium finishers, rounding out his worst season in a decade.

So, another world title for Michael, but he was made to fight for it and the revised points system led to a close battle in both the drivers' and constructors' championships. Eddie Jordan's team ended up ninth overall, and he must have felt that there's no such thing as the luck of the Irish, as the meagre results his team scored would have ranked them fifth using the previous points system.

CONSTRUCTORS' CUP 2003

	Make	Pts
1	**Ferrari**	158
2	**Williams-BMW**	144
3	**McLaren-Mercedes**	142
4	**Renault**	88
5	**BAR-Honda**	26
6	**Sauber-Petronas**	19
7	**Jaguar**	18
8	**Toyota**	16
9	**Jordan-Ford**	13

TECHNICAL INNOVATION

HANS Device

From the start of 2003, all Formula One drivers had to wear the HANS device - a special collar designed to protect the neck in an accident. Developed in the USA, the Head and Neck Protection System's chief purpose was to reduce the risk of injury through violent movement of a driver's head and neck in an accident when the car suddenly decelerates as it strikes a solid object. With g-forces of 100g being recorded in momentary peaks during severe impacts, a head and helmet weighing 7.5kg when stationary can obviously be a weapon in its own right when pulling away from the driver's restrained body that is held in place by his six-point safety harness. The HANS device is a horseshoe-shaped collar that rests on the back of the driver's shoulders and is fastened both to his harness at the front and to both sides of his helmet from the rear by a pair of flexible tethers. Although aware of their benefit, many drivers baulked at wearing them at first as they found that they restricted head movement. However, after minor modification, the HANS device is now here to stay.

DRIVERS' WORLD CHAMPIONSHIP 2003

	Driver (NATIONALITY)	Make	Pts
1	**Michael Schumacher** (GER)	Ferrari	93
2	**Kimi Raikkonen** (FIN)	McLaren-Mercedes	91
3	**Juan Pablo Montoya** (COL)	Williams-BMW	82
4	**Rubens Barrichello** (BRA)	Ferrari	65
5	**Ralf Schumacher** (GER)	Williams-BMW	58
6	**Fernando Alonso** (SPA)	Renault	55
7	**David Coulthard** (GB)	McLaren-Mercedes	51
8	**Jarno Trulli** (ITA)	Renault	33
9	**Jenson Button** (GB)	BAR-Honda	18
10	**Mark Webber** (AUS)	Jaguar	17

All scores counted

2004

No one could touch Michael Schumacher in 2004 as he racked up 13 wins from 18 starts en route to his seventh drivers' title, with not one of his opponents able to live with the Ferrari/Bridgestone combination, although BAR pushed them hard.

GREAT RACE

Brazilian Grand Prix 2004

Michael Schumacher was a bit-part player in the season's final race. He qualified only eighth and an engine change dropped him to 18th. Instead, pole went to his team-mate Rubens Barrichello, so perhaps this was finally going to be his day on his home circuit. Wrong, as Kimi Raikkonen powered from third to first on the opening lap, passing Juan Pablo Montoya's Williams before the first corner and Barrichello's Ferrari out of the second, with Felipe Massa and Jenson Button further demoting Montoya. Running with a lighter fuel load, Barrichello re-passed Raikkonen for the lead on the fourth lap, but then began a scramble for dry tyres, with intermediates - the tyre of choice at the start of the race - no longer the things to have. Raikkonen was one of the first to pit, but Montoya was right on his tail as they left the pits and the Colombian moved ahead of the Finn into Subida do Lago. Fernando Alonso was in the lead, though, as he'd started the race on dry tyres. When he finally pitted on lap 18, Montoya took over and, vitally, held the upper hand all the way to the finish line, rounding out his Williams career with a win.

Renaults to the fore: Jarno Trulli leads his team-mate Fernando Alonso up the hill at Monaco

Never has a team or driver exerted such control over the grand prix scene. Certainly, McLaren's Kimi Raikkonen, aided by a revised points system that made finishing second almost as good as a win, had pushed Michael Schumacher through most of 2003 but, in 2004, McLaren's revival faltered and fell on its face. Only the upwardly mobile BAR team could challenge the Italian outfit, albeit without recording a race victory. Indeed, with Rubens Barrichello wining twice in the (very much) number two Ferrari, that left only three wins to be shared between the other nine teams. Jarno Trulli won for Renault at Monaco, Raikkonen for McLaren at Spa-Francorchamps and Juan Pablo Montoya, on his final outing for Williams, at Interlagos.

In short, Ferrari and tyre supplier Bridgestone were just too good for their rivals and, after Schumacher had won the first five grands prix, it came as little surprise that the Italian constructor waltzed off with its sixth consecutive constructors' title. Critics had pointed out how in the previous campaign Ferrari and Bridgestone had conducted considerably more mileage in testing than any other team, but this time round Toyota and Williams edged ahead of them, despite the fact that Ferrari test driver Luca Badoer still came out on top, covering close on

14,000 miles in his 83 days of testing. With budget aplenty, albeit less than Toyota's, Ferrari were out on their own.

Perennial Ferrari challengers McLaren and Williams ended up with egg on their faces, especially McLaren, who produced their second less-than-perfect chassis in two years, triggering much time-consuming and focus-shifting work midseason to bring it up to speed towards the end of the season. Williams decided a radical leap would be the way to propel them back to the glory years of the 1990s and opted for a high-nose and twin-keel front for its BMW-powered chassis. Ugly can be effective, but not in the case of this "walrus nose" and they, like McLaren, lost time reverting to a traditional front-end format. Still, at least the extra work put in by both McLaren and Williams produced winning cars, something that eluded the team that pressed Ferrari hardest: BAR.

In their stead, it was left to Renault to take up the challenge, with Fernando Alonso finishing third behind the Ferraris at the Australian season-opener, before BAR's Jenson Button used Honda's increasingly powerful engine to come on strong in the next two races and record consecutive podium finishes. The second of these was held in Bahrain, one of two countries that was to host

Advantage BAR: Jenson Button resists Michael Schumacher's challenge for the lead at Imola

a grand prix for the first time as Bernie Ecclestone's desire to see a true World Championship was realized. The other newcomer to the grand prix scene was China, with both Hermann Tilke-designed circuits really impressing.

As the wins racked up, Schuamcher's bid "faltered" at Monaco when he clashed with Montoya in the tunnel when running behind the safety car, leaving the way clear for Trulli to score a victory for Renault and a long-overdue win for the underrated Italian. Ironically, the safety car had been deployed after Trulli's team-mate Fernando Alonso crashed in the tunnel. Schumacher had the grace to say that, even if he had avoided the clash with Montoya, Trulli would probably have won the race anyway.

That Schumacher bounced back to win the next seven rounds, with Barrichello finishing second in three of these, simply rubbed salt into their

rivals' wounds. Such was his dominance that the great German wrapped up the title at the Belgian GP, round 14 of 18, but the headlines on that day were filled by the driver who beat him across the line, as Raikkonen gave McLaren's updated, Mercedes-engined MP4-19B its first win, with Schumacher second.

Perhaps because the pressure was then off, Schumacher followed up with two weak races in a row. First he spun down the order in the opening laps at Monza, before powering back through to second place as his Bridgestones found the track conditions to their liking, and then, on Formula One's first visit to Shanghai, he floundered around to finish 12th. Ferrari still had the last laugh, though, as Barrichello triumphed in both – as he tended to when Ferrari let him off the leash once Michael had the drivers' title in the bag. Schumacher made amends with win number 13 in the Japanese GP.

This spurt of points made it clear to Button that third place would be as high as he could rank overall, but the Briton had worked wonders for BAR, boosted by ever-stronger engines from Honda, as he and Takuma Sato gathered the points to outscore Renault, who inexplicably ditched Trulli for the final three races of the campaign and replaced him with Jacques Villeneuve – back from a year out. Button's year contained four second-place finishes and six thirds, but it was troubled by a "will he, won't he?" debacle as he hesitated about joining Williams.

The last laugh went to Montoya and Williams, as the Colombian won a hugely exciting championship-closer with his soon-to-be team-mate Raikkonen at Interlagos, a race where Barrichello was frustrated when victory in his home race escaped him yet again. Despite his victory in Belgium, Raikkonen could only rank seventh overall and his McLaren team-mate David Coulthard fared even worse, stumbling to tenth in the rankings, before being dropped to make way for Montoya for 2005. McLaren, the 1998 champions, ended the year in fifth overall, behind Williams, who lost Ralf Schumacher for six races after he suffered a back injury in a monumental collision with the wall in the US GP at Indianapolis; Antonio Pizzonia proved more effective

than Marc Gene as a stand-in for the German. However, Ralf raced impressively to second place at Suzuka on his second race back.

Sauber continued to carve a steady furrow, but at least they scored more points than they had done in 2003, something that was beyond Jaguar Racing as it crumbled and folded – a fate that also befell Jordan, when their ownership changed over the winter as the teams prepared for the 2005 season. Between them was Toyota, with the best-funded team in the paddock still trying to find its feet.

Finally, behind the scenes, there was more battling between Bernie Ecclestone and the manufacturers, who had pooled their interests under the banner of the Grand Prix Working Committee as they tried to land a larger slice of the financial pie.

CONSTRUCTORS' CUP 2004

	Make	Pts
1	**Ferrari**	262
2	**BAR-Honda**	119
3	**Renault**	105
4	**Williams-BMW**	88
5	**McLaren-Mercedes**	69
6	**Sauber-Petronas**	34
7	**Jaguar-Cosworth**	10
8	**Toyota**	9
9	**Jordan-Ford**	5
10	**Minardi-Cosworth**	1

DRIVERS' WORLD CHAMPIONSHIP 2004

	Driver (NATIONALITY)	Make	Pts
1	**Michael Schumacher** (GER)	Ferrari	148
2	**Rubens Barrichello** (BRA)	Ferrari	114
3	**Jenson Button** (GBR)	BAR-Honda	85
4	**Fernando Alonso** (SPA)	Renault	59
5	**Juan Pablo Montoya** (COL)	Williams-BMW	58
6	**Jarno Trulli** (ITA)	Renault	46
7	**Kimi Raikkonen** (FIN)	McLaren-Mercedes	45
8	**Takuma Sato** (JAP)	BAR-Honda	34
9	**Ralf Schumacher** (GER)	Williams-BMW	24
10	**David Coulthard** (GBR)	McLaren-Mercedes	24

All scores counted

2005

Michael Schumacher's domination of the grand prix scene came to an end after a five-year run and he could only manage one win as Renault and McLaren scrapped for the honours, with Fernando Alonso beating Kimi Raikkonen to claim his first world title for the French manufacturer.

Renault R25

Designer: **Tim Densham**   Years raced: **2005**
Grand prix wins: **8**   Pole positions: **7**   Fastest laps: **3**
Engine type: **Renault V10**
Engine size/power: **2998cc/950bhp at 19,000rpm**

There will be some who might argue that McLaren's MP4-20 was a superior car but, as a package that also included the engine, Renault's R25 has to come out ahead, especially when one considers its accelerating form in the final races of the season. This car was the fruit of many years of development work, as Renault fought back from its cul-de-sac of developing a wide-angle V10. More conservative with its 72-degree V-angle, the R25 engine gave the team the "oomph" it was seeking and Tim Densham's tidy chassis was considerably easier to drive than its immediate predecessor. A winner on its debut in the hands of Giancarlo Fisichella, Fernando Alonso did the rest and pipped McLaren`s Kimi Raikkonen to the title.

Those who say a change is as good as a rest were correct, as not only were F1 fans treated to a near season-long tussle for honours – between both drivers and teams – but there was the added twist that whichever driver came out on top would become world champion for the first time, bringing to an end five years of Michael Schumacher domination.

The teams in question were Renault and McLaren-Mercedes, both of whom were far more potent than they had been in 2004, and the dicing drivers were Renault's Fernando Alonso and McLaren's Kimi Raikkonen. Renault and Alonso won the day, but the contest ran until the final stages of the season. It was like the ushering in of a new age, but only fools would think that Schumacher had become a spent force. However, for the first time in years, the German didn't have a competitive package, largely because the Bridgestone tyres on his Ferrari were no match for the Michelins in producing a quick qualifying lap. The Japanese tyre manufacturer had been conservative on tyre choice as, for 2005, drivers now had to nurse a set of tyres through qualifying as well as the entire grand prix, with pitstops only for refuelling. Quite simply, Michelin got to grips with this change far better than their rivals. Ferrari were also hampered by

the fact that only two other teams were on Bridgestones, and these were backmarkers Jordan and Minardi.

Along with this rule change, there was yet another alteration in the qualifying format – which aggregated sessions on Saturday and Sunday morning (although, by the seventh round, this had reverted to a single session on Saturday). In addition, the permitted aero package was limited by as much as 25 per cent by raising the minimum height of the front wing. What's more, engines now had to last two meetings rather than one, with the same ten-place grid demotion if an engine change had to be undertaken.

Finally, the World Championship gained a 19th grand prix, with Turkey hosting for the first time.

The vagaries that two-part qualifying could produce were apparent at the opening round in Australia, when rain struck during the first session and left reigning champion Michael Schumacher down in 18th place out of 20 – five behind Alonso, with McLaren's Juan Pablo Montoya and Raikkonen in ninth and tenth. Making the most of pole, Giancarlo Fisichella dominated for Renault and was initially chased by Jarno Trulli, giving Toyota its most impressive outing to date before tyre problems set in. The Italian's problems elevated David Coulthard, the ex-

McLaren man, who gave Red Bull Racing – formerly Jaguar Racing – a dream start. He slipped to fourth, demoted by Alonso, who showed stunning form in his climb through the ranks to third place. Michael Schumacher didn't see the finish, having blocked Nick Heidfeld's Williams and taken both cars out.

Alonso then rattled off wins in Malaysia and Bahrain, with Renault sending shockwaves through the paddock by saying that they hadn't even run their V10 at full revs up to this point. Trulli and Toyota continued to shine with second place in both of these races and with the Italian leaving team-mate Ralf Schumacher in his wake.

Feeling Bullish: David Coulthard gave Red Bull Racing a dream start by running second in the early laps. Here, he holds off Mark Webber's Williams

McLaren were to rue their weak start to the campaign, with Raikkonen managing just a third place and a sixth in the first three races. He was 19 adrift of Alonso; the same margin by which he would lose the title to the Spaniard. Montoya claimed a sixth and a fourth, but then had to stand down for rounds three and four, with the team's test drivers acquitting themselves well as Pedro de la Rosa entertained in finishing fifth in Bahrain and Alex Wurz fourth – third following Jenson Button's disqualification – at Imola.

The start of the European season, and the second race of Ferrari's 2005 challenger rather than its updated 2004 car, suggested the Prancing Horses might yet feature during the campaign, with Michael chasing Alonso all the way to the finish, albeit only after Raikkonen had retired. It was at this race that BAR, runners-up overall to Ferrari in 2004, appeared to have turned the corner after a pointless first three races, with Button finishing third and Takuma Sato fifth, only for both to be disqualified – and the team subsequently barred from the next two grands prix – for having run underweight.

Then, at the fifth time of asking, in Spain, McLaren got its act together, having amended the MP4-20's suspension so it was more effective

in qualifying trim. Raikkonen was in a class of his own, but Alonso was still able to gather eight points for finishing second. Things didn't go so well for Alonso in Monaco, as the R25 ate its tyres and he fell back in the closing stages behind the Williams duo, with Nick Heidfeld taking second place.

Raikkonen ought to have known it wasn't to be his year when he lost out to Alonso on the final lap of the European GP (see box-out), although he did win in Canada at the expense of Montoya, who wasn't called into the pits in time when a safety car was deployed when he was leading the race.

The United States GP stands out as a pinnacle of folly in which politics took over. Outwardly, it appeared to be down to Ralf Schumacher crashing his Toyota into the Turn 13 wall and

Michelin saying it couldn't guarantee the safety of its tyres. That the seven teams on their tyres didn't race was thought to be more down to the FIA not wanting to do a deal with them, as these were the teams who were holding out over the FIA's plans for the future of the World Championship. Either way, the sport lost and Ferrari claimed its only "win" of 2005.

Renault and McLaren diced it out for the remainder of the sum§mer, with McLaren and Raikkonen generally having the upper hand, but mechanical failures cost the Finn dear. Engine failure in practice at Silverstone dropped him from pole to 11th; then he was forced to retire from the lead at Hockenheim. Bouncing back with wins in Belgium and Turkey, he chipped away at Alonso's lead, but another ten-place grid penalty in Italy hurt his chances. A further win at Spa gave him hope, but Renault's decision

to develop its engine right through to the final round, even though V10s were being dropped after 2005, paid off and Alonso's third place at Interlagos, behind Montoya and Raikkonen, secured him the title.

Raikkonen reasserted himself by taking the lead from Fisichella on the final lap at Suzuka, but a final Alonso win in China meant Renault would be constructors' champion, too.

Toyota deserve a mention for making progress, while Williams and BMW brought their fractious partnership to a close. Peter Sauber was feted at the final round, as it was his last race in charge of his eponymous team before BMW took over for 2006. Minardi, too, would never be the same again, as Paul Stoddart sold out to Red Bull and the famous Italian team would be renamed as Scuderia Toro Rosso.

Youngest Champion: Fernando Alonso shares a podium with fellow young guns Trulli and Raikkonen

CONSTRUCTORS' CUP 2005

	Make	Pts
1	**Renault**	191
2	**McLaren-Mercedes**	182
3	**Ferrari**	100
4	**Toyota**	88
5	**Williams-BMW**	66
6	**BAR-Honda**	38
7	**Red Bull-Cosworth**	34
8	**Sauber-Petronas**	20
9	**Jordan-Toyota**	12
10	**Minardi-Cosworth**	7

GREAT RACE

European Grand Prix 2005

Fernando Alonso arrived at the Nurburgring with 49 points to his name, but Kimi Raikkonen – on 27 points – looked to have the on-track advantage. Nick Heidfeld claimed pole for Williams on engine partner BMW's home ground, but it was soon clear that this had been due to a light fuel load. Raikkonen was second on the grid and Alonso sixth. All hell broke loose at the opening corner after Raikkonen reached it ahead of Heidfeld. Mark Webber and Juan Pablo Montoya clashed, Ralf Schumacher tagged Alonso, Felipe Massa clipped Takuma Sato and David Coulthard leapt from 12th to fourth. Had he not been stung for speeding in the pitlane, he could have claimed Red Bull's first podium. As it was, the race boiled down to Raikkonen leading from Alonso, but the Finn flat-spotted a tyre and Alonso began to close. It was all set for a final-lap head to head when the vibrations on the McLaren caused its suspension to fail at the first corner and the Finn was left without a point as his rival gleefully claimed all ten.

DRIVERS' WORLD CHAMPIONSHIP 2005

	Driver (NATIONALITY)	Make	Pts
1	**Fernando Alonso** (SPA)	Renault	133
2	**Kimi Raikkonen** (FIN)	McLaren-Mercedes	112
3	**Michael Schumacher** (GER)	Ferrari	62
4	**Juan Pablo Montoya** (COL)	McLaren-Mercedes	60
5	**Giancarlo Fisichella** (ITA)	Renault	58
6	**Ralf Schumacher** (GER)	Toyota	45
7	**Jarno Trulli** (ITA)	Toyota	43
8	**Rubens Barrichello** (BRA)	Ferrari	38
9	**Jenson Button** (GBR)	BAR-Honda	37
10	**Mark Webber** (AUS)	Williams-BMW	36

All scores counted

2006

Fernando Alonso made it two drivers' titles in a row, but Michael Schumacher and Ferrari really made the Renault ace fight for it, with the German great announcing his retirement from the sport. Honda was delighted as Jenson Button gave it its first win since 1967, while McLaren was frustrated as it endured a winless season.

Ferrari 248

Designer: **Aldo Costa**   Years raced: **2006**
Grand Prix wins: **9**   Pole positions: **7**   Fastest laps: **9**
Engine type: **Ferrari V8**
Engine size/power: **2398cc/785bhp at 20,000rpm**

Renault won the drivers' and constructors' titles, so perhaps this accolade should go to its R26, but it was the remarkable return to form after a weak 2005 season and its progress through 2006 that earns the red beauty from Maranello the top plaudits. The chief reason for this resurgence is that the rule stating that tyres must last an entire race had been rescinded and the first Ferrari designed by Aldo Costa after an interim season when he shared the design duties with Rory Byrne responded by proving competitive in race form on its Bridgestones. Early-season engine problems led to a drop in revs that could only be regained, at first for qualifying only, and then for the races as well, as the new V8's development programme was worked through. The progress was clear to see as Michael Schumacher gave the car its first win at the fourth round, fittingly in Italy at Imola, before adding another next time out. From July on, he and Felipe Massa won seven of the remaining nine races.

Formula One has long had periods of dominance by one team or other, but there's nothing like a rule change or two to upset the order. For 2006, tyres were permitted to be changed during a race once again, helping Ferrari and Bridgestone to get back to the front, while engines had to be downsized from 3000cc V10s to 2400cc V8s, with all of the attached ramifications of this change. So, it's safe to say that the designers and engineers had to work extra hard preparing their 2006 machines.

Proving the worth of their championship-winning credentials, Renault were fast from the outset, with Fernando Alonso and team-mate Giancarlo Fisichella winning the first three races between them. Reigning champion Alonso kept up the pressure and was 25 points clear after completing the first half of the 18-race season with victory in the Canadian GP. But then Michael Schumacher put aside the "will he, won't he?" rumours about his retirement from the cockpit and got stuck into winning. Down and down came the gap to the point that he pulled level on points with two races remaining and a record-extending eighth world title was very much on the cards. But then something all but unheard of during his 11 years with Ferrari happened when he was leading the Japanese GP: his engine blew. This didn't just cost him the 10 points he failed to score, but it added a further two to Alonso's tally as he was elevated from second place. Leaving the Spaniard with a 10-point lead heading to the final round at Interlagos, all Alonso had to do was to be sure that he scored a minimum of one point, just in case Schumacher won there. On this occasion, there was nothing he could do about Felipe Massa on his home track and second place behind the Brazilian was enough to help a jubilant Alonso claim his second straight title. In truth, though, the day belonged to Michael Schumacher as he signed out with a drive so majestic that it went a long way to wiping out the blot left on his record by his unsporting, track-blocking manoeuvre in qualifying at Monaco. He didn't win, but his drive back from the tail of the field – after a tyre-puncturing clash with Fisichella early on – was astonishing and he climbed all the way back to fourth.

While Renault and Ferrari tussled over the honours, and Fisichella and Massa attempted to come out from their team-mates' shadows, McLaren just weren't quite up to the challenge and their lead driver Kimi Raikkonen was the first to come unstuck in the new-for-2006 qualifying format. This was first time out, in Bahrain, when a wishbone failure in the first of the three qualifying segments meant that he was one of the six drivers eliminated at the 15-minute mark. Six more would be forced to qualify from 11th to 16th if they were at the bottom of the timesheets after the second qualifying segment was brought to a close after a further 15 minutes. Starting 22nd wasn't the dream way to get his season underway and he wasn't to be the only potential frontrunner who would find himself restricted to the rear of the grid. The flashes of

The Best of Rivals: Michael Schumacher gets the better of Fernando Alonso in front of the *tifosi* at Imola, but the Spaniard claimed a second straight title for Renault

National Colours: Felipe Massa wore special overalls for his home race in Brazil, and won

speed were there, but a pair of second places were his best results in a season interrupted by the departure of team-mate Juan Pablo Montoya who quit Formula One to head Stateside for a new career in NASCAR stock cars. Replacement Pedro de la Rosa failed to set the pulse racing.

Honda expected less, but Jenson Button finally rewarded the input of all from Honda and predecessors BAR by winning in Hungary. Being on the podium at the final race, in Brazil, showed that this was no flash in the pan. Team-mate Rubens Barrichello was never as comfortable with the Honda RA106.

BMW money propelled Sauber forward and this was another team that came on as the campaign progressed, most notably when Robert Kubica was brought in, precipitating Jacques Villeneuve's retirement from the sport's top table, and raced to third place at Monza, on only his third outing, matching Nick Heidfeld's finishing position in Hungary.

For all its vast financial input, Toyota slipped backwards despite the best efforts of Jarno Trulli and Ralf Schumacher, with internal tension aplenty as technical director Mike Gascoyne was fired after only three races. This echoed the fate of Geoff Willis who was ousted from Honda a few races later, emphasizing that Japanese corporate culture doesn't always fit with the feisty, individual ways of the sport's top brains.

Red Bull were blessed by David Coulthard's drive to third place at Monaco, but offered little else as they backed off their development programme so that they could start preparing for 2007. The team began with Christian Klien but replaced him with Robert Doornbos before the season was out, albeit with no change in their results.

To be reviewing Williams's season so far down the order shows how this once great team had a torrid time as it had to make do with running a non-works engine rather than a manufacturer-supplied one. Cosworth's efforts with its V8 were much admired, but their budget was tiny against their rivals, and reliability was an issue, scuppering Mark Webber's powerful drive in Monaco when he was set for third place or perhaps even better.

Under former grand prix winner Gerhard Berger, Scuderia Toro Rosso – the team that had been Minardi until Red Bull money bought it out for 2006 – were given permission to run rev-restricted V10 engines, which caused some unrest, but brought just one point when Vitantonio Liuzzi raced to eighth place at Indianapolis. Team-mate Scott Speed raced to a pair of 10th-place finishes, but he was denied a point for eighth place at the Australian GP when he was made to add 25 seconds to his race time for overtaking David Coulthard under yellow flags.

One of the two remaining teams started its season as MF1 Racing, having been Jordan as recently as 2005, and ended it as Spyker after being bought out by Michiel Mol and being renamed after the Dutch sportscar manufacturer. Not surprisingly, neither Christijan Albers or Tiago Monteiro managed to score a point.

The newest kids on the block were Super Aguri, a team formed by former racer Aguri Suzuki at the 11th hour, principally to stem criticism in Japan that Takuma Sato had been kicked out of BAR just as it became rebranded as Honda Racing. Its first car, an updated 2002 Arrows, was way off the pace after it was brought to the opening round in Bahrain with next to no testing, but the team's own car at least brought the team off the back of the grid at the final round as Sato raced to 10th place. In support, Yuji Ide proved out of his depth, with the more competent Franck Montagny and Sakon Yamamoto struggling along with Sato as they waited for the arrival of much-needed development parts.

CONSTRUCTORS' CUP 2006

	Make	Pts
1	Renault	206
2	Ferrari	201
3	McLaren-Mercedes	110
4	Honda	86
5	BMW Sauber	36
6	Toyota	35
7	Red Bull-Ferrari	16
8	Williams-Cosworth	11
9	Toro Rosso-Cosworth	1

GREAT RACE

Hungarian Grand Prix 2006

This was a race with something for everyone. To the fan, it was full of intrigue and changes in the story line. To Honda, it put them back in the driving seat for the first time in their second attack on Formula One since they'd taken control of BAR as the Japanese manufacturer landed its first win since 1967. Most of all, it helped Jenson Button chalk up his first F1 win at his 114th attempt. That he pulled this off from 14th on the grid gives lie to what an unusual race this was. The conditions were tricky, with a damp track at the start, but usual front-runners Fernando Alonso and Michael Schumacher had been awarded 2-second penalties for driving misdemeanours and would start 15th and 11th respectively, so Kimi Raikkonen led away for McLaren. Yet the Finn came unstuck when team-mate Pedro de la Rosa closed in on him and Raikkonen failed to notice Vitantonio Liuzzi slowing to let him by, vaulting over the Red Bull. By not pitting until very late, Alonso was then looking to have pulled off a masterstroke, but a wheel-nut came loose as he left his stop and he crashed out, leaving Button clear to win, which he did from de la Rosa by half a minute.

DRIVERS' WORLD CHAMPIONSHIP 2006

	Driver (NATIONALITY)	Make	Pts
1	Fernando Alonso (SPA)	Renault	134
2	Michael Schumacher (GER)	Ferrari	121
3	Felipe Massa (BRA)	Ferrari	80
4	Giancarlo Fisichella (ITA)	Renault	72
5	Kimi Raikkonen (FIN)	McLaren-Mercedes	65
6	Jenson Button (GBR)	Honda	56
7	Rubens Barrichello (BRA)	Honda	30
8	Juan Pablo Montoya (COL)	McLaren-Mercedes	26
9	Nick Heidfeld (GER)	BMW Sauber	23
10	Ralf Schumacher (GER)	Toyota	20

All scores counted

2007

Inter-team battles and intra-team battles marked this campaign as a classic. The title fight went all the way to the final round and ended up with a driver leaping from third in the rankings to first. That driver was Ferrari's Kimi Raikkonen, who edged out McLaren's warring duo of Fernando Alonso and rookie Lewis Hamilton.

Keeping the Best for Last: Ferrari's Kimi Raikkonen enjoyed a tremendous run of three wins in the final four rounds, capping it by snatching the title from Lewis Hamilton at the final round in Brazil

The first suggestion that this was going to be a special season was when McLaren signed double World Champion Fernando Alonso from Renault to lead its attack following Kimi Raikkonen's departure to Ferrari. Then, even before the first corner at the opening grand prix, in Melbourne, McLaren's rookie Lewis Hamilton showed emphatically that he wanted to be part of the equation. He started fourth, got blocked by Robert Kubica's BMW Sauber and then jinked out not only around the Pole but around the outside of Alonso too. The journalists in the press room whooped with delight.

The day, however, belonged to Raikkonen and Ferrari as they showed that they had got to grips best with Bridgestone's new spec tyres, with Alonso getting past Hamilton for a two-three finish for McLaren. Formula One had proved immediately that it didn't have to rely on Michael Schumacher, who had retired at the end of 2006, for its star quality.

Fabulous racing followed, but the season was far from all sweetness and light as it was to be haunted by Alonso falling out with his team, furious that he wasn't de facto number one, something that McLaren prides itself on never granting. He was to

return to Renault for 2008. On top of this, McLaren became embroiled in an espionage scandal after Ferrari technical drawings were found in the possession of its chief designer Mike Coughlan, supposedly passed to him by Ferrari Race & Test Team Manager Nigel Stepney. The FIA levied a $100m fine and the annulment of McLaren's Constructors' Championship points. To add a twist to this, Renault was also said to have another team's technical information – McLaren's – but escaped punishment.

Early in the year, there was no trace of this and fans enjoyed Ferrari and McLaren scrapping for wins, with Alonso helping McLaren to victory second time out, in Malaysia, with Hamilton resisting Raikkonen for second. Then the pendulum swung the other way as Felipe Massa won in Bahrain and Spain.

McLaren bounced back at Monaco, Alonso keeping Hamilton behind him for victory, to the disappointment of the British press. They didn't have to wait long for the 22-year-old's first win, as he achieved that next time out, in Canada, in a race interrupted by safety car incursions.

The possibility of Formula One's first rookie World Champion increased when Hamilton resisted

a challenge from Alonso for victory at Indianapolis. By now, Alonso was starting to feel insecure, as Hamilton was much loved within the team, having been part of its set-up for a decade since being mentored by Dennis when still a kart racer.

Raikkonen was 26 points down after the US GP, but he came good again at Magny-Cours then followed that up with victory at Silverstone, much to the disappointment of the legions of new fans who turned up there to watch Hamilton start from pole

before sliding back behind Raikkonen and Alonso. Hamilton's advantage was whittled away further when Alonso won at the Nurburgring.

It was in Hungary that civil war broke out at McLaren, with Hamilton going back on a team decision in qualifying about letting Alonso past to complete an extra fuel-burning lap, then Alonso blocking the pit until he could be sure that Hamilton wouldn't be able to take on fresh tyres in time for a final qualifying run. With Alonso put back five places on the grid, Hamilton led all the way and kept Raikkonen behind him to claim his third win.

Hamilton's luck ran out in Turkey when a puncture dropped him from third to fifth. Massa raced to his second straight win there with Raikkonen second, Ferrari closed the gap to McLaren to 11 points. A one-two for McLaren at Monza should have opened this out, but their points had been scrapped, leaving Ferrari way clear. Then the balance tipped again, and Ferrari came up trumps at Spa-Francorchamps, and Raikkonen's win ahead of Massa moved him within 13 points of Hamilton. This seemed academic, though, when Formula One returned to Fuji Speedway for the first time since 1977 and Hamilton scored a classy win in streaming wet conditions, leaving him 12 points clear even of Alonso – who crashed – with two races to go.

A desire to try to help Hamilton wrap it up at the penultimate race at Shanghai, blew up in McLaren's face when they kept him out as they waited to see which way the weather would change. Then, pitting on threadbare tyres, he slid into the pit entry gravel trap and was out. Victory for Raikkonen would have been of no consequence

Fast from the Start: Lewis Hamilton slotted in well at McLaren and was a race winner by the sixth round

had Hamilton simply been brought in earlier and settled for second, but it kept the title battle open.

So, to Interlagos they went, with Hamilton four points clear of Alonso and Raikkonen seven points down, but it soon unravelled for Hamilton (see box-out), and so it was that Raikkonen stole the title and McLaren was left with both of its drivers one point short. With McLaren sent to the back, BMW Sauber ended the year ranked second. Mario Theissen's team's best result was Nick Heideld's second place in Canada, on a day of mixed emotions after Kubica's mighty shunt. Amazingly, the Pole missed only one race before returning to add a pair of fourth-place finishes.

Having done the double in 2006, Renault went backwards and it was only when rookie Heikki Kovalainen got up to speed in the second half of the year, taking second in Japan, that the team shone, while Giancarlo Fisichella's form dropped away.

Williams ranked fourth, but it was disappointed by its inconsistent form, with the highlight not coming from Nico Rosberg, but from veteran Alexander Wurz, who snatched third in the much-shuffled Canadian GP.

Changing from Ferrari engines to Renaults didn't help Red Bull Racing, as both Mark Webber and David Coulthard retired too frequently, wasting the RB3s' speed, with Webber's third at the Nurburgring their best result, although he was deprived of second at Fuji when Sebastian Vettel took him out behind the safety car.

Toyota continued to baffle as its considerable funding failed to produce results for Jarno Trulli and Ralf

Schumacher. How embarrassed they must have felt when Scuderia Toro Rosso, the team that had been Minardi to the end of 2005, showed superior form as the season came to an end. Vettel ran third before crashing at Fuji, then finished fourth and sixth at Shanghai, Vettel ahead of Vitantonio Liuzzi. Honda tumbled from fourth in 2006 to eighth, scoring just four points through the best efforts of Jenson Button and Rubens Barrichello. And Super Aguri, the second-year team to which it supplied engines, could have outshone it by taking a podium in Canada. However, this chance was missed when Anthony Davidson bent his front wing on a marmot, although Takuma Sato provoked a smile when he overtook Raikkonen on merit late in the race en route to sixth.

CONSTRUCTORS' CUP 2007

	Make	Pts
1	**Ferrari**	204
2	**BMW Sauber**	101
3	**Renault**	51
4	**Williams-Toyota**	33
5	**Red Bull-Renault**	24
6	**Toyota**	13
7	**Toro Rosso-Ferrari**	8
8	**Honda**	6
9	**Super Aguri-Honda**	4
10	**Spyker-Ferrari**	1

* McLaren-Mercedes' points annulled by FIA for alleged espionage

GREAT RACE

Brazilian Grand Prix 2007

The season finale at Interlagos will long be remembered for the way that the stage was set for F1's first rookie World Champion to be crowned or, at the very least, his team-mate to pick up the pieces, only for a dark horse to beat them both by a solitary point. The protagonists in this exquisite piece of drama were, respectively, Lewis Hamilton and Fernando Alonso for McLaren and Ferrari's Kimi Raikkonen. Sixteen rounds had been held and Hamilton was four points clear of Alonso with Raikkonen was three points further in arrears. When Felipe Massa put the second Ferrari on pole for his home race, Hamilton wasn't worried, as he was second fastest. It didn't matter, hugely, when he was outsprinted to the first turn by Raikkonen. But the Finn had to lift to avoid clipping his team-mate. Hamilton lifted too and Alonso demoted him to fourth, but then the red mist descended and he tried to get back past three corners later, ran wide and fell to eighth. To be sure of the title, Hamilton had to finish fifth or higher and was all set to take this on lap 7 when his MP4-22 suddenly slowed and lost 40s before he as talked through procedures to restart it and got going again. From 18th, Hamilton fought back to seventh, but it wasn't enough, and Massa let Raikkonen through to take the win he needed to be champion.

DRIVERS' WORLD CHAMPIONSHIP 2007

	Driver (NATIONALITY)	Make	Pts
1	**Kimi Raikkonen** (FIN)	Ferrari	110
2	**Lewis Hamilton** (GBR)	McLaren-Mercedes	109
3	**Fernando Alonso** (SPA)	McLaren-Mercedes	109
4	**Felipe Massa** (BRA)	Ferrari	94
5	**Nick Heidfeld** (GER)	BMW Sauber	61
6	**Robert Kubica** (POL)	BMW Sauber	39
7	**Heikki Kovalainen** (FIN)	Renault	30
8	**Giancarlo Fisichella** (ITA)	Renault	21
9	**Nico Rosberg** (GER)	Williams-Toyota	20
10	**David Coulthard** (GBR)	Red Bull-Renault	14

All scores counted

2008

If 2007 had been close, 2008's finale was better still, the championship sorted only in the final 20 seconds when Lewis Hamilton regained a position and took the title ahead of Ferrari's Felipe Massa. BMW Sauber scored its first win, and as Scuderia Toro Rosso, while Super Aguri folded after just four rounds.

Sport is all about endeavour and emotion as it deals in both success and failure. Just watching the final lap of the last race was proof of that. The television cameras caught it all as Felipe Massa swept to victory to overhaul Lewis Hamilton for the title. His family leapt with joy, only to be brought back to earth when, some 20s later, Hamilton came across Timo Glock's Toyota, struggling on dry-weather tyres on a track becoming ever wetter, and swept past with one corner to go to claim the place

he needed to be champion. Small wonder that Hamilton could hardly believe that he'd hauled back a title that, like in 2007, had been his to lose, and so broke Fernando Alonso's record to become the youngest World Champion, at 23 years and 300 days.

There were important rule changes for 2008, with the banning of electronic driver aids, something that many felt would reveal the truly talented drivers after years of traction control and anti-lock brakes

obscuring the issue. Other changes included gearboxes having to last for four grands prix and all teams running with a standardized engine brain, ECU.

There were also two new street venues, around the docks in Valencia and in front of the central business district in Singapore, with the latter hosting Formula One's first night race. Still smarting from the espionage charge that cost it $100m plus its constructors' points from 2007, McLaren was happy again when Hamilton stormed to victory in the opening round in Australia. Reigning champion Kimi Raikkonen had to start 16th after a fuel pump problem and made it back to sixth before a late engine failure left him eighth. Nick Heidfeld showed that BMW Sauber had moved up another gear by claiming second, with Williams' Nico Rosberg not far behind for his first podium. McLaren's new signing, Heikki Kovalainen, ought to have been next, but he hit his pitlane limiter after passing Alonso's Renault and so returned to fifth. Massa retired the other Ferrari, also with engine failure.

Ferrari needed a better second race, in Sepang, and they got this when Raikkonen won as he pleased, with BMW Sauber taking another

second place, this time through Robert Kubica. Ferrari won again in Bahrain, with Massa beating Raikkonen, and Hamilton colliding with Alonso. Then Raikkonen triumphed at Barcelona, with McLaren's day made worse when Kovalainen suffered a major shunt due to a wheel failure. Massa gave Ferrari four on the trot by winning in Turkey for the third year, with Hamilton having to use a three-stop strategy to stay close.

It thus came as a relief to McLaren when it rediscovered winning form at Monaco, although Hamilton was lucky as he suffered a puncture, and pitting then turned out to be the ideal strategy on a day of changeable weather.

Good luck turned to bad in Canada, when a safety car period wrecked a race that Hamilton was dominating and he clashed with Raikkonen who had jumped him in the pits and was stationary by a red light at the pit exit. Kubica, who could also have been hit, was left clear to take BMW Sauber's first win, with Heidfeld second. A 10-place grid penalty for the following race in France hurt Hamilton further, especially as he picked up a drivethrough and failed to score as Massa passed Raikkonen's slowing car to win.

A year of celebration: Lewis Hamilton and McLaren won the opening race together and then four more as they raced to the drivers' title

Hamilton responded in the best way by winning a very wet British GP (see box-out). He then won at Hockenheim when he led with ease but the arrival of a safety car forced him to put on a remarkable charge, even to pass Renault's one-stopping Nelson Piquet Jr who found himself in the lead, from 17th. Massa went around the outside at the first turn in Hungary to take the lead. His bravery wasn't rewarded, as his engine failed. It wasn't Hamilton who benefitted, though, as he'd had a puncture, but Kovalainen. Valencia was next and an easy win for Massa ahead of Hamilton brought the Brazilian back into the reckoning.

Then came a race at Spa that produced magnificent action as rain fell in the closing laps. Hamilton fought with Raikkonen before getting by to win, with Raikkonen later spinning off, but he was denied victory for failing to drop back sufficiently after passing with all four wheels off the circuit at the final chicane. Penalized 25s, this gifted victory to Massa and dropped Hamilton behind Heidfeld.

If the sport felt sullied by the stewards' ruling, it was washed clean with three days of rain at Monza that produced another new winner. This was Toro Rosso's Sebastian Vettel, who started from pole then won as he pleased, keeping Kovalainen in his wake to become the youngest ever winner, at 21 years and 73 days.

Then, after a season playing catch-up, Renault came good. The first of its wins came at Singapore when Alonso looked good for pole, but had a fuel line come off. Starting 15th, he was making little progress, but made an early pitstop and found himself in the lead when team-mate Piquet Jr crashed and brought out the safety car. Early leader Massa provided fireworks too, when he left his pitstop with the fuelhose attached.

Alonso struck again, at Fuji, but this time on merit in a race in which Hamilton pushed Raikkonen wide into Turn 1, earning himself a drivethrough. Massa picked up one as well for spinning Hamilton a lap later. Victory at Shanghai left Hamilton with a seven-point advantage going to the final round, with Massa lucky that Raikkonen let him through from third.

With fifth at Interlagos enough to ensure that he would be champion, Hamilton was fourth with seven laps to go when rain returned. Massa was doing all he could by leading. Glock shot up the order by not pitting and demoted Hamilton to fifth. With two laps to go, Vettel forced his way past and Hamilton was set to fail again, but it all came good with one corner to go.

Kubica – many critics' driver of the year – was deprived of third in the rankings by mistakenly starting on dry tyres after a deluge, letting Raikkonen equal his tally but rank higher as he'd won twice. Kovalainen ended up seventh overall and knew he'd have to improve in 2009.

Alonso's eternal drive for glory and Renault's improved form moved him to fifth overall, with Piquet Jr not impressing greatly. Toyota had another insipid season, although sparkling qualifier Trulli and Glock both took podium finishes.

Toro Rosso finished a strong sixth, embarrassing not just for parent team Red Bull but also Williams and Honda. Toro Rosso's points came through Vettel's win at Monza, with Sebastien Bourdais often unlucky. Mark Webber and David Coulthard deserved better with Red Bull, but their Renault-powered version of Adrian Newey's design was not as competitive. Rosberg – second at Singapore – and Kazuki Nakajima suffered fluctuating form with Williams.

At least they weren't driving for Honda, as Rubens Barrichello and Jenson Button were again made to look stupid by a difficult car, with Barrichello at least grabbing third in the wet at Silverstone. Spyker, renamed Force India by billionaire Vijay Mallya, would have to wait for 2009 for the fruits of their investment to be realized after the highlight of a possible fourth place at Monaco for Adrian Sutil was denied when Raikkonen clipped him.

CONSTRUCTORS' CUP 2008

	Make	Pts
1	Ferrari	172
2	McLaren-Mercedes	151
3	BMW Sauber	135
4	Renault	80
5	Toyota	56
6	Toro Rosso-Ferrari	39
7	Red Bull-Renault	29
8	Williams-Toyota	26
9	Honda	14

GREAT RACE

British Grand Prix 2008

Rain has long made grands prix more exciting. The rain that hit Silverstone was something else, though, being so heavy that cars were spinning off left, right and centre. And, through it all, Lewis Hamilton sailed supreme to vault from fourth in the Drivers' Championship to equal first. A McLaren started from pole, but it was team-mate Heikki Kovalainen's, with Hamilton fourth. But, keeping his McLaren in line on standing water, he was soon up to second, having demoted Kimi Raikkonen and Mark Webber before the first corner. Webber was to spin when trying to repass Raikkonen at Chapel. Four laps of sitting in Kovalainen's spray was enough for Hamilton and he dived into the lead at Stowe. Six laps later, Kovalainen spun at Abbey and Raikkonen grabbed second. Then, with the track drying, Raikkonen closed in on Hamilton. When they pitted on lap 21, Ferrari's decision to leave Raikkonen on intermediates backfired as Hamilton's new intermediates let him pull away by 6s per lap. On lap 27, Kovalainen caught Raikkonen, but fumbled his move into Luffield and Nick Heidfeld passed both. Then the rain became torrential on lap 35 and cars were sliding off everywhere, with Rubens Barrichello calling in for extreme wets and soaring from ninth to an eventual third behind Heidfeld. So big was Hamilton's lead that he could afford to fit a final set of intermediates as the rain eased, knowing that his lead was so great that he could react to any changes in the weather. He won by 1m09s.

DRIVERS' WORLD CHAMPIONSHIP 2008

	Driver (NATIONALITY)	Make	Pts
1	**Lewis Hamilton** (GBR)	McLaren-Mercedes	98
2	**Felipe Massa** (BRA)	Ferrari	97
3	**Kimi Raikkonen** (FIN)	Ferrari	75
4	**Robert Kubica** (POL)	BMW Sauber	75
5	**Fernando Alonso** (SPA)	Renault	61
6	**Nick Heidfeld** (GER)	BMW Sauber	60
7	**Heikki Kovalainen** (FIN)	McLaren-Mercedes	53
8	**Sebastian Vettel** (GER)	Toro Rosso-Ferrari	35
9	**Jarno Trulli** (ITA)	Toyota	31
10	**Timo Glock** (GER)	Toyota	25

All scores counted

2009

Rule changes often alter the balance in F1, but few would have predicted that Jenson Button would at last become a multiple winner and lift the title, and that he would do this in a team that was saved with just four weeks to go before the start of the season.

What a difference a year makes. Rubens Barrichello and Jenson Button were down at the end of 2008 after a lacklustre campaign with Honda had left them ranked 14th and 18th respectively. Two weeks later, the bottom fell out of their world when the Japanese manufacturer pulled the plug on its F1 operation.

Yet, not only did former technical director Ross Brawn and chief executive officer Nick Fry save the team, but the car taken over by the renamed Brawn GP was taken to eight wins to give Button the drivers' title and the team the constructors' title. Ferrari, McLaren and BMW Sauber, the pace-setters in 2008, were reduced to supporting roles. This story wouldn't have reached its extraordinary conclusion had there not been another roll of the dice. This was supplied by big changes to the technical rules. Chief among these was the lowering and widening of the front wing, with the drivers given the scope to alter its main flap's angle around each lap. The rear wing was made 25cm narrower and mounted higher and the winglets and bargeboards were banned, all with a view to slashing downforce and thus making it easier for a driver to follow another car and be close enough to try to overtake. Engine revs were cut by 1,000rpm to 18,000rpm to keep

costs under control and slick tyres were reintroduced.

So, there was plenty to keep the designers busy, with one further twist in the introduction of KERS, an energy retrieval system that would store energy produced by braking then release it when the driver started accelerating, adding extra power for overtaking. This carried a weight penalty, but some teams worked it to their advantage.

The biggest advantage of all was enjoyed by three teams – Brawn, Toyota and Williams – who guessed correctly that a second diffuser would be permitted. The other teams were outraged and protested, but Brawn had implemented this best and Button rocketed to six wins in the first seven races. With not quite half a season gone, the title was his to lose.

On the driving front, there was remarkable consistency, with Brawn, previously Honda, keeping on Barrichello and Button. Ferrari retained Felipe Massa and Kimi Raikkonen, McLaren did likewise with Lewis Hamilton and Heikki Kovalainen, BMW Sauber continued with Nick Heidfeld and Robert Kubica and Renault stuck with Fernando Alonso and Nelson Piquet Jr. Of the few changes, Sebastian Vettel joined Mark Webber at Red Bull Racing and

was replaced at Scuderia Toro Rosso by Sebastien Buemi.

It was clear that a recalibration of expectation was going to be required when the white Brawns filled the front row for the season-opening race in Melbourne. Button was then never headed, while Barrichello's car had its anti-stall kick in and he was swamped

by the pack, being hit from behind. Having fallen to seventh place, he was still competitive enough to work his way back to a second, leaving their rivals fuming.

When the sport's governing body overthrew their rivals' protests about double diffusers, Brawn made the most of the time lag until they too

Brawn BGP 001

Designers: **Loic Bigois, Jorg Zander & Ben Wood**   Year raced: **2009**
Grand Prix wins: **8**   Pole positions: **5**   Fastest laps: **4**
Engine type: **Mercedes V10**
Engine size/power: **2400cc/720bhp at 18,000rpm**

Opinion will be divided as to the greatness of the Brawn BGP 001, as some critics will point to the fact that it stole a march on most of its rivals in the opening races of the 2009 season by guessing correctly that a double diffuser would be acceptable. This gave Brawn an early advantage before rivals developed a double diffuser for their cars. However, that both Brawn drivers were still in there fighting for honours in the final round is tribute enough to this rebranded team that had been pulled back from the brink at the 11th hour after Honda quit F1. Fortunately for drivers Jenson Button and Rubens Barrichello, Ross Brawn had convinced Honda that its RA108 was uncompetitive early in 2008, so work was well advanced on the 2009 car that was going to be running to new rules – wider front wings, smaller rear wings, winglets and a return to slick tyres – when Honda pulled the plug. Even with having to change things to fit a Mercedes engine, these hours in the wind tunnel had not been wasted and Button in particular was able to make it work, winning six of the first seven races. Later in the year, as Red Bull in particular hit form, Barrichello was the more effective, his more aggressive style getting more heat into the BGP 001's tyres. The Red Bull RB5 was faster for much of the year, but this Brawn deserves credit for being honed in difficult times and hanging on.

Red Bulls to the Fore: Sebastian Vettel leads Red Bull Racing team-mate Mark Webber at Abu Dhabi

would have working double diffusers, with Button winning a race in a deluge in Malaysia, finishing third behind Vettel and Webber in another storm in Shanghai and then grabbing win number three in Bahrain.

By the time of the Spanish GP, their rivals were getting up to speed with their revised cars, but Button won again, in a race that Barrichello was convinced ought to have been his. Button was victorious in Monaco, also ahead of Barrichello, then Button pressured Vettel into a first-lap mistake to win in Turkey.

Red Bull was the team that had reacted the best and Vettel drove to a dominant victory at Silverstone ahead of Webber as Button fell flat in front of his home crowd and could finish only sixth. Then, having been woefully off the pace in pre-season testing and been forced into throwing change after change at its cars, McLaren hit the pace at the German GP. However, after a KERS-accelerated start that saw Button briefly nose ahead of Barrichello into the first corner, Hamilton was hit by Webber, picked up a puncture and had to pit. Webber

went on to have his day of days, claiming his first win as Barrichello slid to sixth before blaming his team for 'costing him the race' after a faulty fuel rig meant they couldn't put in enough fuel to change him to a two-stop strategy. Hamilton's patience was rewarded with victory next time out in Hungary and it became clear that McLaren had the best car on twisty circuits, whereas Red Bull's advantage lay at circuits with high-speed corners. The meeting was run in shock as Massa had suffered serious head injuries after being hit by a spring dropped by Barrichello's car in qualifying.

Earning his just rewards, Barrichello beat them all to win on the streets of Valencia, this his first win since his Ferrari days in 2004. Much of the attention was focused, however, on Renault, as the team was set to be made to miss the event after Alonso's car had been sent back out after a pitstop in Hungary with a wheel still loose. However, worse was to follow when team principal Flavio Briatore and engineering chief Pat Symonds were banned for their roles in the alleged race-fixing incident when Piquet Jr's crash in the 2008 Singapore GP helped Alonso pull off a surprise win. That Piquet Jr gave evidence against the team after he was dropped from their line-up after the Hungarian GP.

As the season progressed it became clear that Button's points lead was being eroded and he could do little, save at Monza where he finished

Turkish Delight: Jenson Button made it five wins from seven races to set up his drivers' title

second behind Barrichello. Hamilton then dominated in Singapore as Glock claimed a good second for Toyota, but fifth for Button, just one place behind Vettel and one ahead of Barrichello, kept him in the driving seat.

There was talk that Button was bottling it under pressure and Vettel did his utmost to unsettle him by winning at Suzuka, with Trulli scoring another second for Toyota. This wouldn't be enough for Toyota, though, and it quit before the year was out. Then came Brazil, where Button fought from 14th to fifth to land the title as Barrichello slipped down the order.

The final round was held at F1's newest venue, the stunning Yas Marina circuit in Abu Dhabi. Held in the evening so that the race would enjoy both daylight and floodlit night, Vettel laid down a marker for 2010 by winning as he pleased.

CONSTRUCTORS' CUP 2009

	Make	Pts
1	**Brawn-Mercedes**	172
2	**Red Bull-Renault**	153.5
3	**McLaren-Mercedes**	71
4	**Ferrari**	70
5	**Toyota**	59.5
6	**BMW Sauber**	36
7	**Williams-Toyota**	34.5
8	**Renault**	26
9	**Force India-Mercedes**	13
10	**Toro Rosso-Ferrari**	8

GREAT RACE
Brazilian Grand Prix 2009

The 2007 Brazilian GP had been one of the most dramatic grands prix ever as Lewis Hamilton failed to claim the title and Kimi Raikkonen took it. In 2008, Hamilton made amends in the final few hundred metres. This time around, the title was settled at Interlagos again, but without such highs and lows. With this race and one more in which to extend or protect his 14-point lead over team-mate Rubens Barrichello, Jenson Button was looking good, but he qualified only 14th. Barrichello was 10th in Q2 and so scraped into the final qualifying session and magnified the scenario by taking pole. Barrichello knew that he'd have to win in front of his home crowd to have a shot at the title, and he survived the tricky first corner and led away as those behind him clashed, but Button had also started well and avoided the carnage and gained five places on the first lap. With Mark Webber staying out six laps longer than Barrichello before his first pit stop, emphasizing how light Barrichello had had to run to claim pole, the Red Bull driver took the lead and stayed there to the finish. Robert Kubica worked his way forward from eighth to second and Hamilton was promoted to third when Barrichello had a puncture. However, the driver who did the most overtaking was none other than Button, who showed his desire to land the title with a round to spare, and fifth place was enough for that.

DRIVERS' WORLD CHAMPIONSHIP 2009

	Driver (NATIONALITY)	Make	Pts
1	**Jenson Button** (GBR)	Brawn-Mercedes	95
2	**Sebastian Vettel** (GER)	Red Bull-Renault	84
3	**Rubens Barrichello** (BRA)	Brawn-Mercedes	77
4	**Mark Webber** (AUS)	Red Bull-Renault	69.5
5	**Lewis Hamilton** (GBR)	McLaren-Mercedes	49
6	**Kimi Raikkonen** (FIN)	Ferrari	48
7	**Nico Rosberg** (GER)	Williams-Toyota	34.5
8	**Jarno Trulli** (ITA)	Toyota	32.5
9	**Fernando Alonso** (SPA)	Renault	26
10	**Timo Glock** (GER)	Toyota	24

All scores counted

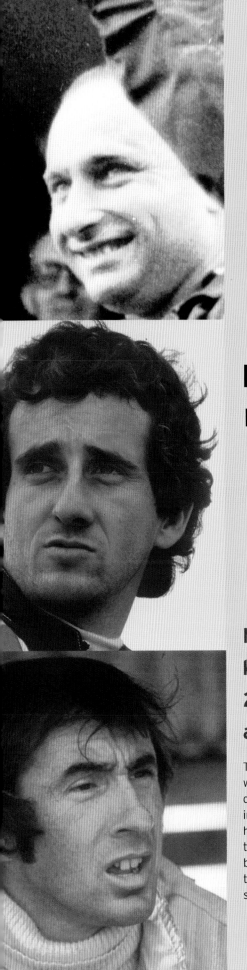

PART 2:
THE GREAT DRIVERS

Motor racing fans have thrilled to the exploits of the speed kings of Formula One down the years. Here is a selection of 200 of the fastest of them all, with the greatest picked out and given a page each throughout this chapter.

There are myriad drivers who have won races, lost races, starred and disappointed in Formula One since its inception in 1950. The drivers featured here range from grand prix winners to those who intermittently shone but who failed in their quest to hit the top and to others who have their own stories to tell. After all, Eddie Irvine may be recalled more in years to come for being punched on the chin by Ayrton Senna on his debut rather than for his best drives for Ferrari, even though he came within a race of being World Champion in 1999.

Everyone listed in the following pages had a dream. Some achieved it, others did not. Indeed, it is immensely sad how many were killed in their bid for glory.

Thankfully, racing is far safer today than when drivers used to race in short-sleeved cotton shirts, flat caps and perhaps a jaunty neckerchief.

All statistics are correct to the end of the 2009 World Championship.

Michele Alboreto

Nationality: Italian
Born: 1956
Died: 2001

This dignified Italian had a long and frustrating Formula One career that petered out in 1994 when he followed a phalanx of his former rivals into the world of touring cars. Second in the 1979 Italian Formula Three series, Michele won the European crown in 1980. Formula Two followed in 1981, but Michele so impressed Tyrrell with a one-off drive at the San Marino Grand Prix that they gave him a contract until the end of 1983. During the next three years he won twice, both times on North American soil. His second win – at Detroit in 1983 – was a landmark, as it was the last win for a normally aspirated engine before the turbo cars completed their stranglehold. Ferrari followed from 1984 to 1988, and he won on his third outing, at Zolder, helping him to fourth place overall at the end of the season. A pair of wins helped Michele to second overall in 1985, but thereafter his career tailed off. He returned to Tyrrell in 1989, then crossed to Larrousse mid-season. Three thin years with Footwork followed before

his worst year: 1993, with the Scuderia Italia team. The car was a beast, and Michele failed to qualify five times. A year with Minardi restored his pride, but he headed off to join the German Touring Car Championship at the controls of a works Alfa Romeo. Moving on to sports cars, Michele was killed at Lausitzring in 2001 when his Audi flipped during testing.

○ 194 Grands Prix, 5 wins (Caesars Palace GP 1982, US GP 1983, Belgian GP 1984, Canadian GP 1985, German GP 1985)
○ No drivers' title (best result – 2nd overall 1985)

Jean Alesi

Nationality: French
Born: 1964

Born in France of Sicilian parents, Jean was viewed as an outsider until he started to shine in the junior formulae, and only then was he considered a Frenchman. Running with next to no sponsorship, he starred in the 1986 French Formula Three Championship, finishing second to Yannick Dalmas. He went one better in 1987 before moving up to Formula 3000 in 1988. Halfway through his second year in this category, a vacancy came up at Tyrrell for the French Grand Prix and

team boss Eddie Jordan propelled Jean into the seat. Jean responded in style, taking fourth place. In the first race of 1990, Jean swapped the lead with Ayrton Senna's McLaren, finishing second. Another second came at Monaco. Jean joined Ferrari in 1991, and, despite endless promise, it was not until the Canadian Grand Prix in 1995 that he finally won.

He should also have won in Italy, and drove a belter in the wet at the Nurburgring. Jean moved to Benetton in 1996 and had his best ever year, finishing fourth overall, despite not winning a race, then staying on for 1997 before joining Sauber for 1998.

A spell with Prost in 2000 was added to by a mid-season switch to Jordan in 2001, after which he left Formula One to race for Mercedes in the German Touring Car Championship with great effect.

○ 201 Grands Prix, 1 win (Canadian GP 1995)
○ No drivers' title (best result – 4th overall 1996)

Philippe Alliot

Nationality: French
Born: 1954

Philippe began his career with three years of racing in the French Formule Renault series, claiming the title in 1978. Formula Three proved a harder nut to crack, for it took him four years before he moved on to Formula Two for 1983, before spending two years with the struggling RAM team in Formula One.

He then moved to Ligier for the second half of 1986, before joining the Larrousse Lola team, for whom he raced for three seasons, scoring points on four occasions. A return to Ligier in 1990 was fruitless and it curtailed his Formula One career. However, he bounced back with Larrousse in 1993 and scored his only fifth place, at the San Marino Grand Prix. Hopes of a grand prix swansong with McLaren in 1994 thanks to French engine supplier Peugeot were dashed when team boss Ron Dennis chose Martin Brundle instead, even though

Philippe had a run-out in place of the suspended Mika Hakkinen in Hungary. Following his retirement he has raced touring cars.

○ 109 Grands Prix, no wins (best result – 5th San Marino GP 1993)
○ No drivers' title (best result – 16th overall 1987)

Fernando Alonso

SEE PAGE 124

Chris Amon

Nationality: New Zealander
Born: 1943

This affable Kiwi did everything in Formula One except win a race, or a World Championship one at least. Chris was spotted by team owner Reg Parnell and invited to contest the 1963 Formula One season, arriving in Europe while still a baby-faced 19-year-old and claiming his first points finish before his 21st birthday.

Parnell's death left Chris in limbo in 1965 and 1966, but Ferrari signed him for 1967 and he went straight in with third place at Monaco. A win would surely follow. Wrong. Second at Brands Hatch in 1968 was the best he could do. A move to the fledgling March team for 1970 enabled Chris to win a Formula One race – the International Trophy at Silverstone – but, sadly for him, this was a non-championship affair. His championship season saw him finish second twice and seventh overall.

A two-year spell at Matra was his next period of gainful employment and it produced victory first time out, in the Argentinian Grand Prix, but this was another non-championship race.

It almost went right at Clermont-Ferrand in 1972. Almost but not quite. The race was virtually his for the taking when he suffered a puncture.

A season with Tecno in 1973 produced nothing and a move to run his own car in 1974 proved even less successful. A few races for the rather under-financed Ensign team in 1975-76 reminded people of his speed, but his flashes of genius came to little. This was a talent wasted.

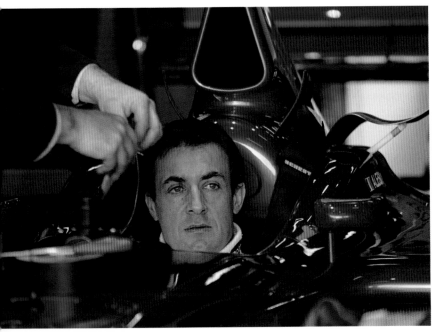

The Outsider: Jean Alesi at the wheel of his Prost before the Spanish Grand Prix, 2001

Champagne Moment: René Arnoux pops his cork after winning the Brazilian Grand Prix in 1980

○ 96 Grands Prix, no wins (best result – 2nd British GP 1968, Belgian GP 1970, French GP 1970)
○ No drivers' title (best result – 4th overall 1967)

Mario Andretti
SEE PAGE 125

Michael Andretti
Nationality: American
Born: 1962

Michael, son of Mario, ripped through the junior ranks of American racing, winning the Formula Super Vee and Formula Atlantic titles en route to graduating to the IndyCar scene in 1984. He was second in 1986, 1987 and 1990, before finally claiming the IndyCar title in 1991. Egged on by his father, Michael tried Formula One with McLaren in 1993. What a disaster! It seemed that, if there was an accident, he was in it. This is unfair, however, for he had the mighty Ayrton Senna as a team-mate and a McLaren chassis that did not want to play the game. Perhaps one of his biggest mistakes was attempting to commute from the US, since he never really became part of the team and he was replaced after peaking with a third-place finish in the Italian Grand Prix. Winning ways came back on his return to IndyCar, giving

Reynard a victory on its first race in the formula and then doing the same for Swift in 1998. Michael hung up his helmet midway through the 2003 season and now runs one of the top teams in the Indy Racing League.
○ 13 Grands Prix, no wins (best result – 3rd Italian GP 1993)
○ No drivers' title (best result – 11th overall 1993)

René Arnoux
Nationality: French
Born: 1948

One of the fruits of a government-backed scheme to unearth French talent in the 1970s, René did all the right things as he rocketed into Formula One. It was only when he reached the highest echelon that he started to run off the rails. His speed was never in question, simply his application. He beat future Formula One rival Patrick Tambay to take the French Formule Renault title in 1973. An abortive move to the European Formula 5000 Championship in 1974 was followed by a return to the French ladder to stardom in Formule Super Renault in 1975. He duly won the title and progressed to Formula Two in 1976, being pipped to the title in the final round by Jean-Pierre Jabouille. He went one better in 1977. Then came Formula One, albeit

with a slow start in 1978 with the fledgling Martini team. It folded mid-season and René had a couple of runs for Surtees. However, it all came right for 1979 and he joined Jabouille in the Renault works team. A brace of wins at the start of 1980 pushed him into the limelight, but his form faded until he won the 1982 French Grand Prix against team orders ahead of team favourite Alain Prost. René moved to Ferrari for 1983, winning three times as he was placed third overall behind Nelson Piquet and Prost. These were to be his last wins, though, and he was shown the door after the first race of 1985. He was back in 1986, this time with Ligier, with whom he raced for four seasons, but produced next to no results after the first of these. Since retiring from F1, René has been involved with the extremely successful DAMS Formula 3000 team.
○ 149 Grands Prix, 7 wins (Brazilian GP 1980, South African GP 1980, French GP 1982, Italian GP 1982, Canadian GP 1983, German GP 1983, Dutch GP 1983)
○ No drivers' title (best result – 3rd overall 1983)

Peter Arundell
Nationality: British
Born: 1933

Peter Arundell shone like a star, but his career became unstuck when he had a major accident in a Formula Two race at Reims and he was never as quick again. Strong form in the junior categories earned Peter the attention of Lotus boss Colin Chapman, who snapped him up for Formula Junior and he won the 1962 British title. Although anxious to move into Formula One, he waited to make his break with Lotus, and thus had to spend 1963 contesting non-championship Formula One races in addition to Formula Junior. For 1964, though, Peter was in Formula One with Lotus. Third in his first two races, at Monaco and then Zandvoort, he had driven in only four races when he spun during the concurrent Formula Two race at Reims and was T-boned

by Richie Ginther. Thrown from the cockpit, he suffered numerous broken bones and it was two years before he was fit for F1 again. His return season with Lotus yielded just one sixth-place finish and his career fizzled out.
○ 11 Grands Prix, no wins (best result – 3rd Monaco GP 1964, Dutch GP 1964)
○ No drivers' title (best result – 8th overall 1964)

Alberto Ascari
Nationality: Italian
Born: 1918
Died: 1955

Alberto was Mr Superstition – a great racing driver, a double World Champion, but also a man ruled by lucky charms and coincidence.

Born into a motor racing family, he soon turned to motorized competition, starting with motorcycles. After the interruption of the Second World War, Alberto had his first taste of grand prix racing in 1947. He was chosen to lead the Ferrari team in the 1950 Formula One World Championship, in which he placed fifth overall.

In 1952, although Alberto missed the first race, he won the Belgian, French, British, German, Dutch and Italian Grands Prix and duly took the title. Alberto kept this winning streak going into 1953, taking the first three races and then two more later in the year as he motored to his second consecutive world title. However, Alberto was soon to perish in a freak accident when testing a sports car at Monza. Acknowledging Alberto's attention to numbers and dates, it is uncanny to note that, like his father, he died on the 26th of a month, at the age of 36, at the exit of a fast left-hander, four days after walking away from an accident.
○ 31 Grands Prix, 13 wins (German GP 1951, Italian GP 1951, Belgian GP 1952, French GP 1952, British GP 1952, German GP 1952, Dutch GP 1952, Italian GP 1952, Argentinian GP 1953, Belgian GP 1953, British GP 1953, Dutch GP 1953, Swiss GP 1953)
○ World Champion 1952 and 1953

FERNANDO ALONSO
He Reigns in Spain

This is the driver who broke Michael Schumacher's five-year title-winning streak. Seen through the eyes of his fellow countrymen, he's also the driver who finally put Spain on the F1 map.

Having begun racing karts at the age of three, it's safe to say that Fernando started young. That he collected titles at the same rate as his contemporaries collected football stickers really marked him out. In 1996, he added a world title to his Spanish honours, so it's no surprise that Adrian Campos, a wealthy Spaniard with a weak F1 CV from the late 1980s, snapped him up and propelled him into car racing, as the driver who might finally give Spanish fans their first hero since Alfonso de Portago in the 1950s.

To say that Fernando was an instant hit is an understatement, as he claimed the Euro Open by Nissan series, taking six wins en route to the title. Formula 3000 was next – much sooner than most drivers' ascent through the junior ranks – and he astonished everyone with his dominant win in the final round at Spa-Francorchamps, the result elevating him to fourth overall.

With Flavio Briatore managing his career, a deal was made for Fernando to race for Minardi – it meant that he had reached F1 before he was 20.

After an exemplary first year with the under-funded team, Flavio moved Fernando to be test driver for his own team, Renault, in 2002 and the mileage he put in stood him in good stead when he landed a race seat for 2003.

Fernando's sheer ability floored everyone, as pole on his second outing, in Malaysia, was followed by his first podium visit, for third. Another third followed in Brazil, but it was his battle for the lead in Spain with Michael Schumacher that drove his fans wild. There were too many retirements for Fernando's to be a title challenge, but he was able to claim a flawless win in Hungary, making him the then youngest driver to win a grand prix.

Fernando failed to win in 2004, struggling with a Renault that was tricky to drive, but he progressed from sixth overall the previous year to fourth, claiming one second and three thirds as Michael Schumacher dominated.

Everything came together in 2005 – the Renault R25 was a major improvement – and a drive through the field to third in Australia showed great promise that was realized by winning the next three races at Sepang, Bahrain and Imola. Kimi Raikkonen then came good for McLaren, but Fernando scored well wherever possible and he took victory when Raikkonen's suspension collapsed on the final lap at the Nurburgring. Fernando kept giving 100% and a late-season performance gain from Renault was all that was needed for Fernando to claim the crown with two races to run.

Fernando was crowned World Champion again in 2006, but he was made to fight even harder by Ferrari and Michael Schumacher, making his victory all the sweeter as he moved on to McLaren for 2007.

This was a troubled year as he clashed with team boss Ron Dennis as he felt Lewis Hamilton was not playing second fiddle to him. The fall-out from this was a return to Renault, a team that had lost its competitive edge. A fortunate win in Singapore was followed by another in Japan, but matters declined in 2009 and he failed to get close to winning.

Fernando spent the majority of 2005 battling with Kimi Raikkonen for outright honours

° 140 Grands prix, 21 wins
° World Champion 2005 and 2006

1981	1990	1994	1996	1998	2000	2002	2004	2006	2008
Born 29 July in Oviedo, Asturias, Spain	Asturias and Basque Cadet Kart champion	Spanish Junior Kart champion for the second time	World and Spanish Junior Kart champion	Spanish Inter-A Kart champion. Second in European series	Advances to Formula 3000. Tests for Minardi	Contracted to Flavio Briatore, he acts as test driver for the Renault F1 team	No more wins with Renault, but Fernando improves to fourth overall	Made to fight by Schumacher, but makes it two F1 titles on the trot, winning seven races	Returns to Renault and wins twice, but slips to fifth overall

1988	1993	1995	1997	2001	2003	2005	2007	2009
Asturias Rookie Kart champion	Spanish Junior Kart champion	Spanish Junior Kart champion and third in World series	Italian and Spanish Inter-A Kart champion	Steps up to Formula One with Minardi, finishing tenth in Germany	Joins Renault's and scores first grand prix win in Hungary and ranks sixth overall	Three wins in first four races sets him up to win title with two races to go	Moves to McLaren and wins four times, but ends up third after strife with team	A season of struggling, ranking ninth overall

MARIO ANDRETTI
Mr Versatile

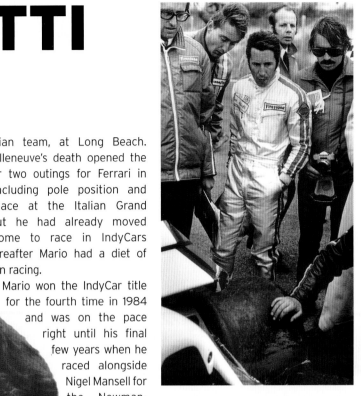

Here is a man who wanted to race more than almost any man before him – or since. And this will to race stayed with Mario until his retirement at the end of 1994, helping him achieve one of the most comprehensive career tallies of all time.

An immigrant from Italy, Mario knew that he wanted to race even before leaving for the US. He and elder brother Aldo then found a way to race sprint cars on the local dirt ovals. "Super Wop", as he was known, graduated to IndyCar racing in 1964.

In his first full season, in 1965, he amazed the establishment not only by finishing third in the Indy 500, but also by winning the title. Another title followed in 1966 and a third in 1969, but, by the time of the third crown, he had already achieved an ambition by making his Formula One debut (for Lotus) at the end of 1968. Again Mario upset the establishment, for he qualified on pole first time out at Watkins Glen.

A mixed Formula One programme followed from 1969 to 1974 with Lotus, March, Ferrari – including victory in the 1971 South African Grand Prix – and Parnelli, as he split his time with IndyCar and sports car racing before he joined the grand prix circus full-time with Parnelli in 1975.

Parnelli folded early in 1976 and Mario joined the team that had given him his Formula One break: Lotus. It was in a poor state, but he and boss Colin Chapman rebuilt it, winning the famously wet Japanese Grand Prix.

More progress was made in 1977 and Mario was crowned world champion in 1978 after winning six races, albeit saddened by the death of team-mate Ronnie Peterson in the Italian Grand Prix. Two more years followed with Lotus, but it was a team on the slide and, for 1981, he moved across to race for Alfa Romeo, with a best result of fourth in his first outing for the Italian team, at Long Beach. Gilles Villeneuve's death opened the door for two outings for Ferrari in 1982, including pole position and third place at the Italian Grand Prix, but he had already moved back home to race in IndyCars and thereafter Mario had a diet of American racing.

Mario won the IndyCar title for the fourth time in 1984 and was on the pace right until his final few years when he raced alongside Nigel Mansell for the Newman-Haas team in the early 1990s. Mario made the occasional foray to the Le Mans 24 Hours, a race that had always eluded him, finishing second there in 1995, a year after he quit IndyCar racing for good.

For a driver who had avoided being hurt in accidents, Mario nearly came unstuck in 2003 when he ventured out for son Michael's team in practice for the Indy 500 and had a massive aerial flip. Fortunately he escaped from this little misdemeanour without injury, but it could easily have been the end.

- o **128 Grands Prix, 12 wins**
- o **World Champion 1978**

Left: Mario Andretti in a moment of reflection
Above: in his role as driver for Ferrari at the Dutch Grand Prix in Zandvoort, 1971

1940	1964	1966	1968	1970	1975	1977	1979	1981	1984	1994
Born 28 February in Montona, Italy	US Sprint Car Champion. Made IndyCar debut	IndyCar Champion again, with eight wins	IndyCar runner-up again. Formula One debut with Lotus at end of year. On pole for US GP	Five races for March. Won sports car races at Sebring and Watkins Glen in a Ferrari	Full Formula One programme for Parnelli, fourth in the Swedish GP	Arrival of ground-effects Lotus 78 led to four wins and third overall	Lotus lost its way and he fell to tenth overall	Moved to Alfa Romeo, but scored only three points	IndyCar Champion, with six wins, joined on grid by elder son Michael	Troubled final season of IndyCar racing

1958	1965	1967	1969	1971	1976	1978	1980	1982	1995
Started racing on American dirt track scene	IndyCar Champion for Dean Van Lines team	IndyCar runner-up. Won Daytona 500 NASCAR race and Sebring 12 Hours sports car race	Three races for Lotus. IndyCar Champion again and won Indy 500	Won South African GP on debut for Ferrari and ranked eighth overall	Victory in season-closing Japanese GP for Lotus helped Mario to sixth overall	World Champion with six wins for Lotus	Another troubled year produced just one point for Lotus	One race for Williams and two for Ferrari, taking third at Italian GP. Concentrated on IndyCars for first time since 1974	Second in Le Mans 24 Hours

Changing Gear: Richard Attwood gets ready to climb into the cockpit of his Reg Parnell Lotus-BRM

Richard Attwood

Nationality: British
Born: 1940

After an apprenticeship in Formula Junior, during which he won the Monaco support race in 1963, followed by an unhappy period with a limited Formula One programme with BRM in 1964, Richard went on to enjoy a shot at the big time with a Reg Parnell Racing Lotus-BRM in 1965, collecting a couple of sixth places. However, he raced sports cars for the next two seasons before joining BRM, replacing Mike Spence. His second place first time out, at Monaco, amazed all and sundry. Sadly, this form was never repeated and he was to race sports cars from then on, winning the Le Mans 24 Hours for Porsche in 1970. He continues to star on the historic racing scene.

○ 17 Grands Prix, no wins (best result – 2nd Monaco GP 1968)
○ No drivers' title (best result – 13th overall 1968 and 1969)

Luca Badoer

Nationality: Italian
Born: 1971

Luca starred in Italian Formula Three, before moving on to Formula 3000 and winning the title at his first go.

He made his Formula One debut with the uncompetitive Scuderia Italia team in 1993, where more often than not he outpaced his team-mate, Michele Alboreto. Luca sat on the sidelines in 1994, but was back with Minardi in 1995 and was equal to team-mates Pierluigi Martini and Pedro Lamy. He drove for Forti in 1996 until the team collapsed. Luca then became Ferrari's test driver before returning to racing with Minardi in 1999, breaking down when he retired from fourth place at the Nurburgring. He continued as Ferrari's test driver, but his reputation took a battering when he stood in for Felipe Massa in 2009

○ 44 Grands Prix, no wins (best result – 7th San Marino GP 1993)
○ No drivers' title

Giancarlo Baghetti

Nationality: Italian
Born: 1934

It is unlikely that anyone will ever match his feat of winning on his grand prix debut. Yet this is what happened when he joined Ferrari for the 1961 French Grand Prix at Reims. He raced sports cars before Formula Junior tempted Giancarlo to try his hand at single-seaters in 1958. Success in this propelled him to Ferrari in 1961, when he won the non-championship Syracuse and Naples Grands Prix. Then came his big day at Reims, where he resisted everything that Porsche's Dan Gurney threw at him. A limited season with Ferrari in 1962 was followed by a spell with the Italian ATS team in 1963 and another racing a Centro Sud BRM in 1964.

○ 21 Grands Prix, 1 win (French GP 1961)
○ No drivers' title (best result – 9th overall 1961)

Julian Bailey

Nationality: British
Born: 1961

One of the quickest of the quick in British club racing in the early 1980s, Julian overcame a huge shunt to win the Formula Ford Festival in 1982. Lack of cash restricted his movement upwards, but he made it to Formula Three by 1985 and on to Formula 3000 by 1987, where he won once, at Brands Hatch. Julian finally made it to Formula One in 1988, racing for Tyrrell, but he chose a year when Tyrrell was not competitive; he often failed to qualify and collected no points. It looked as though he had had his shot and missed. Ever resourceful, Julian raised the money to buy a seat at Lotus in 1991 and scored his best finish, a sixth place at the San Marino Grand Prix, before his money ran out after four races. Since then he has raced in both touring cars and sports cars.

○ 7 Grands Prix, no wins (best result – 6th San Marino GP 1991)
○ No drivers' title (best result – 18th overall 1991)

Mauro Baldi

Nationality: Italian
Born: 1954

Several seasons at the front end of the grid in the European Formula Three Championship in the late 1970s saw Mauro come on strong to win the prestigious Monaco Formula Three race in 1980. Electing to stay on for a fourth year of Formula Three in 1981, he won the European title and then bypassed Formula Two to join the Arrows Formula One team for 1982. His first points came at the Dutch Grand Prix. A move to the works Alfa Romeo team for 1983 was not a success, however, and Mauro was not invited to stay on, so found himself with the new Spirit team in 1984. This was floundering by early 1985, and since then Mauro has raced with great success in sports cars, winning the 1990 world title in a Sauber-run Mercedes. In 1994, Mauro won the Le Mans 24 Hours, sharing a Dauer Porsche with Yannick Dalmas and Hurley Haywood.

○ 36 Grands Prix, no wins (best result – 5th Dutch GP 1983)
○ No drivers' title (best result – 16th overall 1983)

Lorenzo Bandini

Nationality: Italian
Born: 1935
Died: 1967

Lorenzo's racing career started in saloon cars loaned to him by the owner of the garage at which he was a mechanic. By 1959 he was on the grid for the new Formula Junior category, and his form over the next two seasons was enough to attract the attention of Ferrari. He was pipped for a vacant seat early in 1961 by compatriot Giancarlo Baghetti. Scuderia Centro Sud handed him his Formula One debut in a Cooper-Maserati and he drove well enough to secure a seat at Ferrari for 1962.

Lorenzo was third at his first attempt, at Monaco. Despite only occasionally being selected by the team, he also won the non championship Mediterranean Grand

Prix. Dropped in 1963, he was soon back at Ferrari after Willy Mairesse was injured – he even won the Le Mans 24 Hours for the marque.

Lorenzo's only grand prix victory came in 1964 when he triumphed in Austria at Zeltweg – he ended the season fourth overall, three places behind his team-mate, John Surtees.

Monaco was to prove his happiest hunting ground in 1965 and 1966 – with second places – and it was in the second half of 1966 that he finally became Ferrari's number one driver.

Monaco was also to prove his undoing. Running second behind Denny Hulme's Brabham during the 1967 Monaco Grand Prix, Lorenzo's Ferrari clipped the barriers at the chicane and flipped. The car caught fire instantly and Lorenzo was terribly burned while an inadequately equipped crew of marshals extricated him. He died of his injuries within a week.

○ 42 Grands Prix, 1 win (Austrian GP 1964)
○ No drivers' title (best result – 4th overall 1964)

Rubens Barrichello
Nationality: Brazilian
Born: 1972

After collecting five karting titles, Rubens arrived in Europe at 17 and won the GM Euroseries. He then pipped David Coulthard to the 1991 British Formula Three title, then had to make do with third in Formula 3000 but was in Formula One before his 21st birthday when Jordan snapped him up. Rubens almost took second on his third outing, the European Grand Prix, but fuel feed problems hit. He finished third at TI Circuit in 1994, claimed pole in the wet at Spa and also finished fourth five times.

Usually outpaced by team-mate Eddie Irvine in 1995, Rubens peaked with a second in Canada. After little progress in 1996, he turned to Stewart, coming second at Monaco. His third year with Stewart was better as he led in Brazil, took pole at Magny-Cours and third at Imola and the Nurburgring to rank seventh, but he went to Ferrari

for 2000, scoring his first win at Hockenheim. Showing stronger form in 2001, Rubens pushed McLaren's David Coulthard for the runner's-up position. Ferrari dominated in 2002 and Rubens won four of the 17 rounds to Michael Schumacher's 11, to be runner-up. Life was harder in 2003 and Rubens fell to fourth although winning twice. His form was stronger in 2004, finishing as runner-up to Michael but, after a troubled 2005, Rubens joined Honda for 2006. This failed to revive his career, and again he had to watch as a team-mate, Jenson Button, gave his team its first win, just as he had to do when Johnny Herbert broke Stewart's duck in 1999. Things went downhill in 2007 and 2008, save for third in the wet at Silverstone.

Then came 2009 when his F1 career was saved by Brawn GP rising from Honda's ashes. Better still, he was in a competitive car and victory at Valencia was his first in five years. Another win,

at Monza, helped him rank third and he moved to Williams for 2010, extending his record as F1's most experienced driver.

○ 287 Grands Prix, 11 wins (German GP 2000, European GP 2002, Hungarian GP 2002, Italian GP 2002, US GP 2002, British GP 2003, Japanese GP 2003, Italian GP 2004, Chinese GP 2004, European GP 2009, Italian GP 2009)
○ No drivers' title (best result – 2nd overall 2002 and 2004)

Jean Behra
Nationality: French
Born: 1921
Died: 1959

After a career racing motorcycles, "Jeannot" switched to four-wheeled competition in 1949 and graduated to Formula One with Gordini in 1952, a year in which he won the non-championship Reims Grand Prix ahead of the best of the Ferraris, earning him the devotion of his home fans. Tenth

overall in his first season, he stayed with Gordini for two more years, but became frustrated by many car breakages and moved on to Maserati for 1955.

He kicked off with non-championship wins at Pau and Bordeaux and backed this up with many sports car wins, but success still eluded him in the World Championship.

Fourth overall in 1956, he scored his best-ever grand prix result in Argentina in 1957 when he finished second to team-mate Juan Manuel Fangio. Heading for victory in the British Grand Prix, he was thwarted by clutch failure and his career dipped from then on.

A drive for BRM in 1958 yielded nothing and so the offer to join Ferrari was eagerly accepted. Sadly, he was killed in a sports car race at Avus.

○ 52 Grands Prix, no wins (best result – 2nd Argentinian GP 1956, Argentinian GP 1957)
○ No drivers' title (best result – 4th overall 1956)

Red Machine: Rubens Barrichello qualifies his Ferrari on the front row for the US Grand Prix, Indianapolis, September 2003, but he wasn't to finish the race

Derek Bell

Nationality: British
Born: 1941

Very few British drivers have driven in Formula One for Ferrari. However, of those who have, few have failed to make their mark in the sport's top category. Derek was one of the unlucky ones. Propelled through the junior formulae first by his charismatic stepfather and then by Peter Westbury, Derek starred in Formula Two, catching the eye of Enzo Ferrari who signed him up for the last few grands prix of 1968. However, no regular drives followed, and the next three years saw him turn out for three different teams in only four grands prix, peaking with sixth place at the 1970 US Grand Prix for Surtees. Things looked better for 1972 when he managed five races for the Martini team, but the move bought no success, so he rejoined Surtees for 1974, qualifying only once. He then looked to sports cars for his glory and has won the Le Mans 24 Hours five times.

○ 9 Grands Prix, no wins (best result – 6th US GP 1970)
○ No drivers' title (best result – 22nd overall 1970)

Stefan Bellof

Nationality: German
Born: 1957
Died: 1985

Germany had long been aware of its failure to win the World Championship and, if Stefan Bellof had not been killed in a sports car race in 1985, it could all have been very different. Exciting is a description that does not really do justice to Stefan's driving: it was electrifying. He was, in short, a joy to watch – on the ragged edge of control where others would long previously have lost it.

Fresh out of karting, he won the German Formula Ford Championship, vaulted to Formula Three for 1981 and was third overall. Moving up to Formula Two in 1982, he drove with great success for the Maurer team, winning the first two races. However, results tailed off, with retirements blunting his achievement. So a second Formula Two season became essential, dovetailed with sports car races for the works Porsche team. He made it to Formula One in 1984 with Tyrrell and was challenging for victory at Monaco before heavy rain stopped play when he was third, thwarting both him and Ayrton Senna as they closed on Alain Prost. However, the Tyrrell team was found to have committed a technical irregularity and all his points were removed for the 1984 season.

At least Stefan was able to enjoy winning six times for Porsche en route to claiming the world title. For 1985 he found the Tyrrell to be less competitive, and had only a fourth and a sixth to his name when he overstepped the mark in a sports car race at Spa, failing in a crazy attempt to overtake in the daunting Eau Rouge corner. He died instantly.

○ 20 Grands Prix, no wins (best result – 4th US East GP 1985)
○ No drivers' title (best result – 15th overall 1985)

Jean-Pierre Beltoise

Nationality: French
Born: 1937

Hugely successful as a motorcycle racer, Jean-Pierre first raced a car in 1963, and indeed his early sports car races nearly cost him the movement in one of his arms after a crash at Reims in 1964. However, he fought back to win the French Formula Three title in 1965 for Matra, and embellished this with victory in the Monaco Formula Three race in 1966, and several months later made his grand prix debut, winning the Formula Two class in the German Grand Prix. It was not until 1968 that he was given his first run in a grand prix in a Formula One car, still with Matra. This produced fifth place, however, and he was allowed to continue, soon exceeding this result with second at the Dutch Grand Prix. His progress continued into 1969 and a further second place helped him to fifth overall in the championship. He stayed on with Matra for 1970 and 1971, but things turned sour when he was threatened with the suspension of his license following the death of Ignazio Giunti after an incident involving Jean-Pierre in a sports car race in Argentina. Then, in 1972, it all came right – at Monaco at least, when he won in torrential conditions for BRM. That was his only ever win, however, and he faded from Formula One after two further seasons with BRM.

○ 86 Grands Prix, 1 win (Monaco GP 1972)
○ No drivers' title (best result – 5th overall 1969)

Gerhard Berger

Nationality: Austrian
Born: 1959

Gerhard started racing Alfasuds, but Formula Three soon followed; as did success as he chased Ivan Capelli for the European title in 1984. At the end of that year he had a shot at Formula One with ATS, finishing sixth on his second outing, even though he was not eligible for points.

Things looked good for 1985, but Gerhard broke his neck in a road accident. Defying doctors' orders, he was up and about far ahead of their predictions and joined Arrows for 1985, scoring points in the final two races. A move to the new Benetton team in 1986 produced his first win, in Mexico, and helped Gerhard land a ride with Ferrari for 1987. Again he peaked at the end of the year, this time with two wins.

Another win and more consistent scoring saw him to third overall in 1988, and then came his final season with Ferrari – where he failed to finish a race until September. Angered by this lack of mechanical fortitude, Gerhard moved to McLaren for 1990 to drive alongside Ayrton Senna. Seldom as quick as Senna, at least he taught the Brazilian to smile and Gerhard was a regular front-runner until the end of 1992 when he returned to Ferrari. The pressure of leading Ferrari through its longest non-winning streak was huge, but he brought this to a close at the 1994 German Grand Prix. He should have added to this in the Australian Grand Prix, but he ran wide, letting Nigel Mansell through, yet finished second to ensure he ended up third overall. Unable to live with Williams and Benetton in 1995, Gerhard brought his Ferrari home

Tired Out: Derek Bell dabbled in Formula One but enjoyed consistent success in the Le Mans 24 Hours

third six times. Electing not to stay on, he headed back to Benetton in 1996, but the wins did not come, as shown when his engine blew when leading in Germany. A strong second in Brazil was a false dawn in 1997, but he sprung back from missing three races with sinus trouble to win from pole in Germany and then announced his retirement. He later ran BMW's Formula One programme from 1998 to 2003.

○ 210 Grands Prix, 10 wins (Mexican GP 1986, Japanese GP 1987, Australian GP 1987, Italian GP 1988, Portuguese GP 1989, Japanese GP 1991, Canadian GP 1992, Australian GP 1992, German GP 1994, German GP 1997)
○ No drivers' title (best result - 3rd overall 1988 and 1994)

Eric Bernard
Nationality: French
Born: 1964
After victory in the national kart series, Eric beat Jean Alesi to win the prestigious Winfield school scholarship in 1983, launching him into Formule Renault. A strong run in this was followed by title success in 1985 that boosted him into Formula Three, in which he finished second to Alesi in 1987. Formula 3000 was another category that took two bites, with Eric finishing third overall for DAMS in 1989. His two Formula One outings that year for Larrousse were backed up with a full-time ride for 1990, with Eric claiming fourth at the British Grand Prix. A weak 1991 season followed, and it was curtailed when he broke a leg in Japan. To many this would have been the end, but Eric fought back and returned to the Ligier team in 1994, peaking with third place at the German Grand Prix, his only scoring drive of the year. However, as rookie team-mate Olivier Panis outpaced him more often than not, it spelt the end of Eric's Formula One career.
○ 45 Grands Prix, no wins (best result - 3rd German GP 1994)
○ No drivers' title (best result - 13th : 1990)

The Nearly Man: Gerhard Berger won a total of 10 GPs but never managed to take the world title

Lucien Bianchi
Nationality: Belgian
Born: 1934
Died: 1969
Born into an Italian family that was tempted to Belgium to work for racing driver Johnny Claes, Lucien cut his teeth in sports cars and rallying before moving on to single-seaters in 1959. The first grand prix for which he qualified was, fittingly, the Belgian in 1960 and he drove his Cooper into the points, finishing sixth. However, he dropped back to sports cars, and it was not until 1968 that Lucien had a decent crack at Formula One, with the little-fancied BRM-powered Cooper. His highlight that year came when he won the Le Mans 24 Hours and it was to sports cars that he turned in 1969, but they later claimed his life at Le Mans.
○ 17 Grands Prix, no wins (best result - 3rd Monaco GP 1968)
○ No drivers' title (best result - 17th overall 1968)

"B Bira"
Nationality: Thai
Born: 1914
Died: 1985
Prince Birabongse Bhanuban, a colourful figure on the European social scene in the mid-1930s, was also a car fanatic from an early age and, when at school in England, made it his ambition to become a racing driver. He eventually graduated to a mighty ERA, but his career was interrupted by the Second World War, after which he won various Formula Two races before making his Formula One debut in 1950 for Maserati, finishing fifth at Monaco and then fourth in the Swiss Grand Prix. Running in Maserati, then Gordini, then Connaught, then Maserati again, "B Bira" raced on until the start of 1955 when he retired.
○ 19 Grands Prix, no wins (best result - 4th Swiss GP 1950, French GP 1954)
○ No drivers' title (best result - 4th: 1956)

Mark Blundell
Nationality: British
Born: 1966
When Mark first arrived in Formula Ford aged 17, he was already a remarkably seasoned competitor after many years of racing in motocross. Armed with family wealth and the "will to win", he contested 70 races that year.

This propelled him into Formula Ford 2000 for the next two seasons, racing with - and often beating - rivals such as Damon Hill, Johnny Herbert and Bertrand Gachot.

Most people would then have gone to Formula Three in 1987, but not Mark, who leapt directly to Formula 3000 without passing Go. A chance to drive for the works Lola team came his way in 1988, but this bombed after he had achieved second place in the first round.

Staying on for 1989, he had an even worse season, but sports cars came to his rescue and he drove with great speed for the works Nissan team.

A test-driving role at Williams followed in 1990, and Mark made his Formula One racing debut with Brabham in 1991. He was not an overnight success. Dropping to sports cars again in 1992, he was back in Formula One with Ligier in 1993 and scored third place first time out, ending up tenth overall.

A move to Tyrrell in 1994 saw Mark suffer at the hands of Japanese team-mate Ukyo Katayama, raising cries of unfair treatment but, whichever way you look at it, it cost him the chance to stay on for 1995. Drafted into the McLaren line-up when Nigel Mansell could not fit into the car, he got the drive for keeps when Mansell quit.

Mark brought the tricky car home in the points six times, but lost out in the chase for a Sauber ride in 1996, and moved on to become a race-winner in IndyCars in 1997.
○ 61 Grands Prix, no wins (best result - 3rd South African GP 1993, German GP 1993, Spanish GP 1994)
○ No drivers' title (best result - 10th overall 1993 and 1995)

Raul Boesel

Nationality: Brazilian
Born: 1957

Raul came second in the British Formula Ford series in 1980. Making sure that he scored points rather than throw them away in a win-or-bust approach, Raul finished third in the British Formula Three championship and leapt into Formula One for 1982. However, the March team was not the one to be with that year and his best result was eighth at the Belgian Grand Prix. Frustrated, he moved to Ligier for 1983 and went one better with seventh place in the US Grand Prix West. However, no points came his way and Raul headed to IndyCars. A period racing for the Jaguar sports car team netted Raul the 1987 world title, but he returned to IndyCars in the 1990s.

○ 23 Grands Prix, no wins (best result – 7th US West GP 1983)
○ No drivers' title

Felice Bonetto

Nationality: Italian
Born: 1903
Died: 1953

The average age of drivers in the inaugural Formula One World Championship race in 1950, held at Silverstone, was almost double the age of today's grid and when Felice made his debut in the Swiss Grand Prix that year he was five days short of 47. A star in the long, heroic Italian road races of the 1930s, his move to Formula One came with Ferrari, for whom he shone in several non-championship races. He entered his own Maserati in several grands prix in 1950 and drove a works Alfa Romeo in 1951, finishing third in the Italian Grand Prix.

A move to sports cars followed, but he returned to Formula One at the end of 1952 but was tragically killed on the Carrera Panamericana road race through Mexico.

○ 15 Grands Prix, no wins (best result – 3rd Italian GP 1951, Dutch GP 1953)
○ No drivers' title (best result – 8th overall 1951)

Joakim Bonnier

Nationality: Swedish
Born: 1930
Died: 1972

Having begun his career in rallying and then having honed his skills in ice races, Jo was awarded the Swedish Alfa Romeo franchise and used its Disco Volante in sports car races.

He bought a Maserati 250F with which to race in Formula One, starting at the 1956 Italian Grand Prix.

Jo's first full season came in 1958 and his results improved when he moved to BRM, taking fourth in the Moroccan Grand Prix – his victory at Zandvoort in 1959 marked the end of BRM's long wait for a grand prix win. That was his golden moment, and the following year-and-a-half produced only three fifth places.

He raced a Porsche in 1961–62, but tended to be overshadowed by team-mate Dan Gurney. Jo was held in high esteem by his fellow drivers, and he founded the Grand Prix Drivers' Association which began to campaign to make circuits safer.

Three years with Rob Walker's team, driving Coopers and Brabhams, saw a number of fifth and sixth places and, though Joakim chipped away with his own privately entered Coopers and McLarens until 1971 that was his lot. He was killed at Le Mans in 1972.

○ 102 Grands Prix, 1 win (Dutch GP 1959)
○ No drivers' title (best result – 8th overall 1959)

One Hit Wonder: Jo Bonnier took part in over 100 grands prix and won one, the Dutch GP in 1959

Slim Borgudd

Nationality: Swedish
Born: 1946

Slim used the money he gained from his musical exploits as Abba's drummer to go racing. He contested the 1978 European Formula Three series and he finished third overall in 1979, a year when Alain Prost was champion.

Practically the whole of 1980 was spent trying to raise the cash to race in Formula One, and so he made his debut in 1981 with ATS, scoring his solitary point for his sixth place in the British Grand Prix. His money ran out after only three races with Tyrrell in 1982 and Slim's greatest success since was in truck racing.

○ 10 Grands Prix, no wins (best result – 6th British GP 1981)
○ No drivers' title (best result – 18th overall 1981)

Jean-Christophe Boullion

Nationality: French
Born: 1969

Jean-Christophe flew in Formula Ford, then showed great pace in French Formula Three and consequently won the Formula 3000 title in 1994 for the DAMS team.

He matched the pace of Damon Hill and David Coulthard as Williams' test driver, but was given a chance to race at Sauber when Karl Wendlinger was dropped before Monaco in 1995. Occasionally quick and often erratic, he was soon dropped and has since raced sports cars with success.

○ 11 Grands Prix, no wins (best result – 5th German GP 1995)
○ No drivers' title (best result – 16th overall 1995)

Thierry Boutsen

Nationality: Belgian
Born: 1957

Thierry rocketed through Formula Ford. His maiden year in Formula Three, in the heady days of 1979, was not so sweet, but he finally came good and landed a works ride for 1980, finishing second overall to Michele Alboreto. Formula Two

Victory Rites: Ayrton Senna congratulates Thierry Boutsen after the bustling Belgian pipped him to the post in the Hungarian Grand Prix, 1990

followed and he was second again, this time to Geoff Lees, but he had done enough to impress. And so Thierry made it to Formula One for 1983 with Arrows, with whom he stayed until 1986, peaking with second place at Imola in 1985.

Thierry moved to Benetton in 1987. Five third places in 1988 helped him to fourth overall – his best placing in the championship.

A move to Williams in 1989 yielded two victories, both in the wet, and although he won again in 1990, holding off massive pressure from the Brazilian Ayrton Senna in Hungary, his contract with Williams was not renewed. Thierry moved to Ligier for 1991 and 1992, which proved a costly mistake, the team being off the pace even with Renault engines.

When Ivan Capelli was sacked by Jordan in 1993, Thierry moved into the vacancy, but he did not last the season. He has since raced touring cars and sports cars.

○ 163 Grands Prix, 3 wins (Canadian GP 1989, Australian GP 1989, Hungarian GP 1990)

○ No drivers' title (best result – 4th overall 1988)

David **Brabham**

Nationality: Australian
Born: 1965

Youngest of Sir Jack Brabham's three sons, David considered racing only after spending a summer watching his brother Geoff race in the US. As soon as he returned to Australia he started in single-seaters, then joined his parents in England and was an instant hit in Formula Three. He won a long, hard fight with Allan McNish for the 1989 title and backed this up by winning the Macau Grand Prix, the unofficial world final for Formula Three. David made his Formula One debut in 1990 when Middlebridge, the team that was set to run him in Formula 3000, bought the Brabham Grand Prix team, an outfit that had been sold off by his father when he retired from racing in 1970. However, the car was not a gem and David was dropped at the end of the year, turning successfully to sports cars. After a spell with Jaguar and then Toyota, he made it back to Formula One with the formation of the Simtek team in 1994. It was a ghastly year, for team-mate Roland Ratzenberger was killed at Imola and David showed inner strength to remotivate the team. Fighting from the back of the grid,

he gave it his all, with a best finish of tenth, but he could not find the money to continue and became a works BMW touring car driver, then moved to sports cars with Panoz.

○ 24 Grands Prix, no wins (best result – 10th Spanish GP 1994)

○ No drivers' title

Jack **Brabham**

SEE PAGE 132

Vittorio **Brambilla**

Nationality: Italian
Born: 1937

Born in Monza, he raced motorcycles, then karts, before joining his brother Tino in Formula Three in 1968. Despite not competing in all the rounds, Vittorio finished second overall and went one better in 1969. The brothers teamed up in Formula Two in 1970, but Vittorio spent much of the year blowing engines in his efforts to keep up with drivers in newer machinery. Occasional quick drives were not enough, especially with Vittorio junking several chassis, and money was too tight for success to follow. Only when Beta Tools agreed to finance him in 1973 did he make progress. He took Beta Tools to Formula One in 1974

with March and he scored his first point before the year was out. His second season promised so much, with pole in Sweden, but offered frequent retirements until he held it all together to win the Austrian Grand Prix after a downpour. Seconds after crossing the finish line, Vittorio punched the air with delight and crashed. He moved to Surtees in 1977 and did poorly, with the exception of a fourth place in Belgium. Then came disaster in the 1978 Italian Grand Prix when he was struck on the head in the accident that was to inflict fatal injuries on Ronnie Peterson. It was a year later that Vittorio was back in the cockpit, returning at Monza for Alfa-Romeo. But the old speed was not there and he retired from Formula One after just a handful more races.

○ 74 Grands Prix, 1 win (Austrian GP 1975)

○ No drivers' title (best result – 11th overall 1975)

Tony **Brise**

Nationality: British
Born: 1952
Died: 1975

Tony could have been a British World Champion, but he died in the same light aircraft accident that claimed the life of Graham Hill. Encouraged by his father, a former racer, Tony started in karts at the age of ten and shone in Formula Ford, finishing second in the 1971 British series. Moving up to Formula Three in 1972 was not a great success, since he had the wrong car. However, he picked up a drive with the GRD team for 1973 and won the British title ahead of Alan Jones and Jacques Laffite. For 1974 Tony tried Formula Atlantic with a works Modus and finished third overall. Hill signed him up for Formula One for 1975, and Tony did great things with what was clearly not a very quick car, getting it into the points in Sweden, but that plane crash denied us the knowledge of just how far he could have gone.

○ 10 Grands Prix, no wins (best result – 6th Swedish GP 1975)

○ No drivers' title (best result – 19th overall 1975)

JACK BRABHAM
An Uncompromising Man

Known as "Black Jack", Brabham's nickname reflected his demeanour rather than an affinity with the gaming tables. As uncompromising as they come, he combined dedication and determination with a shrewd nature and the mechanical know-how to forge a remarkable career.

Jack was behind the wheel of a family car by the age of 12. New South Wales champion in his first season, Jack forged an alliance with Ron Tauranac, with whom he would later form Brabham. When the authorities objected to sponsorship on his Cooper, Brabham went overseas and shone in the 1954 New Zealand Grand Prix.

Persuaded to go to Europe, Jack became associated with John Cooper and made his World Championship debut in the 1955 British Grand Prix. By 1959 the Coopers, with 2.5-litre Climax engines, were a force, driven by Jack, Stirling Moss, Maurice Trintignant, Bruce McLaren and Masten Gregory.

Although Moss took pole for the season-opener at Monaco, it was Jack who won. He may not have been the quickest of drivers, but he was consistent. He won again at Aintree and sealed the championship at Sebring by pushing his car to the finish in fourth place after running out of fuel. In 1960, Jack won a second title for Cooper, his campaign including five straight wins. For 1961, there was a new 1.5-litre formula and Ferrari leapt to the fore. Ever shrewd, Jack saw the potential for production racing cars and, with Tauranac, formed Motor Racing Developments. The first

Brabham made its debut in 1962, and a fourth at Watkins Glen brought the first points ever for a driver in a car of his own manufacture.

Dan Gurney joined Jack and, although they won non-championship races at Solitude and Zeltweg, they did not win a pukka grand prix until Rouen in 1964 when Gurney took the

The Wizard of Oz: Jack Brabham is a study in concentration as he prepares for battle at Brands Hatch

chequered flag. The demands of the business sent Jack into semi-retirement in 1965, but he came back full-time in 1966 and, at Reims, finally won in a Brabham, and went on to clinch his third title.

Beaten into second place by team-mate Denny Hulme in 1967, Jack signed Jochen Rindt for 1968, but there were problems with the Repco engine and Rindt left for Lotus. Jack was then joined by Jacky Ickx. Jack broke an ankle when testing, but Ickx finished second overall to Jackie Stewart and was snapped up by Ferrari. Having his aces poached was becoming tedious for Jack and he was determined that 1970 would be his final year. It started well, with victory at Kyalami, and the season produced two incredible races in which Jack lost out to Rindt on the last lap. At Monaco he was pursued relentlessly and went straight on at the final hairpin. He reversed out and finished second, but never had his face looked blacker. Then, at Brands Hatch, he ran out of fuel and again Rindt came past to win. Jack hung up his helmet after that year's Mexican Grand Prix, 16 seasons after his Aintree debut.

○ **126 Grands Prix, 14 wins**

○ **World Champion 1959, 1960 and 1966**

1926	1953	1957	1959	1960	1964	1967	1971
Born 2 April in Hurstville, Australia	Australian Hill Climb Champion in a Cooper	Did five grands prix for Cooper. Broken fuel pump cost him third at Monaco	Won at Monaco and Aintree to claim World Championship, also helping Cooper to constructors' title	World Champion again thanks to five straight wins mid-season	Dan Gurney gave Brabham its first win, in French GP, but Jack's best was a pair of seconds	Team-mate Denny Hulme became World Champion, Jack's two wins leaving him as runner-up	Retired from driving and ran cars for Graham Hill and Tim Schenken before selling team to Bernie Ecclestone

1948	1955	1958	1962	1966	1970
Started racing in Midget class, going on to build his own cars	Fourth in non-championship New Zealand GP then tried his luck in British GP. Won non-championship Australian GP	Won non-championship New Zealand GP then raced full Formula One season for Cooper, his best result being fourth at Monaco	Formed team with long-time designer and friend Ron Tauranac, racing a Lotus until Brabham chassis was ready	Became first World Champion in a car bearing his name, with four wins. Awarded the OBE	Won in South Africa, but hit last lap problems to lose at Monaco and Brands Hatch, leaving him fifth overall

Chris Bristow

Nationality: British
Born: 1937
Died: 1960

After starting in an MG special, Chris was helped into more competitive equipment by his father in 1957, and his form in 1958 led him to be signed up by the British Racing Partnership for 1959. This offered him the chance to race single-seaters as well as sports cars, and he made his grand prix debut in the British Grand Prix, albeit in Formula Two equipment. The death of team-mate Harry Schell pitched Chris into the role of team leader shortly after the BRP put him into Formula One with a Yeoman Credit Racing Cooper. Sadly, he suffered a fatal accident in the Belgian Grand Prix on a dark day at Spa that also claimed the life of compatriot Alan Stacey.

○ 4 Grands Prix, no wins (best result – 10th British GP 1959)
○ No drivers' title

Tony Brooks

Nationality: British
Born: 1932

Tony Brooks was a driver of consummate skill. If he had not been bitten by the racing bug he would have gone on to become a dentist, dabbling in sports cars as a pleasant distraction from his studies. However, in 1955 he went abroad and raced a Connaught. In only his second race, the non-championship but nevertheless well-attended Syracuse Grand Prix, he thrashed all comers – it was the first win by a British driver in a British car since 1924. World Championship Formula One followed in 1956 with BRM, but his season was foreshortened when he was thrown from his car at Silverstone and broke his jaw. Vanwall signed him up for 1957 and second place first time out, at Monaco, was followed by victory at the British Grand Prix, an event in which he started but handed over his car mid-race to Stirling Moss as he was suffering from leg injuries sustained during the Le Mans 24 Hours. Staying

Mind Your Toes: Tony Brooks flies past a trio of rather casual bystanders at the Nurburgring in 1958

with Vanwall for 1958, he was tipped by the retiring Juan Manuel Fangio as the likely World Champion, but though Tony won three times – each time on the real drivers' circuits – he wound up third overall. Ferrari signed him for 1959 and Tony won twice more, ending the year second to Jack Brabham. A deal to rejoin Vanwall for 1960 fell through when the team elected not to rejoin the fray and Tony regrets taking a ride in one of Yeoman Credit Racing's Coopers instead of opting for a sabbatical. Moving on to BRM for 1961 was not as competitive as he would have liked, but Tony rounded off his career with third place in the United States Grand Prix and then retired to run a motor business. He was one of the all-time greats, consistently showing that he had what it took to shine, but no car with which to do so.

○ 38 Grands Prix, 6 wins (British GP 1957, Belgian GP 1958, German GP 1958, Italian GP 1958, French GP 1959, German GP 1959)
○ No drivers' title (best result – 2nd overall 1959)

Martin Brundle

Nationality: British
Born: 1959

How a driver who made Ayrton Senna work so hard for the British Formula Three title could race in Formula One for a decade and not score a win is a mystery. Senna had whipped all comers in the first half of 1983, but Martin became the quicker of the two in his Eddie Jordan Racing Ralt and took the title down to the wire. Ken

Tyrrell was not slow to identify this talent and signed Martin for 1984. He was fifth in his first grand prix, in Brazil. Coming second in Detroit behind Nelson Piquet propelled Martin to the brink, but a race later he broke his ankles at Dallas. In addition, Tyrrell was adjudged to have been running illegal cars, and the team's results were scrapped.

He had four points-scoring drives in 1986, but his career took a dive when he chose to join Zakspeed in 1987. It was hopeless and Martin was left without a drive in 1988. Fortunately, he raced for Jaguar and won the World Sports Car Championship, as well as having a one-off drive for Williams at Spa. He drove for Brabham in 1989, but this was not the team it had once been and he went back to sports cars for 1990, winning the Le Mans 24 Hours.

A return to Brabham for 1991 was not a success either as their Yamaha engines were weak. Then came his break: a ride at Benetton for 1992, but Michael Schumacher soon proved himself team leader as Martin struggled to finish races.

From San Marino on, though, he scored points in all but one race to rank sixth overall, usually racing better than Schumacher in the process. A move to Ligier in 1993 brought more regular points scores and seventh overall. Then it looked as though he was out of a top ride for 1994, but he hung in there for a McLaren seat and claimed it at the last minute. Again no wins came, but Martin was twice on the podium and ended the season in seventh overall. He had to share the second Ligier with Aguri Suzuki in 1995 and his best drive came when he chased David Coulthard for third at Magny-Cours. A ride with Jordan for 1996 promised more than it delivered. He is now the expert voice in BBC television's commentary booth.

○ 158 Grands Prix, no wins (best result – 2nd Italian GP 1992, Monaco GP 1994)
○ No drivers' title (best result – 6th overall 1992)

Jenson Button

Nationality: British

Born: 1980

European Super A karting champion in 1997, Jenson moved into Formula Ford at 18, won the 1998 British title and the Formula Ford Festival. On pole for his first Formula Three race in 1999, he had the less competitive Renault engine and ended the year third overall. He then shone in a test for the Prost Formula One team, but was signed by Williams after a shoot-out with Bruno Junqueira. Jenson raced to six points-scoring results, sometimes ahead of team-mate Ralf Schumacher, but lost his ride to Juan Pablo Montoya, heading to Benetton, on-loan. A troubled 2001 season was spent as Renault developed its wide-angle V10.

In 2002, when the Benetton team changed its name to Renault, Jenson lost third on the final lap of the Malaysian Grand Prix as his car limped to the finish.

He moved to BAR for 2003. Jacques Villeneuve didn't welcome him, but Jenson collected two fourths, Villeneuve just a sixth. Team leader in 2004, Jenson was seldom off the podium, albeit failing to win. Ranked third, he was then only ninth in 2005, but with Honda taking control for 2006 he had great hopes and took victory in the wet in Hungary.

The next two campaigns were sapping, with just fifth in Shanghai in 2007 and sixth in Spain in 2008. So, 2009 could hardly have been more different as the salvage operation that turned Honda into Brawn produced the best car and Jenson won six of the first seven races and was crowned World Champion with a round to go. He then joined Lewis Hamilton at McLaren for 2010.

° **171 Grands Prix, 7 wins (Hungarian GP 2006, Australian GP 2009, Malaysian GP 2009, Bahrain GP 2009, Spanish GP 2009, Monaco GP 2009, Turkish GP 2009)**

° **World Champion 2009**

This Space for Hire: Jenson Button wears his logos with pride before the Australian Grand Prix, 2003

Alex Caffi

Nationality: Italian

Born: 1964

Ever the bridesmaid, Alex was second in the Italian Formula Three series in 1984 and 1985, then third in 1986. His Formula One break came in 1987 when he drove the unwieldy Osella. His fortune was better in 1988 with a Scuderia Italia Dallara. Staying on for 1989, he took fourth place at Monaco and was then running fifth at Phoenix (having been second earlier on) when team-mate Andrea de Cesaris tipped him into the wall.

Alex moved to Arrows in 1990, but it was not a success. Staying with the team, now renamed Footwork, he found his chances were hampered by heavy and uncompetitive Porsche engines and then by a jaw-breaking road accident. He qualified only twice on his return. Just when he thought it could get no worse, it did: he joined the new Andrea Moda team for 1992. He quit after two races and elected to race in touring cars in Italy and Spain.

° **56 Grands Prix, no wins (best result – 4th Monaco GP 1989)**

° **No drivers' title (best result – 16th overall 1989 and 1990)**

Ivan Capelli

Nationality: Italian

Born: 1963

Hot from karting, Ivan went direct to Formula Three and dominated the Italian series at his second attempt, in 1983. Staying with Enzo Coloni's team for 1984, he won the Monaco race and later the European Championship ahead of Gerhard Berger and Johnny Dumfries. A limited Formula 3000 campaign in 1985 produced a win at the Osterreichring and promoted Ivan to the Tyrrell Formula One team for a couple of races. Amazingly, he was fourth on his second outing, in Australia, yet no offer for 1986 was forthcoming.

So Ivan returned to Formula 3000, winning the title for Genoa Racing. He joined March for 1987 and claimed a point at Monaco, but 1988 was better, as he was in the points six times, chasing Alain Prost's McLaren in Portugal before settling for second.

The 1989 season was an unmitigated disaster, as the March chassis handled like a pig, but 1990 was much better and Ivan led the French Grand Prix for 46 laps before Alain Prost pushed his Ferrari ahead with just three laps to go. After a troubled season in 1991 he was signed for Ferrari for 1992, but points were few and far between, and after just two races for Jordan in 1993, he was fired. He now commentates for Italian television.

° **92 Grands Prix, no wins (best result – 2nd Portuguese GP 1988, French GP 1990)**

° **No drivers' title (best result – 7th overall 1988)**

Eugenio Castellotti

Nationality: Italian

Born: 1930

Died: 1957

Eugenio cut a swathe through European sports car racing in the early 1950s. He made his Formula One debut at the 1955 Argentinian Grand Prix with Lancia and swept to second place on his second outing, at Monaco. On the death of team-mate Alberto Ascari, he became team leader and scored points three more times to be third overall. Continuing with the Lancia-Ferrari set-up in 1956, Eugenio was second in the French Grand Prix and finished sixth overall in the championship. He won the legendary Mille Miglia road race to make up for his disappointment with his Formula One results. Eugenio was only to race in one more grand prix, however, being killed when testing for Ferrari at its Modena testing circuit in early 1957.

○ 14 Grands Prix, no wins (best result – 2nd Monaco GP 1955, French GP 1956)

○ No drivers' title (best result – 3rd overall 1955)

Johnny Cecotto

Nationality: Venezuelan

Born: 1956

After becoming the youngest ever 350cc motorcycle World Champion, Johnny swapped across to four wheels with a drive in Formula Two in 1980. By 1982 he was a front-runner, only losing out on the title to works March team-mate Corrado Fabi when dropped scores were taken into consideration.

His Formula One debut came in 1983 when he joined the little Theodore team, amazingly finishing in sixth place in his second race, at Long Beach. No more points followed, and he moved to Toleman for 1984, but his single-seater career was cut short with a leg-breaking shunt at Brands Hatch. Subsequently, Johnny has won numerous titles in touring car racing in both Italy and Germany.

○ 18 Grands Prix, no wins (best result – 6th US West GP 1983)

○ No drivers' title (best result – 19th: 1983)

François Cevert

Nationality: French

Born: 1944

Died: 1973

Fate struck a cruel blow when it claimed the life of this talented Frenchman at the 1973 US Grand Prix, for he was poised to assume Jackie Stewart's role as Tyrrell team leader and thus make a bid to become the first French World Champion. French Formula Three champion in 1968, François was

promoted by Tecno to its Formula Two squad and finished third overall in 1969. Tyrrell snapped him up for 1970 and put him under the tutelage of Stewart. François was twice second in 1971 before winning the final race of the season, at Watkins Glen, the track that would later claim his life. This helped him to third overall behind Stewart and Ferrari's Jacky Ickx. In 1973 he was second six times, three times behind Stewart. Then then came that fateful day in upper New York State...

○ 47 Grands Prix, 1 win (US GP 1971)

○ No drivers' title (best result – 3rd: 1971)

Eddie Cheever

Nationality: American

Born: 1958

Eddie shone in Formula Three and then in Formula Two and was looking to jump into Formula One at the end of 1977 at the age of 19. A seat at Ferrari seemed a possibility, but Gilles Villeneuve got there first. Eddie rolled out for Theodore and had a one-off ride for Hesketh in 1978, but elected

to return to Formula Two, and it was not until 1980 that he graduated full-time, with the new Osella team. Sadly, the Italian team was out of its depth and he was able to show his hand only when he moved to Tyrrell in 1981, putting in five points-scoring drives. He hit the podium in 1982 with Ligier, peaking with second at Detroit and this helped him land a ride for 1983.

Two years with the Benetton-Alfa Romeo team and three with Arrows came next, but the star was fading and Eddie headed to Indy Cars, winning the 1998 Indy 500 before eventually stepping down from driving in 2003 to concentrate on running his own team.

○ 132 Grands Prix, no wins (best result – 2nd US GP 1982, Canadian GP 1983)

○ No drivers' title (best result – 6th: 1983)

Louis Chiron

Nationality: Monegasque

Born: 1899

Died: 1979

Louis scored more than a dozen grands prix wins before the Second World War and several more after it. Nicknamed "The Old Fox" in deference to his advanced age and wily tactics, he was on the grid for the first World Championship race in 1950, driving a works Maserati. Third place at his native Monte Carlo was his best result that year, and indeed was the best of his championship career. The unreliability of the Lago-Talbot he raced in 1951 wasted that year, and it signalled the end of his serious bid for Formula One glory.

○ 15 Grands Prix, no wins (best result – 3rd Monaco GP 1950)

○ No drivers' title (best result – 9th: 1950)

Jim Clark

SEE PAGE 136

Peter Collins

Nationality: British

Born: 1931

Died: 1958

The tricks learned in three years of Formula 500 racing were to stand Peter in good stead throughout his

Passing the Ton: American Eddie Cheever took part in 132 grands prix but failed to win – he came in second twice. Here he's pictured in an Osella

JIM CLARK
A Smooth Operator

An unassuming man out of the cockpit, Jim was a genius in one. When enthusiasts get together to debate who was the greatest driver ever, he invariably enters into the discussion alongside Ayrton Senna and Michael Schumacher.

The son of a farmer, Jim had his first contact with racing when his eldest sister married a local racer who took him to Charterhall. Shortly after his 17th birthday, garage owner Jock McBain advised him to enter an auto test. He won it.

After a number of rallies, Ian Scott-Watson lent Jim a DKW for his first race. For 1957, Scott-Watson bought a Porsche and Jim became serious.

McBain re-formed the Border Reivers team for 1958 and bought an ex-Archie Scott-Brown Jaguar D-type and Jim scored 12 wins from 20 starts.

However, Jim had a chastening experience at Spa. He was entered in a sports car race and Scott-Brown was killed when he was caught out by changing conditions. It sowed the seeds of a career-long dislike for the place, but it was not strong enough to prevent him winning four Belgian Grands Prix there.

When Scott-Watson bought a Lotus Elite and Jim scrapped with Colin Chapman on his first visit to Brands Hatch, Chapman's new Lotus company was in its embryonic stages. But, when a Formula One deal with Aston Martin failed to materialize, he joined Lotus to drive in Formula Two and Formula Junior in 1960. He won immediately and Chapman entered him in the Dutch Grand Prix, where he ran fifth before retiring. Then it was Spa, and the jinx struck again. Team-mate Stirling Moss broke both his legs in practice. Then, in the race, Jim was first to reach Chris Bristow's crash. Then team-mate Alan Stacey was killed when a bird flew into his face.

Jim overcame the experience and by 1961 was a full-time grand prix driver. That year, however, he was involved in the accident that killed Wolfgang von Trips and 13 spectators at Monza and the authorities sought to blame him for the tragedy.

Chapman produced the Lotus 25 for 1962 and Jim scored his first grand prix win with it. He battled down to the wire with Graham Hill for the title before losing out at the final round when his car broke. Jim was untouchable in 1963 and took seven wins from ten starts. He also finished second in the Indy 500, to the astonishment of the American establishment. Five wins in 1965 gave Jim a second title and he also won the Indy 500.

With the new 3-litre formula introduced for 1966, Lotus did not have the engines to mount a bid and it was not until the Cosworth DFV was introduced in 1967 that Jim was the man to beat again, giving the engine a debut win at Zandvoort and pushing Denny Hulme hard for the title.

Jim started 1968 by winning in South Africa. Then, driving in a Formula Two race at Hockenheim, his car flew off the road and he was killed instantly.

○ **72 Grands Prix, 25 wins**
○ **World Champion 1963 and 1965**

The Victor's Wave: Jim Clark after coming first in the Kentish Hundred Trophy, Brands Hatch, 1960

1936
Born 4 March in Kilmany, Fifeshire, Scotland

1956
Competed in his first circuit race in an unlikely DKW race saloon

1959
Made single-seater debut in Formula Junior and was invited to join the Aston Martin Formula One team, but it never got off the ground

1961
Lotus was no match for Ferrari and his best was two thirds. Involved in Wolfgang von Trips' fatal crash at Monza

1963
World Champion, winning seven of the ten grands prix.

1965
World Champion for a second time thanks to six wins in first six races. Won Indy 500

1967
Arrival of Ford DFV led to four wins and he ended year third overall. Awarded an OBE

1953
Took part in an auto test and won it, later trying rallying

1958
Took 12 wins from 20 races in a Border Reivers Jaguar D-type

1960
Started in Lotus's Formula Junior team, but was promoted to Formula One and finished with third in Portuguese GP. Third in Le Mans 24 Hours

1962
Won Belgian, British and US GPs. Only car failure when leading final round kept him from the title

1964
Poor reliability from Climax engine left him third overall despite three wins. Led Indy 500 but retired

1966
Lotus struggled at introduction of 3-litre rules and he won once. Runner-up in Indy 500

1968
Won season-opening South African GP, but was killed in Formula Two race at Hockenheim

career, and he made a big impression when he moved up to Formula Two with HWM in 1952. Sadly, the cars were not reliable, but Aston Martin was sufficiently impressed to sign him for its sports car team. A ride with BRM in 1955 was limited by the late arrival of its new car. However, Ferrari signed Peter for 1956. Two wins, in Belgium and France, followed, helping Peter finish third overall behind Juan Manuel Fangio and Stirling Moss. The following year was not so good, and he failed to win as his Lancia-Ferrari was outclassed by the rival Maseratis and Vanwalls. Peter was back on form with the advent of Ferrari's classic Dino 246 Grand Prix car in 1958. Cruelly, just a fortnight after he stormed home ahead of Hawthorn in the British Grand Prix, he was killed in the German Grand Prix at the Nurburgring when chasing Tony Brooks' Vanwall for the lead.

○ 32 Grands Prix, 3 wins (Belgian GP 1956, French GP 1956, British GP 1958)
○ No drivers' title (best result – 3rd overall 1956)

Erik Comas

Nationality: French
Born: 1963

Too many talented drivers from one country arriving at the top will spoil one another's chances. Thus Erik found himself competing with Jean Alesi and Eric Bernard. Erik won the French Formule Renault title in 1986 and then suffered from being number two to Bernard in Formula Three. Thus, it was not until his second year in Formula Three, in 1988, that he won the French title. Formula 3000 saw Erik partner Bernard again. He scored more points, but lost the title to Alesi by the smallest of margins. Yet again he stayed on for a repeat, winning the 1990 crown. Two years in Formula One with Ligier were his reward, but he scored no points in 1991. He scored in Canada, France and Germany in 1992, then Erik had a huge shunt at Spa from which he was lucky to escape alive. Larrousse was his home for the next two years, but a trio of sixth places was

his paltry reward. He has since earned good money racing sports cars in Japan, winning the GT title for Nissan in both 1998 and 1999.

○ 59 Grands Prix, no wins (best result – 5th French GP 1982)
○ No drivers' title (best result – 11th 1992)

David Coulthard

Nationality: British
Born: 1971

After a successful kart career, David graduated to Formula Ford in 1989 and became the first winner of the McLaren/Autosport Young Driver award, being granted a run in a Formula One car. Beaten by Rubens Barrichello in the 1990 GM Euroseries and the 1991 British Formula Three series, he finished only ninth in Formula 3000 for Paul Stewart Racing in 1992. He won at Enna in 1993 to rank third. A greater success though, was his role as Williams test driver. No ride was forthcoming for 1994, so it was back to Formula 3000. Second in the opening race was followed by Ayrton Senna's death at Imola and thus David moved up to Formula One. He soon got on

to Damon Hill's pace and peaked with second in Portugal. David raced on at Williams in 1995, winning in Portugal and also leading in Belgium and Italy to end up third overall, but contractual obligations moved him to McLaren for 1996, where he and Hakkinen struggled to keep up with the Williams drivers.

David won first time out in 1997, however, later adding a win at Monza. Strong form at the start of 1998 laid the way open for a title battle with Hakkinen, but he slipped into a support role and once again finished up third. Winning only once dropped him to fourth in 1999, but three wins in 2000 gave him a shot at the title before his form dipped and he ended up third again. A strong start to 2001 produced two wins, but Michael Schumacher soon left him in his wake and he ended the year as runner-up. David held the upper hand over rookie team-mate Kimi Raikkonen in 2002, albeit winning only once, and could have won the first three races in 2003, but came away with just one win and was blown away in qualifying and ended the year seventh, five places behind his team-

mate. And so it was that 2004 was David's last year at McLaren and it was troubled for he and Raikkonen.

Moving to Red Bull Racing, formerly Jaguar, in 2005 was a welcome change and he revived his reputation as a real racer. This was made plain to all when he raced to a surprise third at Monte Carlo in 2006. Fourth in Japan was his highlight in 2007, then he used his experience to finish third in Canada in 2008. But, with young guns on the rise, he crossed over to be a TV pundit in 2009.

° 247 Grands Prix, 13 wins (Portuguese GP 1995, Australian GP 1997, Italian GP 1997, San Marino GP 1998, British GP 1999, Belgian GP 1999, British GP 2000, Monaco GP 2000, French GP 2000, Brazilian GP 2001, Austrian GP 2001, Monaco GP 2002, Australian GP 2003)
° No drivers' title (best result – 2nd overall 2001)

Piers Courage

Nationality: British
Born: 1942
Died: 1970

Heir to the Courage brewing fortunes, Piers cared little for brewing and

The Flying Scotsman: David Coulthard accelerates out of a hairpin as he puts his McLaren through its paces in preparation for the 2003 Monaco Grand Prix

chose to race cars instead. Since his father refused to give him financial support he had to make his own way in racing. With Jonathan Williams he formed Anglo-Swiss Racing and went after Formula Three glory across Europe. It was a hand-to-mouth existence, with both men looking to survive on their prize money. A more professional approach was employed in 1965 and Piers started to win races. However, he had a tendency to spin away good positions, and it was not until 1968 that he was given a proper crack at Formula One after shining in the Tasman series in New Zealand. Piers was given his break by Tim Parnell who asked him to drive a BRM, and was in the points before the year was out. For 1969 he teamed up with Frank Williams and he was promptly second at Monaco, matching this with second in the US Grand Prix. For the following season Williams ran him in a de Tomaso, but it was not a patch on the Brabham he used in 1969. However, Piers was then killed in a fiery accident in the Dutch Grand Prix.

○ 28 Grands Prix, no wins (best result – 2nd Monaco GP 1969, US GP 1969)
○ No drivers' title (best result – 8th 1969)

Yannick Dalmas

Nationality: French
Born: 1961

Yannick was French Formule Renault champion in 1984 and landed a top drive in Formula Three for 1985 with the crack ORECA team, finishing second overall. In time-honoured fashion, he stayed on to become team leader and won the title in 1986. Formula 3000 was next and Yannick won twice, but poor results elsewere left him fifth overall. Before the year was out, however, he had his first taste of Formula One with the Larrousse Camels team, scoring fifth place at his third attempt. However, he was adjudged not to have competed in enough grands prix to be eligible for points. Staying on with the team in 1988, he was not at his best, which he put down to ill health. Back with

Larrousse in 1989, things were even worse and Yannick was forced out of the team to make way for Michele Alboreto. He picked up a ride with the tiny French AGS team, but often failed to make it through pre-qualifying. The 1990 season was only slightly better. Career salvation came with a drive in the Peugeot sports car team, and Yannick won the Le Mans 24 Hours in 1992. Since 1993 it has been mainly a diet of touring cars for Yannick, but his trips to Le Mans have yielded three further wins – in 1994, 1995 and 1999.

○ 23 Grands Prix, no wins (best result – 7th Monaco GP 1988, US GP 1988)
○ No drivers' title

Derek Daly

Nationality: Irish
Born: 1953

Derek was Irish Formula Ford champion in 1975, Formula Ford Festival winner in 1976 and won the BP British Formula Three crown in 1977. He kicked off his Formula One career with the Hesketh team in 1978 by leading until spinning off in a very wet International Trophy race at Silverstone. His form in the World Championship was not so good, as he failed to qualify on all three outings. Crossing to Ensign was an improvement, and he scored a point before the year was out. A move to Tyrrell halfway through 1979 preceded a full season with Tyrrell in 1980 and his most spectacular shunt of all on the

Irish Motormouth: Derek Daly back in 1982

opening lap of the Monaco Grand Prix when he became airborne and landed right on his team-mate, Jean-Pierre Jarier. His ride with March did not yield a point in 1981. A ride with Theodore in 1982 looked equally dire, but Carlos Reutemann quit suddenly and Derek was asked to take his place at Williams alongside Keke Rosberg. The Finn went on to win the title, while the Irishman never made it to the podium and quit Formula One for IndyCars. Despite a leg-smashing shunt in 1984, Derek went on racing in IndyCars and then sports cars until 1992, and has since become a respected television commentator stateside.

○ 49 Grands Prix, no wins (best result – 4th Argentinian GP 1980, British GP 1980)
○ No drivers' title (best result – 10th 1980)

Cristiano da Matta

Nationality: Brazilian
Born: 1973

Born into a racing family, with his father Antonio a multiple Brazilian touring car champion, Cristiano was racing karts as soon as he was old enough. Brazilian champion in 1991, he claimed the Brazilian Formula Ford and Formula Three titles before heading to race in British Formula Three in 1995. He ranked eighth in that and then eighth in Formula 3000, but it was only when he headed to the United States in 1997 that his career regained momentum, as Cristiano ranked third in Indy Lights before winning the title the following year. This propelled him into IndyCars and he was a race winner in 2000 before winning the 2002 ChampCar crown for Newman-Haas Racing. Doing so with a Toyota engine helped him impress the manufacturer enough to offer him a crack in its F1 team in 2003. He did not disappoint, leading the British Grand Prix after an early scramble of the order. His best results were a pair of sixth-place finishes and he collected another sixth in 2004 before trying ChampCar in which he won at Portland in 2005, then escaped with head injuries in 2006 after being hit by a deer at Road America

○ 28 Grands Prix, no wins (best result – 6th Spanish GP 2003, German GP 2003, 2004 Monaco GP)
○ No drivers' title (best result – 13th 2003)

Christian Danner

Nationality: German
Born: 1958

Christian first came to prominence when he raced a BMW M1 in 1980. BMW signed him on a three-year contract and placed him in the works March Formula Two team for 1981, despite his having no single-seater experience. It took him until the end of 1983 to get on to the pace. Driving for Bob Sparshott, he was the inaugural Formula 3000 champion in 1985 and was given two Formula One outings by Zakspeed. A move to Osella for 1986 produced little and Christian joined Arrows mid-season, hitting the points in Austria. Returning to Zakspeed in 1987, he had little to cheer about. Christian's final shot at Formula One was with the new Rial team in 1989 and he came fourth at Phoenix, but only qualified once thereafter, and quit again for touring cars.

○ 36 Grands Prix, no wins (best result – 4th US GP 1989)
○ No drivers' title (best result – 18th overall 1986)

Elio de Angelis

Nationality: Italian
Born: 1958
Died: 1986

Very few drivers have reached Formula One as early in life as Elio did, for he had a full-time ride when he was just 20. Coming from a wealthy family, he cut his teeth on karts, then blasted into Formula Three, pipping Piercarlo Ghinzani to the 1977 Italian crown. He then won the 1978 Monaco Formula Three race, but had little to shout about in Formula Two. Family backing propelled him into Formula One for 1979 with Shadow. Elio picked up a fourth place at Watkins Glen, but the car was never really competitive. He

The Narrowest of Margins: Elio de Angelis pips Keke Rosberg's Williams to the post by five-hundredths of a second to win the Austrian Grand Prix in 1982

joined Lotus for 1980 and made the most of the superior equipment to finish second in his second outing, in Brazil. The following year showed consistent points scoring, then, in Austria in 1982, he had his first win, by a nose, from Keke Rosberg's Williams. A change to Renault engines scuppered 1983, but 1984 was much better and Elio ended up third overall. A second win was picked up in San Marino in 1985, and he led the title race awhile before falling back to fifth at season's end. Elio moved to Brabham for 1986 and it was while testing at Paul Ricard that he crashed and died.

∘ 108 Grands Prix, 2 wins (Austrian GP 1982, San Marino GP 1985)

∘ No drivers' title (best result – 3rd overall 1984)

Andrea de Cesaris

Nationality: Italian
Born: 1959

Andrea's passage to Formula One was eased by strong Marlboro connections. However, along the way, he was world karting champion, finished second to Chico Serra in the 1979 British Formula Three series and placed fifth for Ron Dennis's Project Four Formula Two team.

Before 1980 was out Andrea made his Formula One debut with Alfa Romeo. He drove for McLaren in 1981, but was he wild! By the season's end, he had scored but one point and junked numerous chassis.

Without powerful backers, his F1 career would have ended there and then, particularly if the other drivers had been given a say. He simply scared them all with his highly unpredictable driving.

However, Andrea spent 1982 and 1983 with Alfa Romeo. He came third at Monaco in 1982 but he could have won. Lying second going on to the final lap behind Didier Pironi, he was

gifted the lead when the Ferrari's electrics failed but, cruelly, Andrea had run out of fuel.

Andrea led again, at Spa in 1983, but his engine blew, and even though he scored two second places, he was on to pastures new – Ligier – for 1984. Two seasons with the French team produced little, so then Andrea went to Minardi, then Brabham, then Rial, then Dallara, then Jordan, then Tyrrell, Jordan again and finally to Sauber before his Formula One days ended in 1994 with Andrea the second-most-experienced Formula One driver ever, behind Riccardo Patrese. But still with no win...

∘ 208 Grands Prix, no wins (best result – 2nd German GP 1983, South African GP 1983)

∘ No drivers' title (best result – 8th overall 1983)

Emmanuel de Graffenried

Nationality: Swiss
Born: 1914

"Toulo", or Baron de Graffenried to be correct, was one of the stars in the post-war years, winning the 1949 British Grand Prix in a Maserati. He drove the same car when the World Championship began in 1950 and struggled against his rivals' newer equipment. Alfa Romeo gave him a run at the non-championship Geneva Grand Prix and he came second. Alfa signed him for 1951. In 1952 and 1953, he raced with a Maserati, coming fourth in the 1953 Belgian Grand Prix – his best result. He also won the non-championship Syracuse Grand Prix.

∘ 22 Grands Prix, no wins (best result – 4th Belgian GP 1953)

∘ No drivers' title (best result – 8th overall 1953)

Pedro de la Rosa

Nationality: Spanish
Born: 1971

Spanish Formula Ford champion in 1990, Pedro won the British and European Formula Renault titles in 1991. A strong first year of Formula Three suggested a title bid in 1994, but weak Renault engines wrecked that. He dominated Japanese Formula Three in 1995. Formula Nippon champion in 1997, he became Jordan's test driver before landing a full-time ride with Arrows in 1999, scoring on his debut.

Pedro ran third twice in 2000, but mechanical failure forced him out. Joining Jaguar in mid-2001, he scored twice, but his second season was pointless, and Pedro became a test driver for McLaren, being rewarded with one outing at Bahrain in 2005, then eight more in 2006 when Juan Pablo Montoya quit, finishing a career-best second in Hungary. Remaining as McLaren test driver paid off when he lined up his racing return with BMW Sauber for 2010.

° 71 Grands Prix, no wins (best result – 2nd Hungarian GP 2006)

° No drivers' title (best result – 11th overall 2006)

Patrick Depailler

Nationality: French
Born: 1944
Died: 1980

For years it looked as though this little Frenchman would always be bridesmaid and never the bride in Formula One. Then, at the Monaco Grand Prix in 1978, after collecting a frustrating total of eight second places, he finally came good to climb the top step on the podium.

Patrick had a lengthy but muddled schooling in Formula Three and Formula Two that saw him step back down to Formula Three in 1971 and claim the French title. Armed with this, he won the Monaco Formula Three race and was rewarded with two Formula One outings by Tyrrell, finishing seventh at Watkins Glen.

However, he spent the rest of the year in Formula Two, and 1973 and 1974, when he won the European title. But 1974 was also his first full season of Formula One. Patrick did well, too, with a second place in Sweden. The next four years were spent driving with Tyrrell, with points scores aplenty, but only that one win at Monaco to his name.

A move to Ligier in 1979 brought another win, in Spain, and he joined Alfa Romeo for 1980, but when testing before that year's German Grand Prix, Patrick crashed fatally.
○ 95 Grands Prix, 2 wins (Monaco GP 1978, Spanish GP 1979)
○ No drivers' title (best result – 4th overall 1976)

Pedro Diniz

Nationality: Brazilian
Born: 1970

This charming Brazilian will never be allowed to forget that he bought his way into Formula One. Formula Three was followed by two years in Formula 3000 that produced the odd flash of speed.

Pedro bought his way into the Forti Corse team when it first arrived in Formula One in 1995, then moved to Ligier for 1996, and on to Arrows in 1997, where he was sometimes faster than team-mate Damon Hill and where he also pushed Mika Salo hard in 1998.

Moving to Sauber in 1999, Pedro was sixth three times, but failed to score in 2000, making several driving mistakes that earned him the scorn of his rivals. His family's bid to take over the Prost team failed in 2001.
○ 99 Grands Prix, no wins (best result – 5th Luxembourg GP 1997, Belgian GP 1998)
○ No drivers' title (best result – 13th overall 1998)

Lost in Translation: Mark Donohue was Mr Successful in American racing but failed to dominate F1

Martin Donnelly

Nationality: British
Born: 1964

One of the stars of the British scene in the 1980s, this Ulsterman was quick both in Formula Ford 2000 and then in Formula Three. Halfway through 1988, he jumped up to Formula 3000, scoring two wins and two second places from four outings for Eddie Jordan Racing to place third overall. Staying on in Formula 3000 in 1989 was not proving so successful, but Martin took the opportunity to make his Formula One debut in France for Arrows. A full-time ride with Lotus was his reward for 1990 and Martin was doing increasingly well, matching the pace of experienced team-mate Derek Warwick, when he had a huge shunt in qualifying for the Spanish Grand Prix. His car disintegrated and Martin was left in the the track strapped only to his seat. His injuries were horrific, but he fought back to health, even having a test in a Formula 3000 car, but he has since focused on managing teams on the British single-seater scene.
○ 13 Grands Prix, no wins (best result – 7th Hungarian GP 1990)
○ No drivers' title

Mark Donohue

Nationality: American
Born: 1937
Died: 1975

Mr Successful in American racing, Mark never made the grade in Formula One. His early career was financed by sports car driver Walt Hansgen, but then Roger Penske signed him up. This pair won the TransAm title and the Daytona 24 Hours in 1968 and 1969, then took second place in the 1970 Indy 500, won the TransAm series again, led the Indy 500 and won an IndyCar race. Mark made his Formula One debut in a Penske-entered McLaren in the Canadian Grand Prix, finishing third. He won the Indy 500 in 1972, but was injured by crashing his CanAm Porsche.

Using the same turbocharged Porsche, he stormed the 1973 CanAm series, then announced his retirement, but returned when Penske decided to go to Formula One in 1974. The Penske chassis was not a success and it was replaced with a March after Mark had scored one fifth place. He was fifth first time out in the March, but a crash in practice for the Austrian Grand Prix left him unconscious. He apppeared to recover, but died from a brain haemorrhage two days later.
○ 14 Grands Prix, no wins (best result – 3rd Canadian GP 1971)
○ No drivers' title (best result – 15th overall 1975)

Johnny Dumfries

Nationality: British
Born: 1958

Johnny tried to pass himself off as a painter and decorator when he started in Formula Ford, certain that if people discovered he was the Marquis of Bute, they would make life hard for him. He won the 1984 British Formula Three title and came third in a close-fought European series. His crack at Formula 3000 with the Onyx team in 1985 was less successful and he quit mid-season. Help was at hand, though, as Ayrton Senna did not want Derek Warwick to join him at Lotus in 1986, convinced that the team could not run cars for two topline drivers. So, amid a furore, Warwick was turned away and Dumfries found himself in Formula One. He was very much the team's number two, and lost his drive when Lotus signed to use Honda engines in 1987 and a Japanese driver came as part of the deal. A spell in sports cars followed, and he won the 1988 Le Mans 24 Hours for Jaguar. He has run a historic festival on his family estate in Scotland since 2002.

○ 15 Grands Prix, no wins (best result – 5th Hungarian GP 1986)
○ No drivers' title (best result – 13th overall 1986)

Guy Edwards

Nationality: British
Born: 1942

Guy gained a reputation more as a sponsorship-chaser than for his driving. He scored his best results in the European 2-litre sports car series and in Formula 5000. In 1974 he got his break in Formula One with the Embassy Hill team, but it was not a front-runner. In 1976 he came back with a Penthouse-sponsored Hesketh, but found this even further off the pace and retired to the Aurora British Formula One series in which he had far more success. Since hanging up his helmet, he has worked as a sponsorship consultant, linking Silk Cut to the Jaguar sports car team before taking his portfolio to Lotus. This was not a success and the team folded at the end of 1994 with massive debts.

○ 11 Grands Prix, no wins (best result – 7th Swedish GP 1974)
○ No drivers' title

Vic Elford

Nationality: British
Born: 1935

A winner in rallies, rallycross and sports cars, Vic was no slouch either when it came to Formula One machinery. He had a very good year in 1968, for he won the Monte Carlo Rally, the Daytona 24 Hours, the Targa Florio and the Nurburgring 1,000kms, and, on top of those victories, he made his Formula One debut, albeit in a Cooper when Coopers were no longer the cars to have.

Somehow, he carried one around to a fourth- and a fifth-place finish. A privately entered McLaren followed for 1969, but Vic hit some debris in the German Grand Prix, crashed and broke his arm, putting his career into a downward spiral. Since 1974 he has run a racing school in the US.

○ 13 Grands Prix, no wins (best result – 4th French GP 1968)
○ No drivers' title (best result – 13th overall 1969)

Harald Ertl

Nationality: Austrian
Born: 1948
Died: 1982

This bearded Austrian journalist worked his way through the German Formula Vee, Super Vee and then Formula Three series before turning to touring cars, where he won the Tourist Trophy for BMW at Silverstone in 1973.

His Formula One break took a long time to arrive. It wasn't until 1975 that he finally landed a ride in a privately entered Hesketh. But Harald continued to plug away for the next two seasons with the Hesketh team and also raced concurrently in Formula Two. Then, in 1978, he changed across to an Ensign, but had little success and elected to race in the radical Group 5 series in Germany. Sadly, Harald lost his life in a light aircraft crash in 1982.

○ 18 Grands Prix, no wins (best result – 7th British GP 1976)
○ No drivers' title

One Season Only: Johnny Dumfries was Ayrton Senna's team-mate in 1986, but lost his ride when the team did a deal with Honda

Like Father Like Son: Teo Fabi, pictured here in his Benetton B187-Ford at the 1987 British Grand Prix at Silverstone, is now using his experience to help his son Stefano progress in the world of Formula Three

Philippe **Etancelin**

Nationality: French
Born: 1896
Died: 1981

A prosperous farmer and wool merchant, "Phi Phi" was another of the over-50s gang who lined up on the grid at Silverstone in 1950 for the first-ever World Championship round. It was a different world back then.

Famed for his back-to-front cloth cap, he had starred for Bugatti in the 1930s and had won the Le Mans 24 Hours for Alfa Romeo in 1934, with Luigi Chinetti. The following year he was injured in an accident when his car overturned.

He raced an aged Lago-Talbot in 1950, yet still scored two fifth place finishes, before retiring from the World Championship in 1952.

o 12 Grands Prix, no wins (best result – 5th French GP 1950, Italian GP 1950)
o No drivers' title (best result – 13th overall 1950)

Teo **Fabi**

Nationality: Italian
Born: 1955

European karting champion in 1975, he duly graduated through Formula Three to land a ride in Formula Two for 1979. Despite a mixed season, he was signed to lead the works March squad in 1980, finishing third behind the dominant Tolemans. Set for a move with March to Formula One for 1981, he lost the drive to Derek Daly and so went to the US and shone in the CanAm sports car series. Teo got his Formula One break in 1982, though, with Toleman. It was a wretched year and he was glad when long-time backer Robin Herd helped him land an IndyCar ride for 1983. Teo claimed pole for the Indy 500 and notched up four wins. Back in Formula One in 1984, with Brabham, he scored his first points with third place around the streets of Detroit. His first pole came with Toleman in 1985, at the

Nurburgring, but he retired with clutch failure. Indeed, Teo retired most races. Toleman metamorphosed into the Benetton team in 1986, and Teo took two more poles near the end of the year, again without results to match this expertise in qualifying in the wild days of turbocharged engines that would hold together only for a few pumped-up laps. The 1987 season was more successful in terms of gathering points, but it was to be Teo's last in Formula One, as he moved back to IndyCars. He chose to drive the Porsche project car. It did not work, so he went sports car racing and won the 1991 world title for Jaguar. He drifted back to IndyCars, but has since returned to Italy and oversaw his son Stefano's ascent to Formula Three.

o 64 Grands Prix, no wins (best result – 3rd US GP East 1984, Austrian GP 1987)
o No drivers' title (best result – 9th overall 1987)

Luigi **Fagioli**

Nationality: Italian
Born: 1898
Died: 1952

One of the top names in Italian racing in the golden days of the 1930s, Luigi was a race winner for Maserati, Alfa Romeo and then Auto Union. He was almost 52 when the World Championship began in 1950. His maturity helped him collect points aplenty, with four second places, to finish third overall.

Being asked in 1951 to hand his car over to Fangio during the French Grand Prix was too much for Luigi and, even though Fangio went on to win, he quit Formula One that very instant. A career in sports cars came to an end in 1952 when he crashed at Monaco and died of his injuries.

o 7 Grands Prix, 1 win (French GP 1951, shared with Fangio)
o No drivers' title (best result – 3rd overall 1950)

JUAN MANUEL FANGIO
Five-Times Champion

Juan Manuel came to be known universally as "the maestro". He won five world titles and 24 races from 51 starts. He was noted for being able to win a race at the slowest possible speed and, although older than his rivals, had enormous staying power, with Stirling Moss the only driver capable of giving him a hard time.

Born in Balcarce, Argentina, he was the son of an Italian immigrant and had his first taste of racing while riding as a mechanic in a Chevrolet driven by a customer of the garage where he worked. After military service, Juan Manuel started to drive in long and hazardous road races. He enjoyed great success until wartime restrictions intervened.

Racing returned in 1947 and he was intrigued by visiting Italians Achille Varzi and Luigi Villoresi. The Argentine Automobile Club had bought two Maseratis to be driven against them and one was entrusted to him.

Juan Manuel was highly impressed by the European scene, but he came close to quitting before achieving anything as, on his return home to Argentina, he crashed in a road race and his co-driver was killed.

With the backing of the Perón regime, Juan Manuel was sent to Europe and started winning regularly in 1949. As Alfa Romeo prepared for the first World Championship in 1950, Fangio was given a drive. He was pipped to the title by team-mate Nino Farina, but gained the first of his five World Championships the following season.

The Alfa 159 was now past its sell-by date so Juan Manuel moved to Maserati. He then broke his neck in an accident at Monza, which kept him out of action until 1953. When he returned with Maserati, the scene was dominated by Ferrari.

Juan Manuel won the first couple of races in 1954 with Maserati, but Mercedes poached him to head their team. He won another four races that year before taking a second title in 1955 with four victories.

At the end of 1955 Mercedes withdrew because of the Le Mans disaster and Juan Manuel joined Ferrari. The championship became a race between himself, team-mate, Peter Collins and Maserati's Stirling Moss. At Monza, Collins handed his car over after Juan Manuel's had failed, guaranteeing the Argentinian a fourth title.

He returned to Maserati in 1957 and won the championship for the last time. The race that clinched it was his greatest: the German Grand Prix at the Nurburgring. Ferrari had Collins and Mike Hawthorn against him and Maserati tried starting Juan Manuel with a light fuel load so that he could build up a lead, refuel and get out in front. However, a slow stop meant that he was 45 seconds down when he rejoined and he had to drive like a man possessed. Although carrying a heavier fuel load, he took six seconds per lap out of them, blasting past Collins with a lap and a half to go, and then forcing his way past Hawthorn.

In 1958, Juan Manuel was fourth in his home grand prix and then drove his last race in the French Grand Prix, where he also finished fourth.

- 51 Grands Prix, 24 wins
- World Champion 1951, 1954, 1955, 1956 and 1957

Heading For Number One: "The Maestro" wins at Reims for Alfa Romeo en route to the 1951 title

1911	1940	1949	1951	1952	1954	1957	1995
Born 24 June in Balcarce, Argentina	Won the Gran Premio del Nacional in a works Chevrolet	Won Mar del Plata GP and then headed for Europe, where he won five of the lesser grands prix, but his form was noted	Won three grands prix again, but this time it was enough to make him World Champion	Took six wins in non-championship South American races, but broke his neck in the Monza GP and missed the season	World Champion for Mercedes, winning first two races in a Maserati before Mercedes was ready, then adding four more victories	Returned to Maserati and four wins in the first five races set him up for his fifth title	Died on 17 July at home in Argentina

1928	1948	1950	1953	1955	1956	1958
Road racing in Argentina, without his parents' knowledge	Turned to single-seaters to take on visiting Europeans. Was sponsored by Perón's government to race in Europe	Runner-up to Alfa Romeo team-mate Giuseppe Farina, winning three rounds and four non-championship races	Joined Maserati and finished second to Ferrari's Alberto Ascari, despite not winning until final round. Won the Carrera Panamericana	World Champion again for Mercedes, winning four of the six races	Had to overcome Moss's Maserati before claiming his fourth title, winning three times	Ran own Maserati in two grands prix, but, after finishing fourth in the French GP, he retired

GIUSEPPE FARINA
The First World Champion

"Nino" Farina is the name at the top of the list of Formula One history as he was the winner of the inaugural World Championship, in 1950. He should also be recalled, however, as one of the sport's most prolific crashers.

He started in hill climbs in the early-1930s, but crashed first time out and hospitalized himself. "Nino" progressed to circuit racing the following year with a Maserati, then raced an Alfa Romeo under the tutelage of the great Tazio Nuvolari. He made mistakes aplenty in an age when mistakes were frequently punished with a fatal outcome, but kept coming back for more and became a grand prix winner at Naples in 1937. "Nino" won the Italian drivers' title in 1937, 1938 and 1939, all for Alfa Romeo, with increasing success in assorted grands prix around Europe where he gave chase to the dominant works entries from Auto Union and Mercedes, thus putting himself into a strong position to land a top drive when the Second World War ended.

He won the Grand Prix des Nations in Geneva for Alfa Romeo when racing resumed in 1946, but had a disagreement and quit the works team.

After several years of racing privately entered Maseratis and works Ferraris and enjoying continued success in the assorted grands prix that made up the free-form calendar, "Nino" rejoined Alfa Romeo for 1950 and was duly rewarded when he won that first ever World Championship title - winning three of the year's grand

Say It with Flowers: Farina is jubilant after winning the British Grand Prix at Silverstone, May 1950

total of six grands prix in the process.

A model to other colleagues with his straight-arm driving style, "Nino" could not match the pace of his team-mate Juan Manuel Fangio in 1951 and ended up fourth overall, having won only the Belgian Grand Prix. For 1952

he joined Ferrari, but this did not produce a race win - apart from ones in the non-championship races that proliferated back then - until the 1953 German Grand Prix, as he was overshadowed by Ferrari team-mate Alberto Ascari.

Engulfed in flames in a sports car race at Monza at the start of 1954, shortly after opening his campaign with second place in the Argentinian Grand Prix and breaking an arm in a crash in the Mille Miglia, "Nino" had to take time off to recover from his burns and was not back in the cockpit until 1955. However, this return did not last long as he was unable to live with the pain when racing and had to dose himself with morphine. So, "Nino" elected to retire midway through the season.

Sadly, he was unable to stay away and dabbled with the Indy 500 in 1956, failing to qualify, then broke a collarbone in practice for a sports car race. He entered a car for the Indy 500 in 1957, but his driver Keith Andrews was killed in practice and so "Nino" quit the sport. Well, almost, as he was killed in a car crash on the way to the French Grand Prix nine years later, at the age of 59.

- **33 Grands Prix, 5 wins**
- **World Champion 1950**

1906	1936	1940	1950	1952	1955	1966
Born 30 October in Turin, Italy	Joined Alfa Romeo line-up, run by Scuderia Ferrari. Finished second in Mille Miglia	Won the Tripoli GP and was second in the Mille Miglia, but the Second World War intervened	Rejoined Alfa Romeo and became first World Champion when he won three times and overcame intra-team challenge with Fangio	Joined Ferrari and finished as runner-up to Alberto Ascari. Triumphed in non-championship Monza GP and Goodwood's Woodcote Cup	Still in pain, he ranked fifth overall for Ferrari, but retired at the end of the year because of his burns	Died in a road accident on his way to the French GP

1932	1939	1946	1951	1953	1954	1956
Started competing in hill climbs, but crashed first time out and broke a shoulder	Won three grands prix and claimed third consecutive Italian drivers' title. Led Swiss Grand Prix	Resumed racing and won Grand Prix des Nations in Geneva. Quit Alfa Romeo team after a disagreement	Won only once for Alfa Romeo as Fangio dominated and he fell to fourth overall	Won German GP for Ferrari and finished third overall, also winning six non-championship races	Became Ferrari team leader, but curtailed year by breaking arm in Mille Miglia. Then his Ferrari burst into flames in a sports car race at Monza and his legs were burned	Made comeback to race in the Indy 500, but project failed

Sealed With a Kiss: Ginacarlo Fisichella shows his delight at winning for Renault in Malaysia 2006

Giancarlo Fisichella

Nationality: Italian
Born: 1973

Italian Formula Three champion in 1994, Giancarlo was groomed by Alfa Romeo in 1995 and 1996 in the International Touring Car Championship. But he also got a crack at Formula One with Minardi. Moving to Jordan for 1997 saw him lead in Germany then finish second at Spa. Giancarlo took two seconds for Benetton in 1998 and was second at Montreal in 1999, but Benetton lost ground. He was on the podium again in 2000, but 2001 was a struggle with an underpowered Renault engine. A swap with Jarno Trulli took him back to Jordan for 2002, but with an unreliable Honda engine. Ford power was even more disappointing

in 2003, save for Brazil where rain, then a stoppage, left him the victor. Tired of waiting for an opening with a top team, Giancarlo moved to Sauber for 2004, but a hop on to Renault for 2005 was rewarded with victory in the opening round, although team-mate Fernando Alonso generally put him in the shade, as he did in 2006 when Giancarlo again won but once as Alonso took the title for a second year in a row. With Alonso moving to McLaren, 2007 ought to have been better, but he slipped to eighth.

It was all-change for 2008 as Giancarlo moved to Force India. There were no points, but a more competitive car in 2009 helped him to pole and second place in Belgium before he fulfilled a dream by crossing over to finish the year with Ferrari.

° 231 Grands Prix, 3 wins (Brazilian GP 2003, Australian GP 2005, Malaysian GP 2006)
° No drivers' title (best result – 4th overall 2006)

Christian Fittipaldi

Nationality: Brazilian
Born: 1971

Son of Wilson Fittipaldi and nephew of Emerson, Christian raced in British Formula Three in 1990, peaking with victory in the final round, ahead of his team-mate Mika Hakkinen. Christian was Formula 3000 champion at his first attempt with Pacific in 1991. And so he found himself in Formula One in 1992, joining Minardi. He kicked off 1993 with fourth in Brazil, but this form was not repeated and his most famed move was his attempt to pass Pierluigi Martini at the finish at Monza, with Christian clipping his team-mate's car and flipping before landing on his remaining wheels. Two more fourth places followed for Footwork in 1994, but Christian was soon to become disaffected and decided on a transfer to the IndyCar circuit for 1995. Looking for a change of scene, he has since started racing in NASCAR's top stock car category.

° 40 Grands Prix, no wins (best result – 4th South African GP 1993, Pacific GP 1994, German GP 1994)
° No drivers' title (best result – 13th overall 1993)

Emerson Fittipaldi

SEE PAGE 146

Wilson Fittipaldi

Nationality: Brazilian
Born: 1943

He may have started racing first, but he was almost immediately overshadowed by his younger brother Emerson. He followed Emerson to Europe, but his foray was not so successful and he did not return there until 1970 to race in Formula Three. Formula Two followed in 1971 and Wilson raced in Formula One for the first time in 1972 with Brabham. Two

Wilson Fittipaldi with Carlos Reutemann in Austria, 1972

seasons yielded two points-scoring drives, and he lost third place in the 1973 Monaco Grand Prix when his car failed to pick up its fuel. And so Wilson quit Formula One in 1974. He was back a year later, though, with his own Brazilian-built car. It was not a success and he retired to run Emerson in the team for the next five years.

° 36 Grands Prix, no wins (best result – 5th German GP 1973)
° No drivers' title (best result – 15th overall 1973)

Ron Flockhart

Nationality: British
Born: 1923
Died: 1962

Ron came to prominence on the British scene when he started racing an ERA in the early 1950s. He made his grand prix debut at Silverstone in 1954, then came home third in a Connaught in the 1956 Italian Grand Prix. He also won the Le Mans 24 Hours that year, and the next, before landing a full-time ride with BRM in 1959. The results he desired did not follow, however, and Ron went off to become a pilot. He died in 1962, crashing in Australia while practising

EMERSON FITTIPALDI
The First Fast Brazilian

Emerson will be remembered by many for his trademark sunglasses and sideburns, but it is for his remarkable rise to the top that others will remember him. Indeed, it was only with the phenomenon started by Kimi Raikkonen in the 21st century that we have witnessed anything similar. It is safe to say that few people have ever achieved as much as fast in motor racing as Emerson. His early career was meteoric.

Inspired by his father who was a sports commentator, Emerson started on 50cc motorbikes, then followed his older brother Wilson into karts and both progressed to cars, racing, of all things, a Renault Gordini.

Having trounced the opposition in Brazil, winning the national Formula Vee championship, Emerson moved to Europe in 1969. He bought a Formula Ford car and just could not stop winning. Racing school proprietor Jim Russell recognized his talent and signed Emerson to race his Formula Three Lotus. He duly won the Lombank Formula Three title that year and Lotus signed him for its Formula Two team for 1970 and, in mid-season, team boss Colin Chapman hurried Emerson into Formula One, partly to forestall rival team managers from signing him.

Proving that he was a fast learner even at the sport's highest level, he won fifth time out, at Watkins Glen, giving Lotus a much-needed boost after the death of lead driver Jochen Rindt at the previous race.

No victories followed in 1971, with a best of second place in the Austrian Grand Prix, but Emerson still claimed the 1972 title and in

Bad Career Move: joining the family business must have been Emerson's biggest mistake

so doing became the youngest champion of all time.

Runner-up to Jackie Stewart in 1973, he moved to McLaren and won the 1974 title, following this by finishing as runner-up to Niki Lauda in 1975.

Then, however, something happened to derail this golden career: he left McLaren to join brother Wilson's team, Copersucar for 1976. Emerson's

brilliance coaxed the car into a top-three position twice over the next five years, but his talents were wasted in generally inferior equipment and he called it a day.

Demoralized and needing a change of scenery, as he was now without hope of driving for a top team again, Emerson quit at the end of 1980. However, he did not stay in retirement for long as he was invited to race in a sports car race in 1984 and enjoyed it so much that he accepted an invitation to race in the Long Beach IndyCar race. Finishing fifth in that convinced him to race full-time again and he was back on the victory trail in 1985 for Patrick Racing, going on to become champion in 1989, having won the Indy 500.

Emerson won the big race again in 1993, this time for Penske, and remained one of the big names stateside, continuing to outpace drivers half his age, including his nephew Christian, until he injured his back in a massive accident at Michigan in 1996. This took him out of racing, but any thoughts that Emerson had of a return were scotched when he suffered further back injuries in a light aircraft accident the following year.

○ **144 Grands Prix, 14 wins**
○ **World Champion 1972 and 1974**

1946	1969	1972	1974	1976	1980	1989	1996
Born 12 December in Saõ Paulo, Brazil	Headed to Britain, immediately impressed in Formula Ford and was put into Formula Three by racing school boss Jim Russell	Won five grands prix to become World Champion. Also won four non-championship races	Joined McLaren and became World Champion again by winning the Brazilian, Belgian and Canadian GPs	Raced for brother's Copersucar team, and fifth on grid for Brazilian GP was to be his best over the next five years with team	Third at Long Beach was sole highlight and he quit	Scored five wins, including Indy 500, to win Indy Car title	Injured his back in accident at Michigan and sat out the rest of year

	1967	1970		1973	1975	1978	1984	1993	2003
	Won Brazilian Formula Vee Championship	Third in European Formula Two for Lotus. Also made Formula One debut with Lotus and won fourth race, the US GP		Won three of first four races, but none thereafter and ended year as runner-up to Tyrrell's Jackie Stewart	Won Argentinian GP but only won British GP after that and was runner-up to Niki Lauda	Second place in the Brazilian GP and five other point-scoring drives helped Emerson finish ninth overall	Invited to drive in sports car race and liked it so much he turned out in Long Beach Indy Car race, finishing fifth	Won the Indy 500 for Penske and added two more wins to be runner-up to Nigel Mansell	Entered own team – Fittipaldi Dingmann Racing – in Champ Cars

for a record attempt on the London to Sydney route.
- 13 Grands Prix, no wins (best result – 3rd French GP 1956)
- No drivers' title (best result – 11th overall 1956)

George Follmer

Nationality: American
Born: 1934

Formula One seemed a long way from George's ambitions during his lengthy spell racing sports cars in the US. However, at the age of 39, he found himself making his grand prix debut, for Shadow. This came in 1973 and he ran the whole season, peaking with third place second time out, at the Spanish Grand Prix. At the end of the year he returned to the US scene, racing again in the CanAm sports car series and then winning the 1976 TransAm title in a Porsche.
- 12 Grands Prix, no wins (best result – 3rd Spanish GP 1973)
- No drivers' title (best result – 13th overall 1973)

Heinz-Harald Frentzen

Nationality: German
Born: 1967

Heinz-Harald graduated from karting to Formula Ford. He raced in the 1988 GM Euroseries, giving Mika Hakkinen a hard time in the final two rounds. He was then second in German Formula Three in 1989, behind Karl Wendlinger but ahead of Michael Schumacher. A move into sports cars with the Mercedes junior team followed.

He drove in Formula 3000 at the same time, but it did not propel him to Formula One, so he raced in Japanese Formula 3000. Good form clinched a ride with Sauber for 1994. He drove some storming races in 1995 against superior cars, coming third at Monza. Replacing Damon Hill at Williams in 1997, he won at Imola, but no wins followed and he moved to Jordan for 1999. Victories at Magny-Cours and Monza ranked him third overall, but his 2000 campaign was less satisfactory as he had to settle for a pair of

A Bigger Splash: Jordan boss Eddie Jordan is drenched in champagne by runner-up Ralf Schumacher and winner Heinz-Harald Frentzen (centre) at Monza, 1999

thirds. Jordan dropped him during 2001 and a shift to Prost saved his career, but the team folded and Heinz-Harald was snapped up by Arrows for 2002. This was no dream move, though, as the team folded before the year was out. After standing in at Sauber for one race, he joined them full-time for 2003. Yet, despite finishing a surprise third at the rain-hit US Grand Prix, he was dropped at season's end.
- 158 Grands Prix, 3 wins (San Marino GP 1997, French GP 1999, Italian GP 1999)
- No drivers' title (best result – 2nd overall 1997)

Paul Frère

Nationality: Belgian
Born: 1917

A motoring journalist who came good, Paul was always eager to retain his training and race for fun. With remarkably little experience beyond racing an MG, he found himself driving an HWM in the 1952 Belgian Grand Prix and he came fifth...

Paul was in and out of drives in the latter half of the 1950s and thus his second-place finish for Ferrari at Spa in 1956 was the utmost surprise. He also managed to win the Le Mans 24 Hours in 1960.
- 11 Grands Prix, no wins (best result – 2nd Belgian GP 1956)
- No drivers' title (best result – 7th overall 1956)

Bertrand Gachot

Nationality: Belgian
Born: 1962

A cosmopolitan mixture of Belgian, French and Luxembourgeois, Bertrand was the first driver to race under the flag of the European Community. Trained when in karting never to cede a corner to another driver, even if it meant crashing himself, he gained the reputation of being uncompromising. Bertrand was a contemporary of Mark Blundell, Damon Hill and Johnny Herbert in British Formula Ford in the mid-1980s, and he finished as the runner-up to Herbert in the 1987 British Formula Three Championship, before graduating to Formula 3000 and then straight on to Formula One in 1989. Unfortunately, Bernard joined the Moneytron Onyx team and seldom qualified. An even worse year followed in 1990 when he drove the overweight, Subaru-powered Coloni. Salvation came in 1991, from Jordan. And all was going well, including fifth place in Canada, when Bertrand was jailed for spraying CS gas in the face of a London taxi driver. Back with Larrousse in 1992, he struggled through 1994 with Pacific as a shareholder of the team.

He was forced to stand down when funds ran short in 1995.

○ 42 Grands Prix, no wins (best result – 5th Canadian GP 1991)

○ No drivers' title (best result – 12th overall 1991)

Howden Ganley

Nationality: New Zealander
Born: 1941

Lacking racing opportunities in New Zealand, Howden came to England at the age of 19 and found employment as a mechanic. That was in 1961, and it was not until 1967 that he had earned enough for a real crack at Formula Three. Success was slow in coming, and only in 1970 did he enter the limelight by finishing second to Peter Gethin in the Formula 5000 Championship. This helped him land a Formula One ride with BRM for 1971. Points were scored before the end of the year, and Howden stayed with BRM for 1972, albeit with little improvement in form, although he did finish second in the Le Mans 24 Hours. Changing to Frank Williams' young team in 1973 failed to help since the Iso chassis was no world beater, and he quit the sport's top category after two races with March and two non-qualifiying runs with the Japanese Maki chassis in 1974. Howden joined forces with fellow Formula One racer Tim Schenken to form the Tiga (Tim/Ganley) race car manufacturing company.

○ 35 Grands Prix, no wins (best result – 4th US GP 1971, German GP 1972)

○ No drivers' title (best result – 12th overall 1972)

Olivier Gendebien

Nationality: Belgian
Born: 1924

Olivier met up with a rally driver while he was working in the Belgian Congo and agreed to try his luck as a co-driver on his return to Europe in the mid-1950s. Their performances led to the offer of a works Ferrari sports car drive, backed up with selected Formula One outings. Amazingly,

Olivier placed fifth on his debut, the 1956 Argentinian Grand Prix. By and large, though, such Formula One outings were limited and his success was restricted to sports cars: indeed, he won the Le Mans 24 Hours an incredible four times between 1958 and 1962. It was not until 1960 that he got a fair run, with a Yeoman Credit Cooper. Immediately the results came, with third place in Belgium followed by a second-place finish in the French Grand Prix. However, after driving for a mixture of teams in 1961, he quit for sports cars.

○ 14 Grands Prix, no wins (best result – 2nd French GP 1960)

○ No drivers' title (best result – 6th overall 1960)

Peter Gethin

Nationality: British
Born: 1940

A hundredth of a second was the advantage Peter had over Ronnie Peterson when he scored his one and only grand prix win, at Monza in 1971. It was the blink of an eye, but the moment of a lifetime. Having chosen not to follow his father and become a jockey, Peter served his apprenticeship in club racing instead, starting in 1962 in a Lotus 7. In Formula Three by 1965, he raced in Europe and graduation did not come until 1968. The formation of Formula 5000 in 1969 gave him the boost he needed in a semi-works McLaren. He won the title, and repeated the feat in 1970. By the time of the second title, though, he had a handful of grands prix under his belt, having been seconded into the McLaren line-up after Bruce McLaren's death, scoring once. He failed to score for McLaren in 1971, but changed to BRM and scored his famous win in Italy. He was only to finish in the points on one more occasion. Peter won the Pau Grand Prix for Formula Two cars and raced on in Formula 5000 until 1977.

○ 30 Grands Prix, 1 win (Italian GP 1971)

○ No drivers' title (best result – 9th overall 1971)

Piercarlo Ghinzani

Nationality: Italian
Born: 1952

It was through the clinching of deals that Piercarlo extended his Formula One career from 1981 to 1989 with a points tally of just two... Considering he started in motor racing in 1970, his rise to Formula One was very slow. It took him until 1973 to reach Formula Three. He won the European title in 1977 and moved on to Formula Two. A Formula One ride was clinched in 1981 when he joined Osella, and he stayed with the team until mid-1985 when he crossed over to Toleman, scoring his only points at Dallas in 1984. He was back with Osella in 1986; then Ligier, Zakspeed and Osella – for a third time – before he finally called it a day.

○ 76 Grands Prix, no wins (best result – 5th US GP 1984)

○ No drivers' title (best result – 19th overall 1984)

Bruno Giacomelli

Nationality: Italian
Born: 1952

There was something about Bruno that appealed to both team managers (his speed), the press (his approachability) and fans (he

Three-Way Appeal: Bruno Giacomelli

looked so cuddly). He was first seen in Britain in 1976 when he did all he could to stop Rupert Keegan from winning the Formula Three title. March showed faith in him and Bruno raced for Robin Herd's team in 1977 in Formula Two, also making his Formula One debut for McLaren at Monza. McLaren briefly ran Bruno again in 1978, and then he joined Alfa Romeo, for whom he raced until the end of 1982, never landing the results to match the speed. A year with Toleman followed, before a six-year lay-off that was interspersed with sports car and IndyCar races and then a fruitless bid to qualify for the Life in 1990.

○ 69 Grands Prix, no wins (best result – 3rd Caesars Palace GP 1981)

○ No drivers' title (best result – 15th overall 1981)

Richie Ginther

Nationality: American
Born: 1930
Died: 1989

With the exception of Dan Gurney and Phil Hill, Richie was the only American Formula One driver to succeed in the 1960s. He made his name racing a Porsche in the late 1950s. This earned him a works Ferrari sports car contract and brought him to Europe for 1960. He drove in only three grands prix that year, scoring each time, peaking with second at Monza.

Another second place followed in 1961, at Monaco, and another at the same venue in 1962 when he had joined BRM. Over the next two years he was second another five times, but that vital win finally came, for him and for Honda, in Mexico in 1965.

He quit racing in 1967, later dropping out to live in a camper van before dying of a heart attack in 1989.

○ 52 Grands Prix, 1 win (Mexican GP 1965)

○ No drivers' title (best result – 2nd overall 1963)

Those Were the Days: Jose Froilan Gonzalez, aka the "Pampas Bull", sweeps to victory in the 1954 Daily Express International Trophy at Silverstone, one of many non-championship races of the time

Ignazio **Giunti**

Nationality: Italian
Born: 1941
Died: 1971

Ignazio gained his competitive instinct in hill climbs in the mid-1960s and was soon elevated to racing sports cars. He joined the Ferrari Formula One line-up for 1970 alongside Jacky Ickx and Clay Regazzoni. He did enough to stay on for 1971, by finishing fourth at Spa, but he was killed in a freak accident in a sports car race at Buenos Aires when he hit Jean-Pierre Beltoise's stranded Matra.

○ 4 Grands Prix, no wins (best result - 4th Belgian GP 1970)
○ No drivers' title (best result - 17th overall 1970)

Timo **Glock**

Nationality: German
Born: 1982

It's hard enough to get into Formula One, but harder still to get back in once you've lost your drive. However, Timo is clearly made of stern stuff, as he recovered from losing his ride after half a season with Jordan in 2004. Undeterred, the German tried IndyCar racing and went well, but reckoned that GP2 was the only route back to Formula One and duly won that title at his second attempt in 2007. Signed by Toyota, Timo finished second for the Japanese manufacturer in Hungary in 2008 and in Singapore in 2009.

° 36 Grands Prix, 0 wins (best result - 2nd Hungarian GP 2008, Singapore GP 2009)
° No drivers' title (best result - 10th overall 2008 and 2009)

Jose Froilan **Gonzalez**

Nationality: Argentinian
Born: 1922

The "Pampas Bull", as Froilan was known, was a real character, built more like an all-in wrestler than a jockey. He made his Formula One debut in the Monaco Grand Prix, racing a Maserati for the Scuderia Argentina team in place of compatriot Juan Manuel Fangio who had crossed over to Alfa Romeo. No results came his way in 1950, but 1951 was better, for he joined Ferrari and his exuberant, sideways-is-best style saw him on the podium for each of the five races he drove for the team, winning the British Grand Prix.

Indeed, this was Ferrari's first victory in a World Championship grand prix. He backed this up by winning the non-championship Pescara Grand Prix, but signed for Maserati for 1952. No wins followed, so he went back to Ferrari in 1954 and again won the British Grand Prix, also winning three non-championship races, the Le Mans 24 Hours and several other sports car races. Indeed, had it not been for Fangio, he would have been World Champion.

○ 26 Grands Prix, 2 wins (British GP 1951, British GP 1954)
○ No drivers' title (best result - 2nd overall 1954)

Masten **Gregory**

Nationality: American
Born: 1932
Died: 1985

Family wealth made Masten's progress easy. If he wanted to race a car, he bought it. Having raced sports cars in the mid-1950s with growing confidence, he took the plunge and went to Formula One in 1957 with a Scuderia Centro Sud Maserati, coming third on his debut at Monaco. Finishing in the points each time out, he placed sixth overall at season's end and this was to prove his best year. Racing for Cooper in 1959 as number three to Jack Brabham and Bruce McLaren, Masten came second in the Portuguese Grand Prix, but then he crashed in a sports car race and was injured. Indeed, when Masten came to look for a Formula One ride for 1960, his reputation as a crasher went against him, and this led to him racing Cooper and then Lotus cars for four seasons with little success. He signed off with four races in a privately entered BRM in 1965, but it was in sports cars that he earned his glory, winning the Le Mans 24 Hours in 1965 with Jochen Rindt. Many other wins followed before he retired from racing in 1971, before he was felled by a heart attack at the age of 53.

∘ **38 Grands Prix, no wins (best result – 2nd Portuguese GP 1959)**
∘ **No drivers' title (best result – 6th overall 1957)**

Olivier **Grouillard**

Nationality: French
Born: 1958

After winning the French Formula Three title in 1984 at his second attempt, with the topline ORECA team, Olivier progressed with the team to Formula 3000 and showed well, but it was to be four years before he scored two wins for the GDBA team and ended up second overall to Roberto Moreno. He thus graduated from motor racing's second division, landing a ride with Ligier for 1989. Fittingly, Olivier scored his first points on home soil, but the next three seasons – spent with Osella, Fondmetal and then Tyrrell – produced nothing. Nothing, that is, except regular fist-shaking from other drivers as he wandered into their path when they were on a flier in qualifying, or

obstructed the leaders as they came up to lap him. No one was sad to see Olivier go and try his luck in IndyCars but, after failing in that, he returned to Europe and was a frequent winner in a McLaren in GT races in 1995 and 1996.

∘ **41 Grands Prix, no wins (best result – 6th French GP 1989)**
∘ **No drivers' title (best result – 26th overall 1989)**

Mauricio **Gugelmin**

Nationality: Brazilian
Born: 1963

A friend of Ayrton Senna, Mauricio followed him to Britain. Echoing Ayrton's moves, he drove for West Surrey Racing in Formula Three and won the 1985 title plus the Macau Grand Prix. West Surrey decided to move up to Formula 3000 with Mauricio in 1986, but this proved a disaster. Mauricio transferred to the works Ralt team in 1987 and won first time out, but dropped to fourth overall by year's end. However, this

was enough to earn him a Formula One drive for 1988 with the Leyton House March team. For the next four years Mauricio was synonymous with the team's aquamarine colours. Results were mixed, but highlights included third place in Brazil in 1989 and running second in France behind team-mate Ivan Capelli in 1990 before retiring. Then Capelli fell back to second right at the end. The team folded and so Mauricio moved to the new Jordan team for 1992, but the Yamaha engine was gutless and this sounded the death knell of Mauricio's Formula One career. He headed off to become an IndyCar regular and a race winner in 1997.

∘ **74 Grands Prix, no wins (best result – 3rd Brazilian GP 1989)**
∘ **No drivers' title (best result – 13th overall 1988)**

Dan **Gurney**

Nationality: American
Born: 1931

To many fans, Dan is the greatest

American ever to have raced in Formula One, even though the statistics tell a different story. What made Dan stand out was that he built his own car – the Eagle – and won in that. A spell in the army in Korea intervened before he bought himself a Triumph TR2 and raced it. Over the next few years the cars became more exotic and Dan more successful, earning an invitation to race in Europe for Ferrari in 1958. He landed a contract to race Formula One for the team in 1959, with Enzo no doubt aware of the sales value of having American attention focused on Ferrari.

And so began a long Formula One career, which he kicked off with second place behind team-mate Tony Brooks in the German Grand Prix. However, he moved to BRM for 1960 and then on to Porsche for 1961. With reliability he had only dreamt of at BRM, he finished third overall despite not winning a race. Staying on for 1962, though, he did get to the top step of the podium, at the French Grand Prix. Indeed, Rouen was a happy stamping ground for Dan, for his next win came there in 1964, his second year with Brabham. And he rounded out that year with another win, in Mexico. Ironically, both 1963 and 1965 saw him in the points more often, frequently challenging Jim Clark.

Then Dan bit the bullet and built his own cars for 1966. The Eagle came good in 1967, with Weslake power in place of Climax, and Dan brought this beautiful car home first in Belgium, but all too often it broke. He won the Le Mans 24 Hours for Ford with AJ Foyt. Success for Dan was later to come outside Formula One, with second in the Indy 500 in both 1968 and 1969. Following the death of Bruce McLaren, he returned to Formula One with McLaren's team.

∘ **86 Grands Prix, 4 wins (French GP 1962, French GP 1964, Mexican GP 1964, Belgian GP 1967)**
∘ **No drivers' title (best result – 3rd overall 1961)**

The Greatest American in F1? Dan Gurney built his own car, the Eagle, and won a grand prix in it

MIKA HAKKINEN
The Original Ice Man

Think Mika and F1 fans think McLaren, immense natural speed and an almost freakishly cool demeanour. Nothing, it seemed, excited him. Well, not until he claimed the world title that his skills deserved in 1998 and then it was as though the blue touch paper had been ignited as the emotions came tumbling out. One of the fastest drivers ever seen in Formula One had finally been rewarded.

After winning the Finnish karting title, Mika bought compatriot JJ Lehto's Formula Ford car and broke most of his lap records en route to the 1987 Scandinavian title. He then won the GM Euroseries in 1988 and graduated to British Formula Three. After a troubled season with a team new to the category, Mika joined established experts West Surrey Racing in 1990 and beat fellow Finn Mika Salo to the title. He also took time out to win on visits to the German and Italian championships and looked to have confirmed himself as the best driver at that level when he was almost stroking victory in the Macau Grand Prix, until trying a move to pass Michael Schumacher on the final lap. They touched and Mika was out of the race. He was inconsolable as he had not needed to be in front at the finish of the second part of this race for an aggregate victory. They would meet again...

Demonstrably without need of further coaching on the way to the top, Mika jumped direct to Formula One with Lotus, running with the big names on his debut at Phoenix until mechanical gremlins struck. In 1992 he peaked with fourth place in Hungary, but mechanical failures were too frequent for his manager Keke Rosberg's liking and so he signed for McLaren for 1993, banking on Ayrton Senna retiring from the sport. Trouble was, he decided to race on and Mika was left as test driver. However, he got to drive before the year was out as Michael Andretti went back to Indy Cars and Mika shattered the opinion of every expert when he outqualified Senna at Estoril at his first attempt. This ensured Mika a ride for 1994 and he raced to second place in Belgium and five thirds.

The MP4/10 was a beast in the first part of 1995, and it was only when the MP4/10B arrived that he scored two seconds. Mika suffered head injuries in Australia, but he bounced back to shine in 1996 and 1997 whenever the McLaren was competitive, achieving his first win at Jerez after disappointments at Silverstone and the Nurburgring.

Then it all came right in 1998, a season he started with victory in Australia, and he went on to win seven more times to beat Michael Schumacher at the final round to clinch the title. He was champion again in 1999, but was thwarted in 2000 as Ferrari came on strong and he won just four races for McLaren to be edged into second place by Schumacher.

Upset by mechanical failures early in 2001, Mika appeared dispirited, but bounced back to win twice before taking a sabbatical in 2002 that turned into full-time retirement.

○ **162 Grands Prix, 20 wins**
○ **World Champion 1998 and 1999**

Blasting Off: Hakkinen gets off to a flying start in the Australian Grand Prix, the first race of 1999

1968	1987	1990	1992	1994	1995	1998	2000	2002
Born 28 September in Helsinki, Finland	Finnish, Nordic and Swedish Formula Ford champion	British Formula Three champion ahead of Mika Salo with nine wins	Took two fourth-place finishes for Lotus and ranked eighth overall	Ranked fourth after visiting podium six times, although never as a winner	Arrival of Mercedes engines brought promise but no wins. Suffered head injuries at season-ending Australian GP	Won eight races to pip Michael Schumacher at final round to be World Champion	Runner-up to Michael Schumacher, winning Spanish, Austrian, Hungarian and Belgian GPs	Announced his retirement from motor racing

1986	1988	1991	1993	1997	1999	2001
Finnish, Nordic and Swedish karting champion	Formula Opel Euroseries champion and runner-up in British series	Leapt to Formula One with Lotus. Fifth on third outing in little-fancied car	Gambled on Senna quitting and joined McLaren, but Senna stayed on and Mika sat on sidelines until Michael Andretti was dropped. Immediately outqualified Senna	Fifth overall again, but finally scored a win, doing so in final race at Jerez	World Champion again, this time only winning five times to beat Ferrari's Eddie Irvine at final round	Fifth overall, with two wins, as he struggled to maintain enthusiasm. Elected to take a sabbatical

From Two Wheels to Four: Mike Hailwood

Mike Hailwood

Nationality: British
Born: 1941
Died: 1981

Best known as a nine-time motorcycle world champion, and 12-time winner of the Isle of Man's Tourist Trophy, Mike moved to four-wheeled sport in 1963 in Formula Junior. He was invited to move to Formula One in 1964, driving a Lotus for Reg Parnell. At the end of 1967 he chose to concentrate on cars, taking part in many sports car events, then winning in Formula 5000 in a car entered by another former motorcycling world champion, John Surtees. Mike returned to Formula One in 1971 with Surtees, finishing fourth at Monza. Second place in the 1972 Italian Grand Prix was his best result and his Formula One career was brought to an end when he crashed his McLaren in the 1974 German Grand Prix, breaking a leg. He dabbled with motorcycles until 1979. Then, he and his two children were killed in a road accident in 1981.

° 50 Grands Prix, no wins (best result – 2nd Italian GP 1972)
° No drivers' title (best result – 8th overall 1972)

Mika Hakkinen

SEE PAGE 151

Lewis Hamilton

SEE PAGE 153

Mike Hawthorn

SEE PAGE 154

Nick Heidfeld

Nationality: German
Born: 1977

After landing the German Formula Three title in 1997, he was snapped up by Mercedes for its driver development programme, he was given plenty of track time with McLaren and placed in Formula 3000 with the McLaren junior team. All that came between him and the 1998 title was one small slip, with the honours going to Juan Pablo Montoya. He walked it in 1999 and thus earned his Formula One break for 2000, albeit with lacklustre Prost. No points came his way, but he was the equal of team-mate Jean Alesi and Peter Sauber signed him for 2001. Points started to flow, with third in the 2001 Brazilian Grand Prix helping him to rank seventh. Then, at the end of 2003 after two more middling seasons in which he did his best in less than sparkling chassis,

Sauber changed both its drivers and, with a change in the rules making Nick too experienced to be a test driver, he found himself on the sidelines, with a Jordan drive his only salvation. It made for a tricky season, but he drove well enough to land a ride with Williams for 2005, taking two seconds and pole at the Nurburgring before returning to Sauber (as BMW) for 2006. The 2007 was a valediction as he started it with three fourths and peaked with second in Canada to rank fifth. He scored four seconds in 2008, yet still no wins, but 2009 was a disappointment as the car was less competitive, apart from in the wet at Sepang where he came second.

° 169 Grands Prix, no wins (best result – 2nd Monaco GP 2005, European GP 2005, Canadian GP 2007, Australian GP 2008, Canadian GP 2008, British GP 2008, Belgian GP 2008, Malaysian GP 2009)
° No drivers' title (best result – 5th 2007)

Johnny Herbert

Nationality: British
Born: 1964

Karting hotshot Johnny starred in Formula Ford before Eddie Jordan signed him for Formula Three in 1987,

where he promptly won the British title. He was set for the 1988 Formula 3000 title when he suffered horrendous leg injuries at Brands Hatch on the day he had signed a Benetton F1 contract. He finished an amazing fourth on his F1 debut in Brazil, but his shattered heels could not cope with braking and he was dropped.

His next mentor was Peter Collins, who signed him for Lotus for 1990, and there Johnny stayed until 1994. A move to Benetton in 1995 was seen as Johnny's big chance, but the team focused on Michael Schumacher. Johnny inherited wins at Silverstone and Monza, though, to end up fourth overall. He raced for Sauber in 1996 and pushed team-mate Heinz-Harald Frentzen, becoming the team's number one for 1997. Joined by Jean Alesi in 1998, he continued to shine despite having little hope of victory, but moved on to Stewart for 1999, scoring a surprise win in a wet/dry race at the Nurburgring.

After a farewell season in 2000, Johnny achieved successes racing for Audi in the US and finishing second at Le Mans for Bentley in 2003.

Great British Hope: former karting hotshot Johnny Herbert at the wheel of his Lotus in the Japanese Grand Prix in his first season, 1990

LEWIS HAMILTON
The Youngest F1 Champion

Lewis is the driver for which the World Championship had been waiting. Once in Formula One, he didn't disappoint, coming within a point of being the first true rookie World Champion. Then, in his second season, he was given the sport's most coveted title: World Champion. So, in a sweep, not only did he reinvigorate the sport, but he brought in new interest then kept the drama going long enough to ensure that they were hooked.

It's not just Lewis's speed that marked him out in the junior reaches of karting, but his confidence. Driven on by his father, Anthony, who held down three jobs to finance Lewis's racing, Lewis won title after title. However, it was what he did at an awards ceremony that made everything else happen. He approached McLaren boss Ron Dennis and, cheekily, suggested that he ought to back him. Nothing ventured, nothing gained" has never been more true, as McLaren financed his ascent through the top classes of karting, in which he became World Champion, and then into car racing.

Using this backing to good effect, Lewis collected titles in each of the three building block formulae, topping out in 2006 when he won the GP2 crown.

So, by 2007, he was a Formula One driver, paired up at McLaren with no less a driver than double World Champion Fernando Alonso. When he overtook the Spaniard on the run to the first corner in the opening race at Melbourne, everyone sat up and paid attention. Here was a driver even better than his reputation. Such was Lewis's form that he was indignant when the team wouldn't let him have a crack at Alonso for victory at Monaco, but he was ready next time out and scored his first win at his sixth attempt in Canada. He won again the following weekend, at Indianapolis, then added wins in Hungary and Japan to open out a 12-point over lead Alonso with two races to go. But this failed to yield the title as Ferrari's Kimi Raikkonen won the final two races and he was slowed in the final round in Brazil by a gearbox problem and seventh place left him a point adrift.

The final round in 2008 was no less dramatic as Lewis again arrived at Interlagos in front, this time with a seven-point lead over Ferrari's Felipe Massa, having scored wins at Melbourne, Monaco, Silverstone and Hockenheim. With just seven laps to go, when running fourth, which was enough to become champion if Massa

Shining Star: Lewis Hamilton's incredible story helped reinvigorate the public's interest in F1.

remained in the lead to the finish, rain struck. In the scramble, Vettel passed him and as Massa took the chequered flag he had been edged out, but he came across Timo Glock's dry-shod Toyota in the final sweep, passed it and was champion...

After that, 2009 was an anti-climax with McLaren not producing a competitive car. However, he showed his talent and determination with wins in Hungary and Singapore.

○ **52 Grands Prix, 11 wins**
○ **World Champion 2008**

1985	1998	2002	2005	2007	2008
Born 7 January in Stevenage, England	Gets himself onto McLaren's books	Takes to car racing, starting with Formula Renault in which he finished third in British series	European Formula Three champion for ASM team with 15 wins. Starts Formula One testing with McLaren	Wins four times and is runner-up in rookie F1 year with McLaren, a point shy of Kimi Raikkonen	Takes another five wins, but this time the drivers' title by a point from Felipe Massa

1995	2000	2003	2004	2006	2009
British Cadet Kart Champion	World Kart Champion	British Formula Renault champion with 10 wins for Manor Motorsport	Steps up to Formula Three, but ranks fifth in European series	GP2 champion with ART Grand Prix, winning five races	McLaren is off the pace but advances and Lewis wins twice to rank fifth

MIKE HAWTHORN
The First British Champion

Tall, blond, bullish and never without a cap and bow tie, this flamboyant man gave the British public the international success it craved in the 1950s.

Being brought up on the spectator banks at Brooklands fired his enthusiasm for racing and so, with his father's assistance, Mike entered the world of competition at the 1950 Brighton speed trials.

By 1952 he had graduated to single-seaters and had won his first race in a Formula Two Cooper-Bristol at Goodwood, even beating a similarly mounted Juan Manuel Fangio later in the day. This was to be the making of Mike and his grand prix debut followed, with an extremely competitive fourth place in the Belgian Grand Prix at Spa-Francorchamps behind the Ferraris. He went one better in the British Grand Prix and ranked fourth overall at the year's end.

Having heard glowing reports back from Luigi Villoresi, who Mike had impressed with his flamboyant driving of his little Cooper in the wet at Boreham, Enzo Ferrari offered Mike a works drive for 1953, which Mike accepted. Having watched and learned from his considerably more experienced team-mates, Mike came good on his fourth outing for the team, winning the French Grand Prix in a spectacular slipstreaming battle with Maserati's Juan Manuel Fangio at Reims. This and two more podium finishes helped him rank fourth overall, showing that Britain had a driver who could truly challenge for honours. He also won the International Trophy and the Ulster Trophy as well as the Spa 24 Hours sports car race with Ferrari team-mate Giuseppe Farina.

Mike had a mixed year in 1954, suffering burns in a crash at Syracuse, but he rounded it out with victory in the Spanish Grand Prix to leave him ranked third overall at Pedralbes.

Mike's racing was then limited by his father's death, so he quit Ferrari to be closer to home to look after the family garage business. Racing for Vanwall in 1955, he was less than impressed with both the car and the team so he returned to Ferrari after two races but found the team had been eclipsed by Mercedes. His 1955 season will always be remembered for his involvement in an accident in the Le Mans 24 Hours that sent Pierre Levegh's Mercedes into the crowd, killing 80 people.

Racing for BRM in 1956 was less than satisfactory, so Mike returned again to Ferrari for 1957 and finished second in the German Grand Prix. Then it all came right in 1958. Although he won only once, to the four wins of Vanwall's Stirling Moss and the three of Tony Brooks, his consistent scoring – with five second places – was enough to make him Britain's first World Champion.

Mike then retired, planning both to expand the family garage business and to get married, only to be killed in a road accident in 1959. It was later revealed he was suffering from a kidney illness that would have precluded further racing. No driver since has cut such a dash.

Cutting a Dash: Mike Hawthorn struggles for speed in a Vanwall during the 1955 Monaco Grand Prix

○ **45 Grands Prix, 3 wins**
○ **World Champion 1958**

1929	1950	1952	1954	1956	1958
Born 10 April in Mexborough, England	Contested the Brighton speed trials in a Riley Ulster	Tested Formula Two Connaughts and HWMs, but raced a Cooper, winning on debut at Goodwood. Fourth on World Championship debut at Spa, then third at Silverstone	Badly burned in non-championship Syracuse GP, but bounced back to win Spanish GP for Ferrari and rank third	Third in opening race, in Argentina, in a Maserati, but then had mix-and-match year as he swapped between this, a BRM and a Vanwall	World Champion, Britain's first, pipping Stirling Moss despite scoring only one win to Moss's four. Death of Peter Collins and a kidney ailment made him quit

1946	1951	1953	1955	1957	1959
Started taking part in motorcycle trials and scrambles	Went circuit racing in a Riley Sprite and soon started winning, including the Leinster Trophy race	Joined Ferrari then won three non-championship races before pipping Fangio to victory in French GP. Scored in every race to rank fourth	Left Ferrari to run garage business after father's death. Raced for Vanwall, but was not competitive so rejoined Ferrari. Won Le Mans for Jaguar but involved in accident that killed 80 spectators	Returned for a third spell with Ferrari and was fourth overall again after coming second in German GP	Killed in a car crash just outside Guildford

DAMON HILL
His Father's Son

No family can match the Hills, as it is the only family to date to have produced a World Champion son to follow in the wheel tracks of a World Champion father – Damon hit the high note in 1996 after Graham was champion both in 1962 and 1968.

Aged only 15 when father Graham died in a light aircraft crash, Damon prefered motorbikes and did not take to cars until 1983. Having shown useful speed in Formula Ford in 1985 against the likes of Bertrand Gachot and OJohnny Herbert, he advanced to Formula Three the following year. Wins started to flow in 1987 and Damon finished third overall in 1988 behind JJ Lehto and Gary Brabham.

Three seasons of Formula 3000 followed, with the second seeing Damon lead race after race in his Middlebridge Lola in 1990 before retiring. The most important event, though, was signing a testing deal with Williams in 1991.

There was no opening in Williams' race line-up for 1992, though, so Damon made his Formula One debut for Brabham. The car was less than competitive, though, and he qualified just twice. All was not lost, however, as Damon gained useful test mileage for Williams and the team signed him for 1993. With the three-time champion Alain Prost as team-mate, Damon truly had someone to judge himself against and showed his skills. Having been robbed of wins in Britain and Germany, he made his breakthrough with victory at the Hungarian Grand Prix and followed this with wins in Belgium and Italy to rank third overall.

Prost was dropped to make way for Ayrton Senna for 1994 and Damon was thrust into the role of team leader on Ayrton's death in the fourth race of the campaign.

Just as his father had before him, he had to heal a team in mourning (Lotus lost Jim Clark in 1968) and achieved a morale-boosting win in Spain. The year became fraught with Michael Schumacher's disqualifications and Damon closed the gap by winning four more races. Victory in Japan set the stage for a last round shoot-out, and Michael's chop that took Damon out in Australia was seen the world over.

Despite winning two of the first three races in 1995, Damon won only twice more, to end up second again after several shunts with Schumacher.

His dream was realized in 1996, though, when Damon started with four wins from the first five races. However, a mid-season dip and the winning progress of his team-mate Jacques Villeneuve saw the title race go to the final round in Japan. There Damon controlled the race for his eighth win and took the crown.

With the top seats already filled, he joined Arrows for 1997. The season was going nowhere when Damon led until the final lap in Hungary, salvaging second place as his gearbox failed.

Wanting more, he headed for Jordan for 1998, and there he turned around a team in trouble into a winning outfit by the 13th race, at Spa-Francorchamps. His second year with Jordan was a poor one, so he retired.

○ **115 Grands Prix, 22 wins**
○ **World Champion 1996**

In the Blood: Damon Hill wins the San Marino Grand Prix in 1996, the year he became World Champion

1960	1984	1986	1990	1993	1995	1996	1997
Born 17 September 1960 in Hampstead, London	Combined racing on two wheels and four, winning more than 40 350cc races	Stepped up to British Formula Three, finished ninth overall	Full Formula 3000 campaign saw him lead five times for Middlebridge but never win	Two second places in first three races for Williams, then won three in a row late in season to rank third overall	Second head-to-head with Schumacher and again Damon ended up runner-up, this time with four wins	Became only driver yet to be a second generation World Champion, winning eight grands prix to outscore team-mate Jacques Villeneuve	Raced for Arrows and led Hungarian GP until final lap. Still finished second but ranked only 12th

	1979	1985	1988	1992	1994		1998	1999
	Started racing motorcycles	Full season of Formula Ford, finishing third in Esso series	Third overall in British Formula Three. Also second in Macau street race and made two Formula 3000 outings	Moved up to Formula One with Brabham. Failed to qualify six times out of eight, but testing form landed him race seat for 1993	Became team leader after Senna's death and won six rounds to go for title at final round, only for Michael Schumacher to drive into him		Joined Jordan and gave team first win at Belgian GP. Late flurry of points helped him rank sixth	Fourth place at Imola was his best result in a torrid season and he quit at year's end

GRAHAM HILL
Mr Determination

Determined, intense, record-breaking, humorous, he was the perfect ambassador for the sport. All this and much more has been said of Graham, the only man to have won the triple crown of World Championship, Indy 500 and the Le Mans 24 Hours.

It has become something of a cliché to say that he was a man who worked at his driving rather than being imbued with natural ability, but Graham did not pass his driving test until he was 24. That same year, he attended a racing school at Brands Hatch and was hooked.

He immediately started working as a mechanic at the school, racing in one of its cars in lieu of payment. Then Graham met Colin Chapman and worked for him as he built up Lotus. Graham built his own Lotus for 1956 and became a works driver in 1958, making his grand prix debut at Monaco. He ran fourth before a wheel parted company with the car. Graham later became synonymous with Monaco as he won there five times.

Disenchanted with the fragility of Chapman's Lotuses, Graham left for BRM for 1960, a year in which he finished third at Zandvoort. After a lacklustre second year, 1962 was better as, equipped with a new V8, he won the Dutch, German and Italian Grands Prix to set up a South African finale with Jim Clark. Clark led but, when the Lotus broke, Graham snatched both victory and the title.

He was runner-up to Clark, John Surtees and Clark again in 1963, 1964 and 1965 respectively. His defeat by Surtees was particularly galling as he had scored more points than the former motorcyclist, but lost out by a point when dropped scores were considered. Graham won the Indianapolis 500 in 1966, but there was a slice of good fortune involved, as Jackie Stewart led convincingly until he was robbed by a technical problem. After a troubled 1966 – the first year of the new 3-litre Formula – Graham was tempted back to Lotus as team-mate to Clark, who narrowly missed out on the title to Denny Hulme. However, the Lotus 49-Cosworth looked promising. Clark started 1968 well enough, winning in South Africa, but was killed in a Formula Two race. The Scot's death devastated Chapman, but Graham put the team back on course by winning in Spain. He fought a three-way tussle with Stewart's Matra and Hulme's McLaren, winning his second crown with victory in the season finale.

Graham was outpaced by team-mate Jochen Rindt in 1969. Then, at Watkins Glen, he spun and popped his seatbelt. Unable to refasten it, he resumed but crashed and was thrown out, breaking his legs. He was determined to return, but was never as fast again.

Having won Le Mans for Matra in 1972, Graham raced on until mid-1975 when he elected to retire to concentrate on team management. Tragically, piloting his plane back from a test at Paul Ricard, he hit a tree on the approach to Elstree and was killed along with protégé Tony Brise, the team manager, designer and two mechanics.

- 176 Grands Prix, 14 wins
- World Champion 1962 and 1968

The Quintessential Englishman: Hill was charm itself and the perfect ambassador for Formula One

1929	1957	1960	1963	1965	1966	1968	1969	1972	1975
Born 15 February in Hampstead, England	Raced a Cooper and a Lotus in Formula Two	Went to BRM looking for a more reliable car, but did not find one, though third in Monaco was a highlight	Scored the first of Monaco wins and added victory in US GP, but ended year as runner-up	Runner-up for BRM for third straight year, yet again winning Monaco and US GPs	BRM struggled with change to 3-litre engines. Won Indy 500 in a Lola as a consolation	World Champion for a second time after becoming team leader on Clark's death	Won in Monaco for fifth time, but ended year by breaking legs at US GP	Won Le Mans 24 Hours in a Matra. Fifth in Italian GP	Retired from racing after failing to qualify at Monaco, then was killed in plane crash

1954	1958	1962	1964	1967	1971	1973
Attended racing school at Brands Hatch	When Lotus moved into Formula One, so did he, but mechanical failures restricted him to one sixth-place finish	Scored two non-championship wins then won Dutch GP. Three further wins made him World Champion	Won Monaco and US GPs again and was runner-up again. Also won Reims 12 Hours and was second at Le Mans	Joined Clark at Lotus and was second in Monaco and US GPs	Joined Brabham and won non-championship International Trophy race	Bought a pair of Shadow chassis and formed his own Formula One team

DENNY HULME
The Bear from New Zealand

Solid, honest and hard-working are all descriptions of Denny Hulme and to see the travails he experienced en route to Formula One makes one appreciate just how easy the hotshots of today have it as they are guided to Formula One with seemingly little more than a hop, a skip and a jump.

Perhaps as a result of these hardships, Denny was known as "The Bear" for his taciturn manner fast and temper, but those close to him held him in huge esteem. He was a racer's racer, with nothing flash about him in any way.

Denny started racing at the age of 20 in 1956, hill climbing an MG TF. Success followed on the tracks, advancing to racing a Cooper single-seater in 1959 and, after winning a "Driver to Europe" scholarship, quit New Zealand for Europe in 1960 to race in Formula Junior all over the continent. Needing money, he went to work at Jack Brabham's garage in 1961, and so started a long relationship with his fellow Antipodean.

Having raced well in a Ken Tyrrell-run works Cooper in Formula Junior in 1962, Denny moved across to race a Brabham later in the year and this relationship was to continue right the way through until the end of 1967.

Denny finished second to Brabham in the 1964 Formula Two series, and he joined his boss's Formula One team for 1965. His first season was solid enough, with his best result a fourth place in the French Grand Prix at Clermont-Ferrand. With Brabham having seemingly found itself the engine most suited to the introduction of the 3-litre engine formula in 1966, Denny and Jack were strong. Yet, retirements hit Denny hard and he ended up with a second place and three thirds in his nine outings, although these were sufficient for him to end the year as runner-up to his team boss.

Denny's best-ever campaign came the following year, 1967, as he not only scored his first win, at Monaco, but notched up another at the Nurburgring and pipped Brabham to the crown.

Having also raced in the CanAm sports car series for compatriot Bruce McLaren's team in 1967, Denny moved across to the McLaren team for his Formula One racing in 1968 as well. And he stayed with the team until he retired from Formula One seven years later, scoring six more wins, two of which came in 1968 as he ranked third overall behind Graham Hill and Jackie Stewart. After a strong 1972 campaign

that yielded a win, at Kyalami, two second-place finishes and four thirds, Denny's final win was in the Swedish Grand Prix of 1973, the first year of the classic McLaren M23 chassis.

During this time Denny also continued to race with huge success

in CanAm, clinching the title in both 1968 and 1970. Denny returned to racing, only for fun, in the 1990s and died of a heart attack while racing a touring car at Bathurst.

○ **112 Grands Prix, 8 wins**
○ **World Champion 1967**

The Man Who Broke the Bank at Monte Carlo: Denny Hulme strikes gold in the Monaco Grand Prix, 1967

1936	1960	1966	1967	1969	1971	1973	1974
Born 18 June in Nelson, New Zealand	Won New Zealand's "Driver to Europe" scholarship and starred in Formula Junior	Ranked fourth in Formula One, with second in British GP his best result. Second in Le Mans 24 Hours for Ford. Won Tourist Trophy	World Champion thanks to wins in Monaco and German GPs. Also second in CanAm series and fourth in Indy 500	Sixth in F1, with only one win, also dropping to second in CanAm behind Bruce McLaren	Weak season, peaking with two fourth places as he ranked only ninth. CanAm runner-up behind team-mate Peter Revson	Won Swedish GP for McLaren, but slipped to sixth overall	Won Argentinian GP and was second in Austria, but fell to seventh overall and quit Formula One

1956	1963	1965	1968	1970	1972	1992
Made competition debut in local hill climb in an MG TF, then took it racing	Starred in Formula Junior for Brabham	Made Formula One debut with Brabham, coming fourth on second outing, the French GP. Won Tourist Trophy	Joined McLaren and won International Trophy then Italian and Canadian GPs to rank third overall. Won CanAm title for McLaren	Fourth overall in Formula One with McLaren, with no wins. Was CanAm champion for a second time	Won the South African GP and ended year third overall thanks to six other podium visits. Continued to win races in CanAm	Had heart attack and died in Bathurst touring car race in Australia

JAMES HUNT
The Face of the 1970s

Few drivers in the history of Formula One have ever done as much as James Hunt to put the sport in the public eye. It just so happened that his long fair hair, devil-may-care attitude and will to win caught the public's imagination at a time when Formula One was having to fight its corner. Indeed, after he claimed his world title after an epic season in 1976, British broadcasters even decided that it might be worth their while to televise the races...

In many ways something of a latter-day Mike Hawthorn, James left a trail of crashed cars behind him when he raced Minis, Formula Ford and Formula Three, earning the "Hunt the Shunt" sobriquet. He was also seldom far away when controversy raised its head, such as when he showed some handy boxing skills after a collision in a televised race on the now defunct Crystal Palace circuit in 1971.

Fortunately, James's raw talent was obvious and he was spotted by the wealthy Lord Hesketh in 1972. The young aristocrat then introduced some much needed funds and helped James to continue in Formula Two.

They stuck together into 1973 and James then stepped up into Formula One, finishing third in the non-championship Race of Champions at Brands Hatch in a hired Surtees. He then produced some great drives in a customer March, particularly his run to second place behind Ronnie Peterson in the US Grand Prix.

Running its own Hesketh chassis in 1974, in patriotic red, white and blue livery of course, and with no ghastly sponsorship stickers, thank you very much, the team rattled the establishment. They were far more than merely playboys, however, as James claimed a trio of third places. Then, in 1975, he won the International Trophy at Silverstone and that vital first World Championship race win came in the Dutch Grand Prix after a battle with no less a talent than Ferrari's reigning World Champion, Niki Lauda.

Hunt the Shunt: James Hunt takes the chequered flag to win the Dutch Grand Prix at Zandvoort, 1976

The newspapers chose to concentrate on his womanizing and anti-establishment antics, but, while this irked James, it helped Formula One gain a popular image in Britain. This was rewarded in 1976 when James moved to McLaren after Emerson Fittipaldi quit to join his family team, scored six wins and took the title amid a downpour in the final race, in Japan, helped when friend and rival Niki Lauda pulled into the pits and said that it was too dangerous to race. James stayed out and clinched the third place he needed to lift the crown.

He won three more times for McLaren and then, after a fruitless 1978 season in which McLaren was left behind as ground-effects transformed the face of Formula One, he drove for Wolf in 1979.

However, he soon became disenchanted and retired mid-season, no longer keen to take risks in a car that had no chance of victory.

James then moved seamlessly into the commentary box, as his laconic style made him the perfect foil for Murray Walker. His death, of a heart attack, in 1993 shocked everyone in the racing world.

- **92 Grands Prix, 10 wins**
- **World Champion 1976**

1947	1968	1970	1973	1975	1976	1978	1993
Born 29 August in Belmont, Surrey, England	Graduated to Formula Ford and started winning from his second outing	Scored strong Formula Three wins at Rouen and Zolder, but his many crashes earned him the nickname "Hunt the Shunt"	Destroyed Hesketh's Formula Two car so team advanced to Formula One with a March and James was second in end-of-year US GP	Scored breakthrough win in Dutch GP and rose to be ranked fourth overall	Replaced Emerson Fittipaldi at McLaren and became World Champion after six wins and an epic battle with Niki Lauda	No wins at all in final season with McLaren, with third in French GP his best showing	Died of a heart attack in June at home in Wimbledon

1967	1969	1971	1972	1974	1977	1979
Made racing debut in a Mini	Advanced to Formula Three then Formula Two	Raced a semi-works March in Formula Three	Had full works ride with March but went and joined forces with Lord Hesketh who pushed him back into Formula Two with some success	Ran in Hesketh's own chassis and was eighth overall again. Won International Trophy	Won British, US East and Japanese GPs for McLaren, but fell back to fifth overall	Moved over to race for Wolf but quit after Monaco GP and went on to form television commentary partnership with Murray Walker

Lift-off: all four wheels leave the tarmac as Jacky Ickx jumps his F2 Matra at the Nurburgring, 1967

○ 162 Grands Prix, 3 wins (British GP 1995, Italian GP 1995, European GP 1999)
○ No drivers' title (best result – 4th 1995)

Damon Hill
SEE PAGE 155

Graham Hill
SEE PAGE 156

Phil Hill
Nationality: American
Born: 1927
Died: 2008

Mario Andretti is the most famous American World Champion, but he wasn't the first. That was Phil Hill 17 years earlier, in 1961 with Ferrari. Amazingly, this was his one strong season and he only came through to claim the title at the penultimate round after team-mate Wolfgang von Trips had been killed in an accident early in that race at Monza. Phil won the US sports car championship in 1955, and caught Enzo Ferrari's eye. He signed up for a few European races in 1956. Anxious to advance to Ferrari's Formula One squad in 1958, Phil became frustrated when Enzo insisted he was more cut out for sports cars. However, Phil was given a run in a few grands prix and peaked with third in Ferrari's home race at Monza. He had his first full season in 1959, struggling with a front-engined 246, but took two seconds. The first of Phil's three wins came in 1960 at Monza, but 1961 was to be his best season as Ferrari had the best car and engine. Phil took his "Sharknose" Ferrari to victory at Spa and Monza. Phil moved on to less successful times at ATS in 1963 and Cooper before he returned to sports cars. Ill health forced him to retire.

○ 48 Grands Prix, 3 wins (Italian GP 1960, Belgian GP 1961, Italian GP 1961)
○ World Champion 1961

Denny Hulme
SEE PAGE 157

James Hunt
SEE PAGE 158

Jacky Ickx
Nationality: Belgian
Born: 1945

Jacky started on motorcycles then turned to saloons in 1965, twice winning the Spa 24 Hours. However, he caught the eye of Formula One team boss Ken Tyrrell who put him into his Formula Three team. Jacky was fast straight away, but his Matra lacked reliability. Tyrrell promoted him to Formula Two for 1966. He won three races in 1967, even having the audacity to qualify third for the German Grand Prix when pitched in against more powerful Formula One cars. Running fourth in this race before his suspension broke ensured that he was promoted to Formula One for 1968, with Ferrari. He was fourth overall in his first season, winning the French Grand Prix. He moved to Brabham in 1969 and won twice more, also winning the Le Mans 24 Hours, yet there was nothing he could do to keep the title from Jackie Stewart. Back with Ferrari in 1970, he won three times, but was second again. Three more years with Ferrari became ever more frustrating as the Italian cars were no match for the cars from Tyrrell and Lotus. He joined Lotus for 1974, just as that team's fortunes started to slide and Ferrari's improved. The twilight of his career was spent with Williams, Ensign and Ligier, leaving Jacky to draw satisfaction from his record tally of six wins in the Le Mans 24 Hours. He has since been involved with the modernization of Spa-Francorchamps.

○ 116 Grands Prix, 8 wins (French GP 1968, German GP 1969, Canadian GP 1969, Austrian GP 1970, Canadian GP 1970, Mexican GP 1970, Dutch GP 1971, German GP 1972)
○ No drivers' title (best result – 2nd overall 1969 and 1970)

Eddie Irvine
Nationality: British
Born: 1965

Ayrton Senna took exception to this Ulsterman on his grand prix debut in Japan in 1993, punching him for having the audacity to re-pass him after being lapped. So, Eddie had made his mark. British Formula Ford champion in 1987, he shone in Formula Three in 1988 then moved up to Formula 3000 with Pacific in 1989. Signed by Eddie Jordan for 1990, he was third overall, winning at Hockenheim. Eddie then raced sports cars and Formula 3000 in Japan for the next three years, before Jordan asked him to make that Formula One debut at Suzuka, where he came sixth. He was teamed with Rubens Barrichello in 1994, but was involved in a huge accident in the first round that saw him banned for a race. His attitude at the hearing led to this being extended to three races.

By 1995, Eddie's "badboy" reputation was behind him, and although he often qualified well, mechanical failures restricted his scoring, but he was third in Canada. It all came good with Ferrari in 1997, with second in Argentina. He was a valuable number two in 1998, then became a winner in 1999. However, his chance came when Michael Schumacher broke a leg and he became team leader. Three further wins took him to the final round in front, but Mika Hakkinen won to take the title. Eddie moved to Jaguar for 2000, looking forward to being number one from the first year of Jaguar's Formula One adventure. However, the team had a poor year and his best result was fourth at Monaco. This was improved upon by a surprise third at Monaco in 2001, but progress was slow and, although he collected third at Monza in 2002, it was to be Eddie's Formula One swansong.

○ 147 Grands Prix, 4 wins (Australian GP 1999, Austrian GP 1999, German GP 1999, Malaysian GP 1999)
○ No drivers' title (best result – 2nd 1999)

Jean-Pierre Jabouille
Nationality: French
Born: 1942

Jean-Pierre earned himself a permanent place in F1 history when he scored the first victory for a turbocharged car. After a successful career in Formula Two, he had made his Formula One debut in a one-off drive for Frank Williams in the 1974 French Grand Prix. He would only taste success at Renault, for whom he began his full-time grand prix career in 1977, after being involved in the turbo car's development from the beginning. He won one further grand prix, in Austria in 1980, before breaking a leg in that year's Canadian race.

○ 49 Grands Prix, 2 wins (French GP 1979, Austrian GP 1980)
○ No drivers' title (best result – 8th overall 1980)

On the Move: Jean-Pierre Jarier in his Ligier at the Dutch Grand Prix, Zandvoort 1983, his final year in Formula One in a thwarted career

Jean-Pierre Jarier

Nationality: French
Born: 1946

Jean-Pierre raced in 134 grands prix between 1973 and 1983 but, despite being both fast and brave, he never won one. He was at his best for the Shadow team in the mid-1970s, and lost the 1975 Brazilian Grand Prix only when a fuel-metering unit forced him to retire. Similarly, when a chance to revive his career came with Lotus in 1978, he was dominating the Canadian Grand Prix before brake problems intervened. Early in his career he had a reputation for wildness, but he brought himself under control and won the Formula Two title for the works March-BMW team in 1973, two years after he made his Formula One debut, also for March, before moving to Shadow.

After 1978 his career began to go slowly downhill. Two years with Tyrrell provided him no breakthrough and, after a disastrous time with Osella and then Ligier in the early 1980s, Formula One left him behind at the end of 1983. He revived his fortunes in the mid-1990s racing sports cars.

○ 134 Grands Prix, No wins (best result – 3rd Monaco GP 1974, South African GP 1979, British GP 1979)
○ No drivers' title (best result – 10th overall 1979 and 1980)

Stefan Johansson

Nationality: Swedish
Born: 1956

After winning the British Formula Three Championship in 1980 and being a leading figure in Formula Two in the early 1980s, the genial and popular Swede clearly had Formula One potential, but it was not until mid-1983 that he made his debut with the fledgling Spirit-Honda team.

Honda switched its engine to Williams in 1984, and Stefan had to put up with a few guest drives for Tyrrell and Toleman, for whom he looked set to be the number one driver in 1985 before a dispute over tyres left him without a drive. Ferrari provided him with a lifeline, hiring Stefan to replace René Arnoux.

The Swede earned two second places in 1985, and impressed enough to be kept on for 1986, when a succession of mechanical problems and bad luck led to him being replaced by Gerhard Berger for 1987. Stefan went to McLaren, but he was outpaced by Alain Prost and dropped for Ayrton Senna for 1988. He moved to IndyCars in 1991 and has run teams in sports cars, Indy Lights and IndyCars. He was still racing sports cars himself in 2003, encouraged no doubt by winning the Sebring 12 Hours and then Le Mans 24 Hours in 1997.

○ 79 Grands Prix, no wins (best result – 2nd Canadian GP 1985, US GP 1985, Belgian GP 1987, German GP 1987)
○ No drivers' title (best result – 5th overall 1986)

Alan Jones
SEE PAGE 161

Ukyo Katayama

Nationality: Japanese
Born: 1963

The best grand prix driver to come out of Japan, Ukyo looked out of his depth in Formula One, but some stirring drives for Tyrrell in 1994, where he usually had the measure of his team-mate Mark Blundell, gave the lie to that. Ukyo won junior single-seater titles in Japan in 1983-84 and then came to Europe to race in Formule Renault and Formula Three in 1986 and 1987. He went back to Japan to race in Formula 3000 in 1988, and won the title in 1991. His Formula One debut came with Larrousse in 1992, and he showed well against Bertrand Gachot. A terrible year followed, however, and many thought his tiny physique would mean that he would never be strong enough to drive a modern Formula One car. However, in 1994 it became clear that a strong talent and speed were allied to his sunny personality. Ukyo had a thin season in 1995, failing to score a single point as Tyrrell struggled to keep up with the richer teams. He also had a huge accident in Portugal. Sadly, 1996 was no better, and he moved on to Minardi for 1997 before quitting at the end of the year to go mountain climbing with the occasional race at Le Mans.

○ 95 Grands Prix, no wins (best result – 5th Brazilian GP 1994, San Marino GP 1994)
○ No drivers' title (best result – 17th overall 1994)

Rupert Keegan

Nationality: British
Born: 1955

Rupert was a fun-loving playboy who also possessed a fair amount of talent. He won the British Formula Three Championship in 1976 and graduated to Formula One the following year.

The Hesketh he drove was one of the worst cars of the year, but to his credit Rupert managed to qualify for every race he entered.

A season with the ailing Surtees team in 1978 was less successful, and he had to step back to win the British Formula One series in 1979. His return to Formula One in 1980 with a RAM Williams, and briefly in 1982 with March, brought little reward.

○ 25 Grands Prix, no wins (best result – 7th Austrian GP 1977)
○ No drivers' title

ALAN JONES
Williams' Hard Man

Alan remains a legend at Williams, the driver to whom all other drivers since have had to measure up. He was the no-nonsense racer who so shaped the way that Sir Frank Williams and team co-founder Patrick Head think, appreciating neither wimps nor whingers. More than that, Alan was the driver with whom the team first made its breakthrough into the Formula One front line and the man who won the team its first World Championship.

Ever since his father Stan raced in Australia in the 1950s, young Alan had decided he wanted to be World Champion. Having watched his father win the (then non-championship) Australian Grand Prix in their native Melbourne in 1959, Alan demonstrated that the will to win was in his genes as he took to kart racing with gusto. As soon as he was old enough, he ditched the kart and went racing in a Mini and later a Formula Two Cooper. Travelling to England to advance his career in 1967, Alan found that he could not even afford to race in Formula Ford, so returned home to Australia.

Three years later, Alan was back in Europe once more – he and his compatriot Brian McGuire financed their racing in Formula Three as they went along by selling used cars.

This was how Alan operated for three years. After a strong 1973 season, his career was saved as Harry Stiller entered him in Formula Atlantic. Stiller kept backing him and took Alan into Formula One in 1975, using a privately entered Hesketh, but he was then left in the lurch when Stiller closed the team.

Fortunately, Graham Hill's team snapped him up to replace the injured Rolf Stommelen and were rewarded when he raced to fifth place in the German Grand Prix.

Alan's car was more famous than he was in 1976 as he ran in a works Surtees carrying Durex condom sponsorship. Apart from finishing second in the Race of Champions, his best result was fourth place in the Japanese Grand Prix and Alan had earned himself a reputation as a hard-trying charger.

He landed a drive with Shadow in 1977 after Tom Pryce was killed at Kyalami and, almost from nowhere, won the Austrian Grand Prix, despite having started from 14th on the grid.

It was with Williams that his career took off. Driving their first purpose-built chassis in 1978, Alan produced some excellent drives and these were the precursor to success in 1979 when he won four grands prix in Patrick Head's ground-effect FW07. Indeed, a lack of reliability in the first half of the season prevented an assault on the title. No such mistakes were made in 1980, when five wins helped Alan storm to a title that he came close to retaining in 1981.

Alan quit at the end of 1981, made a brief return for Arrows in 1983, and a full-time one with the Haas Lola team in late 1985 and 1986. The car was poor, however, and Alan retired from Formula One for good. He has since raced touring cars and commentated on Australian television.

- **116 Grands Prix, 12 wins**
- **World Champion 1980**

Winning ways: Alan Jones holds the trophy aloft after winning the British Grand Prix at Brands Hatch, 1980

1946	1963	1973	1975	1977	1979	1980	1986
Born 2 November in Melbourne, Australia	Was Australian karting champion then moved up to race a Mini	Second overall behind Tony Brise in John Player Formula Three series	Formula One debut in a Stiller-entered Hesketh then joined Graham Hill's Embassy Racing team in place of injured Rolf Stommelen	Joined Shadow after Tom Pryce's death and won the Austrian GP, going on to rank seventh overall	Williams FW07 was best car, but it did not arrive until mid-season. Thereafter, Alan won four times to rank third	World Champion for Williams after winning in Argentinian, French, British, Canadian and US East GPs	Full season with Team Haas produced a fourth place in the Austrian GP, then when team folded, he returned home to become a pithy television commentator

1959	1970	1974	1976	1978	1981	1983
Watched his father, Stan, win the non-championship Australian GP	Second crack at Europe, starting a four-year spell in Formula Three	Advanced to Formula Atlantic and won races for Harry Stiller, shining in a Formula 5000 outing	Second in non-championship Race of Champions for Surtees then peaked with fourth in Japanese GP. Won two North American Formula 5000 races	Joined Williams and collected a second-place finish in the US GP	Won first and last grands prix of season to rank third, then retired	Bored, he raced Porsches in Australia then finished third in Race of Champions and had a one-off appearance for Arrows at Long Beach

Christian Klien

Nationality: Austrian
Born: 1983

Like his contemporaries, Christian was a karting champion. Progressing to the German Formula BMW Junior Cup at 16, he ranked fourth and moved up to Formula BMW in 2000. He ranked third in only his second attempt in 2001, but winning the 2002 German Formula Renault title earned him a ride in the 2003 European Formula Three championship. By far the best rookie in that year's series, he notched up three wins, including the Marlboro Masters international invitation race at Zandvoort, but had to settle for the runner-up slot in the end-of-season rankings behind Formula One test driver Ryan Briscoe. His selection as the second driver for Jaguar Racing for 2004 was still a surprise, though, but Christian matured, peaking with a best result of sixth. Retained for 2005, in a driver-alternation scheme with Vitantonio Liuzzi when the team had become Red Bull Racing, Christian won their battle and collected a fifth-place finish in the Chinese GP. However, he was turfed out before the 2006 season was over and has been snapped up by Honda as a test driver.

○ 48 Grands prix, no wins (best result - 5th Chinese GP 2005)

○ No drivers' title (best result - 15th overall 2005)

Heikki Kovalainen

Nationality: Finnish
Born: 1981

One to watch in the junior categories, what marked Heikki out was beating Michael Schumacher in the final of the multi-discipline Race of Champions in 2004. Runner-up to Nico Rosberg in GP2 in 2005, he became a test driver for Renault and stepped up to a race seat in 2007. After taking a while to find his form, he placed fourth in Canada and second in Suzuka. McLaren signed

Arriving with a Bang: Robert Kubicka burst onto the scene for BMW midway through 2006

him for 2008 and he claimed his one win at the Hungaroring. However, through the season and then 2009, he was very much in team-mate Lewis Hamilton's shadow and had to turn to reborn Lotus in 2010.

○ 52 Grands Prix, 1 win (Hungarian GP 2008)

○ No drivers' title (best result – 7th overall 2007 and 2008)

Robert Kubica

Nationality: Polish
Born: 1984

Promoted into the BMW Sauber A Renault development driver from 2002, Robert was World Series by

Renault champion in 2005 then promoted into the BMW Sauber Formula One team in place of Jacques Villeneuve in mid-2006. By his third outing, at Monza, he was on the podium. In 2007, he scored 11 times, and survived a huge accident in Canada. The 2008 season was better still and he won the Canadian GP en route to ranking fourth. However, the team's form dropped in 2009 and he returned to Renault.

○ 57 Grands Prix, 1 win (Canadian GP 2008)

○ No drivers' title (best result - 4th overall 2008)

Jacques Laffite

Nationality: French
Born: 1943

Jacques' impish sense of humour and irreverence, allied to a considerable talent behind the wheel, brightened the grand prix scene for more than a decade during the 1970s and 1980s. Having won the French Formula Three and European Formula Two titles in the early 1970s, Jacques made his grand prix debut for the Williams team in 1974. He and team boss Frank Williams got on well, and Jacques helped keep the team afloat by taking a timely second place in the German Grand Prix in 1975. The following year he joined the new Ligier team and they developed well together, until Jacques finally tasted victory in 1977 in Sweden. No more wins followed until 1979 when the team switched from Matra V12 power to a Cosworth V8. Jacques and the JS11 won the first two races of the season, but he did not win again until mid-1980. A return to Matra power in 1981 saw him take two wins and make a late-season push for the title, but after a dreadful 1982 he left to drive for Williams in 1983. Usually, though, he was overshadowed in the uncompetitive cars by team-mate Keke Rosberg, and he returned to Ligier in 1985. The cars were quick, and Jacques went with them all the way, scoring a number of podium finishes and briefly leading the Detroit Grand Prix in 1986. However, an accident at the British Grand Prix ended his Formula One career. He has since raced touring cars and contested a sports car campaign partnering Jean-Pierre Jabouille in a Morgan in 2007.' Then add: 'He did the same again for AutoGT Racing 2008, then raced the VW Scirocco Cup in 2010.'

○ 175 Grands Prix, 6 wins (Swedish GP 1977, Argentinian GP 1979, Brazilian GP 1979, German GP 1980, Austrian GP 1981, Canadian GP 1981)

○ No drivers' title (best result – 4th overall 1979, 1980 and 1981)

Nicola Larini

Nationality: Italian
Born: 1964

Nicola won the Italian Formula Three title with Coloni in 1986, before moving up to Formula One with the team in late 1987. He switched to Osella in 1988-89, when some brilliant drives in weak machinery earned him a seat at Ligier for 1990. Unfortunately, neither this car nor the Lamborghini he drove in 1991 were competitive, and he left Formula One. Nicola won the Italian touring car title with Alfa Romeo in 1992, and went on to dominate the highly competitive German series in 1993. As the Ferrari's test driver, he subbed for an injured Jean Alesi in early 1994, finishing second in the San Marino Grand Prix before Alesi returned. He was back in Formula One with Sauber in 1997, but was dropped after five races and races touring cars to this day, now for – Chevrolet.

o **49 Grands Prix, no wins (best result – 2nd San Marino GP 1994)**
o **No drivers' title (best result– 14th overall 1994)**

Niki Lauda

SEE PAGE 164

JJ Lehto

Nationality: Finnish
Born: 1966

Great success was forecast for JJ (real name Jyrki Jarvilehto) who had won the European, Scandinavian and Finnish Formula Ford 1600 titles by 1986. When he came to Britain in 1987 he dominated the national and European Formula Ford 2000 scene before winning the closely fought British Formula Three series in 1988. Formula 3000 was a less fruitful hunting ground, but he established a respected Formula One reputation with drives at Onyx, Dallara and Sauber between 1989 and 1993 before landing a seat at Benetton in 1994.

JJ broke his neck in a pre-season testing accident and, though he was close to the pace of team-mate Michael Schumacher, the deaths of friend Roland Ratzenberger and Ayrton Senna affected him deeply, and when it was clear that his neck still was not completely healed Benetton dropped him. He raced in the German Touring Car Championship in 1995 and 1996 and then became the world's top sports car driver when leading McLaren's GT attack against the Mercedes in 1997. After a year in IndyCars in 1998, he returned to sports cars with BMW in 1999, winning the Sebring 12 Hours. He shared a Champion Racing Audi with Johnny Herbert with much success in the American Le Mans Series in 2003.

o **60 Grands Prix, no wins (best result – 3rd San Marino GP 1991)**
o **No drivers' title (best result –12th overall 1991)**

Stuart Lewis-Evans

Nationality: British
Born: 1930
Died: 1958

His career statistics don't add up to much, but that belies a rare talent. This frail man was a leading exponent of Formula Three before being given his Formula One debut by Connaught at the end of 1956. After showing well in the Connaught early in 1957, he was signed by Vanwall to partner its two stars, Stirling Moss and Tony Brooks. Stuart put in some truly brilliant performances, but in World Championship races, although his flair and finesse were evident, he had only a fifth place at Pescara to show for his efforts by the end of the year. Nevertheless, he won considerable admiration from his team-mates, and played a crucial role in helping Vanwall to win the first Constructors' title, in 1958. He was on the threshold of a splendid Formula One career, but he crashed heavily in the 1958 Moroccan Grand Prix, and suffered severe burns in the ensuing fire. He died six days later.

o **14 Grands Prix, no wins (best result – 3rd Belgian GP 1958, Portuguese GP 1958)**
o **No drivers' title (best result – 9th overall 1958)**

Vitantonio Liuzzi

Nationality: Italian
Born: 1981

Good in karts, strong in Formula 3000, Vitantonio muscled his way into Formula One with Red Bull Racing in 2005. Two years were then spent at Scuderia Toro Rosso, losing fourth place in Canada due to debris from Robert Kubica's accident being trapped under his car. Then he lost out in 2008 before returning to Formula One with Force India for the last five races of 2009 after Giancarlo Fisichella moved across to Ferrari, earning a fulltime ride for 2010.

o **44 Grands Prix, 0 wins (best result – Chinese GP 2007)**
o **No drivers' title (best result – 18th overall 2007)**

Promise Unfulfilled: JJ Lehto beside his Benetton before the Portuguese Grand Prix at Estoril in 1994

NIKI LAUDA
Comeback Hero

Great Survivor: Niki Lauda at the height of his powers in 1975 when he helped put Ferrari back on the map

At the end of 1976 Niki had missed out on the world title following a horrific accident in which he nearly died, but this gritty Austrian had become one of the sport's great survivors.

He began in hill climbs and then, with a bank loan, Niki bought himself a place in the March Formula Two team in 1971. He was more than just a rich kid, however, as, at Rouen, he had to be given the "slow" signal to prevent him beating team-mate Ronnie Peterson.

Niki made an inauspicious Formula One debut at the Osterreichring in 1971 and arranged to buy himself a March Formula One ride for 1972, but his loan was stopped, so Niki persuaded the bank to spread the deal over five years. The trouble was, the March was a lemon. However, for 1973 he was offered the third BRM alongside Jean-Pierre Beltoise and Clay Regazzoni. Both were winners and things looked up when he outpaced them. BRM even started to pay him so Niki could maintain his bank payments. He led in Canada and attracted the attention of Ferrari. By 1974 Niki was with the Italian team and did much to restore their fortunes.

Niki won at Jarama and Zandvoort and looked favourite for the title. He then dominated at Brands Hatch until a puncture forced him to pit, only to find the pit exit blocked. Then he crashed on the first lap at the Nurburgring and hit oil when leading in Canada. Critics questioned his temperament. In 1975, Niki dominated, putting Ferrari back on top. His championship year included wins in Monaco, Belgium and Sweden.

In 1976, it looked certain that he would win back-to-back titles as he won four of the first six races, but, at the Nurburgring, he crashed and his car burst into flames. Niki was pulled out by three fellow drivers, but his life hung in the balance and he was administered the last rites. Incredibly, he came back, scarred, at Monza, where he turned in a heroic drive to fourth. A strong run by James Hunt threatened his lead and, in the last race at Fuji, Niki pulled out after a lap in appalling conditions, his burned eyelids unable to blink in the spray. Hunt finished third and took the title by a point.

Ferrari had signed Carlos Reutemann to lead the team in 1977, but, with feisty determination, Niki won at Kyalami. Further wins in Holland and Germany gave him his title back. Angered at Ferrari politics, Niki left for Brabham, where he did not enjoy similar success. He did win in Sweden, though, beating the all-conquering Lotus 79s with the BT46B "fan car". Niki quit at the end of 1979, but he was back in 1982, winning twice for McLaren. It was the beginning of the turbo era and McLaren lagged behind until it got hold of TAG-Porsche power. Niki used his craft in 1984 to overcome team-mate Alain Prost, ending up a half-point ahead.

Niki's final year was 1985, and he knew he would not be able to hold Prost again, although he did beat the Frenchman at Zandvoort to record his last triumph.

- **171 Grands Prix, 25 wins**
- **World Champion 1975, 1977 and 1984**

1949	1969	1973	1975	1976	1978	1982	1985	2001
Born 22 February in Vienna, Austria	Took to Mini racing but soon moved into single-seaters in Formula Vee	Joined BRM and scored fifth place in Belgian GP	Came good with five wins to be World Champion for Ferrari	With five wins and heading for a second title he crashed in the German GP. Although terribly burned, he just lost out to James Hunt	Moved to Brabham and won Swedish GP in Brabham "fan car". Also won Italian GP to rank fourth overall	Returned to racing with McLaren and won at Long Beach and Brands Hatch to rank fifth	Won only the Dutch GP and ranked tenth as Prost walked the title, then retired from racing	Took over Ford's Premier Performance Division and ran team until end of 2002

1968	1971	1974	1977	1979	1984	1992
Contested hill climbs in a Mini	Moved up to Formula Two and made Formula One debut in home race with a rented March	Moved over to Ferrari and won the Spanish and Dutch GPs to rank fourth overall	Won three times, in South Africa, Germany and Holland, to be World Champion again for Ferrari	Weak season with Brabham caused him to quit before end of year. Went off to set up a charter airline	World Champion for a third time, winning five grands prix to pip McLaren team-mate Alain Prost by half a point	Rejoined Ferrari in a consultancy role that continued through until 1999

Team Builder: Bruce McLaren pictured in 1964 after he formed his own company which went on to dominate the CanAm sports series for the rest of the decade

Lella Lombardi

Nationality: Italian
Born: 1943
Died: 1992

Lella is the only woman to date to finish in the top six in a grand prix, in Spain in 1975. Spells in Formula Monza and Formula Three in Italy led to a Formula 5000 programme in 1974, when she finished fourth in the championship, and that earned her a full season in Formula One in a March in 1975, when she also finished seventh in the German Grand Prix. Lella then dropped out of Formula One, but continued her career in sports cars. She died of cancer in 1992.

○ 12 Grands Prix, no wins (best result – 6th Spanish GP 1975)
○ No drivers' title (best result – 21st overall 1975)

John Love

Nationality: Zimbabwean
Born: 1924

John partnered Tony Maggs in Ken Tyrrells' Formula Junior team in 1961 and then won the 1962 British Touring Car Championship in a works Mini Cooper.

An abortive attempt to race Formula One in Europe in 1964 led to his return to South Africa where he not only won the first of his six South African Formula One titles at the end of that year but also raced regularly in the country's World Championship Grand Prix.

His results were relatively patchy as he kept finding himself in outmoded equipment, but in 1967 he came close to causing one of the greatest upsets of all time when

only a precautionary late pit stop for fuel lost him the race, dropping him to second place. Thereafter he shone in the South African Springbok sports car series.

○ 9 Grands Prix, no wins (best result – 2nd South African GP 1967)
○ No drivers' title (best result – 11th overall 1967)

Brett Lunger

Nationality: American
Born: 1945

An heir to the wealthy DuPont family, Brett's early racing career was interrupted by a spell in Vietnam in the American army.

He resumed in Formula 5000 in 1971, tried Formula Two in Europe in 1972 and then moved up to Formula One in 1975 as James Hunt's team-

mate at Hesketh. Brett switched to Surtees in 1976, and drove a private McLaren in 1977-78, with minimal impact.

○ 34 Grands Prix, no wins (best result – 7th Belgian GP 1977)
○ No drivers' title

Bruce McLaren

Nationality: New Zealander
Born: 1937
Died: 1970

A talented driver and the man who established what is now the second most successful grand prix team of all time, he arrived on the Formula One scene in 1959 with a series of assured performances with Cooper before winning the final race of the year.

After winning the first grand prix of 1960, McLaren slipped into a supporting role to reigning champion Jack Brabham, eventually becoming team leader in 1961 when Brabham left. However, after several frustrating seasons, which had been briefly enlivened by winning the 1962 Monaco Grand Prix, Bruce formed his own team in 1964. In partnership with abrasive American Teddy Mayer, the tolerant, popular McLaren built his company into a successful, professional outfit with a reputation for technical excellence.

In 1968 he enticed his friend Denny Hulme, the reigning world champion, to join him and, while Hulme set the pace in Formula One, McLarens dominated the American CanAm sports car series for the rest of the decade. Bruce continued to race in Formula One, and occasionally shone, winning the 1968 Belgian Grand Prix, and dominating the Race of Champions the same year. As his team had a reputation for consistency and safety, it was ironic that he should die while testing one of his CanAm cars at Goodwood in 1970.

○ 101 Grands Prix, 4 wins (US GP 1959, Argentinian GP 1960, Monaco GP 1962, Belgian GP 1968)
○ No drivers' title (best result – 2nd overall 1960)

Tony Maggs

Nationality: South African

Born: 1937

Tony came to prominence in 1961 driving for Ken Tyrrell's Formula Junior team when he shared the European Formula Junior title with Jo Schlesser.

He was snapped up by Cooper for 1962-63 and, although he finished second in the French Grand Prix both years, he was replaced by Phil Hill and moved to drive a BRM for Scuderia Centro Sud. He drove his final grand prix in South Africa in 1965, then raced in sports cars until he killed a boy in a crash and quit the sport.

○ **25 Grands Prix, no wins (best result – 2nd French GP 1962, French GP 1963)**

○ **No drivers' title (best result – 7th 1962)**

Umberto Maglioli

Nationality: Italian

Born: 1928

An accomplished sports car driver and the winner of the Carrera Panamericana in 1954, Umberto only drove occasionally in grands prix as a junior driver for Ferrari in the mid-1950s, followed by three races for Maserati in 1956.

Leg injuries interrupted his career, but he won the 1959 Sebring 12 Hours, and repeated this feat again in 1964. He won the 1968 Targa Florio driving a Porsche, and was victorious on the Sicilian road circuit in 1953 and 1956.

○ **10 Grands Prix, no wins (best result – 3rd Italian GP 1954, Argentinian GP 1955)**

○ **No drivers' title (best result – 18th overall 1954)**

Jan Magnussen

Nationality: Danish

Born: 1973

A double World Kart Champion, Jan won the Formula Ford Festival in 1992. He walked away with the 1994 British Formula Three series, with 14 wins in 18 races for Paul Stewart Racing. McLaren signed him as test driver for 1995, while Mercedes fielded him in the International Touring Car series. Jan finished runner-up to Bernd Schneider.

Born Under a Bad Sign: Willy Mairesse was famous for the number of lurid accidents he was involved in throughout his career. Later he took his own life

He got his Formula One break when he stood in at McLaren for the 1995 Pacific Grand Prix when Mika Hakkinen had appendicitis, but then moved Stateside to race the IndyCar circuit with Penske. Jackie Stewart brought him back to Formula One when he signed him for Stewart Grand Prix for 1997, with Jan enduring a run of engine failures.

With his form in early 1998 sketchy, he was replaced by Jos Verstappen and has since returned to the US to race sports cars. He also races touring cars at home in Denmark and won the 2003 title.

○ **25 Grands Prix, no wins (best result – 6th Canadian GP 1998)**

○ **No drivers' title (best result – 15th overall 1998)**

Willy Mairesse

Nationality: Belgian

Born: 1928

Died: 1969

Willy was famous for his lurid accidents. Ferrari signed him in 1960, and he was in and out of Formula One until he was signed up as number two to John Surtees in 1963. He ended his grand prix career after crashing out of the German Grand Prix. He raced in sports cars until 1968, when he crashed in a Ford GT40 at Le Mans after a door flew open, and he suffered head injuries. He was ill for a year and, realizing there was no place for him in racing, killed himself.

○ **12 Grands Prix, no wins (best result – 4th Italian GP 1962)**

○ **No drivers' title (best result – 14th overall 1962)**

NIGEL MANSELL
The People's Champion

The world's most dramatic driver and the most courageous. Late in his career, he was one of the very fastest, too and, although he moaned a lot, the public loved him.

In his early racing days, Nigel thought he was the best and could not understand why others refused to see this. Even when he had been given a shot at Formula One in 1980 few took him seriously. What they should have heeded was that he drove most of his debut with fuel burning his skin.

The 1986 season was a low for Nigel. Despite five wins, the year ended in disappointment at the Australian Grand Prix when his Williams' left rear tyre exploded. In 1987, he was in a fight for the title with team-mate Nelson Piquet. Heading for the penultimate race in Japan, Nigel had beaten Piquet in Mexico yet was lying 12 points behind. However, he came to grief in qualifying, injuring his back and finishing his season.

Nigel made a bold move in 1989, when he joined Ferrari. This most English of men was not expected to blend into the Italian outfit, but he did, earning the adoration of the *tifosi* by winning first time out, in Brazil.

Alain Prost joined Ferrari in 1990 and this soon fazed Nigel, convincing him Prost was getting better equipment. He won only once, after chopping across Prost's bows entering the first corner at Estoril. This forced Prost to slow and he fell to fifth, losing the title to Senna. So it was back to Williams for 1991 and back to winning ways. Indeed, Nigel won five races, yet still had to play second fiddle to Ayrton Senna.

Finally, Nigel got it all right in 1992. Not only did he win nine times, but he completed the year with almost double the points of the driver who came second, team-mate Riccardo Patrese. There is no doubt that he drove magnificently, but his Williams-Renault was the class of the field and Nigel impressed no one by refusing to acknowledge this technical superiority.

Amazingly, by the time Nigel clinched the title with five races to go, it was clear that Williams did not want to retain him: Prost was going to join for 1993 and Senna had offered his services for nothing. Not wishing to be a team-mate of either, Nigel decided to try IndyCar racing with the Newman-Haas team. He won the first race, then crashed heavily when he tried a banked oval for the first time.

He was back up to speed for the Indianapolis 500 and nearly won that, too, only dropping to third in the closing laps. Nigel learned from his mistakes and won next time out. Two more wins followed on the ovals, putting him into a points lead he was never to lose. He was the only driver in Formula One to clinch the IndyCar title back to back – a true world champion.

Sadly, the Lola was no longer the chassis to have in 1994 and rival Penske cleaned up. So Nigel returned to Formula One mid-season with Williams, winning the Australian Grand Prix. In 1995 he joined McLaren, but never settled, and quit after two races.

○ **187 Grands Prix, 31 wins**
○ **World Champion 1992**

World at his Feet: Mansell waves to the crowd after winning the San Marino Grand Prix in 1992

1953	1977	1981	1985	1987	1991	1993	1995
Born 8 August in Upton-on-Severn, England	British Formula Ford champion	Signed by Lotus for a full campaign, Nigel finished third at Zolder and fourth at Caesars Palace	Joined Williams and rose to sixth overall, winning the final two races	Runner-up for Williams again, this time to team-mate Nelson Piquet, even though he outscored him by six wins to three	Drive at Williams prevented him from retiring and he won five grands prix to be runner-up	Quit Formula One for IndyCar racing and won title with Newman/Haas Racing even though he endured massive shunt early in season	Made two outings for McLaren, but did not fit car properly and entered retirement for good to run a golf course near Exeter

1969	1980	1984	1986	1989	1992	1994
Member of British junior karting team	Raced for Honda in Formula Two, but given Formula One break by Lotus	Broke into top-ten overall for first time with two thirds, but crashed out of lead at Monaco	Pipped to title in finale when he had a blow-out in Adelaide and Prost claimed crown. Won five grands prix	Joined Ferrari and won on his debut in Brazil. Another win in Hungary helped him rank fourth overall	World Champion with massive domination by winning nine of the 16 grands prix. Dropped by Williams at end of year	Second season in Indy Cars was not such a success, but Nigel took in four races for Williams and won the Australian GP

Robert Manzon

Nationality: French
Born: 1917

After being one of the rising stars in the immediate post-war years, Robert was a mainstay of the Gordini team in the early 1950s, despite the fact that it was an era dominated by Maserati, Ferrari and then Mercedes. He did put in some excellent performances, however, including third places in the 1952 Belgian Grand Prix and at Reims in 1954, driving a privately entered Ferrari in the latter. After winning the Pescara sports car race for Gordini against the more powerful Ferraris in 1956, Robert retired to run the family business.

○ 28 Grands Prix, no wins (best result – 3rd Belgian GP 1952, French GP 1954)
○ No drivers' title (best result – 6th overall 1952)

Onofre Marimon

Nationality: Argentinian
Born: 1923
Died: 1954

A protégé of Juan Manuel Fangio, Onofre joined the works Maserati team in 1953 after showing great promise. He stood in for Fangio in some early-season non-championship races, and when Fangio left to join Mercedes he found himself effectively leading the team. He finished an excellent third in the British Grand Prix, ahead of Fangio, and seemed destined for great things, but he was killed instantly in a crash at the Nurburgring during practice for the German Grand Prix in 1954.

○ 11 Grands Prix, no wins (best result – 3rd Belgian GP 1953, British GP 1954)
○ No drivers' title (best result – 11th overall 1953)

Pierluigi Martini

Nationality: Italian
Born: 1961

Perennially underrated, Pierluigi became a respected member of the grand prix fraternity. After winning the European Formula Three title in 1983 and failing to qualify a Toleman at the 1984 Italian Grand Prix, the inexperienced Martini suffered an appalling debut season in Formula One with the uncompetitive Minardi-Motori Moderni team. However, a step back to Formula 3000 saw him return in 1988 a changed man, and in 1989 he was at his best in Formula One, briefly leading the Portuguese Grand Prix and qualifying an amazing third in Australia. Following that he was consigned to the midfield, alternating between the Minardi and Scuderia Italia teams. Pierluigi missed the first half of 1993, when he was dropped by Scuderia Italia, but returned with Minardi until a cash crisis saw him dropped in the middle of 1995. Racing in sports cars brought him victory at Le Mans in 1999 with Yannick Dalmas and Jo Winkelhock in a works BMW.

○ 119 Grands Prix, no wins (best result – 4th San Marino GP 1991, Portuguese GP 1991)
○ No drivers' title (best result – 11th 1991)

Jochen Mass

Nationality: German
Born: 1946

Jochen graduated to Formula One with Surtees after strong showings in the European Touring Car Championship – he was champion in 1972 – and Formula Two in which he was runner-up to Jean-Pierre Jarier in 1973 before making his Formula One debut with Surtees. He ran a full campaign for Surtees in 1974 and then moved to McLaren in 1975, where he was an excellent number two to Emerson Fittipaldi and won the Spanish Grand Prix. However, he then dropped into a subordinate role after James Hunt arrived in 1976, as he could not match the Englishman's pace on the track. Jochen moved to ATS in 1978, but broke a leg in a test at Silverstone. He drove for Arrows in 1979-80, had a year off in 1981 and returned for an uncompetitive season with March in 1982, after which he concentrated on sports cars, winning the Le Mans 24 Hours for Mercedes in 1989. The following year he acted as tutor to the company's young stars, including Michael Schumacher, before retiring at the end of 1991.

○ 105 Grands Prix, 1 win (Spanish GP 1975)
○ No drivers' title (best result – 7th 1975)

Felipe Massa

Nationality: Brazilian
Born: 1981

Few really knew who Felipe was when he was signed by Sauber to race for them in 2002. Further investigation showed that he had won the Brazilian Formula Chevrolet title in 1999, the European and Italian Formula Renault title in 2000 and the second division

Mass Movement: German driver Jochen Mass on the way to his maiden – his one and only – grand prix win in a McLaren at Barcelona in 1975

Euro Formula 3000 title (not the FIA International one) in 2001.

But he benefited from the Swiss team casting its nets wide to see if they could land another hotshot to match the previous year's charge, Kimi Raikkonen. Teamed with Nick Heidfeld, he was often every bit as quick but he was too wild for Sauber's taste and was dropped after taking a fifth and two sixths. Then Ferrari signed him as a test driver for 2003 then, amusingly, placed the now more mature Felipe back with Sauber – to whom it supplied engines – for 2004. Fourth place at Spa was followed by fourth in Canada in 2005.

Then he became a Ferrari driver in 2006 and went increasingly well alongside Michael Schumacher, winning in Turkey then Brazil to rank third. For a few seconds, he was World Champion in 2008, but then Lewis Hamilton passed Timo Glok to take the points he needed for the crown.

The 2009 season was even more cruel as his campaign was curtailed by a head injury at the Hungarian GP. But he survived to come back for 2010.

○ 122 Grands Prix, 11 wins (2006 Turkish GP, Brazilian GP, 2007 Bahrain GP, Spanish GP, Turkish GP, 2008 Bahrain GP, Turkish GP, French GP, European GP, Belgian GP, Brazilian GP)

* No drivers' title (best result – 2nd 2008)

Arturo Merzario

Nationality: Italian
Born: 1943

Little Arturo made his name in sports cars before joining Ferrari in 1970. By 1972 he had put in enough promising performances to be promoted to the grand prix team mid-season.

His feistiness served him well through Ferrari's nadir in 1973. It also appealed to Frank Williams, who signed Arturo in 1974. He took a couple of good points finishes, but things did not go well the following year, and he quit mid-season. He drove a works March in 1976, and ran his own private March in 1977 before setting up his own team in 1978. The car, however, was a disaster and he wound

The Resistible Rise of Little Arturo: Arturo Merzario brings his Ferrari home in sixth place at the British Grand Prix at Brands Hatch in July 1972

up his Formula One career having exhausted most of his funds.

○ 57 Grands Prix, no wins (best result – 4th Brazilian GP 1973, South African GP 1973, Italian GP 1974)

○ No drivers' title (best result – 12th 1973)

John Miles

Nationality: British
Born: 1943

The son of actor Sir Bernard Miles, John began his motor racing career with an extremely successful period in Lotus sports cars during 1966–68. After a brief fling with Formula Two in 1969, he was entrusted by Lotus boss Colin Chapman with the development of the four-wheel drive Lotus 63.

He became Jochen Rindt's number two in 1970 after Graham Hill broke both his legs in an accident, but as

an engineer he was nervous of the fragility of the Lotus 72 and was dropped after Rindt's death in the Italian Grand Prix. This signalled the end of his Formula One career. He later became a road tester and then a development engineer for Lotus Cars.

○ 12 Grands Prix, no wins (best result – 5th South African GP 1970)

○ No drivers' title (best result – 19th 1970)

Stefano Modena

Nationality: Italian
Born: 1963

A splendid year in Formula Three – when he impressed the grand prix community in the support race at Monaco in 1986 – marked him as a man to watch, and he won the Formula 3000 title at his first attempt in 1987. However, his first

three years in Formula One were with tail-end teams, and it was not until he joined Tyrrell in 1991 that his ability became clear.

The car was not quite as good as he expected, however, and, after a great performance at Monaco, when he qualified second to Ayrton Senna, and a superb second in the next race at Montreal, Stefano faded badly.

Despite this disappointment, he was signed up to drive for Jordan in 1992, but the project dramatically failed to gel, and Stefano's Formula One career came to an end. He later shone in touring cars, finally showing the speed that people always knew he possessed.

○ 70 Grands Prix, no wins (best result – 2nd Canadian GP 1991)

○ No drivers' title (best result – 8th 1991)

Tiago Monteiro

Nationality: Portuguese
Born: 1976

Some drivers have "future star" written all over them; others have to work at their craft. Tiago falls into the latter category. Indeed, he didn't arrive in Formula One in 2005 with glowing credentials. Amazingly, by mid-season, he'd changed most people's opinion through using his head and finishing race after race as faster rivals made mistakes. That he got to spray champagne from the podium showed just how bizarre the US GP had been, as he finished third for Jordan in a race where only six cars started, after the Michelin-shod teams had withdrawn. More impressive was his drive to eighth in the Belgian GP. Sadly, there was no repeat in 2006 as the team, known as Midland then Spyker, lagged behind.

Tiago was runner-up in French Formula Three then runner-up in the Formula Dallara Nissan V6 in 2004, and he has headed to the World Touring Car series with SEAT for 2007.

○ **37 Grands Prix, no wins (best result - 3rd US GP 2005)**
○ **No drivers' title (best result - 16th overall 2005)**

Juan Pablo Montoya

Nationality: Colombian
Born: 1975

Fast and feisty, Juan Pablo was seen in the early 2000s as the driver most likely to topple Michael Schumacher. For all his speed, it took the Colombian quite a while to reach Formula One. After racing karts in Colombia, he shone in the US Barber Saab series in 1994, raced in Britain in 1995 then stepped up to Formula Three in 1996. Moving up to Formula 3000 was when he really showed his talent and he not only finished as runner-up, to Ricardo Zonta in 1997, but was also signed by Williams as its test driver. He beat Nick Heidfeld to the 1998 Formula 3000 title but was sent to the USA, winning the Champ Car title at his first attempt. He then won the Indy 500 in 2000 before Williams had a seat free for him in 2001 and he raced to his first grand prix win, at Monza. He moved up from sixth overall in 2001 to third overall in 2002, albeit not winning once in a year that yielded seven poles. Third again in 2003, Juan Pablo did at least win - at Monaco and Hockenheim - as Williams hit form, but he could have been champion, as a drive-through penalty at Indianapolis cost him dear. As it was, his engine failure when leading the Suzuka finale was academic.

He knew through 2004 that he was moving on to McLaren and signed out with a win in Brazil. A shoulder injury interrupted 2005, but Juan Pablo bounced back and won three times, matching Raikkonen for speed. In 2006, though, Juan Pablo lived the first half of the year in Raikkonen's shadow before knocking the pair of them out at the start of the US Grand Prix. He then announced his retirement, claiming disenchantment with Formula One and is now enjoying NASCAR stock racing in the USA.

○ **95 Grands Prix, 7 wins (Italian GP 2001, Monaco GP 2003, German GP 2003, Brazilian GP 2004, British GP 2005, Italian GP 2005, Brazilian GP 2005)**
○ **No drivers' title (best result - 3rd overall 2002 and 2003)**

Roberto Moreno

Nationality: Brazilian
Born: 1959

Roberto's Formula One career was over almost before it started when he failed to qualify a Lotus at the 1982 Dutch Grand Prix. He was to get another chance, but that race handicapped him for a number of years. After finishing second to team-mate Mike Thackwell in European Formula Two in 1984, Roberto moved to IndyCars. A return to Europe in 1987 saw him race in Formula 3000 and he also had a few outings for the fledgling AGS team. He stayed in Formula 3000 in 1988 and won the title impressively. Ferrari awarded him a testing contract and he raced for Coloni, and Eurobrun, before being given his break late in 1990 at Benetton, replacing the injured Alessandro Nannini. A second place behind team-mate Nelson Piquet at Suzuka ensured he was kept on, but he was fired (just after finishing fourth in the Belgian Grand Prix), as Benetton snapped up Michael Schumacher. A year with hapless Andrea Moda in 1992 was less than he deserved. Roberto then suffered with the hopeless Forti Corse team in 1995 and moved back to IndyCars for 1996.

○ **42 Grands Prix, no wins (best result - 2nd Japanese GP 1990)**
○ **No drivers' title (best result - 10th overall 1990 and 1991)**

Stirling Moss

Nationality: British
Born: 1929

People describe Stirling as the best driver never to win a World Championship. And that he was, a talent far greater than many who became champion. At the age of 18 in 1948, Stirling entered local hill-climbs before turning his hand to racing in 1949. Success in Formula Three earned him a ride in HWM's Formula Two car. He also raced sports cars and finished second in the Monte Carlo Rally in 1952. His Formula One outings stood little chance of success

As Good As It Gets: Juan Pablo Montoya after winning the Italian Grand Prix for Williams in 2001

Glittering Prize: the 20-year-old Stirling Moss and his proud parents admire the cup he has just won in the 500cc event before the Monaco GP in 1950

between 1951 and 1953 as he was behind the wheel of British cars that had no answer to the superior Alfa Romeos and Maseratis.

For 1954, Stirling decided that he would widen the net and he approached Mercedes boss Neubauer who suggested Stirling should spend the year showing what he could do in a competitive car. He purchased a Maserati as a result. Taking third place first time out in the Belgian Grand Prix convinced Neubauer to sign him for 1955 to drive alongside Fangio. This teacher-pupil relationship really worked and yielded his first win, when Fangio let him by in the British Grand Prix at Aintree. They ended the season with Fangio claiming the world title for the third time and with Stirling runner-up. Mercedes' decision to withdraw from racing in response to the disaster at Le Mans in 1955, in which more than 80 spectators were killed, took Stirling to Maserati in 1956, for whom he won twice, and he again wound up second overall to Fangio. Back in British machinery

in 1957 with the Vanwall team, he won three times, but still he ended the year in Fangio's wake. Staying with Vanwall in 1958, he was a four-time winner, but was runner-up for the fourth year in succession, losing out at the final hurdle when Mike Hawthorn scrabbled his way past Ferrari team-mate Phil Hill in the Moroccan Grand Prix to claim the extra point he needed to pip Stirling to the World Championship crown.

For 1959 and 1960 Stirling drove assorted cars, but was seen mainly in a Cooper, winning twice in 1959. However, he also raced a Lotus and gave the marque its first ever win at Monaco in 1960. He won again after recovering from leg and back injuries inflicted when he was thrown from his car at Spa-Francorchamps. Ferrari was prepared for rule changes in 1961 and its new engine was the class of the field. Stirling raced with the less powerful Coventry Climax in his Lotus and still managed to win twice. His career was brought to a close in a non-championship meeting at

Goodwood in 1962 when he crashed head-on into an earth bank, incurring head injuries. Stirling recovered, but chose not to return to the cockpit.

○ 66 Grands Prix, 16 wins (British GP 1955, Monaco GP 1956, Italian GP 1956, British GP 1957, Pescara GP 1957, Italian GP 1957, Argentinian GP 1958, Dutch GP 1958, Portuguese GP 1958, Moroccan GP 1958, Portuguese GP 1959, Italian GP 1959, Monaco GP 1960, US GP 1960, Monaco GP 1961, German GP 1961)

○ No drivers' title (best result – 2nd, 1955, 1956, 1957 and 1958)

Luigi Musso

Nationality: Italian
Born: 1924
Died: 1958

Luigi dominated sports car racing in Italy in the early 1950s before buying a Maserati 250F, winning the non-championship Pescara Grand Prix and finishing second in the Spanish Grand Prix in 1954. A string of good results in 1955 saw him join Ferrari for 1956, and he won his first race, the Argentinian Grand Prix, sharing

his Lancia-Ferrari with Juan Manuel Fangio. In 1957 he won the non-championship Marne Grand Prix, but was by now struggling to keep pace with team-mates Mike Hawthorn and Peter Collins. Chasing them at Reims, he ran wide on a long, fast corner, and the car flipped in a ditch. The unfortunate Luigi was killed instantly.

○ 24 Grands Prix, 1 win (Argentinian GP 1956)
○ No drivers' title (best result – 3rd, 1957)

Satoru Nakajima

Nationality: Japanese
Born: 1953

Japan's first regular grand prix driver, Satoru was Honda's representative on the grid in the late 1980s. After a glittering career in Japan, he moved up to Formula One and was made Ayrton Senna's team-mate at Lotus in 1987, when the team first ran Honda engines.

Miles off Senna's pace, Satoru ran much closer to Nelson Piquet in the team in 1988, and in '89 matched his best Formula One result, coming fourth in the torrential rains of Adelaide. Satoru raced for Tyrrell for the next two seasons, before bowing out at the end of 1991 to run teams in both Japanese Formula 3000 (Formula Nippon) and Formula Three.

○ 74 Grands Prix, no wins (best result – 4th British GP 1987, Australian GP 1989)
○ No drivers' title (best result – 11th overall 1987)

Shinji Nakano

Nationality: Japanese
Born: 1971

Raced in British Formula Vauxhall in 1990 before moving to Japanese Formula 3000 in 1992, peaking with sixth place overall in 1996. Family connections helped him secure backing from Mugen to land a Formula One ride with Prost in 1997, and he scored a pair of sixth places before moving to Minardi. A spell in IndyCars followed, but with little success.

○ 33 Grands Prix, no wins (best result – 6th Canadian GP 1997, Hungarian GP 1997)
○ No drivers' title (best result – 16th 1997)

Alessandro Nannini

Nationality: Italian
Born: 1959

Sandro's Formula One career was cut short when an arm was severed in a helicopter accident. Micro-surgery reattached the limb, and Alessandro became a race-winner in the German Touring series. Given his chance in Formula One with Minardi, he was more than a match for Andrea de Cesaris before joining Benetton in 1988, where he sometimes outpaced team-mate Thierry Boutsen. He won in Japan in 1989 when Ayrton Senna was disqualified and, after being outshone by Nelson Piquet, came of age in the second part of 1990. He was pipped by Senna in Germany after a brilliant drive, and lost in Hungary after being elbowed out of the way by Senna. But then, after Sandro finished third in Spain, and a contract with Ferrari was rumoured, came the helicopter crash. Fighting back valiantly, he starred for Alfa Romeo on the international touring car scene until 1997, when he joined Mercedes' works sports car team.

○ 77 Grands Prix, 1 win (Japanese GP 1989)
○ No drivers' title (best result – 6th overall 1989)

Gunnar Nilsson

Nationality: Swedish
Born: 1948
Died: 1978

Gunnar sat in a racing car for the first time in 1973, racing in Formula Super Vee. He was clearly good as he stepped up to Formula Two and promptly finished fourth at the Norsring. Strong form in the German Formula Three series in 1974 earned him a works March ride in the British series in 1975, with Gunnar winning the title. Gunnar tried the more powerful Formula Atlantic series later in the year and won five rounds of that, with Lotus quick to snap him up for its 1976 Formula One line-up. A pair of third-place finishes showed promise and he won the wet 1977 Belgian Grand Prix at Zolder, but then became

Lifting the Trophies: Alessandro Nannini after his only grand prix win at Suzuka in Japan for Benetton in 1989

increasingly inconsistent. No one knew it at the time, but Gunnar was suffering from cancer and, although he signed for the fledgling Arrows team in 1978, he was never well enough to drive the car and he died that autumn.

○ 31 Grands Prix, 1 win (Belgian GP 1977)
○ No drivers' title (best result – 8th overall 1977)

Jackie Oliver

Nationality: British
Born: 1942

Best known as the former boss of the Arrows team, Jackie had a distinguished driving career. Success with Lotus in Formula Two ensured that he was in the right place to be drafted into the grand prix team when Jim Clark was killed in 1968. Jackie crashed in his first two races, but led the British Grand Prix before his transmission failed and, although he rounded off the season with third in Mexico, he was dropped in favour of Jochen Rindt for 1970. He joined BRM for a couple of years, scoring two top-six finishes. Jackie returned to Formula One with the new Shadow team in 1973 and finished third in the Canadian Grand Prix at Mosport Park, although many people think he won

on a day when lap charts were thrown into confusion by a wet/dry race and the use of a pace car. He drove for Shadow in 1977, but by then was heavily involved in the management of the team, which he quit to set up Arrows in 1978, and then sold the team to Tom Walkinshaw in 1996.

○ 50 Grands Prix, no wins (best result – 3rd Mexican GP 1968, Canadian GP 1973)
○ No drivers' title (best result – 13th overall 1968)

Carlos Pace

Nationality: Brazilian
Born: 1944
Died: 1977

Having raced for most of the 1960s in Brazil, where his long-time friends and rivals were the Fittipaldi brothers, Carlos came to Britain in 1970. Success in Formula Three and Formula Two led to a drive with Frank Williams' Formula One team in 1972, for whom he showed well against team leader Henri Pescarolo. He left Williams at the end of the year to join Surtees, where some excellent performances were ruined by poor reliability and in mid-1974 he quit. Soon though, he was snapped up by Bernie Ecclestone's Brabham team, and in 1975 he took

a fine victory in the Brazilian Grand Prix. Second in the 1977 Argentinian Grand Prix boded well, but he was killed in a light aircraft accident.

○ 72 Grands Prix, 1 win (Brazilian GP 1975)
○ No drivers' title (best result – 6th overall 1975)

Jonathan Palmer

Nationality: British
Born: 1956

After dominating the British Formula Three Championship in 1981 and then Formula Two in 1983, Jonathan drove first for RAM and then Zakspeed in Formula One, although he had shown well in a one-off drive with Williams in the 1983 European Grand Prix. He then started a three-year liaison with Tyrrell. In his first season, 1987, he won the Jim Clark Cup as best non-turbo driver, but 1988 was a disaster with a poor car. His career was briefly revitalized by the 018 chassis in 1989, only for him to be overshadowed by Jean Alesi in the latter half of the season. After that, Palmer, with some realistic self-appraisal, decided his career was over. He commentated for the BBC and then formed his own junior formula – Formula Palmer Audi – for 1998. Justin Wilson was his first champion and Jonathan has since helped him reach Formula One, with Minardi and then Jaguar in 2003.

○ **82 Grands Prix, no wins (best result – 4th Australian GP 1987)**

○ **No drivers' title (best result – 11th overall 1987)**

Olivier Panis

Nationality: French
Born: 1966

Second in the French Formula Three Championship in 1991, before graduating to Formula 3000, Olivier chose the wrong chassis in 1992. However, in 1993 he took the title for the DAMS team. His debut Formula One season, with Ligier in 1994, showed admirable consistency, as he finished 15 of the 16 races. His best result was a second in Germany, after half the field had been wiped out on lap one.

Olivier's second season with Ligier was saved by another second in the Adelaide finale. Against the run of play, Olivier won at Monaco in the wet in 1996, but it was a one-off. He stayed on when the team became Prost in 1997, shining on Bridgestone tyres in the early rounds and finishing second in Spain, but he then broke his legs at the following race in Canada.

Two poor seasons followed and he spent 2000 as test driver for McLaren. Ironically, this rejuvenated his career, as he matched the pace of the team's racers David Coulthard and Mika Hakkinen and as a result was signed by BAR for 2001, where he proved the equal of Jacques Villeneuve. A lack of reliability hampered Olivier's 2002 campaign and all he could retrieve was one fifth-place finish. Moving to Toyota for the Japanese manufacturer's second year in Formula One, Olivier had a nightmare of a time through 2003, again seldom around at the end of races, again with a fifth place his top finish. He stays with Toyota for 2004.

○ **141 Grands Prix, 1 win (Monaco GP 1996)**

○ **No drivers' title (best result – 8th overall 1995)**

Massimiliano Papis

Nationality: Italian
Born: 1969

"Mad Max" came to racing from karts. Race-winning form in Formula Three was followed by two years in Formula 3000 that produced just one win, a runaway affair at Barcelona in 1994. He joined Footwork mid-1995 when Gianni Morbidelli's money ran dry and was faster than team-mate Taki Inoue. He was soon dropped, but shone in the 1996 Daytona 24 Hours sports car race in a private Ferrari. He has subsequently raced in Indy Cars and sports cars in the US, winning the Daytona 24 Hours for a second time in 2002.

○ **7 Grands Prix, no wins (best result – 7th Italian GP 1995)**

○ **No drivers' title**

Mike Parkes

Nationality: British
Born: 1931
Died: 1977

Elevated to the Ferrari grand prix team in 1966 after establishing himself as one of the world's leading sports car drivers, a brief Formula One career followed, in which his best results were second to Ludovico Scarfiotti in the 1966 Italian Grand Prix, and victory in the following year's International Trophy race at Silverstone. However, an accident in the 1967 Belgian Grand Prix left Mike lying beside his upturned Ferrari with a broken leg. He went on to manage teams for Fiat and Lancia in touring cars, and was then involved with the Lancia rally team, before he was tragically killed in a road crash in 1977.

○ **6 Grands Prix, no wins (best result – 2nd French GP 1966, Italian GP 1966)**

○ **No drivers' title (best result – 8th 1966)**

Reg Parnell

Nationality: British
Born: 1911
Died: 1964

Although what would have been the best years of his career were taken away by the Second World War, Reg was one of Britain's most respected professionals. Success in a Maserati in domestic events in the late 1940s meant he was invited to drive for the Maserati works team.

He finished an excellent third in the first World Championship grand prix, at Silverstone in a works Alfa Romeo, then drove the "Thinwall Special" Ferrari to a points finish in 1951, after which he raced twice more in British Grands Prix, but concentrated on national events around the world.

○ **6 Grands Prix, no wins (best result – 3rd British GP 1950)**

○ **No drivers' title (best result – 9th 1950)**

Riccardo Patrese

Nationality: Italian
Born: 1954

Although Riccardo was one of the most popular personalities in Formula One in the latter stages of his career, in his youth he was grand prix racing's "enfant terrible".

The personality transformation took place over a decade at the beginning of what turned into Formula One's longest career – 256 grand prix starts. At the beginning he was quick but unruly and, although he led the South African Grand Prix in 1978 in the new Arrows team's second race, success eluded him until he joined Brabham in 1982, when he won the Monaco Grand Prix. He made too many mistakes, though, and in 1983 he threw away the San Marino Grand Prix, but put in a flawless performance to win in South Africa.

In the mid-1980s his career went into a downward spiral, with Alfa Romeo and then Brabham, only for him to be given a chance to revitalize it with Williams in 1988. He forged an excellent working relationship with technical director Patrick Head, and also returned to winning ways, finding a new serenity in simply being lucky enough, as he saw it, to be employed by a top team in a sport he loved. This rejuvenation was never more evident than when Nigel Mansell returned to the team in 1991, and he had to play second fiddle to Riccardo through the first half of the season.

In 1992, though, Riccardo was pushed into the shadows by Mansell and, after a season at Benetton when he could not match Michael Schumacher's pace, Formula One left him behind. Despite offers to return in 1994, he chose to concentrate on touring cars until retiring at the end of 1997.

○ **256 Grands Prix, 6 wins (Monaco GP 1982, South African GP 1983, San Marino GP 1990, Mexican GP 1991, Portuguese GP 1991, Japanese GP 1992)**

○ **No drivers' title (best result – 2nd overall 1992)**

Wild at Heart: Riccardo Patrese was quick but he did not always possess the discipline necessary to win

Ronnie Peterson

Nationality: Swedish
Born: 1944
Died: 1978

Widely regarded as the fastest driver in the world in the mid-1970s, Ronnie's seat-of-the-pants driving style and astonishing car control won him an army of fans. This gentle man made his grand prix debut with the March team in 1970, having scored many successes in Formula Three for the outfit. The following year it became clear that Peterson was a world-class talent when he took four second places, and was runner-up to Jackie Stewart in the World Championship. He would not win a grand prix, however, until he left March to join Lotus in 1973, winning the French, Austrian, Italian and US East Grands Prix in the Lotus 72, and finishing third in the World Championship. He dragged the now-ageing car to three more victories in 1974, but a dreadful 1975 season with Lotus prompted a switch back to March for the following year, when he took one win, before a lucrative offer to drive Ken Tyrrell's six-wheel P34 in 1977 turned into a disaster.

Questions were asked about Ronnie's ability, but he emphatically answered them after returning to Lotus in 1978 as number two to Mario Andretti. Together they dominated the season in the Lotus 79 and, as well as scoring two more superb wins, Ronnie often sat just feet from Andretti's exhausts, his integrity refusing to allow him to break his contract and pass the American. This form was enough to win him an offer to be McLaren's number one driver in 1979, but then tragedy reared its ugly head at the start of the Italian Grand Prix when a multiple shunt left him with serious leg injuries. A bone marrow embolism entered his bloodstream, and the Swede died the following morning, thus depriving Formula One of one of its most electrifying talents.

○ 124 Grands Prix, 10 wins (French GP 1973, Austrian GP 1973, Italian GP 1973, US East GP 1973, Monaco GP 1974, French GP 1974, Italian GP 1974, Italian GP 1976, South African GP 1978, Austrian GP 1978)
○ No drivers' title (2nd overall 1971 and 1978)

Nelson Piquet

SEE PAGE 175

Nelson Piquet Jr

Nationality: Brazilian
Born: 1985

Whether he likes it or not, this son of a triple World Champion will always be associated with "Singaporegate", the matter that was raised after he was dropped by Renault halfway through his second year with them in 2009. He had shown his skills by being British Formula Three champion in 2004, GP2 runner-up in 2006 and finishing second in the 2008 German Grand Prix after an inspired tyre choice. However, when he seemingly was asked by the Renault team to spin out and trigger a safety car that would assist team-mate Fernando Alonso in the 2008 Singapore Grand Prix, he lost his credibility and, most likely, his Formula One future.

○ 28 Grands Prix, 0 wins (best result – 2nd German GP 2008)
○ No drivers' title (best result – 12th overall 2008)

Didier Pironi

Nationality: French
Born: 1952
Died: 1987

Motivated by a burning desire to be France's first World Champion, Didier's cold, calculating approach was disrupted forever in August 1982 when he crashed with extreme violence in practice for the German Grand Prix, badly breaking both his legs and ending his motor racing career. An impressive debut year with Tyrrell in 1978, when his reputation was bolstered by a win at Le Mans in an Alpine-Renault, followed by marking time the following year, led him to a drive with Ligier in 1980, where he comfortably outpaced team leader Jacques Laffite.

Didier scored his first grand prix

The Man Who Would Be King: Didier Pironi in 1981 when Ferrari overalls could be of any colour

win in Belgium that year and was extremely unlucky not to win in Britain, too, following a superb charge through the field. For 1981 he joined Gilles Villeneuve at Ferrari, and for the first time in his career was unable to get on terms with a team-mate.

A sole fourth place was all he could achieve in a year when the brilliant French-Canadian took two wins. Didier was determined that the same fate should not befall him in 1982, when he was at the centre of a tragic sequence of events. He snatched victory against team orders as Villeneuve was cruising to the flag at Imola. Villeneuve was killed in the following race, and now Didier looked set for the world title. He won the Dutch Grand Prix in masterful style, and comfortably led the championship when he arrived in Hockenheim. After the crash came dozens of operations, and although he vowed to return one day, it looked increasingly unlikely. For thrills, Didier turned to powerboat racing. The Frenchman's approach had always been uncompromising and when he hit the wake of an oil tanker without easing off the throttle his boat flipped and Didier and his two crew members were killed instantly.

○ 70 Grands Prix, 3 wins (Belgian GP 1980, San Marino GP 1982, Dutch GP 1982)
○ No drivers' title (best result – 2nd overall 1982)

Emanuele Pirro

Nationality: Italian
Born: 1962

A brilliant touring car driver, Emanuele never quite made the grade in Formula

NELSON PIQUET
Bernie's Brabham Hero

Nelson Piquet, or Nelson Soutomaior to give him his birth name – Piquet was a name invented to conceal his racing from his family – is one of only a handful of three-time World Champions. Although he won the last of these with Williams, he is always associated with success in a Brabham. Think Piquet and people think of a white car with dark blue colour contrasts taking the battle to Williams, Renault and McLaren in the early 1980s and, more often than not, coming out a winner.

Nelson was Brazilian karting champion in 1971 before trying car racing. He wanted to follow the established path to British Formula Three in 1977, but he could not speak English so raced in Europe instead. However, he knew what he had to do for 1978 and learned the language so that he could come to racing's melting pot. He beat Derek Warwick and compatriot Chico Serra to the title. Better still, he made his Formula One debut in a privately entered Ensign, then had three races in a privateer McLaren before being snapped up by Brabham. Bernie Ecclestone's team would be his home from home for the next seven years.

Nelson was immediately quick in 1979, pushing team leader Niki Lauda

hard all the time, and when Lauda retired suddenly towards the end of 1979, Nelson became team leader. The following year saw him win three grands prix and push Alan Jones for the World Championship, which he clinched in 1981, overhauling Carlos Reutemann in the Las Vegas finale.

A switch to BMW turbos by Brabham in 1982 led to poor reliability and only one win, but in 1983 he took a second title, this time snatching it from Alain Prost at the final race, after a late-season push from BMW.

In the following years Brabham slowly drifted away from competitiveness, with Nelson only taking three wins in two years, and he left at the end of 1985 to earn what he saw as his due at Williams. However, a rude shock awaited him there in the form of Nigel Mansell, whom most observers had expected Piquet to outpace easily. Both Nelson and Mansell lost out on the 1986 title race to Prost, and Nelson was not amused by Williams' refusal to ask Mansell to give way to him, which, in his view had allowed Prost to snatch the title. Still, he took a third title in 1987, relying on consistency and reliability after a heavy accident early in the season.

There followed a disastrous two seasons with Lotus, although he went some way to repairing his reputation at Benetton in 1990-91, when he won a further three races. Upon Michael Schumacher's arrival in 1991, Nelson became surplus to Benetton's requirements and, with no leading Formula One drives available, retired from grand prix racing. He entered the Indianapolis 500, but crashed in qualifying, badly damaging his feet.

Many thought the accident would end his career, but Nelson returned to Indy in 1993. His son Nelson Jr was a race winner in British Formula Three in 2003.

o **204 Grands Prix, 23 wins**
o **World Champion 1981, 1983 and 1987**

Boy from Brazil: Piquet in his Lotus at Monaco in 1988, when he failed to win a race as reigning champion

1952	1972	1979	1981	1983	1984	1986	1988	1990	1992
Born 17 August in Rio de Janeiro, Brazil	Turned to cars, racing in Formula Vee and sports cars	Full season with Brabham produced fourth place in Dutch GP	World Champion, winning Argentinian, San Marino and German GPs	World Champion again after winning Brazilian, Italian and European GPs, pipping Renault's Alain Prost to the title	Fell to fifth, despite winning in Montreal and Detroit as McLarens dominated	Joined Williams and won four times to have title shot, but was thwarted by Prost	Honda took engines to Lotus and Nelson went with them, but only managed three third places	Joined Benetton and won final two grands prix, to rank third	Crashed in qualifying for the Indy 500, damaging his feet

1971	1978	1980	1982	1985	1987	1989	1991	2003
Brazilian karting champion	Won British Formula Three title. Formula One debut with Ensign, then privately entered McLaren and Brabham	Won three grands prix, finishing year as runner-up to Alan Jones	Won only in Montreal as team struggled in first year with BMW turbo engines	Struggled on Pirelli tyres and won only once, at Paul Ricard, was eighth overall	World Champion for a third time, winning German, Hungarian and Italian GPs	Made do with trio of fourth-place finishes and fell to eighth overall	Victory in Canada was highlight of final year in Formula One, ranking him sixth	Followed son Nelsinho's Formula Three campaign around Britain

One. After a long apprenticeship in Formula Three, Formula Two and then Formula 3000, in all of which he took several victories, he became McLaren's test driver in 1988, before replacing Johnny Herbert at Benetton halfway through 1989. Emanuele was dropped at year's end, and drove for Dallara for the next two seasons, before going back to touring cars for good. He has raced almost exclusively for Audi right through until 2004, winning the Italian title twice and the German title once and also picked up three wins for the German marque at the Le Mans 24 Hours in 2000, 2001 and 2002, as well as winning the 2001 American Le Mans Series crown.

○ 37 Grands Prix, no wins (best result – 5th Australian GP 1989)
○ No drivers' title (best result – 18th overall 1991)

Alain Prost
SEE PAGE 177

Tom Pryce
Nationality: British
Born: 1949
Died: 1977

Tom moved into Formula One in 1974 with the Shadow team after an excellent Formula Three career, and showed himself to have great natural pace from the beginning, putting the car on the second row of the grid in only his second race. He won the non-championship Race of Champions at Brands Hatch at the start of 1975, but it was an up-and-down year, highlighted by pole at the British Grand Prix and great drives in the German and Austrian races. Financial troubles blighted 1976, but a new sponsor provided fresh hope for 1977. Then, in a bizarre accident, Tom hit a marshal who was crossing the straight just over a blind brow in the middle of the South African Grand Prix. Tom was dead before the car had come to rest.

○ 42 Grands Prix, no wins (best result – 3rd Austrian GP 1975, Brazilian GP 1976)
○ No drivers' title (best result – 10th overall 1975)

Fine Finnish: Kimi Raikkonen after his only Formula One win for McLaren in Sepang, Malaysia in 2003

David Purley
Nationality: British
Born: 1945
Died: 1985

"Purls" will forever be remembered for his efforts to save the life of Roger Williamson trapped in his burning vehicle in the Dutch Grand Prix of 1973, for which he was awarded the George Medal. He had a brief grand prix career, starting in 1973, when he hired a private March with little success in terms of results. He then dropped back to a successful Formula Two season in 1974, and then an excellent two years of Formula 5000 before returning to Formula One in 1977, racing his own Lec chassis. He led the Belgian Grand Prix briefly during a sequence of pit stops, but then his front-line racing career ended with a horrific head-on crash into a wall in practice for the British Grand Prix, which he was lucky to survive. Having proved that he was well enough to drive a Formula One car again, he turned to aerobatics for his thrills, and was killed when his Pitts Special crashed off the Sussex coast in 1985.

○ 7 Grands Prix, no wins (best result – 9th Italian GP 1973)
○ No drivers' title

Kimi Raikkonen
Nationality: Finnish
Born: 1979

Kimi took the shortest of approaches to Formula One, as a few Formula Ford races were followed by landing the British Formula Renault title in 2000, bringing his tally of car races to 23. His manager Steve Robertson urged Sauber to give him a test and gave him a race seat. The FIA put him under probation as he was skipping Formula 3 and Formula 3000, but he proved this unnecessary by finishing sixth on his debut. He collected two

fourths before the year was out. With Mika Hakkinen taking what was, at the time, a sabbatical, Kimi moved to McLaren for 2002 and would have scored his first win in France, but slipped on oil with a few laps to go. The first win came in the second race of 2003, at Sepang, and Kimi was in contention for the title until the final race, losing to Schumacher. McLaren had an uncompetitive 2004 and Kimi won just once, in Belgium. In 2005, a lack of pace in the opening races then a string of grid penalties for engine changes prevented him from beating Fernando Alonso to the world title. A less competitive car kept him out of victory circle in 2006.

A move to Ferrari for 2007 yielded instant dividends as he won the opening round in Australia and three wins in the final four races took him past Lewis Hamilton to be World Champion. His 2008 contained just two wins and he slipped to third overall before he won but once in 2009 and fell to sixth, so he quit for rallying.

○ 157 Grands Prix, 18 wins (Malaysian GP 2003, Belgian GP 2004, Spanish GP 2005, Monaco GP 2005, Canadian GP 2005, Hungarian GP 2005, Turkish GP 2005, Belgian GP 2005, Japanese GP 2005, Australian GP 2007, French GP 2007, British GP 2007, Belgian GP 2007, Chinese GP 2007, Brazilian GP 2007, Malaysian GP 2008, Spanish GP 2008, Belgian GP 2009)
○ World Champion 2007

Brian Redman
Nationality: British
Born: 1937

A top sports car driver, Brian had a low-key grand prix career, which ended prematurely because he did not like the high-pressure atmosphere of Formula One. Making his debut with a Cooper in 1968, he had to withdraw after three races when he broke his arm in a crash at Spa, but he returned sporadically until 1974, in between a succession of superb performances for Ferrari and Porsche in sports car events, in which he continued to compete until the early 1990s.

ALAIN PROST
The Professor

Hailed as the supreme race tactician by some observers and as a political animal by others, Alain won four world titles. Unusually for someone dubbed "The Professor", Alain could have been a professional footballer. Yet a dalliance with karts led to him winning the 1973 world title. The rest, as they say, is history.

Some hold Alain's lack of flamboyance against him, he would rather wait to make his move rather than rushing as though every lap was the last. Detractors would claim that he always worked the team around to his way of thinking, but if he was given the latest equipment ahead of his team-mate it was because he would make better use of it. Through all the carping, Alain kept on winning, with world titles coming his way in 1985, 1986, 1989 and 1993.

Alain bypassed Formula Two to make his Formula One debut in Argentina in 1980. His car, a McLaren, was not one of the quick ones of the time, but he outpaced experienced team-mate John Watson and claimed a point for sixth. Fifth place followed in Brazil, then he broke his wrist in South Africa.

With fortunes improving in the Renault team, it was anxious to sign the best French talent to lead its attack, so Alain drove one of its yellow cars in 1981, fittingly taking the chequered flag at the French GP. Two more wins followed to leave Alain fifth overall. In 1982 he went one place better. Then, in 1983, was runner-up, just two points behind Nelson Piquet.

Fed up with being blamed by the French media for losing out to Piquet, he returned to McLaren. Runner-up to team-mate Niki Lauda by half a point in 1984, Alain gained the world title that he had been threatening to win for so long. And he did the same again in 1986, clinching the crown in the famous three-way shoot-out in Adelaide in which Nigel Mansell had a blow-out. Amid all this drama, Alain completed the race with a fuel gauge long since reading empty. He spent three more years with McLaren, winning his third title in 1989 after a fractious time with Senna at Suzuka.

Their mutual antipathy reared its head again in 1990, when Alain raced for Ferrari. They clashed again at Suzuka and Senna became the champion, with Prost the runner-up. Disillusioned with his car and Ferrari politics in 1991, Alain spoke out once too often and was fired, going off to be a commentator for French television.

However, the lure of racing was too much and he returned for Williams in 1993. An incredible year yielded seven wins and his fourth title. However, news that Senna was to join him in 1994 saw Alain tender his resignation. After a spell as adviser at McLaren, he took over Ligier and renamed it Prost for 1997, but found running a team to be a total nightmare.

- **200 Grands Prix, 51 wins**
- **World Champion 1985, 1986, 1989 and 1993**

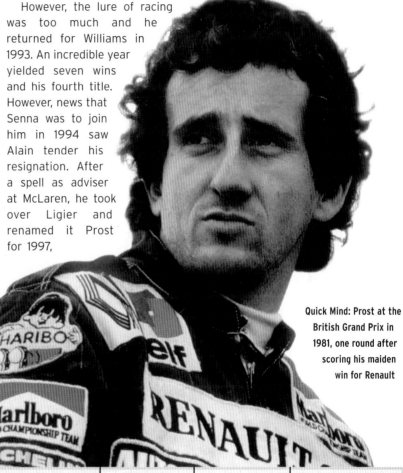

Quick Mind: Prost at the British Grand Prix in 1981, one round after scoring his maiden win for Renault

1955	1976	1980	1983	1985	1986	1989	1991	1997
Born 24 February in Saint Chamond, France	French Formula Renault champion	Sixth on Formula One debut for McLaren in Argentina. Fifth in second race in Brazil was his best result all year	Finished as runner-up to Nelson Piquet, despite winning French, Belgian, British and Austrian GPs	Crowned World Champion after winning five grands prix	World Champion again for McLaren, with four wins, with last of these in Adelaide helping him overhaul Nigel Mansell	World Champion for a third time despite clashing with Senna in penultimate race in Japan	Fired by Ferrari before end of season for criticizing the team. Fifth overall with three second places	Finally bought Ligier and renamed team after himself

1973	1979	1981	1984	1988	1990	1993	2001
World Junior Karting champion	European and French Formula Three Champion, including victory in Monaco Formula Three GP	Joined Renault and won French, Dutch and Italian GPs to rank fifth overall	Rejoined McLaren and won seven grands prix, yet was pipped to title by half a point by team-mate Niki Lauda	Runner-up to team-mate Senna as between them they won all but one of the 16 grands prix	Joined Ferrari and finished as runner-up after Senna returned the compliment in the Japanese GP	Joined Williams and claimed a fourth world title, winning seven grands prix	Prost team folded with second in 1999 European GP its best result

○ 12 Grands Prix, no wins (best result – 3rd Spanish GP 1968)
○ No drivers' title (best result – 12th overall 1972)

Clay Regazzoni

Nationality: Swiss
Born: 1939

Gianclaudio, also known as Clay, became one of Formula One's most respected performers – and also one of its saddest stories.

He made his grand prix debut for Ferrari midway through a remarkably successful Formula Two season in 1970, and proved himself to be an accomplished driver straightaway.

Not only did he take an excellent fourth place on his debut in Britain, and follow it with a second place in Austria, but he also assured himself of a permanent place in the hearts of Ferrari fans when he won the Italian Grand Prix. Clay stayed with the Italian team for another two seasons, before being dropped for 1973, only to return in 1974 alongside Niki Lauda.

He proved the perfect foil for the Austrian, and came close to winning the World Championship in 1974, and supporting Lauda ably for another two years, before he was replaced by Carlos Reutemann for 1977.

Two years in the comparative wilderness with Ensign and Shadow were followed by a splendid return to the limelight in 1979 with Williams – indeed he gave the team its first grand prix win, at Silverstone, before again being replaced by Reutemann and returning to Ensign. However, tragedy was soon to follow. In his fourth race of 1980, the car's throttle jammed open along the flat-out Shoreline Drive at Long Beach, and he careered down an escape road and into a concrete wall at unabated speed. He suffered severe spinal injuries which have kept him partially confined to a wheelchair ever since. His love of the sport, though, remains, and he is a commentator on Swiss television.

○ 132 Grands Prix, 5 wins (Italian GP 1971, German GP 1974, Italian GP 1975, US West

GP 1976, British GP 1979)
○ No drivers' title (best result – 1974)

Carlos Reutemann

Nationality: Argentinian
Born: 1942

Carlos was a supremely talented racing driver, who at his best was untouchable, but he could just as easily turn in a performance of overwhelming mediocrity as he could reduce a field of the best drivers in the world to bit players. Never was this more apparent than at the end of 1981 when, poised on the brink of the World Championship and after clinching pole position in brilliant style, he faded badly to eighth place in a race in which he only had to place ahead of Nelson Piquet – who finished the race semi-conscious in fifth place – to take the title. Carlos made a sensational

Formula One debut in 1972, after placing second to Ronnie Peterson in the European Formula Two Trophy in 1971, putting his Brabham on pole position before finishing seventh. The following season saw him establish himself as a consistent top-liner, and he started 1974 in brilliant style, leading the first two races until mechanical problems intervened, and winning the third, before his form tailed off until August, when he recovered to win the Austrian Grand Prix in brilliant style. Two more up-and-down seasons followed before he joined Ferrari for 1977, where he was overshadowed by Niki Lauda, and 1978, when he was back to his best alongside Gilles Villeneuve. Reutemann took four wins that year, only two less than world champion Mario Andretti in the dominant Lotus 79. A switch to Lotus

Natural Born Talent: Carlos Reutemann on the podium after winning the Austrian Grand Prix, 1974

for 1979 proved ill-judged, but the move to Williams in 1980 was not. He ably backed up Alan Jones to the title that first year, before mounting his own challenge in 1981. For most of the year it looked a certainty that he would tie up the championship well before the end of the season, but then came the almost inevitable slump. He returned in 1982, took an excellent second place in the first race, in South Africa, and then quit after the second. He is now a leading figure in Argentinian politics.

○ 146 Grands Prix, 12 wins (South African GP 1974, Austrian GP 1974, US GP 1974, German GP 1975, Brazilian GP 1977, Brazilian GP 1978, US West GP 1978, British GP 1978, US East GP 1978, Monaco GP 1980, Brazilian GP 1981, Belgian GP 1981)
○ No drivers' title (best result – 2nd 1981)

Peter Revson

Nationality: American
Born: 1939
Died: 1974

After a brief fling with Formula One in 1964, the heir to the Revlon cosmetic fortunes returned to race in sports cars in the US until good performances in Indy Cars attracted the attention of the Formula One fraternity. He guested in a Tyrrell at the US Grand Prix in 1971 before signing up for Yardley McLaren.

He soon proved to be a reliable points-scorer. When the McLaren M23 came on stream in 1973, he took an excellent first victory in the British Grand Prix, grabbing the initiative in the wet early stages and heading an intense four-car battle towards the end. Another win followed in the confused and wet Canadian race. He left McLaren after he was offered only a third car in 1974 and switched to Shadow, but he was killed in testing for the South African Grand Prix at Kyalami when the front suspension failed and the car hit the barriers.

○ 30 Grands Prix, 2 wins (British GP 1973, Canadian GP 1973)
○ No drivers' title (best result – 5th overall 1972 and 1973)

JOCHEN RINDT
The Posthumous Champion

Some World Champions are admired for making the most of the equipment given to them and winning races. Some stand out for other reasons and Jochen is one who stands out for his all-or-nothing attitude and his aggressive driving style that left onlookers in no doubt that he was giving 100 per cent. He was nothing if not entertaining.

The early years of his competition career were spent taking part in hill climbs from 1960 in his native Austria and then racing in an Alfa Romeo Giulietta followed by Formula Junior. Anxious to progress, Jochen contested the non-championship Austrian Grand Prix in 1963. However, it was when he took to Formula Two the following year that people started to sit up and pay attention, especially when Jochen shone at Crystal Palace.

His incredible car control enabled him to dominate Formula Two throughout the 1960s, but the Austrian found success in Formula One much harder to come by. He made his World Championship debut in Austria's first championship round, before returning for a full campaign in 1965 with Cooper, for whom he performed with enthusiasm but little success – except for a pair of second-

place finishes at Spa-Francorchamps and Watkins Glen in 1966. Having had enough of the chassis and its underpowered Maserati engine, Jochen left at the end of 1967.

During his spell with Cooper, Jochen scored a surprise win at the Le Mans 24 Hours in 1965, sharing a Ferrari with Masten Gregory. Victories were otherwise confined to Formula Two, a category in which he continued to race alongside his Formula One duties.

A move to Brabham as a replacement for Denny Hulme in 1968 looked a shrewd one, given that the team had won the last two World Championships, but its new Repco engine was a failure, and Jochen had only two third places to show for his two years with the team when he joined Lotus in 1969.

After feeling secure with the engineering standards at Brabham, Jochen did not trust Lotus boss

Colin Chapman to anything like the same extent, and a broken rear wing when he was heading for his first victory, at Silverstone, did little to bolster his confidence.

Nevertheless, the Rindt-Chapman relationship did eventually gel, and he took his first win in the US Grand Prix at the end of 1969. Another win followed in the venerable Lotus 49 at Monaco in 1970, thanks to a last-lap fumble by Jack Brabham, before Chapman unveiled the sleek Lotus 72. The car took Jochen to four consecutive victories at Zandvoort, Clermont-Ferrand, Brands Hatch and Hockenheim in the summer of 1970, but although he was on course for the World Championship, he felt increasingly unsafe after the deaths of his friends Piers Courage and Bruce McLaren.

Tragically, in practice for the Italian Grand Prix at Monza, Jochen's fears were realized, and he was killed, thus becoming motor racing's only posthumous World Champion when Jacky Ickx failed to overhaul his points total in the remaining three races of the season, despite winning two of them.

○ **60 Grands Prix, 6 wins**
○ **World Champion 1970**

Mr 100 Per Cent: Rindt in the cockpit of his Lotus at the Dutch Grand Prix, Zandvoort, 1970

1942	1962	1964	1966	1968	1969
Born 18 April, Mainz-am-Rhein, Germany	Made circuit racing debut in an Alfa Romeo Giulietta	Starred in Formula Two at Crystal Palace then made World Championship debut in the Austrian GP in a Rob Walker Brabham	Second in Belgian and US GPs helped Jochen rank third overall in Formula One. His only wins were in concurrent Formula Two races	Joined Brabham and was third twice. Again starred in Formula Two, winning six races	Moved to Lotus and was rewarded with second at Monaco and then his first win, in the US GP to rank fourth

1960	1963	1965	1967	1970
Entered hill climbs and rallies in a Simca Montlhery	Raced a Formula Junior Cooper, earning a reputation for his sideways style and speed. Made Formula One debut in the non-championship Austrian GP	Contested a full season with Cooper, finishing fourth in German GP. Also won Le Mans 24 Hours in a Ferrari with Masten Gregory	Regretted having a three-year deal with Cooper as it struggled and he scored but two fourths. However, he won nine Formula Two races	Became World Champion posthumously, having been killed in practice at Monza after winning five of the previous rounds. Jacky Ickx failed to overhaul his points total

Mexican Wunderkind: Ricardo Rodriguez who signed for Ferrari at 19 and tragically died in the Mexican Grand Prix before his talent could be fulfilled

non-championship Mexican Grand Prix – his home race – Ricardo drove Rob Walker's Lotus instead and, trying to snatch back pole, he went into the Peraltada corner too fast, ran out of road on the exit and was killed.

○ 5 Grands Prix, no wins (best result – 4th Belgian GP 1962)

○ No drivers' title (best result – 12th, 1962)

Keke Rosberg

SEE PAGE 181

Nico Rosberg

Nationality: German
Born: 1985

Nico proved that talent can be inherited by winning the German Formula BMW and GP2 titles before making his Formula One debut for Williams in 2006. Keke's son set the fastest lap of the race on his debut, in Bahrain, but that was to be his best result. His form in 2007 was inconclusive. Then 2008 bamboozled as he started it with third in Australia and seldom scored again before finishing second in Singapore. In 2009, he produced a run of fourths, fifths and sixths. Then Nico joined Mercedes for 2010.

° 70 Grands Prix, no wins (best result – 2nd Singapore GP 2008)

° No drivers' title (best result - 7th 2009)

Pedro Rodriguez

Nationality: Mexican
Born: 1940
Died: 1971

Pedro and his younger brother Ricardo were indulged with high-performance cars from an early age by their wealthy father, and first came to the notice of the European racing fraternity in a Ferrari at Le Mans in 1960, where they almost won. However, while Ricardo shot straight into the works Ferrari Formula One team, Pedro's career needed a long time to take off, before he finally got a full-time drive with Cooper in 1967. Thanks to his car's reliability and to heavy attrition he won his first race for the team, switching to BRM in 1968, where his spirited driving lifted the team's morale after the death

of Mike Spence at Indianapolis. He had a part-time role in Formula One in 1969, before returning to BRM in 1970, where he took one of the all-time classic victories, beating off race-long pressure from Chris Amon's March.

This eccentric, who went everywhere with his famous deerstalker hat and bottle of Tabasco sauce for use at the world's finest restaurants, was now at the top of his game. He was acknowledged as a wet weather ace, and had established himself as the world's leading sports car driver. Halfway through 1971, which looked set to offer Pedro even more success, he accepted an offer to drive in an insignificant Interseries race in Germany. While he was dicing for the lead, a slower car edged him into the

wall and his Ferrari burst into flames. The Mexican sadly died shortly after he was extricated from the wreck.

○ 55 Grands Prix, 2 wins (South African GP 1967, Belgian GP 1970)

○ No drivers' title (best result – 6th overall 1967 and 1968)

Ricardo Rodriguez

Nationality: Mexican
Born: 1942
Died: 1962

Thought by many to have had even more talent than his brother Pedro, Ricardo qualified an astonishing second on the grid at his first grand prix, at Monza, when he was just 19 years old. Ferrari signed him for 1962, but he did not drive in every race. Angry that Ferrari did not enter the

Louis Rosier

Nationality: French
Born: 1905
Died: 1956

Louis' career was disrupted by the Second World War, but he won some non-championship grands prix for Talbot. When the first ever World Championship started in 1950, his Talbot played second fiddle to Alfa Romeo, but Louis picked up points and won the Le Mans 24 Hours. He won the 1951 non-championship Dutch and Bordeaux Grands Prix, until he was killed in a crash at Montlhery.

○ 38 Grands Prix, no wins (best result – 3rd Swiss GP 1950, Belgian GP 1950)

○ No drivers' title (best result – 4th overall 1950)

KEKE ROSBERG
One Can Be Enough

Keke only won one grand prix in his championship-winning year, but that was enough as a record 11 drivers shared visits to the winner's circle during that year's 16 races. However, do not hold this solitary win against him for Keke was more than worth a world title in a career that entertained more than most.

Perhaps an image that better conjures up Keke as most remember him is the stubbing out of his ever-present cigarette before climbing aboard his Honda turbo-powered Williams at Silverstone in 1985 and going out to risk everything as he claimed pole at a then-record speed of over 160mph. It was the epitome of an all-or-nothing lap. No wonder he was held in such esteem by his contemp-oraries – bravery only starts to cover what he did.

Success in Formula One was a long time coming for this affable Finn, and he achieved what he achieved often in spite of his machinery. But how he worked at keeping his career momentum going, working harder than almost any driver before or since as he criss-crossed the globe in an attempt to keep the wins coming. Take 1977, for example, the year before he made the big time, when he won the

Formula Pacific Tasman series in New Zealand, then took in the European Formula Two season, interspersing the races with those making up the North American formula Atlantic. Few would have taken on such an onerous amount of travel, but Keke needed the prize money. He made it to Formula One in 1978 after winning the Tasman series

again and then shocking everyone by beating the established stars in the International Trophy at Silverstone in streaming conditions. Until 1982, though, when Williams signed him to replace Alan Jones, he was never given top-rate equipment. However, as shown by winning that 1982 title, he made the most of his chance. In

1983, Williams lagged behind the turbo-powered teams, but Keke took an inspired win at Monaco. Although Williams had the Honda turbo in 1984, its FW09 was unable to match the McLarens, and Keke had to make do with an inspired win at scorching Dallas when most of his rivals collapsed with heat exhaustion or crashed on the crumbling track. By the end of the year he decided he would retire after a further two years. Two wins followed in 1985 for Williams, and then Keke switched to McLaren for his final year, where he was surprised by the pace of team-mate Alain Prost. "I thought I was the fastest driver in the world," he said, "until I came here." There were no wins, but he retired while leading his final race, the Australian Grand Prix.

Keke did return to the sport, though, first as a manager to JJ Lehto and Mika Hakkinen, helping them take their first steps on the international racing scene and then as a driver again with Peugeot in sports cars in 1991. Touring cars followed, racing for Mercedes and subsequently Opel, before setting up his own Formula Three team for which son Nico raced in the European series in 2003.

o **114 Grands Prix, 5 wins**
o **World Champion 1982**

Royal Blessing: Rosberg receives his trophy after winning the Monaco Grand Prix for Williams in 1983

1948	1977	1979	1982	1984	1991	2003
Born 6 December in Stockholm, Sweden	Won Tasman series then returned to European Formula Two. Won at Enna, ranked sixth. Fourth overall in North American Formula Atlantic	Raced in CanAm sports car series, but returned to Formula One when James Hunt quit Wolf team	Leaped at chance to replace Alan Jones at Williams and became team leader when Carlos Reutemann quit after two races. Won the Swiss GP at Dijon-Prenois and three second places helped him become World Champion	Williams' first turbo car was a brutal one, but Keke tamed Honda's horses and won in Dallas to rank eighth overall	Raced for Peugeot in World Sports Car series, winning rounds at Magny-Cours and Mexico City	Oversaw son Nico's Formula Three campaign alongside his semi-works Mercedes touring car team

1973	1978	1980	1983	1985	1986	1992
European and Scandinavian Formula Vee champion	Won Tasman series again, then made his mark in Formula One by winning the wet International Trophy race in a Theodore. Also raced an ATS and a Wolf	Stayed with Wolf as it meta-morphosed into Fittipaldi. Third place at Kyalami helped him rank tenth overall	Won Monaco GP, but struggled against rival teams with turbo-engined cars and fell to fifth overall	Won US GP in Detroit and later Australian GP to rank third overall	Joined McLaren. Took second at Monaco then ended Formula One career by retiring from lead in Australian GP	Raced in German Touring Car series for Mercedes, then formed own team to run cars for Opel, then Nissan, then Mercedes

Restless Talent: Mika Salo made his comeback with the all-new Toyota team in 2002

Ricardo Rosset

Nationality: Brazilian
Born: 1968

Ricardo was not thought special when he raced in British Formula Three in 1993, but he won a race in 1994, then won first time out in Formula 3000, finishing runner-up to team-mate Vincenzo Sospiri. He moved to Formula One in 1996, but struggled as number two at Arrows. It got worse in 1997 with Lola pulling out after the first round, then he struggled with the declining Tyrrell team through 1998.

○ **26 Grands Prix, no wins (best result - 8th Hungarian GP 1996, Canadian GP 1998)**
○ **No drivers' title**

Luís Pérez Sala

Nationality: Spanish
Born: 1959

Success in Formula 3000 was never matched in Formula One. Luís took two wins in F3000 in both 1986 and 1987, was second to Stefano Modena in the championship in the latter year, and looked promising when he stepped up to Formula One with Minardi in 1988. When Pierluigi Martini joined the team he was overshadowed. He went on to race in the Spanish Touring Car Championship.

○ **26 Grands Prix, no wins (best result - 6th British GP 1989)**
○ **No drivers' title (best result - 26th overall 1989)**

Eliseo Salazar

Nationality: Chilean
Born: 1954

Most famous for being kicked and punched live on television by Nelson Piquet after the two had collided in the 1982 German Grand Prix, Eliseo showed well in Formula Three and the British Formula One series before joining struggling March and then Ensign in 1981. Success did not come any easier with ATS in 1982 when he was overshadowed by team-mate Manfred Winkelhock and, after a few brief appearances with the RAM team in 1983, he was out of a drive. Eliseo moved to race in IndyCars in the 1990s, racing for AJ Foyt in the 2002 Indy Racing League.

○ **24 Grands Prix, no wins (best result - 5th San Marino GP 1982)**
○ **No drivers' title (best result - 18th overall 1981)**

Mika Salo

Nationality: Finnish
Born: 1966

Like his compatriots JJ Lehto and Mika Hakkinen, Mika Salo was European Formula Ford champion. He caught up with Hakkinen in British Formula Three, and the pair jousted for the 1990 crown, with Hakkinen scraping home.

With Formula 3000 teams lining up to sign Salo, he was found guilty of drink-driving and was effectively banished to Japan, where he stayed until 1994, racing in Formula 3000, when he joined the dying Lotus team for the last two races. He did enough to impress Tyrrell to sign him for the 1995 season and shocked everyone by running third in the opening race.

A couple of fifth places in 1995 were repeated in 1996. Talked of as a Ferrari driver in 1997, Mika stayed with Tyrrell, but then moved to Arrows for 1998 and was let down by a weak engine. A stand-in for BAR and Ferrari in 1999, he even handed victory at Hockenheim to Ferrari team-mate Eddie Irvine. He scored six points for Sauber in 2000 and headed the Toyota team for 2002.

This was seen as a big chance for Mika, but he grew restless as the team stuttered and was not dismayed to be bought out of the second year of his contract.

○ **94 Grands Prix, no wins (best result - 2nd German GP 1999)**
○ **No drivers' title (best result - 10th overall 1999)**

Roy Salvadori

Nationality: British
Born: 1922

In a Formula One career spanning ten years, Roy was perpetually overshadowed by his fellow countrymen, but he was a splendid driver, especially in sports cars, and his finest hour came with a victory in the 1959 Le Mans 24 Hours for Aston Martin. Concentrating on sports cars in the mid-1950s, when he was a member of the factory Aston Martin team, Roy hit the grand prix front line with Cooper in 1957. He then switched to Aston Martin's unsuccessful grand prix assault just as Cooper became the team to beat in Formula One. Roy later drove a privately entered Cooper, almost winning the 1961 US Grand Prix, before retiring from Formula One in 1962 and from sports car racing a couple of years later.

○ **47 Grands Prix, no wins (best result - 2nd German GP 1958)**
○ **No drivers' title (best result - 4th overall 1958)**

Rising son: Takuma Sato is Japan's best hope yet

Takuma Sato

Nationality: Japanese
Born: 1977

Having won a racing scholarship at Suzuka, Takuma headed to Britain in 1998, shining in Formula Vauxhall and then Formula Three in 2000 before beating Anthony Davidson to the 2001 title with 12 wins. A seat with Jordan was next and he sent his home crowd wild with his first points by finishing fifth in Japan. There was no seat free in 2003, so Takuma tested for Honda-supplied BAR team and was promoted in place of Jacques Villeneuve for 2004. While team-mate Jenson Button was almost always on the podium in 2004, Takuma managed just one visit, in the USA, but his form dwindled through 2005 and he was dropped from the line-up for 2006 and was saved only by the Honda-encouraged formation of Super Aguri Racing. Eighth in Spain in 2007 was a boost, but sixth in Canada was better still as it included overtaking Fernando Alonso's McLaren. However, the team collapsed after just four races in 2008, leaving Takuma out of Formula One.
○ 91 Grands Prix (best result - 3rd United States GP 2004)
○ No drivers' title (best result - 8th overall 2004)

Ludovico Scarfiotti

Nationality: Italian
Born: 1933
Died: 1968

The nephew of the former Fiat boss Gianni Agnelli, Ludovico assured himself immortality in the annals of Italian motor racing when he won the 1966 Italian Grand Prix for Ferrari. A master at hill climbs, Ludovico made his Formula One debut in the 1963 Dutch Grand Prix just a fortnight after winning Le Mans with Lorenzo Bandini.

After sporadic appearances for Ferrari throughout the next couple of years, Ludovico was expected to appear full time in 1967 following the Monza win, but was dropped in

Master of Hill Climbs: Ludovico Scarfiotti won national fame by winning the Italian Grand Prix in 1966

favour of Chris Amon. However, when Bandini was killed and Ferrari team-mate Mike Parkes was badly injured, he almost gave up. He returned in 1968 with Cooper, but was killed when he crashed during a hill climb in Germany.
○ 10 Grands Prix, 1 win (Italian GP 1966)
○ No drivers' title (best result - 10th overall 1966)

Jody Scheckter

SEE PAGE 184

Harry Schell

Nationality: American
Born: 1921
Died: 1960

This French-born American was one of the extroverts of the 1950s' scene. He was destined to race as his father, and later his mother ran Ecurie Bleue. Harry made his World Championship debut in 1950, but started to make his mark in 1953 when he joined Gordini, and was even more impressive in 1954, driving a Maserati. He was employed by both Vanwall and Maserati in 1955 and gave the first showing of Vanwall's potential in 1956 when he snapped at the heels of the Ferraris in the French Grand Prix. He also won the non-championship Grand Prix de Caen in a Ferrari in 1956 and was employed as support for Juan Manuel Fangio at Maserati in 1957, before moving to BRM in 1958, taking a career-best second place in the Dutch Grand Prix.

He was driving a private Cooper when he crashed and died in the wet in practice for the Silverstone International Trophy in 1960.
○ 56 Grands Prix, no wins (best result - 2nd Dutch GP 1958)
○ No drivers' title (best result - 5th overall 1958)

Tim Schenken

Nationality: Australian
Born: 1942

After a successful career in the junior categories - in which he won 42 British Formula Ford races in 1968 alone, as well as the British Formula Three crown that year - and after a mixed season of Formula Two, Tim made his Formula One debut for Frank Williams' de Tomaso team in 1970, following the death of Piers Courage.

He was then signed to partner Graham Hill at Brabham, and overshadowed the former World Champion for most of the year, finishing third in Austria. A move to Surtees in 1972 proved to be a mistake, however, and effectively ended any chances he might have had of landing a top Formula One drive. He then drove the uncompetitive Trojan in 1974 before concentrating on sports cars and retiring in 1977. He later formed a company for building racing cars with racer Howden Ganley.
○ 34 Grands Prix, no wins (best result - 3rd Austrian GP 1971)
○ No drivers' title (best result - 14th overall 1971)

Michael Schumacher

SEE PAGE 185

JODY SCHECKTER
From Wild to Wealthy

Jody burst on to the Formula One scene amid recriminations and controversy, but retired eight years later a World Champion and, surprisingly to some, as a respected elder statesman, having matured considerably from his early days.

Having started out by racing karts and then motorcycles in his native South Africa, like his elder brother Ian, cars came next and after a spell in saloon racing and the obligatory period in the army doing National Service, Jody tried his hand at Formula Ford, doing well enough to win the Sunshine Series' Driver to Europe prize. And this is how this very fast but very wild youngster arrived at Brands Hatch in 1971.

Jody took pole on his first appearance, in the race supporting the Race of Champions, then spun but still finished second. A series of similarly exciting encounters followed before Jody decided to make the step up to Formula Three. Amazingly, he was a winner at this higher level before the year was out.

It was impossible not to notice this whirlwind and McLaren had his name on a Formula Two contract for 1972. He won just the once, at Crystal Palace, but the team decided that

he was ready for a shot at Formula One and so Jody made his World Championship debut at the US Grand Prix in which he finished ninth.

A second season of Formula Two followed, with McLaren fielding him in five grands prix, but, despite his dazzling progress, which saw him leading the French Grand Prix, there were demands that he be banned after he had caused a multiple pile-up

that brought the British Grand Prix to a halt two weeks later.

Jody moved to Tyrrell for 1974, replacing the retired Jackie Stewart, and began to lose his wild edge, taking two wins and third place in the World Championship. The following year was not so successful, but he made the six-wheel P34 a serious proposition in 1976, and again finished third in the title race.

Jody risked switching to the new Wolf team in 1977, but it paid off with three victories and the runner-up spot in the World Championship. However, after a poor year in 1978, he moved to Ferrari with the express intention of becoming World Champion.

He shrugged off the shock of being beaten by team-mate Gilles Villeneuve in the new 312T4's first two races, and knuckled down to a season of solid results and three wins.

Although Villeneuve was often quicker than Jody, it was Jody's regular scoring that ensured a narrow victory in the World Championship, secured by victory at Monza with Villeneuve dutifully trailing him. With the title under his belt, 1980 was a disaster. The new Ferrari 312T5 was off the pace and Jody, bemused and demoralized, decided to retire, safe, at the end of the season.

He then disappeared from the sport and went off to start a firearms training system business in the US. This grew and grew and, when he sold it, he became an extremely wealthy man. Jody now watches over the career of his son Tomas and runs a large organic farm in Hampshire.

o **112 Grands Prix, 10 wins**
o **World Champion 1979**

Human Whirlwind: Scheckter took a series of calculated gambles which had a habit of paying off...

1950	1970	1972	1974	1975	1977	1978	1980
Born 29 January in East London, South Africa	Moved up to Formula Ford, spinning 14 times in first race	Graduated to Formula Two with McLaren, winning at Crystal Palace. Then made Formula One debut for team in US GP	Joined Tyrrell and won Swedish and British GPs and was second in Monaco and German GPs to be third overall	Stayed on with Tyrrell and won South African GP, much to delight of the local fans, ranking seventh overall	Moved to new Wolf team and won first time out in Argentinian GP. Added wins in Monaco and Canadian GPs to be runner-up to Niki Lauda	Second season with Wolf was not so successful as he failed to win any races and fell to seventh overall	Ferrari produced a dog of a car and Jody scored just two points and retired from racing at end of year

1968	1971	1973	1976	1979	1996
Raced a Renault R8 in saloon races after trying karts and motorbikes	Won prize drive in Formula Ford race supporting the Race of Champions at Brands Hatch. Moved up to British Formula Three and won eight races	Made assorted Formula One outings and led French GP. Then came the British GP when he lost control and triggered a 20-car accident. Won North American Formula 5000 series	Gave Tyrrell's six-wheeled P34 its first win, in Sweden, and was also second four times to be third overall	Move to Ferrari brought the world title, with wins in Belgian, Monaco and Italian GPs to head his number two, Gilles Villeneuve	Back on racing scene guiding the careers of his two sons

MICHAEL SCHUMACHER
A Man for All Seasons

With a record seven world titles to his name by the age of 35, Michael is an all-time great. No driver has proved as focused on every ingredient required for a winning mix.

When Michael started winning for Benetton a year after his Formula One debut, he didn't have a car to match those from Williams or McLaren, but his titles in 1994 and 1995 were proof of his driving skills. However, it's the manner in which he has helped transform Ferrari for which he's held in the highest regard. His partnership with supremo Jean Todt is one of the greatest ever, with leading roles for technical boss Ross Brawn and chief designer Rory Byrne, both of whom followed him from Benetton.

Michael was guided from karts to cars by Willi Weber. After a promising first year in 1988, he advanced to Formula Three. German champion in 1990, also winning the Macau street race after a clash with Mika Hakkinen, Michael was given his Formula One debut by Jordan in Belgium in 1991 after Bertrand Gachot was jailed. He was then swapped by Benetton for Roberto Moreno.

Michael's first win came in Belgium in 1992. Another followed in 1993,

Before he won eight times in 1994. The season came to a head in Australia when he clipped a wall and took out Damon Hill. In so doing, he claimed the title. His 1995 title came in a more acceptable manner as he beat Hill's superior Williams nine times.

Moving to Ferrari in 1996, Michael joined a team that had forgotten how to win. Three wins were his reward. He added five more in 1997, but his hopes were dashed when he crashed into Jacques Villeneuve in the final race and was charged with overly robust driving.

The title battle also went to the final round in 1998, but Hakkinen won. A broken leg ruined 1999. However, in 2000, Michael became the first Ferrari driver since Jody Scheckter in 1979 to be World Champion. In 2001, Michael won nine races and wrapped up the title with four rounds to run. That was nothing compared to 2002 when he raced to 11 wins from 17 rounds, and was confirmed champion as early as July.

After equalling Fangio's record of five titles in 2002, Michael moved clear in 2003, winning six times. However, a new points system ensured that the title race went to the final round. This late in the day Michael endured a string of problems but claimed the result he required to beat McLaren's Kimi Raikkonen by two points.

The 2004 season was all-Michael, as he won 13 times for title number seven. But 2005 was a wake-up call as Ferrari was off the pace on its Bridgestones and he won just once, in the widely boycotted US GP. With talk of retirement hanging over him, Michael raced to seven wins in 2006 and only just failed to beat Fernando Alonso to the title before standing down.

The next three years were spent in retirement, and a neck injury precluded him standing in for the injured Felipe Massa at Ferrari in 2009, but Michael returned full-time with Mercedes in 2010.

° 250 Grands Prix, 91 wins
° World Champion 1994, 1995, 2000, 2001, 2002, 2003 and 2004

Simply the Best: Michael Schumacher

1969	1991	1993	1995	1997	1999	2001	2003	2006
Born 3 January in Hurth-Hermuhlheim, Germany	Second in Japanese Formula 3000 race. Made F1 debut with Jordan, was then poached to join Benetton, scoring immediately	One win, in Portugal, and eight other top-three finishes helped him to fourth overall	World Champion again, this time recording nine wins to outscore Williams's Damon Hill	Disgraced by his antics in finale when he swerved into Jacques Villeneuve's Williams. Won five times in season.	Breaking a leg at British GP caused him to miss six races. Won at Imola and Monaco	World Champion for fourth time, again with nine wins	World Champion for sixth time	Retires from F1 after adding another seven wins, to reach 91

1990	1992	1994	1996	1998	2000	2002	2004
German Formula Three Champion, also beating Mika Hakkinen to win at Macau. Raced for Mercedes in World Sports Car Championship	Scored first win on anniversary of his debut. Three third places helped him rank third	Won first four races. Disqualified from the British and Belgian GPs, but four more wins meant he took title by a point	Moved to Ferrari and did well to rank third with two wins as car was not pick of pack	Runner-up to Hakkinen, scoring six wins but losing out at final round	World Champion for third time, but first time for Ferrari, with nine wins	World Champion for fifth time, wrapping it up at 11th of 17 rounds. Scored 11 wins	Extends record to seventh F1 title

Keeping It in the Family: Ralf Schumacher started off in karts like his brother Michael and worked his way up. This picture is from the German Grand Prix, 2003

Ralf Schumacher

Nationality: German
Born: 1975

Like his elder brother Michael before him, Ralf was all but brought up on karts as their father Rolf ran a kart circuit. He graduated to car racing at the age of 17 in 1992. Ralf progressed from Formel Junior to Formula Three in 1994 and his first win helped Ralf to third overall behind Jorg Muller and Alex Wurz. Runner-up to Norberto Fontana in 1995, this duo met again in Japanese Formula 3000 in 1996, and Ralf showed that he could master these more powerful cars by taking the title at the final round, even though he crashed out of the race. Ralf stepped up to Formula One with Jordan in 1997 and showed raw speed. However, he upset the team by knocking team-mate Giancarlo Fisichella out of second place in Argentina en route

to third. Staying on with Jordan in 1998, Ralf peaked with second place behind team-mate Damon Hill in Belgium. Moving on to Williams for 1999, his new-found maturity shone through as he scored 11 times in 16 races, peaking with a second-place finish at Monza. Ralf drove even better in 2000, ranking fifth overall, but he was given a scare by the pace of his rookie team-mate Jenson Button. Ralf came of age in 2001 by scoring his first win after outrunning the McLarens at Imola. Then he won again at Montreal, this time beating brother Michael in a straight fight. His third win came on home ground at Hockenheim, inheriting victory when team-mate Juan Pablo Montoya hit trouble. The 2002 season was one that started well with a somewhat fortunate win in the second race, in Malaysia, but his form was somewhat

erratic, although winning again would have been tough as Ferrari was so dominant. He doubled that tally to win twice in 2003, doing so with masterful drives in consecutive races mid-season, but his form was again too patchy to enable him to mount a challenge for the title.

○ **115 Grands Prix, 6 wins (San Marino GP 2001, Canadian GP 2001, German GP 2001, Malaysian GP 2002, European GP 2003, French GP 2003)**

○ **No drivers' title (best result – 4th overall 2001 & 2002)**

Ayrton Senna

SEE PAGE 187

Johnny Servoz-Gavin

Nationality: French
Born: 1942
Died: 2006

After proving wild in Formula Two,

Johnny was given a Formula One break in 1968 when an accident to Jackie Stewart saw him drafted into Ken Tyrrell's Matra team at Monaco. He qualified second, and led before thumping a barrier on the first lap.

Returning for Monza, he came in second, and he was retained by Matra for 1969, and went on to win the Formula Two title. He signed as Stewart's team-mate for Tyrrell for 1970 but, after failing to qualify at Monaco, he retired, blaming an eye injury from a road accident for his loss of pace.

○ **12 Grands Prix, no wins (best result – 2nd Italian GP 1968)**

○ **No drivers' title (best result – 13th, 1968)**

Jo Siffert

Nationality: Swiss
Born: 1936
Died: 1971

Jo began his Formula One career in 1962, the year in a which he was also joint European Formula Junior champion, but despite picking up several top-six finishes, success eluded him until 1968. The reason for this change of fortune was that, in his fourth year with Rob Walker's team, the popular Swiss driver had front-line equipment at his disposal for the first time in the form of a Lotus 49.

Jo duly won the British Grand Prix at Brands Hatch and was then offered a ride with Ferrari for 1970. However, Porsche, for whom he raced in sports cars, was determined to hang on to him and paid for a season in a works March. This proved a disaster as the team overextended itself in its first year in Formula One and he was delighted to join BRM alongside Pedro Rodriguez for 1971.

After Rodriguez was killed mid-summer, Jo buoyed the team's spirits with a superb win in Austria, only to die in a non-championship race at Brands Hatch the same year.

○ **96 Grands Prix, 2 wins (British GP 1968, Austrian GP 1971)**

○ **No drivers' title (best result – 4th overall 1971)**

AYRTON SENNA
The Fastest Ever

Ayrton was a genius, a tyrant, a benevolent and humble person, yet arrogant too, a man who divided opinion like no other. But there was one thing that no one could deny: he was the fastest driver the world has ever seen.

Ayrton won kart races from the moment he started competing at the age of 13. He was Brazilian champion as soon as he was old enough to race in the senior category.

Then, when he came to Britain to race in Formula Ford 1600 in 1981, it took him only until his third race to score his first win. But Ayrton couldn't adapt to being away from Brazil, so he went back to São Paulo. Then he changed his mind and returned to Britain to win the British and European Formula Ford 2000 titles.

Ayrton won the final British Formula Three round of 1983 against Martin Brundle to claim the title and the Formula One tests with McLaren and Williams that came with it. They were impressed, but neither signed him, leaving him to settle for a ride with little-fancied Toleman for 1984.

A move to Lotus for 1985 brought Ayrton's first win, in torrential conditions, at Estoril. Another win followed and he ended the year fourth overall. Moves were made to introduce Derek Warwick as his team-mate for 1986, but Ayrton balked at this, earning flak from the media. He duly won twice and was fourth overall again. Then, at Monaco in 1987, he scored his fifth win, starting his love affair with the street circuit. He was to win there on five more occasions, but his rate of progress was insufficient, so he joined McLaren in 1988. Eight wins and the title were his reward. The next few years were his purple patch, with second overall in 1989 being followed by world titles in both 1990 and 1991.

For 1994, with Nigel Mansell racing in the US and Alain Prost having quit, the way was clear for what many saw as the creation of the ultimate partnership: Ayrton, Williams and Renault engines. The season kicked off in Brazil with pole, but Ayrton was overtaken by Benetton's Michael Schumacher at their first fuel stops and he spun off trying to make up lost ground. Matters looked to be improving in round two at Aida in Japan, as Ayrton was on pole again, but he was hit from behind by Mika Hakkinen at the first corner and forced out. Schumacher won both races. Then came Imola.

Ayrton was in front after a restart and he was being pressured by Schumacher. Then, at the start of the second lap, after the cars had been released, Ayrton's Williams speared right at Tamburello, hit the wall and came to rest on the side of the track. For an instant Ayrton moved, then he became still. His death was the extinction of perhaps the man who came as close to perfection in his chosen pursuit as any driver in history.

- **161 Grands Prix, 41 wins**
- **World Champion 1988, 1990 and 1991**

Speed King: Senna savours his moment of triumph at the Japanese Grand Prix, Suzuka, in 1993

1960	1980	1983	1985	1986	1988	1990	1993
Born 21 March in Saõ Paulo, Brazil	Runner-up in World Karting final and Brazilian Champion for second year in a row	Graduated to Formula Three and won final round against Martin Brundle to claim the prestigious British title	Moved to Lotus and won Portuguese and Belgian GPs to finish fourth overall	Resisted moves to have Derek Warwick join him at Lotus. Took two more wins to be fourth overall again	In McLaren, he found a team that could meet his needs. Won eight grands prix to claim first title	Became World Champion again, with six wins, again clashing with Prost in Japanese GP	Produced drive of his life to win at Donington in European GP and added four more wins to be runner-up to Prost's Williams

1977	1981	1982	1984	1987	1989	1991	1994
South American Karting Champion	Moved to England and won the British Formula Ford 1600 series	Back in Brazil and sponsored by a local bank, won 22 races along with the championship	Made Formula One debut with Toleman and finished second at Monaco to rank ninth overall	Won Monaco GP, prompting his love affair with the circuit. Ended year third overall	Won six grands prix, but was runner-up after clashing with team-mate Alain Prost	Made it three world titles with another seven wins	Joined Williams with high expectations, but failed to a win before he crashed to his death in San Marino GP

Raymond Sommer

Nationality: French
Born: 1906
Died: 1950

Raymond was a key figure of the inter-war period of racing, especially in sports cars, where he won Le Mans in both 1931 and 1932, first with Luigi Chinetti and then with the legendary Tazio Nuvolari. Eschewing driving for teams in Formula One because of the constraints they put on him, Raymond delighted in taking on the mighty Ferrari and Mercedes teams and beating them as often as possible. After the war he consolidated his reputation for no-holds-barred racing with an excellent fourth place at Monaco in 1950 in a Formula Two Ferrari, before being killed in a non-championship race at Cadours towards the end of the year.

○ 5 Grands Prix, no wins (best result – 4th Monaco GP 1950)
○ No drivers' title (best result – 13th overall 1950)

Mike Spence

Nationality: British
Born: 1936
Died: 1968

Mike began his Formula One career as Jim Clark's team-mate at Lotus and, although he was overshadowed by the great Scot, often ran competitively in his two years at Lotus, peaking with third place in Mexico in 1965. Mike switched to a semi-works BRM drive in 1966, before being promoted to the full works team in 1967. That year he also raced the radical Chaparral sports car with some success. He seemed on the threshold of grand prix success, but died of head injuries following an accident at Indianapolis where, ironically, he was replacing Clark, who had been killed the previous month in a Formula Two race at Hockenheim.

○ 36 Grands Prix, no wins (best result – 3rd Mexican GP 1965)
○ No drivers' title (best result – 8th overall 1965)

Jackie Stewart

SEE PAGE 189

Rolf Stommelen

Nationality: German
Born: 1943
Died: 1983

After making his name taming the Porsche 917 sports car, Rolf entered Formula One with Brabham in 1970. From the off, he showed great promise with four top-six finishes, but seasons with Surtees and then the ugly Eifelland March all but destroyed his Formula One career.

An occasional drive with Brabham in 1974 provided a lifeline, and he was offered a drive with the Hill team for 1975, only to be injured in a crash at the Spanish Grand Prix, when his car flew into the crowd and killed four spectators.

When Rolf returned later in the year, he was off-form and was mainly away from Formula One until spending a season as an also-ran with Arrows in 1978, after which he returned to sports cars. He was killed in a crash at Riverside, California in 1983.

○ 54 Grands Prix, no wins (best result – 3rd Austrian GP 1970)
○ No drivers' title (best result – 11th overall 1970)

Philippe Streiff

Nationality: French
Born: 1955

This tall, serious Frenchman made his debut with a Renault in the 1984 Portuguese Grand Prix. Halfway through 1985, he replaced Andrea de Cesaris at Ligier, scoring an excellent third place at the end-of-year Australian Grand Prix.

Philippe's first full year came with Tyrrell in 1986, and he spent the next two years with the British team, for whom he was usually outpaced by his team-mates.

A move to AGS in 1988 revitalized him, and he impressed with some excellent drives, including a superb showing in qualifying at Imola.

He was to stay with AGS in 1989, but a heavy crash in testing at Jacarepagua left him paralysed.

○ 54 Grands Prix, no wins (best result – 3rd Australian GP 1985)
○ No drivers' title (best result – 13th overall 1986)

Piratical Privateer: the maverick Raymond Sommer in his CTA-Arsenal which was forced to retire on the first lap of its debut in the French GP, 1947

JACKIE STEWART
A Sponsor's Dream

Think of Jackie Stewart and you think of a blue Tyrrell notching up win after win, you think of sunglasses and sideburns, but you also think of a champion with a business brain.

World Champion in 1969, 1971 and 1973, he also possessed great commercial acumen. Having seen too many of his friends and contemporaries die, Jackie wanted Formula One to be made safer and for drivers to be better remunerated for the risks they took. He had found himself trapped in his inverted car at the Belgian Grand Prix in 1966, soaked in petrol. Thankful that no spark ignited, he began a safety crusade.

Jackie was a top marksman, but failed to qualify to represent Britain in the 1960 Olympics. Perhaps this spurred him to follow his brother, Jimmy, into racing. Whatever the reason, his early races for Ecurie Ecosse demonstrated that Jackie was special. Ken Tyrrell placed him in his Formula Three car and victories soon followed. He was pressed to sign for Lotus for 1965 but he turned them down and joined BRM instead.

Very few drivers win races in their first season of Formula One, but Jackie did, triumphing on his eighth outing, the Italian Grand Prix, which helped

him end up third overall behind Jim Clark and team-mate Graham Hill.

Jackie kicked off 1966 in the best possible style by winning at Monaco. However, the BRM was not competitive again as Brabham took control and Jackie did not win again until the 1968 Dutch Grand Prix, when he was reunited with Tyrrell.

Six years out of Jackie's nine-year spell in Formula One were spent driving for Ken. At first this was in a Ford-powered Matra, and the engine powered him to three victories in 1968. The combination's second year was even more successful, with Jackie winning six races and the title – the sixth for a Briton since Graham Hill won it in 1962.

In 1970, the Matra was replaced by a March, but he could not live with Jochen Rindt's Lotus or the Ferraris. So, in 1971, Jackie went and did battle in a Tyrrell chassis. Perfecting the art of driving a storming opening lap and then controlling the race, Jackie won six times in 1971.

The following year yielded four wins, but he was beaten to the title by Lotus' Emerson Fittipaldi. Then, in 1973, he had five wins in the bag when he reached Watkins Glen, intending for this to be his final race. After the

death of team-mate François Cevert in qualifying, Tyrrell withdrew his entry. His record of 27 grand prix wins (from 99 starts) was to stand until beaten by Alain Prost in 1987 (in his 118th start).

Jackie combined forces in 1997 with his elder son Paul – who had run a successful team in Formula Three – to enter the Stewart Grand Prix team with

Ford power and Rubens Barrichello and Jan Magnussen in 1997. A second place was their best result all year, but Johnny Herbert gave Stewart its first win at the Nurburgring in 1999 before the team was sold to Ford and re-badged as Jaguar for 2000.

- **99 Grands Prix, 27 wins**
- **World Champion 1969, 1971 and 1973**

Swinging Sixties Icon: Jackie Stewart stands beside his Tyrrell-run March at Zandvoort in 1970

1939	1961	1964	1966	1968	1970	1972	1997
Born 11 June in Milton, Scotland	Took up circuit racing with a Marcos sports car	Ken Tyrrell signed him for Formula Three. He won his first race then turned down Formula One contracts from Cooper and Lotus	Won Tasman series, then Monaco GP, but BRM's H16 engine ruined second half of year. Came close to winning Indy 500	Won three races in a Tyrrell-run Matra, but injured wrist in Formula Two race and missed two, leaving him runner-up to Lotus's Graham Hill	Won Race of Champions again and Spanish GP in a Tyrrell-run March, but had to wait for Tyrrell chassis. Ranked fifth overall	Troubled by an ulcer, Jackie was off form, missing Belgian GP, but still won four races to be runner-up to Lotus's Fittipaldi	Launched Stewart Grand Prix Formula One team

1959	1963	1965	1967	1969	1971	1973
Member of British clay-pigeon shooting team	Won two races in a Jaguar and was entered by Ecurie Ecosse in a Tojeiro, then a Cooper Monaco, winning at Goodwood	Made World Championship debut with BRM after coming second in Race of Champions and winning International Trophy. Won Italian GP to be third overall	Collected a second and a third in just two finishes. Kept his hand in with four Formula Two wins	Winning six races, Jackie walked away with the World Championship. He also won Race of Champions	Tyrrell shone, and Jackie won six grands prix to be crowned champion for a second time.	World Champion for third time. He won five races but quit before US GP as team-mate François Cevert was killed in practice

Hans-Joachim Stuck

Nationality: German

Born: 1951

The son of pre-war ace Hans Stuck, Hans Jr's natural talent rarely seemed to find full expression in Formula One. Already a touring car ace when he made his grand prix debut in 1974 with March, Hans Jr proved somewhat inconsistent in the following three years. When Carlos Pace was killed early in 1977, Hans replaced him in the Brabham line-up, and scored superb third places at the German and Austrian Grands Prix.

He proceeded to lead the end-of-season US Grand Prix only to slide off in the soaking conditions. Hans drove for Shadow in 1978 and ATS in 1979, but rarely featured prominently, before moving to a very successful career in sports cars, which included winning the 1985 world title and the Le Mans 24 Hours in both 1986 and 1987, all with Porsche partner Derek Bell. Since then, Hans won the German touring car title with Audi in 1990.

○ 74 Grands Prix, no wins (best result - 3rd German GP 1977, Austrian GP 1977)

○ No drivers' title (best result - 11th overall 1977)

Troubled Start: Marc Surer during his Formula One debut at the US Grand Prix, Watkins Glen, 1979, before he retired from the circuit with engine trouble

Danny Sullivan

Nationality: American

Born: 1950

One of the few Americans in Europe in the 1970s, Danny finished second to Gunnar Nilsson in British Formula Three in 1975. Following strong performances in Formula Atlantic all around the world, Danny headed home and raced in the CanAm sports car series before making a surprise move to Formula One in 1983.

Racing for Tyrrell, Danny finished second in the non-championship Race of Champions at Brands Hatch then raced to fifth place at Monaco. However, he raced IndyCars in 1984, winning three races, before winning the Indy 500 for Penske in 1985. Overall IndyCar champion in 1988, he raced on into the 1990s, also in sports

cars and is now masterminding a Red Bull-backed American driver search programme.

○ 15 Grands Prix, no wins (best result - 5th Monaco GP 1983)

○ No drivers' title (best result - 17th overall 1983)

Marc Surer

Nationality: Swiss

Born: 1952

Promoted to Formula One after winning the 1979 European Formula Two title, Marc raced three times with Ensign in 1979, before moving to ATS in 1980 and badly damaging his ankles in a crash at the South African Grand Prix. In 1982, when he was driving for Arrows, he crashed in testing again, but, once fit, he drove for Arrows until the end of 1984, earning admiration for his often skilled performances.

Marc was finally given the chance to show his ability in Formula One when he replaced François Hesnault in a Brabham alongside Nelson Piquet in 1985, before moving back to Arrows in 1986.

Marc's career ended when he crashed a Ford RS200 rally car heavily. His co-driver was killed and Surer himself was badly burned. After running BMW's touring car project, he has since become a television commentator.

John Surtees

SEE PAGE 189

Aguri Suzuki

Nationality: Japanese

Born: 1960

Aguri is Japan's most successful grand prix driver. After winning the

Japanese Formula 3000 title in 1988, a dreadful first year in Formula One in 1989, in which he failed to qualify for Zakspeed, was erased by some superb drives for Larrousse in 1990, including a finish that brought him to the podium at his home grand prix.

However, a financially strapped season with Larrousse did nothing to help his reputation, which was damaged further by two years with Footwork, when he was outpaced by Michele Alboreto and Derek Warwick.

He signed a contract to race with Ligier in 1995, albeit sharing the drive with Martin Brundle who proved faster. Aguri now fields a team in the Indy Racing League.

○ 64 Grands Prix, no wins (best result - 3rd Japanese GP 1990)

○ No drivers' title (best result - 10th overall 1990)

JOHN SURTEES
A Champion on Two and Four

John is assured a place in the history books as the only man to have won the World Championship on both motorcyles and in cars, but there is more to this remarkable man than that, as he also went on to build his own cars and ran his own team to a very high standard – albeit not high enough by his own exacting standards.

Having won seven world motorcycle titles between 1956 and 1960, making his name on Nortons and then starring on MV Agustas, John took time out in 1959 to take a look at a move to four-wheeled competition by testing for Aston Martin and Vanwall. However, he showed his real talent by winning on his four-wheeled debut in a Ken Tyrrell-run Formula Junior Cooper in 1960 and Lotus boss Colin Chapman invited him to drive for his grand prix team when the races did not clash with his motorcycle commitments. John did not disappoint, finishing in an amazing second place on only his second outing in the British Grand Prix at Silverstone and taking pole position in Portugal, where he dominated the race until damaging a radiator.

A move to Ferrari for 1963 was the kick-start for success, and John took his first win at the Nurburgring. In 1964 he secured two more wins and snatched the world title at a nail-biting final race, in Mexico, in which the destiny of the championship first slipped from Clark's hands, then from Graham Hill's before finally falling into John's grasp as he finished second behind Dan Gurney's Brabham.

John's 1965 season was disrupted when he had a heavy crash in a Lola CanAm car, but his doggedness and determination pulled him through and he returned to Ferrari for 1966. He always excelled on the classic road circuits, and Spa-Francorchamps that year was no exception, with John taking a superb victory in the Belgian Grand Prix after an intense battle with Jochen Rindt. That, however, was followed by a falling-out with team manager Eugenio Dragoni and John drove for Cooper until the end of the season. He cocked a snook at Ferrari by winning the final race, in Mexico, before spending a difficult couple of years developing Honda's challenge, which included a victory in the 1967 Italian Grand Prix.

John signed for BRM for 1969, but it was a trying year, made worse by medical problems that were a long-term effect of the CanAm crash. By now he had made up his mind to start his own team, where he would not need to compromise his ideas on the technical approach. The team was not the success he had hoped for, however, even though John won the Gold Cup twice and Mike Hailwood won the Formula Two crown in 1972, the year in which he also finished second in the Italian Grand Prix. John retired from driving at the end of that season. That elusive first win never came the team's way and it ceased competing at the end of 1978, a decision hastened by the onset of medical problems.

⚬ **111 Grands Prix, 6 wins**
⚬ **World Champion 1964**

Doubling Up: Surtees took seven world motorcycle championships before moving on to four wheels

1934	1956	1961	1963	1965	1967	1970
Born 11 February in Tatsfield, Surrey, England	Became World Champion on an MV Agusta and followed this with six more world titles over the next three years	Regretted his decision to spurn Lotus as he fought his Yeoman Credit Cooper to just two fifth places	Scored his first World Championship win for Ferrari, in the German GP, and also won non-points Mediterranean and Rand GPs and two sports car races	Arrival of Ferrari's flat-12 hampered his year and second in season-opening South African GP remained his best result. Won Nurburgring 1,000kms	Joined Honda and developed its Lola-derived chassis well enough to win Italian GP and ended season fourth overall	Surtees fielded a McLaren, then a chassis of its own, with fifth its best result until it won non-championship Gold Cup at Oulton Park

1951	1960	1962	1964	1966	1968	1969	1972
Started racing motorcycles	Tried a Formula Junior Cooper then Lotus gave him a shot at Formula One. He finished second in the British GP, just four months after his first car race	Raced his Bowmaker Racing Lola to fourth overall after finishing second at the British and German GPs	World Champion for Ferrari thanks to wins in German and Italian GPs and three other second places	Won Monza 1,000kms then Belgian GP, but fell out with Ferrari and raced for Cooper, winning Mexican GP. Won CanAm title	Stuck it out with Honda, but second in French GP was his best finish	Moved to BRM and had a trying season that convinced him to run his own outfit	Made final two grand prix outings. Team soldiered on until the end of 1978

Toranosuke Takagi

Nationality: Japanese
Born: 1974

Formula Nippon champion in 1997, Toranosuke was blindingly fast in his first year with Tyrrell in 1998, but he crashed too much.

A move to Arrows for 1999 produced a seventh place, but he stepped back to Formula Nippon in 2000 to rediscover his form. He won almost every race to be champion and signed to race for Toyota in IndyCars. He continues in the Indy Racing League, still both competitive and erratic.

○ **32 Grands Prix, no wins (best result – 7th Australian GP 1999)**
○ **No drivers' title**

Patrick Tambay

Nationality: French
Born: 1949

After success in Formula Two, Patrick made his grand prix debut, for Ensign, at the same time as Gilles Villeneuve made his debut for McLaren. Villeneuve was to become a close friend, but McLaren preferred to run Patrick in 1978, while Villeneuve went to Ferrari. Patrick came off the worse, though, as McLaren slumped into a period of uncompetitiveness. He was replaced by Alain Prost and went to the US where he won the CanAm title. He returned to Formula One in 1981 with Theodore and then Ligier, but was dropped at the end of the season.

In 1982 he announced his retirement from Formula One, but was recalled by Ferrari after Villeneuve's death. He won the German Grand Prix before taking an emotional win at the 1983 San Marino Grand Prix. He challenged for the world title that year, but was dropped by Ferrari at the end of it.

In subsequent spells with Renault and the Haas-Lola teams, this immensely popular man never had a car worthy of his considerable talent. Ever urbane, Patrick is now one of the faces of Formula One on French television.

○ **114 Grands Prix, 2 wins (German GP 1982, San Marino GP 1983)**
○ **No drivers' title (best result – 4th overall 1983)**

Gabriele Tarquini

Nationality: Italian
Born: 1962

Hugely underrated, Gabriele never had a Formula One car to match his ability. He caused a sensation in 1985 when, as reigning World Karting Champion, he went straight to Formula 3000 and became a front-runner. Yet it wasn't until 1988 that he got to Formula One with Coloni. Drafted in at AGS to replace the injured Philippe Streiff in 1989, Gabriele scored a point at Mexico, but AGS slipped further down the grid over the next two years. He drove for Fondmetal in 1992, but success was thwarted by financial problems, and the team dropped out of Formula One. Gabriele has since made a reputation for himself in touring cars, winning the British title in 1994 for Alfa Romeo. Touring cars continue to be a happy hunting ground and Gabriele clinched the European title for Alfa Romeo in 2003.

○ **38 Grands Prix, no wins (best result – 6th Mexican GP 1989)**
○ **No drivers' title (best result – 26th overall 1989)**

Piero Taruffi

Nationality: Italian
Born: 1906
Died: 1989

Piero was in his 40s when the World Championship started in 1950, having made his debut 20 years earlier on the Mille Miglia. He finished second in the Swiss Grand Prix for Ferrari in 1951 and scored his only grand prix win in the same race a year later, also coming second in the British Grand Prix. Piero then concentrated on sports cars with Lancia in 1953 and won the Targa Florio the following year before dropping back into Formula One for Mercedes in 1955, finishing second in the Italian Grand Prix. After winning the 1957 Mille Miglia, he hung up his helmet and opened a racing school.

○ **18 Grands Prix, 1 win (Swiss GP 1952)**
○ **No drivers' title (best result – 3rd overall 1952)**

Gallic Charm: Patrick Tambay on the podium, between René Arnoux (second and left) and Keke Rosberg (third), after winning the German Grand Prix in 1982

Trevor Taylor

Nationality: British
Born: 1936

Drafted into the Lotus Formula One team, Formula Three and Formula Junior hotshot Trevor was compared to team-mate Jim Clark – and like every other driver of the era he was found wanting. Given a full season in 1962, he came second in the Dutch Grand Prix.

A succession of accidents took their toll, however, and then a poor season with BRP effectively finished his Formula One career at the end of 1964.

○ 27 Grands Prix, no wins (best result – 2nd Dutch GP 1962)
○ No drivers' title (best result – 10th overall 1962)

Mike Thackwell

Nationality: New Zealander
Born: 1961

Mike became the youngest ever grand prix driver when he started the 1980 Canadian Grand Prix for Tyrrell aged just 19, but his career never really managed to take off.

Back to Formula Two in 1981, a huge accident at Thruxton stalled Mike's progress, and although he fought back to win the 1984 Formula Two crown, he dropped out of the sport entirely shortly afterwards.

○ 2 Grands Prix, no wins (best result – retired both races)
○ No drivers' title

Maurice Trintignant

Nationality: French
Born: 1917

Maurice was a top driver when racing resumed after the Second World War finished in 1945.

By then, he was something of a street racing specialist and won at Monaco for Ferrari in 1955 and then at the same venue in a Rob Walker Racing Cooper three years later.

He also won three non-championship races in the 1950s and the Le Mans 24 Hours in 1954. When he briefly replaced Stirling Moss in

The Full Monte: Renault's Jarno Trulli on his way to fourth place in qualifying for the Monaco Grand Prix in 2003. A grand prix win still eludes him

1962, he was still sprightly enough to show Jim Clark the way at the non-championship race at Pau, but it proved to be his last competitive year and he quit in 1964.

○ 82 Grands Prix, 2 wins (Monaco GP 1955, Monaco GP 1958)
○ No drivers' title (best result – 4th overall 1954 and 1955)

Jarno Trulli

Nationality: Italian
Born: 1974

Benetton boss Flavio Briatore was so sure of the ability of the 1994 World Kart Champion that he paid for Jarno to go direct to German Formula Three midway through 1995. Jarno won the final two races and became champion in 1996. Briatore put him with Minardi for 1997, but his break came when he subbed for Olivier Panis at Prost and led in Austria. He stayed on with Prost until the end of 1999, peaking with second in the European Grand Prix before joining Jordan.

This move was blighted by mechanical failure, but he showed flashes of class. It was the same story in 2001 as his Jordan let him down as he was heading for points. He did, however, twice finish fourth to rank equal seventh.

He was then involved in a straight swap for 2002 with Giancarlo Fisichella – another driver run by Briatore – heading to the emerging Renault team. He appeared to suffer

the luck of 1960s' star Chris Amon, with almost every top drive scuppered by mechanical failure, with two fourths his best showings. As Fernando Alonso hogged the glory in 2003, Jarno at least made the podium at the German Grand Prix. That elusive first win came his way in 2004, though, with a fine run in Monaco. Dropped for 2005, he popped up again with Toyota and collected two second-place finishes before enduring a trying 2006 season. After minimal gain in 2007, Jarno finished third at Magny-Cours in 2008. Things improved further in 2009 when he rose to eighth overall, peaking with second at Suzuka before Toyota quit.

○ 219 Grands Prix, 1 win (Monaco GP 2004)
○ No drivers' title (best result – 6th, 2004)

Sebastian Vettel

Nationality: German

Born: 1987

A star in the junior formulae, Sebastian was soon the leading light in Red Bull's talent search and he jumped from the World Series by Renault to Formula One mid-2007 when Jacques Villeneuve was dropped by BMW Sauber. He scored a point on his debut, then did seven races for Scuderia Toro Rosso. He hit Mark Webber behind the safety car at Fuji, but made amends by finishing fourth in China. Victory in the wet at Monza in 2008 earned Sebastian his stripes and he was promoted to Red Bull Racing for 2009, then winning four times to be runner-up to Jenson Button.

° **43 Grands Prix, 5 wins (Italian GP 2008, Chinese GP 2009, British GP 2009, Japanese GP 2009, Abu Dhabi GP 2009)**
° **No drivers' title (best result - 2nd overall 2009)**

Jos Verstappen

Nationality: Dutch

Born: 1972

Jos shone in the GM Euroseries in 1992 before winning the 1993 German Formula Three title. Snapped up by Benetton for 1994, he was thrown in at the deep end when JJ Lehto broke his neck in testing. He survived a pit fire in Germany and then finished third in Hungary. Driving for Simtek in 1995, Jos qualified mid-grid in Argentina, Imola and Spain, but it all came to nought when Simtek ran out of cash. He then struggled first with Arrows in 1996 and then with Tyrrell in 1997, before joining the Stewart team midway through 1998.

Dropped for 1999, he was back with Arrows in 2000 and came fourth at Monza. Strong showings early in 2001 were largely down to the fact that he started light; and this was because his Arrows could not carry a full fuel load.

However, he was to score just once, taking sixth at the A1-Ring, then lost his drive with Arrows just before the start of the 2002 season. Back in harness in 2003, Jos raced for Minardi

Sheer Talent: Gilles Villeneuve at the US Grand Prix West at Long Beach, which he won in 1979, a year in which he took the chequered flag three times

and peaked with a ninth place for the backmarking team.

° **107 Grands Prix, no wins (best result - 3rd Hungarian GP 1994)**
° **No drivers' title (best result - 10th overall 1994)**

Gilles Villeneuve

Nationality: Canadian

Born: 1950

Died: 1982

Some thought Gilles personified everything good about motor racing; his natural speed and spectacular style complemented by an open, irreverent character. Others said his flamboyance bordered on the reckless.

He dominated the Canadian Formula Atlantic scene, and wiped the floor at an invitation race at Trois-Rivieres at the end of 1976 that included World Champion James Hunt. That led to a drive with McLaren in the 1977 British Grand Prix, where he stunned everyone by running on the pace of the leaders in a two-year-old car. Unfathomably, McLaren did not take up an option on his services, but Ferrari signed him to replace Lauda at the end of 1977.

Gilles stayed with Ferrari until the end of his career. He scored his first win, on home soil in Canada, in 1978, and would have been World Champion in 1979, when he won three grands

prix, had he not honourably stood by team orders at the Italian Grand Prix and sat behind team-mate Jody Scheckter, who took the title instead. Then followed two years in hugely inferior cars (although he had two opportunistic wins in 1981) until in 1982 he finally had the equipment to win consistently. However, after having victory stolen from under his nose by team-mate Didier Pironi as he was cruising to the flag in the San Marino Grand Prix, Gilles was plunged into turmoil. He pledged never to speak to Pironi again, and, two weeks later, he crashed fatally during practice for the Belgian Grand Prix.

JACQUES VILLENEUVE
A Straight-Talking Man

Jacques became World Champion, but his father Gilles did not. However, due to a career move that went wrong, you can be sure that it will be Gilles' name that stands out when the sport is looked back upon in the years ahead.

Jacques was not particularly interested in racing when his father Gilles was alive, but he took it up and spent three years in Italian Formula Three, starting in 1989 and ranking sixth overall in 1991, albeit still without scoring his first win. A winner at last in 1992, he finished as runner-up in the Japanese Formula Three series.

It was when in Japan that he met up with Craig Pollock, who had taught at his school in Switzerland before moving into sports management, and Pollock suggested that he headed "home", back to North America in 1993. The move paid off as Jacques ranked third in the Toyota Atlantic series.

Jacques' next step was his biggest as he moved up to race in the IndyCar championship and he really raised his game to be named Rookie of the Year in a season that included second place in the Indy 500. Jacques then won the title in 1995 with four wins, including the Indianapolis 500.

Moving to Formula One with Williams for 1996, Jacques came close to equalling Giancarlo Baghetti's feat of winning on his debut, but an engine problem forced him to slow and finish second behind team-mate Damon Hill. He went on to win four times and chased Hill all the way to the final round. Jacques was champion in 1997, with seven wins, surviving an assault by Schumacher at the final round. His title defence in 1998 was ruined by a poor Williams and he ranked fifth.

Jacques then joined Pollock's new BAR team in 1999. Despite bold promises that wins would come, even as early as the team's first race,

On the Road Again: Villeneuve pepares in the garage before the European Grand Prix, 1997

mechanical failure after mechanical failure wrecked his year. Indeed, Jacques did not as much as finish a race until the 12th round. As it was, not a point was scored all year, with his best finish eighth at Monza.

Jacques collected four fourth-place finishes in 2000 to rank seventh overall. On paper, his 2001 campaign with BAR was more successful, with a pair of thirds at Barcelona and at Hockenheim, but both of these came his way largely through the attrition of the front-runners.

By the end of the year, Jacques was dispirited. To make matters worse, a palace coup saw Pollock deposed and David Richards took over the team. It was too late for Jacques to find another ride for 2002 so he stayed on. The following two years offered a gradual improvement in form, but they provided little in the way of cheer, particularly in 2003, when he scoffed at the credentials of incoming Jenson Button, only to be outraced and outscored by him. On hearing that he was to be replaced by Takuma Sato for 2004, Jacques declined to contest the Japanese Grand Prix and his Formula One career was over.

∘ **99 Grands Prix, 11 wins**
∘ **World Champion 1997**

1971	1991	1993	1995	1997	1999	2001	2003
Born 9 April in Saint Jean-sur-Richlieu, Quebec, Canada	Sixth in Italian Formula Three series	Manager Craig Pollock coaxed him to race in Formula Atlantic and Jacques became champion	IndyCar champion with Team Green, taking four wins, including the Indy 500	World Champion, but only after surviving collision with Michael Schumacher at final round at Jerez. Won seven grands prix	Moved to Pollock's all-new BAR team and failed even to finish a race until the 12th round. His best result was an eighth place	Reached podium with third place at Spanish GP and again at German GP, ranking equal seventh	Dropped by BAR at end of year after scoring just six points to team-mate Jenson Button's 18

1988	1992	1994	1996	1998	2000	2002
Made racing debut in Italian Group N saloon series	Moved to Japanese Formula Three and was runner-up. Also raced sports cars in Japan	Stepped up to Indy Cars with Forsythe-Green. Rookie of the Year, winning at Road America. Also second in Indy 500	Formula One with Williams. First win came at European GP then added three more to be runner-up to Damon Hill	Third year was a tough one after withdrawal of works Renault engines and he failed to win a race	Second season with BAR yielded four fourth places and seventh overall	Struggled with BAR, with best result fourth at French GP, slipping to equal 12th overall

◦ **67 Grands Prix, 6 wins (Canadian GP 1978, South African GP 1979, US West GP 1979, US East GP 1979, Monaco GP 1981, Spanish GP 1981)**
◦ **No drivers' title (best result – 2nd, 1979)**

Jacques Villeneuve
SEE PAGE 195

Luigi Villoresi
Nationality: Italian
Born: 1909

A successful grand prix driver in the golden days before the Second World War, Luigi was marginally past his peak by the time the World Championship came to be founded, although he was still quick enough to win the 1949 Dutch Grand Prix.

After years with Maserati and Alfa Romeo, Luigi had moved to Ferrari in 1949 to encourage the career of his young friend Alberto Ascari, whom he recognized as having a far greater talent than his own. Luigi pulled out of Formula One temporarily after Ascari's death in 1955, returning in 1956 for Maserati, only to crash badly at the non-championship Rome Grand Prix and retire.

◦ **31 Grands Prix, no wins (best result – 2nd Argentinian GP 1953, Belgian GP 1953)**
◦ **No drivers' title (best result – 5th overall 1951 and 1953)**

Wolfgang von Trips
Nationality: German
Born: 1928
Died: 1961

Until Michael Schumacher won the World Championship in 1994, von Trips was Germany's most successful grand prix driver. Always quick, he shrugged off the reputation as a crasher he had garnered in his early career when he rejoined Ferrari in 1960. A number of top-six placings that year were followed by a determined assault on the World Championship in 1961.

Two wins and two second places from six races had him bang on target as he arrived at Monza for the Italian Grand Prix. However, after taking pole, he made a poor start and, trying to protect his position on the first lap, collided with Jim Clark. His car crashed into the crowd, killing 14 spectators. Von Trips also died, leaving team-mate Phil Hill to clinch a bitter world title.

◦ **27 Grands Prix, 2 wins (Dutch GP 1961, British GP 1961)**
◦ **No drivers' title (best result – 2nd overall 1961)**

Derek Warwick
Nationality: British
Born: 1954

It seems inconceivable that Derek could spend ten years in Formula One and still not win a grand prix. Regarded as a better prospect than Nigel Mansell in the early stages of his career, he appeared to have success in his grasp when he was signed to replace Alain Prost at Renault in 1984. The French team was in terminal decline, however, and, when he was blocked from joining Lotus in 1986 by Ayrton Senna, he temporarily left Formula One, only to return, for Brabham, after the death of Elio de Angelis.

Leading Light: Wolfgang von Trips was the German master who showed Michael Schumacher the way

After three promising, but fruitless, years with Arrows, then an even worse one at Lotus, Derek quit Formula One for success in sports cars – in which he was World Champion in 1991 – before returning for another fruitless year with Footwork in 1993. But still the cards did not fall for him, and in 1994 Formula One passed him by.

◦ **147 Grands Prix, no wins (best result – 2nd Belgian GP 1984, British GP 1984)**
◦ **No drivers' title (best result – 7th overall 1984 and 1988)**

John Watson
Nationality: British
Born: 1946

On his day, John could drive quite superbly, but those days did not come as often as he would have liked. After a slow rise through the single-seater echelons, he broke into Formula One in 1973, and drove for a number of middle-ranking teams until getting his break with Penske in mid-1975. He took a splendid victory for the team in the 1976 Austrian Grand Prix, and was signed to Brabham for the 1977-78 seasons, when a number of good results failed to translate into wins.

He then spent a frustrating couple of seasons with McLaren before profiting from the arrival of John Barnard and Ron Dennis in 1981.

He was a World Championship contender when Niki Lauda returned from retirement in 1982 and, although somewhat overshadowed by the Austrian in 1983, John still managed a brilliant victory in that year's Long Beach Grand Prix. The sacking of Prost by Renault in 1983 was the death knell for John's career. Prost took his McLaren drive, and he was unable to find a seat for 1984.

A brief return in 1985 was disappointing, and he enjoyed success in sports cars before setting up his own racing school at Silverstone. He is now a television commentator.

◦ **152 Grands Prix, 5 wins (Austrian GP 1976, British GP 1981, Belgian GP 1982, Detroit GP 1982, US West GP 1983)**
◦ **No drivers' title (best result – 2nd 1982)**

Will to Win: Mark Webber celebrates with Minardi boss Paul Stoddart after clinching fifth place on his debut in the Australian Grand Prix at the Albert Park Circuit, Melbourne, 2002

Mark Webber

Nationality: Australian
Born: 1976

A hotshot in Formula Ford in Australia then Britain, Mark was a winner in Formula Three and in Formula 3000 after a two-year break as a works Mercedes sports car driver, he finished second to Justin Wilson in 2001. But his biggest break was Flavio Briatore signing him as Renault's test driver. He joined Minardi for 2002 and had a dream debut by finishing fifth in the opening race. Jaguar snapped him up for 2003 and Mark galvanized the team by qualifying third in Brazil and scoring points seven times. He qualified well again in 2004, but points were harder to come by. Mark's move to Williams for 2005 was meant to launch his career, but the team fell out with BMW, leaving his podium at

Monaco a highlight. The streets of Monte Carlo could have been a high point in 2006, but third or better was lost when his engine failed and Mark was hoping for better things with Red Bull. Top results didn't come straight away in 2007, but he was third at the Nurburgring. Then, in 2008, he had a consistent time, but the fireworks were saved for 2009, a year that Mark started in pain because he'd broken a leg and a shoulder. Yet, he was to follow second in Shanghai with wins in Germany and Brazil.

° **139 Grands Prix, 2 wins (German GP 2009, Brazilian GP 2009)**
° **No drivers' title (best result – 4th overall 2009)**

Karl Wendlinger

Nationality: Austrian
Born: 1968

Winner of the 1989 German Formula Three title, he joined the Mercedes sports car junior team in 1990 and then impressed enormously for the underfinanced March team in 1992, before joining Sauber for 1993. A serious crash at Monaco in 1994 left him in a coma for 19 days and took Formula One to the political brink after the tragic deaths of Ayrton Senna and Roland Ratzenberger two weeks earlier.

He made his racing comeback for Sauber in 1995, but was not up to the task and was dropped after four races, with just a 13th place to show for his efforts.

○ **41 Grands Prix, no wins (best result – 4th Canadian GP 1992, Italian GP 1993, San Marino GP 1994)**
○ **No drivers' title (best result – 11th overall 1993)**

Ken Wharton

Nationality: British
Born: 1916
Died: 1957

Ken made his Formula One debut in an old-fashioned Frazer-Nash at the 1952 Swiss Grand Prix and finished fourth, but that was to be the best result of his entire career.

A consistent finisher through 1953 and 1954, he called it a day in Formula One after an unproductive year for Vanwall in 1956, in which he received burns in an accident in the International Trophy at Silverstone. Wharton was killed in a crash in a Ferrari sports car in New Zealand in 1957.

○ **15 Grands Prix, no wins (best result – 4th Swiss GP 1952)**
○ **No drivers' title (best result – 13th overall 1952)**

Investing for the Future: Justin Wilson sold shares against his future earnings and won a ride for Jaguar in the German Grand Prix, Hockenheim, 2003

Peter Whitehead

Nationality: British
Born: 1914
Died: 1958

This wealthy businessman who was robbed of victory in the 1949 French Grand Prix when problems with the gearbox dropped him to third, raced on in Formula One, netting a couple of top-ten places in Ferraris until the end of 1952, by which time he was finding success in sports car events. Thereafter, he raced in Formula One only in the British Grand Prix, and pulled out in 1954. He was killed when his half-brother Graham crashed the car in which both were competing in the 1958 Tour de France.

○ 10 Grands Prix, no wins (best result – 3rd French GP 1950)
○ No drivers' title (best result – 9th overall 1950)

Roger Williamson

Nationality: British
Born: 1948
Died: 1973

A protégé of successful Midlands businessman and racing enthusiast Tom Wheatcroft, who is the owner of the Donington Park circuit, Roger was a frequent race-winner in Formula Three and Formula Two. Wheatcroft wanted to fund him in a full season of Formula One in 1974, and they dipped their toes in the water in 1973 with a March.

But Roger was taken out of the British Grand Prix in a multiple-shunt on the first lap. And then it happened again at Zandvoort: a suspension failure caused him to crash.

The car came to a halt upside down and on fire and, apart from David Purley, no one intervened to try to rescue him. As the marshals stood by, Roger burned to death in front of millions of television viewers.

○ 2 Grands Prix, no wins (best result – retired from both races)
○ No drivers' title

Justin Wilson

Nationality: British
Born: 1978

Selling shares against your future earnings is a bold step, but it is one that Justin took to get his Formula One break with Minardi in 2003. Ever short of cash, he was not able to graduate to Formula Three in 1998, so went instead to Formula Palmer Audi and won the title. The prize put up by series mastermind and former racer Jonathan Palmer was a season in Formula 3000. Fast from the off in this the top feeder category, he beat Mark Webber in a straight fight for the title in 2001. It was at this point that Justin faced a problem other than lack of cash as he tried to break into Formula One: his six-foot-three-inch frame was thought to be too tall. However, Minardi took him on for 2003 and Justin wowed onlookers by overtaking eight cars on the opening lap of the first race in Australia. More feisty drives followed and Justin's break came when Antonio Pizzonia was dropped and he joined Jaguar for the final five races of the season. Sadly, three of these ended in retirement and he lost his ride to Christian Klien for 2004, since becoming a regular race winner in Champ Cars.

○ 16 Grands Prix, no wins (best result – 8th United States GP 2003)
○ No drivers' title (best result – 19th overall 2003)

Manfred Winkelhock

Nationality: German
Born: 1952
Died: 1985

Manfred was backed by BMW as he rose racing's ladder. He spent most of his Formula One career with ATS and RAM, rarely enjoying the chance to shine, but his reflexes and bravery were used to good effect at the Detroit Grand Prix in 1982, when he qualified fifth. A good drive in a Porsche sports car provided him with some welcome success, but he was killed in an accident at the Mosport Park 1,000km race in 1985.

○ 47 Grands Prix, no wins (best result – 5th Brazilian GP 1982)
○ No drivers' title (best result – 22nd overall 1982)

Alexander **Wurz**

Nationality: Austrian
Born: 1974

The third generation of a racing family, Alex was the German Formula Ford champion in 1992, then runner-up in German Formula Three in 1994. He raced in the International Touring Car series in 1996, when he also won the Le Mans 24 Hours. Test driver for Benetton in 1997, Alex got his Formula One break when Gerhard Berger was ill, finishing third on his third outing. After a spectacular year with Benetton in 1998, he struggled in 1999 and 2000 as the team favoured Giancarlo Fisichella. He signed as McLaren test driver for 2001, staying on the sidelines until asked to sub for Montoya at Imola in 2005, finishing third. He quit McLaren to join Williams for 2006, claiming third in Canada in 2007, then stepped down to be Honda test driver in 2008.

○ 53 Grands Prix, no wins (best result – 3rd British GP 1997, San Marino GP 2005)
○ No drivers' title (best result – 8th 1998)

Alessandro **Zanardi**

Nationality: Italian
Born: 1966

In the same season he lost the Formula 3000 title to Christian Fittipaldi, Alessandro made his Formula One debut with Jordan.

He became a Benetton test driver in 1992, moved on to race for Lotus in 1993 and was lucky to survive a huge accident at Spa, after which he was replaced by Pedro Lamy.

He won his seat back in 1994, but had no drive in 1995. Moving to IndyCars, he was runner-up in 1996 and then champion in both 1997 and 1998. However, his Formula One return with Williams in 1999 was a disaster, producing no points.

In 2001 Alessandro lost both of his legs in a crash in an IndyCar race in Germany. Happily he is now walking again, even racing in touring cars.

○ 41 Grands Prix, no wins (best result – 6th Brazilian GP 1993)
○ No drivers' title (best result – 20th, 1993)

Ricardo **Zonta**

Nationality: Brazilian
Born: 1976

Ricardo won the South American Formula Three crown in 1995, then landed a Formula 3000 ride for 1996 and rounded out the year with two wins. He duly won the title in 1997. Mercedes signed him for 1998 and he won the FIA GT title for them. A Formula One ride for BAR produced no points, but he progressed in 2000, although tension with Jacques Villeneuve led to his dismissal. Ricardo won the Dallara Nissan World Series in 2002, before becoming test driver for Toyota's Formula One team in 2003.

○ 29 Grands Prix, no wins (best result – 6th Australian GP 2000, Italian GP 2000, US GP 2000)
○ No drivers' title (best result – 14th overall 2000)

DRIVERS' RECORDS

It's no easy task comparing drivers across the ages, but these lists of stats highlight those who shone, up to the end of 2009.

MOST GRANDS PRIX STARTS

286 Rubens Barrichello BRA
256 Riccardo Patrese ITA
250 Michael Schumacher GER
247 David Coulthard GBR
230 Giancarlo Fisichella ITA
218 Jarno Trulli ITA
210 Gerhard Berger AUT
208 Andrea de Cesaris ITA
204 Nelson Piquet BRA
201 Jean Alesi FRA
199 Alain Prost FRA
194 Michele Alboreto ITA
187 Nigel Mansell GBR
180 Ralf Schumacher GER
176 Graham Hill GBR
175 Jacques Laffite FRA
171 Jenson Button GBR
    Niki Lauda AUT
169 Nick Heidfeld GER
165 Jacques Villeneuve CAN
164 Thierry Boutsen BEL
162 Mika Hakkinen FIN
    Johnny Herbert GBR
161 Ayrton Senna BRA
159 Heinz-Harald Frentzen GER
158 Martin Brundle GBR
    Olivier Panis FRA
157 Kimi Raikkonen FIN
152 John Watson GBR
149 René Arnoux FRA
147 Eddie Irvine GBR
    Derek Warwick GBR
146 Carlos Reutemann ARG
144 Emerson Fittipaldi BRA
140 Fernando Alonso ESP
139 Mark Webber AUS
135 Jean-Pierre Jarier FRA
132 Eddie Cheever USA

    Clay Regazzoni SUI
128 Mario Andretti USA
126 Jack Brabham AUS
123 Ronnie Peterson SWE
119 Pierluigi Martini ITA
116 Damon Hill GBR
    Jacky Ickx BEL
    Alan Jones AUS
115 Felipe Massa BRA

MOST GRANDS PRIX WINS

91 Michael Schumacher GER
51 Alain Prost FRA
41 Ayrton Senna BRA
31 Nigel Mansell GBR
27 Jackie Stewart GBR
25 Jim Clark GBR
   Niki Lauda AUT
24 Juan Manuel Fangio ARG
23 Nelson Piquet BRA
22 Damon Hill GBR
21 Fernando Alonso ESP
20 Mika Hakkinen FIN
18 Kimi Raikkonen FIN
16 Stirling Moss GBR
14 Jack Brabham AUS
   Emerson Fittipaldi BRA
   Graham Hill GBR
13 Alberto Ascari ITA
   David Coulthard GBR
12 Mario Andretti USA
   Alan Jones AUS
   Carlos Reutemann ARG
11 Rubens Barrichello BRA
   Lewis Hamilton GBR
   Felipe Massa BRA
   Jacques Villeneuve CAN
10 Gerhard Berger AUT
   James Hunt GBR

The only man ever to become World Champion on both two wheels and four, British ace John Surtees is almost dwarfed by his massive victor's garland as he celebrates winning the German Grand Prix for Ferrari around Nurburgring's 14-mile Nordschleife in 1964, his title-winning season

Top: Ayrton Senna is greeted by the Lotus team at a drenched Estoril after scoring the first of his 41 wins in the 1985 Portuguese GP. Above: Juan Manuel Fangio leads the way at Monaco in 1950, with his Alfa Romeo separated from Alberto Ascari's chasing Ferrari by Bob Gerard's aged ERA

	Ronnie Peterson SWE	
	Jody Scheckter RSA	
8	Denny Hulme NZL	
	Jacky Ickx BEL	

MOST WINS IN ONE SEASON

13	Michael Schumacher GER	2004
11	Michael Schumacher GER	2002
9	Nigel Mansell GBR	1992
	Michael Schumacher GER	1995
	Michael Schumacher GER	2000
	Michael Schumacher GER	2001
8	Mika Hakkinen FIN	1998
	Damon Hill GBR	1996
	Michael Schumacher GER	1994
	Ayrton Senna BRA	1988
7	Fernando Alonso SPA	2005
	Fernando Alonso SPA	2006
	Jim Clark GBR	1963
	Alain Prost FRA	1984
	Alain Prost FRA	1988
	Alain Prost FRA	1993
	Kimi Raikonen FIN	2005
	Michael Schumacher GER	2006
	Ayrton Senna BRA	1991
	Jacques Villeneuve CAN	1997
6	Mario Andretti USA	1978
	Alberto Ascari ITA	1952
	Jenson Button GBR	2009
	Jim Clark GBR	1965
	Juan Manuel Fangio ARG	1954
	Damon Hill GBR	1994
	James Hunt GBR	1976
	Nigel Mansell GBR	1987
	Felipe Massa BRA	2008
	Kimi Raikkonen FIN	2007
	Michael Schumacher GER	1998
	Michael Schumacher GER	2003
	Ayrton Senna BRA	1989
	Ayrton Senna BRA	1990

MOST CONSECUTIVE WINS

9	Alberto Ascari ITA	1952
	Alberto Ascari ITA	1953
7	Michael Schumacher GER	2004
6	Michael Schumacher GER	2000
	Michael Schumacher GER	2001
5	Jack Brabham AUS	1960
	Jim Clark GBR	1965
	Nigel Mansell GBR	1992
4	Jack Brabham AUS	1966
	Jenson Button GBR	2009
	Jim Clark GBR	1963

	Juan Manuel Fangio ARG	1953
	Juan Manuel Fangio ARG	1954
	Damon Hill GBR	1995
	Damon Hill GBR	1996
	Alain Prost FRA	1993
	Jochen Rindt AUT	1970
	Michael Schumacher GER	1994
	Michael Schumacher GER	2002
	Ayrton Senna BRA	1988
	Ayrton Senna BRA	1991

STARTS WITHOUT A WIN

208	Andrea de Cesaris ITA
169	Nick Heidfeld GER
158	Martin Brundle GBR
147	Derek Warwick GBR
135	Jean-Pierre Jarier FRA
132	Eddie Cheever USA
119	Pierluigi Martini ITA
111	Mika Salo FIN
109	Philippe Alliot FRA
107	Jos Verstappen NED
99	Pedro Diniz BRA
97	Chris Amon NZL
95	Ukyo Katayama JAP

MOST FASTEST LAPS

75	Michael Schumacher GER
41	Alain Prost FRA
35	Kimi Raikkonen FIN
30	Nigel Mansell GBR
28	Jim Clark GBR
25	Mika Hakkinen FIN
24	Niki Lauda AUT
23	Juan Manuel Fangio ARG
	Nelson Piquet BRA
21	Gerhard Berger AUT
19	Damon Hill GBR
	Stirling Moss GBR
	Ayrton Senna BRA
18	David Coulthard GBR
17	Rubens Barrichello BRA
15	Clay Regazzoni SUI
	Jackie Stewart GBR
14	Jacky Ickx BEL
13	Fernando Alonso ESP
	Alberto Ascari ITA
	Alan Jones AUS
	Riccardo Patrese ITA
12	Rene Arnoux FRA
	Jack Brabham AUS
	Felipe Massa BRA
	Juan Pablo Montoya COL

MOST POLE POSITIONS

68	Michael Schumacher GER
65	Ayrton Senna BRA
33	Jim Clark GBR
	Alain Prost FRA
32	Nigel Mansell GBR
29	Juan Manuel Fangio ARG
26	Mika Hakkinen FIN
24	Niki Lauda AUT
	Nelson Piquet BRA
20	Damon Hill GBR
18	Mario Andretti USA
	René Arnoux FRA
17	Fernando Alonso SPA
	Lewis Hamilton GBR
	Jackie Stewart GBR
16	Stirling Moss GBR
	Kimi Raikonen FIN
15	Felipe Massa BRA
14	Alberto Ascari ITA
	Rubens Barrichello BRA
	James Hunt GBR

	Ronnie Peterson SWE
13	Jack Brabham AUS
	Graham Hill GBR
	Jacky Ickx BEL
	Juan Pablo Montoya COL
	Jacques Villeneuve CAN

MOST POINTS

This figure is the gross tally, i.e. includes scores that were later dropped

1369	Michael Schumacher GER
798.5	Alain Prost FRA
614	Ayrton Senna BRA
607	Rubens Barrichello BRA
579	Kimi Raikonen FIN
577	Fernando Alonso SPA
535	David Coulthard GBR
485.5	Nelson Piquet BRA
482	Nigel Mansell GBR
420.5	Niki Lauda AUT
420	Mika Hakkinen FIN
385	Gerhard Berger AUT
360	Damon Hill GBR
	Jackie Stewart GBR

329	Ralf Schumacher GER
326	Jenson Button GBR
320	Felipe Massa BRA
310	Carlos Reutemann ARG
307	Juan Pablo Montoya COL
289	Graham Hill GBR
281	Emerson Fittipaldi BRA
	Riccardo Patrese ITA
277.5	Juan Manuel Fangio ARG

MOST DRIVERS' TITLES

7	Michael Schumacher GER
5	Juan Manuel Fangio ARG
4	Alain Prost FRA
3	Jack Brabham AUS
	Niki Lauda AUT
	Nelson Piquet BRA
	Ayrton Senna BRA
	Jackie Stewart GBR
2	Alberto Ascari ITA
	Jim Clark GBR
	Emerson Fittipaldi BRA
	Mika Hakkinen FIN

	Graham Hill GBR
1	Mario Andretti USA
	Jenson Button GBR
	Giuseppe Farina ITA
	Lewis Hamilton GBR
	Mike Hawthorn GBR
	Damon Hill GBR
	Phil Hill USA
	Denis Hulme NZL
	James Hunt GBR
	Alan Jones AUS
	Nigel Mansell GBR
	Kimi Raikkonen FIN
	Jochen Rindt AUT
	Keke Rosberg FIN
	Jody Scheckter RSA
	John Surtees GBR
	Jacques Villeneuve CAN

Above: Renault's Alain Prost sprays the bubbly after taking his first grand prix win, in the 1981 French GP, with Nelson Piquet second and John Watson third.

WORLD CHAMPION DRIVERS

Here is the roll call of the drivers who have earned the sport's ultimate accolade.

1950 GIUSEPPE FARINA ALFA ROMEO	**1965** JIM CLARK LOTUS	**1980** ALAN JONES WILLIAMS	**1995** MICHAEL SCHUMACHER BENETTON
1951 JUAN MANUEL FANGIO ALFA ROMEO	**1966** JACK BRABHAM BRABHAM	**1981** NELSON PIQUET BRABHAM	**1996** DAMON HILL WILLIAMS
1952 ALBERTO ASCARI FERRARI	**1967** DENNY HULME BRABHAM	**1982** KEKE ROSBERG WILLIAMS	**1997** JACQUES VILLENEUVE WILLIAMS
1953 ALBERTO ASCARI FERRARI	**1968** GRAHAM HILL LOTUS	**1983** NELSON PIQUET BRABHAM	**1998** MIKA HAKKINEN McLAREN
1954 JUAN MANUEL FANGIO MASERATI & MERCEDES	**1969** JACKIE STEWART MATRA	**1984** NIKI LAUDA McLAREN	**1999** MIKA HAKKINEN McLAREN
1955 JUAN MANUEL FANGIO MERCEDES	**1970** JOCHEN RINDT LOTUS	**1985** ALAIN PROST McLAREN	**2000** MICHAEL SCHUMACHER FERRARI
1956 JUAN MANUEL FANGIO FERRARI	**1971** JACKIE STEWART TYRRELL	**1986** ALAIN PROST McLAREN	**2001** MICHAEL SCHUMACHER FERRARI
1957 JUAN MANUEL FANGIO MASERATI	**1972** EMERSON FITTIPALDI LOTUS	**1987** NELSON PIQUET WILLIAMS	**2002** MICHAEL SCHUMACHER FERRARI
1958 MIKE HAWTHORN FERRARI	**1973** JACKIE STEWART TYRRELL	**1988** AYRTON SENNA McLAREN	**2003** MICHAEL SCHUMACHER FERRARI
1959 JACK BRABHAM COOPER	**1974** EMERSON FITTIPALDI McLAREN	**1989** ALAIN PROST McLAREN	**2004** MICHAEL SCHUMACHER FERRARI
1960 JACK BRABHAM COOPER	**1975** NIKI LAUDA FERRARI	**1990** AYRTON SENNA McLAREN	**2005** FERNANDO ALONSO RENAULT
1961 PHIL HILL FERRARI	**1976** JAMES HUNT McLAREN	**1991** AYRTON SENNA McLAREN	**2006** FERNANDO ALONSO RENAULT
1962 GRAHAM HILL BRM	**1977** NIKI LAUDA FERRARI	**1992** NIGEL MANSELL WILLIAMS	**2007** KIMI RAIKKONEN FERRARI
1963 JIM CLARK LOTUS	**1978** MARIO ANDRETTI LOTUS	**1993** ALAIN PROST WILLIAMS	**2008** LEWIS HAMILTON McLAREN
1964 JOHN SURTEES FERRARI	**1979** JODY SCHECKTER FERRARI	**1994** MICHAEL SCHUMACHER BENETTON	**2009** JENSON BUTTON BRAWN

A Wealth of Experience: Formula One drivers were rather older in the 1950s than they are today, as shown by this line-up at Monza of Juan Manuel Fangio, Giuseppe Farina, Felice Bonetto and Baron Emmanuel de Graffenried

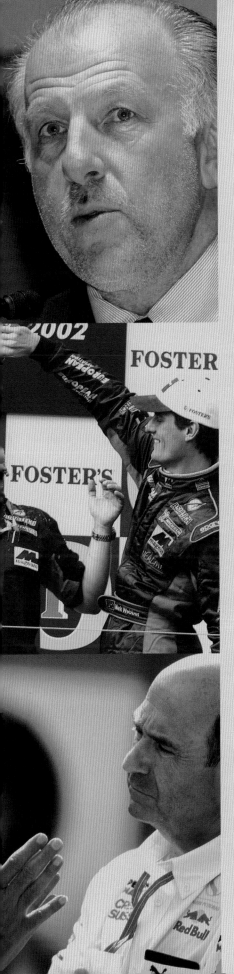

PART 3:

THE
CONSTRUCTORS

Ferrari ruled the roost at the start of the 21st century, but it hasn't always been so. This chapter examines the varied ingredients of the teams that are striving to topple them and the history of those who have shone but fallen from the roster.

The trophy cabinets at Ferrari and McLaren are bulging with silverware, with space set aside for future hauls, but there are other constructors that have been, at one time or another, at the top of F1's tree. This chapter takes a look, therefore, not only at the 10 teams that currently contest the World Championship, but also those such as Alfa Romeo, Maserati, Cooper, BRM, Lotus, Brabham and Tyrrell that set the pace before them.

Much as all teams involved in Formula One seek to take the chequered flag first, many only see it when it's being held statically, signalling the end of the race rather than a chance to visit the podium. So this chapter also looks at the likes of Hesketh, March and Wolf, teams that won the occasional grand prix, but never quite became world champions in a sport where the difference between success and failure can be the blink of an eye.

All statistics in this book are correct to the end of the 2009 World Championship.

FERRARI

FORMULA ONE RECORD

Country of origin: Italy   Date of foundation: **1946**
Active years in Formula One: from **1950**
Constructors' Cup victories: **1961, 1964, 1975, 1976, 1977, 1979, 1982, 1983, 1999, 2000, 2001, 2002, 2003, 2004, 2007, 2008**

Ferrari is Formula One's most famous team, bar none. Wherever a grand prix is held, Ferrari flags waved from the grandstands outnumber all the others put together. If Ferrari was a football team, it would be Manchester United – a team followed the world over.

After fielding semi-works Alfa Romeos before World War Two, Enzo Ferrari emerged as a force in his own right, with his team carrying the fight to the Alfa Romeos with the Ferrari 375 in 1951 – a year in which Jose Froilan Gonzalez gave the team its first win, in the 1951 British Grand Prix. However, Ferrari lost out to Alfa Romeo in the final race. The FIA then ran grands prix to 2-litre rules from 1952, but Ferrari was well prepared for the change and Alberto Ascari dominated both the 1952 and 1953 World Championships for them. Indeed, after Piero Taruffi won the opening race of 1952, Ascari won the next nine races before his team-mate Mike Hawthorn won the French Grand Prix in 1953. He then won two of the next three races, with another team-mate, Giuseppe Farina, claiming the other, before Maserati's Juan Manuel Fangio won the final round in Italy, preventing a clean sweep of two full seasons.

The next change of regulations, to 2.5-litre engines for 1954, knocked Ferrari off the top, as Maserati and Mercedes assumed control, even though Ferrari drivers Gonzalez, Hawthorn, Maurice Trintignant, Luigi Musso, Fangio and Peter Collins all recorded grand prix wins. That was before 1957, when Ferrari failed to win a race for the first time since 1950.

The Tipo 146 put Ferrari back on the map in 1958, the car being christened Dino, after Enzo Ferrari's son. Many believe Stirling Moss was the true champion that year, as he won the most races, but the crown fell to Hawthorn in the final round in Morocco.

After the mid-engined Coopers dominated both the 1959 and 1960 campaigns, Ferrari was back in front in 1961, fully prepared for new 1.5-litre regulations with the Tipo 156 "shark-nose". The cars dominated but tragedy struck when Wolfgang von Trips was killed at Monza after a clash with Jim Clark. Team-mate, Phil Hill, went on to clinch the title.

John Surtees took another title for Ferrari in 1964, and so became the only man to win world titles on both two wheels and four. However, 1966's new 3-litre rules led to Ferrari struggling to match first Brabham's Repco engine then Ford's DFV, whose introduction, at the 1967 Dutch Grand Prix, triggered a change in Formula One's balance of power.

Although Jacky Ickx came close for Ferrari in 1970, it wasn't until 1974 that the team looked like championship contenders again. Niki Lauda was quick but inexperienced, losing out to McLaren's Emerson Fittipaldi. However, Lauda made amends by taking the flat-12 312T to the title the following year, and he would have retained his title in 1976 had it not been for his near-fatal accident at the Nurburgring. He lost out to James Hunt by a point, but regained the World Champion's crown with great consistency in a magnificent comeback in 1977.

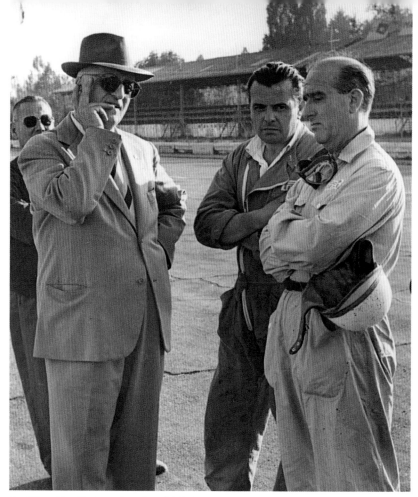

Head Horse Man: big cheese Enzo Ferrari talks to driver Giuseppe Farina during testing in 1953

In 1979, Jody Scheckter beat his spectacular young Ferrari team-mate Gilles Villeneuve to the championship with the Ferrari 312T4, but the following season's T5 was a disaster, as everybody but Ferrari began to master ground-effect aerodynamics.

By now, 1.5-litre turbocharged engines were taking over from 3-litre normally aspirated ones and Ferrari fitted turbo power to its 126C. It was a handful, but Villeneuve managed

---

VIP

Enzo Ferrari

Born in 1898, Enzo became involved in motor racing as a driver, but he went on to found Formula One's most famous and most successful team. His greatest win behind the wheel was in the Coppa Acerbo at Pescara in 1924, but he turned to team management, running Alfa Romeo's team from 1930 to 1937. They fell out and the first car racing under the Ferrari name appeared in 1946. Success followed as it took on and beat Alfa Romeo, much to Enzo's delight. Famed for worshipping his cars rather than his drivers, Enzo gained a useful injection of cash when, in 1969, Fiat bought both his Formula One and sports car teams and its road car subsidiary. Enzo remained at the helm, though, an enigmatic character with dark glasses who was often frustrated by Fiat executives' attempts at interference. Indeed, the team appeared to be its own worst enemy until Niki Lauda and Luca di Montezemolo took it by the scruff of its neck and modernized it in the mid-1970s. Enzo died in 1988, with Cesare Fiorio taking over the running of the team.

to score remarkable wins with it at Monaco and Jarama in 1981.

Ferrari employed British designer Harvey Postlethwaite and the resulting Ferrari 126C2 was the class of the field in 1982. However, Villeneuve was killed in practice at Zolder and Didier Pironi was injured in a crash in qualifying at Hockenheim.

Michele Alboreto was competitive in 1985 and Alain Prost won five races in 1990, losing to Senna in controversial circumstances in Japan, but then the wins dried up until Gerhard Berger claimed one in 1994 and then Jean Alesi did the same the following year. Both were reaping the fruits of Jean Todt's involvement as the team chief who had joined the team midway through 1993 had immediately started to pull the various strands together to give the team a structure.

The arrival of Michael Schumacher in 1996, as Alesi and Berger moved in the opposite direction to race for Benetton, wasn't met with delight by the *tifosi*. Neither was the signing of Eddie Irvine from Jordan. However, the way that Schumacher galvanized the team earned their respect, with his trio of wins in that first year taking him to third place overall and helping Ferrari finish second in the Constructors' Championship. It proved that he could take Ferrari back to the front.

That he came within a whisker of winning the 1997 title made them like him more, although the way he barged Jacques Villeneuve at the final race at Jerez saddened them. However, the German's herculean bid to overhaul McLaren's Mika Hakkinen in 1998 made them love him forever, even though he came up short.

Schumacher's 1999 challenge was wrecked when he suffered a broken leg in a crash during the British Grand Prix. However, Irvine took over, supported by stand-in Mika Salo, and won three rounds to take the title race to the final round before he lost out to Hakkinen. Ferrari did come away with the constructors' title, though, its first since 1983.

Red Procession: Jody Scheckter leads from Gilles Villeneuve during the 1979 Italian Grand Prix at Monza. They finished first and second

Fully fit again in 2000, Schumacher got the better of Hakkinen, winning nine times to become World Champion, Ferrari's first since Jody Scheckter 21 years earlier. With Irvine moving to Jaguar, Rubens Barrichello joined from Stewart and won once at Hockenheim. The 2001 season produced a third straight constructors' title, as Schumacher won nine grands prix to be champion again.

That was nothing compared to what happened in 2002, when Schumacher wrapped the title up by July. He went on to collect 11 wins, with Barrichello winning four, leaving their rivals with just two wins between them. Their tally of 221 points was 129 clear of the next best team, Williams. It was less of a cakewalk in 2003 as Williams and McLaren fought back, but again Schumacher took the drivers' title - albeit by only two points from McLaren's Kimi Raikkonen - and guided Ferrari to its fifth straight constructors' crown, edging out Williams. Schumacher's tally was six wins, as the wins were shared around between seven drivers, with Barrichello coming on strong to win twice. There were occasions in 2003 when the Brazilian more than matched the German, which is perhaps why his contract was extended to keep him at Ferrari until the end of 2006.

The 2004 season stands out as one of Ferrari's greatest, with Schumacher winning 13 times and Barrichello taking a pair of wins. Ferrari's tally was double runner-up BAR's score. Conversely, 2005 was a disaster as a rule change left Ferrari struggling on its Bridgestones as Renault and McLaren took control.

The Schumacher-Todt-Brawn-Byrne axis broke up when Schumacher announced his retirement in 2006 as he pushed Fernando Alonso for the title. Brawn said he'd be taking a sabbatical, too, and would never return to Ferrari..

Kimi Raikkonen joined Felipe Massa in the driving line-up for 2007, won the opening round then used a late-season burst to steal the title from Lewis Hamilton at the final round in Brazil.

Stefano Domenicali took over from Jean Todt for 2008 and the team continued in a strong vein, with Massa being pipped to the title by Hamilton by one point, with Raikkonen third.

This form wasn't continued into 2009, as Raikkonen appeared to lose interest and Massa suffered a serious head injury, but there was cause for optimism as Fernando Alonso was arriving for 2010.

VIP
Jean Todt

A small man of large achievement, Jean began his competition career as a rally co-driver in 1966 and sat alongside runner-up Guy Frequelin as their Talbot team won the manufacturers' crown in 1981. A move into team management followed with Peugeot Talbot Sport in 1982 and he masterminded the development of Peugeot's 205 Turbo 16 that dominated the 1985 and 1986 World Rally seasons before taking Peugeot to dominance in the Paris-Dakar rally raids. He took over all Peugeot motor sport in 1987, and the team won the World Sports Car Championship crown as well as the first of two Le Mans 24 Hours wins, in 1992. Attracted by his success, Ferrari signed Jean to lead its Formula One team in 1993, and he used his analytical mind to focus on the best way of making this giant team work effectively. He succeeded and, thanks to the combined talents of Michael Schumacher, designer Rory Byrne, engine guru Paolo Martinelli and technical director Ross Brawn, the team hit the top in 1999 and has stayed there ever since.

McLAREN

FORMULA ONE RECORD

Country of origin: **Great Britain**   Date of foundation: **1963**
Active years in Formula One: **from 1966**
Constructors' Cup victories: **1974, 1984, 1985, 1988, 1989, 1990, 1991, 1998**

Bruce McLaren is the man behind the McLaren name. He won a New Zealand scholarship to race in Europe in 1958 and his results in Formula Two Coopers earned him a place in Cooper's grand prix team in 1959. At Sebring that year, he became the then youngest grand prix winner, aged 22, a record beaten only in 2003 by Fernando Alonso.

He formed Bruce McLaren Motor Racing and built his own cars. His first Formula One chassis, the M2B, was designed by Robin Herd and was built in 1966. Unfortunately, the first year of the 3-litre engine formula meant suitable power units were hard to find and McLaren used an underpowered Serenissima.

Before Herd moved on at the start of 1968, he penned the M7 to take the new Ford Cosworth DFV engine. Bruce gave the car a win on its debut in the Race of Champions at Brands Hatch and later won the Belgian Grand Prix. Reigning World Champion Denny Hulme won in Italy and Canada to take the title race down to the wire before losing out to Graham Hill in the final round, leaving McLaren second behind only Lotus.

In 1969, Bruce matched Hulme's 1968 achievement in ranking third.

Bruce and Denny were also sweeping all before them in the North American CanAm sports car series, winning the 1967, 1968, 1969 and 1970 titles, in the process, earning huge amounts of prize money that helped subsidize the Formula One team. McLaren also built CanAm cars for others to race. Tragically, Bruce was killed while testing a CanAm car at Goodwood in June 1970, so it's not surprising that 1970 and 1971 were winless in Formula One as Teddy Mayer attempted to right the ship. However, the American did a good job as Hulme took his M19 to one win in 1972. It was the arrival of the Gordon Coppuck-penned M23 in 1973, though, that saved the team. It was to win 16 races and its drivers would claim two world titles over the next four years. Hulme and Peter Revson raced to three of these wins in 1973. Then Emerson Fittipaldi joined from Lotus in 1974 and became McLaren's first World Champion, claiming three

wins en route to his crown. That year also saw Marlboro's appearance as McLaren's sponsor, an association that would continue until 1996.

Fittipaldi lost out to Ferrari's Niki Lauda in 1975, then jumped ship to race for his family's Copersucar team in 1976, so the team did an 11th-hour deal for James Hunt to move across from Hesketh to replace him. And, after one of Formula One's most dramatic seasons, the Englishman took the title by a solitary point, edging out Lauda. Hunt won three more races in 1977, but Lauda reclaimed the title.

McLaren was caught out when Lotus introduced ground-effect technology and then failed to catch up as fast as its rivals did. From 1978 to 1980, the team ranked no higher than seventh. It was only in 1981 that McLaren started winning again.

The foundations of the McLaren greatest years were laid when Mayer sold part of the company to Project Four boss Ron Dennis, who stepped up from Formula Two, bringing meticulous attention to detail. Designer John Barnard penned one of the Formula One classics, the carbonfibre MP4, and this relaunched the team, with John Watson winning the 1981 British Grand Prix. For 1982, Dennis persuaded Niki Lauda out of retirement and he won at Long Beach and Brands Hatch. The Ford-engined team struggled against those using the emerging turbocharged engines in 1983, but the debut of a TAG-badged Porsche V6 turbo showed promise.

For 1984, Dennis swooped when Alain Prost became available and he and Lauda dominated, with Alain winning seven races to Niki's five. The Austrian took the title, though, by half a point. Prost made amends in 1985 and won another title in 1986, despite the Williams-Honda combination of Nigel Mansell and Nelson Piquet being in a superior car.

For 1988, Dennis had the ultimate superteam: Prost, Ayrton Senna and Honda engines. Senna won the first of his three titles in four years,

Southern Star: long-time McLaren stalwart Denny Hulme powers his McLaren M19 to victory in the South African Grand Prix at Kyalami in 1972

McLaren One-Two: Ayrton Senna and Alain Prost share the Monaco podium in 1989 with Brabham's lapped Stefano Modena. Joy is in short supply

although Prost left for Ferrari as World Champion in 1989. His replacement, Gerhard Berger, was fast but soon realized that Senna was the fastest of his age. Honda's withdrawal in 1992 rendered McLaren impotent, but Senna still took five wins with Ford power in 1993 before joining Williams.

Ford gave way to Peugeot for 1994, but the French engines spent the year blowing up and it was with relief that McLaren did a deal with Mercedes for 1995. This also failed to bring a victory, though Mika Hakkinen twice finished second. The 1996 season was also winless, but Mercedes was making progress, with both Hakkinen and David Coulthard making visits to the podium. Resplendent in the silver and grey livery of new sponsor West, this improvement continued in 1997 as Coulthard won twice and Hakkinen was victorious in the final race.

This was nothing compared to 1998, when McLaren started the year with a car and engine combination that was the class of the field as Formula One started its first year on grooved

tyres. The MP4-13 was the first McLaren designed by Adrian Newey and Hakkinen won eight times to be champion, and Coulthard won once to rank third, helping McLaren to its first constructors' title since 1991.

Hakkinen took the title again in 1999, again winning at the final round, this time ahead of Ferrari's Eddie Irvine, although Dennis was frustrated when Ferrari pipped the team to the Constructors' Cup. Hakkinen lost out to Schumacher in 2000, then Coulthard outraced his Finnish team-mate in 2001, but his early-season challenge fell away and Schumacher was champion again.

Hakkinen took 2002 off, with Kimi Raikkonen joining from Sauber. Hakkinen then decided that he would rather retire and his compatriot blossomed, but neither he nor Coulthard could match Schumacher. McLaren started 2003 well, but the drivers failed to win again after the first two races, although Raikkonen lost out to Schumacher by only two points at the final round.

To many, the most important

change in 2004 was McLaren's move, including its supercar building arm, into an architectural masterpiece outside Woking, drawing all of its strands under one roof. Yet the team's form dipped and many blamed the move for making the team take its eye off the ball.

In 2005, though, Raikkonen ought to have been world champion and

McLaren the champion team, but reliability problems cost them dear and Fernando Alonso and Renault outflanked them, as they did in 2006 when Raikkonen failed to take even one win and Juan Pablo Montoya quit.

It was all change for 2007, with reigning World Champion Alonso and long-time McLaren protégé Lewis Hamilton filling the seats. They worked well together, but once Hamilton started winning in his rookie year the atmosphere changed and Alonso fell out with Dennis. But they kept winning races and Hamilton ought to have been champion but fumbled the final few races and it lipped away by a point. Worse than that, the team were dissqualified from the Constructor's Championship and fined as one of its employees was found in possession of Ferrari documentation.

McLaren bounced back in 2008 and Hamilton held his nerve to pip Felipe Massa to the title in the final third of the lap of the last race of the year in Brazil.

The 2009 campaign got off to an awful start, with the MP4-24 way off the pace, but the team responded and the car was setting the pace before the year was out, with Hamilton winning twice to rank fifth. More momentous than this, Dennis handed over the reins to Martin Whitmarsh, ending an era.

VIP
Ron Dennis

Much is made of the fact that Ron started as a mechanic, but it is this and his subsequent climb to running the most important team in Formula One after Ferrari that make him such a clear-thinking operator. Having begun in Formula One with Cooper in 1966, he moved to Brabham and stayed until forming his own team, Rondel, in 1971. This operated in Formula Two, but gained its break by running cars in the Formula One-supporting BMW Procar series for BMW M1 sports cars in the late 1970s, by which time it had become Project Four. Having landed backing from Marlboro, Dennis merged with McLaren in 1980 to form McLaren International and his professional approach put McLaren back on a winning track, making it the dominant team of the 1980s with Niki Lauda, Alain Prost and Ayrton Senna all winning drivers' titles. Entering into partnership with Mercedes did more than put the team back to the top, as McLaren built a supercar at its new headquarters in Woking for Mercedes. Ron dropped his Formula One involvement at the start of 2009 to focus on the next generation supercar.

WILLIAMS

FORMULA ONE RECORD

Country of origin: **Great Britain**   Date of foundation: **1968**
Active years in Formula One: **from 1972**
Constructors' Cup victories: **1980, 1981, 1986, 1987, 1992, 1993, 1994, 1996, 1997**

Like McLaren, Williams established itself in Formula One thanks to the availability of the Ford Cosworth DFV. This very affordable, yet competitive power unit offered the team the chance to build towards a future that has been glorious, that would see it dominate the sport for periods in the 1980s and 1990s.

Sir Frank Williams is proof that determination will triumph over adversity. A talented driver, he reached Formula Three before he hung up his helmet, then ran fellow racer Piers Courage in Formula Two in 1968. Working well together, they stepped up to Formula One with a Brabham in 1969. A fine second place behind Graham Hill at Monaco caught the attention of De Tomaso and so Williams ran their car in 1970. The collaboration ended in tragedy when Courage died at Zandvoort.

Williams ran paying drivers in an assortment of cars, with Jacques Laffite's second place in the 1975 German Grand Prix at the Nurburgring the highlight, before he founded Williams Grand Prix Engineering with up-and-coming engineer Patrick Head in 1977. Williams attracted Saudi Arabian backing and Head's nimble FW06 allowed Alan Jones to turn in some fine drives in 1978.

Head produced the ground-effects FW07 in 1979, and Clay Regazzoni scored the team's first win at Silverstone before Jones dominated the second half of the season. The Australian was teamed with Carlos Reutemann in 1980, winning five times to Reutemann's one as he claimed the title and Williams took the Constructors' title for the first time. Nelson Piquet beat Jones to be champion in 1981, but Williams were again the constructors' champions. Jones then retired, temporarily as it happens, but the team has never been able to find a driver that represents its values of focus and cussed determination so well again.

By 1982, turbocharged engines were too strong for normally-aspirated rivals, but Keke Rosberg managed to give the Ford Cosworth engine its final championship success, albeit through consistency rather than wins, as 1982 was the amazing year in which 11 drivers shared the 16 grands prix, with World Champion Rosberg winning just the Swiss Grand Prix at Dijon.

Williams then forged an alliance with Honda. The V6 turbo was brutal and heavy, but constant development meant that by the end of 1985, with Nigel Mansell driving, they were the ones to beat. Although Nelson Piquet and Mansell were the class of the field in 1986, Alain Prost's McLaren stole the title when Mansell suffered an exploding tyre in the final round.

However, this last-round robbery was nothing compared to an even bigger blow that hit just before the start of the season when Frank was paralysed in a car crash, leaving him wheelchair-bound.

In addition, there was tension between their drivers in 1987 as Mansell outpaced Piquet, yet the Brazilian's consistency took him to his third world title. The 1988 season was a watershed using normally-aspirated Judds, with Mansell jumping at the chance to join Ferrari after a massive drop off from nine wins in 1987 to none in 1988. A deal with Renault then brought Williams back as a major force although, with Riccardo Patrese and Thierry Boutsen on the books, the team lacked a top-line driver and the pair recorded just two wins in both 1989 and 1990. Head's FW14 was superb through 1991, but the returning Mansell lost out to Senna's McLaren because of gearbox problems.

By 1992, Williams had mastered active suspension and their car was dominant, perhaps more so than any before as Mansell won nine races, including the first five on the trot, and romped to the title. After a contractual dispute, though, the Englishman left to seek further glory on the Indy Car championship trail. This was not to be the last time that Williams bade farewell to a driver as soon as he had become World Champion. Alain Prost, with two world titles already to his name, proved a more than capable replacement and duly won the second consecutive drivers' and constructors' double for Williams, with Damon Hill adding three wins to Prost's seven.

Feat of Clay: Regazzoni took over at Silverstone in 1979 after team-mate Alan Jones dropped out and raced on to score Williams' maiden victory

With Prost also not being kept on, Williams signed three-time champion Ayrton Senna from McLaren for 1994, with the team further bolstered by the signing of a major sponsorship deal with Rothmans. Tragically, the great Brazilian died in the third round at Imola as he battled for the lead with new rival Michael Schumacher. With the team's test driver David Coulthard drafted in as a replacement, Hill saved a sad year by challenging Schumacher for the drivers' title, only losing out in the final round at Adelaide. Williams, though, won the constructors' crown for the third year in succession.

It was always going to be harder for Williams in 1995, with Benetton also running with the pace-setting Renault engines, but the team must have expected more than its tally of five wins – with four for Hill and one for Coulthard – as poor race tactics cost them dear and Schumacher made it two titles in succession for Benetton.

In 1996, reigning IndyCar champion Jacques Villeneuve was drafted in and he and Hill won all but four of the races, with Hill lifting the world title before, in now time-honoured fashion, defending his title with another team. Villeneuve became Williams' seventh World Champion in 1997, but only after a clash with Schumacher at the Jerez finale.

Acceleration: Ralf Schumacher leads Williams team-mate Montoya into the first corner of the French GP in 2003 on his way to an impressive victory

The loss of works Renault engines at the end of 1997 cost Williams dear as they were outstripped by McLaren and Ferrari in 1998 – and very nearly by Jordan and Benetton as well – as Villeneuve and Heinz-Harald Frentzen collected just a trio of thirds.

It was all-change for 1999 as Ralf Schumacher and reigning IndyCar champion Alessandro Zanardi signed up.

While Ralf shone, Formula One returnee Zanardi did not, and he was replaced by novice Jenson Button. It was in 2000 that real progress was made, as BMW took over as the team's engine partner, bringing the finance and ambition that any manufacturer needs for success.

By 2001, the engine was the most powerful of all, helping Ralf and Juan Pablo Montoya push McLaren hard in Ferrari's wake, taking three wins and one win respectively. Despite seven pole positions in 2002, however, Montoya failed to win a round, but consistent scoring left him third behind to Michael Schumacher. With Ralf fourth overall, Williams ranked second to Ferrari. In 2003, they could have gone one better, but a slow start then a faltering finish to their campaign left them second to Ferrari again, with Montoya third overall, his hopes floundering when he was penalized at the US Grand Prix and then retired from the lead in the Suzuka finale. Ralf also won twice, but ended up fifth overall.

For 2004, the FW26 made the other teams nervous with its unusual nose treatment, but it flopped and

had to be replaced, leaving the drivers struggling, although Montoya won the final race of the year in Brazil.

Out-and-out war with BMW in 2005 brought their relationship to a close, although the highlights included having both drivers on the podium at Monaco and pole position for Nick Heidfeld at the Nurburgring.

Racing with non-works Cosworth power in 2006 produced flashes of promise, but no concrete results for Mark Webber or Nico Rosberg. Things went better with Toyota engines in 2007 and Williams vaulted from eight to fourth overall, with Rosberg scoring consistently and Alexander Wurz grabbing a surprise third place in Canada. So, in comparison, 2008 was a disaster as the team fell to eighth overall, with little to cheer apart from Rosberg's third in Australia and second in Singapore.

Rosberg had his best season in 2009, but Kazuki Nakajima added not one point to Nico's 34.5, leaving the team seventh.

Then, for 2010, an entirely new driver line-up was selected

BRAWN GP

FORMULA ONE RECORD

Country of origin: **Japan, then Great Britain** Date of foundation: **1962**
Active years in Formula One: **1964-68 as Honda, 1999-2005 as BAR, from 2006 as Honda Racing, from 2009 as Brawn GP**
Constructors' Cup victories: **2009**

This is a story of three teams spread across two periods of activity with a 31-year gap in the middle and drawn together by a common thread: Honda engines.

Then, after Honda quit in 2008, the team was resurrected for 2009 as Brawn GP, Mercedes engines were fitted and it was the pick of the crop, winning the constructors' title as Jenson Button became drivers' champion.

Honda grew rapidly after World War Two, establishing itself in the motorcycle field before electing to enter Formula One in 1964. The man responsible for this was Yoshio Nakamura and the first Honda Formula One car was the RA271, fitted with a transverse V12 engine. It made its debut in the German GP, driven by Ronnie Bucknum, but retired with four laps to go when the steering failed. Bucknum ran fifth at Monza before the engine overheated.

Honda recruited Richie Ginther in 1965 and the RA272 showed promise on the faster circuits. Reliability was poor, but there was a sweetener at the final race, in Mexico, where Ginther led all the way for Japan's first F1 win.

Honda then had to evolve, as Formula One adopted new 3-litre engines for 1966. Soichiro Honda gave the go-ahead for a new car equipped with a powerful V12, but the Honda weighed in at more than 200kg over the limit.

For 1967, Nakamura persuaded John Surtees to join. Having seen what Honda could do in motorcycling, Surtees figured it would be only a matter of time before they achieved similar success, but the RA273 was still overweight and his best result was third in South Africa. At Monza, though, the RA300 appeared. Lola had been involved in its construction and it was built at Surtees' factory, but it still used the Honda V12 and became known as "the Hondola".

That 1967 Italian GP was a classic: Dan Gurney led before his clutch failed, then Jim Clark took over until he had a puncture. He rejoined a lap down, slipstreamed past the leaders and began making up the lost ground. Incredibly, he managed it and passed Brabham for the lead with just a few laps to go. Then he ran out of fuel, leaving Brabham to hold off Surtees, who went inside at the Parabolica on the final lap to win.

The 1968 season saw the emphasis on solving Honda's weight problem. The RA301 was developed with Lola's Eric Broadley, but it wasn't ready in time. Honda was also behind on its development of its V12. They then produced an fully Honda-built RA302, with an air-cooled V8, but Surtees didn't like the way it handled and refused to drive it. So Honda took on Jo Schlesser, who lost control of the car on his debut in the French GP. The RA302 speared off the road with a full fuel load and Schlesser died as the car, equipped with magnesium wheels, burned out. Surtees, in the RA301, finished second in the race to Jacky Ickx's Ferrari.

At the end of the year, Honda quit and didn't return until the 1980s, and only then as an engine supplier. Massive investment reaped reward and Honda won successive world titles with Williams in 1996 and 1997 then McLaren between 1988 and 1991. Honda then stayed away until 2000, when it returned to supply engines for BAR, doubling up for 2001 by supplying Jordan too.

British American Racing, led by Craig Pollock, had entered Formula One in 1999, having had a year of running the Tyrrell team. However, there was no mistaking the two enterprises, for BAR was an all-new team that arrived amid a blaze of publicity, easing Tyrrell - a 30-year-old team - into retirement.

Having gained experience after guiding Jacques Villeneuve through the junior categories, Pollock wanted to form his own team. He joined forces with chassis manufacturer Reynard and British American Tobacco. Headquarters were built at Brackley in England and Adrian Reynard led the technical side with Malcolm Oastler as his sidekick, supported by engineer Jock Clear, one of many employees

Becoming Used to Winning: Jenson Button waves to his crew after giving Brawn GP its sixth win in the first seven races of 2009

Advantage Lost: Jenson Button started from pole position at Imola in 2006, but his Honda was usurped instantly by Michael Schumacher and his Ferrari

poached from Williams. BAR signed Formula 3000 champion Ricardo Zonta as number two.

For 1999, BAR joined Williams and Benetton in running Renault-based Mecachrome engines, but these and numerous teething problems meant that Reynard's proud boast that his cars have won the first race every time they have graduated to a more senior formula – including Formula Three, Formula 3000 and IndyCars – couldn't be maintained. Indeed, at the end of their first year, BAR had failed to score a single point.

The drivers remained for 2000, but Pollock had convinced Honda to supply the team with its engines. The return was instant, with Villeneuve and Zonta finishing fourth and sixth in the opening round. More points followed, including fourths at Magny-Cours, the A1-Ring and Indianapolis for Villeneuve. Zonta added sixths at Monza and Indianapolis. However, Zonta knew that he was on the way out of the team, especially after he'd tipped Villeneuve out of the German

GP... BAR finished level on points with Benetton, but had to settle for fifth place on countback.

BAR dropped to sixth in 2001 in a year bolstered by surprise podiums at Barcelona and Hockenheim, when Villeneuve persevered in races of attrition. Then, over the close season, former Benetton boss David Richards replaced Pollock at the helm. The 2002 season was a weak one, but the arrival of Button in 2003 brought hope, and he outstripped Villeneuve – even leading the US GP – to lift the team to fifth overall. Villeneuve knew he was going to be dropped for 2004 to make way for Takuma Sato, so quit a race early.

Ironically, it was in 2004 that BAR got motoring, with Button doing everything but win as Michael Schumacher dominated for Ferrari. Still, Button ended the year third overall, with 10 podium results. Any thoughts that this form would continue into 2005 were dispelled as the car was weak aerodynamically and spent the early races playing catch-up. Then,

just after Button finished third at Imola, a bombshell burst and he and Sato were disqualified and banned from the next two races for running underweight. The Englishman was able to qualify on pole in Canada, but it wasn't until the 10th round, France, that Button scored a point. Thirds in

Germany and Belgium helped, but he was ranked only ninth at year's end and BAR only sixth as Sato collected just one point.

In the background, Honda was taking an ever-increasing role, morphing from engine-suppliers to technical partners, taking over completely for 2006, when the team was re-branded as Honda Racing, with Button joined by Rubens Barrichello. Their form was patchy, but Button was mighty in the wet in Hungary to take both his first win and Honda's first since 1968.

After two poor seasons, Honda pulled out at the end of 2008 and the team rose like a phoenix with technical director Ross Brawn now at the helm for 2009. Barrichello and Button were kept on and scored a one-two in the opening round at Melbourne. Button then carried on this winning streak and added five more, all in the first half of the year, to become champion in Brazil with a round to go. With Barrichello adding a pair of wins, Brawn GP was able to outscore Red Bull to be the constructors' champions too.

At year's end, though, Brawn GP was no more as Mercedes bought the controlling stake and the team was renamed Mercedes GP for 2010.

FORCE INDIA

FORMULA ONE RECORD

Country of origin: **Great Britain**   Date of foundation: **2005**
Active years in Formula One: **as Midland in 2006, as Spyker in 2007, then as Force India from 2008**
Constructors' Cup victories: **none**

The Jordan team was confined to history in 2005 and Midland F1 rose from its ashes, but two more identity changes would follow by 2008 as this once front-running team struggled for survival.

So, it was out with showman Eddie Jordan and in with the ultra-low-profile, Russian steel magnate Alex Shnaider, who had paid £16 million to take ownership.

Underneath, though, a lot of Jordan Grand Prix was still there: the team headquarters at Silverstone and a good deal of the staff, but not as many as required for the continuity that's so important for success. With the inevitable messiness of a change-over year in 2005, when the cars had to run as Jordans and in which money was tight, many good engineers, mechanics and even managers walked – quite a few of them because they didn't enjoying working with Shnaider's lieutenant Colin Kolles, a man with no prior management experience above Formula Three. Sporting director Trevor Carlin walked away too, to be replaced by his right-hand man, Adrian Burgess.

One of the mysteries, though, was why Shnaider was absent from more grands prix than he attended. Whatever, the reason, it made his involvement appear less than whole-hearted, convincing many that he had bought the team simply to try and make a profit by selling it on.

However, this sentiment passed when the likes of former Jordan driver Eddie Irvine were rebuffed, and a new livery for 2006 gave Midland F1 its own identity for the first time.

Looking back at 2005, Kolles could point to the fact that his drivers finished third and fourth at the US Grand Prix, although this only meant that Tiago Monteiro and Narain Karthikeyan had finished behind the Ferraris and ahead of the Minardis, as only six cars started the race. Monteiro's point for eighth place in Belgium was far more impressive, but it's safe to say that other teams would have fared better with the Toyota engines that they were running.

Monteiro gathered the money to stay on for 2006, to be joined by another paying driver, Christijan Albers, who had transferred from Minardi. But their Formula One experience of just one season each failed to propel the team away from the tail of the grid, especially with Minardi having received an influx of cash as it was re-badged as Scuderia Toro Rosso.

It was said that 2006 would be the season that marked just how serious Shnaider and Midland F1 intended to be. On the plus side, they had Toyota V8 engines and chirpy former racer Johnny Herbert as sporting relations manager to make the press feel welcome. Technical director James Key was making quite a name for himself, as was chief designer John McQuilliam, but the lack of interest from the top – Shnaider – and the lack of release of the funds required to become competitive left drivers Monteiro and Albers with little to smile about, their top results a fluky ninth place and two 10th places respectively. By year's end, their lack of testing led to them being outstripped not just by Scuderia Toro Rosso, but also by Super Aguri Racing.

Then in stepped businessman Michiel Mol to buy the team and rename it again, this time after Dutch sports car manufacturer Spyker. This lasted only through 2007, with Adrian Sutil's point for eighth in Japan the only one scored by the orange, Ferrari-powered cars.

For 2008, the team was given its long-term lifeline, a financial injection from Indian industrialist Vijay Mallya and a new name, Force India. However, neither Sutil nor Giancarlo Fisichella was able to score. With Force India's first all-new car coming on stream in 2009, and with Mercedes engines in place of the Ferraris used before, results improved, with Fisichella taking pole and finishing second at Spa then Sutil finishing fourth with a fastest lap at Monza.

VIP
Vijay Mallya

With the Indian economy being one of the driving forces of the world stage at the start of the 21st century and certainly maintaining growth where others faltered, it was always likely that some of this money would make its way to Formula One. That it did so from one of the movers and shakers of this burgeoning economy came as little surprise. That the investor was a racer in his younger years made this injection of funds all the more inevitable. This man was Vijay Mallya, who raced single-seaters in the early 1980s, but it was his position as head of the UB Group that enabled him to become involved. Firstly, he did so through promoting its Kingfisher beer brand on the Benetton cars in 1996, but he wanted more and so bought the ailing Spyker team for 2008. His ambitions were clear. By renaming it Force India this flamboyant individual wanted to take some of Indian's sporting passion away from its staples of cricket and hockey and create a brand with which they could identify. The cars carrying the white, orange and green of the national flag but, as yet, no Indian drivers.

A Force to be Reckoned With: Vitantonio Liuzzi showed good form for the team in 2009

RED BULL RACING

FORMULA ONE RECORD

Country of origin: **Great Britain**   Date of foundation: **2000**
Active years in Formula One: **2000-04 as Jaguar Racing, from 2005 as Red Bull Racing**
Constructors' Cup victories: **none**

The Red Bull energy drink has been an outstanding commercial success since Dietrich Mateschitz started marketing it in the 1980s. As a result, the Austrian with a passion for motorsport sponsored Sauber then, for 2005, took over Jaguar Racing and re-branded it as his own. In an instant, he had the ultimate marketing tool and this has proved so successful that he took over Minardi for 2006 and re-branded that as his own too, as Scuderia Toro Rosso.

This entry, though, is about Jaguar Racing and its metamorphosis into Red Bull Racing. Think Jaguar and most think of its victories in the Le Mans 24 Hours in the 1950s and the 1980s. It was a marque linked inextricably with sports car racing, so it was considered odd that parent company Ford used Jaguar's colours to adorn the team it bought from Jackie Stewart at the end of 1999. Many felt that the Ford oval would have been more appropriate, bearing in mind Ford's illustrious involvement in Formula One since investing in the Cosworth DFV engine that changed the face of the sport.

The Stewart team's three-year spell to 1999 was marked by Rubens Barrichello finishing second in the wet at Monaco in 1997. A poor 1998 followed, before Johnny Herbert won a wet-dry race at the Nurburgring in 1999, with Barrichello third. However, by then, the team had already been sold to Ford.

The team changed little when it was re-badged as Jaguar Racing, save for the fact that Jackie Stewart was now an advisor with Ford executive Neil Ressler taking the helm. Barrichello and Eddie Irvine did a straight swap, with Irvine joining from Ferrari. It was a poor season, with aerodynamics a weak point, although having your team base in Milton Keynes and your wind tunnel in California didn't help. Irvine's fourth at Monaco was one of only two points-scoring drives and Herbert was replaced by Pedro de la Rosa for 2001.

Irvine scored a surprise third at Monaco, but he and de la Rosa collected only minor placings thereafter. By August, though, the team had its third boss, with three-time world champion Niki Lauda now in control.

The aim was to have fewer mechanical failures in 2002, but this wasn't achieved, nor was a superior chassis. Irvine kicked off with fourth in Australia, but this was achieved in a race of attrition. Progress was made, with Irvine finishing third at Monza, a result that lifted Jaguar to seventh overall. De la Rosa was never higher than eighth and he and Irvine were dropped for 2003.

So too was Lauda, who was replaced by Tony Purnell, with David Pitchforth as managing director. Pleasingly, the R4 chassis was finally worthy of Jaguar's Cosworth engines and Mark Webber took the team to uncharted waters, albeit only in qualifying, as his third on the grid in Brazil showed. Sadly, Jaguar would have to settle for seventh overall again.

Jaguar were seventh for a third year in 2004 with Webber's best a sixth at Hockenheim, a result matched two races later by newcomer Christian Klien. Disillusioned, Ford put the team up for sale, but it was only saved at the 11th hour.

Back with a bang in 2005, re-branded as Red Bull Racing and sporting a much bigger budget, it nearly pulled off a shock result at the Australian opener when David Coulthard ran as high as second before finishing fourth. He repeated this result at the Nurburgring. At season's end, the team had finished seventh for the fourth straight year, but was hard on the heels of BAR, who had finished second overall the year before.

It was party time for this party-centred team at Monaco in 2006 when Coulthard raced to third, but the team's rampant ambition was shown by the signing of McLaren's design chief Adrian Newey to pen its 2007 car. With a change to Renault engines as well, results didn't come immediately, but Coulthard and Mark Webber started collecting points.

After a marginal improvement in 2008, the team lifted off in 2009 as new signing Sebastian Vettel won four times to be runner-up to Jenson Button and Webber took two wins to help the team rank second overall.

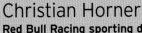

Flying Scot: David Coulthard was a revelation in his Red Bull Racing car in 2006, taking third at Monaco

SCUDERIA TORO ROSSO

FORMULA ONE RECORD

Country of origin: **Italy**   Date of foundation: **1972**
Active years in Formula One: **1985-2005 as Minardi, from 2006 as
Scuderia Toro Rosso**
Constructors' Cup victories: **none**

New Clothes: Minardi changed more than its livery when it metamorphosed into Scuderia Toro Rosso

Tail-end team Minardi was bought by Red Bull drinks magnate Dietrich Mateschitz in 2005 and renamed Scuderia Toro Rosso. For the first time, the team would have a full budget.

From 1974, Fiat dealer Giancarlo Minardi ran cars in Formula Two. Close ties with Ferrari enabled him to field an ex-works Formula One Ferrari in Scuderia Everest colours in 1976. Then, in 1980, he became a constructor, building a Formula Two chassis driven by Alessandro Nannini.

Minardi moved into Formula One in 1985, entering a car for Pierluigi Martini and taking part in the first two races with a Ford Cosworth engine, after which they fitted a Motori Moderni turbo, but it was uncompetitive. Martini was replaced by Andrea de Cesaris and Nannini. They fared little better. The team plugged on in 1987, this time with Adrian Campos in place of de Cesaris. Minardi reverted to Ford power in 1988 and re-signed Martini alongside a more promising Spaniard, Luis Sala.

In 1989, Minardi made it into the top 10, an important step for a small team, as it confers freight benefits. Minardi was delighted when Martini and Sala finished in the points at Silverstone. Then, at Estoril, Martini was fifth and made history for the Faenza team by leading for a lap...

For 1990, Martini was partnered by Paolo Barilla then Gianni Morbidelli, but there were no more points, although 1991 looked positive when Minardi struck an engine deal with Ferrari. The results weren't as spectacular as they'd hoped and Lamborghini V12s were used in 1992 and Christian Fittipaldi scored the team's only point of the season at Suzuka.

Customer Ford HBs produced steady performances through 1993 and 1994, but the loss of a Mugen Honda engine deal to Ligier at the start of 1995 was a big blow. After that, but the team continued in its usual position at the rear of the grid, unearthing Giancarlo Fisichella and Jarno Trulli.

The cruellest fortune struck Luca Badoer when his car broke when he was heading for fourth at the Nurburgring in 1999, although Marc Gene saved the day by finishing sixth. The team was sold to Paul Stoddart for 2001, who moved many of the staff to a new base in England. Fernando Alonso impressed, but the team never came close to scoring.

Their 2002 season was given a dream start in Melbourne when rookie Mark Webber finished fifth in a race of attrition, but it was to be their only score, with the might of the manufacturer-backed teams leaving Minardi to feed off scraps. Minardi's only success in 2003 lay in staying afloat, helped by cash initiatives from the FIA. Gianmaria Bruni and Zsolt Baumgartner were lacklustre in 2004 and the Hungarian scored their only point.

The team's final year as Minardi produced a fifth/sixth finish at the US GP, with Christijan Albers ahead of Patrick Friesacher, but this largely boycotted race produced the team's only points.

For 2006, now known as Scuderia Toro Rosso and run by Gerhard Berger, the team caused friction by running restricted V10s while all rivals had to downgrade to V8s, but Vitantonio Liuzzi scored just one point.

Matters improved in 2007 when Sebastian Vettel was introduced to replace Scott Speed and collected fourth at Shanghai. His form grew better still in 2008 when he qualified on pole in the wet at Monza and raced off to Toro Rosso's first win, helping it rank sixth, above sister team Red Bull from whom it received more than a little chassis assistance.

Vettel's departure to Red Bull weakened the team for 2009 and it fell to the bottom of the pile as rookie Sebastien Buemi outperformed Sebastien Bourdais, but peaked with two seventh place finishes.

VIP

Paul Stoddart

Along with Eddie Jordan, Paul was a typical Formula One privateer, a man with a passion for motor sport and someone who was not scared of a scrap. Successful in the garage business in Melbourne, he made his fortune in the aviation industry, building up European Aviation to the point that it had 25 passenger and cargo jets as well as a massive aviation-spares business. However, racing lured this Australian and he bought up several Tyrrell Formula One chassis that were being sold when the team folded. He ran these for himself and other drivers in historic Formula One circles and soon found himself running a Formula 3000 team before buying the controlling share of Minardi in January 2001. Money was tight from day one, but Paul fought his team's corner, earning respect along the way as few want to see the privateer teams priced out of Formula One to leave it the domain of only the automotive manufacturers. Paul felt that some wanted him out of the way, but he fought on until midway through 2005, when it became clear that Red Bull money would guarantee the jobs of his staff and then, like Jordan, he sold the show.

RENAULT

FORMULA ONE RECORD

Country of origin: **France** Date of foundation: **1898**
Active years in Formula One: **1977-85 and from 2002**
Constructors' Cup victories: **2005, 2006**

Renault took a bold decision to enter the World Championship in 1977 as it was pitching its 1.5-litre turbo engine against 3-litre normally-aspirated opposition at a time when Formula One was the domain of British teams who used customer engines. For a company the size of Renault to do less than win would have been disastrous.

A turbo engine had never been regarded as a feasible proposition, but Renault gained a good deal of turbo experience in sports car racing. The Renault RS01 first appeared at the British Grand Prix, with Jean-Pierre Jabouille driving. The project was hampered by the split of resources with the sports car programme and Renault's preoccupation with winning the Le Mans 24 Hours. Once that was achieved, in 1978, Formula One began to be taken much more seriously.

Renault introduced the RS10 ground-effect cars in 1979 and Jabouille scored a popular first win in the French Grand Prix at Dijon, a race that was also memorable for a last-lap tussle between team-mate René Arnoux and Gilles Villeneuve's Ferrari.

The Renault turbos were devastatingly effective in the altitude of Kyalami, where the normally aspirated cars gasped for breath. Arnoux won there in 1980 and also in Brazil, and it was soon obvious that turbocharging was the way to go. Renault had a head start and for 1981 it signed rookie Alain Prost who took three wins but lost out to Brabham's Nelson Piquet for the crown.

By 1982, BMW and Ferrari had developed turbo engines and were closing the gap. The Ferraris looked probable champions, but Villeneuve was killed in qualifying at Zolder and team-mate Didier Pironi smashed his legs at Hockenheim. Williams's Keke Rosberg ended up as champion with a single win to his name.

Prost had three wins and a 14-point lead in 1983 when the circus got to Austria, but he warned that Piquet and the Brabham-BMW had overtaken the Renault team on development. The championship went down to the wire at Kyalami. Prost dropped out early on and Piquet's Brabham cruised to the title. Prost said what he thought, and was promptly given his marching orders as a result.

Renault took on Derek Warwick and Patrick Tambay for 1984. Warwick led in Brazil, but tangled with Lauda and was forced to retire. With rival engines now just as good, Renault was facing a tough time and there were no more wins as McLaren dominated. After another struggling season when its drivers dubbed their car "tow-car of the year", Renault quit.

The company continued as an engine supplier from 1986 and began its association with Williams in 1989. Nigel Mansell and Alain Prost took drivers' titles in 1992 and 1993, while Williams won the constructors' title for three years in a row before Renault pulled out at the end of 1997.

In 2001, as engine supplier for Benetton, Renault power and reliability increased as the season went on, with Giancarlo Fisichella claiming third at the Belgian Grand Prix. The manufacturer re-badged the team as Renault for 2002, with progress being made as three Jenson Button and Jarno Trulli collected fourths. Trulli got on the podium at the German Grand Prix in 2003, but was outshone by team-mate Fernando Alonso who won in Hungary, giving Renault its first win since 1983.

It was Trulli's turn to win in 2004, at Monaco, but 2005 was the year they had been waiting for, with Fisichella taking the Australian opener before Alonso hit his stride and won seven times to be champion as Renault claimed its first constructors' crown. This was repeated in 2006, again with seven wins, as the Spaniard pipped Michael Schumacher.

With Alonso joining McLaren for 2007, Fisichella became team leader, joined by Heikki Kovalainen, but it was the rookie who came out on top with second in Japan as they guided Renault to third in the rankings.

Alonso returned in 2008 and even scored two wins, but they dropped to fourth overall. Then, troubled in 2009 by talk of it having fixed the 2008 Singapore GP, the team lost team principal Flavio Briatore and engineering chief Pat Symonds and it fell to eighth, with Alonso's third in Singapore its best result.

Wheel of Fortune: Fernando Alonso with Flavio Briatore after the Spaniard's first win in Hungary in 2003

BMW SAUBER

FORMULA ONE RECORD

Country of origin: **Switzerland**   Date of foundation: **1970**
Active years in Formula One: **from 1993-2005, from 2006 as BMW Sauber**
Constructors' Cup victories: **none**

Peter Sauber's first racing experience was in a VW Beetle, but he built his own cars from 1970. Although Sauber finished second in the 2-litre class at Le Mans in 1978, he became better known when he built the Sauber C6 for the Group C sports car category. Sauber entered his first Mercedes-powered car in 1985 and his team went on to set new standards. As the cars became the class of the field, so Mercedes invested more and became an official entrant. In 1989, Sauber-Mercedes won both Le Mans and the World Sports Car series.

Formula One was next, but, in November 1991, Mercedes announced that it wouldn't be making the move with them. It did, however, promise financial and technical support. Harvey Postlethwaite had left Tyrrell to draw the new Sauber C12, but when he heard that Mercedes wasn't going to join in, he quit. Sports

car designer Leo Ress and former McLaren man Steve Nichols were then responsible for development.

The car showed immediate pace, but lacked much of the electronic technology, like active ride. Sauber chose JJ Lehto and Karl Wendlinger as his drivers. Lehto arrived on the recommendation of Nichols, who'd worked with him when he was Ferrari test driver, and Wendlinger had been part of the Mercedes Junior Team in sports cars.

The team made a stunning debut in the 1993 South African Grand Prix when Lehto finished fifth, the first time that a new team had scored points in its first grand prix in 16 years. There may well have been strained relations between the drivers after they collided at Monaco, but there were also solid performances: Lehto was fourth at Imola, Wendlinger fourth at Monza.

Lehto was replaced by Heinz-Harald Frentzen for 1994, and he qualified fifth in Brazil and finished fifth in the Pacific Grand Prix. Then the team suffered a big blow when Wendlinger crashed in practice at Monaco. He fell into a coma and his life hung in the balance before he made a full recovery.

There were also money problems and then Mercedes announced its move to McLaren. However, Ford, having lost Benetton to Renault, agreed an engine-supply deal for 1995 and Frentzen raced to third in the Italian Grand Prix.

Then came the news that Stewart Grand Prix would take over the works Ford engines in 1997. However, in a move that shocked everyone, Sauber landed 1996-spec Ferrari engines for 1997 and re-badged them as Petronas units in deference to the team's sponsor. Third in Hungary was their best result.

Despite the efforts of Jean Alesi in 1998 and 1999, then Mika Salo in 2000, success eluded them. Sauber's 2001 season was its zenith, with Nick Heidfeld finishing third in Brazil and with rookie Kimi Raikkonen also finishing in the points on his debut, helping Sauber to rank fourth.

They ranked fifth in 2002, albeit with Heidfeld and Felipe Massa

scoring only half the 2001 points tally. Frentzen returned in 2003, but apart from third in a jumbled US Grand Prix, he and Heidfeld were midfield men as Sauber slipped to sixth. Giancarlo Fisichella joined for 2004 and finished fourth in Canada, a result matched by Massa in Belgium. The 2005 season, Sauber's last with Petronas power, wasn't good.

The arrival of BMW power and money for 2006 meant that Peter Sauber handed the reins to Mario Theissen. There was then an upswing, with Heidfeld coming third in Hungary and rookie Robert Kubica placing third in only his third race after replacing Jacques Villeneuve.

Record books show that the team finished 2007 as runner-up to Ferrari, but this involved the removal of McLaren's points and the Swiss team's best result was Heidfeld's second place in Canada, a race that Kubica exited in car-destroying style.

The team's first win came in Canada in 2008 when Kubica beat Heidfeld in a one-two finish. With six other second-place finishes, the team ranked third overall.

The 2009 season wasn't as good, with the team falling to sixth and BMW pulling out, leaving Sauber to take up the reins again.

First Victory: Nick Heidfeld leads Robert Kubica at Montreal in 2008, but it was Kubica who took the team's first win

TOYOTA

FORMULA ONE RECORD

Country of origin: **Germany**   Date of foundation: **1993**
Active years in Formula One: **from 2002-2009**
Constructors' Cup victories: **none**

In the Points: Ralf Schumacher showed flashes of form, such as finishing third in Australia in 2006

Toyota became the world's second largest motor manufacturer in 2003, behind General Motors but ahead of Ford for the first time. In terms of profits made, though, it has long been top, and it was with this in mind that plans were put into place to make its first foray into single-seaters for 2002.

Toyota's sporting success had been rooted in rallying, although touring car and sports car racing had also featured in the 1980s and 1990s, albeit with its bids to win the Le Mans 24 Hours having been spiked by the success in 1991 of Mazda.

Aware that Japan is far from the heartland of F1, the company decided it must have a European base. Unusually, it chose to base itself in Germany alongside the headquarters of its ultra-successful rally team, Toyota Team Europe, in Cologne.

The Formula One programme would be run by Ove Andersson, who had run TTE since its inception in 1993 and Toyota's European rally team – on which it was based – since 1975. Experts asked what he knew, but he augmented his knowledge of running a major operation by using Toyota's chequebook to lure the staff he needed. Mika Salo was signed to lead the driving side, supported by Allan McNish, a driver who had impressed Toyota in sports cars but, more importantly, had long been a test driver for McLaren and Benetton. Andersson said that he hoped the team would be good enough to qualify in its first year, but you expected he reckoned on rather more than that.

A clue to the fact that Toyota's huge budget wouldn't spell immediate success came when it was announced that its first car had come from the pen of sports car designer Andre de Cortanze rather than from a recognized Formula One designer. However, he was replaced by ex-Ferrari designer Gustav Brunner before the start of the 2002 season. Whatever the shortcomings of the chassis, the engine behind it was one of the most powerful on the grid. Despite Salo claiming sixth on the team's debut in Australia – admittedly in a race of appreciable attrition – this couldn't hide the fact that the chassis wasn't the best out there and a further sixth place, two races later, was Salo's only other score. McNish was unlucky not to finish sixth in the second round, when a bungled pitstop dropped him to seventh, and this remained his best result. Indeed, the team appeared to lose ground, leaving Toyota equal ninth overall with Arrows and Minardi.

The first car that carried the full Brunner stamp was 2003's TF103 and as Toyota decided that it wanted to gain impetus rather than rely on the experience it had gained, Salo and McNish were replaced by the experienced Olivier Panis and Champ Car champion Cristiano da Matta. The progress made was clear as they advanced to the midfield and even ran one-two after the British Grand Prix was shuffled by a track invader. Their best result was Panis's fifth place at Hockenheim and he later qualified third at Indianapolis. Toyota ended the year eighth overall.

Toyota's 2004 season was weak and da Matta was dropped before the year was out to make way for Ricardo Zonta. However, progress was marked in 2005 as Ralf Schumacher and Jarno Trulli took over and were no strangers to the front end of the grid, with Trulli bagging a pair of second places as Toyota soared to fourth overall.

Toyota dropped to sixth in 2006, with just one podium visit when Ralf finished third in Australia. Yet 2007 marked a further slide away from their target, with the team earning but a pair of sixths.

Toyota enjoyed a far stronger time in 2008, with Trulli and new signing Timo Glock claiming a third and a second respectively as Toyota climbed to fifth. Then came 2009 when Glock finished second in Singapore and then Trulli second at Suzuka, helping Toyota rank fifth again. Everyone thought that this late-season form would keep the manufacturer keen, but it quit at season's end.

BENETTON

FORMULA ONE RECORD

Country of origin: **Italy/Great Britain**   Date of foundation: **1986**
Active years in Formula One: **1986-2001**
Constructors' Cup victories: **1995**

With his base in Italy, Luciano Benetton built a chain of shops selling colourful clothing with a youth appeal. He saw Formula One as the ideal way of promoting them. In the early 1980s, Benetton sponsored Tyrrell, Alfa Romeo and Toleman, which Benetton then bought in 1986, fielding the cars as Benettons.

With turbocharged BMW engines, they were tremendously powerful and Gerhard Berger claimed their first victory in Mexico. Benetton began to emerge in the late 1980s. In 1989 they had Alessandro Nannini as their lead driver supported by Johnny Herbert, but when Flavio Briatore took over as kingpin in the Benetton organization both team boss Peter Collins and Herbert were fired. Briatore replaced Herbert with Emanuele Pirro, which was not the most inspired of moves, but Nannini finished the year with a win in the Japanese Grand Prix after Ayrton Senna was disqualified.

The team signed three-times World Champion Nelson Piquet in 1990, then in the twilight of his Formula One career. Piquet turned in some fine performances, though, and, as before, Benetton picked up the pieces in Japan when Senna and Prost collided.

Benetton's future, however, was shaped by the events of 1991 when a youthful Michael Schumacher burst on to the scene. Already a German Formula Three Champion and Macau winner, Michael was also a member of the Mercedes sports car junior team when he made his Formula One debut in a Jordan at Spa. He stunned the regulars by qualifying seventh.

Benetton had seen enough. After ugly scenes at Monza, the team managed to prise Schumacher away from Jordan and sign him to a long-term contract. Engineering director Tom Walkinshaw had been responsible for running the Jaguar sports car programme and he had first-hand experience of Schumacher's ability.

The German was brilliant from the start. He outpaced Piquet immediately and regularly brought the car home in the points. Benetton realized that it had a future World Champion on its books and Briatore instigated a build programme for a new technical facility in England's Cotswold hills, bringing the operation together under one roof. In 1992, Schumacher was unable to go for the championship because Williams had mastered active suspension first, allowing Nigel Mansell and Riccardo Patrese to finish one-two in the title race. However, Schumacher did score a wonderfully judged first grand prix win at Spa-Francorchamps.

In 1993, Benetton made great strides towards closing the gap with Williams by introducing a semi-automatic gearbox and active suspension. Schumacher did not have traction control until Monaco, though, where he led, but it was too late to stop Prost and Williams marching towards the drivers' and constructors' titles.

However, 1994 was the year. The Benetton B194 was the first chassis to see daylight from the "big four" teams and Ford had done a great job with the Zetec-R V8 engine. Schumacher won the first two races of the year and, when Senna was killed at Imola, he was left as Formula One's top gun. Benetton endured suggestions of illegality, then Schumacher suffered a two-race ban for ignoring a black flag at Silverstone and was thrown out on a technicality at Spa-Francorchamps. He went to Adelaide with a one point lead over Damon Hill and the title was decided when the pair collided.

In 1995, Benetton won the valued Constructors' Cup for the first time as Schumacher won nine grands prix – retaining his World Championship – and Johnny Herbert won two.

Jean Alesi and Gerhard Berger failed to win for Benetton in 1996. Berger took a single win in Germany in 1997, but the old guard were replaced in 1998 by Alex Wurz and Giancarlo Fisichella, with rally boss David Richards at the helm until Rocco Benetton – son of the company owner – took over late in the season. This line-up stayed the same through 1999 and 2000, albeit with Briatore returning in 2000, but no more wins were scored. Hopes that Renault engines would improve the team's form in 2001 were over-optimistic, but the signs were good by season's end as Benetton was transformed into the Renault team for 2002.

First Notch on his Belt: Michael Schumacher races to his maiden Formula One win for Benetton at the 1992 Belgian Grand Prix at Spa-Francorchamps

BRABHAM

FORMULA ONE RECORD

Country of origin: **Great Britain**   Date of foundation: **1961**
Active years in Formula One: **1962-1987 & 1989-1992**
Constructors' Cup victories: **1966, 1967**

Jack Brabham is the only driver to win the World Championship in a car bearing his own name.

Brabham won back-to-back titles for Cooper in 1959-60, but returned home to Australia and struck up a business partnership with Ron Tauranac, an aircraft engineer. They came to England and set up Motor Racing Developments (MRD). The cars were known as MRDs until someone pointed out that, if said rapidly in French, it sounded like something dogs did on the pavement. So, Brabham, although never a man who sought publicity, allowed his own name to be used instead.

The Brabham Racing Organization was formed in 1962, using cars built by MRD. It raced to its first grand prix wins in 1964, when Dan Gurney was first past the flag in both the French and Mexican Grands Prix.

Lotus dominated in 1965, but for the following year there was a new 3-litre formula in Formula One and Brabham had an engine built by the Australian Repco company. With it, Brabham became the first driver to score a win in a car bearing his own name, at the French Grand Prix, and went on to secure his third World Championship title.

The following season saw the introduction of the Cosworth DFV. The new engine won first time out in Jim Clark's Lotus, but consistency allowed Denny Hulme to win a second successive championship for Brabham.

Then the team missed out. Brabham managed to sign up-and-coming Austrian Jochen Rindt for 1968 and there is no doubt that, if the engines had been up to it, Rindt could have prolonged the success. However, the new four-cam Repco was neither quick nor reliable and Rindt left for Lotus at the end of the season.

From a Jack to a King: Jack Brabham in his days as a driver at the Nurburgring in 1966

After Jackie Stewart and Matra dominated in the 1969 season, Brabham, now 44, decided that 1970 would be his final year in Formula One. Tauranac produced his first monocoque Brabham, the BT33, and Jack won the opening race in South Africa. He should have won in Monaco, but allowed himself to be pressured into a mistake at the hairpin on the last lap by a charging Rindt.

Then Lotus upped the ante with its new Type 72. After outdriving Rindt at Brands Hatch, Brabham ran out of fuel on the last lap and that was the end of his challenge that year. Rindt then became the sport's only posthumous champion after an accident at Monza, and Brabham returned to Australia.

After struggling on in 1971, with Graham Hill and Tim Schenken, Tauranac sold the company to Bernie Ecclestone. One of Tauranac's design assistants, South African Gordon Murray, then became responsible for the Brabhams which, instead of taking over an "EM" (Ecclestone/Murray) tag, continued as BTs. Murray's distinctive BT44 was one of the prettiest Formula One cars ever built and it won three races in 1974, all with Argentinian Carlos Reutemann driving.

Ferrari domination with flat-12 engines caused Ecclestone to turn to Alfa Romeo for a similar unit but, despite signing Niki Lauda from Ferrari, the team could not win another championship. Lotus was pioneering aerodynamic wing cars and ground effect and, to counter the suction effect, Murray built a BT46B with a huge fan on the back that sucked the car on to the track. Lauda immediately blew the Lotuses away in the Swedish Grand Prix. It may have been brilliant, but it was rapidly banned.

Nelson Piquet joined the team at the end of 1978 and became a great favourite after Lauda retired the following year. Nelson won the World Championship in a Brabham in both 1981 and 1983, but the Brazilian left at the end of 1985 and Brabham rapidly declined. Elio de Angelis was killed testing the lay-down BT55 and, at the end of 1987, Ecclestone withdrew Brabham from the championship.

The team returned in 1989 after being sold to a Swiss financier who was later jailed for fraud. Its ownership then became even murkier and, although the team raced until 1992, it was an embarrassment to its former self before it disappeared from F1 altogether.

BRM

FORMULA ONE RECORD

Country of origin: **Great Britain**   Date of foundation: **1947**
Active years in Formula One: **1951-1977**
Constructors' Cup victories: **1962**

BRM's roots go back to 1947 when the British Motor Racing Research Trust was formed with the idea of building a British challenger to break the Italian stranglehold.

The man behind it was Raymond Mays, who was the first to bring commercial support to motor racing when he persuaded companies to back his English Racing Automobiles (ERA) efforts in the 1920s and 1930s. The BRM (British Racing Motors) project was a similar idea.

The original BRM team was a co-operative and the plan was to build a two-stage supercharged engine producing 600 brake horsepower. Unfortunately, when the car made its debut, in the non-championship International Trophy at Silverstone, it was a disaster. With Raymond Sommer driving, the car qualified on the back of the grid and broke a drive-shaft on the line. Spectators threw coins at it as it was pushed off.

The research trust lasted until 1952, when Sir Alfred Owen of the Owen Organization took over BRM. No great progress was made until the 1960s, as Cooper and Lotus overtook BRM in the effort to establish Britain at the forefront of the international racing scene.

BRM went into 1962 with just one grand prix victory to its name – the Dutch Grand Prix of 1959 with Jo Bonnier – and an ultimatum from Owen to win the championship or else. Peter Berthon, part of BRM since the start, was no longer on the scene and Tony Rudd, a former Rolls Royce apprentice who had worked for Merlin engines, took over as chief engineer and team manager, doing much work on the new BRM V8 engine.

Graham Hill showed the car's potential by winning the first heat of the Brussels Grand Prix in its debut race and then beat Jim Clark's Lotus by a nose in the International Trophy at Silverstone. He went on to score his first grand prix win in the opening round of the championship.

Hill won again in the German Grand Prix and then finished one-two for BRM with Richie Ginther at Monza. He was now embroiled in a title battle with Clark's Lotus that went right down to the wire in South Africa. Clark took off into the lead with Hill second, but an engine problem put him out and Hill won the World Championship for BRM in the Type P57.

Clark dominated in 1963, but BRM came back with its first monocoque car, the P261, the following year. Hill won two grands prix and was only prevented from taking a second championship by John Surtees's Ferrari in the final race of the season, where Hill's BRM was clobbered by Surtees's young Ferrari team-mate, Lorenzo Bandini. Hill reputedly sent Bandini a "Learn to Drive" manual.

For the new 3-litre formula of 1966, Rudd developed the H16 engine, which was effectively two V8s mounted on top of each other with the cylinder banks opened out to lie horizontally. The complicated engine was not a success despite the team's best efforts, and was replaced by a V12 in 1968.

By this time the BRM chassis was a little long in the tooth. Talented young designer Tony Southgate joined the organization and designed the P153 and P160 chassis, which put BRM back into the winner's circle when Pedro Rodriguez won a close battle with Chris Amon in the 1970 Belgian Grand Prix at Spa-Francorchamps.

The emerging Niki Lauda turned in some promising drives to launch his career with BRM in 1973, but, at the end of the following year, the Owen Organization withdrew its support. Louis Stanley tried to keep the team afloat, but it all fell apart in 1977. The new P207 was late and, when it did arrive, neither Conny Andersson nor Teddy Pilette could qualify it and Rotary Watches withdrew their sponsorship. BRM's final appearance in the World Championship was with Larry Perkins at the wheel at the 1977 South African Grand Prix at Kyalami.

Smile for the Camera: Jo Bonnier sweeping to BRM's first victory in the 1959 Dutch Grand Prix. Photographers don't get as close to the action today...

COOPER

FORMULA ONE RECORD

Country of origin: **Great Britain**   Date of foundation: **1946**
Active years in Formula One: **1950-1969**
Constructors' Cup victories: **1959, 1960**

Cooper was responsible for the switch to rear-engined cars in Formula One, a move that won back-to-back World Championship titles for Jack Brabham in 1959 and 1960.

It all began when Charles Cooper, a racing mechanic before the Second World War, built his son John a 500cc motorcycle-engined racing car. Using a chain-driven JAP engine, the thinking was that the car had to have the power unit close to the driven rear axle, with the cockpit in front.

The cars were very successful and the Cooper Car Company was established to build more of them. Their 500cc Formula Three cars quickly began to dominate, but there were doubts about whether the same principles could be successfully applied with more potent machinery. People were mindful of the difficult rear-engined Auto Unions of the 1930s.

Cooper concentrated on other projects before returning to the mid-engined concept. An experimental Cooper was run by Jack Brabham in the 1955 British Grand Prix, equipped with a 2-litre, six-cylinder Bristol engine. A new 1500cc Formula Two class was due for introduction in 1957 and Cooper geared up for it by putting a Climax engine in the back of a developed version of its earlier chain-driven Formula Three car. Enlarged versions of the cars made a few grand prix appearances during the 1957 season and clearly outhandled the bigger front-engined machinery. However, they were too underpowered to do any serious damage.

For 1958, Rob Walker - heir to the huge Johnny Walker whisky fortune - ordered a new engine from Coventry Climax for a Cooper and recruited Stirling Moss. Moss beat the Ferraris in Argentina in his blue Cooper T45, fooling the Ferraris into thinking he would need a tyre stop but driving cautiously so that he made the finish

Crossing the Tracks: Jack Brabham steers his Cooper to victory in the 1960 Portuguese Grand Prix

without one, although his rubber was worn through to the carcass. It was the first World Championship win by both a rear-engined and privately entered car.

Moss reverted to a Vanwall thereafter, but Maurice Trintignant won in Monte Carlo aboard the Cooper. The cars were still underpowered, but it was clear that the rear-engined concept had merit, although Vanwall recovered and won the constructors' championship.

By 1959, Vanwall had withdrawn from Formula One and Jack Brabham, working closely with John Cooper, helped develop the T51. Coventry-Climax produced a 2.5-litre engine, thus giving Cooper competitive engines for the first time. Brabham won both the Monaco and British Grands Prix and his World Championship win was sealed when team-mate Bruce McLaren became the youngest winner of a grand prix, aged 22, at Sebring.

The United States Grand Prix was new on the calendar that year and Moss had given himself a second successive shot at the title in the

last race of the year by winning the previous two races in Rob Walker's private Cooper. He took off into the lead at Sebring, but retired with a common gearbox failure, leaving the championship to either Brabham or Tony Brooks, who could win for Ferrari if he took the race with Brabham failing to score. Brabham led but ran out of petrol on the final lap, leaving McLaren to beat Trintignant, with Brooks third. New champion Brabham pushed his Cooper across the line in fourth place.

New Coopers were built for 1960 and, after McLaren won the opening race, Brabham scored five consecutive wins to make sure of back-to-back championship wins. Cooper's pioneering devel-opment was overtaken by more sophisticated designs from Ferrari, BRM and Lotus over the following seasons. Cooper fought back with a monocoque chassis in 1966, but engines were not competitive. In addition, John Cooper had been seriously injured driving a Mini Cooper. The marque disappeared from F1 at the end of 1968.

VIP
John Cooper
Son of racing car manufacturer Charles Cooper, John was hooked on racing from an early age and he and his father started building cars for the 500cc Formula Three category after the Second World War, with their order book filling fast after one of their cars won the first race. Their cars appeared in Formula One from 1950 in the hands of privateers, but John gained valuable hands-on experience of running a team in the category when they fielded Jack Brabham in the late 1950s. John took over the team when Charles died in 1964, but was then injured and Ken Tyrrell took control for him. John elected to sell the team in 1965, doing so to the Chipstead Motor Group, leaving him free to concentrate on running a car dealership in Sussex and take royalties for the Mini Cooper S, a high-performance version of the Mini that was a cult car for 40 years. John was awarded the CBE shortly before his death in 2000.

LOTUS

FORMULA ONE RECORD

Country of origin: **Great Britain**   Date of foundation: **1952**
Active years in Formula One: **1958-1994**
Constructors' Cup victories: **1963, 1965, 1968, 1970, 1972, 1973, 1978**

Two of a Kind: Jim Clark with team boss Colin Chapman before the 1963 Dutch Grand Prix

Lotus founder, the late Colin Chapman, has many times been dubbed a genius. Chapman was an enthusiastic member of the 750 Motor Club who took to building his own cars, calling them Lotuses. He founded the Lotus Engineering Company in 1952 with some money he borrowed from his wife to be, Hazel.

Chapman started by building lightweight sports cars before constructing his first single-seater, the Type 12, in 1957, aimed at the new Formula Two category. The more sophisticated Lotus 16 was run in Formula One in 1959, but it proved too fragile.

Chapman followed the mid-engined concept and built the brilliant Lotus 18 for 1960, with Stirling Moss giving the marque its first grand prix win in a Rob Walker-entered car at Monaco.

Lotus really made its name in the 1960s with legendary Scottish driver Jim Clark. Ferrari had been ready for the new 1.5-litre Formula One regulations in 1961, but the British constructors were forced to use stopgap Formula Two Climax engines. Despite that, Stirling Moss scored that historic win at Monaco against Richie Ginther's "shark-nose" Ferrari.

In 1962, Chapman introduced the Lotus 25 monocoque chassis at the Dutch Grand Prix, following the trends of aircraft designs of the day. Clark was unfortunate to lose the title to Graham Hill's BRM, but he made amends the following year. With the car in updated Lotus 33 form, Clark won his second title for Chapman in 1965 – he also won the Indianapolis 500 in the same year.

Jack Brabham's Repco-engined Brabhams were the class of the field in 1966, but, with exclusive use of the new Ford Cosworth DFV in 1967, Lotus hit back hard with the 49.

Tragically, Clark died in a Formula Two race at Hockenheim in April 1968, the first time that Lotus had run in Gold Leaf colours. Chapman was devastated, but Graham Hill provided a tonic by winning the next two grands prix and going on to take the title.

Chapman managed to replace Clark with the fiery young Jochen Rindt, regarded as the quickest driver in F1. The Austrian dominated most of the 1970 season in the brilliant Lotus 72, but died in practice at Monza when a brake shaft broke. Rindt became the sport's first and only posthumous champion.

Emerson Fittipaldi took over as team leader and won another title with the 72 two years later, but Lotus then lost its way until 1977, when it reaped the reward of developing ground-effect principles. Simply stated, venturi tunnels on each side of a slim chassis created a vacuum and sucked the car on to the track.

Mario Andretti won four times with the Lotus 78 in 1977, but he could not stop Lauda's consistent Ferrari taking the title. However, in 1978, the refined Lotus 78 was dominant in the hands of both Andretti and Ronnie Peterson.

Tragically, Andretti's moment of triumph was soured by Peterson's death as a result of injuries sustained in a multiple pile-up at the start of the Italian Grand Prix.

Continuing his reputation for innovative design, Chapman came up with the twin-chassis Lotus 88, but it was banned by the authorities, leaving a seething Chapman threatening to finish with the sport. It was he who gave Nigel Mansell his grand prix break, but in later years Chapman's name was to be tarnished by reports of the De Lorean fraud. Under pressure, he succumbed to a heart attack in 1982.

Lotus was never the same without him. The team enjoyed limited success in the mid-1980s, but even with turbo engines from Renault and Honda then Ayrton Senna in the cockpit, they could do no more than win the occasional race.

Former manager Peter Collins bought his way into the team in 1990, but on 11 September 1994, he had to give up the unequal financial struggle and place the company in administration. It was acquired by David Hunt, brother of 1976 World Champion James, but then folded.

MATRA

FORMULA ONE RECORD

Country of origin: **France**   Date of foundation: **1965**
Active years in Formula One: **1966-1972**
Constructors' Cup victories: **1969**

It was the French Matra company that helped take Jackie Stewart to his first World Championship success in 1969.

Matra was a big French aerospace concern, whose more lucrative products included guided missiles. They knew all about monocoque construction through this involvement in the aircraft industry and they also had a plastics division. Matra supplied car bodies to René Bonnet, who was running Formula Junior monocoque cars until he went bankrupt. At that point, Matra executive Jean-Luc Lagardère decided to form Matra Sports to take over where Bonnet had left off. The Matra Formula Three cars were renowned for high quality workmanship and when Ken Tyrrell went looking for a chassis, he approached Matra.

Tyrrell had already secured the new Cosworth DFV for 1968 and he had Jackie Stewart signed up, with money and support from Dunlop tyres. After two years of running Matra chassis in Formula Two, Tyrrell went Formula One with the MS10 in 1968, adding the Matra name to the World Championship victory roll at the Dutch Grand Prix.

Stewart remained in contention for the championship until the final round in Mexico, where he was pipped by Graham Hill's Lotus.

Matra had funding from Elf and the French government granted them £800,000 to develop its own engine. The French built a V12, which was raced in an MS11 chassis by Jean-Pierre Beltoise. The V12 was not competitive against the Cosworth, however, and for 1969 Beltoise joined Stewart in Tyrrell's DFV-powered team. Matra, meanwhile, concentrated on sports car racing and on developing the V12 engine.

The new Matra MS80 for 1969 was around 15 kilos lighter than the MS10 had been and it allowed Stewart to dominate the season. After winning in South Africa with the MS10, he gave the MS80 a successful debut in the non-championship Race of Champions at Brands Hatch. He then went to Barcelona, where the Matra team scored a fortunate win when both

Lotus 49s suffered failures to their newly introduced high rear wings.

Unfortunately, the Matra broke while Stewart was leading convincingly from pole position around the streets of Monaco, but both team and driver were dominant thereafter. The British Grand Prix, one of the all-time great races, featured a tremendous duel between Stewart's Matra and Rindt's Lotus. Mechanical problems hampered Rindt and Stewart claimed another win.

Monza that year witnessed another epic. The famous track was bereft of chicanes in those days and the Italian Grand Prix was usually a slipstreaming classic. Stewart had selected a top gear ratio ideal for the sprint to the line out of the last corner. Although Rindt passed him going in, Stewart led coming out and headed a four-car blanket finish to seal the World Championship.

Although Matra could bathe in the glory of building the championship-winning chassis, it was very much a British success. Both the team and engine manufacturer were based in England and the driver was Scottish.

France had not been properly represented in Formula One since 1957, and for the 1970 season Matra insisted on using its own V12 engine. Tyrrell and Stewart did not trust the unit, and so bought a March chassis and raced that instead.

Matra's small sports car company had been taken over by Simca, and so a Matra Simca MS120 was raced by Beltoise and Henri Pescarolo in 1970, achieving three third places. Chris Amon replaced Beltoise for 1971 and won a non-championship race in Argentina. However, over the next two seasons, despite sounding glorious, the cars never won a grand prix.

Matra then concentrated on winning the Le Mans 24 Hours and withdrew from Formula One altogether. The V12 engines appeared in a Ligier chassis and Jacques Laffite won the 1977 Swedish Grand Prix with one, but the Matra team never returned.

Splashing to Victory: Jackie Stewart eases his Matra MS10 around a damp Zandvoort en route to the marque's first Formula One victory in 1968

TYRRELL

FORMULA ONE RECORD

Country of origin: **Great Britain**   Date of foundation: **1960**
Active years in Formula One: **1970-1998**
Constructors' Cup victories: **1971**

Numero Uno: Jackie Stewart took 4th place in the 1973 Italian GP, clinching the World Championship

Tyrrell was one of the independent teams that took Formula One to new heights in the early 1970s. Sadly, it was on the skids by the 1980s and failed to see out the 1990s. Ken Tyrrell became captivated by racing in the 1950s. He raced until 1958 before concentrating on management and founding the Tyrrell Racing Team in 1960. Fortuitously, he managed the Cooper Formula One team when John Cooper was injured in a road accident and made a strong impression with his tactical nous. His path to the top, however, was linked to his discovery of a young Scot called Jackie Stewart.

Stewart was given his break when one of Tyrrell's drivers, Timmy Mayer, was killed when racing in the Tasman series early in 1964. Tyrrell was advised to give Stewart a test in one of his Formula Three cars and, when the Scotsman lapped faster than Bruce McLaren, Ken signed him.

Stewart then drove for Tyrrell in Formula Two while spending three years racing in Formula One for BRM. Tyrrell finally got to run him in Formula One in 1968. Using chassis from Matra and the Ford Cosworth DFV, Stewart only lost out on the title to Graham Hill at the final round. In 1969, the Stewart-Matra combination was unbeatable, winning six races en route to collecting both the drivers' and constructors' titles.

With Matra declining to build a car to accept the Cosworth DFV, preferring to use its own V12 engines, which Stewart did not want, it was all change for 1970. As the 1969 Matra chassis no longer conformed to the rules, Tyrrell was forced to run a March chassis. However, he employed Derek Gardner to pen the first Tyrrell chassis which was raced towards the end of the season, and which led both the Canadian and the United States Grands Prix.

Stewart and Tyrrell were dominant in 1971, and the team's French blue livery and Elf signage were seen at the head of almost every grand prix as Stewart collected six wins and his second title. Tyrrell ran a second car, with Francois Cevert winning the final round.

Stewart's 1972 campaign was interrupted after he suffered from an ulcer, but he returned in 1973 to clinch his third title. Stewart had told Tyrrell in April of his intention to retire after the last grand prix. With the title won at Monza, he never got to race, as Cevert died in practice and the team's entry was withdrawn.

In the immediate post-Stewart era, Patrick Depailler and Jody Scheckter won races for Tyrrell and the team developed the P34 six-wheeler for 1976. The theory was that four small wheels at the front would put more rubber onto the road while cutting aerodynamic resistance. Scheckter and Depailler finished one-two at Anderstorp then Ronnie Peterson replaced Scheckter for 1977, but, by then, the P34s were uncompetitive. After finishing second eight times, Depailler finally won, at Monaco in 1978, but the Tyrrell team did not win another grand prix until Michele Alboreto took a win in each of 1982 and 1983 to bring the team's tally since 1970 to 23 wins.

Through the 1980s and early 1990s, the Tyrrell team was a shadow of its former self. The low spot was having its results annulled in 1984 for an alleged technical irregularity, negating the input of rookies Stefan Bellof and Martin Brundle, who had finished third at Monaco and second at Detroit respectively. The high spot was Jean Alesi making the most of Harvey Postlethwaite's 018 and 019 chassis in 1990 to finish second at Phoenix and Monaco.

The 1994 season was Tyrrell's best for years as it ranked sixth. Then Mika Salo ran third on his debut in Brazil in 1995 before suffering cramp, spining and ending up seventh.

The following year was no better and Tyrrell's decline continued into 1997, with Salo and Jos Verstappen struggling.

The 1998 season was the team's last. Tyrrell had been sold to British American Racing so it could gain a championship entry for a team it was setting up to run in 1999. Set up by Jacques Villeneuve's manager Craig Pollock and American manufacturer Reynard, it would include nothing of Tyrrell's heritage. Ken Tyrrell quit once it became clear he would have no influence over driver choice. He died in 2001.

VANWALL

FORMULA ONE RECORD

Country of origin: **Great Britain**   Date of foundation: **1949**
Active years in Formula One: **1954-1960**
Constructors' Cup victories: **1958**

Tony Vandervell was an industrialist, a racing fan and a patriot. One of the original backers of the BRM project, he became frustrated with its lack of progress and went his own way.

Vandervell bought a Ferrari 125 in 1949 with the intention of testing it and helping the BRM learning process. The car ran as a Thin Wall, a Vandervell trade name. After a couple of years of Formula Two rules, the World Championship conformed to a new 2.5-litre formula in 1954. Vandervell commissioned John Cooper to construct a new chassis for a 2-litre, four-cylinder engine built by Vandervell and based on four Norton motorcycle engines. This was developed into a full 2.5-litre unit by 1955.

The car became known as a Vanwall for the first time, a combination of Vandervell's name and his Thin Wall bearing business. However, racing then was dominated by the Mercedes-Benz team and the lone Vanwall was raced by Peter Collins. Harry Schell and Ken Wharton drove in 1955, but there was little to write home about.

In 1956, Vandervell commissioned a new chassis from Colin Chapman. The bodywork was styled by aero-dynamicist Frank Costin and the engine produced a respectable 285 brake horsepower. Vanwall ran the trio of Schell, Maurice Trintignant and Mike Hawthorn as the drivers, but before the World Championship season started, Stirling Moss gave the car a winning debut in the International Trophy race at Silverstone.

In the French Grand Prix, Chapman himself was entered by Vanwall, but his brakes locked up in practice and

he rammed Hawthorn! The brakes could not be repaired and Chapman wasn't able to start the race.

Schell gave the Ferraris a shock in the race, passing Collins and Castellotti, and then getting up alongside race leader Fangio on two occasions.

The 1957 season saw Vanwall emerge as a force to be reckoned with. The team could boast Stirling Moss, along with Tony Brooks and newcomer Stuart Lewis-Evans. The British Grand Prix at Aintree brought the day Vandervell had been waiting for. Moss qualified on pole, with Jean

Behra's Maserati between him and Brooks. Moss took the lead, but Behra hauled him in when the Vanwall started to misfire and Stirling had to pit for attention to an earth lead. The problem remained and so Brooks was called in to hand over his car to Moss, who resumed in ninth place. He was soon up to fourth, behind Lewis-Evans, Hawthorn and Behra, but the gods were looking after him. Behra's flywheel shattered and Hawthorn punctured a tyre on the debris, allowing Moss through to win. It was the first time that a British car had won a major grand prix since 1923 and the first victory by a British car and driver in the British Grand Prix.

The little mid-engined Coopers made a sensational start to the 1958 season, with Vanwall not ready for the hastily arranged Argentinian Grand Prix, but then Moss won in Holland and Brooks in Belgium. Brooks won again in Germany, a win spoiled by Peter Collins's death in a Ferrari. Moss

won in Portugal before Brooks was successful again at Monza.

The World Championship went to the wire in Morocco and was a straight fight between Moss with three wins and Hawthorn's Ferrari with one victory, but five second places. Moss won superbly, but Hawthorn was second, enough to clinch the drivers' title. On the way, however, he had gone off, stalled and push-started his car against the flow of traffic.

He was disqualified but Moss said he had seen him pushing the car only on the pavement, which was permitted. Hawthorn was reinstated, costing Moss the title. Sportsmanship was different then, but at least Vanwall won the constructors' crown.

Team-mate Lewis-Evans died from burns he received in an accident. Vandervell was shaken by this and, in poor health, gave up quit the team in 1959. With the rear-engined revolution on the way, a chapter of British racing history was over.

Victory Salute: Stirling Moss crosses the line first in the British Grand Prix at Aintree in 1957 to gain the first World Championship win for a British car

ALFA ROMEO

FORMULA ONE RECORD

Country of origin: **Italy** Date of foundation: **1909**
Active years in Formula One: **1950-1951 and 1979-1985**
Constructors' Cup victories: **none**

Alfa Romeo was an evocative motor sporting name of the 1920s and 1930s and was also prominent immediately after the Second World War. The name is an emotive one, but the company last won a grand prix in 1951.

Alfa Romeo entered the grand prix arena in 1924. One of the most brilliant designers of the age was Vittorio Jano. After 12 years with Fiat, one of the most successful makes from the sport's early days, Jano was lured to Alfa Romeo in 1923 and his P2 became the standard setter for the next two years. Antonio Ascari won the car's first race, at Cremona, and so crushing was the Italian superiority in the 1925 Belgian Grand Prix at Spa, that Jano actually laid out a quality lunch in the pits and called his drivers in to partake while the mechanics polished the cars. The team then continued with their dominant display!

Their fortunes changed when Ascari was killed in the French Grand Prix at Montlhery, but Alfa Romeo still took the constructors' championship title and added a laurel wreath to its distinctive cloverleaf badge.

Another Jano great was the Alfa Tipo B that made its first appearance in 1932. Between then and 1934, it won every grand prix in which it was entered, driven by the likes of Rudolf Caracciola and the great Tazio Nuvolari, who many rate as the greatest driver of all time. In 1933, Alfa Romeo was nationalized and officially withdrew from the sport, although Ferrari continued to field the cars on a semi-works basis.

Even against the might of the emerging German marques such as Mercedes and Auto Union, Nuvolari managed some mighty feats with the Tipo B, none better than his win in the 1935 German Grand Prix.

Alfa took full control of its racing programme again in 1938, but the war intervened. Put off by the German dominance of grand prix racing in the late 1930s, Gioacchino Columbo designed an Alfa Romeo Tipo 158 for the smaller voiturette class in 1939. It was hidden in a cheese factory while the Germans occupied Italy, but under the new, pragmatic postwar regulations it automatically became a grand prix car and dominated the scene for the remainder of the 1940s. Alfa Romeo enjoyed a string of 26 unbroken wins.

By 1951, some 13 years after it was designed, the supercharged car, now in 159 guise, took Juan Manuel Fangio to his first world title in the final race of the season, the Spanish Grand Prix, in a shoot-out against the Ferraris of Alberto Ascari, Froilan Gonzalez and Piero Taruffi. It was the car's last race and Alfa Romeo then turned its attention to sports car racing.

In the mid-1970s their flat-12 sports-car engine started to attract the interest of the Formula One brigade, who were watching Ferrari dominate proceedings with an engine of similar configuration. Former Ferrari engineer Carlo Chiti was responsible for the engines and he did a deal with Bernie Ecclestone to supply them to the Brabham team.

Autodelta was Chiti's company and the organization that conducted Alfa's racing programme. The Brabham-Alfas started to show good form and, despite a strong union movement that was opposed to rich man's sport, Alfa Romeo was not slow to recognize the possible benefits of its own programme. In 1979, Bruno Giacomelli debuted the ugly-looking Tipo 177 in the Belgian Grand Prix at Zolder.

As Brabham reverted to Ford power, the new Alfa V12 was put into a new Tipo 179 chassis and, with Giacomelli joined by Patrick Depailler for 1980, the outlook was healthier. Sadly, though, Depailler was killed in testing at Hockenheim and, although Giacomelli led the United States Grand Prix at Watkins Glen before the car expired, Alfa Romeo was not destined to enjoy the success of its heyday. Andrea de Cesaris led the Belgian Grand Prix at Spa-Francorchamps in 1983, but the marque did not win another grand prix before quitting again.

Second Time Around: Alfa Romeo returned to Formula One in 1979. This is Bruno Giacomelli in an unwieldy Tipo 179 at the Monaco Grand Prix in 1980

ARROWS

FORMULA ONE RECORD

Country of origin: **Great Britain**   Date of foundation: **1977**
Active years in Formula One: **1978-2002**
Constructors' Cup victories: **none**

Arrows spent 25 years trying to win a grand prix before it finally folded. Ironically, its second race, the South African Grand Prix of 1978, was the nearest it came, when Riccardo Patrese led until his engine died.

Arrows was established when key members of the Shadow team broke away. Shadow had been sponsored by Franco Ambrosio and he became the "AR" of the Arrows name, with the other initials belonging to Alan Rees, former grand prix driver Jackie Oliver plus designers Dave Wass and Tony Southgate. Gunnar Nilsson was to lead the team, but he developed stomach cancer and died less than a year later, so Arrows opted for Patrese as its number one.

After preparing its car in just 60 days, Arrows hit trouble. Shadow believed that the FA1 was a copy of its DN9. The High Court told Arrows that it could not race the car, so the team had to build a replacement, which it managed to do, and continued without even missing a race.

Early Arrows cars raced in the gold livery of the Warsteiner beer company, and the 1979 car, the futuristic-looking A2 "buzz bomb" was much discussed. It was not successful, though, and the team reverted to more conventional thinking for its subsequent cars.

As the 1980s advanced, it was no longer sufficient to bolt on a Ford Cosworth DFV engine to succeed. A manufacturer link became increasingly important to match the turbocharged engines from BMW, Renault and Ferrari. When BMW pulled out, its turbo engines were renamed Megatrons and they were used to good effect by Arrows.

As the 1980s drew to a close, the Japanese Footwork corporation broke into Formula One striking a deal with Oliver. Arrows was renamed Footwork and it looked as though the injection of Japanese funding could move the team to the forefront, especially when a deal for Porsche engines was signed.

Alan Jenkins was design chief after achieving great success with McLaren. Any hopes of a repeat were dispelled when the first 12-cylinder engine (effectively two sixes joined together) arrived. Whereas a typical unit might have weighed 145-150 kilos, the Porsche weighed 210! Footwork soldiered on with Mugen engines and Aguri Suzuki alongside Michele Alboreto, then Derek Warwick.

Jenkins designed the neat FA15 for a customer Ford engine for 1994, but new rules after early-season deaths spoiled the cars. Footwork's Wataru Ohashi reduced his involvement and the team became Arrows again.

An unspectacular 1996 season masked Tom Walkinshaw's arrival as team owner. His signings for 1997 included Damon Hill, Bridgestone tyres and Yamaha engines, but their form was weak, even though reigning World Champion Hill led until the final lap of the Hungarian Grand Prix before falling to second.

For 1998, Arrows built its own engines, with Mika Salo replacing Hill alongside Pedro Diniz, but the engines were the team's downfall and Diniz quit. Pedro de la Rosa scored on his debut in 1999, but that was his only point of the campaign. With financial backing from Orange and using Supertec engines in 2000, Arrows made clear progress, with de la Rosa twice running third and Jos Verstappen finishing fourth at Monza. Changing yet again, weak Asiatech engines limited Arrows to just a single point-scoring result in 2001.

Arrows started the 2002 season with Heinz-Harald Frentzen scoring a pair of sixth-place finishes in the team's promising Ford-powered A23 chassis, but it failed to last the course as its coffers ran dry. Indeed, the team's transporters turned around once they had reached the Hungaroring as talk of take-over bids came to nothing and the curtain came down for good at the next race at Spa-Francorchamps, when the cars were kept in the transporters through the first day of the meeting then returned back to the UK and were not seen again until they were bought at auction in 2003 by Minardi.

HESKETH

FORMULA ONE RECORD

Country of origin: **Great Britain**   Date of foundation: **1972**
Active years in Formula One: **1973-1978**
Constructors' Cup victories: **none**

Cavalier Englishman: James Hunt charges towards second place in the US Grand Prix in 1973

Lord Alexander Hesketh was a larger-than-life extrovert who enjoyed a considerable inheritance and had an extremely good time spending it. Always a racing enthusiast, he was a friend of Anthony "Bubbles" Horsley, who was having little success in Formula Three in the 1970s.

At the same time, James Hunt was trying to make a name for himself. James was quick but down on his luck, having just been fired by the March works team after a disagreement with Max Mosley, when he met Horsley in a muddy field in Belgium. They came to an arrangement for James to drive a Formula Three car, with backing from "The Good Lord", as Hesketh was known.

Hesketh bought a Formula Two Surtees for 1973, but James shunted it in testing and The Good Lord decided he might as well go the whole hog and rented a Formula One Surtees.

Hunt finished third in the Race of Champions at Brands Hatch and Hesketh decided it was time to forget about the junior ranks. He ordered a new March and managed to persuade one of March's young brains, Harvey Postlethwaite, to design a new car, working from Hesketh's Easton Neston estate, close to Silverstone.

Hunt immediately showed great promise: he scored his first point in the French Grand Prix; he was fourth after a stirring drive at Silverstone; and capped the year with a fabulous second behind Ronnie Peterson at Watkins Glen.

In that first year Hesketh was looked on with scorn by the establishment. They partied everywhere, taking butlers, champagne and Rolls-Royces, but all this belied latent talent and their results showed that they had to be taken seriously.

Jackie Stewart's retirement at the end of 1973 created the chance for a new order to establish itself and Hunt was one of those at the forefront. Postlethwaite's Hesketh 308 was ready for the International Trophy at Silverstone in 1974 and James scored a truly popular win. With their teddy bear mascot, Hesketh Racing was catching the public's imagination.

The 1974 season continued Hesketh's promise, but the Ferraris emerged as the cars to beat, even though the title eventually went to Fittipaldi's McLaren. Hunt again finished the year with a tremendous drive at Watkins Glen.

The speed was clearly there and, at Zandvoort in 1975, the team achieved a fantastic first and only win. In a wet-dry race Hunt gambled on an early change to slicks and managed to hold off Niki Lauda's Ferrari for the rest of the race, crossing the line with both fists punching the air.

Hesketh had always run its cars without commercial backing, but even the Lord did not have bottomless pockets and the team's continuation into 1976 was looking a bit dubious.

Hunt was now in demand and, when Fittipaldi unexpectedly left McLaren to set up his own operation with backing from the Brazilian sugar corporation, Hunt was given his seat and went on to win the 1976 World Championship after an epic battle with Lauda.

Hesketh called a halt and the cars were sold off to Frank Williams, who had just gone into what was to prove an ill-advised partnership with Walter Wolf, a Canadian oil millionaire. Thus, Postlethwaite's 308C became the Wolf-Williams.

Horsley kept Hesketh Racing ticking over for a couple of seasons, using updated versions of the old car with paying drivers, and engineer Frank Dernie penned the 308E. Without a driver of Hunt's calibre on the books, however, the motivation of the early days was gone and Hesketh Racing wound down, concentrating on servicing customer Cosworth engines for a time. One of the great chapters of classic British racing romanticism was at an end.

JORDAN

FORMULA ONE RECORD

Country of origin: **Great Britain**   Date of foundation: **1981**
Active years in Formula One: **1991-2005**
Constructors' Cup victories: **none**

Cutting Corners: Damon Hill leads his Jordan team-mate Ralf Schumacher at Spa-Francorchamps en route to the team's maiden F1 victory in the 1998 Belgian GP after a race packed with incident and intrigue

Wheeler-dealer Eddie Jordan was Formula Atlantic champion in his native Ireland and a promising Formula Three driver before he set up Eddie Jordan Racing in 1981. The team came very close to taking the British Formula Three crown in 1983 with Martin Brundle as their driver, after a season-long battle with Ayrton Senna. One of his drivers did win this title, though: Johnny Herbert in 1987. Moving up into Formula 3000, the partnership continued in 1988, but Herbert was injured at Brands Hatch.

Jordan fancied himself as a talent spotter and, after Jean Alesi had been through a tough Formula 3000 campaign in 1988, Eddie offered him a drive in his team in 1989 and Alesi repaid him by winning the title in style.

Jordan then expanded from his Silverstone industrial unit to new premises across the road and formed Jordan Grand Prix for 1991, with Gary Anderson designing the 191, which turned out to be one of the cars of the year. Bertrand Gachot and Andrea de Cesaris were Jordan's drivers, but the season was disrupted when Gachot sprayed CS gas in a London taxi driver's face and ended up in jail. In his place, Jordan gave Michael Schumacher his debut at Spa. Sadly, Jordan couldn't keep hold of Schumacher, who was spirited away to Benetton before the next race.

Jordan had Ford HB engines in 1991 and the team was regularly embarrassing Benetton, the Ford works team. With no guarantee of works engines for 1992, Jordan did a deal with Yamaha, but the V12 was a disaster and the two companies ended the agreement after just one year.

In 1993, Jordan used Brian Hart's new V10 and signed Rubens Barrichello. The Brazilian showed himself to be at home in Formula One almost immediately, equalling Jordan's best fourth-place result. Ivan Capelli, Thierry Boutsen, Marco Apicella and Emanuele Naspetti all drove the second car, before Eddie Irvine did a tremendous job to score a point on his debut with Jordan in Japan.

For 1994, Jordan kept his pairing of promising young drivers, although Irvine had something of a bad-boy reputation, earning a three-race ban for an incident in Brazil. Barrichello finished sixth in the championship, earning the team's first podium in the Pacific GP at Aida and finishing fourth four times. He also scored the team's first pole in wet-dry conditions at Spa.

Jordan stood out behind F1's "big four" – Williams, Ferrari, Benetton and McLaren – and his company earned itself a three-year works engine deal with Peugeot. Promising in qualifying in 1995, Jordan should have profited, but reliability was poor.

Jordan signed Giancarlo Fisichella and Ralf Schumacher for 1997, with the Italian finishing second at Spa.

Damon Hill replaced Fisichella for 1998 and gave Jordan its first win, at Spa, helping the team to a career-best fourth in the Constructors' Cup. They advanced to third overall in 1999, with Heinz-Harald Frentzen winning at both Magny-Cours and Monza, but fell to sixth in 2000 as Frentzen and Jarno Trulli suffered from poor reliability. The arrival of works Honda engines didn't produce a leap forward in 2001, merely a marked tail-off in form. They continued to dwindle in 2002, with Fisichella managing just a trio of fifth places as they slipped from fifth overall to sixth.

Then came 2003, using Ford engines, with Fisichella boosting the increasingly underfinanced team with a shock victory in the accident-shortened Brazilian GP. Even this wasn't awarded until the following week because of confusion over the count-back rule. Such was Jordan's loss of form, that even with points now being awarded all the way back to eighth, Fisichella only scored once more, finishing seventh in the penultimate race.

Talks of take-over bids and financial salvation continued, and it came as little surprise that the team could only finish 2004 in ninth place.

Eddie sold out to Alex Shnaider and his Midland concern at the end of 2004 and stood down, although the team raced on as Jordan through 2005 before being renamed as Midland F1 for 2006 (see page 214). The high point of its final season in a yellow livery came when Tiago Monteiro and Narain Karthikean finished third and fourth respectively in the US GP – the race from which seven teams withdrew just before the start.

Eddie Jordan

A racer first and foremost, but now best known as a showman and an avid drummer who is always good for a juicy quote, Eddie was no fool behind the wheel, shining in Formula Three. However, he decided he wasn't quite the ticket and set up Eddie Jordan Racing in 1980. This became one of the teams to beat in British Formula Three and then International Formula 3000 and helped the careers of many top names in the process, including Martin Brundle, Johnny Herbert and Jean Alesi. However, Eddie's drive and ambition took him into Formula One in 1991 and he is proud that he not only established the team, that it finished that first season an astounding fifth overall and that he turned it into a winner, but also that it's still going today – albeit under a new name – while more illustrious teams have folded. A talent spotter of note, his was the team that gave Michael Schumacher his Formula One break. This was at Spa, the circuit where Damon Hill gave Jordan their maiden victory in 1998. As money became ever tighter, Eddie had to become less of a showman and more of a battler, before being lured out of Formula One by Alex Shnaider's millions.

LIGIER

FORMULA ONE RECORD

Country of origin: **France**   Date of foundation: **1971**
Active years in Formula One: **1976-2001 (from 1997 as Prost)**
Constructors' Cup victories: **none**

Ligier Makes its Mark: Jacques Laffite races to the marque's first win at the 1977 Swedish Grand Prix

Guy Ligier is a former butcher's assistant who was a top rugby player in his native France and made his fortune in the road construction industry. His company was responsible for building French autoroutes.

Always a motor racing enthusiast, Ligier drove Cooper-Maserati and Brabham-Repco Formula One cars in the mid-1960s and then teamed up with his long-standing friend, Jo Schlesser, to drive a pair of Formula Two McLarens in 1968.

Ligier was appalled by Schlesser's death in a fiery accident aboard the new air-cooled Honda in the French Grand Prix at Rouen-les-Essarts. He withdrew from driving and ran a GT programme with a car designed by Frenchman Michel Tetu. All Ligier cars would race with the "JS" model designation in Schlesser's memory.

Ligier achieved second place in the Le Mans 24 Hours in 1975, with

sponsorship from the Gitanes cigarette company, which was keen to move up to Formula One.

France was lacking a national Formula One entrant after the withdrawal of Matra Sports, so talented design engineer Gérard Ducarouge joined from Matra. The first Formula One Ligier, the JS5, arrived on the scene in 1976 and was a distinctive car. Ducarouge persuaded Matra to develop its V12 engine to give the Ligier project more of a Gallic flavour. Jacques Laffite, dominant in Formula Two, was taken on as driver.

The JS5 had a distinctive high airbox that earned the car its "teapot" nickname. Laffite qualified it on pole for the Italian Grand Prix. He won the Swedish Grand Prix in 1977 in the JS7, and this was the first win by a French driver in a French car with a French engine since the modern-day World Championship began in 1950.

The Swedish win was fortunate and it could never be said that the Ligiers looked set to dominate. All that changed in 1979, however, when the team switched to Ford engines and built the ground-effect JS11 with its distinctive aerodynamic kick-ups.

Ground-effect cars were something of a black art. The Lotus 79 had worked superbly in 1978, but the Ligier's JS11 was suddenly the class of the field in 1979. Nobody at Ligier really knew why, but Laffite won the two opening races of the season. Team-mate Patrick Depailler took another victory in Spain, then broke his legs in a hang-gliding accident and was replaced by Jacky Ickx. With the Williams taking over as the best car in the field, Ligier could not maintain its early form, though. Then, for 1980, Ligier signed Didier Pironi, who won in Belgium and drove one of the races of the year at Brands Hatch.

Talk of a tie-up between Ligier and Alain Prost in 1992 came to nothing and Guy Ligier sold the team to financier Cyril de Rouvre.

Ligier looked shaky at the start of 1994, but Benetton's Flavio Briatore bought it, and 1993 Formula 3000

champion Olivier Panis had a fine debut season in which he finished 15 of the 16 races. However, Ligier never managed to capitalize on a three-year deal for Renault's V10s, and changed to Mugens for 1995.

Panis did not drive as well in 1995, but peaked with a lucky second in the season's final race at Adelaide. Martin Brundle did a far better job, but had to share the other car with Japanese driver Aguri Suzuki.

Panis took a surprise win in the wet at Monaco in 1996, but it was all-change for 1997, with Alain Prost taking control and renaming the team eponymously. Panis broke his legs in Montreal, but the team was cheered when stand-in Jarno Trulli led in Austria. However, 1998 was a disaster and the team scored just one point through Trulli.

The Italian again saved the team in 1999, claiming a surprise second place at the Nurburgring. Trulli was replaced by Alesi for 2000, but Prost was at loggerheads with engine supplier Peugeot and the team went nowhere. The 2001 season was Prost's last as, despite points scored by Alesi, its finances were finally exhausted.

Guy Ligier

This four-square and feisty Frenchman had a mien not unlike Tom Walkinshaw: they were both straight-talking and not a little gruff in their pursuit of their aims. Orphaned as a child, Guy bought a bulldozer then entered the construction industry. Once he had retired from rugby, he spent his weekends racing motorbikes and then tried cars, racing in Formula Junior. It was during the week, however, that he built the foundations of his empire, earning a fortune from building motorways. This enabled Guy to race sports cars and even Formula One, with a privately entered Cooper in 1966, scoring his best result of sixth in the 1967 German Grand Prix once he had changed to a Brabham. In the early 1970s, Guy started a company to build sports racing cars before producing his first Formula One car in 1976. This was sponsored by French industry thanks in no small part to a long-time friendship with President Mitterand. Guy sold most of his shares in the team in 1992 and eventually ceased to be involved when it became Prost in 1997.

MARCH

FORMULA ONE RECORD

Country of origin: **Great Britain**   Date of foundation: **1969**
Active years in Formula One: **1970-77, 1981-1982, then 1987-1992**
Constructors' Cup victories: **none**

Japanese Backing: Ivan Capelli who came third in a March at the 1988 Belgian GP, Spa-Francorchamps

The idea of a group of enthusiasts banding together to set up a Formula One team at the same time as selling customer cars, employing the reigning World Champion and taking pole position at their first race seems ludicrous. That, however, is exactly what March did.

The four founding members were former FIA president Max Mosley, Alan Rees, Graham Coaker and Robin Herd. Herd was a highly regarded young designer who had worked at McLaren and designed the stillborn Cosworth four-wheel-drive car. They got together in 1969 and moved into a small factory in Bicester.

Jackie Stewart had just won the World Championship in a Matra. The French company was determined to use its own V12 engines in 1970, though, and neither Stewart nor Ken Tyrrell wanted that. Instead, they were faced with the prospect of finding an alternative chassis.

Enter March. Jumping at the opportunity to grab the reigning World Champion after attempts to lure Jochen Rindt from Lotus had failed, they ended up fielding a works team as well as selling customer cars in Formula One. There were four March 701s on the grid in South Africa.

They also built customer cars for Formula Two, Formula Three and Formula 5000. The works drivers were Chris Amon and Jo Siffert, with backing coming from STP, and a spare car provided for Mario Andretti in selected grands prix.

The 701s were built hurriedly, but that did not stop Amon from winning first time out at the Silverstone International Trophy. Stewart then won the Race of Champions at Brands Hatch and started from pole at Kyalami, with Amon alongside. Jack Brabham's BT33 won the race convincingly, however, while Amon retired and Stewart finished third.

Stewart won in Spain, but the heavy 701 was soon struggling, especially against the new Lotus 72. Stewart left at the end of the year to drive the first Tyrrell.

March signed promising young Swede Ronnie Peterson and Herd came up with the distinctive 711, featuring the famous "dinner plate" front wing. Peterson was highly competitive with the car and, although Stewart was the dominant force for Tyrrell, Ronnie placed second no fewer than six times and ended the season as championship runner-up.

Herd then embarked on the innovative 721X, which featured a gearbox mounted between the engine and the axle in the interests of improved handling. March took no notice when an inexperienced Niki Lauda told them the car was hopeless. Peterson needed considerably longer to come to the same conclusion. March then scrabbled together a replacement 721G, based on its Formula Two car. The "G" designation was an in-house joke, standing for *Guinness Book of Records*, a reflection on how quickly it was thrown together!

March lost Peterson to Lotus for 1973, and, always under both financial and customer time pressure, adopted the policy of fielding beefed-up Formula Two cars in grands prix, generally with pay drivers at the wheel. Although Stewart had won that second race in Spain in 1970, the first "works" victory did not come until 1975 in Austria, when Vittorio Brambilla, "The Monza Gorilla", won a rain-shortened race. He then threw both arms into the air and shunted on the slowing down lap.

Peterson returned in 1976 and won the Italian Grand Prix in the 761 before leaving for Tyrrell. March disappeared from the F1 scene at the end of the following season, returning a decade later with backing from the Japanese Leyton House concern of Akira Akagi.

Ivan Capelli showed flashes of brilliance with Adrian Newey's 881 and CG901 designs, coming second in Portugal in 1988 and second again in France in 1990, this time having led until just before the end of the grand prix. However, March disappeared again, this time for good, at the end of 1992, a year in which it had struggled against a severe shortage of money.

MASERATI

FORMULA ONE RECORD

Country of origin: **Italy**   Date of foundation: **early 1920s**
Active years in Formula One: **1950-1960**
Constructors' Cup victories: **none**

The Maserati brothers were involved in early Italian motor sport before setting up their first manufacturing business, making sparking plugs, before the First World War.

When hostilities ended, Alfieri Maserati raced his own special and then the brothers embarked on building a straight-eight engine for the Diatto Grand Prix car. They bought it and modified it to conform to the 1926 regulations, with Alfieri taking a class win in that year's Targa Florio.

Maserati then did some twin-engined experimentation before building the 8C-2500 and 2800 chassis. The 8CM was built to take the fight to rival Alfa Romeo's P3 and was the start of a rivalry between the two marques that would continue until after the Second World War. Baconin Borzacchini was an early Maserati faithful, and was joined in an 8CM by Tazio Nuvolari in 1933.

One of Alfa Romeo's greats was Giuseppe Campari, who had joined Alfa Romeo in his teens as a test driver. He was a great music and opera lover and was married to the singer Lina Cavalleri. At Monza, Campari said that he would retire at the end of the meeting. Sadly, he was involved in a tussle with Borzacchini's Maserati, during which they both hit a patch of oil and crashed fatally. Bugatti driver Count Czaikowski hit the same spot and he was also killed.

Maserati could not match the German challenge of the mid- and late 1930s and the company was taken over by Cavallieri Adolfo Orsi, with the Maserati brothers remaining as part of the firm. In the early 1940s, Maserati moved from Bologna to Modena.

The Maserati 4CLT was a competitive proposition just after WWII, if a little underpowered. The brothers then began work on a sports car before leaving to found the Osca marque. The engine from this car was the basis of a Formula Two car which became eligible for the World Championship when Formula One fell by the wayside in 1952-53. This was a time of Ferrari domination, but Fangio won for Maserati at the Italian Grand Prix.

Maserati looked good for the newly introduced 2.5-litre formula of 1954, but once again Mercedes was to launch a major onslaught and spoil the Italian party.

Fangio won the first two grands prix for Maserati in 1954, while he waited for the Mercedes programme to come on-stream. He was driving the 250F, which was destined to become the best-known Maserati ever.

The 250F proved a very popular car among privateers and was progressively improved, with various weight-saving exercises being carried out. With Mercedes withdrawing, Stirling Moss won two races for Maserati in 1956, while Fangio took his fourth world title for Ferrari. The next year, Fangio, disgruntled with the politicking at Ferrari, returned to Maserati. He won four races to collect his fifth title. He did it with one of the most memorable comeback drives in motor racing history, at the Nurburgring. With one of the hub nuts lost during his pit stop, Fangio rejoined the race about 45 seconds behind the Ferraris of Mike Hawthorn and Peter Collins. On the last lap, he passed both to win by just over three seconds. Afterwards, he said: "I don't ever want to have to drive like that again."

Maserati also gave Fangio his last grand prix, at Reims in 1958, although by that time the factory team was no more. Despite a successful 1957, Maserati was in big financial trouble and the 250F continued to race only in private hands until it became outmoded by mid-engined development.

Carving up the Field: Stirling Moss powerslides in Maserati's most successful car, the 250F, at the Monaco Grand Prix, 1956, a race that he won

MERCEDES

FORMULA ONE RECORD

Country of origin: **Germany**   Date of foundation: **1906**
Active years in Formula One: **1954-1955**
Constructors' Cup victories: **none**

Casting a Large Shadow: Alfred Neubauer times Fangio on his way to victory in Argentina, 1955

Mercedes has played a significant part in grand prix history, albeit in spectacular bursts. The name dates back to the first grand prix of 1906, but its greatest onslaught came in the early 1930s after Adolf Hitler had risen to power. He wanted to use motor sport to prove the superiority of German engineering and had his transport minister grant a fund for those building grand prix cars, to be shared between Mercedes and Auto Union.

In 1934, both Mercedes and Auto Union missed Monaco so that their cars could make a patriotic debut at Avus in front of 200,000 people, including Hitler. Mercedes suffered engine problems and withdrew rather than risk losing to Alfa Romeo. This was overcome at the Nurburgring as Manfred von Brauchitsch and Luigi Fagioli led and the Italian was quicker, but a German was supposed to win

and team manager Alfred Neubauer signalled Fagioli to slow, after which Fagioli hounded von Brauchitsch until he decided to pull off and let Hans Stuck finish second for Auto Union.

Alfa Romeo then scored a one-two-three in the French Grand Prix before the German teams started a run of victories. Mercedes had Fagioli for 1935, and Achille Varzi signed for Auto Union, where he refused to be partnered by Tazio Nuvolari, who was the top driver of the age. Ironically, the most remembered feature of 1935 is Nuvolari's fantastic drive in the German Grand Prix with an outdated Alfa Romeo P3. After applying relentless pressure, Nuvolari won in front of 300,000 silent Germans as von Brauchitsch's Mercedes blew a tyre on the last lap.

Caracciola and Mercedes suffered at the hands of Auto Union and Bernd Rosemeyer in 1936, but came back in

1937 with a new racing department under Rudi Uhlenhaut and the superb W125. Caracciola took his second European championship.

There was a 3-litre formula for 1938 and Mercedes dominated until the outbreak of World War Two, beaten only a couple of times by Auto Union's Type D, now in the hands of Nuvolari.

Mercedes didn't come back into grand prix racing until 1954, with its W196, which could be run in either open-wheeler or streamlined format. It dominated, with Juan Manuel Fangio winning the French, German, Swiss and Italian Grands Prix.

The domination continued in 1955, when Fangio was joined by Stirling Moss and claimed his third world title. Moss, however, scored an emotional win in the British Grand Prix, which second-placed Fangio insisted was won on merit. The year also contained the Le Mans tragedy: at least 80 spectators and Pierre Levegh died when his Mercedes went into the crowd. Mercedes withdrew at the end of the year and never returned as a constructor.

After supplying engines to Sauber in 1993 and 1994, though, Mercedes signed a multi-year engine supply

deal with McLaren, beginning in 1995. David Coulthard produced Mercedes first "second generation" win in the opening race of 1997, but it was in 1998 that Mercedes took off as Mika Hakkinen clinched the drivers' title and Coulthard helped him guide McLaren-Mercedes to the constructors' title. Hakkinen claimed a second drivers' title in 1999. However, Ferrari edged ahead in the constructors' rankings and stayed ahead until the end of 2004.

Renault edged McLaren in 2005 before McLaren slipped to third in 2006. Then, just as McLaren hit top form in 2007, the team was charged with espionage and its points annulled in a year that yielded eight wins. Lewis Hamilton took the drivers' title for McLaren in 2008 but not, alas for Mercedes, the drivers' title. Then, with Honda having quit, Mercedes offered engines to the team it begat - Brawn GP - for 2009, as well as to Force India. And this led to eight wins and Mercedes' share of a constructors' title for the first time since 1998.

Inspired by this, Mercedes then bought out Brawn and turned it into Mercedes GP for 2010.

VIP

Alfred Neubauer

Few characters have ever cast such a large shadow down a pitlane. Having joined Austro-Daimler in 1922, Alfred raced in that year's Targa Florio. He then tried the Italian Grand Prix in 1924 before stepping back at the end of the 1925 season to manage the Daimler competition department. With the merger of Daimler and Benz in 1926, which later became Mercedes-Benz, he started a relationship that would last until Mercedes withdrew from motor sport 30 years later. His first success was the SSK tourer, with Rudolf Caracciola his standard-bearer. The team's first pukka grand prix car came in 1934 and the people in the pitlane noticed how Alfred ran the show with military precision, his hat always in place, a raincoat his regular uniform over his bulky form, a stopwatch in his hand, but with a smile seldom on his face. The Second World War interrupted the show, but it was firing on all cylinders again – until Mercedes scrapped all motor sport involvement following the Le Mans disaster of 1955.

PENSKE

FORMULA ONE RECORD

Country of origin: **United States**   Date of foundation: **1966**
Active years in Formula One: **1974-1976**
Constructors' Cup victories: **none**

Roger Penske runs what many experts acknowledge as the best racing team in the world. Interestingly, however, his business interests in the United States have caused him to concentrate on domestic racing programmes since his foray into the Formula One world in the mid-1970s.

Penske has won the Indianapolis 500 a record nine times. A measure of the dominance that he has achieved in North America was most graphically illustrated in 1994, when his Marlboro-backed cars finished one-two-three in the IndyCar World Series.

Al Unser Jr took the title, admirably backed up by two-time World Champion Emerson Fittipaldi and young Canadian Paul Tracy, who took the opportunity to test a Benetton Formula One car at the end of that 1994 season.

Penske is entirely self-made, starting off as a tin salesman and building the Penske Corporation into a truly huge conglomerate. He has a seat on the board of Philip Morris, whose Marlboro brand backs his IndyCar team, and he has been involved with the Mercedes motor sport programme. Mercedes is a major stakeholder in Penske's successful Detroit Diesel company and Roger himself owns a 25 per cent share of Ilmor Engineering, which prepares the Mercedes engines for McLaren.

Penske was a promising driver in his own right, but he hung up his helmet at the age of 28 to concentrate on business. Starting his own team, he struck up a hugely successful partnership with experienced American ace Mark Donohue. Penske rented a McLaren M19 in 1971 and Donohue drove it to third place in the wet Canadian Grand Prix. Penske then started to think about a full grand prix effort. He bought a factory at Poole, in Dorset, and recruited Geoff Ferris, who had learned his trade with Ron Tauranac at Brabham, to design him a car.

The first car appeared in late 1974, with the testing done by Donohue, who had retired. The project sparked his enthusiasm, however, and Mark agreed to commit to a full Grand Prix programme with Penske in 1975.

With First National City Bank support and a Cosworth engine, Penske hardly set the world on fire and, midway through the season, replaced the PC1 with a March 751. In practice at the Osterreichring, Donohue suffered a deflating tyre and flew off the road, hitting television station scaffolding. Although at first he appeared to have escaped with a headache, Donohue fell into a coma and subsequently died from his injuries.

Penske signed John Watson and, with Ferris's elegant new PC4, the combination started to run at the front of the field in 1976. By mid-season, Watson was challenging for a win that, somewhat ironically, came at Osterreichring exactly a year after Donohue's death there.

Formula One was enjoying its epic Hunt versus Lauda season and Watson's sudden intrusion was something that Hunt could have done without, as the Austrian lay in a Mannheim hospital trying to recover from his Nurburgring accident. Watson also battled hard with Hunt's McLaren at Zandvoort before retiring.

At the end of 1976, First National City Bank defected to Tyrrell, attracted by the guaranteed exposure generated by the Tyrrell six-wheeler. Penske decided to halt his Formula One campaign and concentrate on the IndyCar scene instead.

Despite the occasional rumour, Penske has never returned to Formula One. In 1994, however, his closeness to Mercedes, through both business and personal friendships, convinced many that he would play an active role in the McLaren-Mercedes link. This, however, has yet to happen.

In Your Mirrors: James Hunt knows that he can't put a foot wrong as he holds off John Watson's Penske for the lead of the Dutch Grand Prix in 1976

PORSCHE

FORMULA ONE RECORD

Country of origin: **Germany**   Date of foundation: **1948**
Active years in Formula One: **1957-1964**
Constructors' Cup victories: **none**

If you ask anyone to think of Porsche, even a dyed-in-the-wool fanatic thinks of sports car racing and the German marque's outstanding successes over the past five decades. What most Formula One fans forget, though, is that Porsche won in Formula One once, too.

Porsche's first involvement with racing came after the Second World War when the company was asked to design a grand prix car for Piero Dusio and Piero Taruffi. This was called the Cistalia Type 360 and was way ahead of its time with its 1.5-litre flat-12 engine mounted behind the driver, independent suspension and four-wheel drive. Sadly, the car proved too complex and was all but stillborn in 1948. Luckily, Porsche also penned a simpler car for Cistalia, the Giacosa, and this sold in sufficient numbers for a one-make series.

Porsche's 356 sports car was the company's bread and butter and it was not long before the car appeared on the track, starting with the Le Mans 24 Hours in 1951. Success soon followed, spawning a line of cars that are still winning races at the start of the 21st century.

A modified Porsche Spyder RSK was entered in Formula Two in 1957 by Edgar Barth, winning first time out at the Nurburgring. Suitably encouraged, Jean Behra had one converted to "central seat" specification and won a Formula Two race at Reims. This spurred Porsche to build a proper single-seater and it was given its debut at Monaco in 1959 by Wolfgang von Trips. Further forays followed with Barth and Hans Herrmann driving in 1960, while Stirling Moss helped Porsche win the Formula Two title. It had become clear, however, that a proper Formula One car would be needed.

The planned eight-cylinder car was not ready for the start of the 1961 season, so Jo Bonnier and Dan Gurney struggled with the four-cylinder 787 model and this was, like everything else, left in the wake of the "shark-nose" Ferraris. Despite this, Gurney was pipped by just 0.1s in the French Grand Prix by Giancarlo Baghetti's Ferrari. He also finished second in the Italian and United States Grands Prix to end the year equal third with Moss, with Porsche ranking third in the Constructors' Cup.

Porsche's eight-cylinder engine made its debut in the first round of 1962 and Gurney ran third until retiring. However, the Porsche 804 was an improvement and he scored his first (and Porsche's only) win in the French Grand Prix at Rouen. He and Bonnier then finished first and second in the non-championship Solitude Grand Prix before Gurney added a third place in the German Grand Prix to finish fifth overall, with Porsche also fifth in the Constructors' Cup. Feeling that to achieve more would cost too much, Porsche quit F1.

Considering sports cars more pertinent to its road car business, Porsche set about winning the Le Mans 24 Hours, which it did for the first time in 1970 when Herrmann shared the winning 917K with Richard Attwood and Porsche has done so more than a dozen times since, being the leading marque in GT racing through to today.

Porsche became involved with Formula One again in the 1980s when one of its engines was badged as a TAG turbo in deference to the corporation that funded it and fitted it in the back of the McLarens. It hit the tracks late in 1983, but it was in 1984 that it made its impact as Niki Lauda and Alain Prost ended the year first and second overall, having scored 12 wins between them.

Prost then won the 1985 and 1986 titles, with the McLaren-TAG combo taking the 1985 constructors' honours. This relationship lasted through 1987, when the Honda used by Williams proved stronger and McLaren dropped Porsche.

Porsche returned in 1991, with Footwork campaigning a Porsche V12. Unfortunately, it was overweight and the team failed to score a point before dropping it to run a Ford engine.

Sitting Tall: Dan Gurney appears to tower over his Porsche 804 in the 1962 German Grand Prix at the Nurburgring, a race in which he finished third

SHADOW

FORMULA ONE RECORD

Country of origin: **United States**   Date of foundation: **1968**
Active years in Formula One: **1973-1980**
Constructors' Cup victories: **none**

Shadow boss Don Nichols was first active on the sports car scene in the United States. Jackie Oliver drove a Shadow CanAm car in 1971 and Nichols persuaded Universal Oil Products (UOP) to back the team.

Oliver regularly ran at the front of the field with the black-painted cars in 1972, and Shadow announced its plans to go to F1 the following year.

Nichols recruited former BRM designer Tony Southgate, with Oliver and veteran American sports car ace George Follmer to drive. Kit cars were supplied to Graham Hill's newly established team.

Nichols set up a British base for his team in Northampton after Southgate had built the first car in the garage of his Lincolnshire home. The Cosworth-powered DN1 was not spectacular, but it ran in the top half of the field regularly.

Oliver drove only the CanAm cars in 1974, winning the championship against thin opposition, while rapid Frenchman Jean-Pierre Jarier and American Peter Revson were drafted into the F1 team. Things looked promising until Revson was killed in a pre-season testing accident at Kyalami. Brian Redman raced briefly, before handing over to Welsh hot-shoe Tom Pryce.

As young drivers fought to establish themselves in the post-Stewart era, it was evident that Shadow had two of the quickest, even if reliability was not all that it might have been.

Pryce won the Race of Champions for Shadow at the beginning of 1975 and Jarier sometimes got very close to

the qualifying pace of Lauda's dominant Ferrari. Still, solid results did not come and the team struggled when UOP withdrew its support at the end of the year. Oliver had now hung up his helmet and was the team's main sponsorship sourcer. The DN5 had become a little long in the tooth, but Southgate's new DN8 looked highly promising. The only problem was that Southgate himself had been lured to Lotus temporarily before returning to Shadow.

Main backing was now coming from Tabatip cigarillos, but Italian financier Franco Ambrosio also became involved until he was jailed on charges of financial irregularity.

Shadow started 1977 with Pryce and Italian Renzo Zorzi, who had sprung a surprise by winning the Monaco Formula Three race in 1976. At Kyalami, though, tragedy struck. Zorzi stopped on the far side of the main straight, just after a hump in the track. There was no problem and he was getting himself out – and trying to extricate his helmet oxygen supply – when a young marshal ran across the track to stand by in case of fire. Pryce crested the brow, killed the marshal instantly and died when he was hit in the face by the fire extinguisher.

Alan Jones replaced Pryce and brought a partial sweetener to a sad year with the team's one and only win.

Niki Lauda was on the way to regaining his title following his accident at the Nurburgring the previous year, when the circus arrived at his home Osterreichring track. In a wet-dry race, Jones outdrove the Austrian and beat the Ferrari into second place.

Financial problems led to a team split in 1977, with Oliver, Alan Rees and Southgate heading off to form their own Arrows set-up. The Arrows A1, looked very similar to Southgate's unfinished drawings for the Shadow DN9. Nichols got a decision in his favour from the High Court which led to Arrows having to build a new car. Meanwhile, John Baldwin finished the DN9 and Shadow continued with Hans Stuck and Clay Regazzoni.

The team ran for the 1979 and 1980 seasons, but the team finally collapsed after failing to qualify for the French Grand Prix in 1980.

Future Champion: Alan Jones takes his maiden grand prix win at the Osterreichring, 1977. This was to be Shadow's only victory before it folded in 1980

STEWART

FORMULA ONE RECORD

Country of origin: **Great Britain**   Date of foundation: **1987**
Active years in Formula One: **1997-1999**
Constructors' Cup victories: **none**

Jackie Stewart and Sir Jack Brabham won three Formula One World Championships apiece. And they both formed their own grand prix teams. Here, though, the similarity between the Scot and the Australian ends. For "Black Jack" started his own team when he was still a racer, indeed clinching his final crown in one of his own cars, back in 1966. In contrast, Jackie waited after he hung up his helmet at the end of 1973 until 1997 to take the plunge, and Formula One had come a long, long way in the interim. Stewart, however, was ready for this, as he had spent the intervening years as a successful businessman.

The main tenet in Stewart's life is that if you do something, you do it properly. And no one is more meticulous than Jackie Stewart. Indeed, he was effectively the first professional Formula One driver. Not because he was the first to be paid for his services, but because he was the very first to embrace the practices and principals that we still regard today as being truly "professional".

It is not entirely correct to say that Stewart Grand Prix had been formed from scratch, though, for Jackie and his elder son Paul had been running Paul Stewart Racing since 1987, moving up very successfully through the ranks from Formula Ford via Formula Three and Formula 3000, fielding the likes of David Coulthard, Gil de Ferran and Jan Magnussen.

For the team's maiden season, it had a tidy chassis penned by former Footwork designer Alan Jenkins, power from Ford's best V10 engine, promisingly competitive tyres from Bridgestone and fine drivers in Rubens Barrichello and Magnussen. However, these ingredients did not come together as the team Stewart would have wished.

High points included Barrichello finding a new lease of life after rather losing the plot at Jordan and stunning everyone by qualifying fifth in Argentina. The flip-side of this was that Magnussen seemed to suffer all of the team's misfortune.

The team was given hope by the way that its Bridgestones appeared to have an advantage over the teams racing on Goodyears whenever it was wet. And so it proved in Monaco, when Barrichello drove an inspired race to not only finish for the first time that year, but to finish second. The wet track became wetter still as the Stewarts cried their eyes out.

Success in Formula One is not a one-year project, though, and the Stewarts were well aware of this. One only has to compare their approach to entering the big time with Lola's flawed bid – which also kicked off at the 1997 Australian Grand Prix – to see that you have to arrive with everything in place.

To start beating the established teams is another matter altogether, though, and the early races of 1998 showed that the corner had yet to be turned. Anxious for some progress, Magnussen was shown the door after scoring a point for the first time, in Canada. Barrichello was fifth that day, just as he had been in Spain. Replacement Jos Verstappen failed to do any better and it became clear that much work would have to be done to push the team up the grid in 1999, with Johnny Herbert being signed in place of Verstappen for this purpose.

Progress was made through 1999, with Barrichello claiming third place in the San Marino Grand Prix. The Brazilian then claimed pole in the wet at Magny-Cours, but only by dint of setting a quick time before the rain came down harder, then raced to third in the wet-dry race. However, the team's day of days came at the Nurburgring, when Herbert and Barrichello read the changing conditions and kept out of trouble to be first and third, enabling the team to edge past Williams to rank fourth overall.

The team was then sold to Ford and rebranded as Jaguar for 2000.

Silver-Plated Success: Johnny Herbert (left) celebrates the team's only grand prix victory along with Jackie Stewart and team-mate Rubens Barrichello

SURTEES

FORMULA ONE RECORD

Country of origin: **Great Britain**   Date of foundation: **1966**
Active years in Formula One: **1970-1978**
Constructors' Cup victories: **none**

John Surtees is the only man to have won World Championships on both two wheels and four. Surtees had his first experience of four wheels in one of Ken Tyrrell's Formula Two Coopers before joining Ferrari in 1963. He took a close World Championship for the Scuderia in 1964, but left suddenly in the middle of 1966.

Surtees did not restrict his racing to Formula One and was an active sports car driver for Ferrari as well, setting up his own small team in association with Lola's Eric Broadley.

Surtees had a huge accident in a Lola CanAm car at Mosport in 1965 when suspension failure pitched him off the track. He was seriously injured, but fought back to fitness and broke the lap record at the Ferrari test track when he returned to the team.

Ferrari team boss Eugenio Dragoni was not convinced about his recovery, however, and was also a mentor of Ferrari's second driver, Lorenzo Bandini, whom Surtees usually shaded without much ado. Despite being favourite to take the championship and winning at Spa-Francorchamps in the teeming rain, Surtees and Dragoni had one run-in too many and John left immediately to join the Cooper-Maserati team.

For the following two seasons, Surtees drove for Honda and then had a year with BRM before deciding to build his own car for 1970.

The first Surtees Grand Prix car made its debut in the British Grand Prix at Brands Hatch, where Surtees ran seventh before retiring. He scored his first points as a Formula One constructor with the TS7 when he finished fifth in the Canadian Grand Prix. His first win came in the non-championship Oulton Park Gold Cup.

The TS9 followed for 1971, with Rolf Stommelen joining Surtees in his last full season as a driver. For 1972, Surtees concentrated on running his team for motorcycle-racing buddy Mike Hailwood and Tim Schenken. Hailwood had made a promising debut for the team the previous year, and shone when he finished second in the Italian Grand Prix.

Surtees' last grand prix was at Monza in 1972 when he debuted the new TS14. Hailwood led the Race of Champions at Brands Hatch with the car in 1973 until he crashed heavily after a mechanical failure. He was then joined by the promising Brazilian driver, Carlos Pace, who finished on the podium in Austria.

The 1974 season was grim. Jochen Mass and Pace started the year, but Carlos soon left and later in the year Derek Bell and Jean-Pierre Jabouille drove. The team was operating on a shoestring and both cars failed to qualify at Monza. Austrian Helmut Koinigg drove a TS16 in the Canadian Grand Prix, finishing ninth, but was killed in a slow-speed accident next time out at Watkins Glen.

John Watson drove for Team Surtees in 1975 before joining Penske. Surtees then did a deal leading to what his cars were probably most famous for: racing in Durex livery. Alan Jones was the first driver and, ironically, the TS19 proved much more competitive than most of the chassis that had gone before. It led to a very public withdrawal of BBC television's cameras from the pre-season non-championship races in Britain.

The TS19s did not actually achieve much in the form of hard results, though, and Vittorio Brambilla was driving one when he was injured in the multiple accident at the start of the 1978 Italian Grand Prix.

René Arnoux looked the most promising driver to try the new TS20 and, with ground-effects technology taking over, Surtees planned the TS21 with that in mind for 1979. Unfortunately, however, sponsors would not commit to the team and so Surtees decided to bring down the curtain on his team's Formula One participation.

On the Pace: talented Brazilian Carlos Pace showed his colours with Surtees. He's pictured at Monaco in 1973, but quit the team midway through 1974

WOLF

FORMULA ONE RECORD

Country of origin: **Great Britain**   Date of foundation: **1975**
Active years in Formula One: **1977-1979**
Constructors' Cup victories: **none**

Walter Wolf was an Austrian who made his fortune in the oil business in Canada. A lifelong racing enthusiast, he used his new-found wealth to forge an involvement in the sport.

Wolf first appeared on the Formula One scene in 1975 and was courted by Frank Williams who, at that time, was still struggling to make an impression on the sport.

Wolf and Williams struck a deal for 1976, but it soon became apparent that Wolf was an autocrat who did not wish to adopt a mere supporting role. The Hesketh team was winding down, so Wolf took on designer Harvey Postlethwaite's very promising 308C chassis and the man himself.

The 1976 season was disastrous. Jacky Ickx was the driver, but he was not impressed with the car and did not gel with Postlethwaite. Williams did not like working for anyone else and decided to cut his links and go his own way with designer Patrick Head.

Wolf had a major reorganization for 1977. He recruited former Lotus team manager Peter Warr to run his team and signed Jody Scheckter from Tyrrell. Postlethwaite's neat Wolf WR1 chassis looked promising and Scheckter took advantage of some good fortune to win on the car's debut in Argentina.

Good luck he may have had, but the WR1 was a good car and the team was well drilled. Scheckter led a great tussle involving Niki Lauda's Ferrari and Mario Andretti's Lotus in Long Beach, only losing out in the closing stages when a tyre went down.

Lauda had won in Monte Carlo the previous two seasons, but Scheckter went to the Principality, where he lived, and outdrove the Ferrari to claim the team's second win.

Scheckter remained in contention for the drivers' title throughout the year, but the crown eventually went to a consistent Lauda. Andretti's

Pack Animal: Walter Wolf waits for Jody Scheckter after he won the Argentinian GP for Wolf, 1977

Lotus was the class of the field, but the American did not have the best of reliability. Scheckter came good at Mosport Park, though, to score an emotional "home" triumph for his team boss.

The form shown by Andretti and Lotus had served a warning that a ground-effects car would be a pre-requisite for success in 1978, and so it proved. The Lotus 79s of Andretti and Ronnie Peterson proved unbeatable. At Wolf, Postlethwaite came up with the WR5, but the team could not add to its victory tally, with a pair of second place finishes in Germany and Canada, being their best results.

Scheckter was becoming disgruntled and he quickly accepted an offer to join Ferrari – where he went on to win the championship the following season. Wolf took on James Hunt, who was also disgruntled with McLaren's inability to crack the ground-effect concept.

On paper, this looked good. Hunt and Postlethwaite, of course, went back to Hesketh's glory days and the new WR7 looked as though it should work. Just like the successful Ligier JS11, it had distinctive aerodynamic kick-ups ahead of the rear wheels and a futuristic shape.

It was a rush to get the car ready in time, however, and the results did not come. Hunt was always aware of his profession's inherent dangers and, with just one finish behind him, he did not want to put his life on the line for a sixth or seventh place. He had the trappings of wealth and announced his sudden retirement mid-season. Wolf then took on the aggressive young Keke Rosberg, but even the exuberant Finn could do little with the recalcitrant car.

A man used to success, Walter Wolf did not take kindly to being an also-ran and folded his team at the end of its fourth season.

VIP

Walter Wolf

Born in Austria, Walter emigrated to Canada at the age of 18 in 1957 with, he says, seven dollars in his pocket. Starting as a labourer on a building site, he rose up the chain of command and then took loans to buy the company when it was about to fold. That was in 1965, and he became a rich man when Montreal attracted the Expo for 1968 and a great deal of construction work was undertaken. He then sold his firm and bought a company working in oil drilling and broking. Walter soon became a multi-millionaire and this enabled him to pursue his childhood love of motor racing, with his impatience for success embodied by the way in which his unsuccessful alliance with Frank Williams, in 1976, led him to flex his chequebook and buy Williams out. Looking to capitalize on the instant success of his Formula One team in 1977, Wolf branched out and ran a two-car team in Formula Three in 1978, giving designer Giampaolo Dallara his break in the category.

CONSTRUCTORS' RECORDS

Ferrari are currently most successful constructor but a host of teams have reigned in the past.

WORLD CHAMPIONS

1958	Vanwall
1959	Cooper-Climax
1960	Cooper-Climax
1961	Ferrari
1962	BRM
1963	Lotus-Climax
1964	Ferrari
1965	Lotus-Climax
1966	Brabham-Repco
1967	Brabham-Repco
1968	Lotus-Ford DFV
1969	Matra-Ford DFV
1970	Lotus-Ford DFV
1971	Tyrrell-Ford DFV
1972	Lotus-Ford DFV
1973	Lotus-Ford DFV
1974	McLaren-Ford DFV
1975	Ferrari
1976	Ferrari
1977	Ferrari
1978	Lotus-Ford DFV
1979	Ferrari
1980	Williams-Ford DFV
1981	Williams-Ford DFV
1982	Ferrari
1983	Ferrari
1984	McLaren-TAG
1985	McLaren-TAG
1986	Williams-Honda
1987	Williams-Honda
1988	McLaren-Honda
1989	McLaren-Honda
1990	McLaren-Honda
1991	McLaren-Honda
1992	Williams-Renault
1993	Williams-Renault
1994	Williams-Renault
1995	Benetton-Renault
1996	Williams-Renault
1997	Williams-Renault
1998	McLaren-Mercedes
1999	Ferrari
2000	Ferrari
2001	Ferrari
2002	Ferrari
2003	Ferrari
2004	Ferrari
2005	Renault
2006	Renault
2007	Ferrari
2008	Ferrari
2009	Brawn-Mercedes

MOST GRANDS PRIX STARTS

793	Ferrari
666	McLaren
585	Williams
490	Lotus
418	Tyrrell
411	Toro Rosso (formerly Minardi)
409	Prost (formerly Ligier)
394	Brabham
383	Arrows
320	Force India (formerly Jordan)
317	Benetton
287	BMW Sauber
263	Renault
230	March
220	Red Bull (formerly Jaguar)

MOST GRANDS PRIX WINS

210	Ferrari
164	McLaren
113	Williams
79	Lotus
35	Brabham
	Renault
27	Benetton
23	Tyrrell
17	BRM
16	Cooper
11	Brawn (formerly Honda)
10	Alfa Romeo
9	Ligier
	Maserati
	Matra
	Mercedes
	Vanwall
6	Red Bull
4	Jordan
3	March
	Wolf
1	BMW Sauber
	Eagle
	Hesketh
	Penske
	Porsche
	Toro Rosso
	Shadow
	Stewart

MOST WINS IN ONE SEASON

Wins	Constructor	Year
15	Ferrari	2002
	Ferrari	2005
	McLaren	1988
12	McLaren	1984
	Williams	1996
11	Benetton	1995
10	Ferrari	2000
	McLaren	1989
	McLaren	2005
	Williams	1992
	Williams	1993
9	Ferrari	2001
	Ferrari	2006
	McLaren	1998
	Williams	1986
	Williams	1987
8	Benetton	1994
	Brawn	2009
	Ferrari	2003
	Ferrari	2007
	Ferrari	2008
	Lotus	1978
	McLaren	1991
	McLaren	2007
	Renault	2005
	Renault	2006
	Williams	1997
7	Ferrari	1952
	Ferrari	1953
	Lotus	1963
	Lotus	1973
	McLaren	1999
	McLaren	2000
	Tyrrell	1971
	Williams	1991
	Williams	1994

MOST FASTEST LAPS

218	Ferrari
137	McLaren
130	Williams
71	Lotus
40	Brabham
35	Benetton
29	Renault
20	Tyrrell
15	BRM
	Maserati
14	Alfa Romeo
13	Cooper
12	Matra
9	Mercedes
	Prost (formerly Ligier)
7	March
6	Red Bull (formerly Jaguar)
	Vanwall
4	Brawn

MOST POLE POSITIONS

203	Ferrari
145	McLaren
125	Williams
107	Lotus
51	Renault
39	Brabham
16	Benetton
14	Tyrrell
12	Alfa Romeo
11	BRM
	Cooper
10	Maserati
9	Brawn (formerly Honda/BAR)
	Prost (formerly Ligier)
8	Mercedes
7	Vanwall
6	Red Bull (formerly Jaguar)
5	March
4	Matra
3	Force India (formerly Jordan)
	Shadow
	Toyota
2	Lancia
1	BMW Sauber
	Toro Rosso

15	McLaren	1988
	McLaren	1989
	Williams	1992
	Williams	1993
13	Ferrari	2008
12	Ferrari	2004
	Lotus	1978
	McLaren	1990
	McLaren	1998
	Williams	1987
	Williams	1995
	Williams	1996
11	Ferrari	2001
	Ferrari	2007
	McLaren	1999
	Williams	1997
10	Ferrari	1974
	Ferrari	2000
	Ferrari	2002
	Lotus	1973
	McLaren	1991
	Renault	1982
9	Brabham	1984
	Ferrari	1975

MOST POINTS

4091.5	Ferrari
3372.5	McLaren
2606	Williams
1352	Lotus
1082	Renault
877.5	Benetton
854	Brabham
617	Tyrrell
504	BMW Sauber
439	BRM
424	Prost (formerly Ligier)
344.5	Red Bull (formerly Jaguar)
333	Cooper
326	Brawn (formerly Honda)
301	Force India (formerly Jordan)
278.5	Toyota
171.5	March
167	Arrows
155	Matra
94	Toro Rosso (formerly Minardi)
79	Wolf

Just Williams: Alan Jones was the driver who put Williams on the map in 1980 and the team loved success so much that it spent the 1980s and then the mid-1990s as the team to beat, notching up nine constructors' titles

PART 4:
FAMOUS CIRCUITS

If a driver can have talent, a car mechanical superiority and a team great organization, can a circuit have class? You bet . . . Formula One grands prix have been held the world over, moving from circuit to circuit, yet some stand out as the greats...

Try Spa-Francorchamps, Monza, the Nurburgring and Silverstone for starters. Then there's that perennial classic, Monaco, with its narrow streets and beautiful people. These circuits stand out from the pack, although new circuits such as Sepang in Malaysia and Yas Marina in the United Arab Emirates offer something a little different.

Everyone has their favourite driver and some have their favourite team. However, almost to a person, Formula One fans have a favourite circuit. The mighty Spa-Francorchamps is

considered the ultimate by many; others opt for the Silverstone layout of the 1970s; while some swear by the Osterreichring or Monaco. So, what is the difference? A very great deal.

When anyone builds a circuit from scratch in the 21st century, you will most likely be able to predict how the corners will be laid out and where the main straight will be located. In this age of circuit safety circuits are now designed to be able to contain the cars and their drivers.

It was not always so. When racing began a century ago, public roads

were used. Permanent circuits did not come into existence until public pressure forced racing off the open road. Perhaps the greatest of purpose-built tracks was that instigated by Hitler just before the Second World War: the Nurburgring. Over 14 miles long, it twisted through the Eifel forest. However, it was thought too dangerous by the mid-1970s and came close to claiming the life of Niki Lauda. This was when the emasculation process began, and now, of the old tracks, only the Monaco street race remains.

THE CIRCUITS

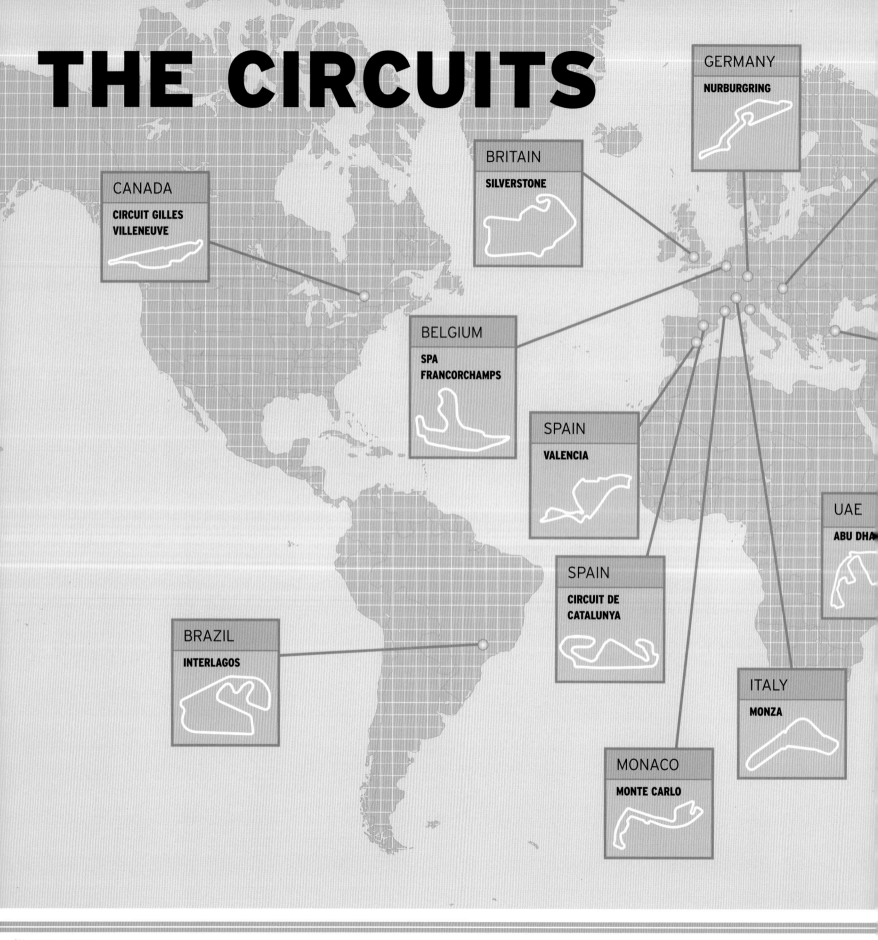

GERMANY
NURBURGRING

BRITAIN
SILVERSTONE

CANADA
CIRCUIT GILLES VILLENEUVE

BELGIUM
SPA FRANCORCHAMPS

SPAIN
VALENCIA

UAE
ABU DHA

SPAIN
CIRCUIT DE CATALUNYA

BRAZIL
INTERLAGOS

ITALY
MONZA

MONACO
MONTE CARLO

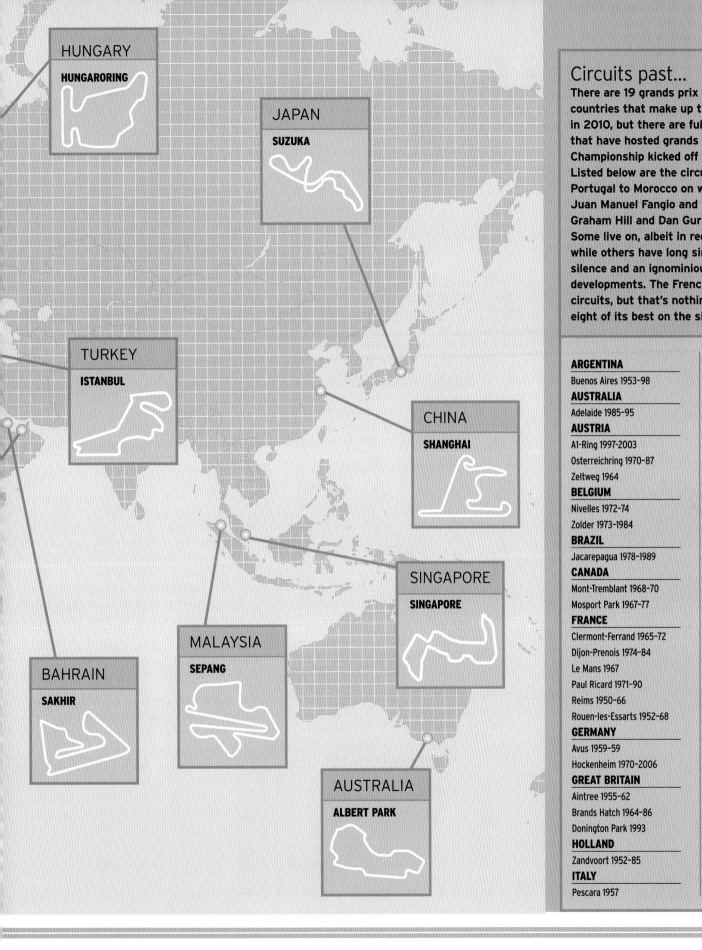

HUNGARY

HUNGARORING

JAPAN

SUZUKA

TURKEY

ISTANBUL

CHINA

SHANGHAI

SINGAPORE

SINGAPORE

MALAYSIA

SEPANG

BAHRAIN

SAKHIR

AUSTRALIA

ALBERT PARK

Circuits past...

There are 19 grands prix divided between 18 countries that make up the World Championship in 2010, but there are fully 46 other circuits that have hosted grands prix since the World Championship kicked off at Silverstone in 1950. Listed below are the circuits from Mexico to Portugal to Morocco on which the greats from Juan Manuel Fangio and Stirling Moss to Graham Hill and Dan Gurney weaved their magic. Some live on, albeit in reduced circumstances, while others have long since been bulldozed into silence and an ignominious end beneath housing developments. The French have six retired circuits, but that's nothing next to the USA with eight of its best on the sidelines.

ARGENTINA
Buenos Aires 1953-98
AUSTRALIA
Adelaide 1985-95
AUSTRIA
A1-Ring 1997-2003
Osterreichring 1970-87
Zeltweg 1964
BELGIUM
Nivelles 1972-74
Zolder 1973-1984
BRAZIL
Jacarepagua 1978-1989
CANADA
Mont-Tremblant 1968-70
Mosport Park 1967-77
FRANCE
Clermont-Ferrand 1965-72
Dijon-Prenois 1974-84
Le Mans 1967
Paul Ricard 1971-90
Reims 1950-66
Rouen-les-Essarts 1952-68
GERMANY
Avus 1959-59
Hockenheim 1970-2006
GREAT BRITAIN
Aintree 1955-62
Brands Hatch 1964-86
Donington Park 1993
HOLLAND
Zandvoort 1952-85
ITALY
Pescara 1957

JAPAN
Aida 1994-95
Suzuka 1987-2006
MEXICO
Mexico City 1963-92
MOROCCO
Ain-Diab 1958
PORTUGAL
Estoril 1984-96
Monsanto 1959
Porto 1958-60
SOUTH AFRICA
East London 1962-65
Kyalami 1967-93
SPAIN
Jarama 1968-81
Jerez 1986-97
Montjuich Park 1969-75
Pedralbes 1951-54
SWEDEN-Anderstorp,
1973-78
SWITZERLAND
Bremgarten 1950-54
UNITED STATES
Dallas 1984
Detroit 1982-88
Las Vegas 1981-82
Long Beach 1976-83
Phoenix 1989-91
Riverside 1960
Sebring 1959
Watkins Glen 1961-80

ARGENTINA

The worldwide success of Juan Manuel Fangio encouraged the popularity of motor racing in Argentina, and it hosted the first World Championship grands prix to be held outside Europe – six years before the first US Grand Prix.

The Buenos Aires track was built with the support of President Juan Perón, who was keen to use Fangio and the sport as publicity tools. Opened in March 1952, the Autódromo Municipal de la Ciudad de Buenos Aires was located on the southern outskirts of the Argentinian capital and featured more than a dozen track configurations, with long straights linked by twists and turns around the pit and paddock area. The earlier races were run without the twists and turns, and lap speeds were correspondingly high. Yet, whatever the layout, the first corner, an "S" after the main straight, has always been a fearsome stretch of track.

It was flat, but challenging. And the view from any of the grandstands was far-reaching, the best vantage point being the one on the old back straight, which also allowed the spectator to see across to the start/finish straight and down to the famous arch at the circuit entrance.

The main hazard in the early days was the crowd, who seemed to have little respect for fast-moving racing cars. As in all South American sporting events, the crowd was always massive and extremely voluble.

The first Argentinian Grand Prix was held in 1953, the fourth year of the championship. Back from plying his trade in Europe, Fangio received a hero's welcome. He had already won the title once, in 1951, and so his popularity at home was enormous. However, he failed to finish, and reigning champion Alberto Ascari took the laurels. The race was overshadowed by a terrible accident involving Farina. The Italian star survived, but nine spectators were killed.

Fangio made amends by winning in 1954 and, indeed, he won three more times in the following three years. It seemed nobody could beat him at home until, in 1958, Stirling Moss triumphed in his Cooper, with Fangio fourth. After one more start at the French Grand Prix, Fangio confirmed his retirement from racing. It was no coincidence that there was no race in Argentina the following year, but it was revived in 1960, when Bruce McLaren gave Cooper another win.

There were no grands prix from 1961 to 1970, and it took the discovery

CIRCUIT DETAILS

BUENOS AIRES
Circuit length: **2.647 miles**
Years race held: **1953-1958, 1960, 1972-1975, 1977-1981, 1995-1998**
Off the grand prix calendar for years, this famous track was eventually given the all-clear for a race in 1995 after its ancient pits were replaced. Sadly, the high-speed lay-out was eschewed and a tight, twisty circuit (derivative number six) used instead.

of a new local hero to encourage its return. The old Autódromo was pressed back into service for a non-championship race in 1971, won by Amon. But all eyes were on the nation's newcomer Carlos Reutemann, who finished third. For 1972 the race was given World Championship status. Reutemann joined Mario Andretti in the history books by taking pole for his first championship grand prix, although Stewart won.

Throughout the 1970s Argentina was the season-opening race, apart from 1976 when political unrest led to its cancellation.

In 1981 there was controversy as Piquet and his "hydraulic suspension" Brabham overcame the new ride-height rules. Reutemann was second, fated never to win at home.

The 1982 event was cancelled and Reutemann, having started the year with Williams, unexpectedly quit racing. Within weeks, Argentina and Britain had gone to war over the Falklands and sport took a back seat.

Argentina became a grand prix venue once again in 1995 and saw a fine win for Damon Hill, with the English driver making it two in a row for Williams in 1996. The Williams domination continued with Jacques Villeneuve's victory in 1997, before Michael Schumacher won there for Ferrari in 1998 after barging David Coulthard's McLaren out of the way.

Chaos at the First Bend: there's smoke everywhere as Michael Schumacher collides with Rubens Barrichello during the Argentinian Grand Prix in 1997

AUSTRALIA

Don't Fence Me In: David Coulthard puts the power down out of Clark at the 2003 Australian GP

CIRCUIT DETAILS

ALBERT PARK
Circuit length: **3.295 miles**   Years race held: **1996 onwards**
Moving the race to Melbourne in 1996 shifted the Australian GP to the start of the Formula One season, thus scuppering Adelaide's traditional end-of-season party. The new parkland circuit, built around a lake, proved popular with the drivers for its fast-flowing nature.

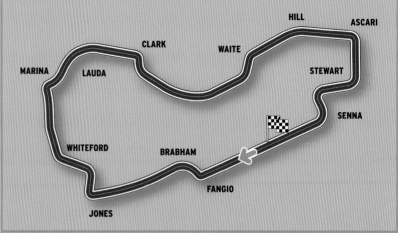

ADELAIDE
Circuit length: **2.347 miles**   Years race held: **1985-1995**
Temporary circuits often come in for a lot of flak for being narrow and failing to offer any points at which overtaking may take place. Not so Adelaide, which offered straights long and wide enough for slipstreaming and banzai outbraking manoeuvres. The South Australian city was small enough to totally embrace the grand prix, its end-of-season parties already part of Formula One folklore. It's still used for touring car races.

Despite the international successes of Jack Brabham and Alan Jones, it wasn't until 1985 that Australia first hosted a World Championship round, in Adelaide.

With the full support of the local government, nothing was left to chance and the Australian race has often been cited as the best-organized event of the year.

The track, used until 1995, ran partly on public roads in and around the Victoria Park horse racing facility. It wasn't a typical street circuit, as it was fast, with long straights punctuated by right-angle turns and some fast kinks. The hairpin at the end of Brabham Straight was a good passing place. Like most street circuits, though, there was no run-off just concrete walls. Spectating was best from the temporary grandstands set up in the park, although hundreds of faces could be spied peering from the surrounding buildings.

Rosberg won the inaugural race, but it was the 1986 event that stands out. Mansell was on course for the drivers' title when one of his rear tyres blew, and millions of television viewers watched as his Williams skated down the escape road in a shower of sparks. Prost won the race for McLaren, and with it his second title.

After a win for Berger in 1987 and a second for Prost in 1988, 1989's race proved memorable. Rain had affected qualifying before, but for the first time it hit the race. The grand prix was stopped after two laps, and Prost declined to restart. With many drivers crashing, including Senna, Boutsen scored a hard-earned win for Williams.

Adelaide had the honour of hosting the 500th grand prix in 1990, and triple World Champion Piquet won for Benetton after a challenge from Mansell. Rain hit again in 1991, the event lasting 14 laps before being red-flagged, with Senna given the win.

Senna and new champion Nigel Mansell collided in 1992, giving Berger his second win before Senna dominated in 1993.

The 1994 event was the first final-round title showdown since 1986 and it ended when Schumacher and Damon Hill collided while fighting for the lead, giving the German the title. Having started from pole, returnee Mansell scored a surprise win after

Berger slipped up. Adelaide held the race for the last time in 1995, with Damon Hill winning by two laps as his rivals hit trouble, including leader David Coulthard hitting the pit wall.

Melbourne took over for 1996, as the season-opener, with a great race at the Albert Park venue. Hill won again, but only after new Williams team-mate Jacques Villeneuve slowed with engine problems.

Coulthard won in 1997, then Mika Hakkinen in 1998 in a controversial McLaren one-two. Hakkinen broke down when leading in 1999 to hand victory to Ferrari's Eddie Irvine, doing so again in 2000 to allow Schumacher to win. Schumacher won again in 2001 after Hakkinen's chase ended with suspension failure

and Coulthard couldn't catch him.

Schumacher made it three on the trot in 2002, with Ralf crashing out at the first corner. Clever strategy gave Coulthard victory in 2003, then Schumacher won again in 2004.

Fisichella won for Renault in 2005, then Renault won again in 2006 through Alonso. It was then Ferrari's turn in 2007 as Raikkonen won the race in which Hamilton announced his arrival on the Formula One stage by finishing third.

Twelve months later, Hamilton was triumphant here for McLaren, then Brawn GP had a remarkable debut in 2009, with Button winning for the team that had been Honda but folded and team-mate Barrichello following him home.

AUSTRIA

Despite its small population, Austria has produced two great World Champions, in Jochen Rindt and Niki Lauda, plus Gerhard Berger. The country also enjoyed one of the fastest and most spectacular circuits that played host to the Austrian Grand Prix from 1970 to 1987 before the race was dropped from the schedule.

The first Austrian Grand Prix was held at the Zeltweg airfield in 1964. Noted for its bumps, the track proved a car breaker, but Lorenzo Bandini's Ferrari survived to win. Being flat and uninteresting, Zeltweg wasn't a popular venue.

The F1 circus returned to the Styrian area in 1970 to a brand-new circuit: the Osterreichring. This was set in mountainous countryside a mile away from Zeltweg. It consisted almost entirely of high-speed sweeps and was one of the fastest on the schedule. It was also the most scenic.

As a spectator venue, it was unrivalled, with those in the know watching at the first corner: the Hella Licht Kurve. The cars would approach this up a steep hill, with a right-hander at the brow. Traversing the hillside, the track rounded a long right-hander, then climbed to the Bosch Kurve, a never-ending right-hander that tipped the track downhill again.

A left-hander brought the track back up to the Rindt Kurve, a double-apex right back to the pit straight. In some places the barrier was alarmingly close to the trackside, while in others drivers had hundreds of metres of grass before anything solid.

Rindt excited the crowd in 1970, but the race was won by Ickx's Ferrari and Rindt would die a few weeks later at Monza. Jo Siffert won for BRM in 1971 then the event gained a tradition of producing an unusual winner.

Perhaps the strangest was in 1975, when rain turned it into a lottery. Italian veteran Vittorio Brambilla was in front when the race was curtailed, and he marked his only grand prix win by crashing after taking the flag.

Sadly, American driver Mark Donohue succumbed to injuries sustained that morning and a chicane was built at the Hella Licht Kurve to slow the cars. Penske gained revenge in 1976 when John Watson scored his first (and Penske's only) win, while in 1977 Alan Jones scored his maiden win, also the only success for Shadow. The 1978 race was hit by rain and Ronnie Peterson survived the carnage to score his final victory. In 1982, the race produced one of the closest finishes ever when Elio de Angelis held off Keke Rosberg by 0.05s.

Lauda finally managed to win at home in 1984. Alain Prost won in 1983, 1985 and 1986, while the 1987 event fell to Nigel Mansell after that race was started three times due to two pile-ups on the narrow grid, and safety concerns contributed to the demise of the event. Finances were also a problem, as was its location so far from major cities and airports.

The race returned in 1997, this time on the truncated A1-Ring circuit at the same venue and Jacques Villeneuve won to put his championship bid back on track. Hakkinen headed Coulthard home in 1998. He expected to do the same in 1999, but Coulthard tipped him into a spin on the first lap and then the Scot was outraced by Ferrari's Irvine. Hakkinen won as he pleased in 2000, then Coulthard triumphed in 2001. That was nothing next to 2002 when Barrichello again was told to back off to let Schumacher by, this time ceding victory. Schumacher won again in 2003, with Barrichello back in third behind Raikkonen. Then Austria lost its grand prix for 2004.

CIRCUIT DETAILS

A1-RING
Circuit length: **2.685 miles**
Years race held: **1997-2003**
The rebuilt A1-Ring track may lack the excitement of the former Osterreichring, on which it is built, but the first bend is very tight over a sharp ridge and never fails to produce drama on the opening lap. The second corner, the Remus Kurve, is even tighter and is the ultimate spectating spot on the circuit. The views around the track are fantastic, thanks to its setting on the side of a mountain in the Styrian region of Austria.

OSTERREICHRING
Circuit length: **3.673 then 3.692 miles**
Years race held: **1970-1987**
The rise and rise of Jochen Rindt made Austria's case to host a grand prix too strong to resist, with its magnificent, mountainside Osterreichring opened for business in 1969. By 1970, Rindt's title-winning year, it had its own grand prix, with its fast, long sweepers a real test of man and machine, especially with the occasional deer wandering out of the surrounding forests. The Bosch Curve was an eye-opener, as were average speeds of 135mph. By 1987, it was considered too unsafe for further use by Formula One.

BAHRAIN

Desert Storm: led by Ferrari, the field brakes for Turn 1 in the first-ever Bahrain Grand Prix in 2004

BAHRAIN INTERNATIONAL CIRCUIT

Circuit length: **3.399 miles**   Years race held: **2004 onwards**

If you thought sand blowing across the track used to be a problem at Zandvoort, that ought to be nothing next to what happens in the deserts of Bahrain... However, at least one half of this plush new venue – it has been modelled so that one half represents the country's deserts, the other its oases – should be sand-free as the sand is kept in check by heavily sprinkled grass verges. Spring weather seems to be good, with dry heat and none of the oppressive humidity that makes the previous grand prix in Malaysia such a nightmare.

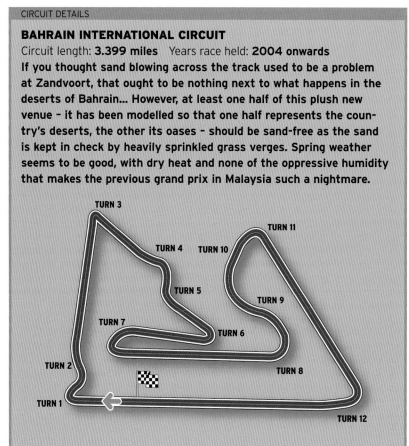

April 2004 was an extremely important date for Formula One as it was the first time that it had raced at a grand prix in the Middle East. The desire in the oil-rich states along the Persian Gulf had been there, with Formula One extremely popular but something that was seen only on television, save for a set of display races in Dubai in the early 1980s.

The only motor sport that had made it within their borders was rallying, with their sandy interiors ideally suited to the desert raid style of rallying seen every January on the Paris-Dakar Rally.

Sporting super state Dubai, home to major golf, tennis and powerboating tournaments, was expected to be the first to coax the World Championship to its shores, but Bahrain beat them to it, scoring a massive PR coup.

Crown Prince Shaikh Salman bin Hamad Al Khalifa is a lifelong fan of motor sport and was instrumental in bringing F1 here, encouraging the government to underwrite its construction costs of $150m. For this, they have got a wonderful new circuit built in the rolling desert alongside a camel farm at Sakhir to the southern end of the largest of Bahrain's 36 islands, 25 miles from the capital Manama. Al Khalifa is keen to use the track for racing all year round, with series run through the winter months attracting drivers from Europe to enjoy the sunshine. In addition to the main circuit, Bahrain International Circuit offers a 1.5 mile inner track, a 2.12 mile outer track, a 1.53 mile oval for testing and a 0.75 mile drag strip.

The circuit comes from the pen of Hermann Tilke, so its emphasis is on tight and technical rather than fast and flowing. Acknowledging that a circuit should display something of the character of the country in which it's located, he has divided the circuit into distinct parts: one being of desert and the other made to have the feel of an oasis. This latter part is the area surrounding the pit, paddock and grandstands, with sprinklers having to run day and night to keep the grass green. Soon after the tight first corner, the track feeds off into the desert section, twisting through rocks and dunes with an interlude in the oasis area down the back straight before more desert and finally back into oasis sector just before the final corner back onto the start/finish straight.

One of the most recognizable features of the circuit is its 10-storey VIP tower that offers a fabulous view of the circuit for up to 5000 people.

The only dark cloud that hung over Bahrain's inaugural race was the threat of terrorism but this did nothing to stop Michael Schumacher's winning ways for Ferrari as he controlled proceedings from start to finish, with team-mate Rubens Barrichello coming home second and Jenson Button finishing in a distant third place for BAR.

Fernando Alonso dominated for Renault in 2005, reaching the finish line way ahead of Toyota's Jarno Trulli, then won again when it was the 2006 season-opener, this time just ahead of Schumacher's Ferrari.

Back to its more regular slot of being the third race on the calendar in 2007, victory was seized by Felipe Massa for Ferrari, with only McLaren's rookie Lewis Hamilton able to keep him in sight.

Then, in 2008, it was Massa again after he demoted BMW Sauber's pole-sitting Robert Kubica at the start and team-mate Kimi Raikkonen pushed the Polish driver back to an eventual this place.

In 2009, it was Button's turn after he advanced from fourth on the grid to pass the lightly-fuelled Toyotas of Trulli and Timo Glock.

BELGIUM

The Belgian Grand Prix has had three homes, but for most only one matters: Spa-Francorchamps, a track that has had two lives: the first until 1970 and then in truncated form after 1983. It has always been regarded as the greatest challenge of the day.

First used in 1924, Spa joined the World Championship at the start, in 1950. Set in the wooded Ardennes hills, it made use of public roads and ran for 8.76-miles, consisting almost entirely of long straights, punctuated by tricky kinks and, occasionally, a proper corner.

The most famous section is just after the pits – a downhill plunge followed by Eau Rouge and Raidillon, a left-right-left flick up and over a hill. The track climbed to the top of the hill at Les Combes and plunged into the valley beyond, with an adverse camber via a long right-hander taken flat-out. The circuit then turned sharp right and climbed all the way back through the woods to the hairpin at

the top, La Source, before dropping back past the pits.

As the track used public roads, trees, lampposts, road signs and houses were among the "natural" hazards. And perhaps the most terrifying aspect of Spa was the weather. The sun could be shining in the pits while rain poured on the far-flung sections. Spa was, in a word, dangerous.

The grand prix ran at Spa from 1950 to 1970, with the exception of three years, and the list of winners shows its propensity for surrendering to the very best. Champions Farina, Ascari and Fangio won there, as did Brabham, Graham Hill and Surtees. The man who made Spa his second home was Clark who won four times.

The danger was ever-present, and in 1960 British youngsters Alan Stacey and Chris Bristow were killed in separate accidents. By 1970, speeds were getting out of hand: Pedro Rodriguez averaged a shade under 150mph. So, a new home was sought,

and two were found. Nivelles, a bland track near Brussels, ran the race in 1972 and 1974. In 1973, the race was run at Zolder, in the Flemish-speaking part of Belgium northwest of Liège. The track broke up badly, but Zolder became home to the grand prix from 1975 to 1982, providing great races. Tragically, it's remembered for claiming Gilles Villeneuve's life in 1982.

The race returned to Spa in 1983, with the track chopped to 4.328 miles by the removal of the most dangerous road section beyond Les Combes.

Like the original track, the new Spa rewarded only the most talented. Senna won five times – including four consecutive wins from 1988 to 1991 – while Prost and Mansell also won. Schumacher took his very first win in 1992, and Hill triumphed in 1993 and 1994 – in the latter year only after Schumacher had been disqualified. The 1995 grand prix produced a win for Berger, Hill won again in 1996, while Schumacher swept all before him in a rain-soaked 1997 race.

The race in 1998 is one that will never be forgotten. First, there was a mass pile-up on the first lap. Then Schumacher threw away victory by slamming into Coulthard when lapping him. And, finally, Hill gave Jordan its first ever win.

Things were less dramatic in 1999 once Coulthard had toughed it out with Hakkinen at the start before sprinting clear to win. Hakkinen was on better form in 2000 and, despite losing ground by staying out too long on wet tyres, came through to win. The star of the 2001 race was Giancarlo Fisichella who took his improving Renault to third behind Schumacher and Coulthard. Schumacher won again in 2002, then there was no race in 2003, but it was welcomed back by all F1 fans for 2004 when Raikkonen won for McLaren. The Finn wa to win again in 2005, in dominant fashion.

After a further year off the calendar, the grand prix circus returned in 2007 and Raikkonen

picked up where he'd left off to win, this time for Ferrari.

The 2008 race was hugely exciting and Hamilton overhauled Massa when rain fell to be first home, but he was penalised for cutting the final chicane, handing victory to Massa.

Fisichella climed a surprise pole for Force India, but lost out in a racelong battle with Ferrari's Raikkonen.

Only the Brave: cars run flat out through the newly revised Eau Rouge, Spa-Francorchamps, 2002

BRAZIL

Tricky When Wet: Rubens Barrichello tip-toes his Ferrari through the first corner sequence in 2003

INTERLAGOS
Circuit length: **2.687 miles**
Years race held: **1973-1977, 1979-1980, 1990 onwards**
Fast, bumpy and a shadow of its former self, this circuit nestles in the heart of Sao Paulo: the home of the late Ayrton Senna. The fervent atmosphere will never be the same there again. The super-fast first corner has been slowed by a chicane. Watch out for overtaking manoeuvres going into Curva 3 at the end of the back straight.

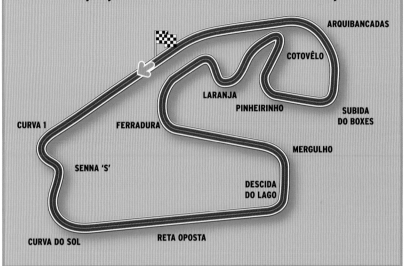

JACAREPAGUA
Circuit length: **3.126 miles**   Years race held: **1978, 1981-1989**
Rio de Janeiro is the romantic capital of Brazil, São Paulo the industrial engine, but it's the latter that is the home of the country's motor racing scene. However, the more glamorous Rio hosted the grand prix almost continuously from 1978 to 1989. The nature of its Jacarepagua track was the reverse of the comparison between the two cities, as it was flat and boring next to Interlagos's swoops. Jacarepagua, home of five wins for Alain Prost, has since been re-developed with the addition of an oval to attract the Indy Car series.

Just as Juan Manuel Fangio boosted the popularity of racing in Argentina, Emerson Fittipaldi's success led to the inauguration of the Brazilian Grand Prix in São Paulo.

Set in the suburbs, running partly around a lake, the circuit had a sweeping "outer" section then a twisty trail through the infield. That added up to an interesting track of 4.946 miles. Spectators had a great view, since the track was set in a natural amphitheatre. Like all circuits in the tropics, Interlagos is bumpy, which can upset the cars in the faster corners.

Brazil held a poorly supported non-championship race in 1972. Fittipaldi led but retired, allowing Carlos Reutemann to win. In 1973 the race had World Championship status and for the rest of the decade would traditionally follow on from Argentina in a season-opening South American double-header. Fittipaldi pleased his fans by winning in 1973 and 1974. Then Pace scored his only victory for Brabham in 1975. Ferrari won through Lauda in 1976, and Reutemann in 1977.

In 1978 the circus moved to Jacarepagua, near Rio de Janeiro. A typical modern track of two straights and a mixture of slow- and medium-speed constant radius corners, it was well constructed and has a scenic backdrop, but lacked the character of Interlagos. Reutemann won again, while Fittipaldi claimed second, the best result of his five-year spell with the Fittipaldi team. The race returned to Interlagos in 1979 but, from 1981 on, it was back at Rio, Prost winning five times in the 1980s, while local hero Piquet triumphed twice, with Mansell winning his first race for Ferrari there in 1989.

That was the last race at Jacarepagua, with the race moving back to Interlagos in 1990. The track had been cut back to 2.687 miles, with the fast, challenging "outer" section all but gone. Fittingly, Prost won the first race. Then, in 1991 Senna became the fourth local star to win the Brazilian Grand Prix, a feat he then repeated in a wet/dry affair in 1993. Mansell won in 1992. The 1994 race marked Senna's first start for Williams, but it didn't work out, and victory went to Schumacher. It was to be Senna's last home race and the mammoth turnout at his funeral a month later showed the depths of emotion that he had stirred in the public. Hill was dominant there for Williams in awful conditions in 1996, and Villeneuve followed suit in 1997. However, no one could get close to McLaren's Hakkinen in 1998 or in 1999. Looking for a hat-trick in 2000, the Finn's McLaren broke down and so Schumacher won for Ferrari. In 2001, Montoya attacked Schumacher, but he was taken out by Jos Verstappen and Coulthard took the honours. Schumacher won in 2002 to shock his rivals with the supremacy of his new car. Then Coulthard ought to have won in 2003, but the race was stopped after Webber crashed, just as Coulthard pitted, and so Fisichella won for Jordan.

Montoya won for Williams in 2004 after a battle with Raikkonen, then won again in 2005 after moving from Willaims to McLaren. Massa delighted his home fans by winning in 2006.

In 2007, Raikkonen won and so defeated Hamilton who failed to beome a rookie World Champion after an early race problem delayed him.

However, Hamilton landed the title in a last round shoot-out in 2008, but he cut it fine, by reclaiming fifth in the final corner to pip race winner Massa.

In 2009, another British driver became World Champion here, as fifth was enough for Button.

Ready for the Off: Michael Schumacher on pole, with Mika Hakkinen, David Coulthard, Jarno Trulli, Heinz-Harald Frentzen and Rubens Barrichello close behind on the grid for Silverstone's British GP in 2001

BRITAIN

While France has had a grand prix since 1906, Britain was a late starter. Despite the fact that the banked Brooklands course opened in 1909, it wasn't until 1926 that it first hosted a grand prix.

Sadly, the two races held there weren't successes. Donington Park hosted races in 1937 and 1938 that were British Grands Prix in all but name, attracting Mercedes and Auto Union to its parkland setting near Derby. Listed merely as Donington Grands Prix, they thrilled with the spectacle of the powerful German cars surging out of the hairpin and flying over the brows.

The British Grand Prix started in 1948 at Silverstone, and the former airfield in Northamptonshire is still the home of the country's premier race. The track has been changed substantially yet on 17 occasions since 1950 the grand prix has taken place at another British circuit.

The track used in 1948 used some of the perimeter roads which would become so familiar, it also had two forays up the wide runways and into what is now the infield.

By the time of the first World Championship race in May 1950, only the perimeter roads were in use, and the track had assumed the 2.927-mile shape which would remain until 1975 and, in subtly modified form, until 1990. It was very fast, and no corner was more testing than Woodcote, the sweeping right-hander which led on to the what eventually became the pit straight.

That 1950 race was the first-ever round of the World Championship, and was held with King George VI in attendance. Alfa Romeo dominated and Farina, who would take the inaugural title, won the race. It was not until 1955 – and a change of venue was made – that the British Grand Prix had a home winner.

The driver was Moss, and the new track Aintree. The RAC decided that it should share the grand prix between Silverstone and the new three-mile circuit around Liverpool's Grand National horse racing course. Aintree was a lot slower than Silverstone. Its great advantage was the facilities, as fans of the car and four-legged racers used the same grandstands.

As in the rest of the 1955 races, Mercedes proved dominant, and Moss added to his growing status by leading team-mate Fangio home. Aintree hosted the grand prix five times, alternating with Silverstone in 1955, 1957, 1959 and 1961, then hanging on to the event for 1962.

Silverstone then had a new rival: Brands Hatch. From 1964 to 1986 the two circuits would alternate. Undulating through the Kent countryside, the 2.65-mile track was extended for the 1964 British Grand Prix, with a loop off into the woods.

It was very different from flat Silverstone, with Paddock Hill Bend, the plunging right-hander after the start, the most popular. The venues may have been different, but the result was the same. Clark won at Aintree in 1962, Silverstone in 1963 and at Brands Hatch in 1964.

Silverstone and Brands Hatch produced memorable races. This started at Silverstone in 1973, when Scheckter spun his McLaren at Woodcote and triggered a pile-up at the start of the second lap. At Brands Hatch in 1974, Lauda led until pitting late in the race with a puncture, only to find the pit exit blocked by people and an official's car.

For 1975, Silverstone made its first important change with the addition of a chicane at Woodcote. That didn't prevent drivers sliding off at nearly every other corner in a rain-hit race, which was stopped early and won by Fittipaldi.

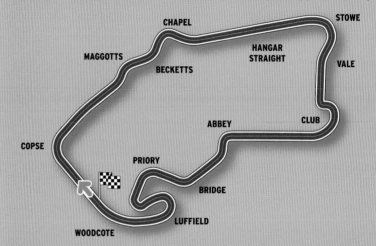

CIRCUIT DETAILS

SILVERSTONE

Circuit length: **2.888 then 2.927 then 2.932 then 2.969 then 3.247 then 3.210 then 3.152 then 3.194 miles**

Years race held: **1950-1954, 1956, 1958, 1960, 1963, 1965, 1967, 1969, 1971, 1973, 1975, 1977, 1979, 1981, 1983, 1985, 1987 onwards**
The home of British motor racing. Once an airfield, it hosted the first ever modern-day grand prix in 1950 and has frequently been transformed since then, largely to slow the cars down. The latest change has emasculated the once mighty Stowe corner, but the new-look "Becketts esses" is the most exciting squiggle in racing.

AINTREE

Circuit length: **3.000 miles**

Years race held: **1955, 1957, 1959, 1961-1962**
Think Aintree and almost all British sports fans think first of the Grand National, that once-a-year horses-over-fences extravaganza of betting. However, in the 1950s, the Liverpool venue also hosted the British Grand Prix, alternating with Silverstone before Brands Hatch took over its slot in 1964. The grandstands were in place already, with great views over much of the circuit spread across the flat land. Stirling Moss scored his first grand prix win here for Mercedes in 1955, and shared victory with Tony Brooks here two years later, to say nothing of winning four non-championship Aintree 200 races as well.

Right Hand Down: Stirling Moss steers his Mercedes into a corner en route to victory in the British Grand Prix at Aintree in 1955

First Chequered Flag: Mansell punches the air after his maiden grand prix win at Brands Hatch, 1985

BRANDS HATCH

Circuit length: **2.650 then 2.614 miles**   Years race held: **1964, 1966, 1968, 1970, 1972, 1974, 1976, 1978, 1980, 1982, 1984-1986**
Loved for its unrivalled amphitheatre cupping much of the lap, this Kent circuit has lost too much ground to make a comeback, as safety standards are more stringent now, meaning that run-off would have to be found for every corner. Alternating with Silverstone between 1966 and 1986, Brands Hatch offered a complete contrast with its dips and curves as well as its contrasting stadium and country sections. Paddock Hill Bend remains one of Formula One's great corners and Clark Curve one of the great places from which to watch a grand prix.

DONINGTON PARK

Circuit length: **2.500 miles**   Year race held: **1993**
Most famous for motorcycle racing these days, this great circuit that hosted the British Grand Prix between 1935 and 1938 has held but one round of the World Championship, the European Grand Prix of 1993. And what a race that was as Ayrton Senna weaved his magic. The circuit provides the downhill Craner Curves and tricky Old Hairpin, with overtaking a regular feature into the Melbourne Corner hairpin.

Brands Hatch also made modifications for 1976, changing the line at Paddock Hill Bend and modifying the straight behind an expanded pit complex. This grand prix went down in history thanks to a first-corner accident triggered by the Ferraris of Lauda and Regazzoni, and also involving Hunt. The Briton won the restart but was later disqualified.

There are other great memories: Hunt battling with Watson in 1977, Reutemann nipping past Lauda in 1978, Regazzoni giving Williams its first win in 1979, Jones beating the flying Ligiers in 1980, Watson avoiding a first-lap skirmish to win for McLaren in 1981 and Warwick hauling his fuel-light "half-tank" Toleman up to second place in 1982.

Brands Hatch boss John Webb managed to secure extra "European Grands Prix" in 1983 and 1985, the second of these giving Mansell his first-ever victory. But the 1986 British Grand Prix proved to be the Kent track's last as Silverstone secured a long-term deal and, although this final race led to another fine win for Mansell, a leg-breaking accident for Laffite underlined that the cars had

outgrown their confines.

Silverstone was not immune to safety concerns. For the 1987 race the 1975 chicane was replaced by a new, much tighter complex well before Woodcote. That year produced one of the best-ever races there, as Mansell defeated team-mate Piquet.

Mansell was always news, finishing second in the wet in 1988 and again after a puncture in 1989. In 1990 he announced a very emotional but temporary retirement after his Ferrari's gearbox had failed.

For 1991, Becketts became a fast set of esses, while Stowe was slowed to a harder right, followed by a new left-hander called Vale, and a much slower Club. After Abbey there was a completely new section: a fast right-hander at Bridge, followed by the double lefts of Priory, and the double rights of Luffield.

Mansell won the first race on the new track, followed it up in 1992, and both times the crowd went berserk. With Nigel gone to America the audience shrank in 1993, and those who turned up went home disappointed after Damon Hill's engine blew and Prost won.

Another major rebuild followed in 1994. Copse was reprofiled, with further modifications at Stowe. A slow complex was introduced at Abbey and Priory was also changed. This time the fans got the result they wanted, victory for Hill after Michael Schumacher was penalized for a start procedure irregularity.

Herbert won for Benetton in 1995 and Villeneuve for Williams in 1996 before making it two out of two in 1997. Schumacher won in strange circumstances in 1998 when he was allowed to keep victory despite taking a stop/go penalty in the pits after crossing the finish line.

Coulthard secured a home win in 1999, in the race in which Schumacher broke a leg, and then overpowered Barrichello to make it two on the trot in 2000. Hakkinen was the man in control of proceedings for McLaren in 2001, ending a 10-month winning drought. Schumacher won in 2002, as he did everywhere that year. But the 2003 race was one of the all-time classics as Barrichello outraced Montoya and Raikkonen.

Schumacher rediscovered his winning touch at Silverstone in

2004, leading Raikkonen's McLaren home with team-mate Barrichello third. Then in 2005 it was Montoya's turn to turn win, for McLaren, ahead of Alonso's Renault.

Alonso went one better in 2006 when he won easily from pole position, with Schumacher finishing second for Ferrari.

Ferrari's form improved in 2007 and Raikkonen was first home to delight the tifosi, as he and Alonso showed their experience to use their tyres better to overhaul the pole-sitting rookie Hamilton.

Rain can always affect play and Hamilton put on a masterclass in his second British Grand Prix in 2008 to dominate for McLaren as others slid and spun everywhere. BMW Sauber's Heidfeld was the best of the rest, finishing more thn a minute adrift.

In 2009, there was talk of the race being moved to Donington Park. On the track, though, Vettel put on a masterclass for Red Bull Racing. ahead of team-mate Webber

Spot of Trouble: James Hunt is one of the drivers involved in a pile-up at the start of the British Grand Prix at Brands Hatch in 1976

CANADA

Canada joined the circus in 1967 and, apart from absences in 1975, 1987 and 2009, has been a regular, with the Canadian fans relying on the Villeneuve's for someone to cheer on, with Jacques following Gilles.

The original home of the Canadian Grand Prix was Mosport Park in eastern Ontario. This magnificent road course undulated through woods and Moss won the first big event in 1961, while its first World Championship race in 1967 was won by Brabham.

Canada alternated the race between its two major circuits: in 1968 and 1970 the race was run at Mont Tremblant in Quebec. It was soon deemed too dangerous. From 1971, Mosport Park took over.

One of Mosport's most memorable races was in 1973, when a deluge caused a pace car to be deployed for the first time. Peter Revson was declared the winner. Three years later, James Hunt scored a superb win as his championship bid built up momentum. Then in 1977, Jody Scheckter gave the Canadian-owned Wolf team its final victory.

Mosport was always regarded as outdated, and for 1978 the race moved to Montreal. Built on the Ile

Notre Dame around the site of Expo 67, it was a cross between a street circuit and a permanent road course, with fiddly slow corners and some fast, barrier-lined sections.

From the start, there's a kink into a hairpin that feeds on to a curving section punctuated by a left-right "S" and then a tight left before a more open right that leads the cars on to the back straight. Another chicane follows before a hairpin then a long straight and a final chicane.

The first race produced the dream result: a maiden win for local hero Villeneuve. In 1981 the race was hit by rain. Villeneuve starred, but Jacques Laffite won for Ligier. The 1982 race was run without Villeneuve, who had been killed at Zolder. The track was renamed in his honour.

The race has the distinction of twice having a "winner" docked a minute for jumping the start. In 1980, Pironi was the culprit, while Berger did the same in 1990. The beneficiaries were Jones and Senna respectively.

Boutsen secured his first victory in 1989 then 1991 had one of the strangest finishes ever, when leader Mansell began celebrating too early and stalled his Williams, letting Piquet

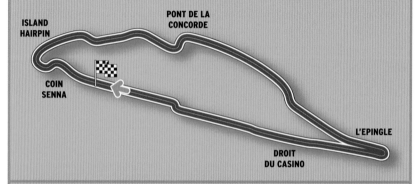
sweep by to score his last victory.

Mansell crashed over the final chicane in 1992 and Berger got revenge. Prost scored his only Canadian success in 1993, while Schumacher won in 1994 when a temporary tyre chicane was added in the aftermath of the Imola tragedies. Hill thwarted Villeneuve's hopes of a home win in 1996, and Schumacher spoiled the party in 1997 when the race was marred by Olivier Panis's leg-breaking accident, with the German winning again for Ferrari in 1998 when both of the McLarens dropped out. Schumacher led again in 1999, but Hakkinen harried him into crashing at the final chicane, the Finn going on to win. Schumacher gained his revenge in 2000. Ralf Schumacher marked his

100th grand prix with victory in 2001 before his brother won the next three, with an outsized brake duct costing Ralf second place in 2004.

Montoya was set for victory for McLaren in 2005, but a pit stop infringement and so team-mate Raikkonen won instead. Michael Schumacher was second that time and afgain in 2006, this time behind Renault's polesitter, Alonso.

Hamilton fans will always recall the 2007 race as it was when he held his cool through four safety car periods to take his first win. He might have won in 2008, too, but he crashed into Raikkonen in a pitlane scramble in a safety car period and left the way clear for Kubica to take his and BMW Sauber's - first win..

Canada Dry: Ralf Schumacher leads the field through the first turn in 2003 as his brother locks up

CHINA

Giant Structure: the start/finish straight is dominated by the grandstand, pit buildings and "bridges"

CIRCUIT DETAILS

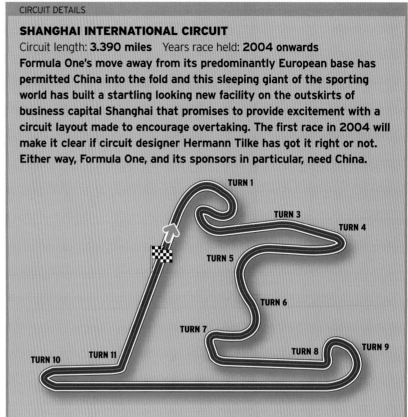

SHANGHAI INTERNATIONAL CIRCUIT

Circuit length: **3.390 miles**   Years race held: **2004 onwards**

Formula One's move away from its predominantly European base has permitted China into the fold and this sleeping giant of the sporting world has built a startling looking new facility on the outskirts of business capital Shanghai that promises to provide excitement with a circuit layout made to encourage overtaking. The first race in 2004 will make it clear if circuit designer Hermann Tilke has got it right or not. Either way, Formula One, and its sponsors in particular, need China.

The attraction of the world's largest population of 1.3 billion people proved too much for Formula One's marketing men and this burgeoning economic giant was given its first grand prix for 2004. Fittingly, it wasn't given to capital Beijing but to economic hotbed, Shanghai.

Typically, an all-new circuit had to be built, but that is the way that it happens now, such are the safety, hospitality and transport facilities demanded by the sport's governing body. Designed by the ubiquitous Hermann Tilke, the circuit is built in the shape of the Chinese character Shang, giving it an unusually long back straight out of a slow corner into a hairpin.

This ought to provide a perfect overtaking spot. The long and ever-tightening first corner looks to be more than a little tricky, too.

In its communist days, China was missing from the motor sport map, with the first action across its thousands of miles being a rally. However, just a stone's throw over the border in the Portuguese enclave Macau, racing had been thriving for 50 years with an annual grand prix, latterly for Formula Three cars around its streets. Indeed, this invitation race became the most prestigious on the Formula Three calendar, outstripping Monaco's. Its cast of winners includes Ayrton Senna, Riccardo Patrese, Michael Schumacher and David Coulthard.

Mainland China then decided to build a circuit of its own, not only to give itself a more cosmopolitan image but also to bring in welcome foreign exchange as it shed its communist past. This circuit was opened at Zhuhai in 1996 after the city in south-west China, situated just 36 miles west of Hong Kong, had hosted an international sports car race around its streets. With aspirations to host a F1 grand prix, the circuit attracted more sports car races, but even though it was nominated as the reserve race for 1998, the facilities were never quite up to scratch as finances were short and the project has lost momentum.

The first grand prix at Shanghai in 2004 went to Ferrari, but not as predicted to Michael Schumacher who was strangely off form. Instead, Rubens Barrichello came out on top after a great three-way battle with BAR's Jenson Button and McLaren's Kimi Raikkonen.

The second grand prix at this stunning facility was all about Renault and Fernando Alonso from start to finish. Raikkonen was best of the rest, with Ralf Schumacher profiting from two safety car periods to rise to third for Toyota. Weirdly, Michael Schumacher was again off form here, crashing out of the race during a safety car period.

Alonso looked set to make it two straight wins in Shanghai in 2006, but a combination of changeable weather, Schumacher hitting form and finding an advantage from his Bridgestone tyres meant that the German won.

Lewis Hamilton arrived in Shanghai with a 12-point championship lead in 2007 and qualified on pole and was fighting for the lead with title rival Raikkonen in wet-dry conditions when he slid into a gravel trap as he tried to enter the pits and was out, with the Finn winning to close the gap with one race to go.

Hamilton was able to make amends in 2008, though, when he took pole position, set fastest lap and motored home to a 15 second victory over Massa, with Raikkonen making it a Ferrari two-three finish.

In 2009, the Chinese Grand Prix was moved to the front of the championship, put third on the calendar, and Sebastian Vettel dominated from pole for Red Bull Racing in the wet, with Mrk Webber second and the rest far behind.

FRANCE

The French Grand Prix has the finest pedigree of any motor race. The sport originated in France with inter-city marathons such as the 1895 Paris-Bordeaux-Paris, and the very first French Grand Prix was run in 1906 at Le Mans. This was one of 11 venues used before the outbreak of the Second World War, by which time the race had found homes in Reims and Montlhery, the banked track outside Paris. Since the French Grand Prix joined the World Championship in 1950, seven tracks have hosted it.

Reims hosted France's first championship event in 1950. Dating back to 1925, it was a five-mile blast along public roads. Reims was best known for its long Thillois straight that made every race into a slipstreamer. Fangio won in 1950 and 1951, taking over Fagioli's car on the latter occasion. One of the best battles was in 1961, when Baghetti overcame strong pressure to win from Gurney on his championship debut. It was also the scene of tragedy: Italian Luigi Musso lost his life there in 1958.

Reims held the grand prix 11 times, with its last in 1966.

As early as 1952 the French authorities were indulging in their habit of moving the race about. In the early years, the only alternative was Rouen-Les-Essarts, which held the race in 1952, 1957, 1962, 1964 and 1968.

Extended to 4.06 miles for 1957, Rouen was another circuit based on public roads, famous for its downhill plunge after the start, which led to the cobbled Nouveau Monde hairpin, with several blind corners to keep the drivers on their toes. Fangio's win in 1957 is regarded as one of his best, while Ickx won in the rain in 1968. That race is best remembered for the death of veteran Schlesser on his debut for Honda, heralding the end of Rouen as a grand prix circuit.

Four tracks hosted the race from 1965 to 1968. In 1967 the race was held, for one time only, on the Le Mans Bugatti circuit, which used a section of the 24 hours track. The race was boring. Competitors didn't like it and neither did the public.

Clermont-Ferrand emerged as the natural heir. The race was first held there in 1965, and returned in 1969, 1970 and 1972. Opened in 1958, this was a magnificent five-mile road course, set in the mountains of the Auvergne. Something of a mini-Nurburgring with twists and turns aplenty, it induced car sickness. It was also known for loose stones alongside the track, which led to punctures and in 1972 cost Austrian Helmut Marko the sight of one eye. That year's race was perhaps the most dramatic, as early leader Chris Amon fought back from a puncture to claim third for Matra behind winner Stewart's Tyrrell.

The French Grand Prix moved to a very different home in 1971. Those dramatic road courses were replaced by a track at Le Castellet, east of Marseilles. Named after Paul Ricard, the aperitif manufacturer who built it, the track was the first of the bland, modern autodromes which would proliferate over the next two decades. Teams liked Ricard as the weather and facilities were good, but the drivers were less impressed, although they appreciated the run-off areas and barriers. In contrast to its predecessors the track was flat and dull, but it did have Signes – a fast right-hander at the end of the long back straight. That and the fast section beyond the pits were real tests.

Paul Ricard would become the grand prix's home for the next 20 years. However, for much of that period the alternating continued. The new second choice, introduced in 1974, was Dijon-Prenois. Initially, this undulating track ran only 2.044 miles, producing a lap time of less than a minute, and thus traffic problems. By the time the race returned in 1977, an extension had been added, bringing it up to 2.361 miles and, thanks to this

Fast Sweepers: the field, led by the Williams-BMW duo, powers its way through Magny-Cours's sinuous opening sequence of turns in the 2003 French GP

sequence of slower corners, the lap time was increased by 13 seconds.

Dijon-Prenois hosted the grand prix five times, in 1974, 1977, 1979, 1981 and 1984, and had a bonus "Swiss Grand Prix" in 1982. Some memorable races took place, notably in 1979 when Jabouille gave Renault its first grand prix win, and Arnoux and Villeneuve battled hard for second. In 1981 a young Prost scored his maiden win in a race split into two by rain.

By the mid-1980s, the governing body was demanding that all grands prix find long-term homes and, with Dijon dropped, Paul Ricard was sole host between 1985 and 1990. Ricard saw tragedy when Elio de Angelis was killed in testing in 1986, after his wing failed approaching the fast sequence after the pits.

For that year's race the track was cut back to 2.353 miles, removing the section where de Angelis crashed, halving the back straight and slowing the approach to Signes. In its last years as a F1 venue Prost was the king of Ricard, winning during 1988-90. The 1989 race is remembered for a first corner crash in which Gugelmin flipped over the pack, while in 1990 Gugelmin and Leyton House team-mate Capelli stunned everyone with their pace, Capelli leading for 45 laps and finishing second.

For 1991 the track was replaced by the French Grand Prix's seventh home since 1950. With support from President Mitterand, the club circuit of Magny-Cours was transformed into a typical modern autodrome, full of slow turns and hairpins but boasting top-class pit and paddock facilities.

The 2.654-mile facility did not offer much of a challenge, apart from the fast left/right sequence after the start. The rest of it was slow, and there was even a chicane that was completely unnecessary as it was directly after a hairpin! That was later removed.

The first race was a good one, with victory going to Mansell after a battle with Prost's Ferrari. Mansell

won again in 1992, a race split by rain. Prost added a third for Williams in 1993, pipping Hill, then Schumacher won in 1994, but most eyes were on Mansell, making a brief comeback. However, he failed to last the distance. Schumacher won again in 1995, but didn't even reach the start in 1996, his Ferrari blowing up on the parade lap, with Hill doing the honours. The German ace was in a class of his own in 1997, then won again in 1998.

The 1999 grand prix was one of the most bizarre as wet qualifying left Barrichello on pole for Stewart. Coulthard powered clear for McLaren, but retired. Then rain hit hard and, as teams changed tyres and Jordan pulled off a coup and put on enough fuel for Frentzen not to make an extra stop, duly winning from Hakkinen. Coulthard overcame Schumacher to win for McLaren in 2000. Schumacher bounced back in 2001, then appeared to be beaten by McLaren's Raikkonen in 2002 until the Finn slid wide on oil and Michael seized the opportunity. Brother Ralf was the class of the field for Williams in 2003.

Dropped for 2004, the race earned a reprieve when the teams voted to agree to an extra race, one above their statutory limit of 17 and Michael Schumacher ran a four-stop strategy to overcome Renault's Alonso. The Spaniard went one better in 2005 to give Renault its first win on home ground for 22 years.

He was unable to make it two in a row in 2006 as he was delayed by Massa, thus letting Ferrari team leader, Michael, escape in a lead that he was never to lose.

Massa might have hoped of winning in 2007, as he started from pole, but he ended up being beaten by his new Ferrari team-mate Raikkonen, with third-placed Hamilton 30 seconds further back.

Then, after years of talking of the race's demise, the 2008 proved to be the last, with Massa heading a Ferrari one-two ahead of Raikkonen.

MAGNY-COURS
Circuit length: **2.654 then 2.641 miles**   Years race held: **1991-2008**
Little-loved venue for one of the traditional grands prix. Uprated from a club circuit at the behest of President Mitterand, it brought income to a rural region, but little in the way of excitement to Formula One. The Adelaide hairpin at the end of the back straight is the best place to watch. The new slow corner just before the pit entrance is not...

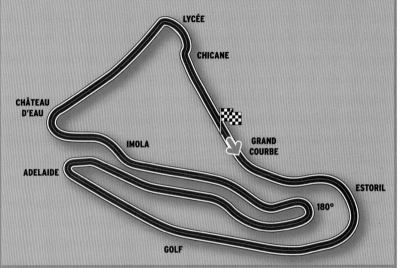

CLERMONT-FERRAND
Circuit length: **5.005 miles**   Years race held: **1965, 1969-1970, 1972**
Seen as France's version of the Nurburgring Nordschleife, this circuit was a rising and falling, serpentine course through the forests above the industrial Massif Central city from which it took its name. Built on a volcanic outcrop, it was a real test of man and machine, with scarcely a straight on which a driver could relax. It closed in 1988, but reopened as Charade, having been chopped back to 2.47 miles.

PAUL RICARD
Circuit length: **3.610 then 2.353 miles**   Years race held: **1971, 1973, 1975-1976, 1978, 1980, 1982-1983, 1985-1990**
The first circuit to carry the name of a sponsor, the pastis magnate who financed the construction of this circuit. Built on an arid plateau east of Marseille, it was fast and open, with its long Mistral Straight and Signes corner a test of bravery. The circuit was chopped after Elio de Angelis died testing there in 1986, with a shorter version used until it was moved, for political reasons, to Magny-Cours in 1991.

REIMS
Circuit length: **4.865 then 4.472 miles**
Years race held: **1950-1951, 1953-1954, 1956, 1958-1961, 1963, 1966**
One of the great circuits, using public roads west of Reims. By the end, it was triangular in shape, with hairpins at two of the corners and long straights in between, down which slipstreaming groups would run before seeing who dared to be latest onto the brakes into the corners. The Hawthorn/Fangio battle of 1953 was one of the greatest races.

GERMANY

Traffic Hold-up: McLaren's Kimi Raikkonen loses control into Hockenheim's first corner in 2003

HOCKENHEIM
Circuit length: **4.219 then 4.227 then 4.234 then 4.239 then 2.842 miles**   Years race held: **1970, 1977-2006, 2008**
No-one has been fond of this place since it claimed Jim Clark's life in 1968. Its high-speed blast through the forest interrupted by three chicanes was considered bland, but there was overtaking aplenty and people grew to like it. For 2002, the circuit was reshaped, the forest blasts lopped off to provide a shorter lap, thus taking the cars past the grandstands in the stadium section more often, ruining the place.

NORDKURVE   EINFAHRT PARABOLICA   SACHS KURVE   SPITZKEHRE   SÜDKURVE   MOBIL 1 KURVE

Until 1976, Germany's Grand Prix was held on the most remarkable circuit of them all: the original Nurburgring Nordschleife. Since then, it has found a home at Hockenheim and the new, shortened Nurburgring.

The first German Grand Prix was held at Berlin's Avus in 1926, and the wet event was blighted by accidents, including one that killed three officials in a timekeeper's box. Safety concerns precipitated a transfer to the Nurburgring – which was somewhat ironic, considering the reputation that the circuit was to acquire.

Work on the 'Ring began in 1925 with its lap lasting 17.58 miles. In later years, the Southern Circuit was excluded and races were held on the 14.17-mile Nordschleife, a sequence of ups and downs, and twisting lefts and rights between pine trees. Much more than Spa-Francorchamps, the 'Ring separated the great from the average. What made the place more daunting was the weather. Even in summer, rain and fog were common,.

The grand prix was held at the 'Ring until World War Two intervened. Racing resumed in 1949, and Germany joined the World Championship in 1951 when 180,000 fans turned up.

Early grands prix confirmed the 'Ring's dual distinction as both a creator and killer of heroes. Ascari had one of his best races in 1952, recovering from a late pit stop to regain the lead from Farina. In 1957 Fangio drove what he regards as his best race, coming back from a slow fuel stop to pass Hawthorn and Collins. But a year later Collins crashed to his death, as had Fangio's protégé, Marimon, in 1954.

The 'Ring was overlooked in favour of Avus in 1959, because crowds had fallen. As in 1926, the track was run up and down a dual carriageway, but it had been shortened and acquired banking at its north end. Uniquely, the race was run over two heats, Brooks winning, but Behra lost his life in a supporting sports car race and Formula One never went back.

The 1960 race was held on the 'Ring's short South circuit, but for 1961 it was both back in the championship and on the familiar, long track. Moss scored his last win.

World Champions Hill, Surtees, Clark, Brabham and Hulme triumphed there in the 1960s, but none more comprehensively than Stewart, who mastered dreadful conditions to win in 1968 by more than four minutes.

Due to an increased emphasis on safety, the Nurburgring underwent major modifications in 1970. Barriers were installed, the track was widened and reprofiled, and run-off areas were created. While this was going on, the grand prix moved to a new venue at Hockenheim, built as a test track for Mercedes. Sadly, it's best known as the place where Clark died in a Formula Two race in 1968. The 4.219-miles lap consisted of two long blasts into and out of the forest, followed by a twisty section in front of huge grandstands. After Clark's death, new barriers made it safer and the 1970 race was an exciting slipstreamer, won by Rindt.

For 1971, the grand prix returned to the 'Ring. Ickx, who had won the previous race there in 1969 in fine style, was again the pacesetter, but he crashed, handing the win to Stewart. The Belgian made amends in 1972.

Despite the modifications the 'Ring remained an anachronism as the cars became faster, and it was fortunate that no one was hurt in 1975 when many suffered punctures. But the following year the track's tenure of the grand prix came to an end as Lauda suffered horrific burns when he crashed on the second lap. While Lauda staged a recovery, the 'Ring did not.

For 1977 the race reverted to Hockenheim, itself modernized by chicanes. Appropriately, the first race was won by Lauda. The track was notable for a high attrition rate, the flat-out blasts proving hard on engines. In addition, the start and the chicanes tended to produce carnage.

In 1980, Hockenheim was again the scene of tragedy, Alfa Romeo driver Patrick Depailler losing his life in a crash in testing at the Ostkurve, the link between the two long straights.

One of the most memorable races came in 1982, by which time a third chicane had been added at the Ostkurve. Pironi was injured in wet practice and in the race Piquet tried to punch Salazar after they collided while Piquet was lapping the Chilean. Pironi's Ferrari team-mate, Tambay, scored an emotional win.

Formula One returned to the 'Ring in 1984, for the European Grand Prix. Built alongside the original, the new 'Ring was a 2.822-mile track with a few interesting corners, but huge run-off areas. Prost won. In 1985, the new 'Ring hosted the German Grand Prix. There was a shunt at the first corner, but Ferrari's Alboreto avoided this to win.

In 1986, the race returned to Hockenheim, which continues to extract a heavy toll on machinery as Piquet won. In 1987, Prost led until a failure with four laps to go, allowing Piquet to win. Then Prost lost sixth gear with two laps to go in 1989, letting Senna through. Senna also won in 1988 and 1990, and Mansell in 1991 and 1992 before Prost scored his first Hockenheim win in 1993 despite a stop/go penalty, taking over when team-mate Damon Hill had a puncture. The 1994 race lost almost half the field in a series of first-lap incidents, before Berger gave Ferrari its first win in four years.

After a ten-year absence, the 'Ring hosted the European Grand Prix in 1995, with Schumacher winning.

Hill made amends at Hockenheim in 1996, and Berger beat Schumacher in 1997. McLaren ruled in 1998, and looked set to repeat this in 1999, but Coulthard picked up a stop/go and Hakkinen was delayed, leaving Salo to cede to Irvine for a Ferrari one-two. McLaren lost out again in 2000 when a spectator got trackside, bringing out the safety car to annul their lead. Then Barrichello performed better in the rain to win for Ferrari. Ralf Schumacher was gifted victory in 2001

when Williams team-mate Montoya was delayed at a pit stop. This was the final race before the circuit was truncated, losing forest sections and order-sorting chicanes.

Michael Schumacher was the first to win on it in his all-conquering 2002 season, before Ralf Schumacher, Barrichello and Raikkonen proved in 2003 that the first corner is still tricky to negotiate. Montoya won by more than a minute for Williams.

Michael Schumacher won again in 2004, but the drive of the race went to BAR's Button, who rose from 13th to second after taking a 10-place grid penalty. Raikkonen retired from the lead in 2005 after a hydraulic leak struck his McLaren, and this led the way for Renault's points leader Alonso, with Montoya a distant second. Michael Schumcher then made it three wins in five years when he led home a Ferrari one-two ahead of Massa in 2006.

With finances dwindling, there was no grand prix at Hockenheim in 2007, but it returned in 2008 and Hamilton won a race in which Glock's accident brought out the safety car and scrambled the order.

With an alternation arrangement in place, it was the Nurburgring's turn to hots the German Grand Prix in 2009 and Red Bull's Mark Webber finally took his first win.

CIRCUIT DETAILS

NURBURGRING
Circuit length: **2.822 then 2.831 then 3.196 miles**
Years race held: **1984-1985, 1995-2007, 2009**
Not to be mistaken with the full-caffeine Nordschleife that of which it makes but a short sector, this circuit was opened in 1984 in a bid to attract Formula One back to the region. It's the very antithesis of the Nordschleife, with run-off aplenty and clear views for driver and fan at every corner. Weather often makes things tricky, but there have been some cracking races, such as in 2003 when Montoya showed "Schumi" how to overtake at the Dunlop hairpin, around the outside...

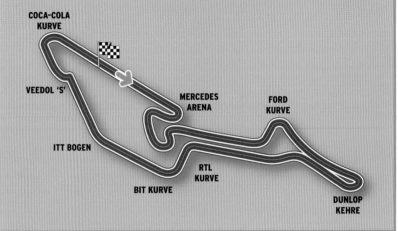

NURBURGRING NORDSCHLEIFE
Circuit length: **14.167 miles**
Years race held: **1951-1954, 1956-1959, 1961-1969, 1971-1976**
The ultimate red meat circuit with more than 100 corners, dipping and bucking its way through the Eifel forest. No driver who was less than supreme ever triumphed here, especially when the capricious weather turned to rain, often with hanging mist for good effect. The sharply-banked Karussel is the most famous corner, but the Flugplatz and the Fuchsrohre were the ones that required the most bravery.

The 'Ring Cycle: Williams ace Juan Pablo Montoya battles with Ferrari's Michael Schumacher at the European Grand Prix at the Nurburgring in 2003

HOLLAND

Together with the Austrian and South African events, the Dutch Grand Prix is one of several classic races which, sad to say, no longer has a place on the World Championship calendar.

Run 30 times between 1952 and 1985, initially in June and latterly in August, every race took place at the same circuit: Zandvoort. Set in sand dunes just a few hundred metres inland from the North Sea, the resort town of Zandvoort was for decades one of the most popular stops on the World Championship tour.

The track itself, opened in 1948, was a clever design which encouraged entertaining racing. A fast and difficult corner on to the long pit straight was followed by the slow right-hander at Tarzan, where heavy braking was required and overtaking opportunities were frequent. One of the most famous corners in racing, it was for years the scene of some exciting action, and occasionally, spectacular accidents. The rest of the track was basically a square, with one side interrupted by a chicane and another by an "S". This loop was later chopped and altered in the name of safety. Sand blowing across the track was a constant hazard.

The list of Dutch Grand Prix winners reads like a Who's Who of motor racing's greats. Ascari won the first two races in 1952-53, while the 1955 event saw a victory for Fangio and the mighty Mercedes team. Moss won for Vanwall in 1958 and Jo Bonnier gave BRM its first victory a year later. All the big names triumphed in the 1960s: Brabham, von Trips, Hill, Clark (four times) and Stewart.

Everyone loved Zandvoort and its holiday atmosphere but, in the early 1970s the track hit the headlines for the wrong reasons. In 1970, Piers Courage died in a fiery accident with the Williams-entered de Tomaso,

and then three years later the same fate befell fellow Englishman Roger Williamson, in only his second race with a privately-entered March.

But while concerns about safety were voiced, the race went on. Lauda registered one of his first triumphs in 1974, and in 1975 Hunt memorably scored his first win for Hesketh. He won again the following year for McLaren after a great battle with Watson. In 1977 Hunt tangled with Andretti, allowing Lauda to win. The 1978 race saw an Andretti/Peterson steamroller performance for Lotus.

The 1979 event is remembered not so much for Jones's victory, but more for the efforts of Villeneuve to drag his three-wheeled Ferrari back to the pits.

The 1983 event was notable for a collision between title contenders Piquet and Prost. Victory went to Arnoux. However, Prost gained his revenge by winning in 1984. The F1 circus visited Zandvoort for the last time in 1985, and the race was a classic, Lauda just holding off Prost for his final victory. The track was coming under threat from developers, and suddenly Holland did not seem like a fashionable place to hold a grand prix. Indeed, the country had never produced a truly competitive driver, which made it hard to justify keeping the race when other venues were applying for dates.

CIRCUIT DETAILS

ZANDVOORT
Circuit length: **2.605 then 2.626 then 2.642 miles**
Years race held: **1952-1953, 1955, 1958-1971, 1973-1985**
One of the most popular circuits of the 1960s and 1970s thanks to Zandvoort's coastal resort status, this was a high-speed track sweeping through the dunes, with sand often blowing onto the track to make handling tricky. The long start/finish straight feeding into the tight Tarzan corner offered a fabulous out-braking point. Sadly, the track claimed the lives of both Piers Courage and Roger Williamson.

Going Dutch: James Hunt leads Niki Lauda at Zandvoort, 1975. It was one of the circuit's epic races and they finished first and second respectively

HUNGARY

Leading the Charge: Fernando Alonso finds himself in space at the start of the 2003 Hungarian GP

CIRCUIT DETAILS

HUNGARORING

Circuit length: **2.494 then 2.469 then 2.722 miles**   Years race held: **1986 onwards**

This was a wasted chance to make motor sport catch on as the Iron Curtain was lifted. It has a beautiful setting in a natural amphitheatre, with spectators able to see much of the track from wherever they watch. But the track is too narrow and twisty for anything other than follow-my-leader processions. Watch for drivers going for a tow down the straight on the run to the only overtaking place: the first corner.

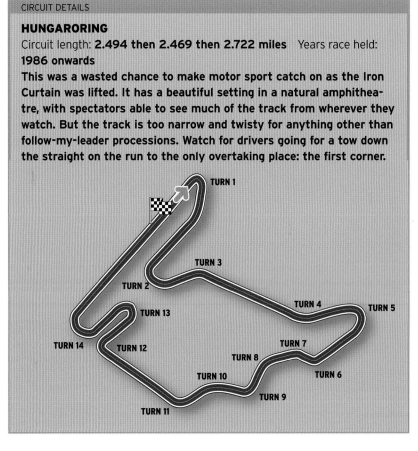

In 1986, Formula One impresario Bernie Ecclestone achieved the unlikely by taking F1 into the Eastern bloc. Built in rolling countryside 12 miles north-east of Budapest, the 2.722-mile Hungaroring is a typical modern autodrome, as its corners are mostly slow and the track is narrow, limiting overtaking opportunities.

For the first three years, the circuit was even slower, for an extra kink had to be built to avoid an underground spring, discovered during construction. For the 1989 race, the problem was solved.

There have been some close races in Hungary, but thanks to the nature of the track, they have rarely featured much overtaking. That said, the inaugural race saw Piquet beat Senna after they swapped places. Piquet won again in 1987 - but only after team-mate Mansell had a wheel nut work loose.

Senna was embroiled in another tight battle in 1988, this time with charging McLaren team-mate Prost, but the Frenchman dropped out with wheel bearing failure just as Senna began to feel the pressure.

The 1989 event was one of the more memorable races. Patrese led until his Williams sprang a water leak, leaving Senna in the lead. Mansell rose from 12th on the grid in his Ferrari and ducked past the Brazilian in a really opportunistic move in traffic.

Senna and Mansell were in the news again in 1990. Boutsen took pole and, against the run of form, led all the way for Williams. He came under strong pressure from Nannini, but there was no way past. The following Senna punted Nannini off, but he could not find a way past Boutsen in the closing laps. Meanwhile, Berger had pushed Mansell out of the way.

Senna won in 1991 after Mansell and Patrese used up the brakes on their Williams-Renaults, and Ayrton triumphed yet again in 1992. Despite a punctured tyre, Mansell came home second and clinched the world title.

Prost was destined never to win in Hungary, and he blew his last attempt in 1993 by stalling on the warm-up lap. Hill stormed to a great maiden victory. Schumacher earned Benetton its first Hungarian win in 1994, as Hill gave chase. But Hill went one better in 1995, then was second again in 1996, behind Villeneuve.

It was so close for Hill in 1997, but his Arrows hit gearbox problems on the last lap and this handed victory to Villeneuve. Then Schumacher raced to one of the all-time great wins in 1998, outracing the superior McLarens by stopping three times to their two-stop strategy. Hakkinen then led all the way the following year, and made it two wins on the trot by keeping Schumacher's Ferrari behind him in 2000. Schumacher struck back in 2001, then sat in team-mate Rubens Barrichello's wake in 2002. In 2003, Alonso proved that he could win for Renault, doing so at just 22. Schumacher won a dull race in 2004, then Raikkonen triumphed in 2005, as team-mate Montoya had to retire.

The 2006 stands out as Hungary's most exciting and Honda came away with the result it had been seeking, a famous victory, with Jenson Button earning the plaudits on a wet-dry day.

Politics overshadowed the 2007 race, as Alonso and Hamilton squabbled at McLaren, but the British driver was the one left smiling after he won, shadowed by Raikkonen.

Heikki Kovalainen scored his breakthrough win here for McLaren in 2008 after poleman Hamilton was passed by Massa at the first corner. Hamilton was scuppered by a puncture, Massa's engine blew and Kovalainen picked up the pieces.

Massa suffered a head injury in qualifying in 2009, then Hamilton won easily ahead of Raikkonen.

ITALY

The name Monza is one of the most evocative in motor sport and it reflects a remarkable heritage. The circuit has hosted the Italian Grand Prix every year since 1950 except 1980, when it was run at Imola.

An Italian Grand Prix had been run for the first time at Brescia in 1921, but Monza, set in a park near Milan, became its rightful home and much of the track used then remains. Monza has always been one of the fastest tracks, even after the addition of chicanes in the early 1970s.

The Italian Grand Prix has a great atmosphere and attracts a massive crowd of Ferrari fans known as the "tifosi". If their team is not winning, they make their feelings known...

The wide pit straight is curtailed by a chicane that usually produces first-lap drama. The Curva Grande right-hander is followed by a second chicane, leading to the Lesmo right-handers that were realigned in 1994 to slow the cars. The track then rushes under the old banked circuit to the Vialone chicane. Then comes the back straight, followed by the Parabolica corner that catapults the cars back on to the start/finish straight again.

Before the chicanes were built, the track was virtually a flat-out blast, encouraging slipstreaming, especially when cars became more "slippery" in the 1960s. However, it was also one of the toughest on machinery, and very often races were decided more by engine longevity than driver skill.

Monza has held some memorable grands prix, but has also had considerable tragedy. In the pre-war races several of the stars of the day lost their lives. Three top drivers were killed in one event in 1933 alone.

Monza was part of the first World Championship in 1950, offering a battle between Alfa Romeo and Ferrari; Farina won for the former.

The first of many dramatic finishes occurred in 1953. It was one of the rare occasions when the lead battle continued to the last lap, not being compromised by mechanical failure. Ascari spun at the last corner, Farina took to the grass and Marimon hit Ascari. The ever canny Fangio was able to steer past the mayhem to win.

A banked section was added for 1955, and a 6.2-mile course was devised, incorporating the original track and the two banked corners. The banking was bumpy and unpopular, and proved notably hard on tyres. Fangio won and Moss triumphed in 1956 before the layout was temporarily abandoned. In the latter race, Collins handed his car to Fangio and in doing so sacrificed his own World Championship hopes to the maestro.

Moss's win started a run of success for English-speaking drivers, who would win every Italian Grand Prix bar one until 1969. Perhaps the most galling loss for the locals came in 1957 when Moss won for Vanwall.

The race was restored to the combined course in 1960, and the British teams boycotted the event. A Ferrari won, this the last victory by any front-engined car, with Phil Hill the first American to win a grand prix. Hill clinched the drivers' title at Monza in 1961, but did so in tragic circumstances after his Ferrari team-mate Wolfgang von Trips and 12 fans were killed.

The grand prix returned to the road course in 1962, and in 1963 an attempt to return to the banked course was abandoned after first practice.

Time and again, races in the 1960s would be spoiled by leading cars dropping out. In 1965 Jackie Stewart scored his first-ever win, and in 1966 Ludovico Scarfiotti led home a Ferrari one-two. The race delivered a photo finish in 1969, Stewart just pulling clear of Rindt, Beltoise and McLaren.

Tragedy returned in 1970 when Rindt lost his life in qualifying.

Into the Funnel: Michael Schumacher leads for Ferrari at the start of the 2003 Italian Grand Prix at Monza as the drivers behind trip over each other

Regazzoni emerged from a great lead battle to score his first win. The following year brought the most sensational finish of any grand prix, as the unrated Gethin led a pack of five across the line by 0.01s.

Monza was ruined in 1972, though, with the introduction of a chicane beyond the pits and another at Vialone. The days of slipstreaming fights were over, and the first "new" race was won by Emerson Fittipaldi.

Peterson emerged as a Monza specialist, winning in 1973, 1974 and 1976, but the track was to claim his life after a pile-up at the start in 1978 left him hospitalized with broken legs, and the Swede died from complications.

Monza was a circuit where the turbo cars could stretch their legs. In 1986, at the peak of the turbo era, Fabi's BMW-powered Benetton blasted to pole position at over 154mph. Remarkably, neither he nor fellow front-row man Prost took up their grid positions after last-minute problems.

Three times in the late 1980s Senna lost out when he seemed to have the race won. In 1987 he went across the grass at the Parabolica, handing Piquet the lead. In 1988 he was leading comfortably when he tangled with backmarker Schlesser, allowing Berger to score the last triumph of Enzo Ferrari's lifetime. Then in 1989 his engine blew with nine laps to go, allowing Prost to win. The Frenchman gave his trophy to the fans in a calculated insult to team boss Ron Dennis. Senna's luck changed when he won in 1990, but the luckiest man that day was Warwick, who survived a huge crash at the Parabolica.

The 1991 event was one of the best, as Senna fought with the Williams pair of Mansell and Patrese. The Italian retired, Senna was forced to take new tyres and Mansell scored a memorable win, but Senna got his own back in 1992 when the Williams duo retired.

As in the 1950s, Monza continued to exert a mechanical toll. Prost was leading in 1993 when engine failure handed the win to team-mate Hill.

He scored a second success in 1994. Since then, Herbert won in 1995, with Michael Schumacher sending the *tifosi* wild in 1996. Coulthard secured his second victory of the year by winning in 1997, but blew up when leading in 1998 and Schumacher passed Hakkinen to head a Ferrari one-two. Hakkinen crashed out of the lead in 1999, much to the delight of the tifosi who'd seen him do the same earlier in the year at Imola – and Frentzen came through to win for Jordan. The 2000 race was marked by a massive first lap crash at the second chicane, with six cars tangling and an airborne wheel killing a marshal.

Schumacher went on to win to send the *tifosi* wild as his title challenge gathered speed. Despite the terrorist attack on New York's Twin Towers the week before, Montoya had reason to smile in 2001 as he scored his first win in his maiden season for Williams. Montoya then set a new outright record pole lap in 2002, at 161.449mph, but he was no match for the Ferraris in the race, Barrichello winning. It was then Schumacher all the way in 2003.

Barrichello was on pole in 2004 and raced clear from pole to win, helped by Schumacher - who had become champion at the previous race - being tipped into a spin on the opening lap and managing to recover only to fifth.

Montoya kept Alonso at bay into the first corner in 2005 and then led all the way to win for McLaren. The team was hopeful of another win in 2006, as Raikkonen led from pole, but Schumacher pitted later and moved through to win. Then Alonso led all the way for McLaren in 2007, followed by team-mate Hamilton.

History was made in 2008 when 21-yer-old Vettel not only took pole for Scuderia Toro Rosso, but dominated a wet race to give it its first win.

In 2009, .Brawn GP enjoyed nits first Monza appearance and Barrichello led Button home for a one-two result for the newly formed team.

CIRCUIT DETAILS

MONZA

Circuit length: **3.915 then 6.214 then 3.573 then 3.588 then 3.604 then 3.625 then 3.585 then 3.600 miles**

Years race held: **1950-1979, 1981 onwards**

To many, this spiritual home of motor racing with its abandoned banked track on the infield is a reminder of bygone days. With long straights and fast corners, it provides the best slipstreaming battles, but its flow is interrupted by chicanes. The Lesmo bends are the biggest test, followed by the entry to the tricky Ascari chicane.

CURVA DI LESMOS · CURVA DEL SERRAGLIO · CURVA PARABOLICA · VARIANTE ASCARI · CURVA DEL VIALONE · VARIANTE DELLA ROGGIA · RETTIFILO TRIBUNE · CURVA GRANDE · PRIMO VARIANTE

Man on the Move: Nigel Mansell had to outrun Ayrton Senna to win the Italian GP at Monza in 1991

JAPAN

Japan's first involvement in Formula One was through Honda, which competed from 1964 to 1968. Yet, it wasn't until 1976 that Japan hosted its first grand prix. This was at Fuji Speedway, a charismatic circuit set on the slopes of Mount Fuji. It was notable for having one of the longest straights in Formula One, linked by a succession of sweeping corners.

The first race there is remembered as the one in which Hunt became champion after Lauda pulled out. Few recall that Andretti gave Lotus its first victory for more than two years.

The sun shone in 1977 and Hunt's final win was overshadowed by the death of several onlookers after Villeneuve vaulted over Peterson's Tyrrell. With the Japanese motor industry showing little interest in the sport, the grand prix was dropped.

It restarted in 1987 at Suzuka, as a result of Honda's successful return to Formula One, this time as an engine supplier. Honda had opened Suzuka in 1963 and it featured a unique – for Formula One – 'figure of eight' layout augmented by a variety of fast and slow bends, including 130R, the flat-out left near the end of the lap.

Suzuka was loved by the drivers, but passing was difficult and it was made even harder when the chicane before the pits was tightened in 1991.

Suzuka's first grand prix is remembered for an accident in practice that ended Mansell's title hopes, handing the honours to team-mate Piquet. The race was won by Berger's McLaren. In 1988, Senna's growing status in Japan was confirmed when he won after recovering from a bad start. He and McLaren team-mate Prost collided at the chicane when battling for the lead in 1989. Senna finished first, but his disqualification handed victory to Nannini. In 1990, Prost (with Ferrari) and Senna tangled again, going off at the first corner.

Senna led again in 1991, when he allowed team-mate Berger past at the last corner to win. In 1992, Patrese took advantage of Mansell's retirement to score his final win. Senna bounced back to win for McLaren in 1993, dominating a wet/dry race. Afterwards he made the headlines by punching debutant Eddie Irvine.

Rain struck in 1994, and a string of accidents caused a pace car period, then a stoppage. After the restart, Damon Hill overcame Schumacher's first-part advantage to score perhaps the hardest-earned win of his career.

Japan earned a second race for 1995. Dubbed the Pacific Grand Prix, it was held at the TI Circuit in Aida. Schumacher won, but a lack of passing meant it wasn't popular.

Suzuka hosted the 1996 finale in which Hill won race and title. Schumacher won in 1997, while his stalling on the grid in 1998 made him begin the restarted race from the back and made it all the easier for Hakkinen to win to wrap up the title. In 1999, Hakkinen won again to clinch the title before a narrow defeat by Schumacher in 2000 meant that he had to make do with being runner-up.

Schumacher triumphed in 2001 and 2002 before having a nervous race in 2003 to collect the point he required for his fourth title in a row after Montoya had broken clear but his hydraulics failed, leaving Barrichello to help team-mate Schumacher by winning from title outsider Raikkonen. Schumacher won again in 2004, leading home brother Ralf's Williams.

Ralf was on pole for Toyota in 2005, but he'd been fuelled light for qualifying and Fisichella took the lead for Renault. However, both were outraced by Raikkonen, who advanced from 17th after a 10-place grid penalty to power his McLaren past Fisichella going onto the final lap to win. In 2006, victory for Alonso helped the Renault driver to close in on his second F1 title after Michael Schumacher's Ferrari lost the lead due to engine failure.

The grand prix went to a revamped Fuji in 2007 and Hamilton mastered very wet conditions to win. Then, in 2008, Hamilton lost his cool and forced Raikkonen wide into the first corner, earning a drivethrough penalty as Alonso won for Renault.

Back at Suzuka in 2009, Vettel closed in on Hamilton in the title race by winning for Red Bull Racing..

Left: A Renault kerb-hops its way through the Casio Triangle in practice for the 2003 Japanese Grand Prix at Suzuka. Right: Adopted favourite Ayrton Senna blasts his McLaren down the straight on his way to victory in 1993

CIRCUIT DETAILS

SUZUKA
Circuit length: **3.641 then 3.617 miles**   Years race held: **1987-2006, 2009**
A really tough and technical circuit, unusual for the fact that it crosses over itself. The crowds are always enormous and chase everything that looks looks like a driver with an autograph book. The toughest corner is 130R at the end of the back straight: it's very fast and very narrow.

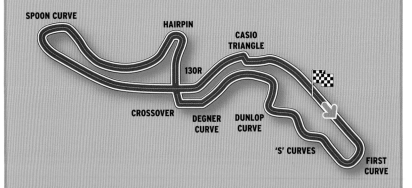

FUJI SPEEDWAY
Circuit length: **2.709 miles**   Years race held: **1976-1977, 2007-2008**
No circuit offers a better backdrop, with the perfect volcanic cone of Mount Fuji rising clear of the forests below. Used only twice by the World Championship, it offered an unusually long start/finish straight fed out of a long, long corner and then coming to an end in a hairpin, making overtaking more than likely. Rain could hit hard, though, and it did in 1976, all but washing the cars off the track. Two chicanes have since spoiled its shape, but this wonderful track is still in use today.

MALAYSIA

Fast Finnish: race winner Kimi Raikkonen crosses the finish line in 2003 as his team goes berserk

CIRCUIT DETAILS

SEPANG
Circuit length: **3.444 miles**   Years race held: **1999 onwards**
A track that tests drivers and engineers, it also tests the mechanics and spectators as soaring temperatures are made worse by debilitating humidity. Fortunately, the giant grandstand has a canopy to provide shade. With Malaysia blessed with natural beauty, many visitors add on a holiday in one of the country's beach resorts. Outbraking is a feature into both the first and last corners, with plenty of track width assisting in this, as do long runs down to both, enabling a driver to tuck in behind the car ahead for a slipstream.

LANGKAWI

PANGKOR LAUT

GENTING

KLIA

SUNWAY LAGOON

BERJAYA TIOMAN

KENYIR LAKE

The World Championship really needed to spread its wings in the 1990s, with its April to September run in Europe bracketed by outings to Australia and Brazil at the start of the year and Japan at the end, with only a visit to Canada in June for variety.

Asia had always been a poor relation, but then Malaysia built a circuit for 1999 so that it could host a round of the World Championship. Sepang was built 30 miles south of capital Kuala Lumpur, with the added advantage of being close to the city's international airport.

It's a mix of tight and sweeping corners combined with an unusually wide track to encourage overtaking. The views from the main grandstand are astonishing, with those on the start/finish straight side able to see almost all of the first half of the lap and those on the rear side of the grandstand enjoying the view over the second half of the lap.

Anyone thinking that this was a case of introducing racing to a country that had watched it only on TV would be wrong, as there had been racing since the 1950s on the streets of Penang and Johore Bahru. In the late 1960s, the Batu Tiga circuit (later known as Shah Alam but also as Selangor) was opened. This was closed in the late 1970s after six children were killed. Reopened in the 1980s, its only World Championship event, a round of the sports car World Championship in 1985, was a failure as the drivers swooned in their cockpits.

With the 1999 title race between Hakkinen and Irvine poised delicately, it was likely that there would be some fireworks for Malaysia's Formula One debut. And so it proved. Schumacher did all he could to assist his Ferrari team-mate by blocking Hakkinen. Irvine duly won, with Hakkinen third, meaning that Irvine would start the final round with a four-point advantage.

The second Malaysian Grand Prix was mercifully without the politics. Sadly, as final round in 2000, it was also run with the title having already been settled in Schumacher's favour. The German then overcame McLaren's Hakkinen and Coulthard before holding off the Scot for victory. He mastered dry-wet-dry conditions to win again in 2001, when the race was brought forward to be the second race on the calendar, leaving the local fans little time to save up for a ticket, explaining why the grandstands were less than full.

Ralf Schumacher won in 2002 after Michael and Montoya collided on lap 1 and Barrichello parked his Ferrari, its engine blown. Even with a stop-go penalty, Montoya made it to second for a Williams one-two. Michael Schumacher had another costly first lap in 2003 when he clashed with Trulli. Alonso was already ahead in the other Renault, chased by

Coulthard, but the Scot was to pull off and the Spaniard to fade, allowing Coulthard's team-mate Raikkonen to score his first grand prix win. Echoing his stunning form in the 2004 opener, Michael Schumacher made it two victories in two races, winning ahead of Montoya and BAR's Button.

The visit in 2005 showed Renault and Alonso's strong form as he scored the first of the seven wins that he'd need for his first drivers' title. Twelve months later, Renault won again, this time with Fisichella heading Alonso home. Alonso bounced back to win in 2007, now driving for McLaren, leading home team-mate Hamilton.

Massa led for Ferrari in 2008, but victory went to team-mate Raikkonen. Massa spun, leaving second to Kubica.

For 2009, it was decided to start the race two hours later to boost the TV audience, but storms hit and darkness fell before a restart could be made, leaving Button as the victor.

MEXICO

The Mexican Grand Prix is unique in that it has twice been a regular grand prix fixture and twice been dumped from the calendar and quickly forgotten.

The race ran in its first form from 1963 to 1970, and had a second lease of life from 1986 to 1992. All events were held on the Hermanos Rodriguez Circuit in the suburbs of Mexico City. The track shared two characteristics with Italy's Monza. Firstly, it was located in a public park. Secondly, it had a fearsomely fast final corner, leading on to a long pit straight. But, unlike Monza's Parabolica, Mexico's Peraltada was slightly banked, which made it even quicker – and even more apt to catch out the unwary. The first corner now has a chicane to slow it before turning right and going into a left-right flick, a hairpin, then a series of "S" bends on to the back straight and that final corner...

Mexico City is shaken regularly by earthquakes, and the tremors contributed to a notoriously bumpy surface which was often criticized. The other unusual factor was its lofty altitude, 7400 ft, to which both men and machines had to adapt.

Much of the inspiration for the grand prix was provided by brothers Ricardo and Pedro Rodriguez. Ricardo lost his life practising for the inaugural non-championship race in 1962, and the track was subsequently named after him. His brother was in the field for the first official grand prix here a year later, and soon matured into one of the top stars of the decade.

Clark won the first championship race in 1963, and a year later Mexico was the scene of a dramatic title showdown, involving Clark, Surtees and Hill. Gurney won the race, but Surtees took the title. In 1965 Ginther gave Honda its first-ever win, while until the end of the 1960s Surtees, Clark, Hill and Hulme each took turns in winning.

Until 1970 the race was firmly established as the season-closer, but that year's race, won by Jacky Ickx, was notorious for the lack of crowd control. Drivers raced between human barriers, and it was a miracle that there were no incidents.

The race was dropped from the schedule for 1971. Pedro Rodriguez was killed in June, and with him went any chance that the Mexican authorities might push for the race to be back on the calendar. Pedro's name was later added to that of his brother in the official title of the circuit.

However, 16 years later, the financial circumstances were right for FOCA and the race was restored, with the track cut from 3.1 to 2.7 miles and suitably uprated with new (but outdated) pits. The Peraltada turn was a wonderful challenge for the modern breed of Formula One cars, but over the years it would be the scene of several huge accidents, many of them on the exit of the corner.

Berger earned maiden wins for himself and the Benetton team in the 1986 event, while Mansell, Prost and Senna won over the next three years. The chicane at the end of the pit straight proved a popular passing place as they picked off backmarkers.

Prost won again in 1990, but the race is best remembered for a daring move by Mansell on Berger – on the outside at Peralta, ensuring a Ferrari one-two. Mansell was again second in 1991, this time behind Patrese.

The last Mexican Grand Prix was held in 1992. Not surprisingly, the Williams-Renault of Mansell – the best "active" car – rode the bumps to perfection and led all the way. Team-mate Patrese finished second. The race disappeared from the calendar in 1993, mainly due to finances.

CIRCUIT DETAILS

MEXICO CITY
Circuit length: **3.107 then 2.747 miles**   Years race held: **1963-1970, 1986-1992**
Crowds spilling onto the verges of this high-speed blast at altitude led to Mexico losing its race after 1970. However, Mexico's capital got its race back in 1986 and held onto it for a further six years. The final corner, the gently-banked 180 degree Peraltada curve, was one of the toughest on the calendar, as Ayrton Senna found out when he tried to take it in sixth gear in 1991 and flipped.

Break for the Border: Nigel Mansell leads team-mate Riccardo Patrese plus Senna, Schumacher and Berger as the Mexican GP gets under way in 1992

MONACO

The Monaco Grand Prix is regarded as the most prestigious event on the calendar. With its casino and yachts, Monaco is still glamorous for the rich and famous, for whom the race is of secondary importance to partying.

Winding its way around the streets of the principality, the track has changed little over the decades, and much of it would be familiar to drivers who raced here in the 1950s.

From Ste Dévote, the track turns up the hill to Casino Square then plunges down to Mirabeau and the tight Grand Hotel (formerly Loews, formerly Station) hairpin. Portier leads on to the seafront, with a tunnel to be negotiated before the harbourside chicane. After that comes Tabac, the Piscine section (which was modified in the 1970s and mid-1990s), then finally the tight right at Rascasse.

With overtaking all but impossible, it's vital to qualify at the front. Yet, the attrition rate is often high, and careful driving can earn points.

The grand prix was first held in 1929, and the pre-war races produced some great battles, with Nuvolari among the winners. Monaco hosted the second-round of the World Championship in 1950, just a week after the opening race at Silverstone. Ten cars were eliminated in a first-lap crash and Fangio scored a famous win.

The grand prix didn't return until 1955 and Monaco has had a race every year since, a record that no other circuit can match. In that 1955 race, the Mercedes effort collapsed and Trintignant scored a surprise win for Ferrari, but it's best remembered for Ascari's flight into the harbour.

Moss won in 1956, when the chicane was tightened, but in 1957 he and fellow Brits Hawthorn and Collins crashed there and Fangio won again. Trintignant scored a second win in 1958 as the opposition faded and he triumphed in a Cooper. Moss lost out to Brabham in 1959 through axle failure then won in 1960. However, his victory in 1961 is the one that stands out, as his underpowered Lotus held off the Ferraris of Ginther and Phil Hill.

Graham Hill then became the king of Monaco. He won five times in all. He first shone at Monaco in 1962, leading until his engine failed, allowing Bruce McLaren to win. He made amends by winning in 1963, 1964 and 1965. On the first two occasions he was helped by problems for Clark, then Clark missed the 1965 race to attend the Indy 500. However, that was perhaps Hill's greatest win, for he had to recover from a trip up the chicane escape road when caught out by a slower car. Hill added further wins in 1968 and 1969.

Stewart scored his first Monaco win in 1966, then winning in 1971 and 1973. Hulme scored his first win there in 1967. But that race was spoiled by the death of Bandini, who crashed at the chicane while in pursuit.

In 1970, Brabham slid into the barrier at the last corner, handing victory to the hard-chasing Rindt. Two years later, the race was run in torrential rain and, against all odds, Beltoise beat the stars to give BRM its final grand prix win. The 1974 race had a pile-up on the run from Ste Dévote to Casino Square, and in its aftermath Peterson scored a fine win in the old Lotus 72, even overcoming a spin.

Lauda was the master of Monaco in the mid-1970s, winning in 1975 (in the wet) and 1976. In 1977 he lost out to Scheckter's Wolf by less than a second, and in 1978 he set a lap record as he chased Depailler, the Frenchman

Playground of the the Beautiful People: Juan Pablo Montoya leads Kimi Raikkonen in a dance round Monte Carlo's harbour during the 2003 Grand Prix

scoring his first grand prix win.

Another thrilling finish took place in 1979, veteran Regazzoni confirming his return to form as he pursued Scheckter's Ferrari. The 1980 race is remembered more for the start. Derek Daly eliminated three other cars as he bounced high over the pack at Ste Dévote. Reutemann scored a canny win as others hit trouble.

Villeneuve added to his growing reputation by winning the 1981 event in the unloved Ferrari 126CK, while 1982 brought one of the most memorable finishes ever. In the closing laps Prost and Daly both crashed, Pironi and de Cesaris ran out of fuel, and Patrese spun – but resumed to score an amazing success.

A virtuoso performance on a damp track earned a great victory for Rosberg in 1983, and in 1984 rain returned in style. Much of the field fell off the road, including Mansell when leading. Amid much controversy, the race was stopped early with leader Prost being caught by newcomer Senna, who was in turn being reeled in by the Tyrrell of fellow rookie Bellof. Prost won again in 1985 after a battle with Alboreto.

In the biggest change since the introduction of the Piscine corners in the early 1970s, the chicane was rebuilt for the 1986 race. It was turned from a high-speed flick into a slow left, right, left sequence. The result was the same, as Prost won. Each race seemed to produce a spectacular crash, and the victim this time was Tambay, who rolled his Haas Lola.

Prost's reign as Monaco's man to beat was almost over. The 1987 race saw Senna pick up his first win with the "active" Lotus, but only after Mansell's Williams-Honda retired.

The following year Senna was in a class of his own but, with a handful of laps to go, he made one of the most publicized mistakes of his career, hitting the barrier just before the tunnel. Prost nipped through to score his fourth (and last) triumph.

For the next five years Senna reigned supreme, winning each year from 1989 to 1993. More often than not, Mansell was his closest challenger, and Senna won the 1992 race after Nigel made a late stop with a loose wheel. And he won in 1993 only after Prost and Schumacher had encountered problems.

The 1994 Monaco race was the first grand prix after Senna's death, and he was missed as Schumacher became the first winner other than Prost and Senna since 1983. There was a surprise first grand prix win for Panis in 1996, but Schumacher returned to win for the third time in 1997 before Hakkinen won for McLaren the following year. Schumacher led all the way in 1999, then streaked clear in 2000, with Coulthard bottled up behind Trulli's Jordan. But his suspension broke, Trulli retired and Coulthard was a clear winner. Schumacher and Barrichello dominated for Ferrari in 2001, then Coulthard got the jump on poleman Montoya in 2002 to win. The Colombian put the record straight in 2003, the last year before the realignment of the track after Piscine and the building of proper pits and a wider pitlane for 2004, when Trulli grabbed pole for Renault and won.

Raikkonen controlled the race in 2005, winning easily from Williams duo Heidfeld and Webber who both passed Alonso in the closing laps as he struggled with rear tyres that had lost grip. Alonso had better fortune in 2006, though, winning easily from Montoya's McLaren. Famously, Schumacher had been fastest in qualifying, but brought the final sesion t oa close by seemingly driving into the barriers and blocking the track before Alonso could complete his last flier. Schumacher got put back to last place on the grid and then did well to reach fifth.

Alonso won again, this time for McLaren, in 2007, with team-mate Hamilton feeling he should have been allowed to make a bid to go for the lead. Hamilton then made sure, winning on a damp track in 2008. It was then all Brawn in 2009 as Button and Barrichello led the Ferraris home.

MONACO

Circuit length: **1.976 then 1.954 then 2.037 then 2.058 then 2.068 then 2.092 miles**   Years race held: **1950, 1955 onwards**

Ever an anachronism in modern day Formula One. Yet this harbourside track nestling in the principality of Monte Carlo corners more glamour than the rest of the grands prix put together. It is incredibly bumpy and narrow, but the cars still hit a heck of a speed as they power out of the tunnel onto the waterfront And the sight of Formula One cars being flung between the barriers in Casino Square never fails to excite.

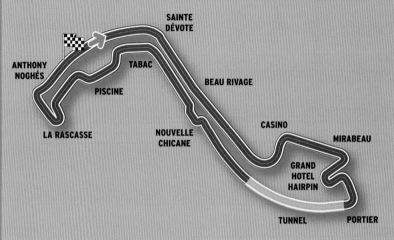

King of the Streets: Ayrton Senna won the Monaco GP in 1989 and every one thereafter until 1993

PORTUGAL

Portugal is a small country which has never had a great Formula One driver, and yet its grand prix was long a well-supported event, often producing drama of the highest order.

The Portuguese Grand Prix had a brief flourish during 1958-60. In the even years it was held on the Oporto street track - where tramlines and cobblestones were among the hazards - and in 1959 it was run at Monsanto, near Lisbon, a tricky parkland venue.

The starting line at Oporto was on the harbour front and, like the modern Macau track, it combined long straights with twisty bits between buildings. Stirling Moss won the first race, while Mike Hawthorn nearly threw away his world title there after driving the wrong way after a spin.

Moss was again class of the field in 1959 in his Cooper. The race was started late to avoid the afternoon heat, and finished after 7pm! Moss, returning from injury, was never really in the hunt in the 1960 Oporto event, which was won by Brabham.

Formula One didn't return for 24 years, this time to a permanent road course near the resort of Estoril. Built in 1972, the 2.70-mile Autodromo do Estoril hosted European Formula Two in the mid-1970s, but had largely been forgotten when it was resurrected and tidied up in 1984.

Featuring up-and-down sweeps through barren, rocky terrain, the lap starts with a flowing right-hander that leads almost immediately into a wicked downhill right-hander and a hairpin. Then it's uphill to another hairpin and down the kinked back straight. A long left-hander, a short straight, then an uphill right-hander lead the track into a series of twists before a long, long right-hander on to the pit straight. Tough on the drivers, it has more overtaking opportunities than most tracks built in recent years.

The 1984 event was held in October and proved to be the championship decider. Prost won the race, but McLaren team-mate Niki Lauda did just enough to win the title - by half a point! The 1985 race was held just seven months later, in April, and Prost was one of several drivers to crash out in torrential conditions. The master on that memorable day was Senna, who collected his first win for Lotus.

After that experiment, the race moved to September. Mansell won in 1986, while Prost triumphed again in 1987 and again in 1988. One of the most controversial races came in 1989, when Mansell was black-flagged after reversing in the pits. He did not respond, and three laps later crashed out of the race with Senna. Berger made Ferrari smile by winning.

Mansell was banned from the next event, but the following year he came back and beat Senna at Estoril - a rare good result during his miserable second season with Ferrari.

Patrese won in 1991, after Mansell lost a wheel leaving the pits! Nigel was later black-flagged, and his title hopes took a major knock. He scored his third success in 1992.

The 1993 race saw Schumacher score his second-ever win for Benetton after the team's superior pit strategy overcame that of Prost and Williams.

In 1994, Damon Hill took full advantage of the absence of a suspended Schumacher by winning. This time the track sported an absurdly slow chicane, corners Nine and Ten, introduced after the Imola tragedies. And it was here that

the McLarens collided in 1996 as Villeneuve raced to victory to take the title race to the final round.

Estoril's race was dropped after 1996 as the safety modifications that had been requested by the sport's governing body hadn't been made.

Michael Schumacher's Benetton is chased by Alain Prost's McLaren at Estoril in 1993 in a race which he went on to win

SAN MARINO

For years, Formula One stuck to the rule that no country could have more than one grand prix, but there was an exception in 1957, when Italy had races at Pescara and Monza.

It was decided in 1976 that the USA was large enough to deserve East and West coast races, and in 1984 it had three events. There was a Swiss Grand Prix at Dijon-Prenois and, since then, Brands Hatch, the Nurburgring, Donington Park, Jerez and Valencia have hosted races under the 'European Grand Prix' title. From 1981 to 2006, Italy ran two grands prix each year, the second taking its title from the principality of San Marino.

The first San Marino Grand Prix was a non-championship race in 1979, a week after the Italian Grand Prix. The venue was Imola. It was built in the 1950s but, like other established circuits joining the Formula One scene, it had to be rebuilt.

The track was set in wooded countryside with up and down sweeps linked by chicanes. Tamburello, the high-speed left-hander shortly after the pits, was a real test. The support of Enzo Ferrari – the track was renamed after his late son Dino – ensured that the race was a success.

Niki Lauda won that first event for Brabham and, after some political manoeuvring, Imola ousted Monza to host the 1980 Italian Grand Prix. For 1981, a compromise was reached, and thereafter both circuits held a race. Piquet won in 1980 and won again in the first and very wet pukka San Marino event the following April.

Imola developed a reputation for drama. The 1982 event was notable for a boycott by the FOCA-supporting teams, and for the start of a feud between winner Pironi and Ferrari team-mate Villeneuve; the Canadian was killed at Zolder a fortnight later. Exactly a year after the feud started, Villeneuve's replacement, Tambay, scored an emotional win here.

Imola is tough on fuel mileage, which was vital in the turbo era. In 1985, Prost ran out on the slowing-down lap and was disqualified for being underweight.

Mansell won in 1987 after team-mate Piquet had a massive accident in qualifying at Tamburello. Berger crashed at the same place in 1989, but Ferrari's worst day at Imola was in 1991: Prost spun off on the warm-up lap and Alesi copied him three laps later. In 1992, Mansell set a record with his fifth straight win, and in 1993 Prost scored another win for Williams.

Imola will always be known for the events of 1994. Ratzenberger died in qualifying and then Senna crashed to his death in the race – at Tamburello.

Hill made Williams smile again by winning in 1996, then Frentzen took his first win in 1997, beating Michael Schumacher, to the flag. In 1998, Coulthard controlled the race for McLaren, then Hakkinen was set to do the same in 1999, but crashed out of the lead, leaving the way clear for Schumacher, with the German winning again in 2000. Ralf Schumacher made his breakthrough for Williams in 2001 after blasting past the McLarens off the line. He had another crack in 2002, but couldn't match the Ferraris, with brother Michael triumphant. Michael won again in 2003 and then again in 2004 as he overcame Honda's pole-starting Button.

Schumacher did his utmost to add the 2005 race to his tally, but Alonso was equal to everything he tried to triumph for Renault after early leader Raikkonen retired his McLaren. There was already speculation that 2006 would be Schumacher's final year, but he was determined to finish off in style and he held off Alonso to win.

CIRCUIT DETAILS

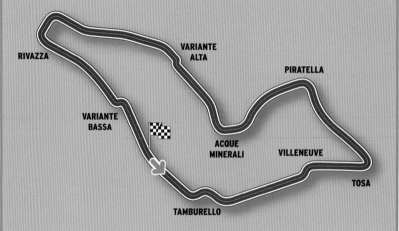

IMOLA
Circuit length: **3.118 then 3.144 then 3.132 then 3.064 miles**
Years race held: **1980-2006**
A fabulous place to watch a grand prix, every grandstand bedecked in banners of Ferrari red and every metre of its perimeter packed by the noisy tifosi, but its memory will always be tainted by the double fatality of Ayrton Senna and Roland Ratzenberger in 1994. Located in beautiful parkland, it has been modified greatly since the accidents, but now has the downhill Acque Minerale restored to its former glory.

Forza Ferrari: Rubens Barrichello leads Ralf Schumacher at the start of the grand prix in 2003

SINGAPORE

Long ago, back in the 1960s, there was racing held in Singapore, but this was around the northern edge of the city along the Thomson Road. However, perhaps spurred into action by neighbouring Malaysia having hosted a grand prix since 1999, Singapore responded to wooing by Formula One driving force Bernie Ecclestone and took the plunge to build a track in the heart of its downtown, in Marina Bay. This would be a track with considerable identity, a track located conveniently to spread F1's global message.

Even more importantly, it was a track built with the express intention of running its races after nightfall, breaking new ground in Formula One. This wasn't just to show the illuminated cityscape to dramatic effect, but to run the grand prix in cooler and less humid conditions in this country on the Equator, much needed as they were by drivers and pit crews alike, and also to ensure that the racing would be live at a time of day that suited the European market.

The inaugural grand prix in 2008 would be the acid test, with many teams worried in advance about the level of light available around the lap and most importantly at the braking zones for the corners, but also at marshalling posts so that drivers could see any warning flags. However, they needn't have worried as the race went off without any problems in these departments and the race will go down in history more for the events that led to victory for Renault's Fernando Alonso who started 15th on the grid and yet vaulted up the order to victory, with his ascent to the front happening after he'd just pitted for fuel and tyres and emerged as the safety car was called out as a car had spun and was sitting in a dangerous position. It was that of his team-mate Nelson Piquet Jr. And it gifted him victory. Amazingly, few seemed too concerned about this until midway through the following year when Piquet Jr was dropped by the team, then spoke out. The ramifications for the team's hierarchy were costly, as team principal Flavio Briatore and engineering chief Pat Symonds were forced out.

Fortunately for all concerned, Singapore's 2009 grand prix at the Marina Bay circuit was more ordered, as Lewis Hamilton dominated for McLaren. Sebastian Vettel should have finished second for Red Bull

Racing, but a penalty for speeding at his second pit stop left him fourth. Another to lose out by speeding in the pits was Nico Rosberg and the Williams driver's race was wrecked as he had to take his drivethrough penalty after a safety car deployment had bunched the field after Force India's Adrian Sutil had collected Nick Heidfeld's BMW Sauber and so he fell to the tail. These two factors helped Timo Glock rise from sixth to second for Toyota, while Alonso was back on the podium, this time with no suggestion of assistance from a team-mate. Many cars had to retire as their brakes weren't up to the task of slowing their cars into the numerous 90-degree corners, with Mark Webber's title challenge taking a knock when his RB5's brakes failed entering Turn 1.

So, with Bernie Ecclestone continuing to cast around for new grand prix venues, Singapore has provided a template for what he wants, a shining example of how a powerful city offers an enticing backdrop for racing. Quite simply, it puts out the message that Formula One is exciting and desirable.

So, with Bernie Ecclestone continuing to look for new grand prix venues, Singapore has provided a example of how a powerful city offers an enticing backdrop for racing.

Finding Light in the Dark: Lewis Hamilton turns in to Turn 1 as he heads for victory on F1's second visit in 2009

SOUTH AFRICA

Three-way Fight: McLaren's Ayrton Senna leads Alain Prost and Michael Schumacher in 1993

CIRCUIT DETAILS

KYALAMI
Circuit length: **2.544 then 2.550 then 2.300 then 2.648 miles** Years race held: **1967-1985, 1992-1993**
Built in 1961, this circuit on the outskirts of Johannesburg took over South Africa's Grand Prix from East London in 1967, offering great corners such as Crowthorn, Barbeque Bend and the Jukskei Sweep. South Africa's apartheid laws eventually made Formula One stay away, but now that they're gone the track has been too chopped to be of interest to Formula One.

EAST LONDON
Circuit length: **2.436 miles** Years race held: **1962-1963, 1965**
Home of the South African Grand Prix from 1934 to 1966, albeit only three times as a World Championship event, this unfashionable port on South Africa's east coast provided an amphitheatre overlooking the Indian Ocean. The lap opened with a couple of kinks followed by a hairpin, Cocobana Corner, followed by a twisty section that led to the tight final corner, Beacon Bend, that fed the cars back onto the start/finish straight. Jim Clark won here three times.

A grand prix was first held in South Africa in the 1930s, but it wasn't until 1962 that the country hosted its first World Championship race.

The original venue was the 2.44-mile seaside track at East London. It was the closing race of a competitive season and the race was won by Hill and, with Jim Clark retiring, the moustachioed Englishman and BRM secured the drivers' and constructors' titles.

The race remained at East London for two more years, but in 1967 moved to a new home at Kyalami, near Johannesburg, and took on a new role as the season opener.

Like so many classic circuits, Kyalami had a long pit straight, preceded by a fast final corner. The undulating 2.54-mile layout included a spectacular downhill run to the tricky first corner, Crowthorne. That led into the Barbeque/Jukskei Kink section, regarded as one of the most dramatic of any grand prix venue.

Pedro Rodriguez won in 1967, but privateer John Love nearly caused the biggest upset of all time by leading – until he had to make a late stop for fuel. In 1970 Jack Brabham scored his last grand prix win, while the following year Mario Andretti took his first.

Tragedy struck twice in the 1970s and both times the Shadow team was involved. American star Peter Revson was killed in testing in 1974, and three years later Welshman Tom Pryce lost his life when he struck a marshal who crossed the pit straight in his path during the race. Lauda won that event – his first victory since his horrific Nurburgring crash.

One of the most exciting Kyalami races came in 1978, when Peterson and Depailler battled for the lead over the last few laps, Ronnie eventually winning and reaffirming that he could still do the job.

The 1979 event saw more excitement as Villeneuve put in a fine wet weather drive, beating his Ferrari team-mate Scheckter (who had won his home race in 1975). Rain struck again in 1981, when the race took place without the "grandee" FISA-aligned teams such as Ferrari, and was outside the championship. That didn't detract from a fine drive by Reutemann.

A controversial pre-practice drivers' strike is what the 1982 event is best remembered for. The race was eventually won by Prost, who recovered in great style after a puncture. For 1983 the race moved to the end of the season, and Prost lost a last-round title showdown to Piquet, although the Brazilian finished only third. Prost was the star in 1984, starting from the back in the spare car and charging through to second, behind team-mate Lauda. The following year Mansell backed up his maiden win at Brands Hatch with a second straight success.

Motor racing had retained links with South Africa far longer than most other international sports, but after the 1985 race the political pressure became so great – particularly in France – that South Africa's grand prix was dropped from the calendar.

However the political climate changed, and in 1992 the race was back, but on a substantially revised Kyalami track.

This included sections of the old track, but not the long start/finish straight. Indeed, it was barely recognizable to the Formula One teams. Something of a bland, modern autodrome, it was slow and lacked the character of the original.

The first "new" race was won by Mansell, and it was as boring as the revised venue suggested. Fortunately, the 1993 event was rather more exciting, as Prost and Senna put on a spectacular show in the early laps. Prost finally came out on top.

That event was a much better advertisement for Kyalami than the previous race, but after a domestic financial wrangle the South African Grand Prix disappeared from the 1994 calendar. If the problems can be overcome, it may return in the future.

SPAIN

Sparks Fly: Nigel Mansell battles wheel to wheel with Ayrton Senna in the 1991 Spanish Grand Prix

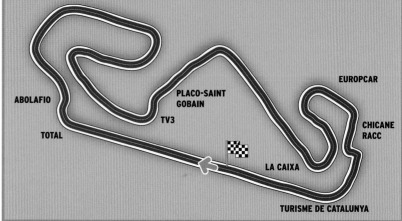
Until Fernando Alonso's breakthrough in 2003, Spain has never had a great grand prix driver, although Alfonso de Portago showed promise in the late 1950s. Yet, the lack of homegrown talent aside, the Spanish Grand Prix has a truly distinguished history.

The race was run in 1951 and 1954 at Pedralbes in the suburbs of Barcelona. Unusually fast and wide for a street venue, it provided Alfa Romeo's Juan Manuel Fangio with his first victory in a World Championship grand prix in 1951. Mike Hawthorn won the second grand prix there for Ferrari three years later.

It was 1968 before Spain next held a grand prix. This then alternated between Jarama and Montjuich Park. On the outskirts of Madrid, Jarama was one of the world's first purpose-built autodromes, designed by John Hugenholtz, the man responsible for Zandvoort and Suzuka. The track consisted of tight, slow corners. In total contrast, Montjuich Park was a

thrilling road circuit, winding up and down for 2.36 miles through a hilltop park in the heart of Barcelona, later home to the main stadium for the 1992 Olympic Games. It had had an earlier incarnation when it hosted the Penya Rhin Grand Prix between 1933 and 1936 then again in 1950, when it was a non-championship event.

Following a trial (non-championship race at Jarama in 1967, won by Clark for Lotus, Graham Hill won the first World Championship round held there for Lotus in 1968 and went on to win that year's drivers' title. In the first Montjuich Park race the following year, both he and Lotus team-mate Rindt suffered wing failures and had huge crashes, as Stewart raced clear to win for Matra. Six years later, an uncannily similar fate befell Stommelen who, by coincidence, was driving a Hill-entered car. After crashes had wiped out much of the field, the German was in the lead of the race when his rear wing failed.

The car cleared a barrier, killing four. McLaren's Mass was declared winner of the curtailed event – it was to be his only win – and the Spanish Grand Prix never returned to Montjuich Park.

Stewart, Emerson Fittipaldi, Lauda, Hunt, Andretti, Depailler and Jones all added their names to the roll of honour at Jarama. However, being narrow and twisty in layout, Jarama rarely produced any overtaking, although that allowed Villeneuve to score a memorable win in 1981, with four cars on the tail of his unwieldy Ferrari, all crossing the finish line covered by just 1.24 seconds! With few tears shed by the drivers, Jarama was dropped after that tedious affair, and it was five years before the Spanish Grand Prix re-emerged, at Jerez, in the far

south of the country. The regional government supported the building of the 2.62-mile track, which was composed of numerous hairpins coupled with a few quick turns on the homeward run behind the pits.

The first grand prix held at Jerez produced a thrilling finish as Lotus ace Senna held off Mansell's Williams by a nose. Annoyingly, subsequent races at Jerez tended to be processional, with comfortable wins for Mansell (1987), Prost (1988 and 1990) and Senna (1989). In 1990, Donnelly suffered life-threatening leg injuries in a horrific crash in qualifying at the fast kink behind the pits. That didn't help Jerez's cause, and by 1991 the race moved to the Circuit de Catalunya, near Barcelona, which was adjudged better than

Follow the Leader: the narrowness of the track helped Ferrari's Gilles Villeneuve hold off Jacques Laffite, John Watson, Carlos Reutemann and Elio de Angelis all the way to the finish in 1981

most, with a long straight past the pits followed by hard braking into the downhill first corner which was good for overtaking.

The first two races at the new Barcelona circuit were hit by rain, and both were won by Mansell for Williams. In 1991, he and Senna (by now in a McLaren) staged a fabulous, if brief, battle for second place, running side-by-side down the straight past the pits. Then Mansell was in a class of his own in 1992, while Prost proved to be a dominant winner for Williams in 1993.

Damon Hill took his revenge, winning for Williams in 1994 after

Michael Schumacher's Benetton hit trouble, then the German won at Jerez on his return from suspension later that year when the southern circuit hosted a race known as the Grand Prix of Europe. He won again in the wet in 1996, but 1997 saw a Jacques Villeneuve double in Spain – and much controversy as Schumacher rammed him in the Jerez season-closer, again run as the Grand Prix of Europe.

There was no race at Jerez in 1998, while the McLarens dominated at Barcelona, Hakkinen ahead of Coulthard. Hakkinen won again in both 1999 and 2000, but lost out on a hat-trick in 2001 when he pulled off

with half a mile to go, handing victory to Schumacher. The Ferrari ace was untouchable in 2002, but had to really attack in 2003 as Renault's local hero Alonso pushed him hard.

The corner at the end of the back straight, La Caixa, was made sharper for 2004, but this failed to produce a new winner as Schumacher won again, albeit after having to overcome the Renault of fast-starting Trulli. Renault was strong again in 2005, but the French team had to give way to McLaren and Raikkonen as the Finn laid down a title challenge and Alonso again had to settle for second place. It all came right for

Alonso in 2006, though, and he won as he pleased after Renault team-mate Fisichella helped keep Michael Schumacher at bay early on.

It was Ferrari versus McLaren in 2007 and the pressure of racing in front of his home fans proved too much for Alonso as he ran wide at the first corner as he tried to pass Massa for the lead, falling to fourth. Massa then controlled the race. Ferrari won again in 2008, this time through Raikkonen, with Kovalainen lucky to scape a huge shunt in his McLaren.

Then, as with so many other early-season races in 2009, victory went to Button in a Brawn GP one-two.

SWITZERLAND

CIRCUIT DETAILS

BREMGARTEN
Circuit length: **4.524 miles**
Years race held: **1950-1954**
This was one of the circuits that the drivers feared the most for, not only was its lap made up of sweeping corners, but the surface was cobbled in places and the track largely overhung by trees that would drop their leaves, making it less than grippy in the wet... Drivers simply had to remember that every corner – save for a few left kinks – was a right-hander, albeit in varying degrees of openness, with the Bethlehem corner soon after the start a 90-degree bend and the final corner, Forsthaus, almost a hairpin.

Careful on the Cobbles: Alfa Romeos to the fore in 1951 as race-winner Juan Manuel Fangio leads his team-mate Giuseppe Farina early in the race

Of the six grands prix held in the first year of the World Championship, excluding the all but separate Indy 500, the Swiss Grand Prix is the only one that hasn't lasted the test of time. Indeed, it ran only from 1950 to 1954 before the violent accident at Le Mans in 1955 that claimed the lives of more than 80 spectators led to the immediate cancellation of all racing in Switzerland, a ban that still stands good today, with only one-at-a-time hillclimb events being permitted.

The very first Swiss Grand Prix was held way back in 1934, using the extremely impressive Bremgarten circuit running through dense forest in the western suburbs of the Swiss capital, Berne. Hans Stuck won on that

occasion for Auto Union. It was Mercedes' turn the following year when Rudolf Caracciola triumphed, before Auto Union struck back through Bernd Rosemeyer in 1936. Thereafter, it was Mercedes territory, with Caracciola bagging a couple more wins before Hermann Lang won the final grand prix there before the interruption of the Second World War.

Back as part of the grand prix circus in 1947, Jean-Pierre Wimille won for Alfa Romeo, with the feat being repeated in 1948, this time with Carlo Felice Trossi as the victorious driver. That race in 1948 was marred by the deaths of Achille Varzi and Christian Kautz. Then Alberto Ascari won

at Bremgarten for Ferrari in 1949, the last visit before the start of the World Championship.

First to win at Bremgarten was the inaugural World Champion Giuseppe Farina for Alfa Romeo after team-mate Juan Manuel Fangio's car hit electrical problems. Fangio bounced back in 1951, when it was the season's opening race, beating Piero Taruffi's Ferrari by almost a minute. Ferrari then claimed the honours in 1952 and 1953 through Taruffi who benefitted from the retirement of team-mate Farina, then Ascari again by more than a minute from Farina. Fangio struck back with Mercedes in 1954 and won what would be the final Swiss Grand Prix there, doing so at

an average speed of a whisker under 100mph, having led every lap and left second-placed Jose Froilan Gonzalez's Ferrari almost a minute behind.

Actually, there was one more Swiss Grand Prix. It was held some 28 years later, in France... This was because racing was still banned in Switzerland, so it was held over the border at Dijon-Prenois. In fact, this was the second Swiss Grand Prix there, as there had been a non-championship event there in 1975, fittingly won by Swiss driver Clay Regazzoni for Ferrari.

For the World Championship event seven years later, by which time a loop had been added to boost the track length, there was another Swiss driver in the field, Marc Surer, but he could qualify his Arrows only 14th before finishing 15th and last, fully four laps behind winner Keke Rosberg's Williams after a lengthy pitstop.

Rosberg was gifted victory when Alain Prost's Renault was slowed by a disintegrating skirt, dropping him to second. This was the Finn's only win all year, but his points tally was still sufficient to claim the drivers' title in the most competitive championship ever, with 11 drivers taking race wins.

TURKEY

Turkey made many Formula One wannabe countries – such as Russia, Egypt and the Lebanon – jealous when they landed a race for 2005.

Then came the serious matter of building a new circuit from scratch. As is now the way the world over, the highly favoured circuit architect Hermann Tilke was brought in to craft a state-of-the-art racing facility of which the country could be proud.

There were certainly problems: a million cubic metres of rock needed to be blasted out of the way, a river ran across the hilly site, budgets for the construction were running over and there was a continual threat of political unrest – stemming from problems with the Kurdish population in the east of the country.

Despite all of these difficulties, though, the Istanbul Park circuit was delivered on time, after employing many thousands of labourers to work around the clock to ensure that it hit its deadline in good time. Indeed, when people arrived for the first race in mid-August, the chief concern was how the drivers and the cars would cope with the rapidly soaring temperatures.

The Turkish Grand Prix organizers could not have wished for a better first race. First up, the drivers loved it, finding the circuit one into which they could really sink their teeth and feel that their talents were rewarded, with its changes of gradient an unexpected bonus. That one corner alone – Turn 8 – had four apexes really marked it out. The downhill esses of Turns 4 and 5 are also a particular treat.

Jenson Button was so moved by the circuit's undulating tarmac that he described it thus: "It's not often that you come to a new circuit and think 'this is mega'. It's a real drivers' circuit, like Suzuka."

The facilities were good too, with the massive towers at either end of the pitlane as the standout features. Certainly, those fortunate enough to watch the racing action from the huge canopied terrace atop each are treated to an amazing view.

It was the racing itself that stood out, though, with Raikkonen putting on a peerless performance as he raced to victory after passing the fast-starting Renault of Fisichella partway round the opening lap. What will be remembered more, though, is what befell McLaren team-mate, Montoya, who was running second and keeping Kimi's title rival Alonso back in third. His first mistake in the closing laps was to chop in front of Monteiro's Jordan after lapping it, clipping its front and spinning. This allowed Alonso to close up onto his tail. Then Montoya ran wide at Turn 8, blaming a broken diffuser, to fall back into third place, losing valuable points in McLaren's attempts to haul in Renault in the Constructors' Cup.

Felipe Massa put his Ferrari on pole in 2006 and benefitted from being ahead of team-mate Michael Schumacher when the cars scrambled to the pits after a safety car period, thus forcing the German to wait. He then went on to win as the delay left Michael behind Alonso.

Massa won again in 2007, with team-mate Raikkonen second and Hamilton's challenge wrecked by a puncture. And he made it three in a row in 2008, with Hamilton just resisting Raikkonen for second.

Massa could finish only sixth in 2009, though, as polesitter Vettel slipped up on lap 1 and Button nipped by to win for Brawn.

CIRCUIT DETAILS

ISTANBUL PARK
Circuit length: **3.317 miles**
Years race held: **2005 onwards**
The lap starts by dipping down to the first corner. Unusually, this is a left-hander as the circuit runs anti-clockwise – Imola and Interlagos are the only other two circuits in Formula One to do so. After a long arc to the right, the sequence of corners from Turn 3 to Turn 6 is twisting before the first straight of note. Out of Turn 9, the track opens out onto a long straight that runs through a kink, Turn 11, before reaching the best overtaking point, the braking zone for the tight left at Turn 12. With the corner onto the start-finish straight also being slow, drivers will look there to hitch a tow down the straight for a possible passing move into Turn 1.

Brave New World: the Istanbul Park circuit impressed all who visited it for its debut grand prix in 2005, with its flowing track and distinctive buildings

UNITED ARAB EMIRATES

CIRCUIT DETAILS

YAS MARINA
Circuit length: **3.429 miles**
Years race held: **2009 onwards**
Designed to be a lap of three parts, the Yas Marina circuit starts with its high-speed stretch down to the first hairpin at Turn 7 then along the longest straight to another at Turn 8. From there, it changes to a twistier, street circuit section, up to Turn 14. At this point, the lap enters its marina section, running alongside the water to the end of its 21-turn lap.

From day to night: Rubens Barrichello's Brawn flashes under the hotel walkway en route to fourth place on Abu Dhabi's grand prix bow

Even after a run of new circuits over the previous decade or so, including Sepang, Shanghai and Istanbul, nothing prepared the Formula One circus for the brand new circuit that greeted them when they arrived in Abu Dhabi for the final round of the 2009 World Championship. The Yas Marina circuit really was something different, its design a mixture of fast and slow accompanied by overwhelmingly extravagant touches such as the section running under the Yas Hotel and the pitlane that rejoined the track via a tunnel. That this most expensive circuit in Formula One history had been pulled off during the worst economic downturn for 80 years proved that

oil-rich countries were still able to stump up for projects for national promotion. Abu Dhabi may have had no connection with or history of motor sport, but it had the financial wherewithal and so it was invited to motor racing's top table. That 14,000 people worked on its construction and it involved 1.6 million tons of earthworks gives an indication of the scale of the project.

The first race there in 2009 was a remarkable one, as it was not only tailormade for the vital European television audience, being held at the right time of day to fit in with their viewing patterns, but it presented the image of being two races, since it started in daylight

and traveled through dusk, making sensational images. Formula One impresario Bernie Ecclestone could not have been more delighted. Even more so, he could now use the Yas Marina circuit as an example of how high the bar could be raised for new construction. Few countries would be able to afford as much to match it, but he had his shining example.

Its inaugural race came without the benefit of being a final round showdown, as Jenson Button had already clinched the drivers' title at the penultimate round, in Brazil. However, Red Bull Racing's Sebastian Vettel was determined not to be kept from being runner-up by the other Brawn GP driver,

Rubens Barrichello. So he gave chase to dominant polesitter Lewis Hamilton's McLaren then took the lead by making his first stop three laps after the Englishman's and was never headed again. When Hamilton dropped out with a brake problem, the reason for him lapping way below his expected pace, Mark Webber claimed the position in the second Red Bull entry, but he was made to work incredibly hard to resist attack after attack by Button in the closing laps. It made for great television images.

With some exciting dicing and 18 of the 20 starters making the finish, it was a good first grand prix for Abu Dhabi, and it certainly made near neighbours Bahrain feel that they might have become part of the World Championship five years earlier, but they had been well and truly trumped by the Yas Marina circuit.

As is the way with a number of the newer, state-funded circuits, the track itself is only part of a complex, with the Yas Marina site having, obviously, a marina, but also five-star hotels, a golf course, luxury housing and most notably a theme park dedicated to Ferrari. These all indicate Abu Dhabi's desire to boost tourism to reduce its reliance on oil for its wealth and the circuit will certainly attract fans to visit.

USA

The United States can lay claim to more grand prix venues than any other country. No fewer than nine circuits have held World Championship races. One year, 1982, there were three events in the USA plus a fourth in Canada. Strangely, Formula One didn't visit the country from 1992 to 1999.

The first US Grand Prix was in 1959 at Sebring, the airfield circuit in Florida famous for its bumpy runways and 12-hour sports car race. Bruce McLaren won and Cooper team-mate Brabham took the title. The event moved across the country in 1960 to Riverside, the dusty Californian road course, with Moss winning.

In 1961, the race found a home. Watkins Glen, an undulating road course in upstate New York, hosted the US Grand Prix until 1980. The event was popular, not least because – in pre-FOCA days – it paid the most prize money... The most famous section of the track was the dramatic uphill esse soon after the start. The inaugural event was won by Innes Ireland, then for the next six years Clark and Hill shared the victories.

The track was extended for 1971, when Cevert scored his first and only win. Two years later, he was killed in qualifying, and a year after that Austrian rookie Koinigg lost his life. Despite the tragedies, the race went on. By 1980, with the turbo era dawning and the cars lapping ever faster, it was clear that the Glen couldn't keep up. After that year's race, won by Jones, F1 never returned.

Chris Pook introduced the US Grand Prix (West) in 1976 on a round-the-houses course at Long Beach. Regazzoni was the first winner and the race became a classic, but after 1983 Pook switched to IndyCars, no longer willing to pay the fees.

In 1981, there was a race at Las Vegas – held quite literally in the car park of the Caesar's Palace hotel. Jones won, but nobody liked the place.

In 1982, Long Beach and Vegas were joined by a race in Detroit. That produced some entertaining races and three wins for Senna. It ran until 1988, when it too joined the IndyCar trail.

Dallas became a venue in 1984 – but it was a disaster, the track falling apart in the heat. It was a one-off...

After the loss of Long Beach, Las Vegas, Dallas and Detroit, Phoenix stepped forward with yet another street event in 1989, despite the presence of a successful IndyCar oval just outside town. The race is best remembered for a fight between Senna and Alesi, who in 1990 produced one of the best dices in years. The 1991 race there was to prove the last.

After a raft or rumours, including potential races in Las Vegas and San Francisco, the US Grand Prix was back on the calendar in 2000, this time at Indianapolis. The track used one of the Speedway's four banked corners, the start/finish straight – in the opposite direction to normal – and a twisting loop around the infield.

Michael Schumacher was the first to win there for Ferrari. Then Hakkinen drove a great race for his final win in 2001, then Schumacher made a mess of trying to stage a photo-finish in 2002, handing victory by 0.011s to Barrichello. Rain intensifying, then easing off, kept changing the order in 2003, with Bridgestone superiority helping Schumacher to outrun Raikkonen's Michelin-shod McLaren. Schumacher did it again in 2004, leading Barrichello in a Ferrari one-two. Then came 2005, for one of F1's darkest days when tyre concerns led all the Michelin runners to pull off after the parade lap, leaving just six cars to go racing, with Schumacher winning from Barrichello again. So, there was a need for a good race in 2006 and Schumacher made it three in a row, ahead of team-mate Massa.

Then came F1's last visit, in 2007, with Hamilton outracing his McLaren team-mate Alonso to take victory.

CIRCUIT DETAILS

INDIANAPOLIS

Circuit length: **2.607 miles**   Years race held: **2000-2007**

Ignore the fact that the Indy 500 was counted as a round of the World Championship from 1950 to 1960, it was only when the Motor Speedway turned some of its massive infield into a circuit that it hosted the US Grand Prix. This started in 2000, with the engineers finding the section of the track that ran around the banking between Turns 1 and 2, in the reverse of the regular direction, something of a challenge. Ferrari has won three of the four races at the Indianapolis Motor Speedway so far, all in front of crowds of close to 300,000.

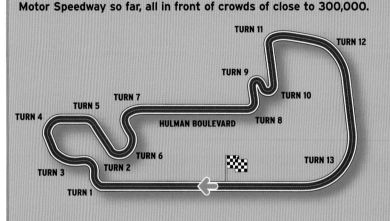

WATKINS GLEN

Circuit length: **2.350 then 2.430 then 3.377 miles**
Years race held: **1961-1980**

No American circuit has hosted the United States Grand Prix for as long, with this upstate New York track enjoying a 20-year tenure that ended in 1980 when street circuits came into favour. The circuit was built in 1956 after a nearby temporary road circuit was considered too dangerous. However, the deaths in consecutive years of Francois Cevert and Helmuth Koinigg proved that the grand prix circuit was none too safe either. Watkins Glen fell into disrepair after losing the grand prix but has since been revived for sports car races.

It's Go, Go, Go: Kimi Raikkonen leads away from the start for McLaren in 2003 with Panis giving chase

INDEX

All page numbers in **bold** refer to major entries